Praise for

"Thanks to Wolff and friends, the cyber-swamp may just have become a little less murky."—*Entertainment Weekly*

"*Net Guide* is the computer world's online *TV Guide*."—*Good Morning America*

"*Net Guide* will keep you from wandering around aimlessly on the Internet, and is full of good ideas for where to pull over."—*Forbes FYI*

"*Net Guide* is the liveliest, most readable online guide yet."—*USA Today*

"What you need to connect."—*Worth Magazine*

"*Net Guide* is the *TV Guide* to Cyberspace!"—Louis Rossetto, publisher/editor, *Wired*

"One of the more complete, well-organized guides to online topics. From photography to the Church of Elvis, you'll find it here."—*PC Magazine*

"The best attempt yet at categorizing and organizing all the great stuff you can find out there. It's the book people keep stealing off my desk."—Joshua Quittner, *New York Newsday*

"It's changed my online life. Get this book!"—Mike Madson, "Computer Bits," Business Radio Network

"My favorite for finding the cool stuff."—*The Louisville Courier-Journal*

"*Net Guide* focuses on the most important aspect of online information—its content. You name it, it's there—from erotica to religion to politics."—Lawrence J. Magid, *San Jose Mercury News*

"Not only did all the existing Net books ignore Cyberspace's entertaining aspects, but they were process-oriented, not content-oriented. Why hadn't someone made a *TV Guide* for the Net? Wolff recognized an opportunity for a new book, and his group wrote *Net Guide*."—Mark Frauenfelder, *Wired*

"Couch potatoes have *TV Guide*. Now Net surfers have *Net Guide*."—*Orange County Register*

"*Net Guide* is one of the best efforts to provide a hot-spot guide to going online."—*Knoxville News-Sentinel*

"Assolutamente indispensabile!"—*L'Espresso*, Italy

"A valuable guide for anyone interested in the recreational uses of personal computers and modems."—Peter H. Lewis, *The New York Times*

"*Net Games* is a good map of the playing fields of Netdom."—*Newsweek*

"This guide to games people play in the ever-expanding Cyberspace shows you exactly where to go."—*Entertainment Weekly*

"The second book in a very good series from Wolff and Random House."—Bob Schwabach, syndicated columnist

"Hot addresses!"—*USA Weekend*

"Move over Parker Brothers and Nintendo—games are now available online. There's something in *Net Games* for everyone from crossword-puzzle addicts to *Dungeons & Dragons* fans."—*Reference Books Bulletin*

"Whether you're a hardened game player or a mere newbie, *Net Games* is the definitive directory for gaming on the Internet."—*.net*

"A wide and devoted following."—*The Wall Street Journal*

"*Net Money* is a superb guide to online business and finance!"—*Hoover's Handbook of American Business*

"[*Net Chat*] is...the best surfer's guide out there."—*Entertainment Weekly*

"A product line of guidebooks for explorers of the Internet."—*Inside Media*

Net Books!

net guide ™

net games ™

net chat ™

net money ™

net trek ™

Coming soon

net sports ™

net tech ™

net music ™

net trek ™

Your Guide to
Trek Life in Cyberspace

A Michael Wolff Book

Kelly Maloni, Ben Greenman,
Kristin Miller, and Jeff Hearn

**For free updates call 1-800-NET-1133
or visit our Website at http://www.ypn.com/**

**RANDOM HOUSE
ELECTRONIC PUBLISHING**

**MICHAEL WOLFF & COMPANY, INC.
DIGITAL PUBLISHING**

New York

4-20-95

*Steve,
Enjoy.
Relax.
Visit other
worlds.
Happy Birthday
Love
Andrea*

The Net Books series is a co-publishing venture of Michael Wolff & Company, Inc., 1633 Broadway, 27th Floor, New York, NY 10019, and Random House Electronic Publishing, a division of Random House, Inc., 201 East 50th Street, New York, NY 10022.

Net Trek has been wholly created and produced by Michael Wolff & Company, Inc. *Net Games*, *Net Chat*, *Net Money*, *Net Tech*, *Net Sports*, NetHead, NetSpeak, and CyberPower are trademarks of Michael Wolff & Company, Inc. All design and production has been done by means of desktop-publishing technology. The text is set in the typefaces Garamond, customized Futura, Zapf Dingbats, Franklin Gothic, Star Trek Font Pack, and Pike.

Published simultaneously in the U.S. by Random House, NY, and Michael Wolff & Company, Inc., and in Canada by Random House of Canada, Ltd.

0 9 8 7 6 5 4 3 2 1

ISBN 0-679-76186-1

The author and publisher have used their best efforts in preparing this book. However, the author and publisher make no warranties of any kind, express or implied, with regard to the documentation contained in this book, and specifically disclaim, without limitation, any implied warranties of merchantability and fitness for a particular purpose with respect to listings in the book, or the techniques described in the book. In no event shall the author or publisher be responsible or liable for any loss of profit or any other commercial damages, including but not limited to special, incidental, consequential, or any other damages in connection with or arising out of furnishing, performance, or use of this book.

All of the photographs and illustrations in this book have been obtained from online sources, and have been included to demonstrate the variety of work that is available on the Net. The caption with each photograph or illustration identifies its online source. Also see sources for uncaptioned images on page 386. Text and images available over the Internet and other online services may be subject to copyright and other rights owned by third parties. Online availability of text and images does not imply that they may be reused without the permission of rights holders, although the Copyright Act does permit certain unauthorized reuse as fair use under 17 U.S.C. §107. Care should be taken to ensure that all necessary rights are cleared prior to reusing material distributed over the Internet and other online services. Information about reuse is available from the institutions that make their materials available online.

Trademarks

A number of entered words in which we have reason to believe trademark, service mark, or other proprietary rights may exist have been designated as such by use of initial capitalization. However, no attempt has been made to designate as trademarks or service marks all personal-computer words or terms in which proprietary rights might exist. The inclusion, exclusion, or definition of a word or term is not intended to affect, or to express any judgment on, the validity or legal status of any proprietary right which may be claimed in that word or term.

Manufactured in the United States of America

New York   Toronto   London   Sydney   Auckland

BOLDLY GO...

It can't get any easier! We've *hotlinked* the thousands of Internet addresses in *Net Trek* for you. Don't bother typing that pesky address, just link to http://www.ypn.com/ and then point and click on the site you want—we'll beam you up!

...TO HTTP://WWW.YPN.COM/

A Michael Wolff Book

Michael Wolff
President and Editor in Chief

Peter Rutten
Creative Director

Kelly Maloni
Managing Editor

Senior Editors: Ben Greenman, Kristin Miller

Art Director: Jeff Hearn

Research Editors: Bill Folsom, Shaun Witten,
Tristan Louis, Kendra Wilhelm

Editorial Assistant: Stephanie Engel

Contributing Editor: Suzanne Charlé

Production Assistant: Linda Pattie

Technical Editor: David Wood

Copy Editors: Julia Curry, Carol Estey, S. Kirk Walsh

Contributing Writers: Joel Furr, Allan Hoffman,
Bill Mason, Miriam Nathan, Jeff Yang

Chief Technology Officer: Stan Norton

Marketing Manager: Bill Folsom

Special thanks:
Random House Electronic Publishing—Tracy Smith,
Mark Dazzo, Alison Biggert, Robin McCorry, Rita Rubin

Peter Ginsberg at Curtis Brown Ltd.

And, once again, Aggy Aed

The editors of *Net Trek* can be reached at Michael Wolff & Company, Inc., 1633 Broadway, 27th Floor, New York, NY 10019, or by voice call at 212-841-1572, fax at 212-841-1539, or email at editors@ypn.com.

Editor's Note

The *Star Trek* phenomenon—seven movies, four television series (five if you count the cartoon), and a multigenerational audience growing geometrically over more than 25 years—is the real stuff of Hollywood (and boardroom) legend.

That legend is about to grow by vast proportions as *Star Trek* becomes the first hit of an altogether new medium—the forums, chat areas, newsgroups, mailing lists, Websites, and FTP archives with their millions of digitized images and sound-bites that comprise the information and entertainment source known as the Net.

Net Trek is a report on this extraordinary entertainment and cultural development. It is a map of a world that others—fans and professionals alike—have built. It is a guide to the vast stores of Trek data that inhabit Cyberspace and supply the Trek canon and fuel the Trek experience. It is a wide-eyed and astonished look at the ever-expanding Trek phenomenon.

Star Trek is to the Net what Milton Berle, Jack Benny, and Ed Sullivan were to television—the standard-bearer that makes it from one medium to another. Trek—its lore and its culture—has made the transition from video and celluloid to digital code and Cyberspace. In so doing, it has begun to define the style, the audience, and the message of the Net. Trek is singularly appropriate to this new interactive medium because it is a culture and an oeuvre driven as much by the participation of its audience as by the contributions of its writers and producers. Trek is "next generation" digital entertainment because it is as dependent on information—the fan-created and fan-administered archives accessible across Cyberspace—as it is on traditional narrative structures.

We have trodden carefully around (and not over) the rights of *Star Trek*'s owners, trusting that they believe—as we do—that the activity on the Net has enhanced, rather than diminished, the value of the franchise. Where we have made reference to trademarks, we have tried to observe the integrity of those marks. Where we have reproduced images—publicity stills, video frames, and Web pages all garnered from the Net—we have done so in an effort to communicate the substance of the medium. Indeed, the images included here are but an infinitesimal fraction of those available on the Internet; commercial services like AOL, CompuServe, Prodigy, and GEnie; and many Trek-related BBSs.

In preparing this book, we have had the help of many of the leading figures and ombudsmen of the Trek community. We owe them a debt of enormous gratitude.

Editor's Note

They include Tim Lynch, whose reviews are a pillar of the online Trek universe; Mike Brown, the Trek world's Vidiot savant; Brigitte Jellinek, who tends the best Trek site in Austria; Andrew Tong, who has his finger on the pulse of all things Trek; Miriam Nathan and Bill "Data" Mason, who oversee AOL's Star Trek Club; Joshua Sean Bell, Treknologist extraordinaire; Kevin Morrison, who helped define Paramount's presence on the Net; Jim Griffith, rec.arts.startrek's Big Dweeb; Arnie Starr, Trek comics inker and GEnie sysop; Mike Hennigan, who maintains GEnie's episode discussions and also serves as eWorld co-sysop; Mark Holtz, the mastermind of Star Trek's List of List; Otto Heuer, super FAQ-man; Phil Kernick, the funniest Trek fan alive; and the dozens of other Cybertrekkers who have guided us home.

Our blunders, however, are our own. If you catch one, if you know of or happen upon sites we missed, if you'd like to help us next time around, or if you just want to nitpick, don't hesitate to drop us a line.

Michael Wolff & Company, Inc.
editors@ypn.com

Contents

Contents

Part 3. Star Trek: The Original Series

Part 4. Star Trek: The Next Generation

Part 5. Star Trek: Deep Space Nine

Part 6. Star Trek: Voyager

Part 7. Real Space

Part 8. Genre: Other Sci-Fi

Appendices

Foreword
Cyberspace—The Final Frontier

Tim Lynch is one of the premier Cybertrekkers—that is, a Trek fan who puts his enthusiasm online. Lynch, 25, is a Los Angeles resident who has been contributing to Net Trek culture since his college days, when he and his roommate Mike Shappe posted weekly reviews of Trek episodes to fledgling Usenet groups. Considered one of online Trek's elder statesmen, Lynch names TNG's "The Inner Light" and "The Measure of a Man" as his favorite Trek episodes.

Almost thirty years after it first aired, *Star Trek* is indisputably the television era's most successful science fiction enterprise (all puns intended). Starting from a position of relative obscurity, Trek has become, in many ways, an integral part of the world's subconscious. Certainly, not everyone is a fan—but you'd be hard-pressed to find someone unaware of it.

There's nothing quite like Trek in that regard— unless, of course, you're talking about the Net. Certainly, it had beginnings at least as humble as *Star Trek's*—and certainly, its expansion has been just as breathtaking. Seven years ago, when I first started my own contributions to the Net (primarily reviews of weekly episodes, which continue to this day), most people had no idea what was meant by the term. Now, thanks to a media explosion, it's difficult to find anyone who hasn't at least heard of the Net.

But the similarities don't stop there. They're philosophical as well as historical. As any good Trek fan can tell you, the show's philosophy of tolerance is often considered its main strength. That philosophy, known as IDIC (or Infinite Diversity in Infinite Combinations), encourages people to acknowledge and respect the differences of others as contributions to a universal dialogue. The Net creates the same effect: since communication is purely typographical, differences become irrelevant, and an opinion about *Deep Space Nine's* quality must be assessed independent of the writer's class, race, religion, location, or physical appearance. You don't even know for certain if a message was posted by a human—who knows what kind of newsfeeds they have on Vulcan?

But Trek and the Net aren't only parallel phenomena. They're also intersecting ones. As the Net has expanded, so has *Star Trek's* presence on it. A decade ago, "net.startrek" was one of the first Usenet groups formed—and now, even confining yourself to Usenet, you could probably spend your entire waking day just reading various facts, opinions, or announcements with a Trek spin (be it convention reports, upcoming schedules, reviews of some of the latest Trek material, or offers of Trek merchandise). As Trek fandom's presence on the Net has grown, Cyberspace has become more and more the preeminent medium for fans' comments, organizations, and entertainments. Want to see an analysis of the Tamarian language? Want to chat about the omnipotent mischief of Q? Go ahead—and when you're finished, there's plenty more where that came from.

My own association with Trek on the Net has for the most part been deeply exciting. The Net acts as a wonderful sounding board—if you actively detested last week's episode of *Voyager*, you can at least enjoy ranting about its flaws afterward. I could describe at length the eternal Usenet debates—on the relative merits of each series, on the role of music in a show, on the value of such Trek concepts as the Prime Directive, on whether gay and lesbian people will (or should) ever be represented in the Trek universe— but I tend to remember the strange moments, such as being greeted in other newsgroups or at conventions with, "oh, you're THAT Tim Lynch!" (It's even stranger when the people who recognize me are on *Star Trek's* writing staff...) While I'd almost certainly be watching *Star Trek* with or without the Net, the connections to other fans and the awareness of the creative forces shaping the series would be lost—and as a result, I wouldn't be enjoying it as much.

This book is your gateway to the Trek universe of the 23rd and 24th centuries, as well as the online culture of the 20th and 21st. Happy hunting.

—Tim Lynch

FAQ

"Frequently Asked Questions" about the Net and Net Trek

1. I always watch *Star Trek* with my friends—never miss an episode or a movie. But I've heard there's more. Where?

The Net, of course, where Star Trek fans from across the globe gather to discuss the shows they love, compile time lines and trivia lists, showcase famous (and favorite) images, act out their Trek fantasies, and publish weekly reviews, newsletters, and fan fiction. Even if you belong to a Trek fan club, go to conventions, and have dinner each week with Rick Berman, there's something for you. The Net offers 24-hour-a-day discussions with an endless stream of fans who never tire of talking Trek.

2. Sounds like a Trek convention.

Actually, many of the traditional practices of Trek fans are being transplanted into the online world. Rather than being mailed to your home, newsletters are being emailed to electronic mailboxes, posted to newsgroups, or published on Web pages. The normal business of a Trek convention—trading rumors with other fans, buying and selling merchandise, even listening to speeches by Trek stars—are all available electronically. William Shatner (Kirk), John de Lancie (Q), and Rick Berman (producer), for instance, have all answered fan questions in live online conferences. And, in the online world, there are no travel plans, no complicated booking arrangements, and almost no costs.

3. Okay. No convention center. But really, where do I go? What is "the Net," anyway?

The Net is the electronic medium spawned by the millions of computers linked (that is, networked) together throughout the world. Known as Cyberspace, the Information Highway, or the Infobahn, the Net encompasses the Internet, a global, noncommercial system with more than 30 million computers communicating through it; the commercial online services, like CompuServe, America Online, Prodigy, GEnie, and eWorld; the thousands of local and regional bulletin-board services (BBSs); the networks of discussion groups, like FidoNet and TrekNet, that are carried out over BBSs; and the discussion groups known as Usenet that traverse the Internet. More and more, the Internet unites all the diverse locations and formats that make up the Net.

4. So, like, I'll really be able to talk to other fans about last night's episode of *Deep Space Nine*?

You sure can. If you visit the main sci-fi message boards on commercial services or the Trek newsgroups on Usenet, you'll find dozens of discussions about every aspect of the episode—its plot, character development, special effects, even minute continuity errors (known in the Trek world as snafus or nitpicks). And if you taped the episode and haven't had a chance to watch the last 15 minutes, don't fret that the Net will ruin your fun— Netiquette encourages Trekkers to post "Spoiler Warnings" when their messages disclose plot secrets. And if last night's show reminded you of a *Next Generation* episode from a few seasons ago or a classic *Trek* from a few decades ago—are they stepping into a temporal distortion again?—you can check out the similarities in one of the many episode guides online, most of which link to reviews, discussions, and archives of images.

- Monthly fee: $8.95
- Free monthly hours: 4
- Hourly fees: $3 (off-prime) or $9.50 (prime time) for 2400 baud; $9 (off-prime) or $12.50 (prime time) for 9600 baud
- Email: feedback@genie.geis.com

Prodigy:
- 800-PRODIGY (voice)
- Value Plan I: $14.95/month includes unlimited core services; 5 hours in plus services, which consist of the bulletin boards, EAASY Sabre, Dow Jones Co. News, and stock quotes; and 30 email messages; additional 'plus' hours cost $2.95 each
- Alternate Plan I: $7.95/month includes 2 hours of core or plus services; additional hours (core or plus) are $2.95/hour
- Alternate Plan II: $19.95/month includes 8 hours of core services; plus services cost an additional $2.95/hour
- Alternate Plan BB: $29.95/month includes 25 hours core and plus services; additional hours are $2.95/hour

Perfect Vision Graphics (PVG):
- 513-233-7993
- Plan I: $65/year includes 1 hour per day
- Plan II: $45/six months includes 30 minutes per day

5. My favorite Trek memories are of the original series. But I can't find anyone who remembers the show, let alone wants to discuss it. Can the Net help?

Can the Net help? Are Vulcans logical? Online Trek has something for everyone—not only resources for fans of *Deep Space Nine*, *The Next Generation*, and *Voyager*, but a wealth of material on the original series. Kirk fans can download a list of his love interests, or a complete account of what William Shatner has been doing since the show went off the air. And if you're interested in pictures that feature the virile and clever young Captain Kirk, you'll never get your fill.

6. I love the Klingons and can't get enough of them. Can the Net help me find my way to the planet Qo'noS?

You can probably even get fairly accurate directions. On the Net, Klingon is a full-fledged culture, with maps, histories, and even a dictionary of phrases as useful as Berlitz guides (yes, you can learn how to say "Where's the bathroom?" in Klingon). From academic discussions of Klingon grammar to formal role-playing games scheduled in live conferences, the Net is crawling with Klingons.

7. Role-playing? What's that?

You're a famous Klingon general dispatched to a summit with the Federation. News arrives that the Romulans are amassing troops along the borders of the Neutral Zone. Do you decide to call for a ship and engage the Romulans in combat, or do you seek a solution through diplomatic channels? Ahh, and it's not a computer you're up against—it's another Trek fan. That's role-playing, and there are plenty of places online to do it, from alt.shared-reality.klingon to AOL's We Are Klingons!

8. Settle a bet. My friend says that Tasha Yar's daughter was born only seven years after Tasha. I say he's wrong. Who's right?

Well, he is. Sorry. To fully explain the life of Tasha Yar, we'd have to resort to a complicated time line full of forks and hairpin turns, loops, and abrupt endings. If you're really curious, you're better off making use of the online resources for this sort of thing, such as the numerous Trek time lines and stardate calendars. There's even a Tasha Yar FAQ that deals more specifically with the odd life of the Ukrainian security officer. In other words, if you're interested, confused, or obsessed with an event in the Trek universe, odds are that other Netters are too. They are likely to have compiled facts, written essays (and translated them into several languages), drawn ASCII diagrams, and participated in online debates on the subject.

9. What about pictures? I collect images of Ferengi. Can I find them online?

Sure you can. Quark, Rom, Nog, even the Grand Nagus himself. And even though it seems counter to Ferengi principles, they won't cost you a dime. The Net is teeming with Trek images—millions of them in thousands of archives and Websites, commercial-service libraries, and bulletin boards. Indeed, the FTP archives listed here represent only a fraction of those that contain Trek materials. Similarly, while there are hundreds of bulletin boards with Trek images for downloading, we have drawn the majority of our pictures from Perfect Vision Graphics BBS (noted throughout *Net Trek* as "PVG") in Dayton, Ohio, which carries an excellent selection of Trek GIFs.

10. You know, I also like *Star Wars*, *Babylon 5*, and *Doctor Who*. Does the Net embrace other sci-fi?

Did you say Star Wars? Babylon 5? Doctor Who? No sooner said than done. In fact, just about every sci-fi television series and feature film, from Lost in Space to Alien to Highlander, has sites on the Net devoted to it—fan discussion, digitized images, and trivia.

11. Browsing, collecting, and playing is great. But is there anything I can bring to the party?

You can bring your own expertise. Hundreds of sci-fi fans participate in online Trek and its relatives, whether as newsgroup regulars or real-time chat personalities. And many of them have designed their own personal Web pages, which link to their favorite sci-fi sites across the Internet.

SENDING EMAIL

I'm on a commercial service. How do I send Internet email? Each of the major commercial services offers Internet email with slight variations in form.

From CompuServe
Enter the CompuServe mail area by choosing the **go** command from the menu and typing **mail** (if you don't have CompuServe's Information Manager software, type **go mail**). If you want to send a message to someone on another commercial service, your email will be routed through the Internet, so you must address it with the prefix **internet:**. Mail to John Doe at America Online, for instance, would be addressed internet:jdoe@aol.com; to John Doe at YPN, it would be addressed internet:jdoe@ ypn.com.

To CompuServe
Use the addressee's CompuServe ID number. If John Doe's ID is 12345,678, you'll address mail to 12345.678@ compuserve. com. Make sure you replace the comma in the CompuServe ID with a period.

From America Online
Use AOL's Internet mail gateway (keyword: **internet**). Then address and send mail as you normally would on any other Internet site, using the jdoe@ service.com address style.

To America Online
Address email to jdoe@aol.com.
→

---

12. How much for all this sci-fi?

Most of the places that are described in this book either have no charge beyond Internet connection fees or are part of the basic services on commercial networks like AOL, Prodigy, eWorld, or CompuServe. There are, of course, some services that carry additional costs—bulletin boards, for instance. Most fees are quite reasonable, but remember to examine costs carefully before plunging into a service. The Net changes.

13. I'm game. What do I need to get started?

A computer and a modem, and a few tricks to find your way around.

14. Can you help me decide what computer and modem I'll need?

If you've bought a computer fairly recently, it's likely that it came with everything you need. But let's assume you have only a PC. In that case you'll also need to get a modem, which will allow your computer to communicate over the phone. So-called 14.4 modems, which transfer data at speeds up to 14,400 bits per second (bps), have become

From GEnie
Use the keyword **mail** and address email to jdoe@service.com@inet#. GEnie's use of two @ symbols is an exception to Internet addressing convention.

To GEnie
Address email to jdoe@genie.geis.com.

From Delphi
Use the command **go mail**, then, at the prompt, type **mail** again. Address mail to Internet "jdoe@service.com" (make sure to include the quotation marks).

To Delphi
Address email to jdoe@delphi.com.

From eWorld
Use the command go email, compose your message, address message to jdoe@service.com, and click on the Send Now button.

To eWorld
Address email to jdoe@eworld.com.

From Prodigy
To send email from Prodigy, first download Prodigy's Mail Manager by using the command **jump: mail manager**. Address mail to jdoe@service. com. Mail Manager is currently available for DOS and Windows only. A Mac version is due soon.

To Prodigy
Address email using the addressee's user ID. For John Doe (user ID: ABCD12A), for example, you would address it abcd12a@prodigy.com.

the latest standard. You should be able to get one for less than $100. (Within a year, however, 14,400 bps will feel like a crawl next to faster speeds of 28,800 bps and higher.) Next, you need a communications program to control the modem. This software will probably come free with your modem, your PC, or—if you're going to sign up somewhere—your online service. Otherwise, you can buy it off the shelf for under $25. Finally, you'll want a telephone line (or maybe even two if you plan on tying up the line a couple of hours per day).

15. What kind of account should I get?

You'll definitely want to be able to get email; certainly want membership in at least one commercial service; and probably want wide access to the Internet.

Here are some of your access choices:

Email Gateway

This is the most basic access you can get. It lets you send and receive messages to and from anyone, anywhere, anytime on the Net. Email gateways are often available via work, school, or the other services listed here.

Commercial Services

Priciest but often easiest, these services have a wealth of material for the online Trekker. The big ones are America Online, CompuServe, and Prodigy. Also popular are GEnie, Delphi, and eWorld. Commercial services are cyber city-states. The large ones have more "residents" (members) than most U.S. cities—enough users, in other words, to support lively discussions among their membership, and enough resources to make a visit worthwhile. They generally require their own special software, which you can buy at any local computer store or by calling the numbers listed in this book. (Hint: Look for the frequent starter-kit giveaways.) AOL, CompuServe, Prodigy, Delphi, and GEnie all provide access to many if not all of Usenet's more than 10,000 newsgroups, and through email you can subscribe to any of the mailing-lists.

Delphi provides access to the Internet's IRC channels.

Internet Providers

There are a growing number of full-service Internet providers (which means they offer email, IRC, FTP, telnet, gopher, WWW, and Usenet access), including Your Personal Network (YPN) run by the editors of this book. In practical terms, the Internet enables you to connect with Paramount's Voyager Website, detailed episode guides, or Vulcan discussions. A dial-up SLIP (serial line Internet protocol) or PPP (point-to-point protocol) account is the most fun you can have through a modem. It is a special service offered by some Internet providers that gets you significantly faster access and the ability to use point-and-click programs for Windows, Macintosh, and other platforms.

BBSs

BBSs range from mom-and-pop, hobbyist computer bulletin boards to large professional services. What the small ones lack in size they often make up for in affordability and homeyness. In fact, many users prefer these scenic roads over the Info

IP SOFTWARE

Most "serial" dial-up connections to the Internet treat your fancy desktop computer as a dumb terminal that requires a lot of typed-out commands. An IP connection, whether through a direct hookup like Ethernet or a dial-up over phone lines, turns your computer into a node on the Net instead of a one-step-removed terminal connection. With an IP link, you can run slick point-and-click programs—often many at once. Macintosh users will need MacTCP and, depending on the kind of IP service you're getting, either Interslip or the more advanced MacPPP. Windows users will need the latest version of WinSock. (The latest versions of programs that run over WinSock can be found at ftp.cica.indiana.edu.) Two all-in-one packages of Internet software that you might want to consider for Windows are Chameleon and WinQVT. Your best bet for these programs is to get your online service to give you these programs preconfigured, as the IP address can be mind-boggling to set up.

Highway. Many of the large Trek BBSs (such as Perfect Vision Graphics BBS) are as rich and diverse as the commercial services. BBSs are easy to get started with, and if you find one with Internet access or an email gateway, you'll get the best of local color and global reach. You'll find BBSs throughout this book. You can also locate local BBSs through the Usenet discussion groups alt.bbs.lists and comp.bbs.misc, the BBS forums of the commercial services, and regional and national BBS lists kept in the file libraries of many BBSs. Once you've found a local BBS, contact the sysop to inquire about the echoes (or conferences) you want. These are the BBS world's equivalent to the Internet's newsgroups. With echoes, you're talking not only to the people on your particular BBS, but also to everyone else on a BBS that carries the echo (in other words, a universe of millions). Even if the discussion of your choice is not on their board yet, many sysops are glad to add an echo that a paying customer has requested. Many, if not most, local BBSs now offer Internet email, as well as live chat, file libraries, and some quirky data base, program, or directory unique to their little corner of Cyberspace.

Direct Network Connection

Look, Ma Bell: no phone lines! The direct network connection is the fast track of college students, computer scientists, and a growing number of employees of high-tech businesses. It puts the user right on the Net, bypassing the phone connections. In other words, it's a damned sight faster.

16. By the way, just exactly how do I send an email?

With email, you can write to anyone on a commercial service, Internet site, or Internet-linked BBS, as well as to those people connected to the Net via email gateways, SLIP, and direct-network connections.

Email addresses have a universal syntax called an Internet address. An Internet address is broken down into four parts: the user's name (e.g., peter), the @ symbol, the computer and/or company name, and what kind of Internet address it is: **net** for network, **com** for a commercial enterprise—as

---

MAIL READERS

Eudora
(Mac and Windows) If the host for your email supports the POP protocol, you're in luck. Eudora makes email even easier than it already was. The commercial upgrade to the free version includes message-filtering for automatically sorting incoming mail, but drops the fun dialog messages (if you start typing without an open window, Eudora beeps, "Unfortunately, no one is listening to keystrokes at the moment. You may as well stop typing." The Windows version requires an IP connection; the Mac version does not.

Pine
(UNIX) Menu-driven with a full-screen editor and spell check. Support of the MIME "metamail" format means that you can "attach" binary files within an email.

Elm
(UNIX, DOS, Windows, OS/2) Programmable "user agent" reader that can also sort, forward, and auto-reply. It does not include its own editor.

Mail
(UNIX) As the name suggests, a no-frills mail program.

with Your Personal Network (ypn.com) and America Online (aol.com)—**edu** for educational institutions, **gov** for government sites, **mil** for military facilities, and **org** for nonprofit and other private organizations. For instance, the creative director of this company, a Trek fan extraordinaire who is known to spend his weekends patrolling the streets of New York City's Greenwich Village dressed as a Klingon, would therefore be peter@ypn.com.

DOWNLOADING WEB BROWSERS

Sites at which you can find Web browsers for downloading, sorted by platform:

Windows

CICA—University of Indiana Windows Archive
ftp://ftp.cica.indiana.edu:/pub/pc/win3/winsock/
mirror site is at
ftp://ftp.cdrom.com:/.5/cica/winsock/

NCSA Mosaic for Windows
ftp.NCSA.uiuc.edu:/PC/Mosaic

WinWeb by Einet
ftp.einet.net:/einet/pc/winweb/

Air Mosaic
ftp.spry.com:/AirMosaicDemo/

Internet Works by Booklink (lite edition only)
ftp.booklink.com:/lite/

Netscape for Windows
ftp.mcom.com:/netscape/windows/
mirrored at
ftp.meer.net:/pub/Netscape/Windows/

Mac

MacWeb by Einet
ftp.einet.net:/einet/mac/macweb/

Netscape for Mac
ftp.mcom.com:/netscape/mac/
mirrored at
ftp.meer.net:/pub/Netscape/Mac/

NCSA Mosaic for Mac
ftp.NCSA.uiuc.edu:/Mac/Mosaic/

University of Texas Mac Archive
ftp://ftp.utexas.edu:/pub/mac/tcpip/

---

17. What about the Web, which I've been hearing so much about?

The World Wide Web is a hypertext-based information structure that now dominates Internet navigation. The Web is like a house where every room has doors to every other room—or, perhaps more accurately, like the interconnections in the human brain. Highlighted words in a document link to other documents that reside on the same machine or on a computer anywhere in the world. You only have to click on the appropriate word or phrase—the Web does the rest. With invisible navigation, you can jump from Andrew Tong's TNG page to a complete episode guide, or from a general list of sci-fi resources at Rutgers to a *Quantum Leap* home page. All the while you've FTPed, telnetted, and gophered with nary a thought to case-sensitive Unix commands or addresses.

Your dial-up Internet provider undoubtedly offers programs to access the Web. Lynx and WWW are pretty much the standard offerings. Usually you choose them by typing **lynx** and **www** and then **<return>**. What you'll get is a "page" with some of the text highlighted. These are the links. Choose a link, hit the return key, and you're off.

If you know exactly where you want to go and don't want to meander through the information, you can type a Web page's address, known as a URL (uniform resource locator), many of which you'll find in this book. With the emergence of new and sophisticated so-called Web browsers (with a graphical point-and-click interface) like Mosaic and NetScape, the Web is starting to look the way it was envisioned—pictures, colored icons, and appetizing text layouts. (See "IP Software" sidebar.)

18. And these newsgroups?

The most widely read bulletin boards are a group of some 10,000-plus "newsgroups" on the Internet, collectively known as Usenet. Usenet newsgroups travel the Internet, collecting thousands of messages a day from whoever wants to "post" to them. More than anything, the newsgroups are the collective, if sometimes Babel-like, voice of the

NEWSREADERS

To read the newsgroups, you use a program called a reader, a standard offering on most online services. There are several types of readers—some let you follow message threads; others organize messages chronologically. You can also use a reader to customize the newsgroup menu to include only the newsgroups you're interested in.

Newswatcher
(Mac) Fancy newsreader. Whole newsgroups can be saved locally in a single file, by article or by thread. Multiple binaries can be automatically decoded—making it possible to grab all of alt.binaries.pictures.supermodels with a couple of clicks. Requires an IP connection.

Nuntius
(Mac) Comparable with Newswatcher, except it can multitask. Some people prefer the way Nuntius grabs the full text of threads; others hate waiting to read the first message. Nuntius also stores newsgroup subjects on your computer—this chews up disk space but accelerates searches through old messages. Requires an IP connection.

Trumpet
(Windows) The most popular Windows newsreader. Thread by subject, date, or author. Like Newswatcher, batch binary extraction. WinNV is also widely used. Available by anonymous FTP from ftp.utas. edu.au in /pc/trumpet/win trump. Requires an IP connection. →

Net—everything is discussed here. And we mean *everything*. While delivered over the Internet, the Usenet collection of newsgroups are not technically part of the Internet. In order to read a newsgroup, you need to go where it is stored. Smaller BBSs that have news feeds sometimes store only a couple dozen newsgroups, while most Internet providers offer thousands. (If there's a group missing that you really want, ask your Internet provider to add the newsgroup back to the subscription list.)

The messages in a newsgroup, called "posts," are listed and numbered chronologically—in other words, in the order in which they were posted. Usenet is not distributed from one central location, which means that a posted message does not appear everywhere instantly. The speed of distribution partly depends on how often providers pick up and post Usenet messages. For a message to appear in every corner of the Net, you'll generally have to wait overnight. If you use the newsgroups a lot, you'll start to notice patterns where messages from some machines take five minutes to appear and others take a day.

You can scan a list of messages before deciding to read a particular message. If someone posts a message that prompts responses, the original and all follow-up messages are called a thread. The subject line of subsequent posts in the thread refers to the subject of the original. For example, if you were to post a message with the subject "A Janeway-Kim romance?" in rec.arts.startrek.current, all responses would read "Re: A Janeway-Kim romance?" In practice, however, topics wander off in many directions.

> **Tin**
> (Unix) Intuitive Unix newsreader that works especially well for scanning newsgroups. You can maintain a subscription list, decode binaries, and search the full text of individual newsgroups. With its help files and easy-to-use menus, this is our favorite Unix newsreader.
>
> **nn (Unix) and rn (Unix)**
> Complex newsreaders (Network News and Read News) favored by Unix-heads.
>
> **trn (Unix)**
> Maps subjects within newsgroups.

19. Mailing lists?

Mailing lists are like newsgroups, except that they are distributed over the Internet email system. The fact that messages show up in your mailbox tends to make the discussion group more intimate, as does the proactive act of subscribing. Mailing lists are often more focused, and they're less vulnerable to irreverent and irrelevant contributions.

To subscribe to a mailing list, send an email to the mailing list's subscription address. Often you will need to include very specific information, which you will find in this book. To unsubscribe, send another message to that same address. If the mailing list is of the listserv or majordomo variety, you can usually unsubscribe by sending the command **signoff <listname>** in the message body. If the mailing list instructs you to write a request to subscribe, you will probably need to write a request to unsubscribe.

20. Echoes or conferences?

L ocal BBSs often carry what are known as echoes or conferences, which are part of messaging networks among BBSs. You'll find several of these networks mentioned throughout the book: FidoNet, RelayNet (RIME), TrekNet, TrekkerNet, WarpSpeed, Ilink, and Smartnet. There are hundreds of BBS conferences in Cyberspace, new ones are added daily, and no BBS carries them all; most don't even carry all the conferences on a single network. Check with local BBSs in your area code to see whether they have the network you want. If they do, but they don't carry the conference you're looking for, ask for it. Most sysops will gladly add a conference for a paying customer. The specialty Trek BBS networks such as TrekNet, TrekkerNet, the Trek File Distribution Network (TFDN), and WarpSpeed are carried on BBSs around the world. We've listed a selection of North American BBSs carrying these networks in an appendix in the back of this book. To get a list of BBSs carrying a particular network, find a BBS carrying the network, go to its file library, and download the information packet about the network.

21. And telnet, FTP, gopher? Can you spell it out?

Telnet:

When you telnet, you're logging on to another computer or network somewhere else on the Internet. You then have access to the programs running on the remote computer. If the site is running a library catalog, you can search the catalog. If it's running a BBS, you can chat with others logged on. If it's running a game, you can challenge an opponent.

Anon-FTP:

FTP (file transfer protocol) is a program that allows you to copy a file from another Internet-connected computer to your own. Hundreds of computers on the Internet allow "anonymous FTP" (anon-ftp). In other words, you don't need a unique password to access them. Just type "anonymous" at the user prompt and type your email address at the password prompt. The range of material available is extraordinary—from scripts to free software to pictures to all sorts of trivia lists! More and more, FTP sites are being accessed from the Web, allowing Net users to view documents before retrieving them. To convert an FTP address to a URL, type **ftp://<ftp server><ftp path>**.

Gopher:

A gopher is a program that turns Internet addresses into menu options. Gophers can perform many Internet functions, including telnetting and downloading files. Gopher addresses throughout this book are useful for finding collections of information and collections of telnet links to Trek sites. Gopher addresses require a port number, and most gopher programs auto-

---

TELNETTING

To telnet, follow this simple four-step process:

1. Log on to your Internet site and locate the telnet program. Since telnet is a widely used feature, you will most likely find it in the main menu of your Internet access provider. On Delphi, for example, telnet is available in the main Internet menu. Just type **telnet.**

2. Once you've started the program, you should see a telnet prompt (for instance, telnet> or telnet:). Type **open <telnet address>**, replacing the bracketed text with the address of the machine you want to reach. (Note: Some systems do not require you to type **open**. Also, don't type the brackets.) Let's say you want to go to TrekMUSE, a center for Trek role-playing at the address grimmy.cnidr.org 1701, so after the telnet prompt you would type **open grimmy.cnidr.org 1701**, or just **grimmy.cnidr.org 1701**. Some telnet addresses do not have port numbers such as the "1701" in our example.   →

matically default to the standard setting of 70 unless otherwise instructed. In this book, any deviations from the standard port number are included in gopher addresses.

22. Any suggestions for first stops on my journey through the world of online Trek?

Well, you might want to start with the sites listed on the first page of the first section, the hubsites to the *Star Trek* universe. Most of these are collections of Trek links, and if you spend some time rooting around you should be able to find a little bit of everything—from the Ferengi Rules of Acquistion to a huge collections of original series soundclips.

3. The telnet program will connect you to the remote computer—in our example, the TrekMUSE server. Once you're connected, you'll see a prompt. Type the remote computer's log-in information as listed in the *Net Trek* entry. The prompt may be as simple as **login** followed by another prompt for a password, or it may ask for information like a character's name, a gender, or the type of creature you'd like to play. If no log-in is needed, the *Net Trek* entry will not list one. Oh, and you may be asked about the type of terminal you're using. If you're unsure, vt-100 is a safe bet.

4. You're logged in. Now just follow the instructions on the screen, which will differ with every telnet site.

23. I keep seeing this TOS. What is it—some sort of weird alien?

No, it's a standard abbreviation. There are many of these abbreviations used throughout this book: UFP (United Federation of Planets), FTL (faster-than-light travel), SFB (Star Fleet Battles), TOS (*Star Trek*, the original series), TAS (*Star Trek*, the animated series), TNG (*Star Trek: The Next Generation*), DS9 (*Star Trek: Deep Space Nine*), VOY (*Star Trek: Voyager*).

24. So, how does the book work?

If you know what kind of Trek information you need, turn to the *Net Trek* index, where every subject and site in the book is listed alphabetically. Of course, you can browse *Net Trek* at your leisure, checking out fan bios, chat listings, and special features as you go.

The book is divided into eight sections:

- Trek Universe
- Trek Phenomenon
- The Original Series
- The Next Generation
- Deep Space Nine
- Voyager
- Real Space
- Genre: Other Sci-Fi

Each part is broken down by subject. Under Universe, you'll find categories on Klingons and Trek Technology; Real Space includes NASA sites and collections of space-photos; and Genre has dozens of other sci-fi series.

The middle sections of the books, those devoted to individual series, are slightly different in their organization. Though they do include ordinary subject pages—The Next Generation has sections on the show's cast, as well as a page on the *Star Trek: Generations* feature film—they also include extensive episode guides.

All entries in *Net Trek* have a name, description, and address. The site name appears first in bold-face. If the entry is a mailing list, "(ml)" immediately follows; if a newsgroup, "(ng)"; and if a BBS, "(bbs)." The description of the site follows.

HOW TO DOWNLOAD

How do I download from a commercial service?
The download command on each of the commercial services may differ slightly depending on the type of computer you use, but in most instances file downloads work as follows:

On **America Online**, once you locate the file you want, select the file name so that it's highlighted. Then select one of two buttons: **download now**, or **download later**. If you choose **download later**, the file will be added to a list of files, all of which you can download when you're done with your America Online session.

On **CompuServe**, if you're browsing a library list (using CompuServe's Information Manager), you can highlight a file you want and select the **retrieve** button to download it immediately. If you want to download it later, select the box next to the file name, then select **yes** when you leave the forum and a window will appear that says download marked files? (If you don't have Information Manager, type **down** and **[return]** at the prompt following the file description.)

On **Delphi**, after you read a file description in the file or database area, there are four commands available—next, **down**, xm, and list. Type down and **[return]** to download the file.

→

After the description, complete address information is provided. A red check mark identifies the name of the network. When you see an arrow, this means that you have another step ahead of you, such as typing a command, searching for a file, subscribing to a mailing list, or typing a Web address (also called a URL). Additional check marks indicate the other networks through which the site is accessible; triple dots indicate another address on the same network; and more arrows mean more steps.

An address is context-sensitive—in other words, it follows the logic of the particular network. So, if the entry includes a Website, the address following the arrow would be a URL that you would type on the command line of your Web browser. If it is a mailing list, the address would be an email address followed by instructions on the exact form of the email message. An entry that includes an FTP, telnet, or gopher address would provide a log-in sequence and a directory path or menu path when necessary.

In a commercial service address, the arrow is followed by the service's transfer word (e.g., keyword, go word, or jump word), which will take you to the site. More arrows lead you along a path to the specific area on the site. IRC addresses indicate what you must type to get to the channel you want once you've connected to the IRC program. The name of a newsgroup entry or BBS echo is also its address, so there is no address information other than the network for these types of sites. (You'll locate the newsgroup or echo at your access provider or BBS.)

On **GEnie**, after you've chosen a file to download, select download a file from the RoundTable library menu. When you see the prompt enter the download request: type the file name and **[return]**. At the next prompt, which asks you to confirm your download, type **d** and **[return]** to download the file. At the next prompt, you'll be asked to choose a download protocol; your best choice, if available with your communications software, is Z-modem (number 4), so type **4** and **[return]**.

How do I download from the Internet?
Using FTP (file transfer protocol). Internet FTP sites open to the public (known as anonymous FTP sites) appear throughout this book, offering dozens of financial and business documents.

To FTP:
1. Log in to your Internet site. Then start the FTP program at that site—in most cases, by typing **ftp** or by choosing it from an Internet menu.
2. When you see the FTP prompt, type **open <ftp. address>** to connect to the other computer. The Star Trek Stories Archive, for example, is at the address ftp.cis.ksu.edu, so you would type **open ftp.cis.ksu.edu**. (By the way, sometimes you'll be asked for just the FTP site name, which means you wouldn't type **open**.)
3. Most FTP sites offer "anonymous login," which means you won't need a personal account or password to access the files.

→

25. What about the cat?

Some people hate cats. But some people love cats. We love cats. Why? Well, we recognize their talents—purring, catching mice, and posing Trek trivia questions. And in that spirit, we've created a trivia feature overseen by our feline mascot, Spot. Each time you see the beast, he'll appear above a trivia box. Try to answer the questions. Then try to answer them while imagining that you have a hair ball. And then, check your answers against the answers in the back of the book (page 359). Hair balls are distracting, aren't they?

26. What about the Episode Guides?

While Trek characters, alien species, and 24th century technology have their fan followings, most Trekkers also have their favorite episodes. On the Net, you can collect episode-specific memorabilia, such as scans of the Doomsday machine, soundclips of Locutus from "The Best of Both Worlds," transcripts of "Ode to Spot" from "Schisms," a review of "All Good Things," and a copy of an archived discussion about *Deep Space Nine*'s "The Maquis." *Net Trek* offers episode guides to TOS, TNG, and DS9, and lists Net resources under many of the episodes. These guides are not comprehensive, but they'll get you started on your hunt. As you go, you'll probably want to add to the listings for your favorite episode, but we hope our list is a good beginning.

When you connect to an anonymous FTP machine, you will be asked for your name with the prompt **name:**. Type **anonymous** after the prompt. Next you'll be asked for your password with the prompt **password:**. Type your email address.

4. Once you're logged in to an FTP site, you can change directories by typing **cd <directory name>**. For example, the Star Trek Stories Archive at ftp.cis.ksu.edu is in /pub/ alt.startrek.creative/stories. After login, type **cd /pub /alt.startrek.creative/ stories** to change to the directory. (To move back up through the directory path you came down, you type **cdup** or **chdirup**.) You must move up one directory at a time.

5. To transfer files from the FTP site to your "home" or "files" directory at your Internet site, use the get command. For example, in the Star Trek Stories Archive, you may run across a must-read parody of the "The Inner Light" with the file name "utterdarkness.txt". Retrieve it by typing the phrase at the prompt **get outerdarkness.txt** and **[return]**. The distinction between the upper- and lowercase in directory and file names is important. Type a lowercase letter when you should have typed uppercase and you'll leave empty-handed.

27. I'm familiar with your normal address style. The episode guide looks different. Am I crazy?

Maybe, but you're right to notice that these addresses are different. In the episode guide, we have devised a a shorthand address system for easy reference. Each address is presented in abbreviated form and keyed to a list of full addresses that appears both on page 21 in the FAQ and in the appendix of the book. Use this master key to construct a full address.

Here are two examples:

1. Tim Lynch's review of the DS9 episode "The Storyteller" is listed with the address ***anon-ftp* <address 24>→strytllr.rev**. This is not the full address, but a base address followed by unique episode information. The full address can be constructed by locating base address 24 in the master key, and then appending the episode-specific segment (strytllr.rev). The full Net address that results from this combination (*anon-ftp* ftp.coe.montana.edu→/pub/mirrors/.startrek/Tim_Lynch_stuff/ds9-1→strytllr.rev) is the exact address of the summary for "The Storyteller."

2. Follow a similar procedure for World Wide Web Uniform Resource Locators (URLs). For instance, Mike "Vidiot" Brown's summary of TNG's "Angel One" is listed with the address ***www* <address 1a>angel1.syn.html**. This is not the full Website address, but the full address can be created by combining the master key's address 1a (http://www.ugcs.caltech.edu:80/~werdna/sttng/synopsis/) with the unique information given in the episode guide address (angel1.syn.html). The full URL that results from this combination (http://www.ugcs.caltech.edu:80/~werdna/sttng/synopsis/angel1.syn.html) is the exact address of the "Angel One" summary.

ADDRESS KEY — Replace the code in the episode guides with the corresponding address

Code	Address
address 1a	http://www.ugcs.caltech.edu:80/~werdna/sttng/synopsis/
address 1b	http://ringo.ssn.flinders.edu.au/vidiot/
address 2	ftp.coe.montana.edu→/pub/mirrors/.startrek/Tim_Lynch_stuff/tng2
address 3	ftp.coe.montana.edu→/pub/mirrors/.startrek/Tim_Lynch_stuff/tng3
address 4	ftp.coe.montana.edu→/pub/mirrors/.startrek/Tim_Lynch_stuff/tng4
address 5	ftp.coe.montana.edu→/pub/mirrors/.startrek/Tim_Lynch_stuff/tng5
address 6	ftp.coe.montana.edu→/pub/mirrors/.startrek/Tim_Lynch_stuff/tng6
address 7	ftp.coe.montana.edu→/pub/mirrors/.startrek/Tim_Lynch_stuff/tng7
address 8	chop.isca.uiowa.edu 8338→General Information→Star Trek Reviews→Star Trek: The Next Generation→Next Generation: Season 2 (1988-1989)
address 9	chop.isca.uiowa.edu 8338→General Information→Star Trek Reviews→Star Trek: The Next Generation→Next Generation: Season 3 (1989-1990)
address 10	chop.isca.uiowa.edu 8338→General Information→Star Trek Reviews→Star Trek: The Next Generation→Next Generation: Season 4 (1990-1991)
address 11	chop.isca.uiowa.edu 8338→General Information→Star Trek Reviews→Star Trek: The Next Generation→Next Generation: Season 5 (1991-1992)
address 12	chop.isca.uiowa.edu 8338→General Information→Star Trek Reviews→Star Trek: The Next Generation→Next Generation: Season 6 (1992-1993)
address 13	chop.isca.uiowa.edu 8338→General Information→Star Trek Reviews→Star Trek: The Next Generation→Next Generation: Season 7 (1993-1994)
address 14	http://www.ugcs.caltech.edu:80/~werdna/sttng/tlynch/
address 15	http://ringo.ssn.flinders.edu.au:80/trekker/tng/1/
address 16	http://ringo.ssn.flinders.edu.au:80/trekker/tng/2/
address 17	http://ringo.ssn.flinders.edu.au:80/trekker/tng/3/
address 18	http://ringo.ssn.flinders.edu.au:80/trekker/tng/4/
address 19	http://ringo.ssn.flinders.edu.au:80/trekker/tng/5/
address 20	http://ringo.ssn.flinders.edu.au:80/trekker/tng/6/
address 21	http://ringo.ssn.flinders.edu.au:80/trekker/tng/7/
address 22	sfrt2→Text and Graphics Library→*Download a file:*
address 23	TFDN Fact Files→*Download a file:*
address 24	ftp.coe.montana.edu→/pub/mirrors/.startrek/Tim_Lynch_stuff/ds9-1
address 25	ftp.coe.montana.edu→/pub/mirrors/.startrek/Tim_Lynch_stuff/ds9-2
address 26	ftp.coe.montana.edu→/pub/mirrors/.startrek/Tim_Lynch_stuff/ds9-3
address 27	chop.isca.uiowa.edu:8338→General Information→Star Trek Reviews→Star Trek: Deep Space Nine→Deep Space Nine: Season 1 (1992-1993)
address 28	chop.isca.uiowa.edu 8338→General Information→Star Trek Reviews→Star Trek: Deep Space Nine→Deep Space Nine: Season 2 (1993-1994)
address 29	chop.isca.uiowa.edu 8338→General Information→Star Trek Reviews→Star Trek: Deep Space Nine→Deep Space Nine: Season 3 (1994-1995)
address 30	http://ringo.ssn.flinders.edu.au:80/trekker/ds9/1/
address 31	http://ringo.ssn.flinders.edu.au:80/trekker/ds9/2/
address 32	http://ringo.ssn.flinders.edu.au:80/trekker/ds9/3/
address 33	ftp.cis.ksu.edu→/pub/pictures/jpg/Startrek
address 34	lajkonik.cyf-kr.edu.pl→/agh/reserve/gifs/startrek
address 35	smaug.cs.hope.edu→/pub/sound/trek

28. I'm a die-hard Trekker, but I do have other interests. What else is on the Net?

Try *Net Guide*, *Net Games*, *Net Chat*, and *Net Money*! You should find them in your bookstore right beside *Net Trek*. And keep an eye out for *Net Sports*, *Net Tech*, and *Net Music*—they're coming soon.

PART 1

TREK UNIVERSE

Trek hubsites

Every Trek fan has his or her own mission. What episode of DS9 is airing next week?

Which episode of TOS aired closest to my birthdate? Where can I get full account of the science of warp speed? How can I compile a list of planets visited by the *Enterprise*? Are there any nude photos of my favorite *Trek* stars? Whatever your needs, they're met on the Net. And the best places to start looking are these hubsites, which offer the best overview of Trek resources online. Check out the huge list of resources for TNG, DS9, and *Voyager* at **Vidiot's Home Page**. Keep in touch with the party line with **Paramount Pictures Star Trek Home Page**. Lose yourself in the endless discussions, libraries, and role-playing games in AOL's **Star Trek Club**. And as you continue on your five-year mission, remember to return to these sites—they're updated regularly and make every attempt to accommodate new additions to the online Trek universe.

On the Net
Across the board

Paramount Pictures Star Trek Home Page See what paramount is planning for the Net universe.

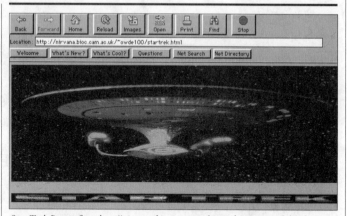

Star Trek Page—from http://nirvana.bioc.cam.ac.uk/~owde100/startrek.html

This page links to all official Paramount resources on the Internet, including the *Voyager* Website. ✓**INTERNET**→*www* http://startrek. paramount.com/

Science Fiction and Fantasy RoundTable 2 The trio of GEnie RoundTables devoted to the science-fiction genre houses some of the best sci-fi discussion in Cyberspace. *Star Trek* fans should transport directly to the second RoundTable.

Twice a week there are live Trek discussions (check out the schedule displayed when you enter), and the message board has categories for each of the current season's episodes, many popular *Trek* novels, each of the *Star Trek* movies, the main *Star Trek* characters and actors, the current year's conventions, and an assortment of other Trek topics ranging from "Klingon Opera" to "The Wormhole Effect."

Be prepared to run into some big names from the Trek universe. Wil Wheaton, who played Wesley Crusher, used to be a regular here. *Trek* graphic designers and authors of the *Star Trek Encyclopedia*, Michael and Denise Okuda, check in fairly often. Armin Shimerman (Quark), Nichelle Nichols (Uhura), George Takei (Sulu), Carel Struyken (Mr. Hom), John de Lancie (Q) and Walter Koenig (Checkov) have all been guests. Some still have accounts.

Tim Dehass, who has written for TNG and *Voyager*, and Dennis Bailey and Lisa White, both writers for TNG, have hosted conference discussions. ✓**GENIE**→*keyword* sfrt2

Star Trek And Guinan thought the Nexus was hard to leave.... With more than a hundred active topics, this is the hub of Trek talk on CompuServe. Suggest that Picard is religious and someone will start citing episodes and scenes where Picard appears to reject the idea of a supreme being. Someone else will mention though, that Picard came from a traditional French family and is probably

Catholic. Soon, another forum member will pipe in, "perhaps by the 24th century, *traditional* French families may not be Catholic."

In other topics, people are trying to find out where and when shows are airing, searching for role-playing games, asking technical questions, reviewing the last episode of DS9, and debating whether or not to forgo cooking entirely and just use a replicator. The *Star Trek* library has a phenomenal amount of Trek images, sound clips, episode guides, FAQs, timelines, interviews and trivia questions. Paradise! ✓**COMPU-SERVE**→*go* sfmedia→*Libraries or* Messages→Star Trek

Star Trek These well-organized areas offer promise—but they're as deserted as Delta Vega, the desolate planet from TOS's "Where No Man Has Gone Before." The Captain's Log section of this forum holds a small selection of FAQs and lists, while the United Federation Library stores images, discussion archives, the newsletter, and other fan-written material. Beam them in, eWorld! ✓**EWORLD**

→sf→Star Trek

Star Trek Information on each *Trek* series, with episode guides, cast information and FAQs for TOS, TNG, DS9 and *Voyager.* ✓**INTERNET**→*www* http://web.city. ac.uk/~cc103/startrek.html

Star Trek BB Young Trek fans and middle-aged mothers, techies and role-players, Brent femmes and Wesley haters—they all have their niche on this bulletin board. Small social clubs have formed around Trek concepts and characters, and members alternate between speaking in character (as a Cardassian or a Trill, for instance) and as themselves. The board has topics for each of the series, a large number of role-playing groups, a social arena (Ten Forward), Trek computer and board games, convention news, and more. ✓**PRODI-GY**→*jump* star trek bb

Star Trek Club One of AOL's most active areas, with several live Trek trivia games each week, a monthly club newsletter, new stories submitted daily by aspiring Trek writers, and passionate dis-

cussions about anything Trek—from aliens to spaceships to DS9 to the Prime Directive. The Club menu features a schedule for the current series, a list of upcoming conventions, a schedule of Club activities, a message board, file libraries, and The Bridge (live chat). If you have any questions, transport to the Promenade and visit the Questions/Help/Datat 1701D topic. ✓**AMERICA ONLINE**→*keyword* trek

Star Trek Newsgroups (rec. arts.startrek*) (ng) It's virtually impossible to surf Usenet without slamming into Trek references, injokes, and cross-posts, whether you're lurking in sci.rocketry or slumming in alt.sex. If you're going to drop a name, you can't go wrong with Kirk, Picard, or (in case you're striving for an air of contempt) Wesley Crusher. And Trek one-liners—"He's dead, Jim," "Beam me up, Scotty," "Make it so!" and "Engage!"—are veritable Usenet mantras. If there is such a thing as a collective Usenet unconscious, then *Trek* has shaped its archetypes.

The heart of Net Trekdom is the rec.arts.startrek.* news hierarchy, which was spun out of the single burgeoning rec.arts.startrek newsgroup in December 1991. The hierarchy isn't organized in a particularly intuitive fashion: there is no rec.arts.startrek.tng, for instance—as much as logic would seem to call for one. Instead, there are two primary groups: rec.arts. startrek.current and rec.arts. startrek.misc.

The former includes discussion of first-run and forthcoming *Trek* shows, books, movies, and paraphernalia; the latter hosts discussion of Trek in general, including remembrances of old *Trek* movies, post-game analysis of old series, and so on. Trekkers (not *Trekkies*

Screenshot from http://www.ftms.com:80/vidiot/

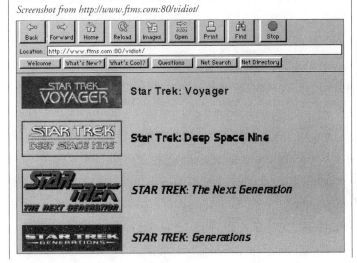

—a quick peek at Otto "Hack-Man" Heuer's rec.arts.startrek. misc FAQ will explain the difference) defend this confusing setup by noting that all the various series, films, novels, and so forth—from TOS to *Voyager*—are facets of the same seamless world. Why split them apart?

So where does discussion about TNG belong, for instance? Well, up until last year, when the series was cancelled, TNG discussion would have landed in either rec.arts.startrek.current or rec. arts.startrek.misc, depending on whether the topic in question was less than four months old. Now that the series no longer releases new episodes, TNG discussion belongs exclusively in rec.arts. startrek.misc (unless you're talking about a new movie based on TNG characters, in which case you can go ahead and post to rec.arts. startrek.current). Does this sound about as straightforward as a Ferengi prenuptial agreement to you? Indeed, Jim.

Frankly, very few people actually take the time to figure out where their posts belong, and most long-running threads are cross-posted to both groups. When in doubt, post wherever you feel comfortable, until someone tells you you shouldn't. For more advanced Net Trekkers, the hierarchy also includes rec.arts. startrek.fandom (fan conventions, politics, and anti-Paramount insurgence), rec.arts.startrek.tech (brain-bending flights of physics and fancy), rec.arts.startrek.info (FAQs, announcements, and press releases) and rec.arts.startrek.reviews (intensely critical analyses of current and past episodes, books, and movies). The last two are moderated; a group overseer filters noise and crank posts.

Avid Trekkers can also find quirkier, non-rec.arts.startrek* fix-

STARNOTES

MONEY IN THE FUTURE

TOS "Catspaw": Lt.(Cmdr?) DeFalco says "I'll bet credits to navy beans we can punch a hole in it."

TOS "Errand of Mercy": Kirk says that the Federation spent a lot of money on their training and it's time they got a return on their investment.

TOS "The Doomsday Machine" (possibly also "Balance of Terror"): Kirk says "Scotty, you've earned your pay for the week." He says the same to Sulu in "The Apple".

TOS "Amok Time": Kirk says "Do you know how much Starfleet has invested in you?", to which Spock begins to reply "twenty-two thousand, two hun...". Might be hours, exercises, food quantity but seems to be money.

ST4: Kirk tells the female lead that there is no money in the future (but he might just mean that they don't have U.S. dollars, or any "hard" cash, which is what she was enquiring about).

TNG "Encounter at Farpoint": Bev Crusher buys a roll of cloth and has her account on the ship billed.

TNG "The Price": There is a bidding war going on for the use of a wormhole, and Picard mentions how much toll the Ferengi might charge if they get the rights to use that wormhole.

TNG "Peak Performance": Riker is playing strategema against Kolrami. Worf whispers to Riker that he has bet a "sizeable amount" on Riker in the ship's pool. He may have made a similar comment about Tasha Yar in "Skin of Evil".

TNG "Unification II": Riker is trying to get info out of the piano player. She said to "drop a few coins in the jar" for info; Riker says he doesn't carry money.

DS9: On the promenade, people can be seen gambling, buying time in the holosuite, buying food, buying drinks, etc. Also, for large cash purchases, the monitary unit seems to be gold-pressed latinum.

DS9 "Past Prologue": The Cardassian merchant wants Bashir to buy a new suit.

—from **rec.arts.startrek.misc FAQ**

es in the alt hierarchy—alt.sex. fetish.startrek, alt.sexy.bald.captains, alt.wesley.crusher.die.die.die among them. Less regimented and more tongue-in-cheek, the alt.trek groups are even more fun than playing hide-the-hairpiece with William Shatner, though they're just as likely to get you a blast in the butt with a phaser set on FLAME. But who cares? Toss on your asbestos away-team gear, beam yourself down, and engage! ✓USENET

Star Trek SIG Until recently this popular Trek hangout on Delphi was a custom forum, owned and run by a Delphi member and, as a result, hidden from view of forum browsers. But Trekkers are used to being underestimated and then bursting onto the scene—and so they did on Delphi. The *Star Trek SIG* is now a main option on the Entertainment menu, and while the Trek archives are unimpressive and sparse, the nightly live Trek talk and steady message-board discussions form an active center for *Trek*, *Babylon 5*, and sci-fi fans in general. The SIG also features direct links to several Usenet and Internet Trek sites. ✓DELPHI→*go* ent sta

The Star Trek Page Links to other Net sites for each of the series, including TOS. There are also links to alien information, ship pictures and descriptions, and large sound and picture archives. ✓INTERNET→*www* http://nirvana.bioc.cam.ac.uk/~owde100/startrek.html

To Boldly Go ...where every Netter wants to go—a site full of *Star Trek* pictures, parodies (several of Commander Riker), and resources. Choose the wormhole option to link to other great Trek Websites. ✓INTERNET→*www* http://

The Star Trek Archive
Updated: Jan 13, 1995

The Star Trek Archive—http://www.ee.umanitoba.ca/~djc/startrek/

www.ksu.edu/~jgs/startrek.html

TrekkerNet With about Twenty sci-fi conferences, this BBS Network is an active discussion center for Trekkers. Join a role-playing game. Get information about upcoming conventions. Read reviews of the latest *Voyager* episode. Debate the decision to use the emotion chip in Data. To participate, find a local BBS carrying Trekker Net echoes (see the appendix on page 360). ✓CHECK LOCAL BULLETIN BOARD SYSTEMS

TrekNet *Star Trek* is one of the most popular topics and board themes in the BBS world and TrekNet unites hundreds of these boards through shared message-based discussions known as TrekNet echoes (or conferences).

The network offers separate echoes devoted to discussions of the Ferengi, Klingons, Romulans, Bajorans, and Vulcans, as well as echoes for picking apart *Trek* books and sharing experiences in Trek clubs—particularly Starfleet. Post a message on the Vulcan echo on your local BBS and TrekNet BBSs across the world will carry

your comment. TrekNet is, in fact, as popular in Europe, Australia and Japan as it is in the U.S.

Three Trek fan clubs—Starfleet, Starfleet Command, and The Federation—have their own echoes on TrekNet, which only members of the fan clubs may read. To participate, find a local BBS carrying TrekNet echoes (see the appendix on page 360). ✓CHECK LOCAL BULLETIN BOARD SYSTEMS

Vidiot Home Page Wouldn't you like to own a house next to Rick Berman or have a friend who worked on the set of *Voyager*? Ahh, for the inside scoop on storylines! Mike Brown's Trek pages often reveal news about upcoming episodes and Paramount decisions, and may be the closest you can get to an inside source.

Each *Trek* series has its own page, with casting news, airdates, images, and episode summaries. If you have a graphical Web browser, be sure to check out the image pages—especially those for the premier episode of *Voyager* and the movie *Generations*. The images take a while to load, but they're well worth it. ✓INTERNET→*www* http://www.ftms.com:80/vidiot/

WarpSPEED Less than a year old, this all-Trek BBS network has a large European membership (the main Hub is in Ireland) and more than fifty conferences. True, the Alien Foods and the Ferengi conferences aren't exactly buzzing, but the Q Continuum, *Deep Space Nine* and the Play-by-Mail conferences are. The range of Trek topics is broad—the Gamma Quadrant for instance, has its own conference—and if it attracts more people, it'll be a Trekkers mecca. To participate, find a local BBS carrying WarpSPEED echoes (see the appendix on page 360). ✓CHECK LOCAL BULLETIN BOARD SYSTEMS

Archives

D. Joseph Creighton's Star Trek Archive A sizeable Web archive that includes ASCII art, mini-FAQs, text descriptions of all *Star Trek* ships, and a wealth of material on technical matters such as relativity, FTL travel, and subspace physics. The archive links to several major Trek sites in Cyberspace. ✓**INTERNET**→*www* http://www.ee.umanitoba.ca/~djc/startrek/

German Star Trek Archive A large collection of Trek FAQs, mini-FAQs and lists (all written in English). The collection covers snafus, alien lists, tech questions, Kirk's loves, transporters, spoilers, filks, and more. All files are compressed with .gz format. ✓**INTERNET**→*anon-ftp* quepasa.cs.tu-berlin.de→/pub/doc/movies+tv-series/StarTrek

Star Trek Archives Lists, lists, lists, including other roles held by Trek characters, books on tape, Trek worlds and locations, ships, TOS and TNG novels, and comic

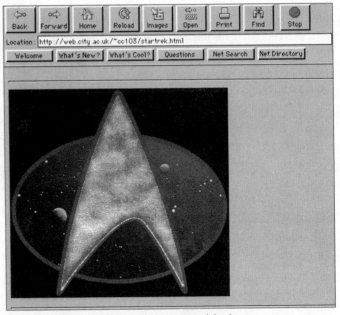

Screenshot from http://web.city.ac.uk/~cc103/startrek.html

books. ✓**INTERNET**→*gopher* gopher. univ-lyon1.fr→Usenet (FAQs [news. answers], stats, docs,..)→Usenet FAQs by newsgroup name→rec→rec.arts.startrek

Star Trek Gopher An impressive Trek gopher that includes a Klingon vocabulary list, a complete set of rules for the Trek drinking game, and lists of stardates, ships, timelines and romances. Not to be missed. ✓**INTERNET**→*gopher* dds. dds.nl→De Bibliotheek→boeken→Mass Media→Star Trek

Star Trek Info Archive Informational postings and announcements about *Trek*, including new sites on the Net, press releases, casting credits, and informative FAQ lists. The articles posted to rec.arts.startrek.info are stored in the format month.day.year.article_number.Z, where article_number is the number of the posting on that particular day. In other words, the fifth article post-

ed on the 20th of February, 1990, would be in the file named 02.20. 90.5.Z. ✓**INTERNET**→*anon-ftp* scam. berkeley.edu→/pub/misc/trek-info

Star Trek Related WWW Sites An index of Websites carrying *Star Trek* resources. Listings are linked to the sites. ✓**INTERNET**→*www* http://gagme.wwa.com/~boba/trek. html

The Trek File Distribution Network In *Star Trek V*, the crew searches for God. On TFDN, you'll find deity in the form of hundreds of Trek-related files. With Trek tech FAQs, parodies, press releases, games and graphics, this is perhaps the ultimate Trek online resource. Each BBS stores the hundreds of continuously updated files in a set of TFDN libraries—usually identified as such with a TFDN prefix. And most BBSs that belong to TFDN allow nonsubscribers to login and download files. So, beam on over to your local board. To participate, find a local BBS carrying TFDN echoes (see the appendix on page 360). ✓ CHECK LOCAL BULLETIN BOARD SYSTEMS

UK Star Trek Archive A small Trek archive with trivia lists, Mark Holtz's list of lists for *Trek* series, and back issues of the European Trek newsletter *Engage*. ✓ INTERNET→*anon-ftp* ftp.doc.ic.ac.uk→ /pub/media/tv/collections/tardis /us/sci-fi/StarTrek/

United Federation Library A library of Trek-related images, discussion archives, icons, ship lists, and episode guides. ✓ EWORLD→ sf→Star Trek→Captain's Log→Conventions List

The World of Star Trek For such an inclusively titled page, this site is short on offerings: Paramount's Short History of *Star Trek*, the Trek FAQ, information on DS9 and TNG, and one link to the monumental Salzburg site. ✓ INTERNET→ *www* http://www.ee.surrey.ac.uk/ Personal/StarTrek.html

FAQs

Captain's Log Lists, guides, and notices eWorld moderators deem to be priority information: DS9 episodes, conventions, character bios, and the Ferengi Rules of Acquisition. ✓ EWORLD→sf→Star Trek →Captain's Log

Holtz' Lists of Lists Mark Holtz has compiled extensive FAQs for *The Original Series*, *The Next Generation*, the *Trek* movies, and *Deep Space Nine*. Also: guides to *The Simpsons* and *Quantum Leap*. ✓ INTERNET→*anon-ftp* ftp.netcom.com →/pub/mhotlz→lol_0494. zip

List of Periodic Postings to rec.arts.startrek * A hypertext version of a list of Trek-related FAQs that often appear on the newsgroup. Several of the list names are linked to sites where the document can be read or retrieved. ✓ INTERNET→*www* http://www. cosy.sbg.ac.at/ftp/pub/trek/lists/ listolis.html

Otto "HACK-MAN" Heur's FAQ Packet With close to 20 mini FAQS covering aliens, snafus, spoilers, stardates, and other topics, this is a must-have collection of Trek information. ✓ TFDN →TFDN Fact Files→*Download a file:* FAQL0694.ZIP ✓ INTERNET→ *anon-ftp* ftp.cis.ksu.edu→/pub/alt. startrek.creative/misc→Heuer. FAQLs.zip

rec.arts.startrek.info (ng) A moderated collection of information about *Star Trek*, including press releases, new episode synopses, and interesting rumors. ✓ USENET

rec.arts.startrek.misc FAQ What are the episodes in which Picard surrenders the ship? What are the forms of money used in the future? And where can you go in the world of back-alley video to see your favorite *Star Trek* actress in the buff? These questions and others are answered. ✓ INTERNET …→*www* http://www.ee.surrey. ac.uk/Personal/STOther/FAQ.html …→*gopher* quepasa.cs.tu-berlin. de→/pub/doc/movies+tv-series/ StarTrek/FAQs→current.gz

Strek-L FAQ Though Strek-L no longer exists, the FAQ (Dec. 1992) still carries useful information: Answers to ten questions, including what "pips" means; how to get in touch with Paramount; and how to sell a *Trek* script or novelization. ✓ INTERNET→*anon-ftp* ftp.cis.ksu.edu →/pub/alt.startrek.creative/info→ strek-l.startrek.faq.zip

TFDN—Star Trek Facts/Info A massive library with an extensive collection of episode reviews from Tim Lynch and Ted Brengle, book reviews, back issues of AOL's Trek newsletter *Dateline*, FAQs and other files, such as a transcript of Avery Brooks's appearance on Prodigy, an explanation of timeloops in *Star Trek* and Mark Holtz's Star Trek List of Lists. All TFDN BBSs carry the same items, though the library sometimes has a different name. ✓**TFDN**→ TFDN Fact Files

More Trek sites

List of Star Trek Websites Divided into major and minor sites, this page lists Trek resources across the Net, including the official Star Trek: Generations home page and the Terry Farrell Internet Fan Club. ✓**INTERNET**→*www* http://gagme.wwa.com/~boba/trek.html

Star Trek Gopher A group of excellent *Star Trek* gopher links, including some to Trek reviews, parodies, fan fiction, TOS sounds, and FAQs. ✓**INTERNET** ...→*gopher* gopher.cs.ttu.edu→Entertainment→Star Trek ...→*gopher* gopher.ocf.berkeley.edu→OCF Online Library →Star_Trek

Star Trek Links This straightforward list of Trek links includes the TrekMUSE web gateway, the Klingon Language Institute's home page, the *Star Trek* page at Dublin City University, Judy Fabian's pictures and sounds archive, and all the Trek newsgroups. ✓**INTERNET**→*www* http://www.maths.tcd.ie/hyplan/s/sj/startrek.html#links

Jellinek's Star Trek Page With a Shatner for every Stewart and more than enough Nimoy to go around, this site includes links to sounds, pictures, episode guides, stories, parodies, comics, and quotes. ✓**INTERNET** ...→*www* http://www.cosy.sbg.ac.at/rec/startrek/star_trek_resources.html ...→*www* http://grimmy.cnidr.org/star_trek_resources.html

---

CYBERTREKKERS

Brigitte Jellinek
Age 24; Salzburg, Austria

Created a formidable Trek Website, Jellinek's Star Trek Page (http://www.cosy.sbg.ac.at/rec/startrek), and spends 30+ hrs/week online

Favorite Characters: Q, Data, Tasha Yar, Ensign Ro, Guinan (or anyone who can make Picard uneasy)

Favorite Episode: "Q Who?" (TNG)

Mission statement: "I used to watch TOS as a child on German TV. It's called 'Raumschiff Enterprise' over here. I've always been a big fan of Mr. Spock. Nowadays I only watch TOS for the comical value. *The Next Generation*, and access to English language TV (via satellite) turned me into a Trekker. I never watch *Trek* alone, I always invite friends over, and we chat, drink tea, watch *Star Trek*, and chat some more. When TNG is over, we'll probably continue meeting once a week to watch old episodes or one of the Movies.

"'Q Who?' featured the Q, the BORG, and Guinan all on one episode—and one of Picard's best speeches. This is probably the closest to classical science fiction *Star Trek* ever got. Don't get me wrong—I like the non-sci-fi episodes too ('Deja Q' for example). But this episode has all the best aspects of *Star Trek*. I also like all the major Picard episodes: 'Best of Both Worlds,' 'Chain of Command,' 'Inner Light,' 'Darmok,' 'Tapestry.' But then I'm always disappointed that after being BORGified and deBORGified, tortured and brainwashed, having been a parent for 20 years, having died....Picard doesn't seem to have changed/grown/learned a thing. Well, that's a TV series for you I guess. I'm a bit doubtful about the whole future of Trek. I don't like *Deep Space 9*, and I haven't seen *Voyager* yet. I don't have any doubts about the future of The Net. It's definitly here to stay and it's getting better every minute. How long will it take until we can meet on the virtual bridge of the *Enterprise* somewhere in cyberspace? Five years? I'm looking forward to that and plan to be part of it when it happens."

Email Address: bjelli@cosy.sbg.ac.at

Trek reference shelf

Throw away your *Webster's*, *Roget's*, and *Bartlett's*, and make room for the reference

guides of the 23rd and 24th centuries. Committed Trek fans *need* their reference materials. Where is the Traveler's homeworld? The answer's waiting in **Star Trek Locations**. Who said "He got turned into a spider and now he has a disease named after him"? **Great Star Trek Quotes** will set your mind at ease. How many stripes does a Starfleet member earn for obtaining the rank of Ambassador? Confirm the fruits of promotion with the **List of Names, Ranks, and Serial Numbers**. And why doesn't Khan Noonian Sing reply to your email? You misspelled his name! Check the **Star Trek Spelling List**.

Location: http://www.ee.umanitoba.ca/~djc/startrek/locations.html

Updated: Jan 24, 1995

Star Trek Locations
by D. Joseph Creighton

Screenshot from http://www.ee.umanitoba.ca./-djc/startrek/locations.html

On the Net

Locations

Range of Type M Planet Characteristics A one-page sheet listing the planetary characteristics of Class M Planets (Earth's class). ✓**TFDN**→TFDN Technical Files→ *Download a file:* PLANETS.ZIP

Star Trek Locations If you find yourself mixing up *Galen IV* and *Galor IV*, if you're confused by *Hansen's Planet* or flummoxed by *Ingraham B*, this is the document for you—a complete atlas to the *Star Trek* universe, with hundreds of planets and interstellar locales,

as well as the episodes or films in which they originally appeared. The Internet sites carry the most updated version of this file. ✓**INTERNET** ...→*www* http://www.ee. umanitoba.ca/~djc/startrek/loca tions.html ...→*anon-ftp* rtfm.mit. edu→/pub/usenet-by-hierarchy/ rec/arts/startrek/misc→STAR_ TREK_LOCATIONS* ...→*gopher* wiretap.spies.com→Wiretap Online Library→Mass Media→Star Trek→ Star Trek Locations ...→*gopher* dds. dds.nl→De Bibliotheek→boeken →Mass Media→Star Trek→Star Trek Locations ✓**GENIE**→*keyword* sfrt2 →Text and Graphics Library→ *Download a file:* 977

WS_Gamma (echo) What's hap-

pening in the Gamma Quadrant? There was a time when the Gamma Quadrant was a big deal—sort of like going to the moon for 1969 earthlings. Now, every DS9 character is hopping a ride through the wormhole. This exotic area of space just isn't inspiring a lot of discussion. ✓**WARPSPEED**

Quotes

Great Star Trek Quotes What makes a great show? Characters, of course. Plots. And memorable quotes. This site collects unforgettable utterances from TOS, TNG, DS9 and all the *Star Trek* films. "Earth. Hitler. 1938." and "All good things come to an end" are here, but as of yet there's no "Khaaaannnnn!" ✓**INTERNET**→ *www* http://www.maths.tcd.ie/hyplan/s/sj/stquotes.html

Trek Quotes Long lists of Trek quotes for the first six seasons of TNG, three seasons of TOS, and each of the first six movies. ✓**INTERNET**→*www* http://www.cosy. sbg.ac.at:80/ftp/pub/trek/quotes/

Spelling

The Star Trek Movies Spelling List Remember Chancellor Gorkhan (or was it Gorkon? or Goarkan?) from *Star Trek VI: The Undiscovered Country*? If it's spelling that's keeping your Trek star from rising, here's a list of characters, races, and locations encountered during the first six *Trek* movies. ✓**INTERNET**→*www* http://www.cosy.sbg.ac.at/ftp/pub/trek/lists/spelling.movies.faq

Star Trek Spelling List The next time you're planning to invite the crew of the Enterprise to a social function download this document, which lists the correct names and spellings for hundreds of characters from the Trek universe. Does the Transit Aid Bajoran in DS9 spell his name *Zaira* or *Zayra*? Are the warriors in "Elaan of Troyius" *Elasians* or *Illyrians*? ✓**INTERNET** ...→*gopher* dds.dds.nl→ De Bibliotheek boeken→Mass Media→Star Trek→Star Trek Spelling List ...→*gopher* wiretap.spies.com →Wiretap Online Library→Mass Media→Star Trek→The Star Trek Spelling List ...→*www* http://www. cosy.sbg.ac.at/ftp/pub/trek/lists/spelling.txt

Who's who

Captains of the Enterprise Captain Pike, sure, and Captains Kirk, Picard and Janeway. But did

ASK SPOT!

a) What solar system did Picard "experience" 1,000 years after its destruction? In what episode?

b) In what solar system did events in the *TOS* episode "The Metamorphosis" take place?

c) In what *TNG* episode, did the Enterprise encounter the planet Reina VI?

d) What planet, since dissolved, did the *TNG* crew visit in the episode "Encounter at Farpoint."

e) In what *TOS* episode was the L-370 system (seven planets) completely destroyed?

(See answers on page 359)

you know about Captain Robert T. April and Captain Kangaroo (sorry! couldn't resist)? This is a complete list of all the brave men (and the one brave woman) who have helmed the Starship *Enterprise*. ✓**COMPUSERVE**→*go* sfmedia→ Libraries→*Search by file name:* CAPTAI.TXT

List of Names, Ranks, and Serial Numbers Lists of the ranks in each *Trek* series. The rank status of several main characters is clarified—"Wes was made an acting ensign by Picard in 'Where No One Has Gone Before,' then made full ensign in 'Menage a Troi' and given a uniform"—and brief character biographies are included. ✓**TFDN**→TFDN Fact Files→*Download a file:* FAQL RANK.ZIP ✓**INTERNET**→*www* http://www.cosy.sbg. ac.at/ftp/pub/trek/lists/namerank. faq

Ranks and Characters Kirk may warn Picard against turning over the Captain's chair for the title of Admiral, but isn't there some middle ground? What comes after Cadet? And how did Miles O'Brien become a Chief? Though this is

not a definitive source of character ranks, it is an archive of a discussion that attempts to resolve inconsistencies of rank within the Trek universe. ✓**AMERICA ONLINE**→ *keyword* trek→MORE...→Star Trek Record Banks→Text/Other Files→ ARCHIVE: Ranks and Characters (filename: RANKCHAR.DOC)

Ranks of Federation Starfleet What rank falls exactly midway between flag rank and commissioned officer rank? Commodore, of course. This exhaustive report on Starfleet ranks and conventions not only lists the entire hierarchy, but also describes the all-important uniform colors and insignias associated with each rank. The site provides examples of characters from each rank (Cadet Wesley Crusher, Ensign Ro Laren, Fleet Captain Christopher Pike), and offers comparison of TOS and TNG ranks. ✓**EWORLD**→sf→Star Trek→United Federation Library→ rank.doc ✓**INTERNET**→*anon-ftp* ftp.cis.ksu.edu→/pub/alt.startrek. creative/misc→rank.doc.zip ...→ *www* http://www.unisuper.com. au/strek/rankdoc.htm

News & reviews

How costly are the special effects in *Voyager*? Where can you find TOS on German tele-

vision? And is it true that James Doohan will be starring in a spinoff TV series called *Scotty: Armed, Drunk, and Mad As Hell*? The online Trek world is full of mavens, gossips, and insiders, and many of them publish electronic newsletters and guides that spill the beans on the shows they love. Keep abreast of Starfleet news with **Voyages: The Star Trek Newsletter**. Review the victories and failures of past seasons with the **Star Trek Episode Guide**. And measure the critical mass with **Star Trek Reviews Electronic Forum** and **Usenet Ratings**.

On the Net

Episode guides

The Complete Star Trek Book, TV, and Film Guides A collection of Trek guides, including the guide to the Pocket Book series, episode guides to the three principal TV series (TOS, TNG, and DS9), and a checklist of all TV and book titles. The files are self-extracting. For Macintosh users. ✓**COMPUSERVE**→*go* sfmedia→ Libraries→*Search by file name:* TREKGU.SEA

Pilot Episodes and Unaired Episodes "Too cerebral" responded network execs when Rodden-

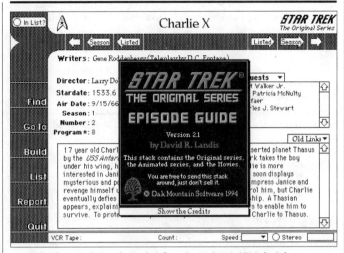

Screenshot from TOS Episode Guide—from CompuServe's SFMedia Library

berry gave them "The Cage" as a pilot episode for TOS. In fact, "The Cage" wasn't aired on television until 20 years later. *Assignment Earth* was created as a spinoff series to TOS, but never got the go ahead. And, then there's the *Trek* that just doesn't make it in the cross-border exchange: "Patterns of Force," in which a planet ends up with a Nazi-like government, was never shown in Germany for obvious reasons. The forgotten, the forbidden, and the first *Trek* episodes are covered in this short FAQ. ✓**INTERNET**→*anon-ftp* quepasa.cs.tu-berlin.de→*/pub/ doc/movies+tv-series/StarTrek/ FAQs*→pilots.gz

Star Trek Episode & Book Checklist A straightforward list of *Trek* television episodes and novels. ✓**COMPUSERVE**→*go* sfmedia →Libraries→*Search by file name:* STLIST.TXT *or* STLIST.ZIP

Star Trek Episodes Guide Three-part episode guide covering TOS, TNG, and DS9. *Voyager* should soon be included. ✓**INTERNET**→ *www* http://www.cis.ohio-state.edu/hypertext/faq/usenet/ star-trek/CS-guide/tv/top.html

Star Trek Guides Austrian Trek fan Brigitte Jellinik has collected links to more than a dozen Trek episode guides and FAQ lists. ✓**INTERNET**→*www* http://www.cosy. sbg.ac.at/rec/startrek/Guides.html

The Star Trek Universe Companion This hypertext guide to the Trek universe is organized by series and alien species. Under the old series, check on the stats (and access ASCII renditions) of Enterprises of the past—from the original USS Enterprise to NCC-1701-C. There are episode guides for both TNG and DS9, an ASCII picture of *Voyager,* and profiles of the Borg and the Klingons.

✓**INTERNET**→*www* http://www.cms. dmu.ac.uk/~it2yh/

Star Trek Viewing Guide Information for each episode of TNG, DS9, and *Voyager* as well as air schedules for DS9 and *Voyager*. ✓**INTERNET**→ *www* http://www. cosy.sbg.ac.at/rec/startrek/Guides. html

Starbase 3—The Complete Trek Database A database of episode descriptions (cast, plot summaries, stardates, airdates, etc.) for all TOS, TNG and DS9 episodes through July 1994. ✓**COMPUSERVE**→*go* sfmedia→Libraries→*Search by file name:* SB3006. ZIP

Newsletters

Dateline: Starfleet (j) Monthly electronic publication with Paramount news, *Trek* TV ratings, lists of new books and comics, convention updates and reports, and *Trek* storyline analysis. All back issues are archived in AOL's Dateline library. ✓**INTERNET**→*email* datelined @aol.com ✍ *Write a request* ✓**AMERICA ONLINE**→*keyword* trek→ MORE...→Star Trek Record Banks→ Text/Other Files→Dateline: Starfleet

Trekker_General (echo) Several of the big Trek newsletters are posted here, including Dateline, RIF, and Engage: the European Star Trek Newsletter. Actor profiles, interview transcripts, episode parodies, and general Trek discussion are also offered. ✓**TREKKERNET**

Voyages: The Star Trek Newsletter (j) A mix of speculation, news, reviews, and features about all the *Trek* series and products. Who's thinking of leaving DS9? What are the best new *Trek* books? And, where can you get the best online Trek demos? AOL Trek

events are also announced here. Editors of the newsletter can be reached through a folder on AOL's Promenade bulletin board. ✓**INTERNET**→*email* voyages1@aol.com ✍ *Write a request* ✓**AMERICA ONLINE**→ *keyword* trek→MORE...→ StarTrek Record Banks→Text/Other Files→TEXT: Voyages: The ST Newsletter # (each issue of the newsletter has a different number)

Nitpicking

Star Trek Snafus Did you notice that in the episode "The Enemy Within," the scratch on Kirk's face switches sides? And when Picard walks into the holodeck in the episode "Ship in a Bottle," he's wearing an open coat with a blue shirt, but when he walks out he's wearing his red shirt? The Trek Gods at Paramount do make mistakes, and Trek fans catch them— nitpicking is a highly regarded vocation in the Trek community. ✓**TFDN**→TFDN Fact Files→*Download a file:* FASQLSNAF.ZIP ✓**INTERNET**→*anon-ftp* quepasa.cs.tu-berlin. de→/pub/doc/movies+tv-series/ StarTrek/misc→snafus.gz ...→ *www* http://www.cosy.sbg.ac.at /ftp/pub/trek/lists/snafu.faq

YATI & OOPS: Inconsistencies & Bloopers Collecting YATI (Yet Another Trek Inconsistency) and OOPS is the avid pastime of many a Trek fan, and the writers, directors, and actors seem more than willing to provide fodder. There are the practical complaints: Troi should have fallen forward when she fainted, not backward (one wag suggested her ample Betazoid bosom precluded this). There are earnest attempts to explain the complexities of the inexplicable, like the Tasha Yar timeline. And how did Klingons evolve forehead bumps between The Original Series and *The Next Gen-*

eration? ✓**GENIE**→*keyword* sfrt2→ SFRT2 Bulletin Board→set 24→read 18

Programming guides

Star Trek Affiliates A national list of local television stations carrying *Star Trek*. ✓**EWORLD**→sf→ Star Trek→Captain's Log→Star Trek Affiliates

Star Trek Air Schedule Schedule of past and upcoming Trek shows with episode name, episode number, and air date. Some episodes are linked to press releases. ✓**INTERNET**→*www* http://www.mit. edu:8001/people/shabby/startrek. html

Upcoming Episodes Science-fiction fan David Henderson keeps a list of upcoming sci-fi episodes for DS9, *Voyager*, and *Babylon 5*, among others. Each listing includes the episode's air date and a very brief plot synopsis. Henderson also collects rumors and interesting tidbits about the series. ✓**INTERNET**→*www* http:// squirrel.bradley.edu/~davidh/scifi. html

Reviews

rec.arts.startrek.reviews (ng) Reviews of *Star Trek* books, episodes, films, and comics. ✓**USENET** *FAQ:* ✓**INTERNET**→*www* http:// www.cosy.sbg.ac.at/ftp/pub/trek/ lists/rec.arts.startrek.reviews.faq

Star Trek Reviews Electronic Forum (ml) If you like Siskel and Ebert, check out the Trekkie version—a mailing list of reviews posted to the rec.arts. startrek.reviews newsgroup. The whole range of *Star Trek* material, from the original series to the latest parody, is fair game for this list's no-holds-barred brand of criticism.

Don't expect puff pieces at this end of the galaxy. Writing about the L.A. Graf novel *Firestorm*, one reviewer said he was "pleasantly surprised" the book ended up being "less than average," having found Graf's previous two novels "at best abysmal." If you disagree, write a review of your own—you'll get the guidelines after you subscribe. ✓**INTERNET**→*email* listserv@cornell.edu ✍ *Type in message body:* subscribe trek-review-l <your full name>

Tim Lynch's Star Trek Reviews

Over the past few years, diehard Trekker and rec.arts.star trek* personality Timothy Lynch has written episode-by-episode reviews of TNG and DS9 shows and posted them to the newsgroup. These sites store a collection of those reviews in addition to a novella-length review of the movie *Generations*. The gopher site lets you search all of Lynch's reviews for specific references—great for finding answers to Spot's questions. The Website includes only TNG reviews. ✓**INTERNET** ...→*gopher* chop.isca.uiowa.edu 8338→General Information→Star Trek Reviews ...→*anon-ftp* ftp.coe.montana.edu→/pub/mirrors/.star trek/Tim_Lynch_stuff ...→*anon-ftp* ftp.alumni.caltech.edu→/pub/tlynch ...→*www* http://www.ugcs.caltech.edu:80/~werdna/sttng/tlynch/

Trekker—Witty Trek Reviews

Phil Kernick's sarcastic reviews of *Star Trek* episodes read like a transcript of the guy sitting next to you on the couch in the common room. Most of the time, he remains endearingly snotty, and entertaining. Sometimes, though, the reviews get a little racy. ✓**INTERNET**→*www* http://ringo.ssn.flinders.edu.au:80/trekker

Usenet Ratings A list of selected episodes, movies, and books with a batting-average style rating (.000-1.000) calculated from polls of Usenet readers. As of now, TNG episode "Shades of Grey" is tagged with the worst rating (.272) while "Yesterday's Enterprise" (.908) tops the list. ✓**INTERNET** ...→*www* http://http1.brunel.ac.uk:8080/~ph93rjh/trekrate.txt ...→*anon-ftp* rtfm.mit.edu→/pub/usenet-by-hierarchy/rec/arts/star trek/misc

≡ **STARNOTES** ≡

"Snafus:

'The Squire of Gothos': Trelane sees Earth history 900 years later, but he talks of Alexander Hamilton's death (1804) and of how he admires Napoleon (whose reign started in 1804). This would put the episode sometime just after 2704. This is more than four centuries too late.

ST6:TUC: In TNG 'Birthright II' Kahless overflowed some ocean with his tears (according to Klingon legend). But in ST6:TUC, Spock states that Klingons have no tear ducts.

ST6:TUC: The cloaked bird of prey is defeated by a gas-seeking torpedo - Lt Uhura having suggested the use of 'the equipment we're carrying to chart gaseous planetary anomolies'.
    At the beginning of the film, it is the Excelsior which is carrying this equipment, not the Enterprise. In fact, the Enterprise is in space dock when Kirk et.al. first set off.
    This was explained by the producers as a mistake that wasn't caught until the movie was nearly released, and it was too late to fix it, so they just left it in, figuring that the nitpickers could rationalize a way around the problem.

'Elementary, Dear Data': Moriarty draws the Enterprise on a piece of paper, and Data immediately proceeds to exit the holodeck holding the piece of holodeck paper. This is in the very episode where the writers 'established' that holodeck matter cannot exist outside of the holodeck.

'Brothers': Data's password doesn't match what was displayed on the screen."

—from **Star Trek Snafus**

The alien players

Here on Earth, we've got the Irish and the Ibos, the Italians, and the Laotians. In space,

it's a little more complicated. Interested in subscribing to a philosophy of logical nonaggression? Prick up your ears and head over to the **Vulcan-L** mailing list. Didn't learn the virtues of selfishness in business school? Study the **Ferengi Rules of Acquisition**. Got a powerful imperialist jones? Drop by AOL's **Cardassians** message board. Affiliating yourself with one particular alien race is a rewarding but difficult process; read the **Frequently Asked Questions About Star Trek Aliens** to make an informed decision. And if you're a twentysomething SWM seeking a 300-year-old slug, pen a mash note to the Trill that thrills, DS9's Jadzia Dax.

Ferengi (video capture)—downloaded from ftp.cis.ksu.edu

On the Net

Across the board

The Cardassians, Romulans & Klingons Who are the baddest in the universe? And, are these the kind of enemies you can identify with? If you'd enjoy being part of an active Klingon club or wish to endlessly analyze Cardassians and Romulans, sign up for Cyberspace's primo alien political-science class. Net seminars are about such questions as: "Is Cardassia more like Iran or pre-WWII

Japan?" and "Has Federation alliance destroyed the spirit of the Klingon empire?" The lack of more "alien" aliens, and an alien home world that isn't run as just another fascist world in space are constant criticisms. ✓**GENIE**→*keyword* sfrt2→SFRT2 Bulletin Board→set 24→read 26

Character/Aliens A decidedly young group of participants with a my-alien-is-better-than-your-alien attitude. One by the name of Lieutenant Commander J. Yar just loves the Romulans. "I think they are the best enemy. They have great ships, too. I love the war bird. Does anyone else feel like this?" The Kirk vs. Picard debate (tougher, sexier, smarter, hairier) also rages here and the Wesley Crusher camps divide based on whether there's any hope for the character. ✓**PRODIGY**→*jump* star

trek bb→Choose a Topic→Character/Aliens

Frequently Asked Questions About Star Trek Aliens To be truly multicultural, try to understand your alien friends. Is the Klingon home world called Kronos, Kling, or Klinzhai? Why do some Ferengis wear headgear? When do Vulcans mate? And, did you know that when a Klingon dies, "other Klingons warn the dead that a warrior is coming by staring into the stiff's eyes and howling upward." We're not all the same, you know. ✓**INTERNET** ...→*anon-ftp* quepasa.cs.tu-berlin.de→/pub/doc/movies+tv-series/StarTrek/FAQs→aliens.gz ...→*www* http://www.unisuper.com.au/strek/t-aliens.htm

Romulans and other Alien Foes Remember when Klingons

STARQUOTES

"I am Locutus of Borg. Resistance is futile. Your life, as it has been, is over. From this time forward you will service...us."—*Best of Both Worlds*

Net Source: Locutus Soundclip—sumex.aim.stanford. edu/info- mac/snd/locutus.hqx

and Romulans were really bad? Regulars in this folder do, and fondly. "Kor was treacherous, I would never turn my back on him—he was the type who would offer you a peace settlement while ordering troops to kill everyone after the document is signed...ahh the good old days." Fans exchange vital information about alien species, particularly the Vulcans, Romulans, and Klingons. (Hint: Romulan fans often sign their posts "Live long and conquer.") ✓**AMERICA ONLINE**→*keyword* trek→ Star Trek Message Board→Classic Trek→Romulans and other Alien Foes

WS_Cult (echo) If they're not talking about transporting Trills, participants in this alien cultures conference are speculating about having sex with Trills or the difference between Vulcans and Romulans. ✓**WARPSPEED**

Bajorans

Bajoran Proverbs Bajoran proverbs by the mouthful, including the profound "Open-mindedness reveals the enemy," "Everything must change," and the ever-popular (and painfully naive) "Love conquers all fear." ✓**INTERNET**→*www* http://web.city.ac.uk /~cc103/proverbs.html

Bajoran Symbols Clip art of Bajoran symbols. ✓**COMPUSERVE** →*go* sfmedia→Libraries→*Search by*

file name: BAJORAN.GIF

Bajorans (echo) Bajorans, recently freed from the tyranny of the Cardassians, find that self-rule is filled with trials and opportunities. Former members of the resistance and Bajoran patriots are welcome to drop by and talk Trek. ✓**TREKNET**

The Bajorans, Ridges and All The intensely spiritual nature of Bajoran society appeals to many in this topic, as does the fervor of their nationalism. Several frequent posters call themselves Bajorans, and often the lines between discussing Bajorans and acting as Bajorans are blurred. Members exchange dress patterns for Bajoran uniforms, debate whether it is "possible to love a terrorist?" (answer: an emphatic "yes."), and map the planet of Bajor for those planning a visit in the near future. ✓**GENIE**→*keyword* sfrt2→SFRT2 Bulletin Board→set 24→ read 27

Borg

A Borg Home Page The Borg links at this site were compiled with an Archie search and represent the most complete set of Borg files on the Net. They include sounds, images, bolo maps, and episode

reviews. ✓**INTERNET**→*www* http:// www.cs.indiana.edu/hyplan/ awooldri/borg/borg.html

The Borg An introductory essay to the species with the hive-computer mind. Though it's rife with typographical errors, this is still a worthwhile site. It includes a photo of the Borg cube ship designed by Rick Sternbach. ✓**INTERNET** →*www* http://www.cms.dmu.ac. uk/~it2yh/borg.html

Borg Collective What's so great about being a Borg besides the joys of assimilation and travel on a cube? Members here have some thoughts about the benefits of collectives, as well as a sense of humor about the hive-minded aliens. ✓**PRODIGY**→*jump* star trek bb→ Choose a Topic→Clubs:Other→ Borg Collective

The Borg Topic The Borg are the aliens that *Next Generation* fans most love to dread, deride, and discuss. Members here ponder whether the horrors of two sociopolitical movements of the 20th century, Nazism and Stalinism, are analogous to collectivism and forced assimilation. They also debate the affects of Hugh's "conversion" on the Borg—are they even scarier now that they are unpredictable? And, somewhat anxiously, they wonder if the Borg have lost their uniqueness as *Star Trek* foes by becoming too much like humans. ✓**GENIE**→*keyword* sfrt2→SFRT2 Bulletin Board →set 27→read 5

Borgisms Offbeat list of hundreds of Borgisms posted on

Usenet: "Cause I'm a Borg, yea, yea, yea," "Even the Borg won't assimilate a Macintosh," "Frankly my dear, you will be assimilated—Butler of Borg," "McBorgs, over half a billion assimilated," "Me and you and a Borg named Hugh," "My other computer is a Borg," etc. Get the picture? ✓**INTERNET**→*anon-ftp* ftp.cis.ksu.edu →/pub/alt.startrek.creative/misc →Borgisms.zip

Borg Jokes A collection of jokes about Borgs. ✓**COMPUSERVE**→*go* sf-media→Libraries→*Search by file name:* BORG.TXT

WS_Borg (echo) The cyborg menace has its own discussion group. Resistance may not be futile, though, since this group hasn't captured many members yet. ✓**WARPSPEED**

Resistance Is Futile (RIF) Newsletter According to its editor, *RIF* is "devoted to *Star Trek* satire, humor, and all things Borgish." With over 500 subscribers, this bimonthly Netzine publishes fan fiction, filks, and *Trek* news with a Borg theme. The not-so-serious topics range from Borg recipes to holiday announcements (Assimilation Week and Schwarzenegger's birthday). ✓**INTERNET**→*email* k.taborn@genie.geis.com ✍ *Write a request*

Cardassians

Cardassians "I would be interested in corresponding with some like-minded Cardassians for once, instead of these people with Federation points of view," writes Gul Alata, Acting Commander of the Green Mansion Fleet on AOL. Bajorans, Cardassians, and members of the

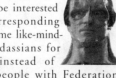

underground battle each other verbally in this topic reserved for Cardie talk but dominated by *Trek* alien role-playing. Writes a Bajoran to Gul Alata, "You came at a time when we had not weapons; a close-to-inexistent military. We trusted. We felt so happy and strong, so together. Then your race came, and we discovered that we were not so indefeatable as we had at first thought. It was a crushing blow." ✓**AMERICA ONLINE** →*keyword* trek→Star Trek Message Boards→Deep Space Nine Board→Cardassians

Cardassians Archive An archive of a discussion about the baddest of the bad guys in the Trek universe, covering Cardassian sex appeal, biology, spirituality, and general villainy. ✓**AMERICA ONLINE**→*keyword* trek→MORE...→ Star Trek Record Banks→Text/Other Files→Upld: 06/18/94→ARCHIVE: "Cardassians" folder (Filename: CARDASSN.TXT)

Cardassians History II A fan's effort to gather information about the Cardassian's orders and military structure (particularly the Obsidian Order). Brief and introductory in nature. ✓**AMERICA ONLINE** →*keyword* trek→MORE...→ Star Trek Record Banks→Text/Other Files→ Upld: 12/06/94→TEXT: Cardassians: Military Orders (Filename: CARDAS.GBK)

WS_Cardas (echo) They're the bad guys of DS9, but Cardies are so darn likable they've inspired a cult following among many Trekkers, especially on this conference. ✓**WARPSPEED**

Dominion

The Dominion Just what are these guys up to? This empire without conscience is like a car

without brakes—it speeds, it swerves, and it attains its aim at all costs. And the Jem'Hadar, the henchmen of the Dominion, "make the Federation's Starfleet look like a cruise line." Will the Dominion atomize the Borg? Over and over again on this conference, fans profess their admiration for clandestine Mafia-like organizations, and many seem eager to blame these shifty types for everything from the demise of a Canadian grocery-store chain to the Kennedy assassination. How can they be stopped? And what about Odo? Is he in for one whopper of an identity crisis? ✓**GENIE**→*keyword* sfrt2→SFRT2 Bulletin Board→ set 28→read 13

Ferengi

Ferengi (echo) While most Ferengi are busy trying to accumulate as much wealth as possible, some drop by this quiet conference to strategize. ✓**TREKNET**

Ferengi Picture of a Ferengi officer. ✓**INTERNET** ...→*anon-ftp* ftp.cis. ksu.edu→/pub/pictures/jpg/Star trek→sttng312.jpg ...→*anon-ftp* la jkonik.cyf-kr.edu.pl→/agh/reserve /gifs/startrek→sttng312.jpg

Ferengi Rules of Acquisition The Ferengi live by the strict code of self-interest. That code is broken down into a variety of rules, listed here next to the name of the character who revealed the particular rule and the episode title. For instance, Rule No. 9: "Opportunity plus instinct equals profit." (Nog, "The Storyteller"). Warm your heart with Rule No. 21: "Never place friendship above profit." (Quark, "Rules of Acquisition"). Ahh, and never forget rule Rule No. 1: "Once you have their money, you never give it back." (Rom, "The Nagus") New rules are added as they're revealed, so check the date on the list. ✓**INTERNET** ...→*gopher* chop.isca.uiowa. edu 8338→General Information→ Star Trek Reviews→Ferengi's Rules of Acquisition ...→*www* http:// www.eeng.dcu.ie/~stdcu/trek/fren rule.html ✓**COMPUSERVE**→*go* sfmedia →Libraries→*Search by file name:* FERENG.RU ✓**DELPHI**→*go* ent sta dat→set ds9→read ferengi rules→

Q (video capture)—downloaded from ftp.cis.klu.edu

down *or* list

Ferengi Rules of Acquisition "Nature decays, but latinum lasts forever." Astro-capitalists gather to enumerate and evaluate the Ferengi Rules of Acquisition. Quiz yourself on the rules or relate how well following No. 33 has worked for you: "It never hurts to suck up to your boss." New rules are added as soon as the show reveals them, and full lists of the rules are posted periodically. ✓**GENIE**→*keyword* sfrt2→SFRT2 Bulletin Board→set 28→read 11

Ferengi Sacred Rules of Acquisition A list of the Ferengi rules known to date and the titles of the episodes in which they were revealed. Rule of Aquisition No. 47: "Don't trust a man wearing a better suit than your own." ✓**E-WORLD**→sf→Star Trek→Captain's Log→Ferengi Rules of Acquisition

Preliminary Ferengi Lexicon An elaborate effort by Timothy Miller, an energetic Internet Trekker, to create the basis of a Ferengi language. The file includes some vocabulary, grammar rules, a phonology, and examples of written Ferengi. ✓**GENIE**→*keyword* sfrt2 →Text and Graphics Library→ *Download a file:* 1330

Rule of Acquisition #112 Sound clip of the 112th Rule of Acquisition. ✓**COMPUSERVE**→*go* sf-media→Libraries→*Search by file name:* ROA112.ZIP

WS_Ferengi (echo) What? Are they giving away cold-pressed latinum on the Promenade? Although there are probably more reasons to dislike a Ferengi than there are Rules of Aquisition, we're still not sure why this conference devoted to discussing Ferengis is so deserted. ✓**WARPSPEED**

Q

WS_Q (echo) Touching on topics from omnipotence to the mystery of Q and his continuum, the conference has a small but steady following. Members are determined to find an acceptable Q theory:

"MAYBE all Q are paradoxes! Never born, never dead!" Or "I don't believe in paradoxes. There must be some explanation for their existence. I think the power can be passed on by birth (Amanda) and it can be given to a person (Riker)." ✓ **WARPSPEED**

Romulans

The Romulan Star Enterprise You may come for Romulan Ale, but you'll probably stay for the camaraderie. The BBS is home to The Romulan Star Empire, an international fan club, and members dial in to exchange news and thoughts on the state of the Empire. ✓ **INTERNET** …→*telnet* romulus. homeworld.com→*bbs* …→*www* http://www.homeworld.com *Support:* ✓ **INTERNET**→*email* info@ Homeworld.com ✍ *Email for automated info*

Romulan Warrior A picture of a rare visitor, a Romulan, to the Enterprise. ✓ **INTERNET** …→*anon-ftp* ftp.cis.ksu.edu→*/pub/pictures/jpg/* Startrek→sttng316.jpg …→*anon-ftp* lajkonik.cyf-kr.edu.pl→*/agh* /reserve/gifs/startrek→sttng316.jpg

Romulans (echo) "Hi Marco! Welcome to the Romulan echo, I am…a Bajoran." Though this introduction seems to hold the potential for an animosity-filled exchange, the conversation stays friendly. But a few messages later, a Romulan is mocking Klingons and a conflicted member replies: "I can't say much against Romulans, because I am half Romulan…but my other Klingon half does not like what he hears

in this echo." Then, a TrekNet member who is writing a Trek novel drops by looking for "information on the structure of the Romulan government, the military, and intelligence." ✓ **TREKNET**

The Romulans Description of the Romulan people, society, and technology from *Starlog ST:TNG Official Magazine Technical Journal.* The feature begins: "First encountered by Starfleet vessels in a battle that took place almost two centuries ago, the Romulans are an aggressive, cunning, territorial people who wish only to expand their share of space by whatever means is necessary…." ✓ **INTERNET**→ *www* http://www.cms.dmu.ac.uk /~it2yh/romulan.html

WS_Romulan (echo) Although rather silent of late, this discussion group is devoted to Romulan culture (there was a movement to construct a Romulan language course). The conference is the base for Romulan sympathizers who wish to participate in an ongoing role-playing game with others in the Klingon, Ferengi and Federation echoes. Remember: Romulans were the Federation's steadfast enemy during the TNG era. ✓ **WARPSPEED**

Trills

The Chills!… **The Frills!…** **The Trills** The Trills: Another good

idea gone wrong? The complexities of the Trill relationship—a series of humanoid hosts inhabited by a 300-year-old slug—leaves viewers with lots of unanswered questions. Who is morally responsible for the actions of the current host? Just what can Trills remember from decade to decade, host to host? What about those complex interior workings of a living being—whose emotions are they, whose gender identity? Does the host ever just want to say 'Hey, bug off'? ✓ **GENIE**→*keyword* sfrt2 →SFRT2 Bulletin Board→set 28→ read 14

The Trill Collection Created to help answer questions about the Trill, this collection of documents treats the symbiont-host relationship as a biological one, and includes newsgroup posts that offer theories on Trill evolution. Timothy Lynch's spoiler review of "Equilibrium" is also available. The collection's architects are looking for articles, sounds, and pictures, as well as any other material pertaining to the Trill species. ✓ **INTERNET**→*www* http://trill.pc.cc. cmu.edu:80/trill.html

Vulcans

alt.fan.surak (ng) The teachings of the Vulcan Surak are debated here. No, not Spock's father Sarek. Surak is a person from ancient Vulcan who, according to the group's FAQ, "created and popularized the philosophies of peace, logic, mastery over one's emotions, and IDIC."

Enter a debate where members theorize about whether a Vulcan's ability to negotiate with other cultures and a Romulan's ability to dominate others are related to their long life spans. Messages to the mailing list Vulcan-l are often echoed in this Vulcan philosophy newsgroup. ✓**USENET**

Intro to Vulcan Philosophy
A very short article originally posted to the Usenet newsgroup alt.startrek.creative. Written in character as a Vulcan Ambassador, the piece argues against claims that Vulcan behavior is often illogical and questions whether Vulcans have any sense of individuality. ✓**TFDN**→TFDN Technical Files→*Download a file:* V_PHIL.ZIP ✓**INTERNET**→*anon-ftp* ftp.cis.ksu.edu→/pub/alt.startrek. creative/misc→VulcanPhilosophy. zip

Location of Vulcan: The Final Word
Copy of a 1991 article from the magazine *Sky & Telescope* in which Gene Roddenberry and three scientists from the Harvard-Smithsonian Center for Astrophysics determined that the star 40 Eridani was the Vulcan sun. ✓**INTERNET**→*gopher* wire tap.spies.com→Wiretap Online Library→Mass Media→Star Trek→Location of Vulcan: The Final Word

Vulcan Woman
Picture of a young Vulcan woman. ✓**INTERNET** ...→*anon-ftp* ftp.cis.ksu.edu→/pub/pictures/jpg/Startrek→sttng089.jpg ...→*anon-ftp* lajkonik.cyf-kr.edu.pl→/agh/reserve/gifs/startrek→sttng089.jpg

Vulcan-L
(ml) Do you fancy yourself a sort of Surak, a man who will lead his society out of violent turmoil into a New Eden of logical precision? Do you have a second eyelid? Or are you just hungry for a little Pon farr? If you've answered yes to any of these questions, you may want to subscribe to the Vulcan mailing list, which discusses issues of Vulcan culture, philosophy, physiology, and technology.

Participants here are at work on a nascent Vulcan language project which builds on a sizable body of Vulcan-oriented *Star Trek* literature (*Spock's World* and *The Vulcan Academy Murders* are the list's favorites). Regular contributors include several students of extraplanetary studies at the Science Academy in the Eridani system (on the planet "which you call Vulcan") who patch into the Internet through subspace frequencies. As in most *Star Trek* forums, members can't resist speaking in character. Those whose ear points have been worn dull through misuse or neglect need not apply. ✓**INTERNET**→*email* majordomo@netcom.com ✍ *Type in message body:* subscribe vulcan-l <your email address>

Vulcans
(echo) A conference that's a light but logical exchange on all matters relating to Vulcans. "What has happened to the Vulcans in the 24th century?" The Vulcans here will do there best to answer. ✓**TREKNET**

WS_Vulcan
(echo) Designated the Vulcan Science Academy, this slow conference is for Trek science topics. It's here that you can speculate about whether a character could get pregnant on the holodeck or ruminate over such seminal questions as: "If you program a computer with a sufficiently complex artificial intelligence program, such that it becomes sentient, are you depriving it of its rights by turning off the computer?" Yup. ✓**WARPSPEED**

You wanna be a Klingon?

In the history of complicated relationships, there are few as turbulent as the on-again,

off-again alliance between the Federation and the Klingon Empire. With their ridged foreheads, tear-duct deficiency (Don't cry for me, Qo'noS), long-standing martial traditions, and short fuses, the Klingons have antagonized Kirk and served under Picard. No alien species in the Trek world is more beloved, especially on the Net. Acquaint yourself with the warrior race on **The Klingons.** Discuss Klingon gender politics on AOL's **We Are Klingons!** message board. And don't forget about the Klingon language, tlhIngan-Hol, a full system of speech and writing developed for the Trek franchise by an actual linguist. You can even peruse a copy of *Hamlet*, the play about that lily-livered smooth-foreheaded Dane, at the **Klingon Shakespeare Restoration Project.**

Klingon death rite (video capture)—downloaded from ftp.cis.ksu.edu

On the Net

Across the board

alt.startrek.klingon (ng) The newsgroup for those who find mainstream *Star Trek* fandom too Milquetoast and sissified—you might call them the Weathermen of the Trekkers. This is a group of irritable idealists who seem to have an insane amount of free time on their hands—enough to have learned Klingon, the velar- and glottar-laden tongue spoken by the warlike aliens. Want to know the Klingon expression for "meter maid?" Apparently someone did, because the newsgroup had a whole thread about it. Alt.startrek. klingon also covers Klingon customs, language, and technology. The highlight of this group is the translations of Klingon dialogue in the movies and TV shows. If the readers here are telling the truth, the Klingons we see on-screen have a very, er, spicy vocabulary. ✓ **USENET**

Bird of Prey (echo) While the conference is for Klingons to convene and discuss any topic of interest—particularly themselves and the Empire—Klingon ships and language are the most active topics. How fast can a Bird of Prey travel? Don't be surprised if a Klingon fan club tries to recruit you while here. ✓ **TREKNET**

Klingon (echo) Do you subscribe to the Klingon point of view? How loud can you scream? Warriors from the Klingon Assault Group (KAG), the Klingon Legion of Assault Warriors (KLAW), and others not yet allied with a Klingon group clash and confer about Klingon history, culture, and Trek story lines. Female Klingons are here looking for mates or role-playing their own positions as warriors. Posts one Klingon sister about her male counterparts, "Just thinking about those ridges…that leather and those buns in spandex…how delectable…." Aggressive admirals, commanders, and other

members of this Klingon conference chat about local Klingon groups: Events, conventions, and club politics are constant topics. As in the Empire itself, infighting on the echo is common, with members rebelling, starting new groups, and attacking each other. "naDev tlhInganpu' tu'lu'!" ("There are Klingons here!") Grrrrr. ✓**FIDONET**

Kronos (the Klingons) The Klingon discussion "We Are Klingons!" became so large, they gave the Klingons a permanent folder on AOL's Star Trek Club. If you've longed to try Boiling Worm Wine and Slimy Tongue Balls, but just can't find the recipes, stop by. A great resource for Klingon warriors-in-training, you can talk about anything here as long as it's Klingon. Are Klingons alien samurai? Well, did you know, for instance, that the Klingon martial art, Mok'bara, is based on tai chi? Or that the Bat'telH, the Klingon "Sword of Honor," is based on an ancient chinese battle sword? You can also get information on Klingon ships, the Klingon Assault Groups, the Klingon Language Institute, and a myriad of other Klingon organizations. ✓**AMERICA ONLINE**→*keyword* trek→Star Trek Message Boards→Kronos (the Klingons)

The Klingon Language FAQ Information on books, tapes, institutes, and Internet resources for learning and speaking the Klingon language. ✓**INTERNET** →*anon-ftp* rtfm.mit.edu→/pub/usenet-by-hierarchy/rec/arts/star trek/klingon→Klingon_language_ FAQ ✓**TFDN**→TFDN Fact Files→*Download a file:* KLINLANG.ZIP

The Klingons A profile of Klingons and the Klingon Empire's relationship with the Federation. ✓**INTERNET**→*www* http://www.cms.dmu.ac.uk/~it2yh/klin.html

WS_Kling (echo) The steady stream of Klingon banter is often posted in both English and tlhIngan Hol on this conference. But not everyone here is certain that translating the Bible into Klingon is so relevant: "Question! How may Klingons read the Bible?" Well, maybe they will now. Club talk is minimal. Members, who seem less die-hard than those on other Klingon conferences, come from around the world; there are a lot of Aussies. When word hit New Zealand that Quark had married a Klingon in "House of Quark," members who hadn't seen the episode yet started to speculate: Could Quark ever hold a seat on the Klingon High Council (brave Ferengi that he is)? ✓**WARPSPEED**

Art & graphics

Klingon Font A Klingon font for Macs. ✓**INTERNET** ...→*anon-ftp* nic.switch.ch→/mirror/info-mac/font

→klingon.hqx ...→*anon-ftp* solo mon.technet.sg→/pub/NUS/zk/mac/font→klingon.hqx

Klingon Graphics Klingon graphics, including rank insignia and Klingon weapons. ✓**COMPUSERVE**→*go* sfmedia→Libraries→*Search by file name:* KLINGO.ZIP

Klinzhai A TrueType version of a Klingon font for Macs. ✓**AMERICA ONLINE**→*keyword* trek→MORE...→Star Trek Record Banks→Text/Other Files→Upld: 07/26/91→Klinzhai, TrueType Klingon Font! (Filename: Klinzhai (TT).sit)

Klinzhai A PostScript version of a Klingon font for Macs. ✓**AMERICA ONLINE**→*keyword* trek→MORE...→Star Trek Record Banks→Text/Other Files→Upld: 06/16/91→Klinzhai, Type 1 Klingon Font! (Filename: Klinzhai.sit)

Fans

Klingon Groups Contact information—for both online and offline Klingon organizations—including the Klingon Language Institute, Klingon Military Academy, Klingon Assault Group, Klingon Honor Division, and A.U.R.O.R.A. (Appreciation and Unity for Robert O'Reilly Alliance). Klingon group members can use the folder for discussion as well. ✓**EWORLD**→sf→Star Trek→Clubs and Conventions→Klingon Groups

The Klingon Empire: A Brief History, Volume 1 A detailed and well-written overview of the Klingons, from prehistorical times to the start of the 24th century. Historical periods are described in chronological order, detailing invasions, philosophical and scientific influences, cults of personality, and so on. ✓**AMERICA ONLINE**→*key-*

word trek→MORE...→Star Trek Record Banks→Text/Other Files→ Upld: 07/20/94→TEXT:Klingon History (Filename: KLN-HIS.TXT)

Klingon: The Warrior Race A profile of Klingons featuring information about their physiology, society, and familial relationships. Descriptions of Klingon starships are also included. One caveat: Though this profile is filled with interesting facts, the grammar and spelling are so atrocious that it's virtually unreadable. ✓ **AMERICA ONLINE**→*keyword* trek→MORE...→ Star Trek Record Banks→Text/Other Files→Upld: 04/10/94→TEXT:Klingon Information (Filename: KL. DOC)

Klingons: The Praxis Legion A brief description of the Praxis legion and a bit-mapped file of its emblem. ✓ **COMPUSERVE**→*go* sfmedia→Libraries→*Search by file name:* PRAXIS.ZIP

Planet Kazh (echo) Orbiting the star Klingonki, Kazh is the home planet of the Klingons. This two-page description of the planet covers its geological history and planetary qualities like its mass (larger than earth), period of revolution, axial tilt, etc. ✓ **TFDN**→TFDN Technical Files→*Download a file:* KAZH. ZIP

Language & literature

Aesop's Fables Even Klingons need moral tales, and this document includes tlhIngan Hol translations of "The Fox and the Crow," "The Goose That Laid the Gold Egg," "The Crow and the Pitcher of Water," and "The Dog and His Shadow." ✓ **INTERNET** ...→*anon-ftp* ftp.kli.org→/pub/ Text/Aesop ...→*gopher* habli.tamu. edu→Aesops Fables

The Klingon Language Institute

General Klingon Writings tlhIngan Hol translations of the George Thorogood's bar-blues "Bad to the Bone," the holiday favorite "Rudolph the Red-Nosed Reindeer," and other songs and stories. ✓ **INTERNET**→*gopher* habli. tamu.edu→General Klingon Writings

HolQeD: Journal of Klingon Language You'll find it in your libraries alongside *Representations* and *Critical Inquiry: HolQeD*, the quarterly journal of Klingon language. And you'll also find it online, sort of: The editors of the publication reprint their table of contents and highlight selected articles for online display. ✓ **INTERNET** →*www* http://www.kli.org/kli/ HolQeD.html

The Klingon Bible Translation Project Gideon, move over. When Klingons stay in hotels, this is the Bible they'll probably have in their rooms, with tlhIngan Hol translations of the Book of Jonah, the gospel according to Mark, the gospel according to John (partial), the 23rd Psalm, and the Lord's Prayer. ✓ **INTERNET** ...→*gopher* habli.

tamu.edu→Klingon Bible Translation Project ...→*anon-ftp* ftp.kli.org→/ pub/Text/KBTP

Klingon Language Guide The introductory guide begins with a summary of the who's who—in Klingon language development, from linguist Marc Okrand on down—reviews the history of Klingon language, and describes the alphabet, syntax, and dialects of the language. ✓ **INTERNET**→*anon-ftp* ftp.cis.ksu.edu→/pub/alt. startrek.creative/misc→Klingon LanguageGuide.zip

Klingon Language Institute Klingon pictures, fonts, parsing programs, and, most impressively, translations of Western classics, including the Bible, Shakespeare, Aesop's fables, Christmas carols, and other songs. ✓ **INTERNET** ...→ *www* http://www.kli.org/KLIhome. html ...→*anon-ftp* ftp.kli.org→/pub

The Klingon Languages Languages? Well, in addition to tlhIngan-Hol, there's Klingonaase—a dialect created by fans of John Ford's *The Final Reflection*—and both tongues are untied at this site. Includes a translation of Shakespeare's sonnet 97 and a link to the Klingon Language Institute. ✓**INTERNET**→*www* http://www.cosy.sbg.ac.at/rec/startrek/Klingon.html

Klingon Shakespeare Restoration Project Neither a borrower nor a Klingon be? With these translations, Klingons and Klingon speakers can learn to speak the speech, trippingly, with translations into tlhIngan Hol of *Much Ado About Nothing, Hamlet,* and sonnets 18, 34, 61, 96, and 97. ✓**INTERNET**→*anon-ftp* ftp.kli.org→/pub/Text/KSRP

Klingonaase Dictionary Klingonaase is a second Klingon language—not the official tlhIngan Hol tongue created by linguist Marc Okrand, but an offshoot derived from John Ford's *The Final Reflection.* This document is a rudimentary English-Klingonaase dictionary. ✓**INTERNET** ...→*anon-ftp* gandalf.rutgers.edu→/pub/sfl→klingonaase.txt ...→*gopher* wiretap.spies.com→Wiretap Online Library→Mass Media→StarTrek→Klingon Vocabulary

Much Ado About Nothing (paghmo' tln mIS) Beatrice and Benedick go for one another's throats in love and spite in this delightful Shakespeare comedy, here translated into the Klingon tongue. ✓**INTERNET** ...→*www* http://www.cosy.sbg.ac.at/ftp/pub/trek/klingonaase/paghmo.txt ...→*gopher* habli.tamu.edu→Klingon Shakespeare Restoration Project→Much Ado About Nothing

tlhIngan-Hol (ml) Immerse yourself in Klingon language and culture. Messages will pour into your mailbox all day and night from members conversing in Klingon and list grammarians,

"→William Shakespeare, Sonnet 97

How like a winter hath my absence been
From thee, the pleasure of the fleeting year!
What freezings have I felt, what dark days seen!
What old December's bareness every where!

And yet this time removed was summer's time;
The teeming autumn, big with rich increase,
Bearing the wanton burden of the prime,
Like widow'd wombs after their lords' decease:

Yet this abundant issue seem'd to me
But hope of orphans and unfather'd fruit;
For summer and his pleasures wait on thee,
And, thou away, the very birds are mute;

Or, if they sing, 'tis with so dull a cheer,
That leaves look pale, dreading the winter's near.

wIlyam SeQpIr. *Sonet*mey bom HutmaHSoch.

Sohvo' bov bIr'e' rur jIDachtaHghach,
qaStaHvIS moDbogh DIS belwI'na', soHbogh.
jISIQ jItaDDI'. jIHDaq jaj Hurgh bach
qanbogh jar wa'maHcha' QIHwI' vIDoHbogh.

'ach bov tuj 'oHpu' tlheDchuqghachmaj nI''e'.
yobqu'ghachmo' yatlh lIngbogh DIrbovchoH,
DIrbotlh 'eq puq law' boghbeHpa'. wanI''e'
rur be'nal chor, Heghpu'DI' be'nal joH.

'ach jIHvaD naH'e' neH luchoSbogh vav
rurlaw' Qapla'vam Dun, DIrbovvetlh laH je,
Duwuvba'mo' bov tuj belwI'mey chav;
bIHoptaHvIS, tamchu' chalHa'DIbaH je.

qoj, chuSchugh bIH, 'ItmoH bIH chuSDI'. vaj,
chISchoH Sor; bIrchoH bov, pay' 'e' luHaj."

—from **Klingon Shakespeare Restoration Project**

pabpo'mey, who are intent on correcting mistakes. (List grammarians are chosen by the list owner.) High Klingon rather than Clipped Klingon is preferred. You may want to introduce yourself to the Klingons on this list when you first subscribe (try and post the

message in Klingon). They're a friendly bunch—for Klingons. ✓**INTERNET**→*email* listserv@kli.org ✍ *Type in message body:* subscribe tlhIngan-Hol <your full name>

Writing Klingon A brief description of the Klingon writing system followed by a picture of the character set. ✓**INTERNET**→*www* http://www.kli.org/kli/plqaD.html

Role-playing

alt.shared-reality.startrek. klingon (ng) In this Klingon role-playing newsgroup users post role-playing style messages in order to collectively create Klingon stories. Messages are expected to be fairly lengthy contributions to the continuing narrative, with a description of your character's role in the story, his or her inner thoughts, life history, plans, and dreams. New characters are welcome; for example, if after reading a series of messages, you would like to create a Klingon crewman in for a drink at the bar, walk into the bar, "note the fistfight between the two drunken officers, pay it no heed, step over the comatose form of Captain Krang on the floor next to the Terran jukebox...," and go on from there.

Warning: Do not develop other people's characters. If his character has been given certain attributes, like motivations, a personal history, and a rank, it is not for you to reveal that the character is a Cardassian spy or wears lacy pink underwear underneath his battle armor. Nor should you turn an opponent into a cringing coward just because it's your turn to write part of the story.

Some of the more dedicated posters to the role-playing group alt.shared-reality.startrek.klingon like to use Klingon language in their postings. Either learn to speak Klingon or take part in one of the English-language threads. When traffic is light it usually gets going again with a good new jumping-off point for the storytelling. ✓**USENET**

PICS & SOUNDS

Dead Klingon Image of a young Klingon killed in battle. ✓**INTERNET** ...→*anon-ftp* ftp. cis.ksu.edu→/pub/pictures/jpg /Startrek→sttng104.jpg ...→ *anon-ftp* lajkonik.cyf-kr.edu.pl→ /agh/reserve/gifs/startrek→ sttng104.jpg

Klingon Image of Klingon broadcast on view screen. ✓**INTERNET** ...→*anon-ftp* ftp.cis.ksu.edu→ /pub/pictures/jpg/Startrek→ sttng105.jpg ...→*anon-ftp* laj konik.cyf-kr.edu.pl→/agh/reserve /gifs/startrek→sttng105.jpg

Klingon High Council Image of four fearsome Klingons, including Gowron, sitting on the high council. ✓**INTERNET**→*anonftp* src.doc.ic.ac.uk→/media/ visual/collections/funet-pics/jpeg /tv+film/StarTrek/tng→Klingon _High_Council.jpg

Klingon Insult Soundclip in the Klingon language of the derisive expression, "Your mother has a smooth forehead!" ✓**INTERNET**→ *www* http://www.kli/sounds/ HabQuch.au

Klingon Warrior Close-up image of an impressive Klingon warrior ready for battle. ✓**INTERNET** ...→*anon-ftp* ftp.cis.ksu.edu→/pub/ pictures/jpg/Startrek →sttng102.jpg ...→*anon-ftp* lajkonik.cyf- kr.edu.pl→ /agh/re serve/gifs/ startrek→ sttng102. jpg

Klingon Warriors Klingon visitors to the Enterprise. ✓**INTERNET**→*anon-ftp* ftp.cis.ksu.edu→/ pub/pictures/jpg/Startrek→sttng 101.jpg

Klingons Worf and Klingon comrades share a traditional ceremonial yell. ✓**INTERNET**→*anon-ftp* ftp.cis.ksu.edu→/pub/pictures/ jpg/Startrek→sttng103.jpg

Lursa In Command A picture of the luscious Lursa—one half of the infamous Klingon sister duo—sitting in high command. ✓**AMERICA ONLINE**→*keyword*→entertainment weekly→generations gallery→lursa in command

Original Klingon Bird of Prey Picture of an original Klingon Bird of Prey. ✓**PVG** dial 513-233- 7993→F→*Download a file:* TOS. GIF

Original Klingon Bird of Prey Picture of three old, original Klingons from TOS. ✓**PVG** *dial* 513-233-7993→F→*Download a file:* PVKLNORG.GIF

Where is the Bathroom? There are those all-important phrases you need to know when traveling to a foreign planet. Here's one: A soundclip in the Klingon language of the vital question, "Where is the bathroom?" ✓**INTERNET**→ *www* http:// www.kli/ sounds/ puchpa% 27.au

Federation diplomacy

Forget NAFTA and NATO. Though trade and military alliances are still important in the

24th century, diplomacy has moved beyond Earth's petty borders. With empires like the Dominion and the Romulans colonizing planets left and right, coalitions such as the UFP (United Federation of Planets) and Starfleet continue to press for peace in the universe, and strategies, such as brinksmanship, balance of power, and deterrence are still very much in evidence. Study the terms of peace treaties with the Klingons and the Romulans. Give yourself an interstellar civics lesson with the **Preamble to the Constitution of the UFP.** Be the Henry Kissinger of the future.

United Federation of Planets

President's Message

Welcome to the United Federation of Planets. It is my hope that these pages will help those who find them to better understand the Federation because understanding is the first step to peace.

UFP Homepage—http://lal.cs.byu.edu/people/black/StarTrek/UFP.html

On the Net

Economics

Hoover's Handbook Company Profiles for the 24th Century Ever wonder about Quark's annual take in bars of latinum? Or, Starfleet's ownership interest in the Utopia Planitia Fleet Yards? If the business side of the Trek universe interests you, the Reference Press, a publisher of business information about 20th century companies, has a selection of humorous *Star Trek*–based company profiles. The profiles follow the standard Hoover's format, but cover such companies as Quark's Inc.

and Mudd & Company (Haaaaarrrrry!) ✓**INTERNET**→ *www* www. hoovers.com ✓**AMERICA ONLINE**→ *keyword* hoover

Starfleet

The Prime Directive The Prime Directive, the philosophical foundation of the Federation and the bane of many a Starfleet officer, is one of the most ardently debated topics in Trekdom. GEnie members agonize over Prime Directive dilemmas almost as much as a 24th-century captain would. What should the punishment be for violating this semi-sacred code? Are there values inherent in the Prime Directive that cannot be quantified? Here anthropologists

argue cultural relativism with pragmatists who favor dispassionate strategic analysis. It isn't even out of the question to be accused of "having internalized Federation values" if you take the Starfleet line. ✓**GENIE**→ *keyword* sfrt2→SFRT2 Bulletin Board→set 24→read 17

Starfleet Command Home Page Introduction to Starfleet command and descriptions of the various branches. ✓**INTERNET**→ *www* http://lal.cs.byu.edu/people /black/StarTrek/starfleet.html

Treaties

Treaty of Peace with the Klingons Compiled from references to the treaty in novels, movies, and televison episodes, this is the Treaty of Peace imposed by the Organians (an advanced life-form that has evolved to the point that they do not need physical bodies) on the Klingons and the United Federation of Planets in the year 2267. The treaty is followed by an explanation of the significance of each of the six conditions. √**TFDN**→TFDN-Star Trek Technology →*Download a file:* ORGANIA.ZIP

Treaty of Peace With the Romulans Text of a treaty established a Neutral Zone between the UFP and the Romulans. √**TFDN**→TFDN-Star Trek Technology→*Download a file:* PEACE.ZIP

UFP

List of Member Planets When you're agreeing to pursue common goals of peace and harmony, it's nice to know who you're harmonizing with, and this page lists the member planets of the United Federation. √**INTERNET**→*www* http://lal.cs.byu.edu/people/black/StarTrek/memplanets.html

Preamble to the Constitution of the UFP "The better to secure and perpetuate mutual friendship and intercourse among the people of the different States in this Union, the free inhabitants of each of these States, paupers, vagabonds, and fugitives from justice excepted, shall be entitled to all privileges and immunities of free citizens in the several States." Change "paupers" and "vagabonds" to "Bajorans" and "Vulcans," and you'll get the picture. √**INTERNET**→*www* http://lal.cs.byu.edu/people/black/StarTrek/fedconstitution/homepage

United Federation of Planets Emblem GIF of the UFP emblem. √**COMPUSERVE**→*go* sfmedia→Libraries→*Search by file name:* UFP.GIF

United Federation of Planets Home Page Though we'll have to wait more than 150 years for the foundation of the UFP, it will be well worth the wait. Because when the Federation is finally founded in 2161, it will attempt to create peaceful coexistence among all the planets of the galaxy. This site defines the mission of the Federation, and includes a description of its Constitution, modeled after several other important political documents, including the Statutes of Alpha III, the Constitution of the United States of America, and the Fundamental Declarations of the Martian Colonies. √**INTERNET**→*www* http://lal.cs.byu.edu/people/black/StarTrek/ufp.html

United Federation of Planets Logo GIF of the Federation's logo. √**COMPUSERVE**→*go* sfmedia→Libraries→*Search by file name:* UFPLOG.GIF

CYBERTREKKERS

Michael L. Brown
Age 46; Madison, WI

Posts Paramount episode press releases to Usenet and archives them at his Website Vidiot's Star Trek Website—http://www.ftms.com:80/. Active participant on rec.arts.startrek* newsgroups.

Trek Offline:	Member of the Official Star Trek Club
Favorite Characters:	Picard and Data
Favorite Episode:	"The Inner Light" (TNG) and "All Good Things" (TNG)
Other Online Interests:	*Babylon 5* and other sci-fi, video, and satellite discussion groups

Mission Statement: "I do not watch the televised repeats of TNG or DS9. I have them all on tape and see them enough each week because of the editing that I do. I record each week's satellite feed and edit out the commercials. I see a new episode a minimum of three times in a week...I even watched the TOS episodes on BBC TV when I was in Scotland during 1972 and 1973. I've watched all of the ST movies, and have them all on wide-screen laserdisc."

Email Address:	brown@ftms.com

Trek time—loops & lines

It's 1995. In less than a year, the Eugenics Wars will rage across the Earth, and the

outlaw Khan and his band of hoods will escape from global authorities and hightail it into space for some cryogenic deep-freeze. Or so the Stardates claim. In fact, keeping track of Trek chronology is one of the most important responsibilities of any serious fan. Is Data older than Picard? Was the USS *Voyager* launched after the crash of the *Enterprise* NCC-1701-D? And how is it that Tasha Yar's daughter was born only seven years after Tasha? Verify events in Trek future history with James Dixon's **Star Trek Timeline**. Read about Gene Roddenberry's design of the Trek calendar in **How the Star Date Came To Be**. And finally, check today's Stardate with **Mac Star Date 1.0.1**. The Trek universe is a complicated place—and an understanding of the 23rd and 24th centuries is only the tip of that growing iceberg called "history." What kind of trek fan would you be, for instance, if you didn't know that Spock and McCoy were trapped in the Ice Age on planet Sarpeidon in the year 2,737 B.C.?

The Guardian of Forever—downloaded from ftp.cis.ksu.edu

On the Net

Date conversion

How the Star Date Came To Be In 1968, smack in the middle of the first run of the first series, Gene Roddenberry took time out of his busy schedule to help author Stephen Whitfield with his book *The Making of Star Trek*. This document is a reprint of Roddenberry's explanation of the stardate. ✓**COMPUSERVE**→*go* sfmedia→Libraries→*Search by file name:* SDATE.TXT

Mac Star Date 1.0.1 Launch the application and today's stardate appears. For Macs. ✓**AMERICA ONLINE**→*keyword* trek→MORE...→ Star Trek Record Banks→Text/Other Files→Upld: 08/22/94 Mac Star Date 1.0.1 (Filename: MacStarDate 1.0.1)

Stardate Converter Program that converts a date into a stardate and vice versa. ✓**COMPUSERVE**→*go* sfmedia→Libraries→*Search by file name:* STARDA.ZIP

Stardates What exactly is a stardate based on? This document calculates stardate units (at 1,000 per year, they clock in at approximately 8.76 hours for a non-leap year) and then illustrates how to convert Stardates into actual years.

January 21, 2363? Well, that's stardate 40057.5, of course. Learn the system and amaze your friends as you render their birthdays in stardates. ✓**INTERNET** ...→*gopher* dds.dds.nl→De Bibliotheek→boeken →Mass Media→Star Trek→Stardates ...→*gopher* wiretap.spies. com→Wiretap Online Library→ Mass Media→Star Trek→Star Trek Stardates

Timeline

A Star Trek Chronology and The Star Trek Future History

A timeline cataloging Trek history through the first five seasons of TNG. This document also contains some fascinating annotation, including speculation on certain confusing temporal matters. Where was the *Enterprise* between 2263 and 2264? What happened during the command of the first captain of the *Enterprise*, Robert T. April? ✓**AMERICA ONLINE**→*keyword* trek→MORE...→Star Trek Record Banks→Text/Other Files Upld: 04/23/94→TEXT: ST Timeline (Filename: TRKLN5)

Frequently Asked Questions about Star Trek Dates and Years

Answers to the most commonly asked questions about the year or stardate of an event (e.g., Gene Roddenberry died in 1991, while the Botany Bay left Earth with Khan in 1996): lists of characters' and actors' ages; and a list of *Star Trek* actors' obituaries. ✓**INTERNET**→*anon-ftp* quepasa. cs.tu-berlin.de→/pub/doc/movies +tv-series/StarTrek/FAQs→dates. gz

Has Star Trek History Been Altered Forever?

A short essay hypothesizing that the TNG episode "Yesterday's Enterprise" created an alternate time that redirected the chronological flow of the series and relocated all ensuing episodes in time. ✓**AMERICA ON-LINE**→*keyword* trek→MORE ...→Star Trek Record Banks→Text/Other Files→Upld: 10/19/94→TEXT: Alternate Timeline (filename: TREKTIME. TXT)

NetTrekker's Ultimate Stardate Guide

A chronology noting the stardates of hundreds of *Trek* adventures, including all events

Sela, Tasha Yar's daughter—downloaded from ftp.cis.ksu.edu

portrayed on television and in movies, books and comics. Adventures are cross-listed if the story used flashbacks, time travel, or visions of the future. Each listing is also tagged with the type of story (e.g., Pocket Books DS9 novel; Animated Series episode). Compiled by Dayton Ward, an active member of AOL's Star Trek club, the list also includes a detailed set of footnotes that often preempt arguments over an event's occurrence. ✓**AMERICA ONLINE**→*keyword* trek→MORE...→Star Trek Record Banks→Text/Other Files→Upld: 12/06/94→TEXT: Ultimate Stardate Guide Ver 1.1 (filename: STAR DATE.ZIP)

Star Trek Chronology Notes

An explanation of how the *Star Trek* Timeline was created. According to the notes, the timeline contributors attempt to collate the chronologies of novels written by different authors, and to use clues given in an episode or novel to suggest other events on the timeline. This page provides an excellent analysis of the time logic, debates, and discrepancies in

the Trek universe. ✓**INTERNET**→ *www* http://www.ugcs.caltech. edu/~werdna/sttng/trek6/trek 6-c.html

Star Trek Timeline

Did Kirk, Spock, and McCoy journey to Earth (TOS, "The City on the Edge of Forever") before or after Frank Oppenhouse was born (TNG, "The Neutral Zone")? What year did James Kirk visit the planet Neural? Make sense out of the tangled chronology of the *Star Trek* series with this timeline, which draws on events from TOS, TNG, DS9, and the feature films. Most of the information is verified by textual evidence, although the author occasionally resorts to speculation. ✓**INTERNET** ...→*gopher* dds. dds.nl→De Bibliotheek→boeken→ Mass Media→Star Trek→Star Trek Timeline ...→*anon-ftp* ftp.cis.ksu. edu→/pub/alt.startrek.creative/ timeline→trek.zip

Star Trek Timeline

Hundreds of events are chronicled on a timeline that begins way back in 9,000,000,000 B.C. and doesn't seem to stop until it's got, well... the future covered. Enter the timeline (created by fan James Dixon) from one of several major events—the creation of the United Federation of Planets, for instance, or Picard's command—and then wade through an incredibly detailed chronology that includes information gathered from all the television shows and most novels and short stories. Links to TNG episode summaries are built. ✓**INTERNET**→*www* http:// www.ugcs.caltech.edu/~werdna/ sttng/trek6.html

Star Trek Timeline

What happened in the universe before Spock and Kirk voyaged through space? Part One of this timeline covers the era between 1996 and

2196—when Joe DiMaggios's hitting streak was broken by Harmon Buck Gin Bokai; Zefram Coch-rane invented the warp drive; and Guinan had her encounter with Q.

Part Two covers important events in the 20th, 21st, and 22nd centuries, including the lives and adventures of the original crew. The third part of the timeline chronicles the voyages of the Enterprise under Picard's command. ✓ **AMERICA ONLINE**→*keyword* trek→ MORE...→Star Trek Record Banks→ Text/Other Files→Upld: 06/27/94- 07/02/94→TEXT: Star Trek Timeline

The Star Trek Timeline One more Trek timeline. Chronicles events in the universe beginning with 597,630 B.C. when a Supernova destroyed the The Tkon Empire through events from the fifth season of TNG. Not incredibly detailed. ✓ **INTERNET**→*www* http:// www.cosy.sbg.ac.at/ftp/pub/trek/ lists/timeline.txt

Time Loops, Yesterday's Enterprise, and Tasha Yar Explained How did Tasha die twice? Questions like this about the episode "Yesterday's Enterprise" came up so often in the rec.arts.startrek* newsgroups that this FAQ was badly needed.

Offering four possible explanations (each of which depends on assumptions as to what timeline is real), the FAQ also examines and explains several other Trek episodes where timeloops were featured. ✓ **INTERNET** ...→*www* http:// www.cosy.sbg.ac.at/ftp/pub/ trek/lists/timeloop.faq ...→*anon-ftp* quepasa.cs.tu-berlin.de→/pub/ doc/movies+tv-series/Star Trek/ FAQs→time.loops.gz ✓ **TFDN**→ TFDN—Trek Fact Files→*Download a file:* faqltime.zip

ASK SPOT!

a) When did the Preservers seed planets, including Earth, with humanoid life?

b) In what year did Spock rescue his son, Zar?

c) When did the Kataanians launch their probe? 1000 B.C., 1368 B.C., 1990 B.C., 2000 B.C.?

d) Did the Eugenics "supermen" seize power across Earth in the 20th or the 21st century?

e) In what year did Cadet Kirk earn a commendation for original thinking by beating the Kobayashi Maru no-win scenario—2150, 2205, 2249? What did he do?

f) Did the planet Medusa (XI Hydrae IV) become the 27th U.F.P. member under Pike's, Kirk's, or Picard's command?

g) What year and stardate did Picard become Locutus of Borg?

h) When did a hologram take control of the *Enterprise NCC-1701-D*'s Holodeck 3? What was the hologram's name?

i) In what year did the United Federation of Planets begin?

j) In what stardate did Captain Spock mind meld with Dr. McCoy, transferring his Katra to the doctor?

k) When was a Romulan peace treaty established?

l) In what year was Scotty born?

m) In what year did Deanna Troi enter and Beverly Crusher graduate from Star Fleet Academy?

n) In what year was the Klingon-Romulan alliance dissolved?

o) In what year did Beverly Crusher and William Riker enter the Starfleet Academy?

p) In what year was the USS *Enterprise* launched from earth under Captain Robert April's command?

(See answers on page 359)

Treknology

What would *Star Trek* be without its technology? A bunch of people in cheesy costumes

(velour at one time) giving melodramatic speeches and jabbing at each other with pointed sticks. From the transporter to the Phaser, from the warp drive to the holodeck, Trek technology has always tried to mix real-world science and pure fantasy, sometimes even anticipating advances of future science. Learn how ships cheat time with the **Relativity and FTL Travel FAQ**. Bone up on wormholes and replicators with the **rec.arts.startrek.tech Reading List**. Trade pointers with other physicists of the 24th century in Prodigy's **Tech Talk**. And do more than just dream about life with a holodeck; figure out how it works with the **Holodeck and Computers FAQ**.

Hawking and peers—http://www.ugcs.caltech.edu/~werdna/sttng/favorites.html #data

On the Net

Across the board

A Matter of Physics Einstein believed that God did not play dice with the universe, but *Star Trek* watchers know by now that the universe is a crapshoot. In the Physics folder, members unravel the Gordian Knot of the *Star Trek* universe and lovingly nitpick—or explain via theory—all the inconsistencies. One debate: How is Warp 13 attained when Warp 10

is supposed to be infinity? Another: How can the molecular beam transport work when the Heisenberg Uncertainty Principle says it shouldn't? Some theories are so convoluted they'd make Stephen Hawking (a Trek fan) blush. A lot of fun for budding physicists. ✓**AMERICA ONLINE**→*keyword* trek→ Star Trek Message Boards→The Neutral Zone

Federation Technology Just another spot in Cyberspace where Trekkers analyze the intricacies of technology that doesn't even exist. Everything from the potential energy uses of black holes posed by aspiring astrophysicists to the ecologically minded viewer's concern about phaser effects on the ecosphere get hearings. "Shouldn't holodecks have been recalled years ago?" asks one board member. It is

not unusual to find equations among the text, or the application of Newtonian physics to Ferengi warp drive. You may even find out how to make a transporter of your own among the many competing theories offered on a daily basis. ✓**GENIE**→*keyword* sfrt2→SFRT2 Bulletin Board→set 24→read 34

Joshua Bell's Star Trek Technology Page A Website from the guy who brought you the Tech mini-FAQs. Several of his FAQs are featured—including the Reading List for Treknology and the FAQ on tranporters and replicators—along with a link to a Trek ASCII archive, and several links to other Trek sites. ✓**INTERNET**→*www* http://www.ucalgary.ca/~jsbell/star_trek.html

Not the Technical Manual Unwilling to limit themselves to the explanations in the *Star Trek Technical Manual*, Usenet regulars theorize endlessly about the technical possibilites of the Trek universe. This manual summarizes many of these discussions, including those on warp speed, holodecks, and transporters. ✓**INTERNET** ...→*anon-ftp* ftp.cis.ksu.edu→/pub/alt. startrek.creative/tech→NotThe TechnicalManual.zip ...→*www* http://www.unisuper.com.au/strek /not-tech.html

rec.arts.sf.science (ng) If you want to discuss hyperspace, intelligence enhancement, or the possibility of receiving phone calls from the future, you've found the right place. The regulars of this newsgroup don't limit their conversations to the pseudoscience of sci-fi. You're as likely to read about relativity as the mechanics of transporter travel. One thread concerned the writing of a "future history." Some of the predictions for the next couple of centuries: genetic tailoring of bacteria, education by virtual reality, the arrival of alien missionaries. This is a friendly and intelligent group of sci-fi-addicted science types, including some youngsters; Damian, an eighth grader into astronomy, posted a question about chaos theory. ✓**USENET**

rec.arts.startrek.tech (ng) The heart of *Star Trek* may well be its human (and alien) relationships, but its soul, surely, is its new machines. Where would *Trek* be without the flash of phasers, the zoom of silver ships, the mix of whimsy and hard science in the Cochrane Drive? Well, it wouldn't be in eternal syndication and box-office nirvana, anyway. Rec.arts. startrek.tech is perhaps the most curious of the rec.arts.startrek* groups, requiring its participants

to find semirational explanations for implausible, and often inconsistent, Treknology. How does a deflector shield work? A warp drive? A phaser? A transporter? (This last one, at least, is easy—it has something to do with Heisenberg Compensators and Annular Confinement Beams.) This is the most male-dominated of the rec.arts. startrek* groups, since it caters expressly to boys-and-their-toys conversation. Still, always an interesting read—not least when RASTers gather together to pound *Star Trek* for tripping itself up with YATIs (Yet Another Technical Inconsistency). Back to the drawing boards. ✓**USENET**

Star Trek Technology How do warp numbers relate to actual velocity? How do you calculate tertiary warp? What is a third-order Cochrane function? A long, highly technical article focused primarily on explaining warp speed and time travel, but also addressing phaser and transporter technology.

Some of the theories expounded contradict the official *Star Trek* canon. The author, Trek fan Leon Myerson, bases much of his analysis on clues from episodes and principles of known physics. Consider the following point: "One of the greatest scientific discoveries made by the original *NCC-Enterprise* was that if a ship went EXTREMELY close to an object of stellar mass while in the normal continuum, then poured on maximum power to force its way to threshold before putting significant distance between itself and the gravity field of the celestial body in question, then the effective threshold velocity could actually be slightly above lightspeed, and the associated time dilation not only extremely large but NEGATIVE."

And then remind yourself that

this is called the "breakaway maneuver," more commonly known as time travel. Cool, huh? ✓**AMERICA ONLINE**→*keyword* trek→MORE...→Star Trek Record Banks→Text/Other Files→Upld: 09/10/93→TEXT: Star Trek Technology (File name: WARPTE2.TXT) ✓**INTERNET**→*gopher* wiretap.spies.com→Wiretap Online Library→Mass Media→Star Trek→Star Trek Technology ...→*gopher* dds.dds.nl→De Bibliotheek→boeken→Mass Media→Star Trek→Star Trek Technology

Tech Talk Help on stardates. An explanation of the emotion chip inplanted in Data. Debate over Klingon ships. All sorts of engaging tech hypotheticals. What, for instance, would you do if the Borg captured Picard again and implanted a device that would explode if Picard was moved off the ship? "Distortion field around Picard and through the transporter," says one member. "The biofilter could easily filter out the explosive," points out another. And, our favorite, "Beam a piece of the ship with him." ✓**PRODIGY**→*jump* star trek bb→Choose a Topic→Tech Talk

Technical Talk Wormholes? Sublight? Atmospheric friction? If that's gibberish to you, lurk awhile before posting here. Regulars know their stuff, and not just when it comes to Trek tech. You're as likely to hear talk of hyperspace and Newton's Laws as arguments about warp drives and shield generators. Sometimes science and the series intersect. "You made mention of DS9 barely holding together when they moved to the wormhole," one person noted. "My question is, why would it have structural problems? They're moving in the vacuum of space, so where would they encounter any pressure like they would moving

through a planet's atmosphere?" Uh, dunno, but the Trekheads seem to have the answers. ✓**DELPHI** →*go* ent sta for set tech

TFDN - Star Trek Technology James Dixon is the star of this library of Trek tech documents. Several of his technical histories and explanations are featured, including articles on cloaking devices, Starfleet ship colouring, the Romulan Peace Treaty, star coordinates, and the trans-warp theory. You can download other interpretations from here, or bypass the warp-speed debate and head for the stardate calculator, the list of locations referred to in *Star Trek*, the HoloDeck FAQ, or one of the several ship lists. All BBSs participating in the Trek File Distribution Network (TFDN) carry the same items although the name of the library may be slightly different on each board. ✓**TFDN**→TFDN — Star Trek Technology

Trekker_Technology (echo) Actual discussion is minimal, but FAQs culled from across the Net are posted here on such topics as the history of NCC starships, technology in *Trek*, and the Ferengi lexicon. ✓**TREKKERNET**

Trektech (echo) Passionate debates about terminal velocity, speculation about the Romulan phase-shifter, and endless analysis of the crash of the Enterprise-D are the types of topics covered here. Ph.D. in physics is not required, just an obsessive interest in understanding the technical capabilities and limits of the Trek universe. ✓**FIDONET** ✓**TREKNET**→TN_Trektech

WS_Eng (echo) Treknology fuels the imagination of many on this conference which alternates between "Gee, wow, imagine that"

entries and the more earnest queries of a role-playing game moderator who is desperate because a player is hung up on the following question: "How long would it take modern Photon Torpedo's to travel a distance of 2000KM?" Founder of the WarpSPEED network, John Buswell, replied: "Straight from our databanks: The maximum cruising velocity will follow the formula $V(max) = v1 + 0.75v1/c$. Where v1 is the launch velocity. Hope that helps. I have mass and range as well, want them?" ✓**WARPSPEED**

Introduction

rec.arts.startrek.tech FAQ Twenty-five Q&A's about Trek technology, including how to calculate warp speed, what the autodestruct sequence entails, and the ins and outs of transporters, holodecks, and replicators. ✓**INTERNET** ...→*anon-ftp* quepasa.cs.tu-berlin.de→/pub/doc/movies+tv-series/StarTrek/FAQs→tech.gz ...→*www* http://www.cosy.sbg.ac.at/ftp/pub/trek/lists/faq_tech.txt ...→*www* http://www.unisuper.com.au/strek/t-tecfaq.html

Rec.arts.startrek.tech Reading List In the mood for episode guides, general reference books, explanations of starship design, or a spaceflight chronology? Download this Treknology bibliography, which identifies dozens of relevant books, offers the FAQ writer's opinion about each book, and includes publisher information, ISBN numbers, and prices for each listing. ✓**COMPUSERVE**→*go* sf-media→Libraries→*Search by file name:* READIN.FAQ ✓**INTERNET**→*www* http://www.ucalgary.ca/~jsbell/faqs/reading-faq.html ...→*anon-ftp* ftp.cc.umanitoba.ca→/startrek/minifaqs→reading-

faq ...→*anon-ftp* rtfm.mit.edu→
/pub/usenet-by-hierarchy/rec/arts
/startrek/tech→Mini-FAQ:_Rec.
arts.startrek.tech_Reading_List

FTL travel

Physics in the 24th Century
Archive of a 1993 discussion on
rec.arts.startrek.tech about subspace communications and faster-
than-light travel. Included is a cutting point-by-point critique of the
Relativity and FTL Travel FAQ.
✓**TFDN**→TFDN - Star Trek Technolo-
gy→*Download a file:* WARPHIST.
ZIP

Relativity and FTL Travel FAQ
A detailed 20-page explanation of
the theory of relativity and faster
than light travel—equations included! This is hard-core scientific
theory, and should be read by experts only. Lesser mathematicians
may suffer eyestrain, dizziness, and
nausea. ✓**INTERNET** ...→*anon-ftp*
rtfm.mit.edu→/pub/usenet-by-

hierarchy/rec/arts/startrek/
tech→Relativity_and_FTL_Travel
...→*anon-ftp* ftp.cc.umanitoba.ca
→/startrek→Relativity_and_FTL.txt

**Warp Factor Versus Light
Speed** A GIF graph comparing
light speed with warp factor.
✓**COMPUSERVE**→*go* sfmedia→Li-
braries→*Search by file name:*
WARP.GIF

Holodeck

**Holodeck and Computers
Mini-FAQ** Answers to almost all
of the questions you have about
holodeck technology. This FAQ
considers issues ranging from eating and weight gain to the ethics
of simulating another person without his or her permission. ✓**INTER-
NET** ...→*www* http://www.ucal
gary.ca/~jsbell/faqs/holodeck-
faq.html ...→*anon-ftp* rtfm.mit.edu
→/pub/usenet-by-hierarchy/rec/
arts/startrek/tech→Mini-FAQ:_
The_Holodeck_and_Computers

...→*anon-ftp* ftp.cc.umanitoba.ca→
/startrek/minifaqs→holodeck-faq
✓**COMPUSERVE**→*go* sfmedia→Li-
braries→*Search by file name:*
HOLODK.FAQ

Medical

Starfleet Medical Files A long
document of 24th century medical
information culled from *Star Trek*
textbooks and *Star Trek* episodes.
To wit: "The function of the pro-
toplaser is to repair all internal and
external bodily damage without
requiring direct access to trauma—eliminating the need to open
the patient, simply to effect repairs." ✓**INTERNET**→*www* http:
//www.eeng.dcu.ie/~stdcu/trek/
med.html

Pictures & sounds

Communicator Badge Picture
of a communicator badge. ✓**COM-
PUSERVE**→*go* sfmedia→Libraries→
Search by file name: STBADG.GIF

ONLINE CYBERTREKKERS

Arnie Starr

Age 40; South Windsor, CT

Ink artist for DC Comics *Star Trek Comic*; regularly attends Trek conventions. Sysop of GEnie's Science Fic-
tion/Fantasy Media RoundTable

"I became a Trek fan when the show first aired, I watched it from day one....When I came online into the
SFRT, I became friends with Wil Wheaton almost immediately, I was into Trek, he was into comics, worked out
fine."

Favorite Series:	All of them—*Voyager* is promising
Favorite Character:	Spock
Favorite Episode:	"The City on the Edge of Forever" (TOS) , "The Inner Light" (TNG), "Darmok" (TNG), and "Blood Oath" (DS9)
Other Interests:	Games, particularly flight sims
Email Address:	starr@genie.geis.com

Technical orders

Tech Order Numbering System Explanation of how to read the Starfleet technical orders number system. ✓**COMPUSERVE**→*go* sfmedia→Libraries→*Search by file name:* TOEXPL.TXT

Transporters

Transporters and Replicators FAQ Answers and hypotheses about transporter technology. "What is a Heisenberg Compensator?" "Does that biofilter gadget work?" And, of course, "Where are you during transport?" ✓**INTERNET** ...→*www* http://www.ucalgary.ca /~jsbell/faqs/transport.html ...→*anon-ftp* ftp.cc.umanitoba.ca→ /startrek/minifaqs→transport-faq ...→*anon-ftp* quepasa.cs.tu-berlin. de→/pub/doc/movies+tv-series /StarTrek/FAQs→transporter.gz ✓**COMPUSERVE**→*go* sfmedia→Libraries→*Search by file name:* TRANSP.FAQ

Warp drive

History of Warp Drive A history of warp drive, reviewing the discovery of warp principles, the development of subspace radio, and the use of Dilithium. Updated in 1993. ✓**TFDN**→TFDN - Star Trek Technology→*Download a file:* WARPHIST.ZIP ✓**AMERICA ONLINE** →*keyword* trek→MORE...→Star Trek Record Banks→Text/Other Files→ Upld: 04/23/94→TEXT: History of Warp Drive (Filename: warp.doc) ✓**INTERNET**→*anon-ftp* ftp.cis.ksu.edu →/pub/alt.startrek.creative/tech→ HistoryOfWarp.zip

Lotus 123 Warp Speed Calculator Calculates in kilometers, light-years, parsecs, and AUs the distance the *Enterprise* could travel at specific warp speeds. For DOS. ✓**COMPUSERVE**→*go* sfmedia→ Libraries→*Search by file name:* WARP.WK1

TransWarp Theory How do you blow up the *Enterprise*? A brief overview of the ship's self-destruct sequences. ✓**TFDN**→TFDN - Star Trek Technology→*Download a file:* TRANSWRP.ZIP

Warp and Subspace Mini-FAQ An attempt to construct a theory of warp-speed travel based almost exclusively on references and information given on the show and in books written about the series. A mixture of formulas and plot summary. ✓**INTERNET** ...→*www* http://www.ucalgary.ca /~jsbell/faqs/warp-faq.html ...→*anon-ftp* rtfm.mit.edu→/pub/ usenet-by-hierarchy/rec/arts/ startrek/tech→Mini-FAQ:_Warp _and_Subspace ...→*anon-ftp* ftp.cc.umanitoba.ca→/startrek/mini faqs→warp-faq ✓**COMPUSERVE**→*go* sfmedia→Libraries→*Search by file name:* WARP.FAQ

Warp Speed Calculator Calculates warp speeds in terms of light speed and in metres per second for all values up to 9.9999. For Windows. ✓**COMPUSERVE**→*go* sfmedia→ Libraries→*Search by file name:* WARPCA.ZIP

Warp Speed Comparison Chart An explanation of the warp speed to light-speed conversion for TOS and TNG starships. Included is a warp speed equivalence chart with a comparison between conventional, transwarp, ultrawarp, and the light-speed multiplier. ✓**AMERICA ONLINE**→*keyword* trek→MORE...→Star Trek Record Banks→Text/Other Files→Upld: 06/12/94→ TEXT: Updated Warp/ Light conversion (Filename: WARP-COM.TXT)

Warp Speed to Light Speed A

brief explanation of how to calculate the warp speed used by the *NCC-1701* in TOS, the *NCC-1701-D* in TNG, and future warp hinted at in TNG's final episode, "All Good Things." ✓**AMERICA ONLINE**→*keyword* trek→MORE...→Star Trek Record Banks→Text/Other Files→Upld: 06/12/94→TEXT: Updated Warp/Light conversion (Filename: WARPLITE.TXT)

Weapons

Weaponry Technology A detailed and easy-to-follow examination of several common weapons used in the Trek universe. Klingon disrupters, Romulan disrupters, photon torpedoes, plasma torpedoes, and plasma disrupters are all covered, while the phasers used by Starfleet, the Cardassians, the Sheliak, and the Tholians are given extra-detailed coverage—the phaser weaponry is, of course, "the most concentrated directed energy weapon among the galactic powers." ✓**AMERICA ONLINE**→*keyword* trek→MORE...→Star Trek Record Banks→Text/Other Files→Upld: 04/19/94→Star Trek clock (Filename: WEAPON.zip)

Wormholes

Wormholes So you've heard of the wormhole near Bajor that leads directly to the Gamma Quadrant. What luck! The long-suffering Bajorans now sit at the hub of intergalactic commerce and activity—it's a new beginning and they owe it all to the wormhole. But what is a wormhole? For the mathematically minded individual, this is a summary of what we know and what has been theorized about wormholes. ✓**INTERNET**→ *anon-ftp* quepasa.cs.tu-berlin.de→ /pub/doc/movies+tv-series/ StarTrek/misc→wormholes.gz

The spacedock

It is probably fair to say that the USS *Enterprise* is the most widely recognized visual

symbol of modern science-fiction. In fact, *Trek* creator Gene Roddenberry often considered the *Enterprise* one of the cast of characters, although most series historians suggest that the ship was not given its own dressing room. In fact, spacecrafts—not only the *Enterprise*, but its Romulan, Klingon, Ferengi, and Borg counterparts—sit at the heart of Trek fandom. Knowing their speed, their size, their weaponry, and their deck plans is mandatory, and the quest for technical minutiae is as endless as the stream of ship-related pictures, animations, and sound files posted in Cyberspace. Learn the science of the infamous **Cloaking Device**. Build your own El-Baz shuttlepod with **Cardboard Models of TNG Shuttles**. And identify those flying objects with a complete checklist of **Active Ships**.

On the Net

Ship lists

The 14 Enterprises A list of 14 ships christened the *Enterprise*. ✓**INTERNET**→*www* http://www.cosy.sbg.ac.at/ftp/pub/trek/lists/enterprises.txt

Star Trek Ships: Expanded
by D. Joseph Creighton

Screenshot from http://www.ee.umanitoba.ca/~djo/startrek/ships.expanded.html

Active Ships A list of every active Starfleet craft in the Trek universe, from the *Magellan NCC-3069* to the *Merrimac NCC-61827*, divided by class; *Ambassador, Antares, Renaissance,* and so on. ✓**INTERNET**→*www* http://lal.cs.byu.edu/people/black/StarTrek/ships.html

Enterprise: A History of the Gallant Ladies of Sea and Space Descriptions of 37 ships (specifications, missions, and historical influences) bearing the name *Enterprise*, both in Earth history and the Trek universe. Did you know that a space shuttle Enterprise is now on display at the Dulles Airport Annex of the National Air and Space Museum? Or that the first Starfleet vessel christened the *Enterprise* will be commissioned in 2123? ✓**COMPUSERVE**

→*go* sfmedia→Libraries→*Search by file name:* EHIST.TXT ✓**INTERNET**→*anon-ftp* ftp.cis.ksu.edu→/pub/alt.startrek.creative/info→Enterprise.zip ...→*www* http://www.unisuper.com.au/strek/enterpri.html

History of Ships Named Enterprise An annotated time line written in 1989 that chronicles both the history of the *Enterprise* and Trek history in general. The plots of episodes and movies are described. ✓**COMPUSERVE**→*go* sfmedia→Libraries→*Search by file name:* STHIS-.TXT

History of the Ships Named Enterprise A time line chronicling vessels bearing the name Enterpise, beginning with the British sailing vessel *HMS Enterprise* of 1616 (which was sent on a fatal mission to find an alternative route to the Orient) and ending with TNG's fourth season and the *Enterprise NCC-1701-D* (which in 2366 underwent major repairs after a Borg attack). ✓**AMERICA ONLINE**→*keyword* trek→MORE...→Star Trek Record Banks→Text/Other Files→Upld: 04/23/94 →TEXT: Enterprise History (Filename: enthist3. doc) ✓**INTERNET**→*www* http://www.unisuper.com.au/strek/historyo.html

Ships of Star Trek An encylopedia of ships in the *Star Trek* universe, including those that have appeared in TOS, TNG, and DS9. Descriptions include information on crew, episodes, and weaponry specs. Did you know that the *Bonaventure* was the first class of Federation ship equipped with warp drive? The eWorld list has been updated more recently. ✓**EWORLD**→sf→Star Trek→United Federation Library→SHIPS.TXT ✓**INTERNET**→*anon-ftp* ftp.cis.ksu.edu→/pub/alt.startrek.creative/info→ShipsOfStartrek.list.zip

Star Trek Ships Remember the *USS Hood* from TNG's episode "The Ultimate Computer"? How about the *USS Grissom* (NCC-636), which was captained by J.T. Esteban and destroyed over Genesis by a Klingon Bird of Prey in ST2? This document includes crew and command information for most of the ships featured in the original series, *The Next Generation, Deep Space Nine*, and the motion pictures. Only the television series and movies are used as sources. The Internet usually has the most updated version of the ship list. ✓**GENIE**→*keyword* sfrt2→Text and Graphics Library→*Download a file:* 978 ✓**INTERNET**→*gopher* wiretap.spies.com→Wiretap Online Library→Mass Media→Star Trek→Star Trek Ship Names ...→*anon-ftp* rtfm.mit.edu→/pub/usenet-by-

hierarchy/rec/arts/startrek/misc →STAR_TREK_SHIPS: _TELEVISION_&_FILM* ...→*www* http://www.cosy.sbg.ac.at/ftp/pub/trek/lists/ships.txt

Star Trek Ships: Expanded If you're a fan of the *USS Horatio* or the Romulan Bird of Prey, you'll want to check out this document. Managed by D. Joseph Creighton and Joshua Sean Bell, this is a list of ships organized by alien race, which ties each craft to the episodes in which they have appeared. ✓**INTERNET** ...→*www* http://www.ee. umanitoba.ca/~djc/startrek/ships.expanded.html ...→*anon-ftp* rtfm.mit.edu→/pub/usenet-by-hierarchy/rec/arts/startrek/misc→STAR_TREK_SHIPS: _EXPANDED_[Updated:_* ...→*www* http://www.unisuper.com.au/strek/t-ships.html

Starfleet's Fleet A list of ships that have appeared on TOS, TNG, DS9, and in the movies. Registry number, ship name, ship class, and the ship's status are included, and the document is easy to import into a database. ✓**COMPUSERVE**→*go* sfmedia→Libraries→*Search by file name:* FLEET.TXT

Cloaking

Cloaking Device Invented by the Romulan Empire and adopted by the Klingon Empire, the cloaking device makes ships invisible. This file describes the history and the effects of cloaking. ✓**TFDN**→TFDN—Technical Files→*Download a file:* CLOAK.ZIP

Discussion of Star Trek Cloaking Devices Ever wonder how *Trek* ships cloak? Well, here's one explanation: "The ship generates a gravitational distortion that causes electromagnetic radiation to curve halfway around the ship before escaping." If high-density tech talk like this makes you want to curve halfway around your PC, be careful approaching this document, in which "all ideas were bounced around within a dedicated panel of Treknicians, including two physicists, a chemist, and a mathematician, with the aid of three ST:TNG Tech Manuals, two VCRs, a large collection of video footage, and a particle in a pear tree." ✓**INTERNET**→*gopher* wiretap.spies.com→Wiretap Online Library →Mass Media→Star Trek Discussion of Star Trek Cloaking Devices

Self-destruct

Destruct Sequence Scenarios How do you blow up the Enterprise? A brief overview of the ship's self-destruct sequences. ✓**TFDN**→TFDN-Star Trek Technology→*Download a file:* ORGANIA.ZIP

Stats & specs

Deck Layout of Federation Vessels Which way to the holodeck? This document details floor plans and layouts for five classes of Federation starships—Constitution, Enterprise, Excelsior, Constellation, and Galaxy—with deck and hull locations for their main areas. ✓**AMERICA ONLINE** →*keyword* trek→MORE...→Star Trek Record Banks→Text/Other Files→Upld: 04/19/94→TEXT: Deck Layout and Breakdown (Filename: DECK.TXT)

Ship Statistics Absolutely-NonCanon Mini-FAQ Ship

specifications and ASCII representations for vessels from several races in the *Star Trek* universe. Missions, ship design, ship size, and system information (warp, impulse, tactical, hospital facilities, etc.) are included. ✓**COMPUSERVE**→*go* sfmedia→Libraries→*Search by file name:* SHIPST.FAQ ✓**INTERNET**→*www* http://www.ucalgary.ca/~jsbell/faqs/shipstats-faq ...→*anon-ftp* ftp.cc.umanitoba.ca→/startrek/minifaqs→ship stats-faq ...→*www* http://www.cosy.sbg.ac.at/ftp/pub/trek/lists/techmini/techmini.faq.05.txt

The Enterprise

The Starship Enterprise The different versions of the *Enterprise*

seem to arouse the same sort of loyalty as models of cars do among the *Road and Track* crowd. There are aesthetic considerations,too: Do you go for the slick high tech of the *Enterprise-D* or the utilitarian look of exposed pipes and valves of the earlier models? The most heated debate ranges around whether or not the *Enterprise* can take anything those damned aliens dish out. ✓**GENIE**→*keyword* sfrt2→SFRT2 Bulletin Board →set 24→read 42

Voyager

Class of Starship Everyone who watches the *Star Trek* series knows who the real star is. She's big, she's graceful, she's sexy, and she's faithful: She's a Federation Starship. Drawing on military naval history, members debate the merits of Starfleet's policy of building bigger and bigger ships (they make bigger and bigger targets). The more aggressive participants hope the new starship will kick everyone's ass, but others maintain that Starfleet is about exploration, not aggression. And what about that new *Voyager*? While the Galaxy Class starship may still be the flagship, this Intrepid Class vessel is capable of going phenomenal distances (good thing, huh!). ✓**AMERICA ONLINE**→*keyword* trek→Star Trek Message Boards→Star Trek Voyager→Class of Starship

CYBERTREKKERS

Joshua Sean Bell

Age 21; Calgary, Alberta

Maintains mini-FAQs on Trek tech and a Website (http://www.ucalgary.ca/~jsbell/star_trek.html)

Time :   70 hrs/week

Other Interests: NarniaMUSH, ASCII art newsgroups, and emailing "my girlfriend who's in Texas"

Favorite Episode: "Yesterday's Enterprise" (TNG) and "Best of Both Worlds, Part I" (TNG)

Mission Statement: "I'd avoided *Star Trek* on the Net for ages but eventually got sucked into rec.arts.startrek.tech when I got a copy of the *TNG Technical Manual*. Started writing, and eventually came up with my Mini-FAQs. I avoid the other groups and all mailing lists because of their sheer volume. And I check out all the Websites. There's a subset of us [on rec.arts.startrek.tech] who have overlapping interpretations of the show, and feed on each other's ideas. Rather nice. Since it is (very!) borderline science, it's actually got an edge to it and can be discussed somewhat rationally.

"The Web will be the next major outgrowth, if I can use 'next' to describe what has already started, of electronic fandom. Interactive sites like Paramount's will become more common; I'm working on my own, and will encourage others to do so as well. I'm very, very pleased that Paramount has done things like the Voyager and Generations sites; I like 'official' information, and we're getting it from our medium for a change. I don't think we'll have much influence on *Star Trek* directly, but it's nice to know that Paramount cares."

Email Address: jsbell@acs.ucalgary.ca

PICTURES OF SHIPS

Across the board

Star Trek Ships Images of the primary ship from each of the series: *NCC-1701*, *NCC-1701-A*, *NCC-1701-C*, *NCC-1701-D*, DS9 station, *Defiant*, and *Voyager*. √INTERNET→*www* http:// everest. cs.uc davis.edu/~hoagland/ Trek.html#ships

Borg

The Borg ship The *Enterprise* encounters an unknown ship—the Borg. √INTERNET ...→*anon-ftp* ftp.cis.ksu.edu→ pub/pictures/jpg/Startrek→ sttng203.jpg ...→*anon-ftp* lajkonik. cyf-kr.edu.pl→/agh/reserve/gifs /star trek→sttng203.jpg

Cardassian

Cardassian Ship Clip art of a Cardassian vessel. √COMPUSERVE→ *go* sfmedia→Libraries→*Search by file name:* CARDAS.GIF

Enterprise

An Enterprise Encounter The *Enterprise* has encountered an unknown vessel. √INTERNET ...→ *anon-ftp* ftp.cis.ksu.edu→/pub/ pictures/jpg/Startrek→sttng323.jpg ...→*anon-ftp* lajkonik.cyf-kr.edu. pl→/agh/reserve/gifs/startrek→ sttng323.jpg

The Enterprise Large shot of the *NCC-1701-D*. √INTERNET→*www* http://lal.cs.byu.edu/people/black /StarTrek/ncc1701d/homepage. html

Enterprise *Enterprise* near a gaseous planet. √INTERNET ...→*anon-ftp* ftp.cis.ksu.edu→/pub/pic tures/jpg/Startrek→sttng100.jpg ...→*anon-ftp* lajkonik.cyf-kr.edu. pl→/agh/reserve/gifs/startrek →sttng100.jpg

Enterprise Image of the *Enterprise* in series opening credits. √INTERNET ...→*anon-ftp* ftp.cis.ksu.edu →/pub/pictures/jpg/Startrek→ sttng05.jpg ...→*anon-ftp* lajkonik. cyf-kr.edu.pl→/agh/reserve/gifs/ startrek→sttng05.jpg

Enterprise Image of *Enterprise* engaging warp engines in opening credits. √INTERNET ...→*anon-ftp* ftp.cis.ksu.edu→/pub/pictures/jpg /Startrek→sttng013.jpg ...→*anon-ftp* lajkonik.cyf-kr.edu.pl→/agh/ reserve/gifs/startrek→sttng013.jpg

The Enterprise The *Enterprise* in orbit. √INTERNET ...→*anon-ftp* ftp. cis.ksu.edu→/pub/pictures/jpg/Star trek→ncc1701b.jpg ...→*anon-ftp* laj konik.cyf-kr.edu.pl→/agh/reserve/ gifs/startrek→ncc1701b.jpg

Enterprise and Alien Ship. The *Enterprise* encounters an alien ship. √INTERNET ...→*anon-ftp* ftp.cis.ksu.edu →/pub /pictures/jpg/Star trek→sttng089.jpg ...→ *anon-ftp* lajkonik.cyf- kr.edu.pl→/agh/reserve/ gifs/startrek→sttng089.jpg

Enterprise and Fleetmate *Enterprise* alongside an older Excelsior-class vessel. √INTERNET ...→ *anon-ftp* ftp.cis.ksu.edu→/pub/pic

tures/jpg/Startrek →sttng038.jpg ...→ *anon-ftp* lajkonik.cyf- kr.edu.pl→/agh/reserve/gifs /startrek→sttng038.jpg

Enterprise and Starfleet vessel. The *Enterprise* has a rendezvous with another Starfleet vessel, possibly the *Crazy Horse*. √INTERNET ...→*anon-ftp* ftp.cis.ksu.edu→ /pub/pictures/jpg/Startrek→ sttng205.jpg ...→*anon-ftp* lajkonik. cyf-kr.edu.pl→/agh/reserve/gifs /startrek→sttng205.jpg

Enterprise Banking around Asteroid An image of the *Enterprise NCC-1701-D* near asteroids. √COMPUSERVE→*go* sfmedia→Libraries→*Search by file name:* EBANK1.GIF

Enterprise D in Space A JPEG image of the *Enterprise NCC-1701-D*. √COMPUSERVE→*go* sfmedia→Libraries→*Search by file name:* ENT-D.JPG

The Enterprise Exploring a New World The *Enterprise* in orbit. √INTERNET ...→*anon-ftp* ftp.cis.ksu.edu→/pub/pictures/jpg /Startrek→sttng202.jpg ...→*anon-ftp* lajkonik.cyf-kr.edu.pl→/agh/ reserve/gifs/startrek→ sttng202.jpg

Enterprise Firing Phasers The original *Enterprise* firing its main phasers. √INTERNET ...→*anon-ftp* ftp.cis.ksu.edu→ /pub/pictures/jpg/Startrek→lg- g22.jpg ...→ *anon-ftp* lajkonik.cyf- kr.edu.pl→/agh/reserve/gifs/ startrek→lg-g22.jpg

PICTURES OF SHIPS

Enterprise GIFs Three external views of the *Enterprise* from TOS. ✓**GENIE**→*keyword* sfrt 1→Text and Graphics Library→ *Download a file:* NCC 1701. ARC

Enterprise Saucer Section Exterior view of *Enterprise* saucer and bridge from opening credits. ✓**INTERNET** ...→*anon-ftp* ftp.cis.ksu.edu →/pub/pictures/jpg/Startrek →sttng002.jpg ...→*anon-ftp* laj konik.cyf-kr.edu.pl→/agh/reserve /gifs/startrek→sttng002.jpg

Enterprise vs 2 Romulan Vessels Can the *Enterprise* hold up against two massive Romulan Warbirds? Find out by consulting this GIF. ✓**COM-PUSERVE**→*go* sfmedia→Libraries→*Search by file name:* ER2.ROMU.GIF

Enterprise-D *USS Enterprise* on its continuing mission. ✓**INTERNET** ...→*anon-ftp* ftp.cis.ksu.edu→/pub /pictures/jpg/Startrek→sttng03. jpg *and* ncc 1701d.jpg ...→*anon-ftp* lajkonik.cyf-kr.edu.pl→/agh/ reserve/gifs/startrek→sttng03.jpg *and* ncc 1701d.jpg

The Enterprises ASCII renderings of the *Enterprise* with specifications. ✓**INTERNET**→*www* http:// www.cms.dmu.ac.uk/~it2yh/pas tent.html

NCC 1701-D Rendezvous Sounds steamy, doesn't it? Find out for yourself by downloading this image of the *Enterprise-D* rendezvousing with an Excelsior

Class Vessel. ✓**COMPUSERVE** →*go* sfmedia→ Libraries→*Search by file name:* ENTS2.GIF

NCC-1701 Another image of the original *Enterprise*. ✓**INTERNET** →*www* http://www.cosy.sbg.ac.at /ftp/pub/trek/pics/NCC 1701.gif

The Original Enterprise Drawing of *NCC-1701*, original *Enterprise*. ✓**INTERNET** ...→*anon-ftp* ftp.cis.ksu.edu→/pub/pictures/jpg/ Startrek→ncc 1701a.jpg ...→*anon-ftp* lajkonik.cyf-kr.edu.pl→/agh /reserve/gifs/startrek→ncc 1701a.jpg

Star Trek NCC-1701 Enterprise Warp Picture Front of the *Enterprise NCC-1701* moving at warp speed. GIF image. ✓**COMPUSERVE**→ *go* sfmedia→Libraries→*Search by file name:* INWARP.GIF

Stern of Enterprise Image of the *Enterprise* in opening credits. ✓**INTERNET** ...→*anon-ftp* ftp.cis.ksu. edu→/pub/pictures/jpg/Startrek →sttng015.jpg ...→*anon-ftp* lajkonik.cyf-kr.edu. pl→/agh/reserve/ gifs/startrek→ sttng015.jpg

TNG MPEG Short animation of the *NCC-1701-D* slowly moving into warp speed. ✓**INTERNET** →*www* http://everest.cs.ucdavis. edu/~hoagland/movies/tng.mpg

TOS Animation Short animation of the *NCC-1701* moving toward a sun. ✓**INTEPNET**→*www* http:// everest.cs.ucdavis.edu/~hoagland

/movies/tosanim.mpg

TOS Enterprise MPEG of the *Enterprise* going to warp. ✓**INTER-NET**→*www* http://www.cms.dmu. ac.uk/~aug/graphics/mpeg/ enterprise.mpeg

The TOS Enterprise Shot of the vessel from the original series. ✓**INTERNET**→*www* http://www. cosy.sbg.ac.at/mirror/httpd/info /star_trek/ncc 1701

TOS Enterprise Another old *Enterprise* image. ✓**INTERNET**→*www* http://www.cosy.sbg.ac.at/ftp /pub/trek/pics/oldenter.jpg

USS Enterprise The *Enterprise* on its continuing mission. ✓**INTER-NET** ...→*anon-ftp* ftp.cis.ksu.edu→ /pub/pictures/jpg/Startrek→sttng 324.jpg ...→*anon-ftp* lajkonik.cyf-kr.edu.pl→/agh/reserve/gifs/ startrek→sttng324.jpg

USS Enterprise Front view of the *Starship*. ✓**INTERNET** ...→*anon-ftp* ftp.cis.ksu.edu→/pub/pictures /jpg/Startrek→sttng 108.jpg ...→ *anon-ftp* lajkonik.cyf-kr.edu.pl→ /agh/reserve/gifs/startrek →sttng 108.jpg

USS Enterprise NCC-1701-D Includes three images of the *Enterprise NCC-1701-D* in the wake of interstellar combat; two of the pictures show the starship separating in order to save the saucer. ✓**COMPUSERVE**→*go* sfmedia →Libraries→ *Search by file name:* BATTLE.SIT

PICTURES OF SHIPS

Ferengi

Enterprise and Ferengi ship *Enterprise* encounters Ferengi warship. ✓**INTERNET** …→*anon-ftp* ftp.cis.ksu.edu→pub/pictures/jpg /Startrek→sttng084.jpg …→*anon-ftp* lajkonik.cyf-kr.edu.pl→/agh/ reserve/gifs/startrek →sttng084.jpg

Klingon

Klingon Bird of Prey Dramatic image of a Klingon Bird of Prey entering warp speed. ✓**COMPUSERVE**→*go* sfmedia→ Libraries→ *Search by file name:* KLINGO.GIF

Klingon Bird of Prey Klingon ship being used for stealth mission in Romulan space. ✓**INTERNET** …→ *anon-ftp* ftp.cis.ksu.edu→pub/pic tures/jpg/Startrek→sttng307.jpg …→*anon-ftp* lajkonik. cyf-kr.edu.pl→ /agh/reserve/gifs/startrek→ sttng307.jpg

Klingon warship Prototype Klingon warship firing upon the *Enterprise-A*. ✓**INTERNET** …→ *anon-ftp* ftp.cis.ksu.edu→pub/pictures/ jpg/Startrek→st-v-06.jpg …→ *anon-ftp* lajkonik.cyf-kr.edu.pl→ /agh/reserve/gifs/startrek→st-v-06.jpg

Klingon Warship Klingon warship approaching the *Enterprise-A*. ✓**INTERNET** …→*anon-ftp* ftp.cis. ksu.edu→pub/pictures/jpg/Star trek→st-v-05.jpg …→*anon-ftp* laj konik.cyf-kr.edu.pl→/agh/reserve /gifs/startrek→st-v-05.jpg

Romulan

Romulan Warbird and the Enterprise GIF of a Romulan ship and the *Enterprise* in a face-off. ✓**COMPUSERVE**→*go* sfmedia→Libraries→*Search by file name:* ROMULA.GIF

Romulan Warbird and the Enterprise Startupscreen Start-up screen of a face-off between the two ships. For the Macintosh. ✓**COMPUSERVE**→*go* sfmedia →Libraries→ *Search by filename:* ROMUL. SIT

Shuttlecraft

Cardboard Models of TNG Shuttles Ulrich Prahn's *Star Trek* Cardboard models with building instructions and pictures in JPEG or GIF formats. PostScript cut out sheets for four different models are currently available, including how-to guidelines for creating scale models of the *El-Baz* shuttlepod and the sophisticated shuttlecraft *Magellan*. ✓**INTERNET**→ *www* http://wwwipd.ira.uka.de /~goetzo/stmodels.html

Shuttlecraft Shuttlecraft approaching a planet. ✓**INTERNET** …→*anon-ftp* ftp.cis.ksu.edu→/pub /pictures/jpg/Startrek→sttng093. jpg …→ *anon-ftp* lajkonik.cyf-kr. edu.pl→/agh/reserve/gifs/startrek →sttng093.jpg

Starfleet

DS9 GIF Image of the station. ✓**COMPUSERVE**→ *go* sfmedia→Libraries→ *Search by file name:* DS9.GIF

Starfleet Vessel Starfleet vessel (possibly an *Enterprise-D* prototype). ✓**INTERNET** …→*anon-ftp* ftp.cis.ksu.edu→/pub/pictures/jpg/ Startrek→sttng032.jpg …→*anon-ftp* lajkonik.cyf-kr.edu.pl→/agh/ reserve/gifs/startrek→sttng032.jpg

The USS Defiant GIF of the ship. ✓**COMPUSERVE**→*go* sfmedia→ Libraries→*Search by file name:* DEF1.GIF

Pre-Enterprise Picture of the *Enterprise*'s predecessor. ✓**PVG** *dial* 513-233-7993→<your username> →<your password>→F→*Download a file:* PVSHIP03.GIF

The ships depicted here are taken from graphics files downloaded from sites listed on these pages. These listings constitute only a fraction of the Trek ship images available in Cyberspace. Every Trek picture archive and commercial service library is filled with artistic renderings and video stills of the starships of the Trek universe.

PART 2

THE
TREK
PHENOMENON

Kirk vs. Picard

There is more heat generated by this debate than in some recent political elections—

probably more difference between the candidates as well. *Entertainment Weekly* listed "Kirk versus Picard" as the single most discussed issue on the information highway—even more than O.J. Yet there appears no hope of resolution: Even the demise (temporary?) of James T. Kirk has only inflamed the partisans. The battle rages on AOL's **Kirk v. Picard** and on every discussion group listed in this book (enough already!). Is this a generational battle? Is it a class thing? Or is it simple a matter of style—Kirk's dashing spontaneity versus Picard's almost professorial bearing? One thing's for certain: it's a no-win situation.

Composite—from CompuServe's Bettman Archives (Kirk) and ftp.cis.ksu.edu (Picard)

On the Net

Across the board

The 2 Esteemed Captains of the USS Enterprise Picture of Picard and Kirk with a space background. ✓**COMPUSERVE**→*go* sfmedia →Libraries→*Search by file name:* CAP2.GIF

Kirk v. Picard Over the last couple of years, countless threads have debated the relative merits of the two captains. This is a collection of some of those lists, including the top 100 reasons why Kirk is

better than Picard and a point-by-point response by Picard fans. Just listen: "Kirk has sex more than once a season." Rejoinder: "Sex with Picard is worth waiting for a whole season." "Kirk never once stood up and had to straighten his shirt." Rejoinder: "Picard never once stood up and had to suck in his gut." "Kirk never asks his bartender for advice." Rejoinder: "Picard never asks his Chief Medical Officer to be bartender." And, that's only three. ✓**INTERNET**→ *anon-ftp* ftp.cis.ksu.edu→/pub/alt. startrek.creative/misc→Kirk.v.Pi card.zip

Kirk v. Picard This debate was spawned by a *TV Guide* question: Who would you rather have defend the Earth—James T. Kirk or Jean-Luc Picard? The discussion quickly breaks into two camps. Kirk lovers find Picard too cerebral, Picard partisans think Kirk lacks diplomatic skills. Is Picard too slow moving or Kirk too prone to insubordination; Kirk too emotional, Picard too reserved? Or is it the type of conflict that makes the difference? Kirk would triumph over the "Gorn or a giant ice-cream cone," but Picard would be the only victor in a battle to the death with "Master

Thespians with perfect diction."
✓**GENIE**→*keyword* sfrt2→Text and Graphics Libraries→*Download a file:* 663

Kirk v. Picard Scan of the *TV Guide* cover featuring Kirk v. Picard. ✓**PVG** *dial* 513-233-7993→<your username>→<your password>→F→*Download a file:* KRKPCRD.GIF

Kirk v. Picard "Picard has had 80-plus years to learn from Kirk's mistakes and build on the things he did right. So sorry Kirk lovers (and I consider myself one)—I'll have to go with Picard." "If it's negotiation, I'll take Picard, but in a battle, give me Kirk any day." The struggle for superiority between TOS and TNG is never as pronounced as it is in the ongoing tussle between the two captains. Who's stronger? Who's smarter? And most importantly, who's balder? Fans in this message board aren't the kind to jump to a conclusion, so even when they admit a certain preference, they go to great pains to justify it, dissecting Kirk's impetuous bravado and Picard's philosophical introspection. ✓**AMERICA ONLINE**→*keyword* scifi→Star Trek/Comics/TV/Star Wars Boards→Star Trek→kirk v. picard

Picard v. Kirk An animation program in which Captain Kirk alters into Captain Picard. Requires a program that runs FLI animations. ✓**COMPUSERVE**→*go* sfmedia→Libraries→*Search by file name:* TREKMO.ZIP

"Star Trek": Kirk encounters Picard The battle between Kirk and Picard plays out in a crude (in more ways than one) but inventive text "animation." If you have a UNIX machine or shell access with your Internet provider, first decode the program with a uude-

coder. Then type: cat startrek2.vt. ✓**INTERNET** …→*gopher* twinbrook.cis.uab.edu→The Continuum→The ASCII Art Bazaar→Animations→"Star Trek": Kirk encounters Picard …→*www* gopher://twinbrook.cis.uab.edu:70/0A/A/startrek.uue

The Top 100 Reasons Kirk Is Better Than Picard Kirk and Picard face off. The list is regularly posted to the rec.arts.startrek* groups. ✓**COMPUSERVE**→*go* sfmedia→Libraries→*Search by file name:* 100.TXT

The Top 100 Reasons Picard Is Better Than Kirk The debate continues. The list in various manifestations is often posted to the rec.arts.startrek* groups. ✓**COMPUSERVE**→*go* sfmedia→Libraries→*Search by file name:* REBUTT.TXT

Who's better: Kirk or Picard The rules of the ring are simple: No kicking, no biting, and may the best captain win. That's "captain" not "actor." Picard and Kirk may not have swapped punches in outer space, but in Cyberspace, and particularly in the *Generations* folder of AOL's *Star Trek* Club, fans constantly fight over the relative merits of the *Enterprise* captains. Kirk's more clever. Picard's a better diplomat. Kirk makes split second decisions and is comfortable in command. Picard has more

control. Quickly, very quickly, the positions get passionate: "Space is a FRONTIER, not a TEA PARTY. It demands a gambling and arrogant nature to get anywhere. Kirk wins the Captain contest hands down." Or, "Picard kicks ass!!" ✓**AMERICA ONLINE**→*keyword* trek→Star Trek Message Boards→Generations (TNG Movie)→Who's better: KIRK or Picard

Kirk's dead

The Death of Capt. James Kirk Angry that their hero has passed on, these Kirk fans check in to remind each other how entertaining Kirk was and—mention more often than not—how misdirected the new series are. Register your complaints about how Kirk died, speculate on whether he really did die, and share some memories. ✓**AMERICA ONLINE**→*keyword* trek→Star Trek Message Boards→Classic Trek→The Death of Capt. James Kirk

Ding Dong; The Kirk Is Dead! Sung to the tune of "Ding-Dong the Witch Is Dead," the parody begins: "Ding-dong, the Kirk is gone./Which old Kirk?/The bald old Kirk./Ding-dong the bald old Kirk is gone." Now, everybody join in. ✓**INTERNET**→*www* http://www.cs.odu.edu/~cashman/humor/ding-dong.html

"Get a life!": Trek humor

It's always fun to play with your food and alien recipes are traded obsssessively in Cyber-

space. WS_Cook is a good place to start collecting them (hint: cooking with another species is considered tasteless—don't give out your recipe for Trill Slug Surprise). Parodies, though, are the main comedy act, with thousands of Trek spoofs posted to the Net. How about a cross-dressing Kirk? An encounter between Picard and the vampire Lestat? There are already enough *Voyager* filks for a debut album: "Now sit right back to hear the tale, the tale of a fateful trip." Check out the **To Boldly Go Where No Man Has Gone Before** Website for a large selection. And, it's not just the fans doing the mocking: a soundclip of Captain Kirk's infamous *Saturday Night Live!* "Get a Life" speech is also available.

"The Trouble with Tribbles"—downloaded from lajkonic.cyf-kr.edu.pl

On the Net

Across the board

Assorted Star Trek Items A strange mix of Trek information and silliness, with an emphasis on the latter. The site includes instructions for the *Star Trek* Drinking Game (two shots everytime Riker says, "You are personally responsible for the captain's safety"

to Worf), and several Trek spoofs including one piece of fiction documenting "The voyages of the starship booby prize" and another following "The voyages of the starship Carbonize" (see the file Star Coke 2). The episode entitled "The Trouble with Tribbles" has its humorous twin, "The Tribble with Troubles." ✓**INTERNET**→*gopher* umcc.umcc.umich.edu→users→ Appleton's Amazing Assorted Arti facts→Assorted Star Trek Items

Good Ol' Geeky Star Trek Stuff In its early stages, the site includes Trek skits (e.g, Microsoft: The Next Generation) and a few soundclips. ✓**INTERNET**→*www* http: //kelp.honors.indiana.edu/%7echr ome/trek/index.html

Star Trek Humor How many *Star Trek* fans does it take to screw in a light bulb? Only one, but you have to wait until the show is over. A grab bag of Trek humor, including limericks, riddles, shuttlecraft bumper stickers, and top ten lists.

✓**GENIE**→*keyword* sfrt2→SFRT2 Bulletin Board→set 35

Star Trek Humor League (ml) Book passage on the USS *Radish* (the fictional ship all list members ride) for nonstop parodies, jokes, and Trek silliness. ✓**INTERNET**→ *email* listserv@nic.surfnet.nl ✍ *Type in message body:* subscribe sthl-l <your full name>

Star Trek Humour A slow but steady trickle of Trek jokes, parodies, and top ten lists. ✓**EWORLD**→ sf→Star Trek→On the Small Screen →Star Trek Humour

Character attacks

alt.ensign.wesley.die.die.die (ng) Have you ever been inspired to kill TNG's annoying child prodigy, Wesley Crusher? Members of this group have—repeatedly and creatively. David wants to unearth the story in which Wesley wired up a console to watch some porno, and he was walking behind counselor Troi and looking at her butt, and she turns around and smacks him." Ahh, that story. Richard sends it to him. When an AOL user posts to the group, suggesting that members are secretly attracted to Wil Wheaton and jealous of him, Frederick responds: "We hate the character, not the actor. In fact, if you had read this group for more than five minutes, you would know that Wil Wheaton knows about this group and thinks it is hilarious. So go away. Log out. This is the information superhighway, and you are about to get run over." Don't expect solidarity here. It's every man for himself and Wesley Crusher is not the only one likely to get beat up. ✓USENET

Filk

alt.startrek.creative (ng) This active group is filled with *Trek* novellas, erotic *Trek* writing, and a huge number of filks—filks about the Borg, Spock, Kirk, the end of TNG, the start of *Voyager*, the Trill named Dax, etc. ✓USENET

End of the Borg "It's the end of the world as we know it (and I feel fine." ✓INTERNET→*anon-ftp* ftp.cis.ksu.edu→/pub/alt.startrek.creative/misc→YetAnotherBorgSong.zip

Filk Songs and Fan Music With a purview much broader than *Star Trek*, this category on GEnie's science-fiction fandom RoundTable is devoted to filkers in both the sci-fi and fantasy genres. Most animated when planning for conventions or just chatting with filking friends, filkers are here not necessarily to exchange filks, but also to meet others with a similar passion. ✓GENIE→*keyword* sfrt3→SFRT3 Bulletin Board→set 15

Filking Although a message board

and library are dedicated to the joys of sci-fi and fantasy filking, the place is often deserted. For newbie filkers, the library holds a few introductions to creating and submitting filks. ✓COMPUSERVE→*go* sflit→Libraries *or* Messages→Filking

Periodic List of Star Trek Music Dozens of lyrical Trek parodies, including the ever popular "Star Trekkin," sung to the tune of "Here we go round the mulberry bush." To wit: "There's Klingons on the starboard bow, starboard bow, starboard bow. There's Klingons on the starboard bow, starboard bow, Jim." ✓INTERNET→*anon-ftp* quepasa.cs.tu-berlin.de→/pub/doc/movies+tv-series/Star Trek→music.gz

Trek_Humor_Filk (echo) You must be funny. Androids other than Data after the emotion-chip replacement need not post. Share your Trek jokes, parodies, or filks. How about a filk called "California Trills?" It's set to the tune of—yup, you guessed it—"California Girls." As for the jokes: "How many Klingons does it take to screw in a light bulb? Two. One to screw in the bulb, the second to kill the first and claim all the glory." A fairly new conference off to a strong start. ✓FIDONET

Food

Are Tribbles Kosher? Hold the mayo! Excerpts from a message thread where eating Tribbles is considered. ✓COMPUSERVE→*go* sf media→Libraries→*Search by file name:* KOSHER.THD

StarTrek Book of Recipes Recipes for food and libations that are referred to in the series. The author improvises for in-

gredients not found on Earth (and makes no claim to any authenticity). Some recipes can't be made, such as Gagh—a dish made of worms not found on Earth and served raw. Riker's lemonade and Picard's Earl Grey tea are less problematic. ✓AMERICA ONLINE→*keyword* trek→MORE...→Star Trek Record Banks→Text/Other Files→Upld: 11/29/94→TEXT:StarTrek Recipe Book (Filename:STKRECIP.TXT)

WS_Cook (echo) "Does anyone know what these ice cream–like things are that you can buy on the promenade? Do you bite it or lick it? Trek chefs sound like Mimi Sheraton, as they critique Troi's chocolate desserts, boast about the strength of Romulan Ale, or debate why data's drink changed color in the episode "Conundrum." ✓WARPSPEED

Get a life

Get a Life—and How to Respond Dos and don'ts for responding to "Get a life" messages on the newsgroup. ✓INTERNET→*www* http://www.cosy.sbg.ac.at/ftp/pub/trek/lists/getalife.txt

Shatner: Get a Life Sound clip from the *Saturday Night Live* skit that Trek fans will never forget—the night Shatner yelled: "Get a life, you

people! For cryin' out loud, it's just a TV show!" Aww, c'mon Bill. ✓**AMERICA ONLINE**→*keyword* winforum→Search the Software Libraries →*Search by file name:* GETALIFE. WAV

Parodies

Kirk GIF from the Simpsons

Image of Kirk from the *Simpsons* episode "Star Trek XII: So Very Tired." ✓**COMPUSERVE**→*go* sfmedia →Libraries→*Search by file name:* TRDKRK.GIF

LCARS: Alexi Kosut's Star Trek Page

While this Web page links to some of the more serious Trek sites on the Net, its focus is on Trek fun. Drop by to read the silly top ten lists, Trek filks, or Alexi Kosut's own fan fiction— "Star Trek: Affliction of Paradise" and "Star Trek: Return to Hellgate." ✓**INTERNET**→*www* http:// www.nueva.pvt.k12.ca.us/~akosut /startrek/

Make It So

Cartoon (in GIF format) of Picard in boxer shorts saying "Mr. Data....Make it sew!" as Data tries to use a sewing machine to mend the captain's uniform. ✓**INTERNET**→*anon-ftp* ftp.iij.ad.jp→ /.3/info-mac/grf→stng-makeitso. hqx

Microsoft Joke

Will Bill Gates someday deserve credit for destroying the Borg? ✓**INTERNET** ...→ *gopher* proper.com→Macintosh Index→Search all the menu titles in the ICI Macintosh Index→*Search by keyword:* joke ...→*www* gopher: //proper.com:70/00/vff/mac/ general/info/sft/star-trek-microsoft -joke.txt

Mock Plot Summaries

Twisted (but recognizable) descriptions of all the original series episodes and the first three seasons of *The Next*

Generation. So, what was the "Miri, Miri" episode about? According to this summary, "The *Enterprise* discovers an Earth-like planet with no adults where everybody gets a certain fatal disease as soon as they reach puberty, so Kirk risks violating the Prime Directive by giving them condoms." ✓**INTERNET**→ *www* http://www.cosy.sbg. ac.at/ftp/pub/trek/fun/treksynopsis-humor.html

Mr. Scott GIF from the Simpsons

Image of a very fat Scotty from the *Simpsons* episode "Star Trek XII: So Very Tired." ✓**COMPUSERVE**→*go* sfmedia→Libraries→ *Search by file name:* FTSCTY.GIF

Next Generation Sketch from 1994 Comic Relief

Transcript of an HBO comedy sketch about *The Next Generation*. ✓**COMPUSERVE**→*go* sfmedia→Libraries→ *Search by file name:* STCOMI.TXT

Star Trek Parodies/Star Trek Stories

Close to 150 episode and character parodies in the Parody directory. The Stories directory also includes humorous works of fan fiction, such as MacEnterprise, BizarreTrek, and BarTrek. Files are compressed. ✓**INTERNET** ...→*anonftp* ftp.std.com→/obi/Star.Trek. Parodies ...→*anon-ftp* ftp.vslib.cz→ /pub/texts/Online-Book-Initiative /Star.Trek.Parodies ...→*anon-ftp* ftp.std.com→/obi/Star.Trek.Stories ...→*anon-ftp* ftp.vslib.cz→/pub /texts/Online-Book-Initiative/ Star.Trek.Stories

Star Trek: The New College Generation

A TNG spoof in the form of a several plays written over the course of three college semesters. The crew of the *Enterprise* reside in a college dormitory: Picard has Beatles posters on his wall and Worf watches *Gorgeous Ladies of Wrestling* on television. Stay tuned.

STARNOTES

"**GAGH**—Gagh is the Klingon name for worms. Gagh cannot be made on Earth. Klingon Ingredients: 1 serving 453.59g Gagh (live) Usually eaten raw. Tips: Don't think about Gagh when eating the other recipes.

BREGIT LUNG—Bregit is a Klingon animal that resembles a Terran dog. Bregit lung is a warrior's food often prepared on Klingon warships. This dish cannot be prepared on Earth, simply because there are no bregits. Klingon Ingredients: 1 serving *2 u Bregit lungs *236.00 ml Bregit blood In a pan, put the lungs and cook in the oven until it darkens. Bathe with the blood. Tips: Usually eaten raw.

SUCK SALT—Suck salt?, think of it as a salty lolly-pop. Terran Ingredients: 1 serving *Sodium Chloride Crystals (as desired) Just eat it! Tips: Don't have too much!"

-from AOL's **StarTrek Book of Recipes**

The Trek Phenomenon *"Get a Life"*: Trek Humor

✓**INTERNET**→*gopher* minerva. acc.virginia.edu→Arts and Sciences →Hereford College→Hereford Col lege Satire→Star Trek: The New College Generation (archive)

Star Trek with the Road Runner What happens when the crew of the *Enterprise* meets the Road Runner? Beep-beep! ✓**COMPUSERVE** →*go* sfmedia→Libraries→*Search by file name:* STROAD.DOC

The Starship Beverly Hills . . . NCC-90210 Have you ever noticed an uncanny resemblance between *Star Trek: The Next Generation* and *Beverly Hills 90210*? Some fans (many of whom formerly frequented Brady Trek discussions) now regularly board The Starship Beverly Hills. What would the ship be like under the command of Luke Perry? He has the high hair of the great Kirk but would the crew look good in faded jeans? Should the universal bad girl, Shannon Dougherty, guest star as a Romulan, Klingon, or Cardassian? ✓**GENIE**→*keyword* sfrt2→SFRT2 Bulletin Board→set 27→read 4

TFDN - Star Trek Parodies (echo) Did you see the episode "Where Everyone Has Gone Before?" How about "Captain, I Shrunk the Wesley!?" And the classic "Time's Toilet?" Television hasn't aired them yet, but this collection of about 200 Trek parodies has a loyal following of readers. All BBSs participating in the Trek File Distribution Network carry the same items, although the name of the library may vary slightly. ✓**TFDN**

Trek Parodies A parody-packed directory with mocking spoofs on each of the television series, beginning with TOS. TNG fans know that Tasha died twice, but that doesn't mean she couldn't be brought back again—see "Ten Ways to Bring Back Tasha Yar." Others up for roasting are "The Inner Light" and "The Best of Both Worlds." Then, there are sagas written about BarTrek, Bubble Gum Trek, Dog Trek, and Nerd Trek. Some Trek fans complain that it's hard to stay awake watching DS9. Perhaps "Deep Snooze 9" will wake them up. ✓**INTERNET**→ *anon-ftp* ftp.cis.ksu.edu→/pub/ alt.startrek.creative/parody

Trek Plots Fan Warren Siege takes on TOS and TNG with parodic plot summaries. "The Galileo Seven-Eleven," in which "Spock takes the shuttlecraft to make a quick stop at a local planet to get a Slurpee, but the natives refuse to accept his Vulcan Express Card"; and then there's "Skin of Evil," in which "the Enterprise is attacked by a being of pure acne." ✓**INTERNET**→*www* http://www.cosy.sbg. ac.at/ftp/pub/trek/fun/trek-synop sis-humor.html

Satire

The Newt Generation Image of Speaker of the House Newt Gingrich as a Borg. ✓**COMPUSERVE** →*go* sfmedia→Libraries→*Search by file name:* NEWTGE.JPG

Humorous Episode Synopsis Remember the TOS episode "Flipside of Paradise"? Well, "Spock gets the girl, so Kirk gets jealous and starts a fight. Spock beats him up, but by then he's no longer in the mood, so they leave the planet." According to the Warren Siegel who compiled synopses for all TOS episodes and the first three seasons of TNG, that's exactly what happened. Not exactly, but close.... ✓**INTERNET**→*www* http://www.cosy.sbg.ac.at/ftp/pub /trek/fun/trek-synopsis-humor.html

Top ten lists

Star Trek Top Ten Lists Enough top ten Trek lists have been written by newsgroup readers to warrant dividing them into categories like "bizarre top ten lists" and "silly top ten lists." Reasons to retire the original crew for good is a *silly* list while signs that the *Enterprise* is crewed by Satan worshipers is considered *bizarre*. So, what are the top ten worries of Picard and the top ten reasons why Riker won't shave? ✓**INTERNET** ...→*gopher* dds.dds.nl→De Bibliotheek→ boeken→Mass Media Star Trek→ Star Trek Top Ten Lists ...→*anon-ftp* ftp.cic.net→/pub/e-serials/archives /ETEXT/pub/Quartz/television/ startrek/→trek-topten.gz ...→*gopher* wiretap.spies.com→Wiretap Online Library→Mass Media→Star Trek→Star Trek Top Ten Lists p.1 *and* Star Trek Top Ten Lists p.2

Star Trek Top Ten Lists A short collection of TNG top ten lists taken from the mailing list Strek-L, including the top ten classes at Starfleet Academy, top 20 uses for Data's detatched head, and the top ten signs you've watched too much *Star Trek.* ✓**INTERNET**→*www* http:// ux1.cso.uiuc.edu/~bunting/ws/lists. html ✓**AMERICA ONLINE**→*keyword* trek→MORE...→Star Trek Record Banks→Text/Other Files→Upld: 06/02/94→TEXT: Star Trek top ten lists (Filename: STTOPTEN.TXT)

To Boldly Go Where No Man Has Ever Gone Before... A humorous list of 20 unlikely *Trek* plotlines. To wit: "Counselor Troi states something other than the blindingly obvious." ✓**INTERNET** ...→*gopher* prism.nmt.edu→Schlake's Humor Archives→s→Star.Trek→to_ boldly_go_where_no_man_has_e ver_gone_before... ...→*anon-ftp* ftp.vslib.cz→/pub/mirrors/OBI/ Nerd.Humor→Star.Trek

Trek University

You can't get a Trek doctorate yet, but it's only a matter of time before college students

will be forced to sit through a lecture entitled **The Undiscovered Country: 1960's Religious Themes in Star Trek**, or read an essay that explores Trek's links to the true nature of the U.S.A. in **Star Trek: The American Dream**. These are the products of college students who'd rather do their theses (and even dissertations) on *Star Trek* than on *Intersubjectivity in Husserl*. Investigate the relationship of the *Enterprise's* mission to the pioneer spirit in **Another Frontier: Voyaging West with Mark Twain and Star Trek's Imperial Subject**. And if its continuing education that you're interested in, get Grandpa hooked on **The Science of Star Trek**. Before you know it, he'll have a warp drive humming out in the garage.

On the Net

Literature

Another Frontier: Voyaging West with Mark Twain and Star Trek's Imperial Subject An essay exploring literary figures in *Star Trek* and focusing on the portrayal of Samuel Clemens in the episode "Time's Arrow." ✓**IN-TERNET**→*gopher* jefferson.village.

Einstein—from http://www.ph. unimelb.edu.au/~gau/einstein.html

virginia.edu→Publications of the Institute→Postmodern Culture→V4 N3, May 1994→Valerie Fulton, "An Other Frontier: Voyaging West with Mark Twain and Star Trek's Imperial Subject"

Pop culture

A Tour of the House of Popular Culture with Star Trek as a Guide An honor's thesis which uses the House of Popular Culture methodology (the author guides you through five rooms, each representing a concept of popular culture). It explores *Star Trek* as a pop-culture phenomenon, with icons, stereotypes, heroes, rituals/events, and arts of Trek. From the emotional power of the *Enterprise* as icon to Kirk as a Kennedyesque heroic figure, the paper extensively references the races, relationships, and story lines of both TOS and TNG. ✓**TFDN**→TFDN — Star Trek Facts→*Download a file:* ST_THES. ZIP

Religion

The Undiscovered Country: 1960s Religious Themes in Star Trek An excerpt from Lafayette College student Dave Learn's honor's thesis. Focusing on the pop culture, politics, and religion of the 1960s, he analyzes the themes and morality of Trek episodes and critiques other interpretations, including Betsy Carpio's argument that Trek "reaffirms traditional Christian beliefs and values." Bibliography included. ✓**INTERNET** ...→*anon-ftp* quepasa. cs.tu-berlin.de→/pub/doc/movies+ tv-series/StarTrek/misc→thesis.gz ...→*anon-ftp* ftp.cic.net→/pub/ e-serials/archives/ETEXT/pub/ Quartz/television/startrek/ ...→ *www* gopher://gopher.cic.net:70/ 00/nircomm/gopher/e-serials/ archives/ETEXT/pub/Quartz/tele vision/startrek/trek-thesis.gz

Science & education

Education on Trek What will education be like in the future? Will the existence of artificial intelligence and other supercomputers make the laborious learning process obsolete? Or will their advance create another generation of unemployable humans, watching the virtual screen as Sally Struthers pitches study-at-home degrees for Xenoaccounting, Earth Standard English, TV/VCR/Holodeck repair. Teachers who are *Star Trek* fans get into full-scale methodological and philosophical debates. ✓**GENIE**→*keyword* sfrt2→SFRT2 Bulletin Board→set 28→read 15

Educational Uses of Peter

David's "Line of Fire" A five-page paper examining the educational potential of the *Trek* novel *Line of Fire* in a science class. ✓**COMPUSERVE**→*go* sfmedia→Libraries→*Search by file name:* PSTONI.GIF

The Science of Star Trek A short hypertext article about the science of the Trek universe with easy-to-understand explanations of Trek tech in the context of scientific principles. Describing replicators, Dr. David Allen Batchelor wrote, "Today, we know how to create microchip circuits and experimental nanometer-scale objects by 'drawing' them on a surface with a beam of atoms. We can also suspend single atoms or small numbers of atoms within a trap made of electromagnetic fields, and experiment on them. That's as close as the replicator is to reality. Making solid matter from a pattern as the replicator appears to do is pretty far beyond present physics." ✓**INTERNET**→*www* http://www.gsfc.nasa.gov/education/just_for_fun/startrek.html

Star Trek: The American Dream A paper written about *Star Trek* and American culture by Peter Müller, a German student of Anglistics and Germanistics at the University of Oldenburg. Müller's paper offers a critical perspective on the way that *Star Trek* addresses dominant themes in American culture, focusing on Puritanism, democracy, frontier, paradise, liberty, equality, and racial balance. Episodes with special relevance are cited and analyzed. ✓**INTERNET**→*www* http://eowyn.informatik.uni-oldenburg.de:8888/startrek/st_and_american_dream.html

Shakespeare

Shakespeare Brief descriptions

" I'm afraid you've got it all wrong, Mister Spock, all of you. I've been monitoring their old-style radio waves. The Imperial spokesman was trying to ridicule their religion, but he couldn't. Don't you see? It's not the sun up in the sky they're worshipping—it's the Son of God."
—**Uhura**, *Bread and Circuses*
Net Source: www.gopher://gopher.cic.net:70/00/nircomm/gopher/
eserials/archives/ETEXT/pub/Quartz/television/startrek/
trek-thesis.gz

of nine episode scenes from *The Next Generation* with Shakespearean references. The descriptions are linked to the actual passage from Shakespeare's works. ✓**INTERNET**→*www* http://www.ugcs.caltech.edu:80/~werdna/sttng/misc1.html#26

Shakespeare References in Star Trek Q's not the only one who thinks that "All the galaxy's a stage." Since Kirk commanded the *Enterprise*, Trek writers have staged Shakespeare in worlds all over the galaxy. This file cites TOS, TAS, TMS, and TNG adventures in which Shakespearean references or story lines have been used. Specific Shakespearean passages are printed. ✓**INTERNET** ...→*www* http://www.cosy.sbg.ac.at/ftp/pub/trek/lists/shakespe.txt ...→*anon-ftp* quepasa.cs.tu-berlin.de→/pub/doc/movies+tv-series/StarTrek/misc→shakespeare.gz

Themes

Apologetics in the 24th Century: Assessing Star Trek Generations An essay commenting on *Star Trek*'s secular humanism and analyzing its successes and failures, particularly in the movie *Generations*. The author wrote the piece from "a Christian world-

and-life view in an attempt to see if the philosophy implied in the movie gives us the answers we're looking for." ✓**COMPUSERVE**→*go* sfmedia→Libraries→*Search by file name:* strek.txt

Essay: The Q This essay, not about the TNG character Q, but about the underlying themes of *Star Trek* (*Q* is taken from the German word *Quelle* which means "source"). It postulates that many *Star Trek* episodes are moving away from the fundamental themes and destroying the Trek genre in the process. ✓**AMERICA ONLINE**→*keyword* trek→MORE...→Star Trek Record Banks→Text/Other Files→Upld: 08/06/94→TEXT:ESSAY—The Q (filename: The Q) ✓**INTERNET**→*anon-ftp* ftp.cis.ksu.edu→/pub/alt.startrek.creative/misc→ST_themes.zip

What Is Star Trek? An introduction to the Star Trek phenomenon with show-by-show descriptions mixed in with some overall Trek history. Did you know that Space Shuttle astronaut Dr. Mae Jemison, the first African-American woman in space, made a cameo appearance on *Star Trek: The Next Generation*? ✓**EWORLD** →sf→Star Trek→Captain's Log→What is Star Trek?

Love & lust in space

Mothers of the future will probably warn their children against getting involved with a

being who might be transported to an alternate universe at any time—it will only lead to heartache. Space exploration and love: Do they mesh? **The Kirk Love FAQ** mathematically proves that James T. Kirk had a commitment problem (.3133 affairs per episode—most of a "low level" of seriousness). Head to AOL's **Worf & Troi** and **Picard & Crusher** to participate in virtual couples therapy for those troubled pairs. If you're of a more lascivious bent, and your interest is in androids, aliens, and all who look fine in spandex uniforms, head to **alt.sex. fetish.startrek** or America online's **Sexy Talk** and let your inhibitions run as wild as a carrier of the Psi2000 virus. And, for those who'd prefer to see their favorite member of Starfleet in the buff (20th-century style), head to the **X-Rated Star Trek Archive**.

Publicity shot—downloaded from PerfectVision Graphics BBS

On the Net

alt.sex.fetish.startrek (ng) Are you curious about which of the ST women have done photo spreads, ah-hem, "out of uniform"? (Denise Crosby, Marina Sirtis, but never Gates McFadden.) Do you wonder which of the male officers on deck has the biggest Ten-Forward? (Apparently, at least as far as TNG is concerned, the Captain's log is most impressive, with No. One a close No. Two.) Ever wished that phasers had a setting marked "stimulate"? Well, then, post haste to alt.sex.fetish.startrek. One of the few sex.fetish groups dominated by female posters, it is a remarkably close-knit community, bound by an intense and absolutely serious lust for the men and women of Trek's past, present, and future. The occasional bin-hex-encoded naughty picture does show up here, but the true draw for most alt.sex.fetish.startrek readers is the titillating conversation, which is equally divided between speculation (what would a sexual interface with Lieutenant Commander Data be like?) and starry-eyed report (I touched Patrick Stewart's hand!).

The undisputed queen of alt. sex.fetish.startrek is New York's Christine Faltz, whose abiding passion for the bald eagle of the spaceways, Jean-Luc Picard—and the actor who plays him—have led her to write a remarkable multi-part epic erotic fantasy entitled "Oh Captain, My Captain." Faltz's

The Trek Phenomenon Love & Lust In Space

exploits have made her something of a star in the Net Trek community, and even beyond it—the *Los Angeles Times* has written about her—but her fame hasn't diminished her ardor. A recent trip with members of the self-styled Patrick Stewart Estrogen Brigade (made up of female Net admirers from across the country) to Stewart's play "A Christmas Carol" led to an actual face-to-face meeting between luster and lustee, with dreamy, weak-in-the-knees results...all of which were then documented in hilarious and heartfelt detail on the group. Impulse thrusters on full, Captain...oh, *Captain...!* ✓**USENET**

alt.sexy.bald.captains (ng) Dominated by a group calling itself the Patrick Stewart Estrogen Brigade ("that's PSEB, with a silent P, as in psychotic," notes one member). Devotees post their desire to "grope him like a piece of meat." Of course, Picard's not the only bald captain to lust after... there's always Captain Stubing. Certainly this is one of the strangest spots on the Net. Amusing territory for lurkers. ✓**USENET**

alt.startrek.creative (ng) Stories and parodies, from "Stormbird: A Klingon Tale" to the X-rated "Friendly Advice." ("Dax seemed oblivious, concentrating all her attention on Odo's tongue. 'Constable, you're cheating,' she gasped. 'Not that I mind, but that's longer than any human tongue I ever felt. But don't stop. Just put it inside me. Oh, yes, there.'") ✓**USENET**

Kirk Love FAQ A list

of Kirk's love relationships in the television series and movies. Adam Cooper, the fan who created the FAQ, rates the sincerity of each relationship on a scale of one to ten. The affair with Sister Edith Keeler (Joan Collins) may rate a ten, but most romances rank closer to the one. ✓**INTERNET**→*anon-ftp* quepasa. cs.tu-berlin.de→/pub/doc/movies +tv-series/StarTrek/misc→kirk-loves.gz

Picard + Crusher We waited seven years for Crusher and Picard to become intimately involved, watching as the two shared each others' thoughts telepathically, ate breakfast together, and saved each others lives. Still, the Picard-Crusher romance just didn't take off, but fans here haven't given up. There's always *Star Trek VIII*. In the meantime, we'll just keep reliving the love scenes in Peter David's novel *Q-Squared* and thinking of baby names. ✓**AMERICA ONLINE**→*keyword* trek→Star Trek Message Boards→The Next Generation→Picard+Crusher

Romance/Love List What would the stars be without love? Empty hunks of cold stone. Wastelands. Worst of all, bad TV. *Star Trek* has always made the most of interstellar romance, whether it's a furtive kiss on the bridge or torrid lovemaking in a private chamber. This list treats the crew like rock stars, tallying sexual and romantic encounters and including an annotation for each rendezvous (of Kirk's Kahn-u-tu paramour Nona in "A Private Little

War," the author writes that "she took him—whether he liked it or not!"). In the end, Kirk is the only true sexual adventurer in the bunch, accounting for more than half of the series' romances. ✓**INTERNET** ...→*www* http://www.cosy. sbg.ac.at/ftp/pub/trek/lists/ romance.txt ...→*anon-ftp* quepasa. cs.tu-berlin.de→/pub/doc/movies+ tv-series/StarTrek/misc→romances. gz ✓**TFDN**→TFDN Facts Files→ *Download a file:* TOSROM.ZIP

Sexy Trek Sometimes raunchy and often slightly twisted, regulars here alternately spin tales about their personal (aka, sexual) involvement with *Star Trek* characters and attack others for doing the same. Lieutenant Illyria, an active contributor on the Neutral Zone message board and a constant target of attack, describes her relationship with the DS9's Doctor Bashir: "We fell in love almost immediately after that strangely magical night, and now he's the only guy I'll ever need or want. :) Julian's a really special person. I hope you know that, Pooh. He really is." Lt. Illyria describes herself as "26" and "definitely NOT a Virgin."

The 14-year-olds are here in force as well: "Have you seen the size of Kira's chest WOW! And that Vulcan's boobs in 'Maquis,' way to go ParaMOUNT!!" Then, there are those who dream of a love scene between Dax and Kira, a menage à trois with Riker, Troi, and Dr. Crusher, and a date with a Betazoid woman. Occasionally, someone will engage in serious soul-searching: "I can't explain it. I'm not usuallly attracted to short-haired masculine women, (Dax would be more my personal style) but when she [Kira] gets angry or indignant about something (sometimes surprise will bring it out), RRRRRrrrrrrrr!" ✓**AMERICA ON-**

Net Trek 73

Love & Lust In Space The T[...]henomenon

LINE→*keyword* Star Trek Message Boards→Star Trek Message Boards →The Neutral Zone→Sexy Trek

Worf & Troi Members are divided: Troi and Worf, or Troi and Riker? "Riker blew it with Troi, but I do hope they find a good mate for him. Just don't break up Worf and Troi to do it." In true Trek fashion, alien culture and attributes play a significant part in the discussion: "I don't find the idea of Worf and Troi romantically involved exciting or even rationally consistent with the way the two species, Betazoids and Klingons, have been created." And, what about the sex? ✓**AMERICA ONLINE** →*keyword* trek→Star Trek Message Boards→The Next Generation→ Worf & Troi

X-Rated Star Trek Archive The dream of Trek is one of equality between men and women, where people are judged by their degrees, wits, ideals, and moral character. Back in the twentieth century, though, things are a little less cerebral, and Trek women are judged by the size of their...well, by the size of their topless portfolios.

This archive houses roughly two dozen topless (and even a few bottomless) shots of Trek women, including photos of Nichelle Nichols (Uhura), Marina Sirtis (Troi), Denise Crosby (Tasha), Kirstie Alley (Saavik), and Terry Farrell (Dax). And though the site is for the most part unregenerately sexist, there are a few slices of beefcake—most notably a coital shot of a grinning Jonathan Frakes on top of Counselor Troi that seems to be taken in Commander Riker's private quarters (this couldn't be a camera trick, could it?). ✓**INTERNET**→*anon-ftp* ftp. netcom.com→/pub/ev/evansc/ pictures

PICS & SOUNDS

A Kiss Dr. Crusher and Captain Picard kissing. ✓**INTERNET**→*anon-ftp* ftp.cis.ksu.edu→/pub/pictures /jpg/Startrek→sttng075.jpg

Barklay Pass Lieutenant Barklay in the episode "The Nth Degree" makes a pass at Troi: "I don't need a counselor. What I need is the company of a charming, intelligent woman." ✓**INTERNET**→ *anon-ftp* smaug.cs. hope.edu→ /pub/sound /trek→barklay- pass

Bite on the Cheek K'Ehleyr to Worf in a soundclip: "Not even a bite on the cheek for old time sake." ✓**INTERNET**→*anon-ftp* smaug.cs. hope.edu→/pub/sound/trek→bite- on-the-cheek

Dr. Crusher and Captain Picard Image of the doctor and captain in an intimate moment. ✓**INTERNET**→*anon-ftp* ftp.cis.ksu. edu→/pub/pictures/jpg/Star trek→sttng076.jpg

Humor and Sex Soundclip of Data: "There may be a correlation between humor and sex. The need for more research is clearly indicated." ✓**INTERNET**→ *anon-ftp* smaug.cs.hope.edu→ /pub/sound/trek→humor-and-sex

Kissing Couple A kiss between Tasha and Data. ✓**INTERNET** ...→*anon-ftp* ftp.cis.ksu.edu→/pub /pictures/jpg/Startrek→sttng064.

jpg ...→*anon-ftp* address 34→ sttng064.jpg

Marina Sirtis Topless Two shots of a topless Sirtis. ✓**COMPUSERVE**→*go* eforum→Libraries→ *Search by file name:* SIRTIS.GIF

Picard/Crusher JPEG image of a sexy love scene between the captain and the doctor in Picard's ready room. ✓**COMPUSERVE**→*go* sf- media→Li- braries→*Search by file name:* NKD NOW.GIF

Riker & Troi Riker invites Troi to dinner, but is turned down. ✓**INTERNET**→*gopher* tiger.acs.appstate.edu→ Tiger's Sound Archive→Star Trek Wav Files→tngagt14.wav

Sexual Organs TNG soundclip: "Commander, tell me about your sexual organs." ✓**INTERNET**→ *gopher* tiger.acs.appstate.edu→ Tiger's Sound Archive→Star Trek Wav Files→st-sex.wav

Tasha Yar in Evening Wear Picture of Tasha Yar uncharacteristically attired—very sexy. ✓**INTERNET**→*anon-ftp* ftp.cis.ksu.edu→ /pub/pictures/jpg/Startrek→ sttng068.jpg→sttng068.jpg

Terry Farrell Terry—topless in a see-through, fishnet bodysuit. ✓**COMPUSERVE**→*go* eforum→Libraries→ *Search by file name:* FARR01.GIF

EROTIC TREK

If you watch closely, you'll notice that the *Enterprise-NCC-1701* is a tingling web of sexual tension. Those hot, hidden glances broadcast between the Captain and Lt. Uhura. The dewy, hungry stares of Nurse Chapel when Spock stalks into the sickbay. And who can forget those enigmatic moments of Kirk-Spock bonding, which suggest that in a more liberated universe these friends and comrades-at-arms might be something more.

The fact is, one of the hidden joys of Trekking (both new and classic) is the picking out the moments of unspoken sexual interplay between its characters. All true Trekkers know it. Some keep it to themselves. Some admit it publicly. Others revel in it. And the most creative of these revellers write Trekkerotica—highly unauthorized pieces of fan-fantasy that bring new meaning to the command "Engage!" Distributed in a vast underground network of 'zines and photocopied broadsheets, Treksex stories were a thriving cottage industry long before the Net became a reality. But with the debut of Usenet, adult BBSs, anonymous ftp sites, and email aliases, Trekkerotica has come out of the plain brown wrapper and found a happy home in Cyberspace.

A steady stream of hot 'n'

sweaty Starfleet stories are posted to the alt.sex.fetish.startrek, alt.sexy.bald.captains, and alt.sex.stories newsgroups, but these mostly focus on close encounters with multiorgasmic aliens or couplings between male and female comrades-at-arms. But the truly imaginative pieces hide in less public areas of the Net. Imagine, for instance, Kirk and Spock, stranded on a deserted planet just as the Vulcan first officer enters Pon farr. If Spock's desire is not consummated, it will kill him—and thus, his human friend must, er, come to his aid. This is a typical plotline from the burgeoning world of Kirk/Spock erotica (known as K/S, or "slash" fiction). Fans have also imagined the birth of passion between Geordi and Data; sadistic encounters with the Q; multi-morphed matings with Odo the shapeshifter; and the brutal, nonconsensual lust of Klingons.

Terry Farrell—downloaded from ftp.netcom.com

Because of their explicit nature, erotic Trek fictions aren't likely to emerge into the public eye any time soon. However, the net.sex.trek world recently took a great leap forward with a *Los Angeles Times* profile of Christine Faltz. Faltz, a 25-year-old resident of Brooklyn, is perhaps the most ardent fan of Patrick Stewart alive—and the sole author of the sprawling, multi-part Trekkerotica epic "Oh Captain, My Captain."

What makes Faltz stand out from the ranks of sex.Trek scribblers, however, is that she has never seen the show: born with congenital microphthalmia, she's been blind since birth. Despite having no idea of the look and feel of Trek except from the descriptions of friends, she was still swept off her feet by *The Next Generation* and its dashing commander. "The first time I 'saw' Trek was in college," she remembers, "I strolled into the room, and I was immediately aware of a captivating voice emanating from the screen, which reminded me vaguely of Sean Connery. To this day, I have no idea what compelled me to stay and watch the rest of that episode—I don't even recall what episode it was." Since then, Faltz has studied Stewart and his Starfleet alter ego with the true devotion of a fan obsessed; she's convinced that he is the

"The denouement of 'Oh Captain, My Captain' features a full-warp ready-room romp with the entire TNG crew."

perfect man, or damn near close enough. "His voice is exceptional; few match it," she says. "And from what I hear—his shoulders, his chest, his arms—and having held his hand, his hands— ooooooooh, boy!"

Faltz had written a few non-Trek pieces of erotica for the newsgroup alt.sex.stories; "Oh Captain, My Captain," her first Trek effort, was posted a few weeks after the end of *The Next Generation*'s syndicated run. "I'd just finished taking the bar exam and was looking for an outlet for a lot of stress," she says. "I missed my weekly dose of Patrick—sure, there were reruns, but I enjoy seeing him in new situations. One night I had a fantastically erotic dream about him and I decided, upon reading a few posts in alt.sex.fetish.startrek that day, to start letting loose." The result: "Oh Captain, My Captain," a wildly imaginative story that's hotter than an overloaded antimatter nacelle. Its denouement features a full-warp ready-room romp with the entire TNG crew (the descriptions of Worf's magnificent member—crested, like his forehead—is particularly vivid).

Readers of "Oh Captain, My Captain" would never guess that Faltz is visually impaired; and while Faltz herself doesn't think her disability has detracted significantly from her enjoyment of the series, she does wish for a fuller experience of the show. "I do feel I could write better fan fiction if I were able to see the characters and the technological aspects of the show. I have no idea, for example, what the *Enterprise* looks like, no idea what the holodeck, the transporter, etcetera, look like. Let's face it—a lot of *Star Trek*'s attraction is its fancy toys and special effects. I'd also like to know what Bajoran nose ridges look like, or Klingon features, the differences between Romulans and Vulcans, and so on. Oh— it would also be nice to see just *how* broad Stewart's shoulders really are. By the Braille method, of course."

Recently, Faltz met Stewart in person, after a performance of his one-man version of *A Christmas Carol* in New York City. She spoke with him briefly, and shook his hand—an incomparable thrill, of course, but one that left her wishing for more. "My husband, Marshall Flax, is a sighted systems administrator at a Wall Street brokerage firm; he knows about my Trek fancies and fetishes, and has given me explicit consent to have one night with Patrick Stewart, whatever happens or doesn't happen," she laughs. "Isn't true love grand? And yes, he's *serious*—just ask him!"

Multi-culti Trek

Keiko O'Brien in DS9's "In The Hands of the Prophets" stirred up a lot of trouble teach-

Groundbreaking scene from "Plato's Stepchildren"—from Perfect Vision Graphics BBS

ing science to Bajorans on the space station—as much trouble as the movement to teach the rainbow curriculum does in the 1990s. Trek has always addressed the divisive issues of our day. Remember the battle between the half-black and half-white alien races? The episode premiered during the height of the Civil Rights Movement in the U.S. But has Trek become too PC? In AOL's **The Neutral Zone: Gay Folk on the Bridge** the discussion focuses on if homosexuality will be "cured" or finally accepted by the 24th century. AOL's **Trekking Afrocentrically** carries on a proud tradition from the early days when Martin Luther King, Jr. convinced actress Nichelle Nichols that she really was breaking barriers as Lieutenant Uhura! **Women Who Love Trek** (in spite of its sometimes blatant sexism) meet to share their pride over Janeway's command and Kira's fortitude. Is this what the Great Bird wanted?

On the Net

Gay Trek

Are Kirk and Spock Lovers?

For years fanzines have speculated about a sexual relationship between Spock and Kirk—bisexual buddies, if you will. The comraderie has always inspired a tremendous response in Trek fans, with fans even now hoping that Kirk will be brought back somehow to help Spock with his mission to influence the Romulan Empire. But, lovers? Most fans don't think so, although, says one, "part of the fun of *Star Trek* is to speculate on all possibilities." And, taking his advice, Todd then writes, "I doubt it [that Spock and Kirk are lovers]…but that doesn't mean I've never fantasized myself into a three-way with them both!"
✓ **AMERICA ONLINE**→*keyword* trek→ Star Trek Message Boards→Classic Trek→Are Kirk and Spock Lovers?

Gay Trek on AOL Equal rights for gays? Sure. Gays in the military? No problem. Gays adopting children? Right on. But gays on *Star Trek*? You gotta be kidding. Boldly going where Starfleet refuses to tread, the various boards dealing with the conspicuous absence of gay characters on *Star Trek* are among the most active and enduring.

The debate is in the realm of unenlightened science fantasy as members speculate that homosexuality is "cured" by the 24th century or the Q Continuum mercifully wipes out homosexuality. But for many gay fans, Paramount is solely to blame for its refusal to develop gay characters. Much discussion centers around the TNG homily on sexual conformity, "The Outcast," and whether or not

Paramount has indeed done its duty. The problem, say the gay fans, is not the lack of a storyline, but that they are not represented in Starfleet at all. When multiculturalism is the writer's Prime Directive, why not? The answer, sad to say, can be found in the postings of many adolescent males who swear they'd stop watching if *Star Trek* introduced a gay crew member. ✓**AMERICA ONLINE** ...→ *keyword* trek→Star Trek Message Boards→Star Trek Voyager→Still No Gays on Trek ...→*keyword* trek →Star Trek Message Boards→Deep Space Nine Board→Gay characters on DS9 ...→*keyword* trek→Star Trek Message Boards→The Neutral Zone→Gay Folk on the Bridge *and* GAY STAR TREK FANS

Race & Trek

Kirk and Uhura Picture of the famous scene from the episode "Plato's Children" where Kirk kisses Uhura—television's first interracial kiss. ✓**PVG** *dial* 513-233-7993 →<your username>→<your password>→F→*Download a file:* plato. gif

Trekking Afrocentrically Although it sits in the Trek Club, discussion in this folder has difficulty moving beyond broad theories of racism, Afrocentricism, and history and into the universe of the 24th century. Discussions often stray—you'll sometimes find more written about the history of ancient Egypt than African culture in Trek. Debates about Cardassian/Bajoran slavery as a metaphor for African slavery in the U.S., and the lack of Afrocentric language, literature, and music in Trek have sparked long discussions. The folder cries for diversity of thought and culture—not just skin color: "Federation species speak English, study (slanted) Earth history, and

even the Klingons in Trek 6 claimed Shakespeare as one of their own. Dull." ✓**AMERICA ONLINE**→*keyword* trek→Star Trek Message Boards→The Neutral Zone→ Trekking Afrocentrically

Women & Trek

Trek Women Trek women: objects of desire or role models for young girls of the 24th century? This message board is evenly divided between wolf whistles (mostly in favor of Jadzia Dax) and feminist manifestos. Is Kira Nerys a perfect balance between feminine serenity and masculine attraction? Was Uhura a token or a vital part of the crew? Did Tasha Yar get offed because "she was a lesbian" or because "Trekland is a testosterone universe and she was

becoming too much woman for them"? And what about Lwaxana Troi's incredible expanding libido? Join the distaff meeting. ✓**AMERICA ONLINE**→*keyword* scifi→Star Trek /Comics/TV/Star Wars Boards →Star Trek→Trek Women

Women Who Love Trek One of the most social communities on the *Star Trek* BB, the women here call each other "Sisters" and "Y's" and the subject (yes, it's about *Trek*) is referred to as "the Cloister." They not only talk about *Star Trek* episodes—often role-playing their conversations—they also try to bring *Star Trek* themes to other discussions and events. How about a Trek Christmas? ✓**PRODIGY**→ *jump* star trek bb→Choose a Topic →Clubs: Other→Women Who Love Trek

The diverse Voyager *crew—from http://www.ftms.com:80/st-voy/*

International Trek

Sure, you can get extra crispy Kentucky Fried Chicken in Krakow, or quench your thirst

with a Diet Coke in Beijing. And there's always that universal love of freedom thing. But what really makes it one small, but happy, planet? Trek, of course! Drop Down Under and read the active **aus.sf. star-trek** for a daily dissection of events in the Trek universe, but don't be surprised if they're chatting about episodes aired seasons ago (they're slightly behind the schedule). And though the Vulcan salute will win friends in any land, **Multi-Lingual Star Trek** provides a handy Trekology phrase book to assist your adventures in worlds beyond your own. *Per andare dove nessuno é mai strato prima d'ora.*

British Starfleet Confederacy

The British Starfleet Confederacy is a non profit making organization that is run by the fans of Star Trek for the fans of Star Trek

Screenshot from http://deeptht.armory.com:80/~bsc

On the Net

Across the board

Multi-Lingual Star Trek So, you want to know how to say "To boldly go where no man has gone before" in Japanese? This document is a compilation of foreign language translations of Trek phrases, most specifically the opening and closing voiceovers. Where were you when "Kohtaaminen avaruudessa" first aired on television? (Hint: that's "Encounter at Farpoint" in Finnish.) ✓**INTERNET** ...→*www* http://www.cosy.sbg.ac.at/ftp/pub/trek/lists/language.txt ...→*anon-ftp* que

pasa.cs.tu-berlin.de→/pub/doc/movies+tv-series/StarTrek/FAQs→multilingual.gz ...→*gopher* umcc.umcc.umich.edu→users→Appleton's Amazing Assorted Artifacts→Assorted Star Trek Items→Multi Lingual Star Trek ...→*gopher* wiretap.spies.com→Wiretap Online Library→Mass Media→Star Trek→Multi Lingual Star Trek

Star Trek Outside North America (echo) Wherever you may be, *Star Trek* is just a remote control click away. Sundays at 4:00 p.m. (Jakarta time) on RCTI in Indonesia, *The Next Generation* is aired. The Army Channel in Korea runs TNG on Tuesday night at 7:55. And, in New Zealand, TNG is shown on Friday night at 9 p.m. For a list of where and when *Trek* episodes are showing, check out this international TV guide. ✓**INTERNET** ...→*www* http://www.cosy.sbg.ac.at/ftp/pub

/trek/lists/startrek.abroad.faq ...→*anon-ftp* quepasa.cs.tu-berlin.de→/pub/doc/movies+tv-series/StarTrek/FAQs→abroad.gz ✓**TFDN** →TFDN Fact Files→*Download a file:* FAQLABRD.ZIP

Australian

aus.sf.star-trek (ng) The Picard and Kirk debate wages here as it does in every Trek discussion group on the Net. Favorite episode discussions and programming listings are common here, too. In fact, about the only difference between the rec.arts.startrek* groups and this one is that the readership is decidely Australian and the volume is much lower. Still, no Trek question goes unanswered. How many patients has Dr. Beverly lost? The answer comes a week later: "19 beings (mostly human)." ✓**USENET**

European

Brigitte Jellinek's Star Trek Page An Austrian Website that includes one of the most comprehensive lists of Trek links in Cyberspace. ✓**INTERNET**→*www* http://www.cosy.sbg.ac.at/rec/startrek/index.html

British Starfleet Confederacy Curious about Trek on the other side of the pond? Well, there are a few minor differences—Kirk and Spock wear bowlers and have waxed moustaches, and the *Enterprise* flies on the left side of space instead of the right. This site, which is the home page of the British nonprofit organization run by and for Trek fans, links to more than 20 *Star Trek* resources, including information about the Pages Star Trek bar in London. ✓**INTERNET**→*www* http://deeptht.armory.com:80/~bsc

Engage/Sci-Fi Zone: The European Star Trek/Science Fiction Mailing List (ml) Over 800 netters subscribe to this biweekly guide to Trek in Europe. Each newsletter is filled with Trek information—from Trek episode spoilers and parodies to reviews of sci-fi Web pages and actor gossip. European convention dates, merchandise updates, video releases, and TV schedules are also covered. The newsletter accepts fiction and news submissions. Each issue is actually a merger of two newsletters—the first devoted to Trek and the second to all things sci-fi. ✓**INTERNET**→*email* listserver@leicester.ac.uk ✍ *Type in message body:* subscribe star trek <your full name> *Archives:* ✓**INTERNET**→*ftp* ftp.doc.ic.ac.uk→/pub/media/tv/collections/tardis/us/sci-fi/StarTrek/engage

English-German Episode Guide A complete episode guide to TOS and the first two seasons of TNG with German and English titles. ✓**COMPUSERVE**→*go* sfmedia→Libraries→*Search by file name:* STGER.TXT

Kurzkritik Star Trek Encyklopädie A description in German of the Simon & Schuster Trek reference book, the *Star Trek Encyclopedia*. The site links to a scan of one of the book's pages. ✓**INTERNET**→*www* http://eowyn.informatik.uni-oldenburg.de:8888/encyklopaedie.html

Star Trek: D.C.U. Irish Trekkers are wired! The birthplace of Miles O'Brien, Chief Engineer on DS9, has a *Star Trek* Club with a home page. The site features links to other *Star Trek* pages and an electronic version of the club's newsletter, "Farpoint." The newsletter not only covers club news, but also announces upcoming conventions in Ireland and England and prints sci-fi and Trek reviews. ✓**INTERNET**→*www* http://www.eeng.dcu.ie/~stdcu/trek

Star Trek Hemmasida A Swedish Trek Website with pages summarizing the storyline and cast for each *Star Trek* series, pictures of all four captains and ships, a programming schedule for TNG in Sweden (you can access a form letter through the site's *Star Trek* Terror page if you you'd like to contact Swedish TV stations about running more *Trek* episodes—TNG is only in its first season there), as well as links to episode summaries, the *Generations* movie home page, the Klingon Language Institute, and several of the best Trek Websites on the Net. Several of the Web pages at this site are available in either Swedish or English. ✓**INTERNET**→*www* http://www.pt.hk-r.se/student/pt94ero/StarTrek.html

The USS Excalibur Homepage This home page is the electronic version of a print newsletter for a British *Star Trek* fan club in Bournemouth, England. This detailed and fascinating Web page links to information about events hosted by the fan club, Trek news and rumors, and Trek humor. ✓**INTERNET**→*www* http://whirligig.ecs.soton.ac.uk/~shd94/index.html

NEWS

chile.ciencia-ficcion(ng) Spanish science-fiction discussion. ✓**USENET**

de.rec.sf.startrek (ng) German Trek discussion. ✓**USENET**

finet.harrastus.startrek (ng) A Finnish Trek group. ✓**USENET**

finet.harrastus.startrek.spocks-hut (ng) Another Finnish Trek group. ✓**USENET**

fj.rec.sf (ng) Japanese sci-fi discussion. ✓**USENET**

fj.rec.sf.startrek (ng) Japanese *Star Trek* discussion group. ✓**USENET**

maus.rec.sf (ng) German science fiction discussion group. ✓**USENET**

ont.sf-lovers (ng) Canadian Trek discussion. ✓**USENET**

zer.z-netz.freizeit.tv.startrek (ng) Very active German Trek discussion group. ✓**USENET**

zer.z-netz.literatur.science-fiction (ng) Science-fiction discussion in German. ✓**USENET**

Ever since Gene Roddenberry designed the original *Enterprise* as a sort of flying United Nations—the Russian Chekov and Japanese Sulu serving alongside the American Kirk, the African-American Uhura, and the human-Vulcan Spock—*Star Trek* has demonstrated a conspicuous respect for international (and even interplanetary) identity. The crew's encounters with alien races frequently encoded concerns about the way that human cultures interact, and the primary mission of the *Star Trek* franchise—from classic *Trek* to *Voyager*—has always been to forgo difference for a more universal humanity, to "explore strange, new worlds" with an eye to their familiarity.

As the show's producers no doubt realize, this world-without-borders mentality has economic implications as well as moral ones. More than any other sci-fi show, *Star Trek* has captured the imaginations (and wallets) of fans across the globe, garnering huge support not only in North America but in Europe, South America, Asia, and Africa. For years, the shows have been shown in Germany and Japan, and at present more than 50 nations enjoy regular broadcasts of one of the three major series.

But these days, worldwide Trek isn't simply a matter of German college kids clustered in a Frankfurt den watching "*Der Zentral-Nervensystemmanipulator*" (that's TOS's "Dagger of the Mind," which Teutonic Trekkers translate as "The Central-Nervous System Manipulator"). These days, Trek fandom is aided and abetted by the Net, which lets cross-cultural communication and contextualization occur at the speed of today's high-tech telecommunications. Trekkers can post to Usenet groups in Australia, Germany, and Canada; browse home pages in Finland and Austria; and visit IRC channels populated by Brits, Poles, Kenyans, and Koreans. On these pages, we have excerpted and/or translated posts from international Trek newsgroups, selecting messages that convey some sense of local flavor without sacrificing the larger aims of Trek culture. As the Finns say, "*Minulla on saanti*" (that's "I have access" to English-speaking humans).

TREK IN GERMANY

>>Hat vielleicht jemand zufaellig Gottschalk´s Late-Nite mit P.S. & B.S. aufgezeichnet und kann
>>mir eine Kopie zukommen lassen? Ich waere auch sehr dankbar fuer ne Kopie. Porto und
>>Kassette werden natuerlich bezahlt.

Vergiss es einfach, die Sendung (na ja, Gottschalk) war so abgrundtief schlecht, du waerst einfach nur enttaeuscht! 1) Du verstehst kaum ein Wort der Schauspieler, englisch und deutsche Synchro uebereinander und das dreifach; 2) Gottschalk praesentierte wieder mal hauptsaechlich Gottschalk; 3) Gottschalk stellte ueberhaupt keine interessanten Fragen; 4) Gottschalk hatte ueberhaupt keine Ahnung; 5) Brent Spiner wurde von Gottschalk fast voellig ignoriert; 6) Das Ganze war sehr kurz (ca. 15 min). Wenn du Gottschalks Bericht von der Oscar-Verleihung gesehen hast, weisst du, was dich erwartet <graus> Kurz und gut: Spar dir das Geld und kauf dir eine ST-Videokassette!

>>Did anybody tape Gottschalk's Late-Nite with P.S. and B.S. [Patrick Stewart and Brent Spiner], and
>>could I get a copy? I would be very grateful. Naturally, I will pay for the cassette and the shipping costs.

Forget about it. The broadcast (or Gottschalk at least) was so abysmal, had you seen it you would just have been dissapointed. 1) It was impossible to understand one word of what was being said with the English and the German synchronization dubbed over it—and that with three people talking! 2) Gottschalk showcased—as usual—primarily Gottschalk; 3) Gottschalk did not ask one single interesting question; 4) Gottschalk clearly didn't have a clue; 5) Brent Spiner was almost completely ignored by Gottschalk; 6) The whole thing was far too short (15 minutes). If you've seen Gottschalk's presentation of the Oscars broadcast, you'll know what to expect <yecchh>. In short: Save your money and buy yourself a ST tape instead!

—from **de.rec.sf.startrek**

TREK IN CHILE

El otro dia vi el capitulo original con el Khan. Lo que pasaba era que rescataban una nave del pasado (o algo asi) y arriba estaba el Khan con una tropa de fieles seguidores que trataban de tomarse el *Enterprise*. Al final, Kirk le daba la opcion de llevarlos a un planeta sin colonizar para que puedieran crear su proipo mundo. La nave que rescataban era el *Botany Bay*. Por eso es que Chekov le dice al otro personaje secundario que deben irse rapido de esa nave, cuando descubre el nombre escrito en la nave.

The other day I saw the original episode with Khan. They were rescuing a ship from the past (or something like that) and onboard were Khan and a group of faithful followers who were trying to take the Enterprise. In the end, Kirk gave them the option of taking them to an uncolonized planet so they could create their own world. The name of the ship they were rescuing was the Botany Bay. That's why Chekov tells the other supporting character that they should leave the ship quickly when he discovers the name written on it.

—from **chile.ciencia-ficcion**

TREK IN AUSTRALIA

Okay Guys, I'm writing about the fact that that the poor people of Bendigo in the state of Victoria, Australia are being prejudiced against because *Star Trek* (all generations) are being omitted from our town. There is a club in Bendigo, you know, where we've seen into the seventh season TNG and third season DS9. We can be just as good as the Melbourneites. In Bendigo we are still wondering what the hell happened to sixth season let alone seventh season. It seems that the video companies are fighting. On TV? We're at the same status as the rest of the country. We're not THAT far behind, which is surprising. We would be if Southern Cross Network (or whatever they call themselves now—Cretins Inc. for all I care) was affiliated with Channel 9.

—from **aus.sf.star-trek**

The archiTreks

Who holds the rights to the dream? Well, Paramount, of course. But, the actors, authors,

artists, and Berman & Company have an impact as well. GEnie's **Star Trek On-Line**, frequented by actual Paramount employees, is an excellent place to get insight into the show's production. **Interview with Richard Arnold** and **The Crew Behind the Crew** illuminate the creative process behind two generations of *Trek*. And the **Star Trek Other Roles** list keeps fans informed about what else their favorite alien—or is that actor?—is starring in.

Avery Brooks, Rick Berman, and Patrick Stewart—from Perfect Vision BBS

On the Net

Canon

Canon vs. Non-Canon If there's one topic more passionately debated than Picard vs. Kirk, it's canon vs. non-canon. This FAQ lists the Trek sources that can be considered canon, from *The Star Trek Chronology* to each of the series. ✓ **INTERNET**→*www* http://www.cosy.sbg.ac.at/ftp/pub/trek/lists/canon.faq

Tech Fandom (echo) The Paramount canon—what is official Trek and what is not—provides the fodder for an endless round of Trek discussions and debates. And just how much can fans influence the canon? Trek fan James Dixon has found two instances where "unofficial" Trek sources were incorporated into the "official" lore and legend of *Star Trek*. ✓ **TFDN**→ TFDN - Star Trek Technology→ TECH_FAN.ZIP

Cast

Actors/Actresses Think of the topic as a hub for Trek fan clubs. John deLancie/Q fans gather in the "4 Q Admirers" subject—one contributor has even met DeLancie and is working on a script with Paramount about the character. Gates McFadden/Beverly Crusher has a "Beverly fans" subject here that's been going on for more than two years. Fans considered "killing Berman" because Gates' role in the movie *Generations* was so small. The DS9 lovely, Dax, has a couple of subjects, as do Picard, Troi, Frakes, Kirk, Julian, Quark, Kira, and even Spot. But the overwhelming fan favorite is Data with dozens of subjects created by adoring fans. Spiner femmes, anyone? Like most fan clubs, once members get to know each other conversation often strays. So don't be surprised if a member finishes her convention report on Marina Sitris and starts talking about the antics of her 18-month-old. Trekkers are mothers, too. ✓ **PRODIGY**→*jump* star trek bb→Choose a Topic→Actors/Actresses

Character List A simple list of actors with recurring roles and the roles they played on each of the Trek series. ✓ **AMERICA ONLINE**→*keyword* trek→MORE...→Star Trek Record Banks→Text/Other Files →Upld: 08/29/94→TEXT:Character List (filename: CHARLIST)

List of Actors' Birthdays for TOS, TNG & DS9 Though most of the *Star Trek* characters were born in the future, the earthling actors and actresses who play them were born in the past. Find out exactly when with this document, which lists the birthdays of many of the actors from TOS, TNG, and DS9. ✓ **COMPUSERVE**→*go* sfmedia→Libraries→*Search by file name:* B-DAYS.TXT

Star Trek Actors' Other Roles

Erika Flores played the character Marissa in the TNG episode "Disaster," but did you know that she also appeared on the pilot episode of the television show *Doctor Quinn, Medicine Woman*? And were you aware that Whoopi Goldberg has acted in roles other than that of the 500-plus-year-old bartender Guinan on TNG? Fifteen parts and growing, this huge list of the "other roles" played by *Star Trek* actors begins with steady actors and then lists guest appearances. The fourth part also traces the appearances of characters that have played roles on more than one of the *Trek* series. ✓**INTERNET** ...→*www* http://www.cosy.sbg. ac.at:80/ftp/pub/trek/lists/Actors-Roles/ ...→*gopher* gopher.univ-lyon1. fr→Usenet (FAQs [news.answers], stats, docs, ..)→Usenet FAQs by newsgroup name→rec→rec.arts. startrek.misc→star-trek→actors-roles ...→*gopher* ugle.unit.no: 8300→faq →rec.answers→Star-Trek→Actors-Roles ...→*anon-ftp* rtfm.mit.edu→ /pub/usenet-by-hierarchy/rec/ arts/startrek/misc→Star_Trek_ Actors*

Star Trek Other Roles

In addition to a complete list of the other roles played by *Star Trek* regulars and guest stars, this document includes information on birthdays, and some interesting trivia. ✓**INTERNET**→*www* http://www.ugcs. caltech.edu/~werdna/sttng/roles1. html

Star Trek: The Actors and Their Characters

Psychoanalysis is a favorite pastime: Is Kira the epitome of the modern woman— never really knowing what she wants, love or career? These topics are archived on a frequent basis, so

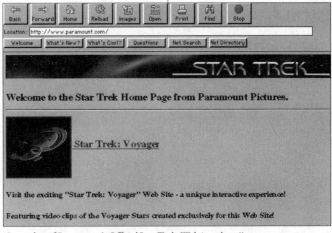

Screenshot of Paramount's Official Star Trek *Website—http://www.paramount.com*

check the library for more anecdotes and analysis. Absolutely every appearance of any actress or actor who played in a *Trek* show is charted in Topic 1. Learn here when to catch Hugh the Borg in an episode of *Blossom*; a Klingon maiden in a pain-relief commercial; or Patrick Stewart as a flamboyant interior decorator in "Jeffrey." In this venue, an actor's role as a Second assistant Romulan is far more important than his Emmy-winning role in any non-*Trek* show. ✓**GENIE**→*keyword* sfrt2→ SFRT2 Bulletin Board→set 32

WS_Char

WS_Char (echo) More than five years after Dr. Pulaski (a Bones clone suggests one member) left and Beverly Crusher returned, members of this conference are still debating the merits of the decision. Obsessing about Trek character development is the pastime of choice here. Low volume. ✓**WARPSPEED**

Paramount

The Crew Behind the Crew

A Q&A session with executive producers Rick Berman, Michael Piller and Jeri Taylor. ✓**INTERNET**

→*www* http://www.ugcs.caltech. edu/~werdna/sttng/iv.prod.html

News/Rumors/Gossip

Berman's been fired! Well, maybe not, but if he were you'd hear it here first. In fact, Berman's firing was announced as a subject with an initial post reading "Ahhhhh, to dream!" Hmmm, questioned another member, maybe he really was. "What time line are you in?" Rumors run rampant on the board ("Anybody else hear the rumor that Patrick Stewart was working on a project with George Lucas that would bridge *Star Trek* and *Star Wars*?") News in the form of airing schedules and notices about upcoming guest stars are also regularly featured. ✓**PRODIGY**→*jump* star trek bb→Choose a Topic→ News/Rumors/Gossip

Paramount Pictures

The official Website for Paramount pictures. Includes a link to the Voyager Website. Praise or complaint about the latest *Voyager* episode? Log 'em here. ✓**INTERNET**→*www* http://www.paramount.com

STAR TREK On-Line!

Keep tabs on this topic for insider discussion

(and jokes) with editors from Pocket Books and production crew members from the series, including Michael and Denise Okuda✓ **GENIE**→*keyword* sfrt2→ SFRT2 Bulletin Board→set 24→read 3

TFDN - Star Trek Credits A library of Paramount ads, promos, and credit lists for each episode of DSN and several TNG episodes. All BBSs participating in the Trek File Distribution Network carry the same items, although the name of the library may be slightly different on each board. ✓ **TFDN**→ TFDN - Star Trek Credits

You and the United Paramount Network Information about the relationship between the UPN and local stations, the schedule, and the programming. ✓ **INTERNET**→*www* http://www.ftms. com:80/vidiot/upn.html

Viacom Online Email Paramount with your thoughts on *Voyager* or Paramount's online presence. ✓ **INTERNET**→*email* voyager@paramount.com

Richard Arnold

Timothy Lynch's Interview with Richard Arnold The complete transcript of an 80 minute interview with Richard Arnold, former assistant to Gene Roddenberry and archivist. Trek reviewer and all-around Trek god on the Net, Timothy Lynch, interviewed Arnold before Gene's death following a storm of anti-Arnold sentiment on Usenet. The lengthy interview covers topics ranging from Gene's relationships with Trek writers to the portrayal of homosexuals on *Star Trek* to Arnold's impressions of many of the leaders in Trek fandom. The interview is divided into five parts, an introduction, and Lynch's own impres-

sions (not favorable) and follow-up information on Richard Arnold. Archives of Usenet discussion about Arnold are downloadable from the same site. ✓ **INTERNET**→*anon-ftp* ftp.coe.montana. edu→/pub/mirrors/startrek/Tim_ Lynch_stuff/richard

Writing

How to Submit Creative Material When TNG was running, Paramount received over 3,000 fan scripts a year and had a 24-hour telephone hot line with information about submitting a TNG script. This guide describes the dos and don'ts of writing for each *Star Trek* series (TNG information may be a bit irrelevant—although there's always *Star Trek VIII*), Pocket Books, DC *Star Trek* comics, Malibu *Deep Space Nine* comics, and Usenet parodies. Hint: You need an agent for Pocket Books and you should first submit a one-page "springboard" outlining your story concept when selling to DC Comics. ✓ **INTERNET** ...→*anon-ftp* quepasa.cs.tu-berlin. de→/pub/doc/movies+tv-series /StarTrek/FAQs→creative.submis sions.gz ...→*anon-ftp* ftp.cis.ksu. edu→/pub/alt.startrek.creative/misc →HowToSubmitCreativeMaterial. zip

Star Trek Novel Guidelines Guidelines compiled by an associate editor at Simon & Schuster's Pocket Books for those interested in writing Trek novels. ✓ **COMPUSERVE**→*go* sfmedia→Libraries→ *Search by file name:* POCKET.TXT

Writers Guide A concise overview of writing for Paramount, including submission guidelines and useful information on agent representation. ✓ **EWORLD**→sf→Star Trek→United Federation Library→ WRITERS.TXT

Sometimes life imitates art. Sometimes art intimidates life. And sometimes life and art work together in perfect harmony. For *Star Trek* fans on the Internet, the last of these three possibilities is the one that warms their heart, especially when they're discussing the ways in which online technology—with its vast reach, incredible variety, and radical democratization of opinion—might galvanize *Trek* fandom. "The Net is Spock's IDIC (Infinite Diversity in Infinite Combinations) realized," says Otto Heuer, the 29-year-old software engineer and self-described "professional hacker" who maintains the rec.arts. startrek FAQs. "With all the millions of people on the Internet, each with a different opinion on any given matter, we literally have an Infinite Diversity in Infinite Combinations."

But there are lumps in the oatmeal of Utopia. And many of those lumps are appearing courtesy of Paramount Pictures, the media giant that owns the *Star Trek* franchise. Though a certain mutual interest is indisputable—"It helps

Rick Berman

Star Trek to have so many people around the world discussing *Star Trek* and it helps Usenet to have a great concept like *Star Trek* to discuss," says Heuer— Paramount has approached online Trek fandom cautiously, with a guarded enthusiasm that often shades into suspicion. While *Babylon 5* creator J. Michael Straczynski makes regular use of Usenet and IRC channels to discuss his show with fans, Paramount's top brass have eschewed the Internet; aside from an occasional commercial-service appearance by William Shatner or Rick Berman, the Trek chat online is exclusively fan-driven.

To some extent, this problem arises from the nature of Usenet posts, the way that the newsgroup world inverts the old saw, "If you don't have anything nice to say, don't say anything at all." Since newsgroups give fans the opportunity to play critic, posts are largely critical, and this may be off-putting to Paramount execs. Rec.arts.startrek.info moderator Jim Griffith explains: "The problem is that with Usenet, every user can be an internationally-read author, critic, or spokesperson. But 1) the users don't handle this

"But when the smoke cleared, nothing had been resolved, and the sleeping media giant was awake—and grumpy."

responsibility well, and 2) those who aren't familiar with the system don't know how to respond to what happens on the Net. So when a typical episode comes out, everyone posts their opinions, 40 percent of which are probably critical. That doesn't mean that 40 percent of the viewers didn't like the episode, but the perception by those producing *Star Trek* is that the Net is out to get them. And they've deliberately avoided dealing with us for that specific reason."

Though Griffith's point is well-taken, the events of the past year suggest that Paramount's wariness is more than a bad case of thin skin. In the summer of 1994, roughly six months before the official theatrical release of *Star Trek: Generations*, a script of the film appeared on rec.arts.startrek.current. "Scripts are driven off various lots all the time," says Mike Brown, whose Vidiot reviews are well-known to online Trek fans. "Until now, these scripts have only made it around via paper, limiting the impact." But after Usenet publication, the leak reached thousands of fans, touching off a series of debates (was the script legitimate? was posting unfair, or even illegal?) and even drawing the attention of Paramount, who

wasted no time contacting those who had posted the script—including one Netter living in the Netherlands.

While online Trekkers acknowledged Paramount's interest in the matter, they defended the electronic medium as a free-speech zone. Andrew Tong, the Caltech undergrad whose TNG pages are among the most impressive sites in all Cyberspace, argued that the law had no place online: "If I were Paramount, I'd prosecute whoever leaked the script," wrote Tong at the time. "I'd think it would be pointless to use lawsuits to stop/punish redistributors."

The reposting of the script in October and November touched off an extended debate on the finer points of copyright law and corporate morality, with some fans defending the dissemination of the script and others deriding it as a clear theft of the writers' work. With the rhetoric flying fast and furious, the Great Generations Script Debates were a wonderful illustration of the Net at its best. But when the smoke cleared, nothing had been resolved, and the sleeping media giant was awake—and grumpy. "The posting really hurt the whole of Trek fandom," says Brown. "Sure, I kept a copy. I probably would have gotten a paper copy anyway. I don't pay for scripts, ever. But the posting of any script doesn't fall into 'rules of Net fair play.' It just isn't a good idea at all." Tim Lynch, whose online TNG, DS9 , and *Voyager* reviews are a staple of Trek culture, makes the point even more emphatically: "Had someone had a copy of the script leaked to them and spilled information from it (a few lines, a plot synopsis, etc.), that'd be the nature of the game—but posting someone else's property verbatim is every bit as much a violation of intellectual property rights as Xeroxing a book would be, in my opinion."

Over the ensuing months, this friction has not lessened, and while many fans suspect that Paramount monitors Internet activity ("I don't *believe* that Paramount representatives are lurking online," says Miriam Nathan, who co-hosts AOL's Star Trek Club Forum, "I *know* they are"), the absence of an official relationship between Trek creators and fans strikes some Trekkers as a travesty. "My newsgroup is the *ideal* place for Paramount to officially announce stuff to the Internet," says Jim Griffith. "News and information without discussion, remember? But as soon as I say 'Usenet,' they say 'thank you very much.' And that hurts both of us."

To be fair, the outlook isn't all that bleak. In the winter of 1995—early

Michael Piller

January, to be precise—*Deep Space Nine* broadcast a two-part episode entitled "Past Tense." The plot? That twenty-first century civilization escaped full-scale class warfare with the help of—that's right—a national computer network known as the Net. Is this Net-to-the-rescue plot twist an olive branch of sorts? Online Trek fans hope so. "I think it's a tremendous possibility that the online world will be the newest source of feedback/ratings for *Star Trek* creators," says AOL's Nathan. "It's instantaneous (pretty much) and it's also an anonymous medium through which they can ask questions, much as we fans do. I also think there's a distinct possibility that the online culture will provide a good grounds for business expansion if the creators have a mind to do that."

And even the most pessimistic of observers do not hestiate to point out that Trek and the Net share a common origin. "*Star Trek* went a long way towards influencing the braintrust of the seventies and eighties, and those same people went on to become founders of the online culture that is emerging," says Jim Griffith. "The big advantage to the online culture is that it has actually managed to unify Trek fandom. It used to be that there was only a sense of community at the convention. Now, people get that sense every time they login."

The Great Bird

And on the eighth day, he created The Original Series. In the continuing debate over the

meaning, purpose, and ideology of the *Star Trek* dream, no other name carries as much weight as Gene Roddenberry's. Invoke Gene to your side in those endless debates over canon and the opposition is silenced. If you were reading the **rec.arts.startrek*** groups when Roddenberry died, you may have been asked by Jim Griffith, moderator of rec.arts.startrek.info, to "sign" an electronic condolence card that was sent to Gene's wife, Majel Barrett: "I asked people to send their names to be added to this, as well as any messages, and I did my best to combine the messages into a single letter, with all of the names at the end. We ended up with 1,300 names from 11 different countries and 44 different states. It was amazing to read some of the stuff people wrote. Gene touched so many people at a time when people really needed his vision." But even if you weren't online then, the memorials remain. Listen to William Shatner eulogize Kirk's creator in a sound file called **Eulogy**. Or read over the transcript of an im-

Gene Roddenberry—downloaded from Perfect Vision Graphics BBS

promptu wake on the night of Roddenberry's death in GEnie's **Science Fiction RoundTable**.

On the Net

Eulogy A sound clip from Shatner's eulogy of Gene Roddenberry: "Very few people have the ability to fire up our imaginations and make us think about the human condition. Gene Roddenberry, the creator of *Star Trek*, was one of those people. He took us where no man has gone before—and beyond. He created a starship, its crew, an entire universe—and brought them to life for millions of people. Without Gene, there would have been no *Star Trek*

computer game or *Star Trek* television series. Gene Roddenberry—born 1921, died 1991. We honor your memory." ✓**TFDN**→TFDN Fact Files→ EULOGY.ZIP

Fallen Great Bird Written to the tune of "Fallen Angel," this filk mourns the loss of Roddenberry with verses like: "Oh Galaxy's Great Bird/ What you put into our hand/ Is a vision of the future/ For we see and understand/ That a dream outlives the dreamer/ That a legend need not die/ As you go to sleep in glory/ Our hearts still seek the sky." ✓**COMPUSERVE**→*go sflit*→Libraries→*Search by file name:* fallen.sng

Gene Roddenberry A Roddenberry picture. ✓**COMPUSERVE**→*go* sf-media→Libraries→*Search by file*

name: GENE 1.GIF

Gene Roddenberry, 1921-1991

Another picture of Roddenberry in GIF format. ✓**COMPUSERVE**→*go* sfmedia→Libraries→ *Search by file name:* GENER1.GIF

Gene Roddenberry (August 19, 1921 - October 24, 1991)

Brief biography from Paramount's press kit of Roddenberry's life and his involvement with *Star Trek*. ✓**INTERNET** ...→*www* http://www. ugcs.caltech.edu/~werdna/sttng/ gene.html ...→*gopher* marvel.loc. gov→Employee Information→Clubs and Organizations→What IF...? LCPA Science Fiction Forum→Miscellaneous Science Fiction/Fantasy and Related Resources→Biographies of Science Fiction/Fantasy Personalities→Gene Roddenberry

Gene Roddenberry Impromptu Wake

Log of a real-time meeting in GEnie's Sci-fi RoundTable the night of Roddenberry's death. ✓**GENIE**→*keyword* sfrt1→Text and Graphics Libraries→*Download a file:* 3010

Gene Roddenberry Obit

Roddenberry's obit as published in the San Diego Comic-Con program book. ✓**GENIE**→*keyword* sfrt1→Text and Graphics Libraries→*Download a file:* 6376

Gene Roddenberry: Who Is He?

The big Kahuna? If you must. The head cheese? A little irreverent, perhaps. The Great Bird? That's better. This document offers an introduction to the life and career of the creator of *Star Trek*, and proves the oft-stated point that "Gene Roddenberry led a life as colorful and exciting as almost any high-adventure fiction." ✓**INTERNET**→*www* http://web.city.ac.uk /~cc103/gene.html

⊧STARNOTES⊧

```
<[R.I.P. Gene ] J.REA1> Hi, Greg. I suppose you
heard the sad news?
<DRIZZAN> Yep. :(
<[Sad Bear] C.BRYANT3> God help me, but I'm
really angry right now...
<[R.I.P. Gene ] J.REA1> Angry? At whom?
<[Sad Bear] C.BRYANT3> I'm angry that such a
man can die... sigh...Sorry if I sound sappy.
<TABITHA> Bear, this man and his vision have
been a part of our lives for as long as a lot
of us can remember. It's ok to feel angry that
he's gone.
<SOARON> Bear - It's fine. A lot of us have
shared the same dream since we first saw Trek.
It's only right to have some angry feelings
mixed in with the sadness we are all sharing.
<TABITHA> I'm pretty angry right now myself;
our local station just ran its piece, and the
female anchor talked like she didn't know what
was going on.
<Elissa> Non-trekkers won't understand what the
fuss is all about.
<[R.I.P. Gene ] J.REA1> The Great Bird is now
one with the Galaxy.
<[Sad Bear] C.BRYANT3> I can remember going to
Europe and stumbling through Germany with only
a year of German. I ended up on a bus by
myself, a pack and a couple of Trek novels... I
was very lonely and no one seemed to pay me any
attention, but someone noticed the book cover
and became very excited saying "Enterprise...
Kirk... Spock"...Suddenly, the world was much
smaller.:)
<[RIPgreatBird] J.REA1> I never met Gene. I
really, really wish I had.
<SOARON> Ellen _ I've watched Trek since I was
five, when it premiered in 1966. I feel pretty
miserable right now. I feel like I did when my
father died.
<[RIPgreatBird] J.REA1> I think the greatest
tribute we can do is to devote our lives to
helping the improvement of the human condition,
so that the 23rd and 24th Centuries will be
more like Gene envisioned them...
<[RIPgreatBird] J.REA1> The Great Bird has been
beamed away from us.

-from GEnie's Log of Gene Roddenberry's
Impromptu Wake
```

Off the screen

Star Trek novels outsell almost all other books in the nation. Learn to read and you

need never be without Picard or Kirk. CompuServe provides plot summaries in the **Star Trek Book Guide** or try the **Star Trek: The Next Generation Novel Compendium.** GEnie's **Star Trek Novels** and eWorld's **Star Trek Fiction** let you converse with actual *Trek* novelists about their work or even get advice on your own prose. Join the virtual reading circles of **Trek_ Books,** where fans meet to discuss and dissect the latest *Trek* tomes. Don't want to waste time reading a dull one? Check out the Usenet community's opinion in **Trek Book Rate Results.** And stay on top of *Trek* comics with the **Star Trek Comics Checklist.**

On the Net

Across the board

Alternative Trek Media You may think *Star Trek* is all novels, movies, and TV. You're wrong. Everything that isn't a novel, movie, or a sanctioned series finds a home here—comic books, parodies, technical manuals, fanzines, and music. Arnie Starr, who inked the classic Trek comics for DC Comics and the original *Next Generation* miniseries, moderates the *Star Trek* in Comics topic. (It's

Book cover—from America Online's Center Stage

inexplicable why there isn't more comics discussion.) This is the category where you can find out the monetary value of your *Star Trek* calendar (it's worth more if it has a special grievous error), or where you can get the incidental music from the Original Series on CD. A lot of fans who market their own Trek memorabilia and collectibles are online here; there are people who produce posters of favorite ships by watching the episodes over and over for technical specifications. Scriptwriting help is offered here, too, including advice on how to work within the Paramount guidelines, pitch your idea, and contend with revisions. The library holds a wealth of previous script production assistance. ✓GE-NIE→*keyword* sfrt2→SFRT2 Bulletin Board→set 34

Books and Comics Don't you think they meant *Star Trek* books and comics when they put this topic in the Trek forum? Sure, Trek books get discussed, but so do books by Asimov, Heinlein, Herbert, Clarke, and the other heroes of sci-fi. People here read, and read widely. Most people think TV and movies when they think *Star Trek,* but here you'll find Treksters bemoaning the rise of books on tape as another sign of mental atrophy: "You need to use your eyes when reading. TV and radio are less cognitively demanding activities." Not all of the regulars agree with that, but even when someone's threatening "a reply that'll fling ya off your keyboard," they say it with a smile. And where else will you see the German poet Friedrich Schiller quoted ("Against stupidity the very gods themselves contend in vain") in a sci-fi forum? One typical discussion centered around reading *Star Trek* books aloud. Those who've tried dramatic readings agree it's difficult shifting from Spock to Scotty in seconds. ✓DELPHI→*go* ent sta for set boo

Star Trek Guides: Books/ Books on Tape/Comics A collection of the popular Net lists devoted to cataloging Trek books, comics, and books on tape. ✓IN-TERNET→*www* http://www.cosy. sbg.ac.at/rec/startrek/Novels.html

Audio

Star Trek Books-On-Tape Whether its Leonard Nimoy and George Takei reading *Spock's World* or Michael Dorn reading

Contamination, listening to *Star Trek* stories is, for many fans, the next best thing to watching. This frequently updated list of *Trek* stories on tape provides title, author, format, and publication date for *Trek* novels (all the series and the movies) and children's *Trek* stories. The addresses and telephone numbers of tape distributors are also attached. ✓**INTERNET** …→*anon-ftp* rtfm.mit.edu→/pub/usenet-by-hierarchy/rec/arts/star-trek/misc→Star_Trek_Books-On-Tape …→*gopher* gopher.univ-lyon1.fr→Usenet (FAQs [news.an swers], stats, docs, ..)→Usenet FAQs by newsgroup name→rec→rec.arts.startrek.misc→star-trek→books-on-tape

"Eat any good books lately?"—Q to Worf
Net Source: Classic TNG Quotes—from AOL's Star Trek Club

Books

Books/Other Print If you're a Riker fan, what's your favorite book? "How about *Fortune's Light*? He seems much more human and even fallible in that one, and he still gets the girl," says Martin. The board often features character-related book topics, but no subject is as popular as the Peter David's best discussions. So, which novel's better? "*Imzadi* was a true labor of love, although *Q-Squared* was excellent," writes Clifford. ✓**PRODIGY**→*jump* star trek bb→Choose a Topic→Books/Other Print

Star Trek Book Guide A two-part summary of *Star Trek* books. Each description includes title, author, publication date, and plot synopsis. Several Bantam Books series, the Ballantine Books Animated Series Adaptations, and the Simon & Schuster Pocket Books series are covered. ✓**INTERNET** …→*gopher* ugle.unit.no 8300→faq →rec.answers→star-trek→CS-guide …→*www* http://www.cis.ohio-state.edu/hypertext/faq/usenet/star-trek/CS-guide/books/top.html ✓**COMPUSERVE**→*go* sfmedia→Li-

braries→*Search by file name:* STBOOK.TXT

Star Trek Fiction In response to a press release posted about Diane Duane's book *Dark Mirror*, the eWorld'er known as Starship wrote: "I've been waiting over 20 years for someone to come up with the bright idea of making a sequel to "Mirror, Mirror" which was always ranked in my top five list of *Star Trek* episodes." Selene jumped in and suggested that Starship watch the DS9 episode "Crossover" with a similar theme. The section includes press releases and reviews of upcoming books as well as general discussion about *Trek* books. DS9 Pocket Book author John Vornholt is an active contributor to the conference. ✓**EWORLD**→sf→Star Trek→Star Trek Fiction

Star Trek Novels You can ask the author of your favorite novel why there weren't more love scenes, or if he could apply stricter adherance to the canon. (Beware, in fact, the ever-present "yes, but is it canon?" debate.) What separates GEnie from other Cyberspace Trek discussions (both in this category and in the RoundTables as a whole) is the large number of published *Trek* authors who are regular contributors, including

Peter David, A.C. Crispin, Brad Ferguson, Daffyd Ab Hugh, Lois Tilton, John Vornholt, and Gene DeWeese. They're giving enthusiasts the lowdown on everything that goes into getting a *Trek* novel into print, including musings on difficulties of writing for an audience with very definite expectations and a large corporation with other specific ideas. The category also features topics devoted to the big Trek reference books, such as the *Star Trek Chronology*, *The Star Trek Encyclopedia*, *The Nitpicker's Guide*, the *Interactive Tech Manual*, and cast member biographies. Primarily, though, it's a place to come and discuss fiction, such as Peter David's *Q-Squared* or upcoming DS9 novels. ✓**GENIE**→*keyword* sfrt2→SFRT2 Bulletin Board→set 23

Star Trek: The Next Generation Novel Compendium Twenty-eight TNG novels are featured with title, author, stardate, characters, races, ships, worlds, and references for each. The compendium has eight appendices summarizing the information in the novels. Appendix D, for instance, is a list of all the worlds encountered in the novels. ✓**INTERNET** …→*anon-ftp* quepasa.cs.tu-berlin. de→/pub/doc/movies+tv-series/StarTrek/Novels/TNG …→*gopher* gopher.univ-lyon1.fr→Usenet (FAQs [news.answers], stats, docs, ..)→ Usenet FAQs by newsgroup name →rec→rec.arts.startrek.misc→novels →tng

Star Trek: The Original Series Novel Compendium *Star Trek* fan Ron Carmen has compiled a multipart compendium with summaries of each of the *Star Trek* Pocket Book novels. Each summary includes lists of the regular and guest characters, alien races, ships, and planets that appear in the book. Summaries also describe plots and document inconsistencies and continuity errors in novels and novelizations. ✓**INTERNET** ...→*anon-ftp* quepasa.cs.tu-berlin. de→/pub/doc/movies+tv-series/ StarTrek/Novels/TOS ...→*gopher* gopher.univ1.fr→Usenet (FAQs [news.answers], stats, docs, ..)→ Usenet FAQs by newsgroup name→rec→rec.arts.startrek.misc →novels→tos ✓**TFDN**→TFDN Facts Files→*Download a file:* TOSNOV. ZIP

TNG Books/Mags Everybody here has a favorite *Trek* book to recommend to other fans, although—you'll be warned—they generally don't comply with the Trek canon. But, given that *Next Generation* episodes are now only in syndication and movies only happen every couple of years, TNG books will be the only steady source for new adventures with Picard and crew. When a high-school English teacher asked for help picking her first *Trek* novel (she loved the episodes "Offspring" and "Inner Light"), a fellow teacher responded: "Being an ex-high-school/university English instructor, I, too, prefer books with strong character development over those with a lot of special effects and 'battle scenes.' My favorite four are *Imzadi* (a MUST read!), *Q-in-Law* (funniest Star

Trek book yet), and *Q-Squared*— all by Peter David—and *Guises of the Mind* (great discussions on religious tolerance and Data's search for God) by Rebecca Neason." ✓**AMERICA ONLINE**→*keyword* trek→ Star Trek Message Boards→The Next Generation→TNG Books/ Mags

Trek Book Rate Results Usenet bibliophiles can rate *Star Trek* novels on a scale of zero to one. Ballots are averaged and new results, along with the batting-average rating, are reposted periodically. As of now, the exciting *The Great Starship Race* garners the highest praise from Trek readers. ✓**INTERNET**→*anon-ftp* rtfm.mit.edu→/pub/ usenet-by-hierarchy/rec/arts/ startrek/misc→TREK_RATE_results_ (BOOKS)

Trek_Books (echo) This online reading circle for talking about *Trek* books—"My passion in life!," according to frequent contributor Linda—generates a steady stream of impressions, criticism, and enthusiasm for the printed version of the Trek universe, with comments coming from around the world. The discussion is open to other

Star Trek Encyclopedia—downloaded from http://www.paramount.com

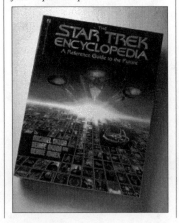

science-fiction novels, but the *Trek* series is the overwhelming favorite. ✓**TREKNET**

Trekker_Books (echo) Although *Trek* books dominate the conference, all sci-fi books are open for discussion. Most of the messages take the form of book reviews, press releases, or FAQs, and fans are generous with their opinions. Before you buy your next Trek story or reference, go here for advice. ✓**TREKKERNET**

Comics

Star Trek Comics Checklist A comprehensive six-part reference guide to *Star Trek* comics, including details on publication dates, authors, illustrators, and story summary. ✓**INTERNET** ...→*anon-ftp* rtfm.mit.edu→/pub/usenet-by-hier archy/rec/arts/star-trek/misc →Star_Trek_Comics_Checklist* ...→*gopher* ugle.unit.no8300 →faq →rec.answers→star-trek→comics-checklist ...→*gopher* gopher.univ-lyon1.fr→Usenet (FAQs [news.answers], stats, docs, ..)→Usenet FAQs by newsgroup name→rec→ rec.arts.startrek.misc→comics-check list

Star Trek/Star Trek: TNG TNG may have filmed its final episode, but the comics keep coming out—and serious fans of the DC *Trek* comics gather in this message folder to speculate about where the inked series is heading and, in the true spirit of comic fandom, make some trades. TOS and DS9 fans are also here, trading, criticizing, and sharing their enthusiasm for the latest issue of their favorite comics series. ✓**AMERICA ONLINE**→*keyword* dc comics→Message Boards→DC Comics Message Board→Star Trek/Star Trek: TNG

Sights & sounds of Trek

Can you hear it? Klaxons sounding "Red Alert, Red Alert." You don't have to rely on

your imagination to relive your favorite Trek sights and sounds any more—the Net provides endless video stills, animations, scanned publicity shots, and soundclips. In fact, images are so pervasive on the Net that it would be difficult to find a large FTP site that didn't have a Trek photo or collection of photos. Try **The Final Frontier** to customize your Mac into a Federation vessel with screensavers, icons, and sound. Search the AOL **Star Trek Graphics File Library**, which houses hundreds of stills—including one of Kirk and that green babe Vina to use for your self-designed Christmas cards. Looking for a job in the wormhole neighborhood? Consider laying out your resume in **Bajoran TrueType**.

Quark (publicity shot)—downloaded from Perfect Vision Graphics BBS

Across the board

Macintosh: The Final Frontier Get Trekked on the Mac. From sounds to dingbats to DS9 fonts to icons to screensavers to an extension that turns your cursor into a Trek symbol, this is a Mac-users Trek heaven. ✓**INTERNET**→*www* http://www.astro.nwu.edu/lentz/ mac/software/mac-trek.html

Fonts & icons

Color Trek Icon Anthology 1.90 S7 More than 200 icons based on *Trek* characters, locations, ships, and other Trekkie things. Tribble icon, anyone? Requires Macintosh with system 7.0+. ✓**AMERICA ONLINE**→*keyword* mac software→Search the Libraries →Search All Libraries→*Search by file name:* Trek Icons Anthology 1.0.sit

The Cool Star Trek Icon An *Enterprise* icon. ✓**COMPUSERVE**→*go* sfmedia→Libraries→*Search by file name:* STARTR.ICO

Star Trek Fonts *Star Trek* font for the Macintosh. ✓**INTERNET**→ *anon-ftp* ftp.u-tokyo.ac.jp→/.1/ mac/umich/system.extensions/font /type1→startrekfonts.cpt.hqx

Star Trek Fonts Family A package of five, including fonts used for Classic *Trek*, *Trek* movies, TNG Crille (for actors credits), and TNG title. Requires a Macintosh and a PostScript or ATM printer. ✓**AMERICA ONLINE**→*keyword* mac software→Search the Libraries→Search All Libraries→*Search by file name:* Star Trek Fonts Family.cpt

Trek Smiley Icons A collection of smiley-face icons modeled after the major races of the Trek universe. ✓**AMERICA ONLINE**→*keyword* mac software→Search the Libraries →Search All Libraries→*Search by file name:* Trek Smileys.sit

Pictures

General Star Trek Images More than 100 Trek images in GIF format, a significant number of them from the movie *Star Trek VI*. A small collection of DS9 photos are also available here. ✓**INTERNET**→*anon-ftp* ftp.sunet.se→/pub/pictures/tv. film/StarTrek

Jellinek's Star Trek Pictures Links to several major archives of Trek images and a small collection of local Trek images, including Dax, Spock, a Bird of Prey, and crew shots from all the series. ✓**INTERNET**→*www* http:// www.cosy.sbg.ac.at/rec/star trek/Pictures.html

Joshua Bell's ASCII Art Archive ASCII artists have created a Klingon knife, the DS9 logo, Spocks, Picards, Kirks, and dozens of ships from empires across the galaxy—Romulan Birds of Prey, Cardassian Warships, *Voyager*, *Reliant*, and several *Enterprises*. ✓**IN-TERNET** ...→*www* http://www.ucal gary.ca/~jsbell/sta.html ...→ *anon-ftp* ftp.cc.umanitoba.ca →/startrek/trek_ascii

Mini-Sound & Pictures Archive A small collection of Trek bitmaps, sounds, and *Voyager* GIFs. ✓**INTERNET**→ *anon-ftp* ftp.netcom.com→/pub/fl /flypba/Up loads

The Movie BBS (bbs) Graphics for fans of all *Star Trek* series. Looking for a portrait of Captain James T. Kirk? How many do you want? How about a collage from, "Best of both worlds?" It's here too. Offstage shots of your favorite actors at conventions? No problem. Klingon ship pictures, complete with specs? You've got it. And if you're get ting tired of graphics, you can also retrieve scripts and Starfleet code books. ☎→*dial* 718-939-5462

Star Trek GIFs Images in GIF format of crew members, including Spock, Kirk, Picard, Beverly, and Data, from both TOS and TNG. ✓**INTERNET**→*gopher* olympus.dcs.hull.ac.uk→Hull CS Research Multimedia Archives→Images→Media→ star_trek_gifs

Star Trek Graphic Files Snapshots of Stewart at conventions, fan renderings of *Voyager* or DS9, VCR stills from favorite episodes, tech diagrams, and more fill this huge library. ✓**AMERICA ONLINE**→*keyword* trek→MORE...→Star Trek Record Banks→Graphic Files

Star Trek Pics Close to a hundred images neatly divided into directories, such as Classic, *Next Generation*, *Deep Space Nine*, and *Voyager*. ✓**INTER-NET**→*www* http://nerys.ti1.tu-har burg.de/startrek/pics.html

Trek ASCII Dozens of ASCII Trek renditions, including the

Romulan insignia, a tricorder, the DS9 logo, and a B'Rel Class Klingon Bird of Prey. ✓**INTERNET**→*anon-ftp* ftp.cis. ksu.edu→/pub/alt.startrek.creative /misc/→trek.ascii.zip

TrekArt, a Gallery of Computer Paintings Information about and sample GIF files from a collection of original art and technical drawings from TOS, TNG, and DS9. ✓**COMPUSERVE**→*go* sfme-dia→Libraries→*Search by file name:* TRKART.ARC

Trekker_Ansi (echo) Trek and sci-fi artists post their ANSI creations. Each message is a different creation: the *Enterprise*, Spock, the Borg, etc. ✓**TREKKERNET**

Screensavers

After Dark Warp Factor 1.3 Screensaver depicting what you might see if you were on the *Enterprise* and looking out a window while traveling at warp speed. For Macs with After Dark 2.0+. ✓**AMERICA ONLINE**→*keyword* mac software→Search the Libraries→Search All Libraries→ *Search by file name:* Warp Factor 1.3_.sit

Star Trek After Dark Screensaver An *Enterprise* screensaver for the Mac. ✓**INTERNET** ...→*anon-ftp* faui43.informatik.uni-erlangen. de→/mounts/epix/public/pub/ Mac/util/screensaver/afterdark→ startrek.sit.hqx ...→*anon-ftp* nic.switch.ch→/mirror/umich-mac/util/screensaver/after dark→startrek.sit.hqx

Star Trek Start-up Screens Three Trek images for Microsoft Windows start-up screens. ✓**COM-PUSERVE**→*go* sfmedia→Libraries→ *Search by file name:* TREKSC.EXE

Sounds

Star Trek Sounds Sounds from both TOS and TNG, including McCoy's "He's dead, Jim," O'Brien's singing, and the computer's announcement of auto-destruction. ✓**INTERNET**→ *www* http://www.cosy.sbg. ac.at/rec/startrek/Sounds.html

TFDN—Star Trek Sounds (echo) Odo asks, "Who the hell are you?" Quark announces, "I love a woman in uniform." The computer responds, "Emergency power engaged." Scotty exclaims, "Captain, we're losing power on the warp engines!" And, McCoy says, "Damn it, Jim!" These are the sounds of *Star Trek,* and there are more than two hundred of them (primarily for IBM compatibles) in this library. All BBSs participating in the Trek File Distribution Network carry the same items although the name of the library may be slightly different on each board. ✓**TFDN**

TOS Pictures

Perfect Vision Graphics BBS (bbs) The Trek file libraries on this BBS dedicated to science-fiction images are extensive and include publicity shots, book cover and magazine scans, video stills, and convention shots. Although there are extensive collections of images for each of the *Trek* series, this BBS may be one of the few Net spots where the original series gets equal billing to TNG. Here you can download Kirk and Uhura's kiss, Kirk covered with Tribbles, a close-up of Captain Pike, an evil Mr. Spock from the Mirror universe, a shot of Lazarus, Spock's love from the Ice Age, and dozens of episode collages. It's a voy-

age worth taking, and, according to 20th century customs, paying for. ✓**PVG** *dial* 513-233-7993→F

TOS Picture Page Images from TOS episodes. Judy Fabian, who designs the page, changes the episode scenes each month. ✓**INTERNET**→*www* http://www.uvm.edu/~jfabian /pictures.html

TOS sounds

Sounds from Star Trek A small collection of TOS sound clips, including the theme and Spock's "most illogical." ✓**INTERNET**→ *www* http:// everest.cs.ucdavis.edu/ ~hoagland/sounds/st/

Star Trek WAV Files (mostly TOS) Small collection of TOS Wav files, including theme music and frequently quoted lines such as "Kirk here" and "I'm a doctor, not a...." Scotty's "Admiral, there be whales here" is also available. ✓**INTERNET**→*gopher* tiger.acs.appstate.edu→Tiger's Sound Archive→Star Trek Wav Files (mostly TOS)

TOS Sounds "Forgive me, doctor, I'm receiving a number of distress calls," is Spock's line in one of the many sound clips available at this gopher. McCoy answers, "I don't doubt it." Kirk opening a captain's log, Kirk rejecting the concept of a no-win situation, and other TOS sound clips for the Macintosh. ✓**INTERNET**→*gopher* gopher. med.umich.edu→Entertainment →Sounds→Star Trek_(TOS)

TOS Sounds Sounds from the original series. Requires a Mac and a HyperCard player. ✓**AMERICA ONLINE**→*keyword*

mac software→Search the Libraries→Search All Libraries→ *Search by file name:* Trek1.sit

Trek Button Sounds These sounds were responsible for creating atmosphere on TOS. Here's a collection of some of the more memorable ones. Requires a Mac and a HyperCard player. ✓**AMERICA ONLINE**→*keyword* mac software →Search the Libraries→Search All Libraries→*Search by file name:* Trek Buttons 3.0.sit

TNG fonts & icons

Next Generation Icons A package of TNG icons of characters and crew members. For Macs running System 7. ✓**INTERNET** ...→*anon-ftp* ftp.u-tokyo.ac.jp→ /.3/info-mac/gui/grf→star-trek-tng-icons.hqx ...→*anon-ftp* nic. switch.ch→/mirror/info-mac/ gui/grf→star-trek-tng-icons.hqx ✓**AMERICA ONLINE**→*keyword* mac software→Search the Libraries→ Search All Libraries→*Search by file name:* Star Trek Nx Generation.sit ✓**EWORLD**→sf→Star Trek→United Federation Library →Trek Icons.sit

Next Generation Icons A package of TNG icons of characters and crew members. For Macs running System 7. ✓**INTERNET** ...→*anon-ftp* ftp.u-tokyo.ac.jp→ /.3/info-mac/gui/grf→star-trek-tng-icons.hqx ...→*anon-ftp* nic. switch.ch→/mirror/info-mac/gui/ grf→star-trek-tng-icons.hqx ✓**AMERICA ONLINE**→*keyword* mac software→Search the Libraries→Search All Libraries→ *Search by file name:* Star Trek Nx Generation.sit ✓**EWORLD**→sf→Star Trek→United Federation Library→ Trek Icons.sit

Star Trek: Next Generation Icons Icons based on 13 TNG

characters and four members of the Borg. For Macs running System 7. ✓**AMERICA ONLINE**→*keyword* mac software→Search the Libraries →Search All Libraries→*Search by file name:* Star Trek - TNG icons.sit

---

Trek Monitors Fonts Font mimmicking the tall, thin font used on the monitors for TNG's *USS Enterprise NCC-1701-D.* On AOL, the first file is a PostScript font, and the second is a TrueType font. For the Macintosh. ✓**AMERICA ONLINE**→*keyword* mac software →Search the Libraries→Search All Libraries→*Search by file name:* TNG MonitorsPS.sit *or* TNG MonitorsTT.sit ✓**INTERNET**→*anon-ftp* nic.switch. ch→/mirror/info-mac/font/tt →tng-monitors.hqx

---

TrueType TNG Fonts Fonts based on those used in TNG, including the Crillee font used in the credits, a dingbat typeface of Klingon-like symbols, and a font similar to the sans serif typeface used on the *Enterprise* control monitors. For Windows 3.1. ✓**AMERICA ONLINE**→*keyword* winforum→ Search the Software Libraries → *Search by file name:* TREKFONT. ZIP

TNG pictures

TNG Images A large collection of TNG's GIFs and JPEGs, including both actor shots, publicity stills, logos, and episode scenes. ✓**INTERNET** ...→*anon-ftp* Danann. hea.ie→/pub/mirrors/funet-pics /tv+film/StarTrek/tng ...→*anon-ftp* ftp.funet.fi→pictures→/pub/pics/ tv+film/StarTrek/tng

---

TNG Trek JPEGs Almost 300 episode stills from the *Next Generation*, particularly the first three seasons. From Tasha seducing Data to Commander Shelby to Worf howling in the Klingon death ritual to the Crystalline Entity, the site has some high quality images in JPEG format. A few original series shots are also available, including Kirk with the Tribbles, and the portal from the City on the Edge of Forever. The "lajkonik" site has a slightly different collection with more original series, but, overall, there's substantial overlap. ✓**INTERNET** ...→*anon-ftp* ftp.cis.ksu.edu→ /pub/pictures/jpg/Startrek ...→*anon-ftp* lajkonik.cyfkr. edu.pl→/agh/reserve/gifs /startrek

TNG sounds

Star Trek: The Next Generation Sounds Sound clips from the first TNG season. Requires a Mac and Hyper-Card player. ✓**AMERICA ONLINE**→ *keyword* mac software→Search the Libraries→Search All Libraries→ *Search by file name:* StarTrek_ TNG.sit

---

Star Trek Wav Files (mostly TNG) Large collection of TNG WAV files, including Q's closing statements in the courtroom in "Encounter at Farpoint," the crew playing poker, Riker inviting Troi to dinner, and Worf's "It is a good day to die...." ✓**INTERNET**→*gopher* tiger.acs.appstate.edu→ Tiger's Sound Archive→Star Trek Wav Files (mostly TNG)

TNG Sound Archive Hear Spock say "fascinating" in a TNG episode, Barclay hit on Troi, and Q tell Worf he'd make a good throw rug. The site holds 125 soundclips for the Macintosh from episodes of *The Next Generation*, particularly Q episodes, "Redemption I and II," "Unification I and II,"

"11001001," "A Matter of Time," "Darmok," "Home Soil," "The Game," "The Nth Degree," "Data's Day," and "Arsenal of Freedom." ✓**INTERNET**→ *anon-ftp* smaug.cs.hope.edu→ /pub/sound/trek

---

Tong's TNG Sounds Enormous collection of TNG sound clips— from ship noises to character dialogue. See the "STTNG_SOUND -INDEX" for a brief description of each clip and its size. ✓**INTERNET** →*www* http://www.ugcs.cal tech.edu:80/~werdna/sttng /sounds/

DS9 fonts & icons

Bajoran TrueType An all-caps font based on the one used in the opening credits of the DS9 series. Dingbats for the Starfleet and Bajoran Provincinal Government emblems are also included. Requires a Mac running System 7 or 6.07 with TrueType INIT. ✓**AMERICA ONLINE**→*keyword* mac software→Search the Libraries→ Search All Libraries→*Search by file name:* Bajoran TT.sit

---

Star Trek Deep Space Nine Icons A collection of DS9 icons including one for each of the seven major characters (Quark, Dax, Kira, Odo, Sisko, Julian, and O'Brien), one Cardassian, and the space station itself. For Macs. ✓**AMERICA ONLINE**→*keyword* mac software→Search the Libraries→ Search All Libraries→*Search by file name:* DS9 icons.sit

---

Star Trek DS9 Icon An icon of the DS9 station for Macs running System 7 and up. ✓**AMERICA ON-LINE**→*keyword* mac software→ Search the Libraries→Search All Libraries→*Search by file name:* DS9 icons.sit

---

DS9 pictures

DS9 Images A small collection of DS9 GIFs and JPEGs, including actor shots and episode scenes. ✓**INTERNET**→*anon-ftp* Danann. hea.ie→/pub/mirrors/funet-pics/ tv+film/StarTrek/ds9

DS9 sounds

Deep Space Nine Sounds Sounds from DS9, including several from the scene where the computer would not comply with any of O'Brien's requests: "unable to comply," "procedure is not recommended," and "warning." O'Brien's response is also available:

"Computer, you and I need to have a little talk." From the DS9 pilot, the following memorable lines are preserved here as sound-clips: Dax's observation that "it is no ordinary wormhole," the beginning of Kira's duty log, and Sisko's "I come from a planet called Earth." In addition, Trek fans get bonus sounds from TNG—Picard lines, such as "Destroy it now!," "It is responding to visual and auditory stimuli...linguistic communication," and "the creature must be destroyed before it destroys us." ✓**INTERNET**→*anon-ftp* sumex-aim.stanford.edu→/info-mac/snd→st-deep-space-nine.hqx *and* st-deep-space-nine-ii.hqx

Voyager pictures

Opening and Closing Credit Images Twenty images from the opening and closing credits of Voyager. ✓**INTERNET**→*www* http://www.ftms.com/st-voy/credits.html

Premiere Episode Images Dozens of video stills of the *Voyager* crew in action. Despite its title, most of these images are taken from the television special *Star Trek Voyager: Inside The New Adventure.* ✓**INTERNET**→*www* http://www.ftms.com/st-voy/premiere.html

CYBERTREKKERS

Jim "The Big Dweeb" Griffith

Age 28; Sunnyvale, CA
Moderator of rec.arts.startrek.info; organized an electronic letter of condolence to Majel Roddenberry, Gene Roddenberry's wife, immediately following Roddenberry's death

Favorite Series: *The Next Generation*
"It came out at a time when special effects technology did justice to the environment that was being portrayed. As great as the original series was, there were just too many moments which were spoiled by the realization that "oh, they froze the film, so that the people wouldn't move while they were transporting them". TNG was the first *Star Trek* series that could portray the *Star Trek* message in a believable fashion. I prefer TNG's stories, but I prefer DSN's characters."

Favorite Characters: Bashir
He doesn't get too moral, and he doesn't overpower you with the force of his personality. He's just a competent, likeable guy who knows his profession but doesn't quite know his place in the universe (but who has a lot of fun trying to figure it out). I think the DSN characters are stronger than those of any other series.

Favorite Episode: "The Inner Light" and "Darmok"
I almost started crying at the end of the "Inner Light" episode. The concept was brilliant, the acting was unmatched, and the writing was convincing and moving. I tend toward the more tragic episodes, because life isn't a nice neat episode which ends happily after 45 minutes.

Other Interests: Newsgroups devoted to movies, television, trivia, gaming, and one or two technical topics.

Mission Statement: "Online culture has actually managed to unify Trek fandom. It used to be that there was only a sense of community at the convention. Now, people get that sense every time they log in."

Email Address: griffith@netcom.com

TrekChat

Trek fans are a nation unto themselves—stalwart, proud, patriotic. But they are also

a nation divided. Between Original Series purists, *Next Generation* aficionados, DS9 fanatics, and hopeful members of the *Voyager* camp, the rhetoric flies fast and furious—Roddenberry vs. Berman, Kirk vs. Picard, along with a broad spectrum of opinions on such topics as morality, technology, and other Trekker treats. The single best source for debate, discussion and Trek-nation town-meetings is the **rec.arts.startrek*** hierarchy, a set of newsgroups that runs the gamut from recent shows to convention information. If you're in the commercial-service state of mind, head over to Prodigy's **Trek** bulletin board, divided into **Show Comparison** and **Show Criticism** for your convenience. And AOL's **The Neutral Zone** weighs in with a volatile mix of rabid partisans and raging iconoclasts. Set course for chat!

The Great Bird celebrates—downloaded from Perfect Vision Graphics BBS

On the Net

Clubs: Other Home to social clubs organized around such Trek concepts as the Borg, Wesley haters, the Dominion, and female fans. Talk Trek and anything else

with like-minded individuals.
✓**PRODIGY**→*jump* star trek bb→ Choose a Topic→Clubs: Other

The Drift Zone The vegan lifestyle. Polarized light. A recipe for cucumber and crab salad. Uh, isn't this part of the Star Trek forum? Well, yes, but it's The Drift Zone—the place to steer the conversation when it veers away from Trek talk. With that said, the Zone doesn't remain Trek-free for long. Even those in the Land of Drift can't do without their hourly Trek fix. Sure, people talk about their cats and the Pentium brouhaha, but they also have a way of moving back to topics relevant to Trek, like whether fans of the old series will start blaming TNG followers for Kirk's death.
✓**DELPHI**→*go* ent sta for→set the

General Discussion - Star Trek You won't get booted from the General Discussion area of Del-

phi's Star Trek forum for topic drift. Whether you're wondering about the effect of zero gravity on sagging breasts or advocating a moment of silence for the death of the Magellan space probe, it's all fair game at this end of the galaxy. Other spots on the Delphi forum advocate adherence to a specific niche of Trek fandom (off-topic talk belongs in the Drift Zone), but not General.

That's not to say the discussion isn't Trek-related. It is, but with a high degree of flexibility. General's got a friendly, anything-goes atmosphere, with discussions about assorted sci-fi books, Trek actors' addresses, and reports of "sniffer" programs snarfing up millions of passwords on the Internet. Tolerate the digression, and you'll actually find your way through to some serious Trek talk. That's especially true when the subject's not limited to a single flavor of Trek, as in discussions of Vulcan names and the number of times various Trek crews have saved the Earth. ✓**DELPHI**→*go* ent sta for→set gen

IRC information and IRC #startrek users list

This site includes addresses for various IRC servers, including EFnet, DALnet, and Undernet, as well as lists of #startrek channel operators and ordinary users. ✓**INTERNET**→*www* http://www.maths.tcd.ie/hyplan/s/sj/www-irc.html

The Neutral Zone

Gene Roddenberry's vision of mankind's future may have been one of peace, but the real Trek universe is filled with hatred, injustice, and passionate differences of opinion. This message board hosts a folder for those who want to crush Wesley Crusher, another for the anti-Ferengi contingent, and still another for those fascinated with homosexual undercurrents on *Star Trek*.

Some of the more bizarre instances of hostility erupt in the People Who Think They're On DS9 folder. It seems like Lt. Illyria (a friend of Bashir's) and some friends have time-traveled back to the 20th century, where they have decided to inhabit the online universe. Unfortunately, people neither believe them nor want them around. ✓**AMERICA ONLINE**→*keyword* trek→ Star Trek Message Boards→The Neutral Zone

On the Small Screen

Trek on TV is the topic—from TOS to *Voyager*. Currently, DS9 dominates discussions, but each series has a message folder along with folders for cross-series topics like Trek humor and Trek themes. And while this isn't the most heavily trafficked Trek discussion spot on the Net, it does help fans channel their energies. ✓**EWORLD**→sf→Star

Trek→ On the Small Screen

The Promenade

Welcome to the Promenade. The Klingon and Starfleet fan clubs each have a discussion folder on this board where members talk Trek. But Starfleet officers and Klingons are not the only ones frequenting the Promenade.

Discussion folders opened here address broad Trek themes, cover Paramount news and gossip, and serve as hubs for trading merchandise, collecting lists, or discussing games (especially the Star Trek Club's popular trivia games). So, if you're a fan of all things Trek and not just a TOS or TNG fan, check out the comings and goings on this board. ✓**AMERICA ONLINE**→*keyword* trek→Star Trek Message Boards→The Promenade

rec.arts.startrek.current/rec.arts.startrek.misc

(ng) These two newsgroups are more or less indistinguishable. In both, you'll find an odd mix of cranky dinos (long time fans), clueless newbies, and occasional emerging lurkers—in short, Infinite Diversity in Infinite Combination—all engaged in heated discourse on the voyages of the starships *Enterprise*, *Excelsior*, *Voyager*, and assorted other vacuum barges.

The most incessant topics? Kirk vs. Picard, of course, although Kirk's recent demise has swung the sympathy vote: "I was beginning to think that I was alone in my preference of Kirk over Picard," says one female rec.arts.startrek.misc'er. "To me, passion is, and has always been, the key. One of the main reasons I prefer TOS to TNG is the pleasure of watching the dynamics of the relationships between Kirk, Spock, and McCoy. On the other hand, Picard always seems to be untouchable; cold and distant even to those he cares for and/or loves." A more satirically-minded fan offers a whole list of reasons to prefer Kirk, including "Kirk doesn't need to 'request' a Bird of Prey, he just takes it" and "at 120+ years, Kirk could beat up an El-Aurian."

The two newsgroups have surprising gender ratios (close to 2:1), which makes for some curious semantic issues: "How come women in Starfleet are called 'Mr.' instead of 'Ms.'?" grouses one female rec.arts.startrek.misc.'er. The question of sexist language is only the tip of the PC iceberg. Indeed, political correctness, or the lack thereof, is the subject of a long-running debate in both newsgroups.

The change in Trek's famous opening monologue—from TOS's "To go where no man has gone before" to TNG's "To go where no one has gone before"—raised the ire of many purists, and the appearance of tokenism regarding captain selection (an African-American for DS9, and a woman for *Voyager*) seemed to confirm suspicions that the PC Patrol had taken the helm at Starship Paramount.

Worse yet was the flap about whether there were black (i.e., non-Caucasian) Vulcans. "I believe in black Vulcans," says one rec.arts.startrek.misc.'er, "mainly because there already has been one: The midwife in the 'Spock's birth' flashback in *Star Trek V: The Final Frontier*. I know the film's painful to watch, but it is canon!" Another fan took a slightly more adverserial approach: "I can handle a black Vulcan. What got me was a reference, I think, in *Entertainment Tonight*, to the first African-American Vulcan! You can have a black Vulcan, but to get an African-American one requires stretching logic just a little bit."

And while the PCing of Trek

Worf: "It is a good day to die, Duras, and the day is not yet over."

—"Sins Of The Father"

Net Source: http://www.cosy.sbg.ac.at/ftp/pub/trek/quotes/st_tng3.txt

has overheated some warp cores, nothing bothers a rec.arts.startrek regular as much as a posting of the infamous "Get a Life!" skit from *Saturday Night Live*, in which guest host William Shatner, playing himself at a Trek convention, mocked Trek faithfuls as narrow-minded dweebs. The skit has been mentioned with such appalling frequency that Taki Kogoma (Captain Gym Z. Quirk) has actually posted a FAQ on how to respond to this particular post.

Ultimately, however, what matters is Trek—in all of its many variations, from the absurd to the sublime. An ongoing discussion over whether there are, in fact, bathrooms on the *Enterprise* has inspired some hilarious exchanges. A thread on 24th-century economics—is there such a thing as money in the Trek universe—has produced some fascinating cross-pollination between Marx and Roddenberry. And there's no better location in Cyberspace for hot information on upcoming Trek doings.

After all, it was on rec.arts.startrek.current that an advanced copy of the *Star Trek: Generations* movie script surfaced, sparking controversy and antagonizing Paramount (see feature, page 87). How much hotter does it get? Strangely enough, no high-level Trek brass seem to read the newsgroups openly. ✓**USENET**

rec.arts.startrek.info (ng) Did

you know that Craig Huxley, who played Captain Kirk's nephew in TOS, is now a record producer whose pet project is a group of singing dogs that howl holiday favorites? Did you want to know? This is the least-visited of all Trek newsgroups, but with postings about series air times and updates from Net Trek luminaries such as Mike "Vidiot" Brown, it remains an interesting source of information. ✓**USENET**

Show Comparison This is where Trek shows, captains, heroes, babes, and villains go head to head. TOS or TNG? Kirk or Picard? Spock or Tuvok? Deanna Troi or Jadzia Dax? And how about the all-important Khan/Soran debate? "Khan was a much more interesting psychopath. Whereas your basic 12-step group probably could have helped Soran out," remarked one member. ✓**PRODIGY**→*jump* star trek bb→ Choose a Topic→Show Comparison

Show Criticism James has a complaint. "It has always bugged me that Kirk and Spock stole the Romulan Cloaking Device in the original series and that Mr. Scott was able to integrate it into the *Enterprise*'s shield system, but that but many years later in the *Next Generation* the Federation has been unable to develop their own cloaking technology. This makes no sense."

And John has an answer, checking in later in the day to remind James of the treaty with the Romulans (covered in such TNG episodes as "Pegasus" and "The Next Phase") that mandated the return of certain technologies. Discussion is usually detailed, sometimes contentious, but always powered by an unquenchable thirst for more Trek detail. ✓**PRODIGY**→*jump* star trek bb→Choose a Topic→Show Criticism

Star Trek One of the most active chat locales in Cyberspace, and also one of the most general. For every specific folder—Wesley Jokes contains howlers such as "Q: What's the difference between Wesley Crusher and a bank-vault deliveryman? A: One saves ships and the other ships safes"—there's a generic one that treats the Trek franchise as a powerful form of benignity that may unlock the secrets to human happiness.

Want to buy *Star Trek* stuff? Feel driven to make a comment on the special-edition rerelease of *Star Trek II: The Wrath of Khan*? Even in the "Star Trek Despisers" thread, there's plenty of opportunity to preach the gospel of Roddenberry: "I was very upset when I heard the news about *Star Trek* going off the air. I watch it faithfully every night. I love the view of the future with no racism. Every show is exciting! :) I DON'T WANT IT TAKEN OFF! Even if they only showed reruns once a week I'd be happier than I am now! To say I'm unhappy is an understatement!" ✓**AMERICA ONLINE**→scifi→Star Trek/Comics/TV/Star Wars Boards →Star Trek

Star Trek (echo) "The E-D was destroyed. But wasn't Riker the captain of the E-D in 'All Good Things'?" Ask a question (silly or not) and someone's ready with an answer. "It being a 'separate reality,' the saucer *could* have been from the original E-D," suggests another conference member. With so much nitpicking left to do, TNG and the movie *Generations* are still active topics of conversation in the echo. DS9 is not living up to the expectations of many conference members—but most of them are not giving up, and it's the main object of discussion. ✓**LINK**

Star Trek (echo) How much of George Takei's stories about Shatner do you believe? Conference members have met both, read both stars' books, and, well, have a few opinions. Notice the differences in the ship bridges on Birds of Prey in *Star Trek III*, *IV*, and *VI*? Sure you did. And, what do you think of the opening music for *Voyager*? All Trek topics, series, movies, and books are open for discussion except for roleplaying and hardcore tech talk. ✓**FIDONET**

CYBERTREKKERS

Mark Arthur Holtz

Age 25; Citrus Heights, CA
Created and maintained the "Star Trek Lists of Lists" and co-moderates the FidoNet echo TREK_VOYAGER.

Trek Offline: "I'm involved with two Sacramento-area fan clubs. On the *USS Oberon NCC-71820*, a Starfleet/Federation-aligned ship, I serve as the Chief Engineeer. The other club I belong to is *Starbase Cosgrove*, an independent fan club, where I serve as Secretary/Treasurer, as well as edit the club newspaper. On both clubs, I have assisted in several activities, including helping out at local conventions and organizing season premiere/finale parties for *Star Trek*."

Favorite Episode: "There are enough favorite episodes to qualify for a List of Lists, and each one for varying reasons, either for a damn good storyline ('Best Of Both Worlds,' 'Yesterday's Enterprise,' 'The City On The Edge Of Forever,' 'The Maquis'), good character interaction ('Measure Of A Man,' 'The Drumhead,' 'The Cage,' 'Duet'), or are simply fun ('The Trouble With Tribbles,' 'The Next Phase')."

Mission Statement: "Eight months after my resignation (from maintaining the lists), I am still getting notes and requests, so one of these days, I'll grab a Super Big Gulp, do a marathon session, and issue a new, up-to-date copy."

Email Address: mholtz@netcom.com

TrekChat The Trek Phenomenon

Star Trek (echo) Fans they are; toadies they're not. When one fan shared his disappointment that *The Next Generation* didn't make good on its Emmy nomination for Best Drama Series (*Picket Fences* won over *NYPD Blue*), he was soon answered with comments like "the seventh season didn't *deserve* to be nominated in the first place. Get some perspective." The small group of conference regulars sometimes drift from discussion of current Trek TV and movies to BBS shop talk, boy-girl flirtation, and stories of real-world vacations. ✓**RELAYNET**

STAR TREK Conference With a slogan more inclusive than America itself ("*Classic Trek, Next Generation, Deep Space Nine* and *Voyager*, all views and opinions are welcome!") this conference allows fans plenty of space to roam across the universe of rhetoric—comparing Tuvok and Spock, celebrating the beauty of Jadzia Dax, expressing grudging admiration for the Ferengi.

Though there's plenty of talk about Deanna Troi, not everyone here is an empath, and sometimes tempers get hotter than a Klingon's blood. But with scheduled Trek talk every Monday at 9:30 pm EST and a second conference room called Ten-Forward, this is definitely one of the friendlier quadrants in Trek space. ✓**COMPUSERVE**→*go* sfmedia→conference→Ten-Forward

Star Trek General Category The catchall in GEnie's huge universe of *Star Trek* chat and news, with categories on costuming, collectibles, dreaming, autographs, bloopers, technology, and museums. So if you want to sell that old pair of William Shatner's underwear or reminisce about your trip to the Trek wing of the Lou-

vre, drop in and start talking. ✓**GENIE**→sfrt2→SFRT2 Bulletin Board→set 24

Star Trek Spoilers If you're not the first on the block to see the new DS9 episode, stay away from this topic—the regulars here will do everything in their power to ruin your enjoyment in advance. On the other hand, if you can't wait to discuss the details with your buddies, this is the place to do it.

You can post all the spoilers you want without having an irate Trekster threaten to abandon you among the Borg. Still, it's best to add a screenful of spoiler warnings before your message as a precaution for those wandering around the wrong part of the galaxy. ✓**DELPHI**→ent sta for→set sta

Star Trek - The Old and New Generation (echo) Trekkers here exchange lines that prove Spock's comic genius, endlessly analyze Kirk's death scene, ask questions about bathrooms on the *Enterprise,* and frequently use the acronym YAGLA (Yet Another God-Like Alien).

In-character discussion is not so common here—you won't find a lot of angry Klingons—but Trek chat is smart and wide-ranging. TNG episode rehashing, analysis of character relationships on DS9, and TOS trivia are equally welcome. ✓**RELAYNET**

#startrek The netizens of #startrek know their Trek lore, but they're just as likely to talk about occupations and end-of-semester anthro papers as their feelings about the latest flick or series. Occasionally, a devoted fan will try to bring the conversation back to *Star Trek* with a question like, "Anyone glad Kirk kicked it in *Generations?*"

Pvall admits he wept. Shocker says, "Picard is better." Pvall agrees ("Kirk is *soo* cheesy"). And then it's back to talk of life offline ("where ya from pilgrim," "where do you work pvall," and so forth). If you want the conversation to stay on Trek, ask a provocative question, like this one: "Don't you totally think Crusher should've married Picard?" Now that'll get things started. ✓**INTERNET**→*irc* /channel #startrek

Ten Forward Come by for a drink with your Star Trek BB friends. The Adult nature of this board doesn't indicate blue Trek, but instead serves as a reminder that participants should strive for a certain maturity. So stop yelling that Romulans are way cooler than Klingons and get down to business—the excercise regiments of Guinan and Sulu, the latest Trek star biography, or peace on Earth.

Such maturity, however, has its costs: the "Adults" have created an ongoing Adult Silly Session with the acronym (A$$), and on the New Ten-Forward, discussion wonders away from Trek into chat about families, holidays, careers, and life in general. Tribble fans, Trek quoters, and Trekkers seeking pen pals are here in force as well. ✓**PRODIGY**→*jump* star trek bb→ten forward

TN_Trek (echo) General Trek chat that comprises all series, all topics, and all kinds of fans. ✓**TREKNET**

WS_10Frwd (echo) Hang out with other off-duty Trek faithfuls in this free-for-all discussion, which ranges over the vast plains of fandom, touching on all important series issues (and some serious real-life topics as well). ✓**WARPSPEED**

Fan fiction

"It was a dark and stormy night in the Gamma Quadrant." Some Trek fans watch their

show. Others want to be a little more active in their appreciation. And those fans end up writing stories. Fan fiction—or fanfic, as it's more commonly known—is everywhere on the Net. The **Star Trek Stories Archive** and **Star Trek Stories** comprise extensive collections of fan stories, and what the material sometimes lacks in quality, it makes up for in enthusiasm. Want to read Borg porn? Interested in speculating on Riker's childhood? Got a great idea for a new *Voyager* episode in which the crew overthrows Janeway and settles on Planet Pitcairn? Just start writing and posting. If you have ideas but no confidence, stop in at AOL's **Trek Writers** for tips. And those who fear that the whole fanfic business has gotten a little too serious should check out the irreverent and hilarious **Hitchhikers' Guide to the Borg**.

On the Net

Across the board

Star Trek Fiction Reviews of upcoming books, discussions with active eWorld member and DS9

Pocketbook author John Vornholt, and general discussions and archives relating to fan fiction. √**EWORLD**→sf→Star Trek→Star Trek Fiction

Archives

Star Trek Fan Stories (echo) Writing Trek stories is almost as big a part of Trek fandom as conventions and, well, watching the shows. This library stores a large collection of original fiction written by Trek fans, including "The Ferengi Gambit," "The Romulan Dawn," and "Enterprise A meets Enterprise D." √**TFDN**→TFDN—Star Trek Fan Stories

Star Trek Parodies A series of parodies and jokes—Trek crossed with classic Warner Bros. cartoons, Trek surrealism, Borg jokes ("What do you call a Borg with a long nose? Cyrano De *Borg*erac"), and other interstellar giggles. √**INTERNET**→*gopher* world.std.com→OBI The Online Book Initiative→The Online Books→Star Trek Parodies

Star Trek Stories Stories and parodies, from the taut suspense of "Purely Alien" (in which Ripley and crew meet up with the TOS *Enterprise*) to the low, low comedy of James "Kibo" Parry's "They Saved Biff's Brane!" ("'Ow! Ow! I got a blister!' shouted Biff. He tried to pop it only to discover it was his eyeball"). √**INTERNET**→*gopher* world.std.com→OBI The Online Book Initiative→The Online Books→ Star Trek Stories

Star Trek Stories Archive Be-

fore the movie *Generations*, there were "Battle of the Ages" and "Enterprise Times Two"—fan versions of a meeting of the old crew and the new crew. And if you're curious to read a different version of the much anticipated Kirk-Picard meeting, you can download these stories from the alt.startrek.creative archives. Fans on Usenet have written a vast amount of Trek fiction over the years and much of it has been archived here. As Paramount attempts to develop the legend of DS9, Netters are simultaneously writing their own storylines with titles like "Flashback," "Changes," "Revenge of the Romulans," and "First Contact." But TNG generates the most fan fiction by far, with a zillion Q storylines and oodles for the Cardassians, Troi, and Data. They may never air on television or be published by Pocket Books but those voyaging through Cyberspace may replicate them (24th century way of saying "download") on their computers. √**INTERNET** …→*anon-ftp* ftp.cis.ksu. edu→/pub/alt.star trek.creative/stories …→*gopher* depot.cis.ksu.edu→ Star Trek Stories

Trek Fan Fiction In the story "Star Trek: Destinies," the author writes "Time is about to meet its end…" In "Nightmares from a Distant Time," the story is one "of loyalty tested, of friendship held, of faith's tenaciousness. It's the story of the heart of a Bajoran…" And, in "Kirk's Other Enterprise," the story suggests an alternative to the movie *Generations* in which Kirk doesn't buy the farm. Written by AOLers, these are just a few of the Trek stories, parodies, and filks archived in the Star Trek Club. ✓**AMERICA ONLINE**→*keyword* trek→MORE...→Star Trek Record Banks→Fiction

Workshops

alt.sex.fetish.startrek (ng) While most Trek sexual fantasies are just short accounts describing last night's dream about Patrick Stewart or Gates McFadden or both, some members take it another step, posting erotic stories and parodies with a *Star Trek* theme. ✓**USENET**

alt.startrek.creative (ng) Stories and parodies, from "Stormbird: A Klingon Tale" to the X-Rated "Friendly Advice." ("Dax seemed oblivious, concentrating all her attention on Odo's tongue. 'Constable, you're cheating,' she gasped, 'not that I mind, but that's longer than any human tongue I ever felt. But don't stop. Just put it inside me. Oh, yes, there.'") In addition, the newsgroup contains discussions of other Trek books and creative achievements, and commentary on the world of fan fiction ("more stories about Guinan," says one woman). ✓**USENET**

Science Fiction RoundTable I Professional as well as aspiring writers frequent this hugely popular writers' roundtable. Covering both the sci-fi and the fantasy genres, the discussions range from writing techniques to writing for specific shows. "Want to write a *Deep Space Nine* novel?"asks John Ordover, who writes Trek books professionally, and the topic grows to several hundred messages. Soon, its *Voyager* counterpart begins. Other topics covering canon, reference materials, and getting a start in Trek writing take off. If you're uncertain as to whether you can join a category labeled private,

email the RoundTable's sysop. ✓**GENIE**→*keyword* sfrt1→SFRT1 Bulletin Board

Star Trek Fan Fiction (Pros Stay Out) The powers that be have closed down much of the interactive fan fiction on this board, but the collaborative efforts remain here for all to enjoy. "Ten Forward Lounge" features the crew of TNG in a romantic thriller; and "The Order of Canopus," in which each character is written by a different person, relates the exploits of a group of space pirates complete with a vampiress and a staff psychologist named Dr. Anna Freud. The Open Mike (Topic 2) gathers filk songs for Trek troubadours—*The Wizard of Oz*'s "If I Only Had a Brain" adapted for Kirk, Spock, and Bones, being one of the classics. "Stinky Star Trek" is a collection of pregnant, and intentionally bad, first lines for Trek novels, and parody runs amok in "TNG meets SNL or is Worf a Girly Man?" (Category 12) and "*Star Trek* Meets *Star Wars*" (Category 19). ✓**GENIE**→*keyword* sfrt2→SRFT2 Bulletin Board→set 36

Trek Writers Discussion for aspiring Trek writers. Flesh out story ideas, strategize about how to get Rick Berman or S&S Pocketbooks to read your stuff, and ask about general writing tips. ✓**AMERICA ONLINE**→*keyword* trek→Star Trek Message Boards→The Promenade →Trek Writers

Writers' Forum On Thursday evening at 10 pm, fan fiction writers gather on the bridge to exchange feedback on each other's writing. The sessions are open to everyone, but if you want to be able to truely participate you need to get on the Trek writers mailing list. Email Elftrek and ask to be

added and each week someone's Trek story (or chapter from the story) will be emailed to you. Scheduled for an hour, Trek talkers linger long after the writing critiques have ended. ✓**AMERICA ONLINE**→*keyword* trek→The Bridge

Sample fiction

Borglemania! A script for the musical production of a simulated Borg attack on the *Enterprise*. All songs are Beatles parodies. ✓**COMPUSERVE**→*go* sfmedia→*Search by file name:* BOR GLE.TXT

Enemy of My Enemy The Romulans investigate whether a new cloaking device will let them enter Federation territory unnoticed. Could this change the balance of power forever? ✓**INTERNET**→*gopher* world.std.com→OBI The Online Book Initiative→The Online Books→Star Trek Stories→Enemy of My Enemy

The Hitchhiker's Guide to the Borg Find out what happens when Arthur, Eddy, and Ford encounter the Borg as they roam the universe in the *Enterprise*. "*The Hitchhiker's Guide to the Galaxy* suggests the following course of action: The best thing to do at this point is to place this copy of the Guide in a safe place, so that it will be of use to whoever may find it in the future, because your hitchhiking days are now over." ✓**COMPUSERVE**→*go* sfmedia→*Search by file name:* HITBRG.TXT

New Trek NCC-1701-H An elaborate description of the *Enterprise-H*, commissioned in 2692 with a crew led by 26-year old Captain Laura Timberman (possibly a distant relevant of Kirk). ✓**COMPUSERVE**→*go* sfmedia→Libraries→*Search by file name:* NEWTRE.TXT

Fan clubs

Masons too secretive? Girl Scouts too goody-goody? Why not join a group where people

will be bound to share your interest in warp drive, Wesley Crusher, and the Prime Directive. The big club names in Trek fandom such as KAG (**Klingon Assault Group**) and **STARFLEET**, the International *Star Trek* fan organization, actively recruit on the Net. Just mention the town you live in and a member of a ship in your area will likely email you. STARFLEET is very active on the Net—the **Starfleet International Home Page** provides a link to its worldwide members in the Net community; and the group also maintains a presence on CompuServe, AOL, eWorld, and GEnie. There are also plenty of conferences that cater to more specific interests—diagnose the Naked Time malady in **TN_Medical**, chat with Odo or Lieutenant Worf wanna-bes on **TN_Security**, or discuss the ins and outs of warp-drive maintenance on **TN_Engineering**. And *Star Trek* fans across the pond may want to end their busy day with a pint of bitter at **Pages Bar**, the only known British *Star Trek* theme pub.

U.S.S. Excalibur NCC 2151-D

Welcome to the Excalibur On-Line Magazine !

Excalibur Online Magazine— http://whirligig.ecs.soton.ac.uk/~shd94/index.html

On the Net

Across the board

Clubs and Conventions A hub of information about role-playing clubs, Trek conventions, Klingon groups, and the STARFLEET fan club—with both online and offline contact information. ✓**EWORLD** →sf→Star Trek→Clubs and Conventions

Group/Club Addresses They come from all corners of the galaxy, searching out fan clubs and actors' addresses. They're looking for "fan clubs based on the Mirror Empire" or they're recruiting for a new Dax fan club (Spot Check?). Dock here when moving to another city and track down informa-

tion about your local Trek organizations. ✓**AMERICA ONLINE**→*keyword* trek→Star Trek Message boards→The Promenade→Group/Club Addresses

Star Trek Fan Clubs and Organizations If you want to take the step from unofficial fan to official fan, Category 27 will be able to help you. STARFLEET International resides in Topic 8, with officials on hand to answer questions and help you get in touch with local organizations; all official STARFLEET news is related in Topic 4. If Starfleet isn't your idea of fun, you can join other Chief Science Officers in discussing 24th century cybergenics or exchange helpful hints for warp drive repair with other Engineers. And for those who like large weapons and bloodshed, drop in to the Klingon club (Topic 15). ✓ **GENIE**→*keyword* sfrt2→SFRT2 Bulletin Board→set 37

TFDN - Star Trek Fandom A small library with subscriptions for fan newsletters and clubs, and information on other Trek BBS networks. All BBSs participating in the Trek File Distribution Network (TFDN) carry the same items, although the name of the library may be slightly different on each board. ✓ **TFDN**

TN_SpecFor/TN_Marines (echo) Members of the STARFLEET Marines International-Corps discuss their fan clubs and STARFLEET organizational politics. ✓ **TREKNET**

Trek_Org (echo) A forum that not only helps *Star Trek* fan clubs disseminate information to their members, but also helps groups advertise for new members. If you tell the conference that you've just moved, you'll be besieged with addresses for local STARFLEET, KLAW, KAG, Federation, or other Trek group chapters. ✓ **TREKNET**

Club officers

TN_Communications Trek communications—from Com badges to subspace communications—is allegedly the topic of conversation but more than 90 percent of the posts involve 20th century communications, particularly *Star Trek* newsletters and fanzines. ✓ **TREKNET**

TN_Engineering (echo) Scotty, LaForge, and O'Brien aren't here, but other would-be Federation engineers come to the conference to discuss ship design and their own Trek engineering ideas. Dominated by members of the STARFLEET fan club. ✓ **TREKNET**

TN_Medical (echo) Since the days when McCoy uttered his famous "Dammit Jim, I'm a Doctor not a..." lines, fans have been intrigued by medicine in the Trek universe. Crusher's and Bashir's adventures have continued to captivate Trekkers, encouraging many to become involved with the medical staffs in their local fan clubs. Fan club members—most belonging to STARFLEET—discuss their ship's medical operations and swap ideas with members of other ships. The Farpoint Station, a local Trek group once posted an open invitation for conference members to check out their medical supply facilities: "We have the most modern replicators in the medical profession. Everything from scanners and hypos, all the way to state-of-the-art diag-beds. After all, to bandage the final frontier, you *will* need a lot of band-aids!" ✓ **TREKNET**

TN_Operations (echo) For those with an interest or involvement in fan club Ship operations. ✓ **TREKNET**

CYBERTREKKERS

Bill Mason

Age 27; Pennsylvania
Hosts the AOL Star Trek Club

"I became a fan when I was around 7 years old and discovered the Animated Star Trek on my TV on Saturday mornings. I am a member of STARFLEET International and one of its local chapters, the USS Thagard."

Time Online: 30-35 hrs/week

Other Interests: General science fiction, comic books, current events, and E-mail chess

Mission Statement: "The conflict with fans of Classic Trek vs. Next Generation seems to have blossomed like it never has—each side being able to be in constant contact with the other seems to have led to escalation of the normal TOS vs. TNG debates to near-warfare at times. Fans on both sides have got to resolve their arguments and live with one another, or I think the Trek culture online will be an unhealthy combative one for some time to come."

Email Address: Data 1701D@aol.com

TN_Science (echo) Some conference members are "currently working on the theory of invisibility" while others want ideas for the science division of their local Trek club's ship. Discussing NASA's programs and alien cultures are also acceptable here. "So, do you think humans could benefit from genetic engineering? Reincorporated intelligence?" Take the conversation from here. ✓**TREKNET**

TN_Security (echo) A curious Trekker and "die-hard security-type-guy" is looking for a local *Star Trek* club. Commander Bev wants to exchange information with security officers in other STARFLEET chapters and clubs. Another security officer is brainstorming about recruiting new members ("Did anyone else recruit in front of theaters when *Generations* opened?") While STARFLEET security types dominate the conference, any topic related to security issues on the show or in local Trek clubs is at risk. ✓**TREK-NET**

Fan friends

TNG E-mail pals Did you ever have pen pals in your youth, kids from distant American cities who spilled their lives onto paper once a week and sent them over to you? It made the world seem like a smaller place, a friendlier place, a place you might actually want to inhabit. That's the theory, more or less, behind AOL's TNG E-mail pals message board, which lets on-line Trek fans input a profile of themselves and their ideal correspondent, and then serves as a kind of clearinghouse for these profiles. Looking for another single mother who dreams of taming Riker? Starved for other Trekkers like yourself? Check in here. **AMERICA ONLINE**→*keyword* trek→

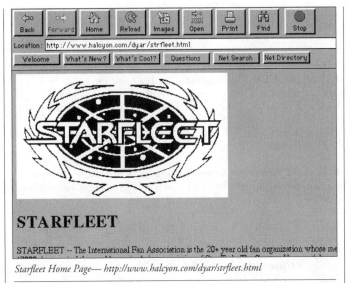

STARFLEET

STARFLEET -- The International Fan Association is the 20+ year old fan organization whose me

Starfleet Home Page— http://www.halcyon.com/dyar/strfleet.html

Star Trek Message Boards→The Next Generation→TNG E-mail pals

Federation

Federation (echo) Members of the Trek fan organization known as the Federation conduct business here and swaps news about fan club activities. Not very active. ✓**TREKNET**

Federation Info A one-page description of the Federation fan club with a snail mail address for contacting the national organization. ✓**AMERICA ONLINE**→*keyword* trek→MORE...→Star Trek Record Banks→Text/Other Files→Upld: 12/09/94 TEXT: Federation→FED INFO.TXT

Foreign

British Starfleet Confederacy Information and application form for the British Starfleet Confederacy, a Trek fan club. ✓**COMPUSERVE** →*go* sfmedia→Libraries→*Search by file name:* FANCLU.TXT

Pages Bar Those Brits know

how to combine their cultural obsessions, and they do so nicely in this site, a Trek-themed pub. ✓**IN-TERNET**→*www* http://deeptht. armory.com:80/~bsc/pages/page-home.html

The USS Excalibur Homepage An electronic version of a newsletter for a *Star Trek* fan club in Bournemouth, England. The page links to information about events, Trek news and rumors, and Trek humor. ✓**INTERNET**→*www* http:// whirligig.ecs.soton.ac.uk/~shd94/ index.html

Klingons

Klingon Assault Group Discussion forum for members of KAG. ✓**AMERICA ONLINE**→*keyword* trek→Star Trek Message Boards→ Klingon Assault Group

Starfleet

STARFLEET Board for STAR-FLEET members to discuss business matters, including election issues, regional complaints, and membership questions. ✓**AMERICA**

Fan Clubs The Trek Phenomenon

ONLINE→*keyword* trek→Star Trek Message Boards→The Promenade →STARFLEET

STARFLEET Descriptions of the STARFLEET fan organization and news about its events. STARFLEET members can gather for discussion here as well. ✓**EWORLD**→sf→Star Trek→Clubs and Conventions→STARFLEET

STARFLEET Academy Courses Application for the STARFLEET Academy and descriptions of its various colleges and schools. But remember—you must be a registered member of the International Star Trek Fan Association to participate. ✓**COMPUSERVE**→*go* sfmedia →Libraries→*Search by file name:* SFACAD.ARC

STARFLEET Chapters List of the chapters of STARFLEET, the International Star Trek Fan Association. ✓**COMPUSERVE**→*go* sfmedia→ Libraries→*Search by file name:* STRFLT.ARC

STARFLEET Echoes (echo) Members of STARFLEET have their own set of conferences on TrekNet BBSs. Find a STARFLEET penpal, perhaps another science officer or one of those security types, in the SF_Penpal echo. During STARFLEET elections, organizational politics can dominate discussions, so a conference has been created to isolate the discussion in SF_Elections. There are also echoes devoted to the Academy (what course are you taking now?), and specific geographic regions. ✓**TREKNET**

STARFLEET International Home Page Looking for a local STARFLEET group? This page breaks down the U.S. and other countries into STARFLEET International's twenty regional groups.

Links are made to regional groups' Web pages, which also contain email addresses for regional coordinators with Net access. Region 7, for instance, has a Website with an FAQ and the names and locations of ships operating in the area. An email address is available for each of the ships if you're interested in contacting them. There are also links to the STARFLEET's FTP site and to affiliated groups. ✓**INTERNET**→*www* http://www.halcyon.com/dyar/strfleet.html

STARFLEET Mailing List (ml) (echo) Members of the list and echo, most of whom belong to STARFLEET (the International Star Trek Fan Association), share information about fleet issues, chapter (ship) operations, and conventions. For Starfleet business, this is the forum to attend. Be forewarned: STARFLEET has a lot of territory to cover and your mailbox is likely to fill quickly with a membership to this list. In fact, if you have access to TrekNet, you may want to just read and post to the echo, which has a bidirectional gateway to the mailing list. ✓**INTERNET**→*email* starfleet-request@panix.com ✍ *Subscribe by request* ✓**TREKNET**

Vessel Registry of STARFLEET Divided by region, this is a comprehensive list of ships and captains (including their snail mail addresses) in the STARFLEET association. ✓**EWORLD**→sf→Star Trek →United Federation Library→VESS_REG.TXT

Starfleet command

Starfleet Command (SFC) (echo) Conferences for members of the fanclub Starfleet Command. Discuss politics, club activities, and positions. ✓**TREKNET**

STARNOTES

"WHAT IS KAG?" "The KLINGON ASSAULT GROUP is a not-for-profit STAR TREK fan organization. There are NO DUES here. Promotions are based solely on merit and level of involvement. Klingon Uniforms aren't required, but to advance within our ranks a uniform will be necessary."

"WHAT DOES KAG DO?" "KAG has Fun. Our members go to fan conventions and intimidate other species. We help charities with food and blood drives, like our 'Feed the Earther' program or the annual 'Blood Feud.' We win costume contests at conventions. We throw excellent parties. We host events like the Dover Peace Conference, a convention for costuming enthusiasts of any species. Or DIS Qujmey: The Year Games...Klingon Olympic games. We share in the richness of Klingon culture and the Klingon Language...and did I mention conventions?"

—from **AOL's Klingon Assault Group Message Board**

Conventions

To boldly go...to Atlantic City? Until Zefram Cochrane's advances make affordable

space travel a reality, we have to make do with terrestrial trips, and Trek fans like nothing so much as a good convention. Want to meet your idol, Terry Farrell? Feel a need to dress up like a Klingon? Just log on, find the nearest convention, and then start putting on that forehead makeup and practicing your lines ("No, Miss Farrell, the pleasure is mine"). **Upcoming Conventions** keeps a good list of events and all the particulars, including guest stars, contact numbers, and prices. **Trekker_Conventions** offers post-occasion analysis so detailed that even fans who didn't make this year's big gathering can feel as if they attended. The Conventions section of **AOL's Star Trek Board** reviews specific events and convention organizers —when there are so many conventions to choose from, you don't want to waste your hard-earned pressed latinum on a dog. And if you've got somewhere to go, but are panicked about the idea of getting all dressed up, **TN_ Costumers** has a vested interest in setting your mind at ease.

Patrick Stewart autographs—downloaded from Perfect Vision Graphics BBS

On the Net

Conventions Message after message devoted to conventions. Anyone going to the Fort Lauderdale show? Do you know when and where Brent Spiner will appear next? And here's the latest info about the *Voyager* Trekon, which will commemorate the maiden voyage of the newest starship. ✓ **PRODIGY**→*jump* start trek bb→ Choose a Topic→Conventions

Trekker_Conventions (echo) Here are the rules: if you go to a convention, take note of everything...everything. Describe the conference, where you sat, what you ate, what questions people asked, who gave autographs, what costumes attendees wore, and most importantly, what the guest stars said and wore. And then file your report online. This conference is filled with obsessively de-tailed convention reports as well as notices, applications, and itineraries for upcoming conventions (from a Mount Holyoke College sci-fi/fantasy gaming convention to a *Star Trek* convention in D.C.). ✓ **TREKKERNET**

TN_Cons (echo) Active conference with convention announcements and news about upcoming events. Not limited to Trek conventions. ✓ **TREKNET**

TN_Cons_Q&A (echo) Ask questions, get answsers, and log gripes about science fiction conventions, particularly Trek cons. Convention organizers and promoters are often lurking, and they're more than willing to respond when needed. ✓ **TREKNET**

TN_Costumers (echo)Everyone here is planning for the next convention, New Year's or Halloween party, or live action role-playing game. And they need a costume. Looking for ideas? Not quite sure where to find the pattern for a *Next Generation* uniform for a newborn baby (10 pounds or less)? You should be able to find someone to help you here. Just tell them what you want: "I think I've about decided to drop the Klingon/Federation cross uniform, and go for a DS9 full uniform (pants, top, undershirt) and to wear a sash with it. BTW...do you make sashes like the one Worf wears? If so, how much? Very interested." ✓**TREKNET**

Conventions William Shatner, in person? No way! Well, yes, it does happen, and to learn the latest about Kirk's appearances, along with those of other *Star Trek* celebs, check out this topic in Delphi's *Star Trek* forum. The traffic's not heavy, but if you stop by now and then, you're likely to hear talk of gatherings with names like Loscon 21, Starbase Indy, and Vulkon. ✓**DELPHI**→ *go* ent sta for→set con

rec.arts.startrek. fandom (ng) Though it's part of the rec. arts.startrek hierarchy, this newsgroup has an agenda all its own, with information and reaction to conventions and other fan events. You'd like to make an announcement about a convention in Florida? Looking for a ride-share to Birmingham for a small DS9 gathering? This newsgroup is filled with information you need to know, along with pictures of Terry Farrell, rumors of a new series starring

Sulu, and reports of Trek stars' appearances on Letterman and Leno. ✓**USENET**

Conventions A chronological listing of convention notices, including location, date, cost, and contact information, as well as the names of guest stars who might (or might not) appear. ✓**INTERNET** →*anon-ftp* rtfm.mit.edu→/pub/ usenet-by-hierarchy/rec/arts/ startrek/info→List_of_Upcoming_ Conventions

Star Trek Conventions From Wishcon IV to FARPOINT, from OKTOBERTREK to VULKON, from a summer 1995 Toronto blowout to an Alaskan theme cruise, *Star Trek* fans love to get together, and many of them love to talk about getting together on GEnie's conventions board. ✓**GENIE**→ *keyword* sfrt2→SFRT2 Bulletin Board→set 33

Upcoming Conventions A list of upcoming Trek conventions and dates, locations, guests, and contact information. ✓**AMERICA ONLINE**→*keyword* trek→Upcoming Conventions ✓**EWORLD** →s→Star Trek→ Captain's Log→ Conventions List

Conventions Pre-convention gossip, convention notices, and post-convention reports and stories fill the messages boards

here. Fans have no mercy when reviewing the conventions and the guest appearances; if you're new to the fandom scene, lurk here for a while. You will almost certainly become more convention-savvy even before donning those Ferengi ears and writing that registration check. ✓**AMERICA ONLINE**→*keyword* trek→ Star Trek Message Boards→The Promenade→ Conventions

Personal Websites

Just as James T. Kirk and the valiant crew of the *Enterprise NCC-1701* explored the

outer reaches of outer space, so have Trek fans explored the outer reaches of Cyberspace. And many of those fans have carved out a niche in the online Trek universe by creating personal Web pages—exquisitely crafted labors of love that both furnish information and foster a sense of community. From the largest projects—**Mike "Vidiot" Brown's Home Page**, **Andrew Tong's ST: TNG Page**, **Brigitte Jellinek's Page**, with its mass of Trekkiana —to the smaller, more intimate sites overseen by fans like Judy Fabian (a classic *Trek* devotee), Robert Lentz, and David Howard Heller, these pages demonstrate a little of what Trekkers bring to Trek.

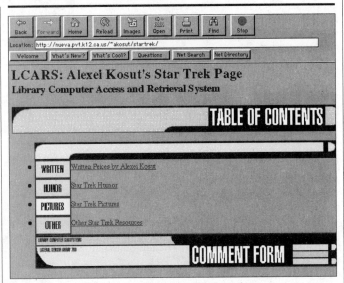

Screenshot—from http://nueva.pvt.k12.ca.us/~akosut/startrek/

On the Net

Alexei Kosut's Home Page Includes fan fiction written by Kosut ("Affliction of Paradise" and "Return to Hellgate"), as well as Trek humor, series pictures, and links to other Trek sites. ✓**INTERNET**→*www* http://nueva.pvt.k12.ca.us/~akosut/startrek/

Andrew Tong's ST: TNG Page When you're talking TNG, you're talking Tong. And when you're talking Tong, you're talking Web pages galore. Fans of TNG are ad-

vised not to miss this page, which serves as a sort of world hub for the series. And fans of Tong should zip over to his non-Trek home page and tour the offerings, which include a page devoted to music video MPEGs. ✓**INTERNET**→*www* http://www.ugcs.caltech.edu:80/~werdna/sttng/

Ayla's Homepage Bare as a female Ferengi, but with lots of tremendous links, including the Kirk and Spock sing-a-long page and a wonderful image of the Defiant. ✓**INTERNET**→*www* http://www.math.ufl.edu/~ayla/trek.html

Brigitte Jellinek's Page One of the premier Trek sites in the world, this massive collection of links, pictures, and sounds is maintained by Salzburg resident Jellinek (that's Bjelli to you). If you get tired of *Star Trek*—far-

fetched, we understand, but still within the realm of possibility— you might want to check out Jellinek's own home page, which includes a picture of the architect herself as well as a sound file of her voice. ✓**INTERNET**→*www* http://www.cosy.sbg.ac.at/rec/startrek/index.html

Bruce's Star Trek Page Collections of FAQs, soundclips, fan fiction, episode guides, cast lists, and more. Besides links to large collections of Trek resources (including the largest collection of TNG episodes and a huge collection of TOS sounds), Bruce also dares to feature the *Generations* script and the Capt. James T. Kirk Sing-a-long page. ✓**INTERNET**→*www* http://www.unisuper.com.au/strek/strek.html

Chris's Homepage This page,

which is devoted to general topics in space and science—engineering and technology, astrophysics and astronomy—also contains links to a number of other *Star Trek* resources, and a nice picture of Captain Picard to top it all off. ✓**INTERNET**→*www* http://128.172.69.103/cworld/Space.html

The Continuum Home Page

The University of Michigan's Trek fans are online and their outpost in Cyberspace is The Continuum Home Page. Great Trek graphics and soundfiles (Want the full overture from *Star Trek VI*?) are available at the site with links to multimedia Trek archives in other corners of the cyber-galaxy. A collection of links to big sites such as the United Federation of Planets page and Cal Tech's Star Trek page are also available. ✓**INTERNET**→ *www* http://www.astro.lsa.umich.edu/users/sewin/Continuum/

The Craziness of David Howard Heller

Somehow self-effacing and self-promoting, this site both lives and dies by the renowned craziness of its creator. Amidst links on Judaism, social justice, and the sincerity-infested folk-rock of the Indigo Girls, the site contains a few Trek sites selected by Heller—most notably the official Paramount *Voyager* page. ✓**INTERNET**→*www* http://escape.com/~indigo/crazy.html

Joshua Sean Bell's Page The primary source for tech questions, including concerns about warp and subspace, transporters and replicators, the holodeck and computers, and ship statistics. The site also includes a reading list for Treknology aficionados, links to other *Star Trek* sites, and a *Star Trek* ASCII art archive. ✓**INTERNET**→ *www* http://www.ucalgary.ca/~jsbell/star_trek.html

Judy Fabian's Page Devoted exclusively to the original series, this page is primarily a revolving catalog of sounds and images. ✓**INTERNET**→*www* http://www.uvm.edu/~jfabian/

Mike "Vidiot" Brown's Home Page The Vidiot savant himself oversees this page, which includes casting news, press releases, airdates, episode summaries, images, and special treats like the Ferengi Rules of Acquisition. And then there are the lavish images. A must for any serious online Trekker. ✓**INTERNET**→*www* http://www.ftms.com:80/vidiot/

Robert Lentz's Star Trek Resources A list of links to Trek parodies, songs, top ten lists, Mac Trek items, the Ferengi Rules of Acquisition, and pages related to Trek science, the Klingon language, the movie *Generations*, and the series *Voyager*. Lentz has also created other Web pages, which you can link to from here, for astronomy, space, and *Babylon 5*. ✓**INTERNET**→*www* http://www.astro.nwu.edu/lentz/sci-fi/star-trek/home-st.html

Roger James Hall Star Trek Page This home page is devoted to TNG, and includes links to a complete episode list, a brief synopsis of the plot of every episode, Tim Lynch reviews, and Usenet ratings for each episode. In addition, Hall's page includes photos of Picard, Riker, and Geordi LaForge, as well as a nice image of the USS *Enterprise NCC 1701-D*. ✓**INTERNET**→ *www* http://http1.brunel.ac.uk:8080/~ph93rjh/sttng.html

Spock's Homebase Links to a collection of sound, image, and FAQ archives, all maintained by Swede Jörgen Nilsson. It just

wouldn't be logical to ignore this site. ✓**INTERNET**→*www* http://www.csd.uu.se:80/~spock/

Steve Norman's Page Maintained by Trek fan Steve Jacobs, this page includes images of the *Deep Space Nine* title screen and the *Star Trek: Generations* title screen, as well as lists of home pages for IRC users, *Star Trek* quotes, and a list of related links. Jacobs describes himself as "a big fan of TNG and DS9" and admits that he enjoyed all six films, but explains that he "never really liked *Star Trek* (The Original Series)." His mission? "To create links from [his] page to other *Star Trek* related pages and FTP sites so you can use this page as a starting point to explore the vast amount of information available through the World Wide Web." ✓**INTERNET**→ *www* http://web.city.ac.uk/~cc103/startrek.html

Vernville Aaron Hamilton's homepage is like a gazette from some backward town where everybody wears suspenders and picks their teeth with splinters from old furniture. Friendly, eccentric, and endearingly self-indulgent, the page includes links to an essay of Hamilton's about spontaneous human combustion, in addition to links to *Star Trek: Voyager* sites. ✓**INTERNET**→*www* http://ug.cs.dal.ca:3400/~hamilton/hamilton.html

Worf's Star Trek Page Maintained by a devout fan of the newer shows—as he explains on his home page, he's not that enamored of TOS—this site contains GIFs of the title screens of DS9 and TNG, as well as links to a handful of other *Star Trek* sites. ✓**INTERNET**→*www* http://www.maths.tcd.ie/hyplan/s/sj/startrek.html

AUTHOR! AUTHOR!

MiSTing Trek on the Net

In the world of fans, there are few as gape-mouthed as Trekkers. And in the world of Trek fan fiction, there's no place like the Net. Fans can now publish their fantasies at the touch of a button, and publish them instantly to a readership of thousands. Every man, woman, or child who invents an adventure for Kirk and Spock, or Picard and company, can be a well-known author in a matter of minutes.

But how "good" is fan fiction? That all depends on what you mean by good. Sometimes, fan writing succeeds wonderfully, demonstrating impressive insight into Trill psychology or crossbreeding *Star Trek* with sci-fi series of decidedly different character (there are *Trek/Galactica* hybrids, *Trek/Babylon 5* hybrids, and even *Trek/Highlander* hybrids). Well-written, powerful, and deliriously unauthorized, these stories make a real contribution to Trek culture, strengthening the canon through challenge.

But for every piece of fan fiction that employs polished and moving prose, there's another piece that comes up short. Way short. Shorter than a Ferengi on Bad Posture Day. With abysmal prose and clichés to spare, these pieces make Danielle Steel look like Nabokov. What should be done with these fanfics? On the one hand, they're a valid form of fan expression, a way for fans to tell their fellow fans stories about the characters they have come to love. On the other hand, bad writing is bad writing—and should be punished accordingly. That's where MiSTing comes in.

MiSTing, of course, refers to Mystery Science Theater 3000, the popular sci-fi comedy show, and more specifically to the show's practice of subjecting creative atrocities to relentless mockery. On MST3K, as it's known to fans, a group of outer-space wiseacres sit around and kibitz about awful movies. Now, MST3K has spawned Mystery Usenet Theater

3000, an Internet version that targets bad newsgroup posts—from get-rick-quick schemes and wacky philosophical musings to sci-fi fan fictions—rather than bad movies.

Take a Net story called "A Gul's Revenge." Please. A TNG fanfic of bottomless banality, the story is full of the overwriting and underplotting that characterizes the worst fan fiction. In the Mystery Usenet Theater 3000 version, created by David Hines, almost every line of the original story is undermined by snide and satiric commentary. Using the MST3K characters to do his dirty work, Hines zeroes in on typos, solecisms, stilted dialogue, confusing plot developments, and vague descriptions—and there are more than enough to go around. To an opening disclaimer that the story "may be copied, distributed, or cross-posted to friends," Hines notes that "it would be more appropriate to distribute to enemies." And this exchange is typical of the irreverence with which the source story is handled:

The Enterprise *is resuming its course to Deep Space Nine after...*
Tom: *Oh, my GOD!!!!!!*
Mike: *What?*
Tom: *He spelled "course" right! He actual-*

ly spelled it *right!*
Mike: *Tom, you're gonna lose your RAM chips....*
Tom: *Oh, forget the Grammar Flamer Sorter Dumper, Mike! He spelled "course" right!!!*
Crow: *I can die now. I've seen it all.*

While the MiSTing of "A Gul's Revenge" may read like a random act of senseless textual violence, such attacks seem to bind the Trek fanfic community closer together, encouraging fans to read each others' work and comment uninhibitedly. Contacted by email, the original author, Stephen Ratliff, says he doesn't mind being the butt of someone else's joke, just so long "as they credit [him] as the author of the work." Now a sophomore at the University of Radford in Virginia, Ratliff admits that "A Gul's Revenge" deserves a certain amount of criticism for its sloppy prose. "I posted it as I wrote it," he says, noting that since then he has written two more Trek fanfics. Ratliff says that the mockery will not dampen his creative spark and that he will continue to forge bravely ahead in the land of fan fiction. "I am plotting out a *Star Trek/ Star Wars* crossover with my brother doing the *Star Wars* side."

"While the MiSTing of 'A Gul's Revenge' may read like a random act of senseless textual violence, it seems to bind the Trek fanfic community closer together."

Gaming in Ten-Forward

Star Trek is fun, and it should stay fun, which is why Trek fans have spent hours devising

games that bring them closer to the show they love. From computer games to board games, role-playing games to card games, drinking games to trivia games, Trek play draws on a variety of skills and yields a variety of pleasures. Want to get sloshed while you're watching Jadzia Dax? Check out the **Star Trek: Deep Space Nine Drinking Game**. Interested in pushing the boundaries of the royal game? **Learn How to Build a 3-D Chess Set**. And if your idea of a good time involves standing on the bridge of a Federation starship and blasting away, then you'll want to visit **SFB Tactics**, which is devoted to discussion of the board game Star Fleet Battles.

Whoopi Goldberg as Guinan (video capture)—downloaded from ftp.cis.ksu.edu

On the Net

Across the board

Games and Collectibles With much talk of collectibles—action figures, late-seventies Trek kitsch—this forum sometimes leaves games behind. But there's plenty of talk of the Next Generation Collectible Card Game, not to mention plenty of vintage Trek board games, roleplaying modules, and state-of-the-art computer games. If you're trying to peddle your version of Trek Candyland—"you are lost in the Gumdrop Forest, and Klingons are trying to roll you for your Pixie Stick"—this may be the place. ✓**DELPHI**→*go* ent sta for set gam

TFDN - Star Trek Games Trek add-ons for *Doom*, dozens of trivia games (Bajoran trivia, Klingon trivia, TOS trivia), Trek tile sets for MahJongg, the rules for 3-D Chess, Trek drinking games, Star Fleet Battles simulator, and Trek characters and equipment for Gurps are just a few of the Trek-oriented games available in this library. ✓**TFDN**→TFDN—Star Trek Games

Trekker_Games (echo) Discuss Trek computer games, trivia games, and drinking games. This conference has low activity, but those who do participate seem to be quite friendly. ✓**TREKKERNET**

WS_Space (echo) Members use this conference to upload their play-by-email game moves. VGA Planets is the consistent favorite. ✓**WARPSPEED**

Drinking games

Star Trek: Deep Space Nine Drinking Game Play with all the conditions listed and you won't make it to the first commercial: there are that many. Drink when someone says "wormhole" or "gold-pressed latinum," when a crew member drinks, when someone uses a holosuite, when a humanoid alien from the other side of the wormhole appears, when Sisko calls Dax "old man," when Kira yells "what the hell is going on?," when Dax smiles at Bashir, when Odo insults Quark, and dozens more. ✓**AMERICA ONLINE** →*keyword* trek→MORE...→Star Trek Record Banks→Text/Other Files→

Upld: 06/03/93→TEXT:Star Trek: Deep Space Nine, The Drinking Game (Filename: DS9DRINK.DOC)

Star Trek TNG: The Drinking Game The favorite of college students everywhere, this game allows large groups of people to watch TNG episodes while they get progressively sloshed. Did someone say "Belay that order"? Take a drink. Are first names used during a scene of sexual tension between crew members? Take two. With intoxication quotas for hundreds of recurrent elements—someone mentions an "Old Earth Saying," a holodeck character becomes aware of his or her own ephemerality, etc.—the game is a great way to get to know the series. One caveat: you may begin to associate Beverly's sweaters with a nasty hangover. ✓ **INTERNET** ...→*www* http://www.cosy.sbg.ac.at/ftp/pub /trek/lists/drinking.txt ...→*gopher* dds.dds.nl→De Bibliotheek→boeken →Mass Media→Star Trek→Star Trek Drinking Game

Star Trek: The Next Generation Drinking Game Another version of the TNG drinking game. Drinks are called for in this game when "Klingons speak English when there aren't any humans in the room," an "ugly new alien race makes an appearance," or "Picard wears his sexy chest-revealing bed clothes." There are thirty-eight Trek actions that result in additional intoxication. ✓ **AMERICA ONLINE**→*keyword* trek→MORE... →Star Trek Record Banks→Text/ Other Files→Upld: 07/10/94→ TEXT:TNG Drinking Game (file-name: TNGDRINK.TXT)

TOS Drinking Game Based on TOS, the game requires players to chug a beer whenever a certain line is spoken or action performed during an episode. If Kirk man-

handles a female, chug a beer. If Kirk says, "beam me up, Scotty," chug a beer. When Spock finds anything fascinating or illogical— you guessed it—chug a beer. The file is a complete list of rules. ✓ **GE-NIE**→*keyword* sfrt2→Text and Graphics Library→*Download a file:* 525

TOS Drinking Game A variant on a drinking game based on TOS. If "Scotty can fix the engines by working on wiring on the bridge," drink. Drink some more if Kirk violates the Prime Directive. And once again if "cheesy trumpet plot resolution is played." ✓ **AMERICA ONLINE**→*keyword* trek→ MORE... →Star Trek Record Banks →Text/ Other Files→Upld: 12/03/94 →TEXT:TOS Drinking Game (Classic Trek Drinking Game)

PC Games

Bajoran Mercenary Adventure A PC role-playing game where the mission is to find the orbs that were stolen by the Cardassian empire. ✓ **AMERICA ONLINE** →*keyword* trek→MORE...→Star Trek Record Banks→Text/Other Files→ Upld: 04/10/94→RPG: Bajoran Adventure (Filename: BAJORRPG .ZIP)

BattleTrek Defeat deadly opponents in this Trek-like game. For Macs with HyperCard. ✓ **AMERICA ONLINE**→*keyword* mac software→ Search the Libraries→Search All Libraries→BattleTrek v2.0.sit

BattleTrek: The Metron Encounter You're captain of the Enterprise and you've been captured by the Metrons and forced into a winner-takes-all battle with a Klingon battlecruiser. Plot taken from the TOS epiode, "The Arena." For IBM compatibles. ✓ **COM-PUSERVE**→*go* sfmedia→Libraries→ *Search by filename:* TREK.ARC

The Classic Star Trek Game For IBM compatibles. ✓ **COM-PUSERVE**→*go* sfmedia→Libraries→ *Search by file name:* TRKEGA.ARC

DoomTrek Change your *Doom* game from a battle against monsters in dungeons to one against aliens on the *Enterprise.* Includes a text file with instructions and a WAD file to patch your version of *Doom.* ✓ **COMPUSERVE**→*go* sfmedia →Libraries→*Search by file name:* DOOMTR.ZIP

Games (Computer/Brd) A topic not only for gaming reviews but also for troubleshooting the games. The *Star Trek Interactive Tech Manual* "looks pretty cool, but is it thorough?" asks one prospective buyer about the multi-media tech program. Several owners respond. But, the warp-like driving force of the topic lies in the gaming strategies and cheats exchanged: "How do you get a phaser when you beam down to Codus Nu VI at the beginning of this game [Star Trek TNG: Sega]? I beam down and get wiped out. When I hit the C button the machine buzzes and tells me there is nothing to get. How do you 'Get' a phaser? The instructions are no help. Is there a book or what? How do you defeat the Romulan Bird of Prey? Help!!" ✓ **PROD-IGY**→*jump* star trek bb→Choose a Topic→Games (Computer/Brd)

Master Trek An enemy fleet of battle cruisers is attacking the galaxy and you must prevent them from taking control. Be aggressive and don't let your fuel run low! For Windows 3.1 with Visual Basic Runtime. ✓ **AMERICA ONLINE** →*keyword* winforum→Search the Software Libraries→*Search by file name:* MSTRTRKS.ZIP

Star Trek Bolo Maps Maps of

different quadrants of the Trek universe that may be used with the shoot-em-up tank game Bolo. For Macs. ✓**AMERICA ONLINE**→*keyword* mac software→Search the Libraries →Search All Libraries→*Search by file name:* Star Trek Bolo.sit

---

Star Trek Game (DOS) Download, unzip, and let 'er rip. ✓**INTERNET**→*anon-ftp* faui43.informatik. uni-erlangen.de→/mounts/epix/ public/pub/pc/msdos/games/Misc →startrek.zip

---

Star Trek Game (Mac) A demo of a Macintosh *Star Trek* game. ✓**INTERNET**→*anon-ftp* ftp.iij.ad.jp→/ .4/mac/umich/game/demo→star trek.sit.hqx

---

Star Trek Simulation Select your ship and your computer opponent's ship and engage in star battles. For IBM compatibles with a CGA. ✓**COMPUSERVE**→*go* sfmedia →Libraries→*Search by file name:* STARIB.ARC

Star Trek: The Next Generation Prevent the Romulans from taking over a vital sector of the universe. For Macintosh with a HyperCard player. ✓**AMERICA ONLINE**→ *keyword* mac software→ Search the Libraries→Search All Libraries→*Search by file name:* ST-TNG.sit

---

Stellar V1.0 Destroy the aliens! Played in a 10x10 matrix with each cell representing a quadrant of the galaxy, you fire photons, protect your ship with shields, travel with warp speed, and dock at starbases to refuel. Based on the original *Star Trek* game written at Dartmouth in the early 1970s. For Windows 3.x. ✓**AMERICA ONLINE** →*keyword* winforum→Search the Software Libraries→*Search by file name:* STELLAR.ZIP

Roleplaying

Ads For Clubs/RPGs What would a Prodigy Bulletin Board be like without members organizing into clubs or roleplaying their interests? One of the hallmarks of the Prodigy BB culture are the electronic social clubs that form on their boards. On the Star Trek BB, there are "clubs" established around each series and roleplaying groups that have emerged as perhaps the most lively and social part of the bulletin board. An ad for the position of bartender on the *USS Voyager* promises uncomplicated fun.

The STNG game draws members by asking if they "miss Jean-Luc, Will, Geordi, Bev, and the rest?" There are a staggering number of RPGs competing for members and this topic is where the groups recruit new members. "Join the Empire. Only the most brave warriors may serve. Name 3 positions most wanted. Qapla." If you have a yearning to be a Klingon, you could email the advertiser expressing your interest or go directly to the appropriate RPG topic.

When a new game is beginning, the game masters will often post a description: "The setting is the solar system, the time period is set during the same year as DS9 is currently operating in. All is well on Earth until a mysterious visitor kidnaps the presidential advisor. Events snowball, and before anyone knows what happened, Earth is under attack by Jem'Hadar ships, a Borg cube, and renegade Romulans. The opening scenes have been set..." When you've found the game you're looking for, head straight for the roleplaying topics. ✓**PRODIGY**→*jump* star trek bb→Choose a Topic→Ads For Clubs/RPGs

STARNOTES

"**+taps+:** Heat the probes have detected another Alien craft
JNimocks: spawn you just lay right here, take it easy
Trek1701: They are dying.
Ens DSIX: Pakled Ship Taking Up An Attck Posture!
Spawn123: lays down
ENSDUKE226: +TAP+, Ack, LJ let's keep those levels down
Cadet LJ: Duke, that would be a good explanation
MAmerson: Captain I can only give you warp 5.7
JNimocks: Working on spawn.
Trek1701: They are clearly not thriving.
Ens DSIX: Something's Happening!
Cadet Knox: Is it safe to beam down?
Vikki Jane: Probes reach positions surrounding the moon and engage their shield generators.
Mamerson: Captain torpedo ready for target on spackled ship.
JNimocks: Spawn needs serious medical attention, help me.
Trek1701: The Pakleds are, to be blunt, slow. They don't have advanced weapons."

—from **America Online's Starfleet Online**

Gaming in Ten-Forward The Trek Phenomenon

alt.starfleet.rpg (ng) Ensign Fred(dy) Krueger of the *USS Excalibur* detects an energy build-up on Mockra IX. "I have never seen such immense energy concentrated in one place," he reports to his superiors. "Perhaps this is a new type of power generator the Borg are after." Meanwhile, Lieutenant Cameron Raeghar of the *USS Caesar Augustus* tests the distortion field and works on modifications to the third warp nacelle. It's a tough job, but somebody's got to do it. In this active role-playing club loosely based on *Star Trek: The Next Generation*, members create characters and weave an action-oriented interactive fiction.

To get started, look for the Starfleet Command document SF.RPG FAQ, frequently posted to the group and available at the newsgoup's Website. (Join the game prepared by first traveling to the Website and reading the FAQ, the Starfleet Manual, an etiquette document, and other helpful guides. Roster lists are also maintained here.) You'll start off as a lowly ensign, newly graduated from Starfleet Academy, but you can move up the ranks quickly, your progress gauged by the skill and frequency of your posts. Become a regular, and you'll be at the front lines in staving off the Borg. √**USENET** *Archives:* √**INTERNET**→ *www* http://rzstud1.rz.uni-karls ruhe.de/~ukea/

Final Frontiers Ferengi? Klingon? Q? Join a race from the *Star Trek: The Next Generation* universe, then an organization, and then work your way up the ranks (from Starfleet cadet to Admiral). The MOO offers flight and combat simulation, an economy, roleplaying, and active discussion groups on the nature of space travel. Be sure to read the game's constitution before beginning. √**IN-**

TERNET→*telnet* trekmoo.microserve. com 2499→connect guest <your full name><your email address> √**INTERNET**→*www* http://www.micro serve.net/~trek/

Starfleet Online (SFOL) So you want to explore the universe? Interested in making friends from distant planets? Consider joining Starfleet. You'll have to attend the academy where you'll learn how to roleplay Trek adventures: an attack by the Borg, a plot contrived by the Romulans, a Klingon trial of honor, a warp drive failure, etc. Even if in an alternate universe (or different Net site), you had risen to the position of captain or admiral, you still have to begin as a cadet here. Drop by the Starfleet Resource Center and the Starfleet Misc Articles archive in Starfleet Online for some background on what SFOL is and what you need to know to get through the Academy. Here in the bowels of the libraries, you'll be able to read the cadet manuals on ships, ranks, races, locations, and technology. And, in the Memory Pine, there's an infinite amount of fan art to enjoy in off-sim times.

If you decide to pursue a career with Starfleet, then just show up at the public room called Starfleet Academy in the People Connection (keyword: pc) during one of the designated academy simulations. (A schedule is posted on the Cadet-Officer Message Center in the SFOL Schedules folder.) Create a Cadet screen name like Cadet Hearn or Cadet Maloni. You and your fellow cadets will be sent an instant message describing a mission and led through a live simulation by a gaming forum host from AOL. After participating in several simulations, you'll probably be good enough to graduate and receive your promotion to Ensign. Notice of your promo-

tion will appear in the graduations listings in the Cadet-Officer Message Center. Then, the adventures begin.

As an Ensign, you're allowed to join advanced simulations in the Final Frontier simulations room (see the Simulations Rooms folder). You'll be asked your preferences for duty positions and will then be assigned to a ship. Promotions occur as your commanding officers decide they are warranted. While simulations happen several times each evening, players also keep in touch and broaden the roleplaying by posting to the message boards. For a quick account of what's happening with many of the ongoing simulations, read the captain's logs or, less formally, the lounge reports in the Starfleet Command message board. Younger would-be members of Starfleet (the Wesley Crushers of the world aside) will probably enjoy the Teen simulations more. Check out the Teen Fleet message board for a sim schedule. √**AMERICA ONLINE**→*key-word* trek→starfleet

Stargame (ml) Will Alison, Selara, and Phantom be able to disengage the control umbilical from the Starbase? That's their task, and to learn the results—or to get a piece of the action yourself—subscribe to this Trek role-playing game, a mailing list in which each member assumes a character and participates in the creation of a complex, multi-threaded virtual world of sci-fi adventure. You never know what's going to happen on a list like this one. You could be asked to review a set of computer logs, ordered to repair the Warp core, or told to work on a "level five diagnostic," whatever that is. If you want to test your ability to write with Kirk-like bravado, this is the place for you. √**INTERNET**→*email* listserv@listserv.

net ✍ *Type in message body:* subscribe stargame <your full name>

StarTrek_RPG/StarTrek/TN_Startrek

(echo) Roleplaying games are ongoing, with Game Masters running their own sessions on these conferences. Send a message to one of the echo moderators to join a game, and then sit back and feel the Trekness coursing through your body. To wit: "As you try to relax in your quarters and ponder the message from Admiral Kirk, the sound of Red Alert Klaxons is heard. Suddenly without waiting for you to acknowledge his presence at the door, your Yeoman enters. 'Commander De Valois, sensors have detected several more Klingon vessels now in the area and decloaking. They've opened fire...'" ✓**FIDONET** ...→Star Trek_RPG ...→ StarTrek ✓**TREKNET**→ TN_Startrek

Trek Sim Manual For Dummies

A manual with advice about Trek roleplaying. ✓**COMPUSERVE**→ *go* sfmedia→Libraries→*Search by file name:* TREKDU.TXT

Trekker_RPG

(echo) "The Away Team member's took up their positions, two covering one of the entrances, the others behind containers. If one fell, another would move up to cover for him...If things got bad enough, they would retreat to the Turbo-lift, if possible, and escape...'About 10 seconds, Sir...,' LaVelle reported, putting his tricorder away again... And counting...'NEXT!'"

If you think you know exactly what should happen next and you can spin a good story, sign up for one of the ongoing Trek roleplaying games in this conference. Usually a game master will describe the time frame the game is set in, the crew positions available, ship stats, and a little background about the plot. You'll then be asked to submit a character profile and wait for your orders. GMs not only announce new games and accept players, but they're also involved in advancing the action of the game and keeping the players in character. Roleplaying here is not complicated or rigid and new players are encouraged to join. ✓**TREKKERNET**

WS_SF_Acad

(echo) At the heart of the WarpSPEED BBS network is a desire to act out the Trek experience. And, it all begins here—the academy. Sign up at the academy by posting a message to this conference with your name, birthdate, today's date, and your area of concentration: science, operations, engineering, or medical. As a cadet, you'll follow a course of lessons over a few months leading up to a final exam. Your grade will determine your rank and then you can choose on which ship you'd like to serve. Each ship has its own private echo. ✓**WARPSPEED**

ST:TNG card games

CCG Website

A home base for the customizable card game, with rules, rule variants, links to other CCG Websites, and checklists. ✓**INTERNET**→*www* http://www.cs.indiana.edu/hyplan/awooldri/st-game.html

Official Card List

Make sure you collect all your Artifacts, and don't leave out the Equipment or Mission cards. ✓**INTERNET**→*anon-ftp* 129.21.204.63→/Wembley/Pub/ST CCG→ Official ST-TNG 363

Simple Cardlist

What's a cardlist? Simple—a list of the cards used in the Star Trek Customizable Card Game. ✓**INTERNET** →*www* http://www.public.iastate. edu/~philborn/st-ccg.html

Star Trek Card Game List

Do you have the Cloaked Mission card? How about the Yridian Shuttle or the Romulan Outpost? Check this very simple list to see what you're missing. Cards are grouped in categories such as Artifact, Dilemma, Equipment, Mission, and Romulan. ✓**AMERICA ONLINE**→ *keyword* trek→MORE... →Star Trek Record Banks→Text/ Other Files→Upld: 11/20/94→ TEXT: Star Trek Card Game List (Filename: STCARDS.TXT)

The Star Trek: The Next Generation Customizable Card Game

FAQ, card checklists, rule variants, pointers to other sources. ✓**INTERNET**→ *www* http://m604 m04.isc.rit.edu/HTML/STCCG_Home.HTML

Star Fleet Battles

SFB Tactics

If you're not seriously into the board game *Star Fleet Battles*, the messages sent to this list will look like a combination of Klingon and theoretical physics. Here's an example: "1 hex/turn == c (Speed of light) == 3e8 m/s." Uh, you lost me. It's not all like that, but there's an awful lot of talk of "positional stabilizers," "relativistic effects," "drone-users vs. direct-fire weapons," and other tactical issues related to the game. "I think the complexity of the rules is what makes SFB," wrote one player. "You have to study, practice, and fight—a lot. It makes SFB a little exclusive." Yet even some SFB fans get fed up with the endless techno-talk: "It's a *game*, for goodness sake." If you're into SFB, or you think you might be, this is a great destination. If not, steer clear—or risk being "photonned" by a techno-weenie with a stash of big weapons. ✓**INTERNET**→

email hcobb@fly2.berkeley.edu

Star Fleet Battles on AOL Not the Net's most active place for SFB talk, AOL's Star Fleet Battles area has been demoted from a forum to a folder. But the faithful press on. "Enough wailing and gnashing of teeth," wrote one of the regulars, following the demise of the SFB Online Forum. "We few diehards can still keep this alive. Anyone have any interesting battles recently? Anyone looking for an interesting opponent?" That's the spirit. Kirk would be proud. But don't waste too much time with pride—it's a static emotion. Activate, and get back to the sort of tactical questions SFB players love to discuss, like the number of shuttles it would take to kill a starbase and the wisdom of narrowing a salvo of photons to range 8. You'll still find periodic SFB online conferences, with orders to "Be there (or we'll send out the Klingon Punishment Brigade)!" ✓**AMERICA ONLINE** →*keyword* gaming→Star Fleet Battles

Star Fleet Battles on CIS An active spot to play games, check out files, and talk tactics. Games get analyzed in great detail, and reps of Amarillo Design Bureau, the makers of *Star Fleet Battles*, hang out here. You'll find regular updates on upcoming products, like *Prime Adventures #1* ("the never-before-known history of how the three Gorn races merged into one") and *Module M Marines* (includes a 48-page rulebook). At monthly conferences, promotions and demotions are announced and everything SFB-related discussed, whether it's "modified victory conditions" or the chance of separating a Gorn saucer (don't count on it). The libraries have a variety of files, like conference transcipts and graphics of SFB ships. You can even pick up "a conversion list

Starfleet Online Logo—downloaded from AOL's Starfleet Online Forum

from SFB hex speed to its equivalent warp speed for fiction." ✓**COMPUSERVE**→*go* pbmgames→Libraries *or* Messages→Board Wargames

Star Fleet Battles on Genie Certainly the place for hardcore SFB fans on the Net, with the game's designer, Steve Cole, online. You'll find lots of topics on everything from "General Star Fleet Announcements" to "Tournament Tactics Discussion." There's talk of SFB products, conventions, rules, and everything else related to the game. It's a great place to find opponents for both face-to-face and play-by-mail games. You can even offer suggestions for the evolution of the game. Of course, if you do, there's a chance they'll be rejected straight from the source. "While many have called for the Black Shark to get a scatter-pack," Cole wrote in response to one player's idea, "I have never supported the idea and the tournament update sheet does not provide it. I think we can let that discussion drop; it's not going to happen." That settles things, doesn't it? If you want to feel like

you're at the center of Star Fleet, head out to this cyber-spot at warp speed. ✓**GENIE** ...→*keyword* scorpia →Games Bulletin Board→set 10 ... →*keyword* sfb (for files)

Tridimensional chess

Klin Zha GIFs of the pieces required to play Klingon Chess and a Windows Write file with the rules of the game. ✓**COMPUSERVE** →*go* sfmedia→Libraries→*Search by file name:* KLNZHA.ZIP

Rules for 3-D Chess Rules for playing the 3-D chess game. Relies heavily on diagrams. ✓**COMPUSERVE**→*go* sfmedia→Libraries→ *Search by file name:* 3DCHES.TXT

Star Trek Tridimensional Chess Another set of rules for the multi-level chess game made popular by Kirk and Spock and continued to be played by members of TNG and DS9. No set of rules for the game were revealed on the show, but Trek fans have come up with their own. ✓**AMERICA ONLINE** →*keyword* trek→MORE...→Star Trek Record Banks→Text/Other Files→

Upld: 04/10/94→TEXT: Tri-Dimensional Chess Rules (Filename: 3DCHES.TXT)

Tri-Dimensional Chess: An Introduction Rules of the official Paramount version of Tri-Dimensional chess. A diagram accompanies the instruction. ✓**AMERICA ONLINE**→*keyword* trek→MORE...→ Star Trek Record Banks→Text/Other Files→Upld: 06/08/94→TEXT: Tri-D Chess Rules (Filename: 3DCHESS.TXT)

Trivia

Star Trek Trivia Chats Do you consider yourself a *Star Trek* trivia expert? Well, then "RED ALERT! Classic Stumper Questions Coming!" The 48 room members quiet down briefly to watch for the upcoming question: "Who did the voice for Alice in Wonderland in 'Once Upon a Planet?'" (Oh no! It's the Trek Animated Series!) Hope you've got the answer because "Hailing Frequencies Closed!" Time's up—did you guess Majel Barrett? Or perhaps Abe Vigoda? The correct answer—which comes from the room host, BirdOf-Prey—is...Nichelle Nichols. BirdOfPrey and Doc Obee, two America Online Star Trek Club forum staffers, host a real-time trivia game every Saturday night at 11:00 PM ET. Another real-time trivia game, based on *The Next Generation* and hosted by Net-Trekker and Data1701D, is held every Friday night at 11:00 PM ET on The Bridge, the Star Trek Club forum's live chat room. Both games are extremely popular, and The Bridge is always filled to capacity, so get there early to get a place onboard. And bring all the trivia books you want—these trivia games will stump even the best! ✓**AMERICA ONLINE**→*keyword* trek→ The Bridge

Trekker_Trivia (echo) How many children did Picard have in his Nexus life? What is the name of the Captain of the Enterprise-B? And what's Odo's specific gravity? Try your hand in Trek Trivialand with this conference. ✓**TREKKERNET**

Trivia This topic is devoted to the minutiae of the Trek universe. List after list of questions are submitted here—some questions provoking discussions; others, quick answers. How old is Guinan? Was Spot a male or a female? And what other felines have spent time in outer space (excluding, of course, the Cat from Outer Space)? ✓**PRODIGY**→*jump* star trek bb→ Choose a Topic→Trivia

20 Questions Star Trek TNG Quick Quiz A twenty-question quiz based on TNG. Question one: "What warp speed, since 'Force of Nature,' are all starships forbidden to exceed unless in emergencies?" ✓**COMPUSERVE**→*go* sfmedia→Libraries→*Search by file name:* QKQUIZ.TXT

Fri/Sat Trivia games info More than three years old, this Trek folder contains a collection of the scoring results of trivia game matches held on the Star Trek Club's Bridge, along with the questions and answers asked during the brain-scorching matches. ✓**AMERICA ONLINE** → *keyword* trek→Star Trek Message Boards→ Star Trek Message Boards→The Promenade→Fri/Sat Trivia games info

Match McCoy's Quotes Match "I'm a doctor" quotes with the right episodes. Fun for kids. ✓**COMPUSERVE**→*go* sfmedia→Libraries→*Search by file name:* MCCOY.TXT

Star Trek 101—Midterm Exam A 20-question exam for diehard Trekkers. True or False: Commander William Riker has slept with more alien robots than Captain James T. Kirk (ret.). ✓**COMPUSERVE**→*go* sfmedia→Libraries→ *Search by file name:* ST101.TXT

Star Trek Quote Game Match a quote with the character who said it. Questions are in the first file, answers in the second. ✓**COMPUSERVE**→*go* sfmedia→Libraries→ *Search by file name:* TREKMA.TXT and MACANR.TXT

Star Trek TOS Episode by Episode Quiz Quiz with a trivia question for every episode of all seven seasons. ✓**COMPUSERVE**→*go* sfmedia→Libraries→ *Search by file name:* EPQUIZ.TXT

TNG Trivia Did you know that LeVar Burton's character, Geordi LaForge, is named after a real *Star Trek* fan named George LaForge who died from muscular dystrophy in 1975? Did you know that if you look closely at the *Enterprise-NCC-1701-D* during the fly-by in the opening credits, you can see someone walking past the windows? Did you know that Stephen Hawking is the only person ever to appear on *Star Trek* as himself? You do now. But you don't know the rest of the fascinating TNG trivia contained at this Website. ✓**INTERNET**→*www* http://www.ee. surrey.ac.uk/Personal/STTNG/misc. html#trivia

TNG Trivia Game V2.0 Parts 1 & 2 A trivia game with two 100-question trivia quizzes, the first devoted to general information and the second focusing on technical trivia. ✓**COMPUSERVE**→*go* sfmedia→Libraries→*Search by file name:* TNG20.ZIP

TrekMUSE

Night after night, recreate the universe of the 24th century in a real-time virtual envi-

ronment on the Net. Board ships, battle enemies, share some ale with a Romulan, and try to outwit a Ferengi. And never mind whether the Ferengi is the guy in the front row of your math class or a doctor in southern Sweden. When humans telnet to this site, they become part of a futuristic milieu drawn from the *Star Trek* TV shows, movies, and books—particularly those based on the *Next Generation*. This quadrant in space, or Cyberspace, is a MUSE, a style of MUD that facilitates roleplaying between Netters and uses automated features such as robots that mimic characters, vehicles, and "monsters."

USS Grissom—*Downloaded from lajkonik.cyf-kr.pl.edu*

Getting Started

When you first log into Trek-MUSE, you'll be classified as an Observer. If after looking around, you decide you'd like a character, use the "+register" command to formally request one. You have to specify the name you want, your email address, and your real name. To get help on the format for doing this, type "help +register." There are two rules to remember: each person can have only one character and you cannot play "feature" characters. This latter rule means that characters who have appeared in Trek movies, books, and TV

shows are not acceptable fantasy incarnations. To put it bluntly: you're not Picard. Once you've registered, your password will be sent to you via email (every hour, on the hour, passwords are sent out by an automated mailer). We strongly suggest that you take an hour or two to read every help topic—type "help topics" for a list of available instructions and background information and "help commands" for a list of commands.

Registered players have to then pick a race. If you're uncertain who you are—feeling a little Klingon on some days, and positively Cardassian on others—you should wander around the Hub area to look at the information available about each race. In addition to known races (Ferengi, Romulans, etc.), TrekMUSE permits players to behave as Independents, members of a small group of merchants and traders not attached to any of the spheres; and joining the Federation is also an option. Once you've picked a race, you'll need to type "signup" in the appropriate

race room. Doing this sets some MUSE properties on your character which indicate your race and what public communication channels you're automatically subscribed to. Klingons, for instance, can speak with Klingons all over the MUSE.

Bright College Years

If you decide to become a member of the Federation, be warned that in order to get very far at all, you'll need to enter Starfleet Academy. You can do this automatically by finding the "registrar yeoman" in the administration building and telling him you want to register, then going over to the training hall, finding a vacant classroom, and taking the automated classes from one of the professorial robots. The classes consist of text that scrolls past on various subjects, followed by a selection of test questions. You have to get 90 percent or better to pass a class, and you have to pass all your classes to go on to the next level. When you've completed your four years of classes, you arrange an internship aboard a ship and serve until you're promoted to ensign. There are, at this time, no provisions for Federation civilians, but, if you'd rather not go the Starfleet route, you can become an Independent and work as a merchant. Don't get exasperated if it takes a while to find your way around at first. Places are spread out to add to the realism. If you've signed with the Federation, just focus on getting to the Academy and then finding the Yeoman in the Adminsitration builiding.

Rank is rather important. Every player is not equal, and you have to earn any promotions you get. For example, just to become a Starfleet ensign, you have to take courses on protocol and rank, and God help you if you show up in a bad mood one day and decide to mouth off to a player who significantly outranks you. There is just as much fun to be had as a low-ranking officer as a higher-up, and a good role-player will realize this and bide his or her time starring off-Broadway, as it were, knowing that in time he or she will have the chance to move to the Great White Way. Within each race, there is a wide range of career options (although there is a broader range of career opportunities with the Federation than the militaristic Gorn).

The training each race puts you through will give you a deep understanding of the era, the milieu, and the system, as well as bringing you up to date on the history of the universe as it's being played out on TrekMUSE. Just reading the "Starfleet History Part III" in the Starfleet Academy classrooms will quickly acquaint you with the long history of cross-border incursions and character demises that have taken place. There are chances to move up: in one battle, the Cardassian leader was aboard a ship which was destroyed, and correspondingly, an awful lot of Cardassians below him got to move up. Once you've gotten through your training, you'll begin to interact significantly with other players, perhaps becoming a member of someone's crew, out exploring, helping to build new starbases, or conducting intelligence missions to assess enemy objectives.

Battle-Ready

Quite a lot of TrekMUSE is automated, in the sense that the MUSE does have merchant ships moving around space without any actual players on board. Combat ships, on the other hand, must have an actual complement of players on board: if you go into battle with fewer than the required three players and lose, you're destroyed, and if you win, your kill doesn't count. Of course, if you go into battle with five crew members and lose, you're still destroyed. Thus, it's essential to have enough qualified crew members along to man the required consoles.

Anything truly significant must take place during so-called "prime hours"—the hours between 4 pm and 11 pm Eastern time. That's when the Directors (the MUSE's "wizard staff"—unkillable, all-powerful, Q-like administrators) are logged in to validate significant achievements like one ship invading Cardassian space and destroying a space station. Furthermore, to steal a ship, you have to have crew of that ship helping you. You can't just run in while a ship is vacant and waltz off with it, because in the real Trek universe, the ship wouldn't really be empty just because its senior officers are in a bar somewhere.

What's a space battle like? If you're on the bridge of the Galileo when it slugs it out with a Cardassian vessel, you'll see the members of the crew reporting on the course of the vessels, distance, speed, and so forth, and you'll hear warnings when the other ship locks on or does damage.

If you *are* a crew member, stationed at one of the consoles, your screen will display the information appropriate to that station. To facilitate role-playing, you'd then report what your station had informed you, just as a helmsman on the *Enterprise* would acknowledge changes in course or the weapons officer would acknowledge a hit by the ship's photon torpedoes. Lest you get the idea that TrekMUSE is nothing but battles, take note that the emphasis here is on the roleplaying and socialization.

Roleplaying the personality of your Gorn, Klingon, Cardassian, or Federation character can be very involved and addictive, and good roleplaying skills must be honed—Gorn players, for example, are expected to play very militaristic warriors; this is not the easiest thing to do without behaving incredibly one-dimensional. And a good roleplaying scene can be done as well in the Ten-Forward lounge as on the bridge. Assigned to the heavy cruiser *Galileo*? Visit the Two-Forward lounge on Deck Two of the ship.

Know Your Character

There's a lot of emphasis placed on the concept of OOC (Out Of Character) and IC (In Character). In other words, if you're a Federation officer and your real-life friend plays a Cardassian, and while chatting OOC your friend tells you that the Cardassians have hidden a bomb aboard Beowulf Station, there's nothing you can do about it in character. ✓ **INTERNET** ...→*telnet* grimmy.cnidr.org 1701 ...→*www* http://grimmy/cnidr. org/trek.html

Netrek

Netrek is almost as old as the original *Star Trek* TV series

and undoubtedly the most popular multiplayer shoot-'em-up on the Internet, with more elaborate playing and programming subcultures than any other game on the Net.

Players can log in over the phone, but all across the world eight-person teams of Netrekkers crowd into underused campus and corporate computer labs to get at the high-powered workstations and network connections that give them an edge in battle. Placed in a world of ships and planets and the "final frontier," tournament-level game play (90 minutes) resembles a Cyberspace version of rugby with dogfights. Teamwork is key, as squadrons fight in formation for control of the galaxy.

Netrek has been through many evolutionary steps. Born in 1972 as *Empire* on a Plato terminal system at the University of Illinois, it was imitated on an IBM mainframe as *Conquest* in the early '80s. These adaptations and others that followed are still in use, including *Netrek*'s immediate predecessor, *Xtrek*. And

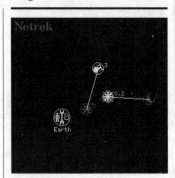

Netrek screenshot—from http://www.cs. vu.nl/~frankn/index.html

even now *Netrek* is giving way to a flashier, more intricate real-time *Star Trek* combat game called *Paradise*.

On the Net

Find a game

Netrek Metaserver You have the software; now log into this server to find a live game. The server tells you who's playing and where. ✓**INTERNET**→*telnet* metaserver.ecst.csuchico.edu 3520 *Info:* ✓**INTERNET**→*www* http://www.cs.umd.edu/users/mwp/Netrek/netrek.html

rec.games.netrek (ng) *Netrek*'s rabid following is evidenced in the daily activity on this newsgroup, the locus of the international *Netrek* community. Newbies pick up connection and strategy tips that are usually buried in the middle of *Netrek* manuals, and old-timers organize and report the results of major battles

they're involved in. The FAQ functions as the *Netrek* manual, but it also points to a host of other useful strategy and tip files that will prevent you from ever actually playing the game if you try to read them all. ✓**USENET** *FAQ:* ✓**INTERNET** ...→*anon-ftp* ftp.csua. berkeley.edu→/pub/netrek→ netrekFAQ ...→*www* http://www. cis.ohio- state.edu/hypertext/faq /usenet/ games/netrek/faq/faq. html

Archives & info

"FTP List" FAQ The guide to all other *Netrek* FAQs. Everything's here, from basic tips to instructions for starting your own *Netrek* server. ✓**INTERNET** ...→*anon-ftp* ftp.csua.berkeley.edu→/pub/netrek →netrekFTP ...→*anon-ftp* rtfm.mit. edu→/pub/usenet/rec.games. netrek→ netrekFTP

Netrek Archives Most files are accessible and browsable via the *Netrek* Web Site. The Carnegie Mellon site has *Netrek* documentation galore: detailed advice for beginners, high-level strategic

STARNOTES

"My GPA has fallen 25% since I started playing Netrek last semester. How do you find time to do your homework and still make Admiral?"

"Nobody's found an answer to this one yet. Just remember that (GPA+kill ratio) is constant."

—from **rec.games. netrek** FAQ

analysis for the experienced. The site archives old *XTrek* files, as well as standard compendiums of rec. games.netrek wisdom. Must-see files include the newbie's guide, Grey Elf's Guide to Planet Taking, and Ship Facts, for the bottom line on torp and plasma velocities. √**INTERNET**→*anon-ftp* ftp.csua.berkeley.edu→/pub/netrek *Info:* √**INTERNET**→*www* http:// obsidian.math.arizona.edu:8080/ ftp.html

Netrek Home Pages If you've got a good enough network connection to play *Netrek*, you've got access to the World Wide Web. Maybe this is why the Web is blanketed with *Netrek* coverage. √**INTERNET** ...→*www* http://obsidi an.math.arizona. edu:8080/netrek. html ...→*www* http://www.cs. cmu.edu:8001/afs/cs/user/jch/ netrek/README.html ...→*www* http://msi.umn.edu/paradise/

Clients

Netrek Client List *Netrek* is a client/server game. The server acts as the host for players who are running client programs. The server coordinates commands from all the players and reports the game situation. There are plenty of *Netrek* servers on the Internet, but you need a client program for your machine (most are X-Windows based, but there are a number of implementations) and a direct connection to the Internet (i.e., you have to have your own IP address), through a dial-up SLIP or PPP account or through a direct network connection. (See the Net Games FAQ and glossary (page 251) for an explanation of these terms.) There is a WWW page listing clients as well as an ac-curate and up-to-date list of pro-grams available from *Netrek* FTP sites. √**INTERNET** ...→*www* http://

www.cs.cmu.edu:8001/afs/cs/user /jch/netrek/ftp-list...→*www* http://obsidian.math.arizona.edu: 8080/client.html

INL

Intercollegiate Netrek League The Intercollegiate Netrek League (INL) organizes team battles with players from all over the world. Elaborate cultures have grown up around the older teams. One championship L.A. team calls it-self Will Riot for Food; the best Seattle team calls itself Lagg U, a play on their once slower net-work connection. Team captains decide on new drafts. Applica-tions are posted on rec.games.ne-trek or sometimes emailed direct-ly to a team captain. Get ac-quainted with the INL by rifling through their files at the FTP site. Documents include current rosters and schedules. √**INTER-NET**→*anon-ftp* ftp.csua.berkeley. edu→/pub/netrek/INL

Newbies

Beginners Must-read file for *Ne-trek* beginners. Anticipates and an-swers newbie questions. √**INTERNET** *www*→http://www.cs.cmu.edu: 8001/afs/cs/user/jch/netrek /beginners.Z

The History of Netrek Leg-endary *Netrek* Ace Andy McFad-den (aka Shadow Spawn) has drafted an authoritative history of *Netrek* that is fascinating reading for players and students of com-puter-game history. Posted regu-larly to rec.games.netrek. √**INTER-NET**→*www* http://obsidian.math. arizona.edu:8080/History.html

Tour of Netrek Take the *Netrek* tour, a walk-through of the Metaserver, with explanations on choosing your "persona" and ship, joining a league, etc. √**INTER-NET**→*www* http://obsidian.math. arizona.edu:8080/nttour.html

NETREK VOCABULARY

DI	Destruction Inflicted. The index for *Netrek*'s scoring and ranking system.
T-mode	Tournament Mode. A "t" signifies that there are enough teams with enough players (the specific number depends on the server you are using) to play a tournament.
ogging	Kamikazi (suicide attack)
genocide	Occurs when a race loses its last planet
pregnant	Carrying armies (said of a ship)
<blank> scum	Name for someone who uses <blank> tac-tic more than you
XTrek	Precursor to *Netrek*
Paradise	*Netrek: The Next Generation.* New ships, new rules, new game.
Netrek For Morons mode (-M)	Newbie help, available on some servers
borg	Robot players, disallowed on standard servers
server god	The person who maintains and often cus-tomizes a *Netrek* server.

Trekware & collectibles

Trek is more than a TV show. It's a way of life, a subculture. And it's also a gold mine.

From action figures to trading cards, from models to a Franklin Mint set, *Star Trek* collectibles are among the most coveted items in the known galaxy, and the Net is full of sites to help fans develop and maintain their collections. Start at one of the large commercial service locations—AOL's imaginatively titled **Where to Buy Star Trek Stuff** or Prodigy's **Memorabilia**. Cater to your own special interests with **Star Trek Modeling**. Visit some of the official sites for merchandise, especially **The Star Trek Store**. And if you want cool Trek merchandise but don't want to leave the comfort of your own computer, check out the selection of Trek shareware and software available for download, including the **Star Trek Clock** and **Starbar**.

Trek action figures—downloaded from Perfect Vision Graphics BBS

On the Net

Across the board

800 Trekker Collectibles An electronic catalog of Trek and other sci-fi products—from the *Voyager* pin to the *Starfleet Technical Manual* to an *X-Files* coffee mug. ✓**INTERNET**→*www* http://www.trekkercom/

Data Base *Star Trek* memorabilia trading post that handles transactions of everything from action figures to rubber stamps. As the forum's mission statement explains, this is the place to "talk about the latest news and reviews of the *Star Trek* universe. After all, that's where the toys come from." ✓**DELPHI**→*go* cus 019

DS9 Buy/Sell/Trade Here's what you won't find here: Benjamin Sisko's wedding gifts, the Odo Shape-Shifter Power Shake, the Jadzia Dax blow-up dolls. Here's what you will find here: just about everything else. ✓**AMERICA ONLINE**→*keyword* trek→Star Trek Message Boards→Deep Space Nine Board→DS9 Buy/Sell/Trade

Games and Collectibles Not the busiest outpost on Delphi's *Star Trek* forum, but a useful one for discussion and news of Trek wares—whether you're wondering what others think of *The Next Generation* card game ("pretty fraggin rad!") or you're trying to unload a *Star Trek* concordance you bought in '76 ("mint condition," with a "stardate wheel that you dial to get to the proper episode"). Stick around, and you may be able to pick up that *Pon farr* chemistry set always wanted. ✓**DELPHI**→*go* ent sta for→ set gam

Memorabilia Scripts, rare magazines and books, Playmates figures, and cards are what keep the real Trek fan interested and in debt. This topic gathers messages which speculate on the next premium collector's item, offers hints on hard-to-find toy parts, and serves as a trading room for all of the above. "Hey everyone! I really need some help with this one."

Which one? Well, it seems Mindy needs sewing patterns for the uniforms worn in *Star Trek VI*. ✓ **PRODIGY**→*jump* star trek bb→ Choose a Topic→Memorabilia

Star Trek Merchandise Order William Shatner's *Star Trek Movie Memories,* or an audio book of Shatner and Leonard Nimoy reading four science-fiction classics. New merchandise appears online as it is released into the real world, with discounts for Delphi members. ✓ **DELPHI**→*go* cus 017→ Shatner Books→Books and Tapes

Star Trek Next Generation - Collectibles & Gifts Features *Star Trek* key rings, clocks, and a lighted halodome (with Klingon warriors shouting orders in their native tongue). Email for more information, or, to order, complete a Web form. ✓ **INTERNET**→*www* http: //diamond.sierra.net:80/trek/

Star Trek-related stuff wanted/for sale Action figures, novelizations, collectibles, videocassettes, and just about every other kind of Trek merchandise available. ✓ **GENIE**→*keyword* sfrt2→ SFRT2 Bulletin Board→set 24→read 20

TN_Swap (echo) Lwaxana Troi, Data as a Romulan, a Ferengi ship, and the DS9 spaceship are just a few of the hundreds of Playmates *Star Trek* figures—perhaps the most collected of all Trek collectibles—coveted on this conference. In addition to Playmates products, the board's participants trade, buy, and sell Trek trading cards, other sci-fi merchandise, and computer equipment in general. ✓ **TREKNET**

TNG Buy/Sell/Trade TNG has generated tons of merchandise—from Playmates action figures to specialty chess sets to collectors' edition of *Next Generation* novelizations. Talk to other fans and collectors. ✓ **AMERICA ONLINE**→*keyword* trek→Star Trek Message Boards→The Next Generation→ TNG Buy/ Sell/Trade

TOS Buy/Sell/Trade The granddaddy of all Trek series has the longest history and also the most precious merchandise. If you want to unload a lobby card from

Trek Commemorative Plate—from Perfect Vision Graphics BBS

Star Trek: The Motion Picture, or you have a movie poster that confirms William Shatner's appearance in *The Brothers Karamazov,* this is the place for you. ✓ **AMERICA ONLINE**→ *keyword* trek→Star Trek Message Boards→Classic Trek→ TOS Buy/Sell/Trade

TREK stuff buy/sell/trade If you're looking for *Star Trek* bedsheets, stationery, or trading cards, this folder is AOL's version of a

Trek marketplace. ✓ **AMERICA ONLINE**→*keyword* trek→Star Trek Message Boards→The Promenade→ TREK stuff buy/seel/trade

Where to Buy Star Trek Stuff A woman writes in to say that her eight-year old daughter is collecting TNG action figures and can't seem to find Commander Riker to complete the set. A fan offers TOS Christmas ornaments to the online world. And other fans lament that convention merchandise is sometimes shoddy. If you're trying to find a playset of the House of Quark, or you just want a pair of dime-store Vulcan ears, this is the message board for you. ✓ **AMERICA ONLINE**→*keyword* scifi→Star Trek/Comics/TV/Star Wars Boards →Star Trek→ Where to buy Star Trek Stuff

Action figures

Playmates Star Trek Collectibles List A collectors's checklist of over a hundred *Star Trek* figurines, and fifteen playsets. ✓ **COMPUSERVE**→*go* collect→Libraries→ *Search by file name:* STARTO.TXT

Playmates Toys Few people understand the unadulterated joy of finding an unopened Playmates figure that you've despaired of getting because you live in the only town in America that doesn't have their Trek-collectibles-act together. Sigh. But here, the success stories just roll in. From Utah: "I just got back from my local toy store with Data in dress uniform and ENSIGN RO!" From Knoxville, Tennessee: "You can find everything at Wal-Mart." And, in Southwest Virginia, there's both success and failure: "Just found the Klingon *Generations* Bird of Prey! It is absolutely BEAUTIFUL. The lights

Commemorating STAR TREK 1987-1994
THE NEXT GENERATION

$2 St. Vincent & The Grenadines
$2 St. Vincent & The Grenadines
$2 St. Vincent & The Grenadines

TNG Stamps from St. Vincent—downloaded from Perfect Vision Graphics BBS

and stand and everything makes it, what I believe, to be the best ship produced yet! Definitely much better than the battle-damaged *Enterprise*." But there's trouble in paradise: "Hugh Borg is not that abundant." Warp 9 to Toys R Us! ✓**AMERICA ONLINE**→ *keyword* trek→Star Trek Message Boards→ The Promenade→PLAYMATES TOYS

Merchandise

Star Trek Calendar An address book and calendar based on the *Generations* movie. ✓**AMERICA ONLINE**→*keyword* hollywood online→ Hollywood Online Store→Star Trek Store→Star Trek PC Calendar/Address Book for Windows *and* Star Trek PC Calendar/Address Book for Macintosh

Models

Star Trek Modeling This topic is decidedly not about the pin-up careers awaiting Data and Bones. Rather, there is a wealth of technical discussion about the construction of personal Starfleets. Those in the know give tips on the best kits. But these mini-engineers are not satisfied just following the instructions. They also trade ideas for model design innovations and

for simulating new universes for their fleet. ✓**GENIE**→ *keyword* sfrt2→SFRT2 Bulletin Board→set 24→Topic 9

WS_Models (echo) Ask for help finding model dealers and parts, or for advice on designing the perfect convention uniform. Warning: the majority of members here are more familiar with the New Zealand market than the U.S. one. ✓**WARPSPEED**

Online stores

Star Trek Store Order the TNG Interactive Tech CD-ROM, a *Generations* poster, the *Star Trek Encyclopedia*, or a communicator pin. GIFs of the products are available for download. ✓**AMERICA ONLINE**→*keyword* hollywood online →Hollywood Online Store→Star Trek Store

Software/shareware

The Captain's Log V.3 An electronic journal designed as a captain's log. Also, displays time and date. Requires a Macintosh and a HyperCard player. ✓**AMERICA ONLINE**→*keyword* trek→MORE...→Star Trek Record Banks→Text/Other Files→Upld: 08/22/94 Captain's

Log 1.3 Journal→Captain's Log 1.3a_.sit

Communicator Trekker telephone dialer with sound and graphics. DOS shareware. ✓**COMPUSERVE**→*go* sfmedia→Libraries→ *Search by file name:* COMMUN. EXE

Star Trek Clock A computer clock with the Starship *Enterprise*'s image on it. Displays time and date. ✓**AMERICA ONLINE**→*keyword* trek→MORE...→Star Trek Record Banks→Text/Other Files→Upld: 07/19/92 Star Trek clock→TREK CLOCK.ZIP

StarBar Displays the time and date in several formats, including *The Next Generation* stardate system and the Julian calendar. ✓**AMERICA ONLINE**→*keyword* trek→ MORE ...→Star Trek Record Banks→ Text/Other Files→Upld: 06/06/93 WINDOWS: Starbar 3.1 →STRBAR31.ZIP

Trading cards

Star Trek: The Next Generation Collectors Cards Trading cards for *The Next Generation* and the movie *Generations*. Customers may order the sets online. ✓**INTERNET**→ *www* http://www2.interpath.net/interweb/skybox/startrek/index.html

Trek Trading Cards Where can you get the best deal on the hologram set of *Next Generation* trading cards? Need only number 27? Topic 19 has the answer. But, trading cards from the shelves of toy stores are not the only business here. There is news of the *Star Trek* Leaf bootleg cards that appeared in England in 1967 and the Russian and Japanese language cards. ✓**GENIE**→*keyword* sfrt2→ SFRT2 Bulletin Board→set 24

PART 3

THE ORIGINAL

Episode guide

What follows is a list of all episodes of the original *Star Trek* in order of airdate, along with relevant Net sites. Addresses are sometimes given in shorthand (*<address x>*); instructions on constructing full addresses appear in the FAQ (page 20), and on the key in the back of the book.

Season 1

The Cage

Episode #1 (pilot)
Writer: Gene Roddenberry
Director: Robert Butler
Stardate: Not Given

Summary: Before Kirk, there was Capt. Christopher Pike, who responded to a distress call and became an exhibit in an alien zoo. The pilot never aired, but pieces were used in "The Menagerie."

The Cage Twenty scenes from the episode. ✓**COMPUSERVE**→*go sf-media*→*Libraries*→*Search by file name:* TREK99.GIF

Captain Pike Picture of Christopher Pike. ✓**PVG** *dial* 513-233-7993→*<your username>*→*<your password>*→*F*→*Download a file:* PVTOS01.GIF

Number One Picture of Number One (played by Majel Barrett). ✓**PVG** *dial* 513-233-7993→*<your username>*→*<your password>*→ *F*→*Download a file:* PVTOS02.GIF

Spock & Pike Picture of Captain Pike and a young Spock. ✓**PVG**

dial 513-233-7993→*<your username>*→*<your password>*→*F*→ *Download a file:* SPKPIKE.GIF

Young Spock A young Spock in the pilot episode. ✓**PVG** *dial* 513-233-7993→*<your username>*→*<your password>*→*F*→*Download a file:* PVTOS10.GIF

The Man Trap

Episode #6 (first episode aired)
Writer: George Clayton
             Johnson
Director: Marc Daniels
Stardate: 1513.1

Summary: A creature nicknamed the salt vampire begins killing crew members for the salt in their bodies.

Kirk and the Salt Vampire Picture of Kirk aiming a phaser at the salt vampire while an angry McCoy tries to protect it. ✓**PVG** *dial* 513-233-7993→ *<your username>*→*<your password>*→*F*→ *Download a file:* TOS-02.GIF

Charlie X

Episode #8
Teleplay: D.C. Fontana
Story: Gene Roddenberry
Director: Lawrence Dobkin
Stardate: 1533.6

Summary: At 17, Charlie Evans, the only survivor of a ship crash on the planet Thasus, is discovered and brought to the *Enterprise*. Having been given telekinetic skills by the Thasians during his solitude, Charlie cannot readjust.

I Wanna Stay Soundclip of

Charlie: "I wanna staaaaaaaay…" ✓**INTERNET**→*www* http://sunsite.sut.ac.jp/multimed/sounds/startrek/i_wanna_stay.au

Never Again Soundclip of Charlie: "I won't do it again. Please, I'll be good, I won't ever do it again!" ✓**INTERNET**→*www* http://sunsite.sut.ac.jp/multimed/sounds/startrek/never_again.au

Charlie X Episode scene. ✓**PVG** *dial* 513-233-7993→*<your username>*→*<your password>*→*F*→ *Download a file:* TOS-06.GIF

Where No Man Has Gone Before

Episode #2 (2nd pilot)
Writer: Samuel A. Peeples
Director: James Goldstone
Stardate: 1312.4

Summary: Most of the original cast makes its first appearance. Commander Gary Mitchell is transformed into something of a deity when an encounter with a force field enhances the psychic powers of some crew members.

Where No Man Has Gone Before Twenty scenes from the episode. ✓**COMPUSERVE**→*go sfmedia*→*Libraries*→*Search by file name:* TREK02.GIF

Dr. Elizabeth Dehner—from CompuServe's Sci-Fi Media Forum

The Naked Time

Episode #7
Writer: John D. F. Black
Director: Marc Daniels
Stardate: 1704.2

Summary: The *Enterprise* is infected by a virus from the planet Psi 2000 that removes the crew members' inhibitions, uncovering thoughts best left hidden.

The Enemy Within

Episode #5
Writer: Richard Matheson
Director: Leo Penn
Stardate: 1672.1

Summary: Talk about multiple-personality disorders. After a transporter malfunction, Kirk is literally split in two, one self brutal and domineering, the other weak and compassionate.

Enemy Within Episode Scene Picture of Kirk, Spock, and Scotty. ✓**PVG** *dial* 513-233-7993→<your username>→<your password>→ F→*Download a file:* OT16.GIF

Kirk on Trial Picture of Captain Kirk on trial. ✓**PVG** *dial* 513-233-7993→ <your username>→<your password>→F→*Download a file:* OTC01.GIF

Mudd's Women

Episode #4
Teleplay: Stephen Kandel
Story: Gene Roddenberry
Director: Harvey Hart
Stardate: 1329.8

Summary: The *Enterprise* rescues Harcourt Fenton Mudd, a space-age con-man, and his three gorgeous female companions. Needing to replenish dilithium crystals, the Enterprise heads to a mining colony where Mudd (whose extensive criminal record has been discovered by Kirk) attempts to trade the women for his freedom. The women's beauty—it is later discovered—is artificial, the result of "the Venus drug."

Mudd and Two Women Image of Harry Mudd sitting at a table with two beautiful women at his side. ✓**PVG** *dial* 513-233-7993→ <your username>→<your password>→F→*Download a file:* TOS-03.GIF

Mudd's Women Scenes Three scenes from the episode, including one with Mudd at the table with two women, another with three women transporting, and a third with Kirk and Mudd together. ✓**PVG** *dial* 513-233-7993→<your username>→<your password>→F→ *Download a file:* MUDDWMN. GIF

What Are Little Girls Made of?

Episode #10
Writer: Robert Bloch
Director: James Goldstone
Stardate: 2712.4

Summary: Dr. Roger Korby, once Nurse Chapel's fiancé, is discovered living in an android body and hatching plans to substitute Federation leaders with android duplicates.

Miri

Episode #12
Writer: Adrian Spies
Director: Vincent McEveety
Stardate: 2713.5

Summary: The *Enterprise* encounters a planet where a virus causes childhood to last hundreds of years, and puberty is a death sentence. The virus was created by adults—all dead now—who were seeking immortality. Dr. McCoy attempts to help Miri, a 300-year-old girl on the verge of puberty, by finding a cure.

"Miri"—from http://www.uvm.edu:80/ ~jfabian

Dagger of the Mind

Episode #11
Written: S. Bar-David
Director: Vincent McEveety
Stardate: 2715.1

Summary: An escaped patient of the Tantalus V penal colony convinces Kirk to investigate the facility's psychiatric treatment program. Is it a revolutionary cure or does it kill with loneliness?

The Corbomite Maneuver

Episode #3
Writer: Jerry Sohl
Director: Joseph Sargent
Stardate: 1512.2

Summary: Balok's ship, the *Fesarius*, captures the *Enterprise*. Unbeknownst to the *Enterprise* crew, this act of aggression is actually meant to gauge the Federation's intentions.

The Enterprise and Fesarius Picture of the *Enterprise* as it encounters alien spaceship in uncharted space. ✓**INTERNET**→*anon-ftp* <address 33>→lg-a21.jpg

The Menagerie, Parts I & II

Episode #16
Writer: Gene Roddenberry
Director: Marc Daniels
Stardate: 3012.4

Summary Part 1: Spock commandeers the *Enterprise* to deliver a maimed Captain Pike to Talos IV, a planet strictly off limits according to Federation regulations but where Pike could live out his life as if he were well. Episodes I and II use footage from the original *Star Trek* pilot, "The Cage."

Summary Part 2: Spock is court-martialled for his illegal flight to Talos IV. The trial scenes tell the story of Captain Pike and "The Cage."

Rigel VII Shot of Rigel VII—planet visited by former *Enterprise* captain Pike. ✓**INTERNET**→*anon-ftp* <address 33>→lg-g8.jpg

---

Starbase 6 Image of the starbase during a visit by the *Enterprise*. ✓**INTERNET**→*anon-ftp* <address 33>→ lg-a3.jpg

---

Vina Picture of Vina, the green Orion slave girl, dancing for Captain Pike of the original *Enterprise*. ✓**INTERNET** ...→*anon-ftp* <address 33>→lg-a15.jpg ...→*anon-ftp* <address 34>→lg-a15.jpg ✓**COMPU-SERVE**→*go* sfmedia→Libraries→ *Search by file name:* STO-01.GIF

Wrong Thinking Soundclip of head Talosian: "Wrong thinking is punishable. Right thinking will be as quickly rewarded." ✓**INTERNET**→ *www* http://sunsite.sut.ac.jp/mul timed/sounds/startrek/wrong_ thinking.au

Your Ship Soundclip of Head Talosian: "Your ship! Release me or we'll destroy it!" ✓**INTERNET**→ *www* http://sunsite.sut.ac.jp/multi med/sounds/startrek/your_ship. au

---

Menagarie Scenes A collage of classic scenes. ✓**PVG** *dial* 513-233-7993→<your username>→<your password>→F→*Download a file:* MENAG01.GIF

Vina—downloaded from CompuServe's Sci-Fi Media Forum

The Conscience of the King

Episode #13
Story :   Barry Trivers
Director: Gerd Oswald
Stardate: 2817.6

Summary: After a Shakespearean drama company comes aboard to entertain the crew, Kirk begins to suspect that the leader is none other than "Kodos the Executioner," who, 20 years earlier, had been responsible for the massacre of half the population of Tarsus IV. The episode borrows heavily from *Macbeth* and *Hamlet*.

The Conscience of the King

Scenes A collage of episode scenes. ✓**PVG** *dial* 513-233-7993→ <your username>→<your password>→F→*Download a file:* KING01.GIF

Scenes from The Conscience of the King Three scenes from the episode, including one of Kirk, Kodos, and Kodos's daughter. ✓**PVG** *dial* 513-233-7993→<your username>→<your password>→F→ *Download a file:* TOS-04.GIF

Balance of Terror

Episode #9
Writer: Paul Schneider
Director: Vincent McEveety
Stardate: 1709.1

Summary: The *Enterprise* encounters an invisible Romulan Bird of Prey and Kirk engages in a battle of wits with its commander.

Romulan Clash Scene with the Romulans. ✓**PVG** *dial* 513-233-7993→<your username>→<your password>→F→*Download a file:* PVBALANC.GIF

Shore Leave

Episode #17
Writer: Theodore Sturgeon
Director: Robert Sparr
Stardate: 3025.3

Summary: An examination of the adage, "be careful what you wish for": The *Enterprise*s' crew's fondest wishes come true when they travel to a planet where an advanced species turns dreams into nightmarish realities.

ASK SPOT!

In what two episodes does Captain Kirk give the order to self-destruct? *(See answers on page 359)*

Shore Leave Scenes Scenes from the episode. ✓**PVG** *dial* 513-233-7993→<your username>→<your password>→F→*Download a file:* SHORE.GIF

The Galileo Seven

Episode #14
Teleplay:	Oliver Crawford & S. Bar-David
Story:	Oliver Crawford
Stardate:	2821.5

Summary: Spock is forced to assume leadership when the *Galileo* shuttlecraft crashes on a hostile planet, stranding its seven occupants. The mantle of command weighs heavily on the logical Vulcan.

Galileo Seven Scenes Three images from the episode "Galileo Seven": one of Spock and Scotty, another of the crew on the shuttlecraft, and another of the Horta throwing rock. ✓**INTERNET** ...→ *www* http://nerys.ti1.tu-harburg.de /startrek/pics/Classic/pvtos13.gif ...→*www* ftp://ftp.informatik.uni-oldenburg.de/pub/startrek/pic tures/tos/pv tos13.gif

The Squire of Gothos

Episode #18
Writer:	Paul Schneider
Director:	Don McDougall
Stardate:	2124.5

Summary: A seemingly all-powerful alien named Trelane captures members of the *Enterprise* crew. They discover to their dismay that they have become the toys of a petulant, god-like child.

The Squire Image of William Campbell as the Squire of Gothos. ✓**PVG** *dial* 513-233-7993→<your username>→<your password>→F→ *Download a file:* CAMPBELL.GIF

Arena

Episode #19
Teleplay:	Gene L. Coon
Story:	Fredric Brown
Director:	Joseph Pevney
Stardate:	3045.6

Summary: After the *Enterprise* engages in a space chase with a Gorn ship, the Metrons transport Kirk and the reptilian Gorn captain to a deserted planet. The sentence: to resolve the conflict through a battle to the death.

Tomorrow Is Yesterday

Episode #21
Writer:	D. C. Fontana
Director:	Michael O'Herlihy
Stardate:	3113.2

Summary: A close encounter with a black star transports the *Enterprise* to the year 1967, and an Air Force pilot reports them as a U.F.O. The *Enterprise* must escape the Air Force and the twentieth century without doing anything that would change the past and thus alter the future.

Court-Martial

Episode #15
Teleplay:	Don M. Mankiewicz & Steven W. Carabatsos
Story:	Don M. Mankiewicz
Director:	Marc Daniels
Stardate:	2947.3

Summary: Kirk is tried for negligence in the death of a crewman. Things don't look good for the commander until Spock takes over the defense, proving that the crewman is not really dead.

Court-Martialed. Picture of Kirk on trial. ✓**PVG** *dial* 513-233-7993→<your username><your

password>→F→*Download a file:* TRIAL2.GIF

The Return of the Archons

Episode #22
Teleplay:	Boris Sobelman
Story:	Gene Roddenberry
Director:	Joseph Pevney
Stardate:	3156.2

STARNOTES

"When 'Let That Be Your Last Battlefield' first aired, I was a kid--8 or 9 years old. Busing for the purpose of integration had just begun in my school district, and the racial climate was terrible--many of the blacks and whites were angry about busing and took it out on each other. Parents fought, mainly with words, and kids fought, mainly with fists. Nothing seemed to matter but the color of your skin. I *hated* it. It was the first time that I was truly afraid to go to school. I had nightmares, especially after seeing LTBYLB--and it *wasn't* because of the writing. If the writing had been decent, perhaps I would be willing to overcome those memories and watch the episode anyway.

—from **AOL's Star Trek Message Board**

Summary: While searching for the starship *Archon*, the *Enterprise* finds a Beta III where a computer named Landru has absolute control over all inhabitants.

Space Seed

Episode #24
Teleplay: Gene L. Coon &
        Carey Wilber
Story: Carey Wilber
Director   Marc Daniels
Stardate: 3141.9

Summary: The *Enterprise* discovers the *S.S. Botany Bay* and its cargo, a group of genetic superhumans who have been sleeping since they fled the "Eugenics Wars" of the late 20th century.

Botany Bay Startupscreen Startupscreen for the Mac of the *Botany Bay* (the ship from 20th century Earth carrying the evil dictator Khan Noonien Singh) and the *Enterprise*. ✓ **COMPUSERVE**→ go sfmedia→Libraries→*Search by file name:* BOTANY.SIT

A Taste of Armageddon

Episode #23
Teleplay: Robert Hamner &
        Gene L. Coon
Story: Robert Hamner
Director: Joseph Pevney
Stardate: 3192.1

Summary: A war simulated by two computers claims the *Enterprise* as a casualty. To force a resolution, Kirk and Spock attempt to show the combatants the horror of total war.

The History of Eminiar VII A description of the events surrounding Eminiar VII's war with Vendikar. ✓ **GENIE**→*keyword* sfrt2→ Text and Graphics Library→*Down-*

load a file: 820

This Side of Paradise

Episode #25
Teleplay: D. C. Fontana
Story: Nathan Butler &
        D. C. Fontana
Director: Ralph Senensky
Stardate: 3417.3

Summary: Space lotus eaters. In order to remain on a planet that produces tranquility-inducing spores, the crew—including the usually rational Mr. Spock—mutinies against the unaffected Kirk.

Spock and Spores Picture of Spock being hit with tranquilizing spores. ✓ **PVG** *dial* 513-233-7993→ <your username>→<your password>→F→*Download a file:* OT03.GIF

Spock's in Love Image of Spock in love. ✓ **PVG** *dial* 513-233-7993→ <your username>→<your password>→F→*Download a file:* OTC09.GIF

The Devil in the Dark

Episode #26
Writer: Gene L. Coon
Director: Joseph Pevney
Stardate: 3196.1

Summary: A distress call brings the *Enterprise* to Janus VI, where miners are being terrorized by a rock-like creature with the ability to dissolve people's bodies. The crew discovers the devil is nothing more than a mother Horta doing what comes naturally—trying to protect her eggs.

Mind Meld In one of the four images on this file, Spock performs a mind-meld with the Horta. ✓ **IN-TERNET** ...→*anon-ftp* ftp.informatik. uni-oldenburg.de→/pub/startrek/

pictures/tos→pvtosqd1.gif ...→ *anon-ftp* ftp.sunet.se→/pub/pic tures/tv.film/StarTrek→ pvtosqd1.gif ...→*anon-ftp* ftp.fu-berlin.de→ /misc/sf/startrek/st-tos/pictures→ pvtosqd1.gif

Spock holds a Horta egg—downloaded from http://www.uvm.edu:80/~jfabian

Errand of Mercy

Episode #27
Writer: Gene L. Coon
Director: John Newland
Stardate: 3198.4

Summary: The warlike Klingons make their first appearance in the Trek universe. Kirk and Spock attempt to broker a peace agreement between Klingons and Organians, who refuse Federation assistance.

The Alternative Factor

Episode #20
Writer: Don Ingalls
Director: Gerd Oswald
Stardate: 3087.6

Summary: The *Enterprise* comes in contact with Lazarus, who, while appearing schizophrenic, is really in mortal combat with his counterpart from an anti-matter universe. The double has gained access through a rip in the space-time continuum.

Lazarus Closeup of Lazarus. ✓ **PVG** *dial* 513-233-7993→<your username>→<your password>→F→ *Download a file:* PVLAZRUS.GIF

The City on the Edge of Forever

Episode #28
Writer: Harlan Ellison
Director: Joseph Pevney
Stardate: 3134.0
Guest Star: Joan Collins

Summary: Rendered paranoid by an accidental overdose of the drug cordrazine, Dr. McCoy escapes through a time portal into Earth of 1930. Kirk and Spock must travel back in order to repair the terrible damage he has done to the future by, ironically, preventing the death of a lovely social worker.

Time Portal Picture of Kirk and Spock outside the time travel portal the Guardian of Forever. ✓**INTERNET**→*anon-ftp* <address 33>→ lg-b12.jpg

Operation Annihilate!

Episode #29
Writer: Steven W. Carabatsos
Director: Herschel Daugherty
Stardate: 3287.2

Summary: The *Enterprise* travels to the beautiful planet of Deneva only to discover that a parasite that destroys the nervous system has infected the inhabitants. Among the casualties are Kirk's brother and sister-in-law. Spock contracts the disease, but survives after being exposed to intense radiation.

Season 2

Amok Time

Episode #34
Writer: Theodore Sturgeon
Director: Joseph Pevney
Stardate: 3372.7

Summary: Responding to the Vulcan mating drive, "pon far," Spock returns to Vulcan to marry his betrothed, T'Pring. She demands that, to prove his worth, Spock fight to the death an opponent of her choosing—Kirk.

Amok Time Scene Scene from the episode. ✓**PVG** *dial* 513-233-7993→<your username>→<your password>→F→Download a file: OT08.GIF

Amok Time Scenes (bbs) Scenes from the episode "Amok Time." ✓**PVG** *dial* 513-233-7993→<your username>→<your password>→F→*Download a file:* AMOK.GIF

Who Mourns for Adonais?

Episode #33
Writer: Gilbert Ralston,
             Gene L. Coon
Director: Marc Daniels
Stardate: 3468.1

Summary: The Greek god Apollo holds members of the *Enterprise* crew hostage, demanding that they worship him.

Adonais In one of the images on this file, a towering Adonais stands over the *Enterprise* crew. ✓**INTERNET** ...→*anon-ftp* ftp.informatik.uni-oldenburg.de→/pub/startrek/pictures/tos→pvtosqd1.gif ...→ *anon-ftp* ftp.sunet.se→/pub/pictures/tv.film/StarTrek→pvtosqd1.gif ...→*anon-ftp* ftp.fu-berlin.de→/misc/sf/startrek/st-tos/pictures→pvtosqd1.gif

Who Mourns for Adonais Collage Nine scenes from the episode. ✓**PVG** *dial* 513-233-7993 →<your username>→<your password>→F→*Download a file:* ST TOS002.GIF

Apollo—from ftp.informatik.uni-oldenburg.de/pub/startrek/pictures/tos

The Changeling

Episode #37
Writer: John Meredyth Lucas
Director: Marc Daniels
Stardate: 3451.9

Summary: The *Nomad*, a probe launched from Earth centuries ago, has been altered by an alien life form and now travels the universe in search of "perfect" life, destroying all that fails to pass muster.

The Nomad Image of Kirk and the *Nomad*. ✓**PVG** *dial* 513-233-7993→<your username>→<your password>→F→*Download a file:* OT18.GIF

Uhura Scene featuring Lt. Uhura. ✓**PVG** *dial* 513-233-7993→<your username>→<your password>→F→*Download a file:* CHNGLNG.GIF

Mirror, Mirror

Episode #39
Writer: Jerome Bixby
Director: Marc Daniels
Stardate: unknown

Summary: A transporter error switches Kirk, McCoy, Scott, and Uhura with their counterparts from a parallel, and evil, universe. The duplicate Spocks work simultaneously to undo the exchange.

Captain Kirk Captain Kirk

checks out Marlena in a black and white GIF. ✓**COMPUSERVE**→*go* sfmedia→Libraries→*Search by file name:* KIRK.GIF

Mr. Spock Image of Mr. Spock from the alternate universe. ✓**COMPUSERVE**→*go* sfmedia→Libraries→*Search by file name:* BAD SPO.GIF

Enterprise Emerges GIF of the *Enterprise*, leaving the negative universe. ✓**PVG** *dial* 513-233-7993→<your username>→<your password>→F→*Download a file:* NEGUNIV. GIF

Mirror Mirror Scene Picture of Kirk and his evil twin. ✓**PVG** *dial* 513-233-7993→<your username>→<your password>→F→*Download a file:* OT01.GIF

Scenes from Mirror, Mirror Nine scenes from the episode. ✓**PVG** *dial* 513-233-7993→<your username>→<your password>→F→*Download a file:* STTOS003.GIF

The Apple

Episode #38
Writer: Max Ehrlich,
             Gene L. Coon
Director: Joseph Pevney
Stardate: 3715.0

Summary: While on the paradisiacal planet of Gamma Trianguli VI, the *Enterprise* earns the enmity of the computer ruler Vaal, which bitterly resents "outside interference" with any of its humanoid subjects.

The Doomsday Machine

Episode #35
Writer: Norman Spinrad
Director: Marc Daniels
Stardate: 4202.9

Summary: After destroying its planet of origin, a huge spaceship travels through the universe annihilating everything in its path, including starships (using their wreckages for fuel).

Doomsday Machine Picture of the Doomsday Machine. ✓**INTERNET**→*anon-ftp* <address 33>→lg-d2.jpg

Doomsday Machine Scenes Sixteen scenes from the episode. ✓**PVG** *dial* 513-233-7993→<your username>→<your password>→F→*Download a file:* STH00.GIF

The Doomsday Machine—downloaded from ftp.cis.ksu.edu

Catspaw

Episode #30
Writer: Robert Bloch
Director: Joseph Pevney
Stardate: 3018.2

Summary: On Pyris VII, a witch and a warlock imprison crew members in a haunted castle. They use magical powers to gain advanced scientific knowledge from the *Enterprise*.

I, Mudd

Episode #41
Writer: Stephen Kandel,
             David Gerrold

Director: Marc Daniels
Stardate: 4513.3

Summary: An android hijacks the *Enterprise* and delivers it to Kirk's old enemy, Harcourt Mudd, who now rules a planet populated by beautiful android women.

Metamorphosis

Episode #31
Writer: Gene L. Coon
Director: Ralph Senensky
Stardate: 3219.4

Summary: The *Galileo* shuttlecraft is mysteriously drawn down to an isolated planet, where Kirk, Spock, and McCoy discover Zefram Cochrane, the inventor of warp drive. Long presumed dead, Cochrane is under the care of a gaseous cloud life-form called "the Companion," which in its love for Cochrane has captured the *Enterprise* crew to alleviate the great scientist's loneliness.

Journey to Babel

Episode #44
Writer: D. C. Fontana
Director: Joseph Pevney
Stardate: 3842.3

Summary: The *Enterprise* transports delegates to a Federation convention. Things begin to go amiss when one of the delegates, Spock's estranged father, falls ill and needs a transfusion.

Friday's Child

Episode #32

ASK SPOT!

In what episode does Dr. McCoy remark, "What am I, a doctor or a moon shuttle conductor?"

(See answers on page 359)

Writer: D. C. Fontana
Director: Joseph Pevney
Stardate: 3497.2

Summary: Negotiations with Klingons over mining rights on Capella IV turn sour when McCoy accidentally offends the hosts, by breaking a cultural taboo when he touches one of the women.

Kirk the Hostage Picture of Captain Kirk as a hostage. ✓**PVG** *dial* 513-233-7993→<*your username*>→<*your password*>→F→ *Download a file:* OTC05.GIF

The Deadly Years

Episode #40
Writer: David P. Harmon
Director: Joseph Pevney
Stardate: 3478.2

Summary: After being exposed to some strange form of radiation, all but Chekov—saved by the adrenalin of shock—suffer from an extreme acceleration in aging. The navigator must discover a cure for his companions as they rapidly pass through senility toward death.

Mind Meld In one of the four images on this file, an unnaturally-aged Kirk leans forward. ✓**INTERNET** ...→*anon-ftp* ftp.informatik.uni-oldenburg.de→/pub/startrek/pictures/tos→pvtosqd1.gif ...→*anon-ftp* ftp.sunet.se→/pub/pictures/tv.film/StarTrek→ pvtosqd1.gif ...→*anon-ftp* ftp.fu-berlin.de→/misc/sf/startrek/st-tos/pictures→pvtosqd1.gif

---

Aging Kirk and McCoy Picture of a rapidly aging Captain Kirk and Dr. McCoy. ✓**PVG** dial 513-233-7993→<*your username*>→<*your password*>→F→*Download a file:* PVTOS12.GIF

Aging Scotty Closeup of an aged Scotty. ✓**PVG** dial 513-233-7993→<*your username*>→<*your password*>→F→*Download a file:* PVSCOTY3.GIF

Obsession

Episode #47
Writer: Art Wallace
Director: Ralph Senensky
Stardate: 3619.2

Summary: Kirk ignores all other duties as he tries to destroy a vampire cloud that lives on the red corpuscles of humans. The cloud killed 200 people during Kirk's first Starfleet assignment, deaths for which he feels some responsibility.

Wolf in the Fold

Episode #36
Writer: Robert Bloch
Director: Joseph Pevney
Stardate: 3614.9

Summary: Scotty is suspected of the brutal slaying of several women. The true slayer is a non-corporeal serial killer, who left a grisly trail of unsolved murders in 19th-century London: Jack the Ripper.

The Trouble with Tribbles

Episode #42
Writer: David Gerrold
Director: Joseph Pevney
Stardate: 4523.3

Summary: While picking up a shipment of grain at K-7, the *Enterprise* acquires from trader Cyrano Jones an adorable furry creature called a Tribble. Unfortunately, Tribbles reproduce at an astounding rate and the ship is soon overrun with the fuzzballs.

Captain Kirk and Tribbles Picture of Kirk buried in tribbles in the *Enterprise* replicator. ✓ **INTERNET** →*anon-ftp* <address 33>→lg-t4.jpg ✓ **COMPUSERVE**→*go* sfmedia→ Libraries→*Search by file name:* CPTKRK.GIF

Uhura & a Tribble Picture of Uhura holding a Tribble. ✓ **PVG** *dial* 513-233-7993→<your username>→<your password>→F→ *Download a file:* UHURA.GIF

The Gamesters of Triskelion

Episode #46
Writer: Margaret Armen
Director: Gene Nelson
Stardate: 3211.7

Summary: Kirk, Uhura, and Chekov are captured and transported to a planet where they must fight to the death as gladiators while the invisible rulers place wagers on the contests.

A Piece of the Action

Episode #49
Teleplay: David P. Harmon & Gene L. Coon
Story: David P. Harmon
Director: James Komack
Stardate: 4598.0

Summary: On a visit to a developing planet, Kirk finds that a previous Federation visit left behind a book glorifying the heyday of the Chicago mobsters—a book the inhabitants have adopted as their social model. Kirk tries to undo the effects of this unfortunate cross-cultural exchange.

The Immunity Syndrome

Episode #48
Writer: Robert Sabaroff
Director: Joseph Pevney
Stardate: 4307.1

Summary: Investigating the destruction of all life in the Gamma 7A star system and the Vulcan ship *Intrepid*, the *Enterprise* discovers that the culprit is a massive amoeba-like creature that feeds on the energy in "life." Spock uses the shuttlecraft to probe the alien.

A Private Little War

Episode #45
Teleplay: Gene Roddenberry
Story: Jud Crucis
Director: Marc Daniels
Stardate: 4211.4

Summary: A peaceful planet's civil debate escalates into violence when the Klingons arm one faction. Kirk must decide whether to preserve equity by arming the other tribe, thus changing their society forever.

Return to Tomorrow

Episode #51
Writer: John Kingsbridge
Director: Ralph Senensky
Stardate: 4768.3

Summary: Disembodied alien minds inhabit Kirk and Spock in order to construct android bodies for themselves. However, when the time comes to return what they have borrowed, the mind in Spock refuses to leave.

Discovering the Beings Image of Spock, Kirk, McCoy, and Dr. Ann Mulhall discovering the preserved minds of three powerful and brilliant survivors of a devastating war more than half a million years ago. ✓ **PVG** *dial* 513-233-7993→<your username>→<your password>→F→*Download a file:* tomrw1.gif

Henoch and Thalassa Picture of Spock (occupied by the mind of Henoch) attempting to seduce Dr. Ann Mulhall (occupied by the mind of Thalassa). ✓ **PVG** *dial* 513-233-7993→<your username>→<your password>→F→*Download a file:* TOMRW2.GIF

Patterns of Force

Episode #52
Writer: John Meredyth Lucas
Director: Vincent McEveety
Stardate: 2534.0

Summary: The *Enterprise* crew discovers that a Federation historian living on a distant planet has disregarded the Prime Directive and undertaken a sinister experiment: To restore order, he has modelled the planet's society on Nazi Germany.

ASK SPOT!

a) What groundbreaking and at the time controversial action occurred in "Plato's Stepchildren?"

b) What is the name of the Tholian commander who first attacked the *Enterprise*?

c) In what episode does Spock say, "For the first time in my life—I was happy"?

(See answers on page 359)

By Any Other Name

Episode #50
Teleplay: D. C. Fontana &
Jerome Bixby
Story: Jerome Bixby
Director: Marc Daniels
Stardate: 4657.5

Summary: Kelvans from the Andromeda galaxy scouting for new colonies take over the *Enterprise* in order to make their journey home.

The Omega Glory

Episode #54
Writer: Gene Roddenberry
Director: Vincent McEveety
Stardate: n/a

Summary: The *Enterprise* stumbles upon the deserted starship *Exeter* orbiting Omega IV. On the planet's surface they discover that the *Exeter's* captain, believing the planet holds the secret to eternal youth, has taken sides in a civil war of Kohms against Yangs, with disastrous results.

The Ultimate Computer

Episode #53
Teleplay: D. C. Fontana
Story: Laurence N. Wolfe
Director: John Meredyth Lucas
Stardate: 4729.4

Summary: The *Enterprise* tests a new computer designed to replace the captain. The inventor, Dr. Richard Daystrom, has built in some unconventional features, and the computer begins playing a war game as if it were real.

Bread and Circuses

Episode #43
Writers: Gene Roddenberry &
Gene L. Coon

Story: John Knebuhl
Director: Ralph Senensky
Stardate: 4040.7

Summary: Kirk, Spock, and McCoy find themselves trapped on a planet that is equipped with space-age technology, but that at the same time echoes the last days of the Roman Empire, with gladiators and lions. The citizens also worship "the sun god."

Assignment: Earth

Episode #55
Teleplay: Art Wallace
Story: Gene Roddenberry &
Art Wallace
Director: Marc Daniels
Stardate: Not Given

Summary: Kirk and Spock travel back in time and join forces with Gary Seven, a human visitor from a far-off galaxy, to help the Earth dodge the dangers of the atomic age, circa 1968 (the same year the show was originally aired).

Assignment Earth (bbs)
Episode scene. ✓**PVG** *dial* 513-233-7993→<your username>→<your password>→F→Download a file:→ASNMNT.GIF

Season 3

Spock's Brain

Episode #61
Writer: Lee Cronin
Director: Marc Daniels
Stardate: 5431.4

Summary: The perils of being too logical: A young woman kidnaps Spock's brain in order to use it to replace the 10,000-year-old operating system that runs her planet.

"Where was I when Star Trek: The Original Series premiered? Hiding in my bedroom because the Salt Monster scared me silly. Hey, I was nine years old and a confirmed scaredy-cat. I made it a point never to be in the same HOUSE, let alone the same room, as a TV set on which 'The Outer Limits' was playing. (Since my dad never missed that show, I spent a lot of time out on the porch.... It took another two weeks and a LOT of assurances from my father that this 'Star Trek' thing was a really good show and not just a monster-of-the-week showcase. That guy with the strange ears put me off for about thirty minutes but after that, I was cool."

"I remember sitting on the floor in front of the coffee table with my head held up by my hands and I don't think that I blinked for the whole hour.... I wrote my first fan letter that night to Leonard Nimoy."

—from GEnie's Star Trek: The Original Series

Brain Gone Soundclip of Dr. McCoy: "His brain is gone!" ✓ **INTERNET**→*www* http://sunsite.sut.ac.jp/multimed/sounds/startrek/brain_gone.au

Restore a Brain Soundclip of Dr. McCoy: "No one can restore a brain!" ✓ **INTERNET**→*www* http://sunsite.sut.ac.jp/multimed/sounds/startrek/restore_brain.au

The Enterprise Incident

Episode #59
Writer: D. C. Fontana
Director: John Meredyth Lucas
Stardate: 5031.3

Summary: Disguised as Romulans, Kirk and Spock board a Romulan vessel with plans to steal a new cloaking device, but run afoul of a powerful woman captain.

Enterprise Incident Scenes Episode scenes. ✓ **PVG** *dial* 513-233-7993→<your username>→<your password>→F→*Download a file:* INCIDNT.GIF

The Paradise Syndrome

Episode #58
Writer: Margaret Armen
Director: Jud Taylor
Stardate: 4842.6

Summary: The *Enterprise* attempts to prevent an asteroid from destroying a planet populated by a culture descended from American Indians. Their mission is complicated when Kirk, suffering from amnesia, marries one of the native women.

And the Children Shall Lead

Episode #60

Writer: Edward J. Lasko
Director: Marvin Chomsky
Stardate: 5029.5
Guest Star: Melvin Belli

Summary: The crew is astonished by a colony of children who are peaceful and contented, despite the fact their parents have been killed. It all becomes clear when they realize that the children are being controlled by Gorgan, a noncorporeal being who murdered the adults and now has designs on the *Enterprise*.

Is There in Truth No Beauty?

Episode #62
Writer: Jean Lisette Aroeste
Director: Ralph Senensky
Stardate: 5630.7

Summary: Kolos, a Medusan so ugly that the sight of him can drive a person mad, comes aboard the *Enterprise* with his escort: a beautiful, blind woman.

Spock and Dr. Jones Image of Spock and Dr. Miranda Jones with red visors standing over the container with the Medusan. ✓ **INTERNET**→*anon-ftp* ftp.informatik.uni-oldenburg.de→/pub/startrek/pictures/tos→sttos02.jpg

Spectre of the Gun

Episode # 56
Writer: Lee Cronin
Director: Vincent McEveety
Stardate: 4385.3

Summary: The *Enterprise* crew finds itself on a mysterious planet, in the midst of a replay of the notorious shoot-out at the O. K. Corral. There's only one problem: they are playing the characters on the losing side.

Day of the Dove

Episode #66
Writer: Jerome Bixby
Director: Marvin Chomsky

Summary: An alien that feeds on hatred plays on the enmity between Klingons and the Federation, hoping to have a memorable, if malevolent, meal. Kirk and the Klingon commander prevent an all-encompassing blood-bath and spoil the alien's feast.

For the World Is Hollow and I Have Touched the Sky

Episode #65
Writer: Rik Vollaerts
Director: Tony Leader
Stardate: 5476.3

Summary: Talk about lovesick. The *Enterprise* discovers that an asteroid about to destroy a Federation planet is a ship full of "sleepers" on their way to a new home. Aboard the dying ship, Dr. McCoy contracts a fatal disease and falls in love.

The Tholian Web

Episode #64
Writer: Judy Burns & Chet Richards
Director: Ralph Senensky
Stardate: 5693.2

Summary: When Kirk disappears into a rift between two universes, the *Enterprise*'s search brings them into Tholian space, where the ship is entrapped in a powerful web-like forcefield.

Trapped Enterprise Picture of the original *Enterprise* caught in the Tholian Web. ✓ **INTERNET**→*anon-ftp* <address 33>→lg-d2.jpg

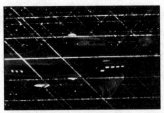

Enterprise caught in the Tholian Web—from anon-ftp <address 33>

Plato's Stepchildren

Episode #67
Writer: Meyer Dolinsky
Director: David Alexander
Stardate: 5784.2

Summary: A bogus distress call leads the *Enterprise* to a planet where the inhabitants use their psychokinetic powers to imprison the crew. But the crew has the last laugh when the ruler's dwarf jester comes to their aid.

Kirk & Uhura Picture of Kirk and Uhura. ✓**PVG** *dial* 513-233-7993→<your username>→<your password>→F→*Download a file:* PLATO.GIF

Wink of an Eye

Episode #68
Teleplay: Arthur Heineann
Story: Lee Cronin
Director: Jud Taylor
Stardate: 5710.5

Summary: The Scalosians, whose accelerated metabolism enables them to travel faster than the human eye can see, kidnap Kirk with hopes that he will breed with Scalosian women and put an end to their planet's rapid depopulation.

The Empath

Episode #63
Writer: Joyce Muskat

Director: John Erman
Stardate: 5121.0

Summary: An exploding star threatens two planets, one of them inhabited by a race of empathic beings. Powerful aliens capable of saving one of the two planets test the empathic race by forcing a mute empath named Gem to prove her race's worth. Gem's test will be her willingness to endure suffering and give her own life for those of strangers—Kirk, Spock, and McCoy—by empathically healing the injuries inflicted on them by the powerful aliens.

Elaan of Troyius

Episode #57
Writer: John Meredyth Lucas
Director: John Meredyth Lucas
Stardate: 4372.5

Summary: The *Enterprise* plays matchmaker to a truculent young woman, Elaan, the Dohlman of Elas, transporting her to Troyius where she is to enter into a marriage to bring peace to the warring planets. Her tears have a powerful effect on men—they fall in love with her. Kirk, of course, falls under her spell. The episode borrows on the play *The Taming of the Shrew* and the myth of Helen of Troy.

Whom Gods Destroy

Episode #71
Written: Lee Erwin
Story: Jerry Sohl, Lee Erwin
Director: Herb Wallerstein
Stardate: 5718.3

Summary: While delivering medicine to an insane asylum on Elbu II, Kirk and Spock encounter a former starship captain with shape-shifting powers who plans to take over the *Enterprise*.

Let that Be Your Last Battlefield

Episode #70
Teleplay: Oliver Crawford
Story: Lee Cronin
Director: Jud Taylor
Stardate: 5730.2

Summary: Clear as black and white. The population of Planet Cheron destroys itself in a violent racial war, in which one side (black on the left, white on the right) battles the other (colors reversed) to the death. The last two survivors carry their deep animosity aboard ship.

The Mark of Gideon

Episode #72
Writer: George F. Slavin & Stanley Adams
Director: Jud Taylor
Stardate: 5423.4

Summary: While attempting to visit the planet Gideon, Kirk suddenly finds himself in a deserted *Enterprise*. He is in reality being held in a duplicate *Enterprise* by the planet's occupants, who believe that he can help save them from their desperate plight of overpopulation.

That Which Survives

Episode #69
Teleplay: John Meredyth Lucas
Story: Michael Richards
Director: Herb Wallerstein
Stardate: n/a
Guest Star: Lee Meriwether

Summary: The *Enterprise* discovers a beautiful woman, Losira, on a deserted planet, only to be terrorized by her: A sentry for a vanished race, she can kill with a touch.

> **"Leave bigotry in your quarters; there's no room for it on the bridge."**
>
> —Kirk, "Balance of Terror"

Net Source: TOS Quote Generator—*http://www.cosy.sbg.ac.at/ftp/pub/trek/quotes/st4_tvh.txt*

The Lights of Zetar

Episode #73
Writer: Jeremy Tarcher &
             Share Lewis
Director: Herb Kenwith
Stardate: 5725.3

Summary: As the *Enterprise* travels to the Federation's library facility, Memory Alpha, Lt. Mira Romaine's body is invaded by pulsating lights, an alien life-form that doesn't want to be displaced.

Requiem for Methuselah

Episode #76
Writer: Jerome Bixby
Director: Murray Golden
Stardate: 5843.7

Summary: While searching for a cure for Rigelian fever, the *Enterprise* comes in contact with Flint, an immortal man who existed in the past as Brahms, da Vinci, and other great artists. In a replay of Pygmalion and Galatea, he creates the "perfect" woman—who proceeds to fall in love with the perennial love-object, Kirk.

The Way to Eden

Episode #75
Teleplay: Arthur Heinemann
Story: Michael Richards &
             Arthur Heinemann
Director: David Alexander
Stardate: 5832.3

Summary: A group, led by a brilliant engineer carrying a deadly disease, has decided to start a new life without technology. To do so, they hijack the *Enterprise* (with little resistance from the crew) to take them to the mythical planet of Eden. But there's a serpent in the garden. The band bear more than a passing resemblance to 20th-century "hippies."

The Cloud Minders

Episode #74
Teleplay: Margaret Armen
Story: David Gerrold & Oliver
             Crawford
Director: Jud Taylor
Stardate: 5818.4

Summary: The *Enterprise* crew travels to Ardana to obtain zenite to battle a botanical plague, only to be embroiled in a terrorist action by a cave-dwelling class of citizens against the overlords who reside in Stratos, a ravishing city in the clouds. Spock becomes involved with the daughter of the leader of the ruling class in the clouds, while Kirk is attracted to the cave-dwelling Vanna.

The Savage Curtain

Episode #77
Teleplay: Gene Roddenberry &
             Arthur Heinemann
Story: Gene Roddenberry
Director: Herschel Daugherty
Stardate: 5906.4

Summary: Beings who want to study good and evil transport Kirk and Spock to a deserted planet where they join forces with Abraham Lincoln and Vulcan hero Surak to battle four evil historical forces.

All Our Yesterdays

Episode #78
Writer: Jean Lisette Aroeste
Director: Marvin Chomsky
Stardate: 5943.7

Summary: Kirk, Spock, and McCoy come to the rescue of inhabitants of Sarpeidon (which is about to be destroyed by a supernova) and find that the race has developed a time machine that will transport individuals to a time period of choice in the planet's history. Kirk gets trapped in a time of witch trials, and Spock and McCoy get trapped in the ice age, where Spock falls in love with Zarabeth, an exile, punished for the crimes of her family. She's destined to live alone for the span of her lifetime, unless Spock stays.

Zarabeth Picture of the lonely Zarabeth. ✓**PVG** *dial* 513-233-7993→ <your username>→<your password>→F→*Download a file:* MHARTLEY.GIF

Turnabout Intruder

Episode #79
Teleplay: Arthur H. Singer
Story   Gene Roddenberry
Director: Herb Wallerstein
Stardate: 5298.5

Summary: Dr. Janice Lester, a Starfleet rival of Kirk's, uses a life-energy transfer device to insert her consciousness into Kirk's body so that she can take control of the *Enterprise*.

Beginning the voyage

Turn on the TV. Watch for the *Enterprise*. Marvel at Kirk and Spock. Dream Gene's

dream. For many *Star Trek* fans, the original series remains the best of the bunch, the one that most successfully combined the conventions of the science-fiction genre with the social vision of the sixties. And many of them are quite vocal about their allegiance. In AOL's **Classic Trek**, the spacey spirit of the series lives on, as it does on Prodigy's **Clubs: Original Series**, Delphi's **TOS—The Original Series**, and GEnie's **Star Trek: The Original Series**. Was Kirk a hero or an antihero? Was Spock the single greatest pointy-eared character in sixties television? And why do some of the aliens look like bit players with throw rugs safety-pinned to their heads? If cartoons are more your speed—bright colors and the voices of the original cast make for hours of incomparable fun—check out the **List of TAS Episodes**, which catalogs every half-hour of the early seventies animated *Star Trek*.

The Enterprise—*downloaded from Perfect Vision Graphics BBS*

On the Net

Classic Trek As one topic thread proudly boasts, "There is only *Star Trek*—all the rest are pale imi-

tations." If you think that Picard and company are pretenders to the throne, spend time in AOL's Classic Trek message board.

Fans are invited to post lists of their three favorite TOS episodes, share their opinions on McCoy, and calculate stardates. One participant even defends the early-seventies animated series as a more canonical show than *Next Generation*: "TAS is more *Star Trek* than the *Next Generation* simply by affiliation of the likes of DC Fontana, David Gerold, and a number of other writers who wrote for the original series, as well as the vocal talents of most of the original cast, save Walter." ✓**AMERICA ONLINE**→*keyword* trek →Star Trek Message Boards→Classic Trek

Clubs: Original Series You may be recruited for a TOS role-playing game here or, perhaps, in some twisted, parallel universe type of theme, you can band together with other evil crew members and plot. ✓**PRODIGY**→*jump* star trek

bb→Choose a Topic→Clubs: Orig Series

Judy Fabian's Star Trek Page Exclusively devoted to the original series, this Website offers a new selection of episode images and soundclips each month. ✓**INTERNET** →*www* http://www.uvm.edu:80 /~jfabian/

rec.arts.startrek.current/rec. arts.startrek.misc (ng) There's the usual grousing from Trek dinos about how much better things were in the "old days" of *Star Trek*: "One problem with TNG and DS9 is that they are prisoners of their special effects. TOS wasn't afraid to show a variety of alien life-forms. TNG is so concerned that everything has to look 'realistic' that every alien ends up as a guy with ridges on his head. There are very few Horta-type aliens on TNG—I mean, almost anything that isn't a guy with forehead ridges. I personally didn't care that the Horta looked like a guy crawling around under a rug. The story

THE ANIMATED SERIES

Guide to Animated Series Episode guide to the animated series that includes credits and plot summaries. ✓**INTERNET**→ *www* http://www.cosy.sbg.ac.at/ftp/pub/trek/guide/star-trek-animated.guide.txt

List of TAS episodes The Tribbles are back, a goddess is sending messages, and—surprise, surprise—the *Enterprise* travels back in time. This is a concise list of episodes in the animated television series with a Trek theme. ✓**INTERNET**→*www* http://www.cosy.sbg.ac.at/ftp/pub/trek/lists/stfafl/tas.txt

Relevance of the Animated Series Only cartoons? Not quite. Most episodes of TAS contributed new information about the Trek universe that later Trek

writers and producers built on, rationalized, or just took for granted. If you haven't watched TAS, this is a quick reference guide to two-dimensional Trek facts and events you probably shouldn't have missed. ✓**TFDN**→ TFDN Technical Files→*Download a file:* TAS.ZIP

Star Trek Animated Series Episode Guide A show history, a list of credits and crew voices, and paragraph-length plot summaries of each episode of Trek's animated series. ✓**INTERNET**→ *anon-ftp* elbereth.rutgers.edu→/pub/sfl→startrek-animated.guide

Trekker_Animated (echo) Dedicated to discussion of *Star Trek: the Animated Series.* Activity is very low and relatively two-dimensional. ✓**TREKKERNET**

25-year-old decisions to ignore the Prime Directive. Consider character motivations and battle strategy (resolution not guaranteed) in the Briefing Room, topic 14. There is even joy in discussing the "Bottom Ten TOS Episodes," glorious and beloved in their failure. Nostalgia and regret run rampant in topic 17 "Season Four, 1969, What If?" What strange new worlds could the *Enterprise* have explored? The guardians of Trek canon feel comfortable here, reveling in the "way it was meant to be." ✓**GENIE**→*keyword* sfrt2→SFRT2 Bulletin Board→set 25

Star Trek: The Original Show The area on eWorld designated for TOS talk, but damned if we could find anyone with anything to say—maybe they're off mind-melding. ✓**EWORLD**→sf→Star Trek→On the Small Screen→Star Trek: The Original Show

TOS—The Original Series If you're tired of hearing a bunch of GenX know-nothings rant about the superiority of Picard over Kirk, head over to Delphi's topic covering the original series. It's one of the few places where you'll find a fan willing to admit having purchased an album with songs sung by Leonard Nimoy and William Shatner. He traded it for "$3 in beer money." Another die-hard fan confessed, "I've STILL got Nimoy's *Outer Space Inner Mind* album!"

The Trekkies here have a true fondness for the original series, and they're not afraid to let their feelings show. "I might occasionally pillory TOS for being a bit too corny and for an overgrown adolescent as captain," one of them said, "but in the end it was a ground-breaking series that forever changed the face of SF TV. That we can still watch TOS nearly 30

was really interesting."

As the granddaddy of the Trek universe, newsgroup posters use TOS often as the touchstone for discussion about Trek's current and future. What has changed? What has stayed the same? And does the center (of the Trek universe) still hold? In most cases, it does—few people on the newsgroups would disagree that the first series has not only stood up to the test of time, but is remarkable in its flexibility and originality.

If there's a cause célèbre among TOSers on the Net, however, it's that of Hikaru Sulu, former lieutenant, current captain of the *Excelsior*. Most readers agree that he and his ship deserve a series, a film, or at the very least a television special or miniseries of their own. "I have long thought a made-for-TV movie featuring cap-

tain Sulu would be an excellent idea," writes one rec.arts.startrek.misc'er. "Certainly it would be fun to bring together various TOS characters as other posters to rec.arts.startrek* have suggested. Whether or not other TOS characters appear, however, I believe that the best use of a Sulu series would be to fill in some of the history in the 70 years between TOS and TNG—perhaps a story involving the much-neglected Romulans, for instance." Now if only Rick Berman read rec.arts.startrek.misc. ✓**USENET**

Star Trek: The Original Series "Where were you when the original *Star Trek* series premiered?" (see topic two for personal responses from Trek fans who define themselves with this lifetime milestone). Reopen discussions about

years later is a testament to the Great Bird's vision." ✓**DELPHI**→*go* ent sta for set tos

Trekker_TOS (echo) Donna tells the conference about a new singing group called the Spock Pistons whose members dress up like Mr. Spock and sing Piston songs. Everybody's talking about Shatner's future, Kirk's love interests, and Kirk's (oops! Shatner's) convention appearances. ✓**TREK-KERNET**

TV: Original Series Not very active, but there's a Chekov fan club, news about the stations airing original episodes, and questions about episodes that fans have recently rewatched. When James pointed out that Kirk's middle initial was written differently ("R" instead of "T") on a tombstone in the episode "Where No Man Has Gone Before," it was confirmed as a Roddenberry error by some and ridiculed as a well-known mistake by others. How could you, James? And how could you, Great Bird? ✓**PRODIGY**→*jump* star trek bb→ Choose a Topic→TV: Original Series

WS_STTOS (echo) Less active than the WarpSPEED conferences on *Deep Space Nine* and *The Next Generation*, this conference occasionally comes to life with speculation about, for instance, the relationship between Dr. McCoy and Mr. Spock or the color of Spock's blood. One serious Vulcan hematologist offers this account of the pointy-eared one: "Spock's blood is copper-based, therefore it is green. If you read the book *Spock's World*. it is discussed how Spock's conception required Genetic Engineering due to Vulcan/Human DNA incompatibility." ✓**WARP-SPEED**

Spock and Kirk—downloaded from ftp. cis.ksu.edu

CYBERTREKKERS

Otto "Hack-Man" Heuer
Age 29; Minneapolis, MN

Maintains more than 20 FAQ lists, Hack-Man's TOS Guide, and Usenet's Trek Rate database

"I get together monthly with a group of people who enjoy Science Fiction to see SF movies or just to sit around and drink."

Favorite Series: TOS & TNG

Favorite Characters: Data, Riker, and Dax

Favorite Episode: "The Best of Both World, Part I "(TNG)

"It was the only TNG episode to use music effectively. It showed that Riker had command presence. The ending actually gave me goose bumps—something no other episode, or any other TV show/movie has been able to do."

Other Online Interests: Pro-wrestling, TV, Video, and Movies.

Mission statement: "I always feel good when I go on a three week vacation and come back to 1000+ email messages from people (newbies thanking me for all the info, long-timers who wonder where I've been, people sending in useful information on the future of *Star Trek*, etc.). I like the fact that there is a worldwide way for people to discuss information on *Star Trek*. I don't think my enjoyment of *Star Trek* in all its flavors would be nearly as great if I didn't have all these people offering different opinions."

Email Address: heuer004@gold.tc.umn.edu

The original crew

The decades since have brought us Picard and Riker, Kira and Dax, but there's nothing

quite like the original *Star Trek* cast for pure entertainment value. Kirk, the cowboy captain, who made impetuosity and libido chic in outer space. Spock, the droll and hyperrational Vulcan. And don't forget the virtual United Nations that served as the supporting cast—Chekov, Sulu, Uhura, Scotty, and McCoy. Whether you want to collect pictures of **Chekov** or recall McCoy's **"I'm a Doctor, Not a..." Sayings**, there are plenty of sites on the Net to meet your needs. And all TOS fans are urged to visit **Spock Goes Kirk**, in which the Vulcan morphs into the Captain thanks to the miracle of modern technology.

TOS crew—downloaded from http://www.cosy.sbg.ac.at/ftp/pub/trek/pics

On the Net

Across the board

Actors Who Played Multiple Roles Did you notice that the troublesome Squire of Gothos looked a lot like the bearer of those troublesome Tribbles, Captain Koloth? This is a list of actors (and their roles) who played more than one role in TOS. ✓**COMPUSERVE**→go sfmedia→Libraries→*Search by file name:* DEJAVU.ZIP

Alphabetical List of Performers in Star Trek (The Original TV Series) Lee Meriwether played Losira in "That Which Survives," Kathryn Hays played Gem in "The Empath," Teri Garr played Roberta Lincoln in "Assignment Earth," Joan Collins played Edith Keeler in "The City on the Edge of Forever," and William Campbell played Captain Koloth in "The Corbomite Maneuver" and Trelane in "Squire of Gothos." But, it's not just the well-known that are listed here. Stuntmen to stars are listed with their guest roles. ✓**AMERICA ONLINE**→keyword trek→MORE...→Star Trek Record Banks→Text/Other Files→Upld: 11/21/93→TEXT: TOS Actor List (Filename: TREK.TXT)

Scott & Kirk Picture of Engineer Montgomery Scott with Captain Kirk. ✓**PVG** *dial* 513-233-7993→F→Download a file: PVTOS09.GIF

TOS Cast Updates What are they doing now? News and gossip about the former crew of the *NCC-1701.* This document is updated through the *Generations* movie. ✓**INTERNET**→www http://www.cgd.ucar.edu/cms/zecca/trek/tos.html

TOS Crew The quintessential picture of the original series crew on the *Enterprise*—from Nurse Chapel to Spock to Chekov—and, of course, Kirk. ✓**INTERNET**→www http://www.cosy.sbg.ac.at/ftp/pub/trek/pics/toscrew.jpg

TOS Picture Publicity shot of the original series crew. ✓**PVG** *dial* 513-233-7993→F→*Download a file:* OLDST.GIF

Kirk

A Young Shatner A young Shatner as Captain Kirk. ✓**COMPUSERVE**→go sfmedia→Libraries→*Search by file name:* PVTRK3.GIF

Ask Mr. Shatner His colleagues haven't said very nice things about him, and curious fans wanted to know—so, are the rumors true?

Obnoxious or not? The questions asked of Shatner on Delphi may not have been that direct or critical, but the controversial actor did discuss his relationship with fellow cast members, his reasons for performing in a public-service announcement for Tourette's Syndrome, his thoughts about Patrick Stewart, and his inspiration for the role of Kirk (Alexander the Great). And, even without Shatner's presence, the discussion goes on. ✓**DELPHI**→*go* ent sta→Ask Shatner

Captain's Log Soundclip of Kirk saying, "Captain's log, stardate 1709.2." ✓**INTERNET**→*gopher* gopher.med.umich.edu→Entertainment →Sounds→Star Trek_(TOS)→cap tain_s_log.au

James T. Kirk Picture of Captain Kirk from TOS. ✓**COMPUSERVE**→*go* sfmedia→Libraries→*Search by file name:* ST04.GIF

Kirk Publicity shot of William Shatner as Kirk. ✓**COMPUSERVE**→*go* bettman→Libraries→*Search by file name:* kirk.gif

No win Sound file of Kirk saying "I don't believe in the no-win scenario." ✓**INTERNET**→*gopher* gopher.med.umich.edu→Entertainment →Sounds→Star Trek_(TOS)→kirk.no win.au

Shatner Biography Biography of Shatner and a picture of him in the role of Captain Kirk. ✓**INTERNET**→*www* http://here.viacom.com /TrekCast.html#Shatner

Shatner Live on Prodigy Two-part transcript of William Shatner's January 1995 appearance on Prodigy. Shatner discusses his experiences with *Star Trek*, his conflicting feelings about the death of Captain Kirk, his *TekWar* books and series, his horses, and his rela-

tionship with cast members. ✓**PRODIGY** →*jump* chat transcripts→ 1Chat Transcripts→ 1/06/95→ William Shatner Part I *and* William Shatner Part 2

Shatner on TV Guide Scan of the 1993 cover of *TV Guide* featuring William Shatner. ✓**PVG** *dial* 513-233-7993→F→*Download a file:* SHTNER.GIF

Star Trek Movie Memories "I assumed they were unbalanced. I assumed they were nerds. And at the risk of repeating my own tired catchphrase, I truly assumed that they needed to 'Get a life!'," writes Shatner about Trek fans in his book *Star Trek Movie Memories*. Not surprisingly, he admits to changing his mind. This is an excerpt from Shatner's latest Trek memoir. ✓**DELPHI**→*go* ent sta sha sta

Wake for Captain James T. Kirk An archive of a live-chat discussion where the passing of Kirk was mourned (by most). ✓**EWORLD** →sf→Star Trek→United Federation Library→Sent: 11/28→10 Fwd - Wake (Filename: Conference Transcript 11/21/94)

William Shatner Publicity shot of William Shatner. ✓**PVG** *dial* 513-233-7993→<your username>→ <your password>→F→Download a file: BILLS.GIF

William Shatner Filmography Captain Kirk and T. J. Hooker! William Shatner starred in a variety of movies outside of his famous role as the captain of the *Enterprise*—from the *Brothers Karamazov* to *Judgement at Nuremberg*—and they're listed here. ✓**INTERNET**→*www* http://www.msstate.edu/Movies/→ Search the database for a person's name.→*Search for the name(s):* shatner, william

Spock

Leonard Nimoy Belts Out a Tune A photo of Nimoy singing. ✓**PVG** *dial* 513-233-7993→F→ *Download a file:* NIMOY2.GIF

Leonard Nimoy Filmography Nimoy has an impressive list of acting credits. He directed *Three Men and a Baby*, acted in *Invasion of the Body Snatchers*, and was the voice of Dr. Jekyll and Mr. Hyde in *The Pagemaster*. For more in-

William Shatner—downloaded from CompuServe's Sci-Fi Media Forum

sight, perform this search. ✓**INTER-NET**→*www* http://www.msstate.edu/Movies/→*Search the database for a person's name*→*Search for the name(s):* nimoy, leonard

Mr. Spock Another picture of the Vulcan, Spock. ✓**COMPUSERVE**→*go* sfmedia→Libraries→*Search by file name:* SPOCK.GIF

Nimoy at a Convention Picture of Leonard Nimoy at a *Star Trek* convention. ✓**PVG** *dial* 513-233-7993→F→*Download a file:* NIM2.GIF

Nimoy in Zombies of The Stratosphere Picture of Leonard Nimoy in the film *Zombies of the Stratosphere.* ✓**PVG** *dial* 513-233-7993→F→*Download a file:* NIMOY 01.GIF

Spock Huge picture of Mr. Spock doing the Vulcan salute. ✓**INTERNET** →*www* http://www.cosy.sbg.ac.at /ftp/pub/trek/pics/spock.jpg

Spock Image of Spock. ✓**COMPUSERVE**→*go* sfmedia→Libraries→ *Search by file name:* SPOCK.GIF

Spock Publicity shot of Leonard Nimoy as Spock. ✓**COMPUSERVE**→ *go* bettman→Libraries→*Search by file name:* SPOCK.GIF

Spock Picture of a much older Spock. ✓**INTERNET**→*anon-ftp* ftp. cis.ksu.edu→/pub/pictures/jpg /Startrek→spock. jpg

Spock Spock stares ahead with intensity. ✓**INTERNET**→*anon-ftp* ftp. cis.ksu.edu→/pub/pictures/jpg/ Startrek→spock1.jpg

Spock Startup Screen A windows start-up screen featuring Mr. Spock. ✓**COMPUSERVE**→*go* sfmedia →Libraries→*Search by file name:* SPOCK.ZIP

Spock (video capture)—downloaded from ftp.cis.ksu.edu

To boldly go... Soundclip of Spock saying the *Star Trek* teaser in *Star Trek II: The Wrath of Khan.* ✓**INTERNET**→*gopher* gopher.med. umich.edu→Entertainment→Sounds →Star Trek_(TOS)→st2-nimoy.au

Spock & Kirk

1967 TV Guide Shot of the cover 1967 *TV Guide* with Kirk and Spock. ✓**PVG** *dial* 513-233-7993→ <your username>→<your password>→F→*Download a file:* STGUIDE.GIF

Entertainment Weekly Cover Scan of the cover with Shatner and Nimoy. ✓**PVG** *dial* 513-233-7993→<your username>→<your password>→F→*Download a file:* ENTERT.GIF

Kirk & Spock Picture of Spock and Kirk on the bridge of the *Enterprise.* ✓**COMPUSERVE**→*go* bettman →Libraries→*Search by file name:* sttrek.gif

Kirk & Spock Sing-a-long Page At the height of their careers as television stars, both

William Shatner and Leonard Nimoy developed delusions of grandeur and embarked on singing careers to prove themselves as multitalented entertainers. This page proves just how wrong their instincts were. With discographies and samples from Shatner and Nimoy's LPs, the Sing-a-long Page answers the oft-asked question, "Who are the two worst singers in the known universe?"

The gold medal goes to William Shatner, whose abysmal renditions of sixties fare, such as "Mr. Tambourine Man" and "Lucy in the Sky With Diamonds," are guaranteed to peel wallpaper at a distance of two hundred yards. Nimoy is a close second, with bonehead attempts at spoken poetry that would make Rod McKuen throw up into his hat. The page includes critical comments—is any other kind possible?—including this marvelous assessment of Nimoy's singing "skills": "Suffering severe delusions of adequacy, Mr. Spock groped for melodies as effortlessly as someone trying to pick up dimes with a catcher's mitt." ✓**INTERNET**→*www* http://www.ama.

caltech.edu/~mrm/kirk.html

Spock Goes Kirk Frames from a morph of Spock to Kirk. ✓**COMPUSERVE**→*go* sfmedia→Libraries→ *Search by file name:* MORPH.GIF

Spock & Kirk Picture of Spock and Kirk. ✓**COMPUSERVE**→*go* sfmedia→Libraries→*Search by file name:* ORTREK.JPG

McCoy

Bones Publicity shot of DeForest Kelley as Bones. ✓**COMPUSERVE**→*go* bettman→Libraries→*Search by file name:* bones.gif

DeForest Kelley Publicity shot of DeForest Kelley. ✓**PVG** *dial* 513-233-7993→<your username>→<your password>→F→Download a file:DEFOREST.GIF

DeForest Kelley Filmography Graduating from Westerns like *Tension at Table Rock, Law and Jake Wade,* and *Gunfight at Comanche Creek.* ✓**INTERNET**→*www* http://www.msstate.edu/Movies/ →Search the database for a person's name→*Search for the name(s):* kelley, deforest

"I'm a Doctor, Not a..." Sayings Pulled from TOS, the

Dr. McCoy on TNG (video capture)— from ftp.cis.ksu.edu

comics, and *Star Trek* novels, this is a list of the variations of this line uttered by Dr. McCoy. ✓**COMPUSERVE**→*go* sfmedia→Libraries→ *Search by file name:* MCCOYQ.TXT

Chekov

Chekov The consensus here is that Chekov rules! Although concerned that he once wore a hairpiece; that he seemed to always be in trouble (awww! ouch! Captain!); and that he (or the actor Walter Koenig) has defected to *Babylon 5,* most of these fans are just completely enamored by their Russian hero. ✓**PRODIGY**→*jump* star trek bb→Choose a Topic→TV: Original Series→Checkov

Chekov Publicity shot of Walter Koenig as Chekov. ✓**COMPUSERVE**→*go* bettman→Libraries→ *Search by file name:* chekho.gif

Chekov Picture of Chekov. ✓**PVG** *dial* 513-233-7993→<your username>→<your password>→F→ Download a file: KOENIG.GIF

Chekov A picture of Walter Koenig at a Mensa convention in 1992. That's right—*Mensa.* ✓**COMPUSERVE**→*go* sfmedia→Libraries→*Search by file name:* CHEKOV.GIF

Walter Koenig Publicity shot of Walter Koenig. ✓**PVG** *dial* 513-233-7993→<your username>→<your password>→F→Download a file: KOENIG.GIF

Walter Koenig Publicity photo of Koenig. ✓**AMERICA ONLINE**→*keyword* center stage→Event Transcripts & Photos→Coliseum & Globe Events→Upld: 11/17/94→ Walter Koenig/PHOTO (Filename: KOENIG.GIF)

Walter Koenig Biography

Walter Koenig—downloaded from America Online's Center Stage Forum

Brief career biography and picture of Koenig in the role of Chekov. ✓**INTERNET**→*www* http://here.via com.com/TrekCast.html#Koenig

Walter Koenig Filmography He played an administrative assistant in *The Questor Tapes,* but is still best known (well, only known) for his role as Chekov on *Star Trek.* ✓**INTERNET**→*www* http: //www.msstate.edu/Movies/→ Search the database for a person's name→*Search for the name(s):* koenig, walter

Walter Koenig of Star Trek A transcript of an AOL center stage event featuring Koenig, who was asked questions about his impressions of the other *Star Trek* shows, his role on *Babylon 5,* and his relationship with other cast members, especially the spotlight-stealing William Shatner . ✓**AMERICA ONLINE**→*keyword* center stage→Event Transcripts & Photos→ Coliseum & Globe Events→Upld: 11/17/94→ Walter Koenig of Star Trek (Filename: AUD1116C.LOG)

Nurse Chapel

Majel Barrett Filmography Originally cast as Number One

for the pilot episode of TOS, later to marry Gene Roddenberry and play the luscious Nurse Chapel and the irrepressible Lwaxana Troi, Barret also accrued a list of non-*Trek* film credits including *A Guide to the Married Men* and *Love in a Goldfish.* Here's the list. ✓**INTERNET**→*www* http://www. msstate.edu/Movies/→*Search the database for a person's name* →*Search for the name(s):* barrett, majel

---

Nurse Chapel & Kirk Scan of Nurse Chapel with Kirk. ✓**PVG** *dial* 513-233-7993→*<your user-name>*→*<your password>*→*F*→ *Download a file:* PVKIRK02.GIF

Scotty

5 Scotty WAVs Five soundclips of Scotty announcing impending disaster. To wit: "If we keep this speed we'll blow up any minute now!" ✓**COMPUSERVE**→*go* sfmedia→ Libraries→*Search by file name:* SCOTTY.ZIP

Doohan Q&A Transcript Transcript of a 1990 interview with Doohan. ✓**COMPUSERVE**→*go* sfme-dia→Libraries→*Search by file name:* SCOTTY.TXT

James Doohan Biography Career biography and picture of Doohan in the role of Scotty. ✓**IN-TERNET**→*www* http://here.viacom. com/TrekCast.html#Doohan

---

James Doohan Filmography You'd think James Doohan would have been able to make a career out of playing Scotty, only Scotty, and nothing but Scotty. You'd be wrong. Doohan has appeared in thousands of Canadian radio pro-grams, hundreds of television shows, including *Bonanza*, and all the *Star Trek* films. ✓**INTERNET** →*www* http://www.msstate.edu

Montgomery Scott, miracle-worker (video capture)—from ftp.cis.ksu.edu

/Movies/→*Search the database for a person's name.*→*Search for the name(s):* doohan, james

---

Newspaper Article About Scotty A 1990 newspaper article in which Doohan discusses the movie *Star Trek VI* and his entire *Star Trek* career. ✓**COMPUSERVE**→*go* sfmedia→Libraries→*Search by file name:* ARTICL. TXT

Picture of Doohan Publicity shot of James Doohan. ✓**PVG** *dial* 513-233-7993→*<your username>* →*<your password>*→*F*→*Download a file:* DOOHAN.GIF

Scotty Picture of a seated Scotty. ✓**INTERNET**→*anon-ftp* ftp.cis.ksu. edu→/pub/pictures/jpg/Startrek/ →scotty.jpg

---

Scotty Beams to Montreal Transcipt of a 1994 Interview with James Doohan published in the *Montreal Gazette.* ✓**COMPUSERVE** →*go* sfmedia→Libraries→ *Search by file name:* SCOTTY.TXT

Sulu

A Biography of Hikaru Sulu Includes information ascertained

from the television series, movies, books, and comics about Sulu. ✓**COMPUSERVE**→*go* sfmedia→Li-braries→*Search by file name:* SULU.BIO

George Takei Publicity shot of Takei. ✓**PVG** *dial* 513-233-7993→ *<your username>*→*<your pass-word>*→*F*→*Download a file:* TMAG. GIF

George Takei Image of George Takei at the 1984 Trek III conven-tion in St. Louis. ✓**COMPUSERVE** →*go* sfmedia→Libraries→*Search by file name:* TAKEI.GIF

George Takei Comments A three-part report on Takei's re-marks to a Trek group in 1989. ✓**COMPUSERVE**→*go* sfmedia→Li-braries→*Search by file name:* TAKEI1.TXT *and* TAKEI2.TXT *and* TAKEI3.TXT

George Takei Filmography Beginning his career with the movie *Ice Palace*, Takei's career in-cludes movies ranging from *The Green Berets* to *Star Trek VI: The Undiscovered Country.* This search will yield a complete list of Takei's movie credits. ✓**INTERNET**→*www*

http://www.msstate.edu/Movies/→Search the database for a person's name.→*Search for the name(s):* takei, george

George Takei Giving Vulcan Salute GIF of Takei at an Oregon Trek convention giving a Vulcan salute. ✓**COMPUSERVE**→*go* sfmedia→Libraries→*Search by file name:* TAK2.GIF

Sulu Photo Promotional shot of Sulu. ✓**COMPUSERVE**→*go* bettman→Libraries→*Search by file name:* sulu.gif

Uhura

A Biography of Nyota Uhura You probably know that Uhura held the rank of lieutenant. But, did you know that she was born at the University of Kenya at Nairobi Hospital? This is a short profile of the TOS character. ✓**COMPUSERVE**→*go* sfmedia→Libraries→*Search by file name:* UHURA.BIO

Beyond Uhura Photo of the cover of Nichelle Nichols' book. ✓**AMERICA ONLINE**→*keyword* center stage→Event Transcripts & Photos→Coliseum & Globe Events→Upld: 10/21/94→UHURA PHOTO (Filename: UHURA.GIF)

Nichelle Nichols *Entertainment Weekly*'s profile of actress Nichelle Nichols and the character Uhura. The short article focuses on why Nichols wanted to quit after the first season. ✓**INTERNET**→*www* http://www.timeinc.com/vibe/decjan94/docs/props.html

Nichelle Nichols in AOL's Center Stage A transcript of Nichols' brief, live appearance in AOL's auditorium. She was promoting her book *Beyond Uhura* and spoke about people who had influenced her—from Martin

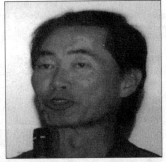

George Takei at a convention—from Perfect Vision Graphics BBS

Luther King to Gene Roddenberry. ✓**AMERICA ONLINE**→*keyword* center stage→Event Transcripts & Photos→Event Transcripts & Photos→Upld: 10/22/94→Nichelle Nichols-BEYOND UHURA (Filename: AUD1021.LOG)

Nichelle Nichols Publicity Shot Publicity picture of Nichelle Nichols. ✓**PVG** *dial* 513-233-7993→<your username>→<your password>→F→*Download a file:* NICHOLS.GIF

Nichols at a Convention Picture of Nichelle Nichols at a *Star Trek* convention. ✓**PVG** *dial* 513-233-7993→F→*Download a file:* NICHOLS4.GIF

Uhura Publicity shot of Nichelle Nichols as Uhura. ✓**COMPUSERVE**→*go* bettman→Libraries→*Search by file name:* uhuru.gif

Uhura Picture of Lieutenant Uhura as communications officer. ✓**PVG** *dial* 513-233-7993→F→*Download a file:* PVTOS08.GIF

Other characters

A Biography of Harry Mudd His name *is* Mudd—and this is his life story, drawn from the episodes in which he appeared ("I, Mudd" and "Mudd's Women"). ✓**COM-**

PUSERVE→*go* sfmedia→Libraries→*Search by file name:* MUDD.BIO

A Biography of Kevin Riley A brief biography of Kevin Riley, the troubled Irish Starfleet officer who sought to avenge his family's death. ✓**COMPUSERVE**→*go* sfmedia→Libraries→*Search by file name:* RILEY.BIO

A Biography of Lt. Saavik Life story of Saavik, a Vulcan/Romulan, who was adopted by Spock's parents. ✓**COMPUSERVE**→*go* sfmedia→Libraries→*Search by file name:* SAAVIK.BIO

A Biography of Winston Kyle What was the story with Mr. Kyle, transporter technician in TOS and communications officer of the starship *Reliant* in the movies? A brief biographical sketch. ✓**COMPUSERVE**→*go* sfmedia→Libraries→*Search by file name:* KYLE.BIO

Khan Close-up of the legendary Ricardo Montalban—not as *Fantasy Island*'s Mr. Rourke but as Khan. ✓**PVG** *dial* 513-233-7993→F→*Download a file:* KHAN.GIF

TOS cast publicity shot—downloaded from lajkonik.cyf-kr.edu.pl

23rd-century guides

From "The Cage" to "Where No Man Has Gone Before," from "The Trouble With Trib-

bles" to "The City on the Edge of Forever," TOS episodes are among the most-beloved sci-fi plots of the past 30 years. Do you remember which episode included the immortal line, "Are you out of your Vulcan mind?" ("Elaan of Troyius.") And did Kirk ever really say, "Beam me up, Scotty" during the series? Make certain that you've seen every single episode by using the **Complete Episode Guide to TOS** from CompuServe as a checklist. Remind yourself of **Favorite Star Trek: The Original Series Quotes**. And use the **Star Trek TOS/TAS List of Lists** to learn how many women were subjected to the loving feelings of Captain James T. Kirk. (Did someone say "Set phaser on 'stud'"?)

Kirk, McCoy, and Spock—downloaded from Perfect Vision Graphics BBS

On the Net

Episode guides

Complete Episode Guide to TOS DOS program that displays extensive episode information in a colorful, convenient format. ✓**COMPUSERVE**→*go* sfmedia→Libraries→*Search by file name:* TOSEP2.ZIP

Hack-Man Episode Guide for the Original Series of Star

Trek An almost 200-page guide to the original series with episode-by-episode plot summaries, commentary, ratings, casting information, airdates, and quotes. The end of the document is a compilation of TOS snafus, a time line, and character profiles. Even the index is interesting, with episodes grouped under hundreds of themes, planets, aliens, and other references to the Trek universe (e.g., Chekov's love interests, money, religion, Romulan episodes, etc.). ✓**INTERNET** ...→*anon-ftp* quepasa.cs.tu-berlin. de→/pub/doc/movies+tv-series/ StarTrek→Hack-Man.TOS.Guide.Z ...→*www* http://www.cosy.sbg. ac.at/rec/startrek/Hackmans. Guide.html

The Original Series Episode

Guide HyperCard Stack A searchable Hypercard stack of the episodes from TOS. Stack includes plot descriptions, the names of scriptwriters and episode directors, cast information, and more. For Macs with a Hypercard player. ✓**AMERICA ONLINE**→*keyword* mac software→Search the Libraries →Search All Libraries→*Search by file name:* Star Trek-TOS Guide 2.0. sea ✓**INTERNET**→*anon-ftp* ftp.u-tokyo.ac.jp→/.1/mac/umich/hyper card/fun→startrektosguide2.0.cpt. hqx ✓**COMPUSERVE**→*go* sfmedia→Libraries→*Search by file name:* TOS21A.SIT

Star Trek (Original) Episode Guide Includes original airdates and short plot summaries for all the episodes of the original series, plus ratings on a star system—surprise!—that range from half a star ("The best part is the opening credits") to five stars ("a Trekkie would be willing to skip a final, to suffer the slings and arrows of outrageous fortune, to cross into the Romulan neutral zone, to boldly go where no man has gone before"). The first five-star episode? "The Trouble With Tribbles," of course. Finding the rest is up to you. ✓**INTERNET** ...→*anon-ftp* elbereth.rutgers.edu→/pub/sfl→star-trek.guide ...→*www* http://www.cosy.sbg.ac.at/ftp/pub/trek/guide/star-trek.guide.txt

Star Trek: The Original Series Episode Guide Every Trekker knows that the pilot episode, "The Cage," in which Captain Pike of the *Enterprise* was replaced with Captain Kirk aired in 1964, but did you know that it was April of 1967 when Dr. McCoy jumped through a time portal and landed up on Earth in the 1930s? November of 1966 when the now-famous two-part episode (a follow-up to the story told in the pilot) "The Menagerie" aired? January of 1968 when escaped lunatics from an asylum on the planet Elba II were beamed aboard the *Enterprise*? This guide lists the name of an episode, the date it aired, the stardate, and a brief synopsis. ✓**INTERNET** ...→*gopher* gopher.univ-lyon1.fr→Usenet (FAQs [news.answers], stats, docs, ..)→Usenet FAQs by newsgroup name →rec→rec.arts.startrek.fandom→star-trek→cs-guide→tv→Star_Trek_Episodes_Guide* ...→*anon-ftp* rtfm.mit.edu→/pub/usenet-by-hierarchy/rec/arts/star-trek/fandom→ Star_Trek_Episodes_Guide*

Star Trek: The Original Series List of Episodes, Plot Descriptions, and Major Characters A short reference with a cast list and episode descriptions. Descriptions include the date an episode aired, the stardate, and a one-liner plot description. In addition, the document lists each instance when McCoy uses the phrase "I'm a Doctor, not a...." ✓**INTERNET**→*anon-ftp* rtfm.mit.edu →/pub/usenet-by-hierarchy /rec/arts/star-trek/misc→STAR TREK_LISTS:_st:tos_ {biweekly}

FAQs & lists

Star Trek TOS/TAS Lists of Lists Nitpicking, trivia, and episode summaries for TOS and TAS. Besides a comprehensive list of actors and characters that have appeared on the series and lists of the species and ships, the list points out plot inconsistencies, traces Kirk's love interests, and groups the episodes by themes. ✓**INTERNET** ...→*anon-ftp* ftp.cc.umanitoba.ca→/startrek/lol→lol.tos ...→*anon-ftp* netcom.com→/pub/mholtz→toslist_0494.Z ...→*anon-ftp* quepasa.cs.tu-berlin.de→/pub/doc/movies+tv-series/StarTrek→/lol_0494→tos0494.txt

TOS FAQ List This quick reference to TOS and TAS lists episodes and stardates for both series. Also included are the meaning of uniform colors, an explanation of stardates, and a description of warp factors. ✓**AMERICA ONLINE**→*keyword* trek→MORE...→Star Trek Record Banks→Text/Other Files→Upld: 06/25/94→TEXT: TOS FAQ List (Filename: TOSFAQ.TXT)

Quotes

Favorite Star Trek: The Original Series Quotes "Captain Pike has illusion, and you have reality. May you find your way as pleasant." So, said the Keeper in a famous line from the early episode "The Menagerie." Here's a list of fan Jeff Koga's favorite Trek quotes from the original series. The list includes quotes from several episodes, but "Errand of Mercy" is so extensively quoted that it almost constitutes a full reprint of the script. Remember Kirk's line in "Errand of Mercy," "I'm a soldier, not a diplomat. I can only tell you the truth"? This list will help jar your memory. ✓**INTERNET**→*www* http://www.cosy.sbg.ac.at:80/ftp/pub/trek/quotes/st_tos.txt

Star Trek Quotes Random quotes generated from the original series. ✓**INTERNET**→*www* http://www.ugcs.caltech.edu/htbin/werdna/fortune?startrek

TOS Automatic Quote Generator A new TOS quote each time you link to the address. ✓**INTERNET** →*www* http://ug.cs.dal.ca:3400/cgi-bin/stfortune

Ratings

TOS Rate Results Usenet readers can rate episodes of TOS on a scale of zero to one. Ballots are averaged and new results are posted periodically. Topping the lists of Trekkers' favorite old series episodes are the classics "The City on the Edge of Forever," "Mirror, Mirror," and "Balance of the Terror." According to this list, if you missed "And the Children Shall Lead," you didn't miss much. ✓**INTERNET**→*anon-ftp* rtfm.mit.edu→/pub/usenet-by-hierarchy/rec/arts/startrek/misc→TREK_RATE_results_(TOS)

Time lines

TOS Timeline A time line tracing each episode, movie, and novel involving the original series crew. ✓**COMPUSERVE**→*go* sfmedia→Libraries→*Search by file name:* PLS207.TXT

Trekking to the movies

Most people account *Star Trek: The Next Generation* as the second Trek series, but to

do so ignores the wildly successful series of feature films that began with 1979's *Star Trek: The Motion Picture.* With large budgets, lavish special effects, and the cooperation of the entire original cast, the movies reached a mass audience the series had not, and the *Star Trek* movie series held its own against such sci-fi movie giants as *Star Wars.* Find out how Trek fans rank the films with **Trek Movie Rate Results**. Moan and groan about the incredibly bad quality of **Star Trek V: The Final Frontier**. And listen enraptured to the entirely fake accent of Ricardo Montalban in the **Khan Soundclip**.

Khan (video capture)—downloaded from Perfect Vision Graphics BBS

On the Net

Across the board

Guide to Movies Cast and guest-star list for the first six *Star Trek* motion pictures. Every player is listed together with a numeric notation for the movie they appeared in. A brief plot synopsis for each film is also included. ✓**INTERNET** →*www* http://www.cosy.sbg.ac.at/ftp/pub/trek/lists/stfafl/movies

---

How Do You Rank the Star Trek Movies? People love to rank things—until their peers tell them that their ordering indicates some incurable form of insanity. Many here have viewed the *Star Trek* movies 30 or 40 times, and they love reciting favorite lines. Participants also spend time analyzing why each movie receives its rank—character development, special effects, acting, directing. The necessity of the Roddenberry touch is also an omnipresent issue. In the end, *The Wrath of Khan* and *Generations* contend for top honors, and there is never really any contest for last place (God knows). This is an active topic, rejuvenated every time one of the films shows on TV or enjoys rerelease on laser disc. ✓**GENIE**→*keyword* sfrt2→SFRT2 Bulletin Board→set 26→read 4

Movies Kirk should have died a more gallant death, suggests one topic member. Well, argues Liza, "Kirk's not dead until McCoy says, 'You're dead, Jim!'" About half of the discussion here is related to the latest *Star Trek* film, *Generations,* but already speculation about *Star Trek VIII* has begun and promises to quickly overwhelm the *Generations* nitpicking. Of course, Trek diehards never get tired of rehashing and rating the old ones. *Wrath of Khan* tops Ralph's and Frank's list while *The Voyage Home* is the avowed favorite of Linda and Philip. ✓**PRODIGY**→*jump* star trek bb→Choose a Topic→Movies

---

rec.arts.startrek.current/rec.arts.startrek.misc (ng) One phrase says it all: Kirk is dead. *Generations,* by breeding a new bloodline for *Star Trek* movies, raised enormous hopes on the Net; but killing off a hero, it also raised a phenomenal tidal wave of anger and not a little denial. Some fans refuse to believe he's really gone—after all, another TOS regular has bitten the stardust and been revived. Others point to a line Kirk drops in that most hated of *Star Trek* movies, *Star Trek V: The Final Frontier*: "I always knew I'd die alone." Since Kirk wasn't alone when he "died," they note—Picard was there—he couldn't be gone for good. The rebuttal: "Kirk is not a psychic. I can't believe a thread this dumb keeps on coming back."

Who knows? The real answer as to Kirk's resurrection lies in that most final of frontiers, the bottom line. In that regard, *Generations* has been a huge success, but among hard-core Trek fans on the Net, *Generations* was a consummate disaster, full of Intrepid-class plot-holes and mediocre characterization. A Net-based petition calling for a protest against Paramount over *Generations* got some support, then died as more rational minds discussed the dubious merits (and effectiveness) of biting the hand that feeds. ✓**USENET**

The Silver Screen & Beyond

While there's a folder for every *Star Trek* movie, *Generations* dominates the area. Still, if you just can't stop talking about Ricardo Montalbam's portrayal of Khan, you can start a thread in the *Star Trek II* folder. ✓**EWORLD**→sf→Star Trek→ The Silver Screen & Beyond

Star Trek Font *Star Trek IX: The Adventues of Me?* Make your own movie posters with this font, which looks similar to the one used for the *Star Trek* movie series. ✓**AMERICA ONLINE**→*keyword* mac software→Search the Libraries→ Search All Libraries→*Search by file name:* Star Trek.sit

Star Trek Movie List of Lists A combination of plot summaries, cast lists, trivia, and nitpicking (lots and lots of nitpicking) about

STARQUOTES

Kirk: "My friends, we've come home."
— **Star Trek IV: The Voyage Home**

Net Source: Quote Generator—http://www.cosy.sbg.ac.at/ftp/pub/trek/quotes/st4_tvh.txt

the first six movies. Did you know that in *Star Trek II: The Wrath of Khan*, "all of the actors who played Khan's men were, at the time, male Chippendale strippers" and that "the blood stain on Kirk's jacket is constantly changing?" ✓**INTERNET** ...→*anon-ftp* ftp.cc. umanitoba.ca→/startrek/lol→lol. tms ...→*anon-ftp* quepasa.cs.tu-berlin.de→/pub/doc/movies+tv-series/StarTrek/lol_0494→tms04 94.txt ...→*anon-ftp* netcom.com →/pub/mholtz→tmslist_0494.Z

Star Trek: The Motion Pictures All seven movies, and non-spoiler discussion of *Generations* so that those of you who missed it in the theaters can have an undisturbed video-rental experience. Find out whether Ricardo Montalban has thought about a prequel to *The Wrath of Khan*, discuss whether the TNG cast will retain its strengths on the big screen, and even speculate about the first DS9 feature (*Dax Soup?*). ✓**GENIE**→*keyword* sfrt2→SFRT2 Bulletin Board→ set 26

TMP—The Motion Pictures Is there anything worse than *Star Trek V: The Final Frontier?* Nope. "ST5 committed a sin worse than the worst. It was boring and stupid." *Generations*, on the other hand, got top ratings from the regulars here, even if some were disappointed with the handling of Kirk's death (one of them wanted him to "simply disappear, like Arthur and other Celtic and Germanic heroes"). The erudite fans

of TMP have high standards. Sure, they'll gab about Kirk's demise like everyone else, but they're also capable of discussing the "canonicity" of these flicks (i.e., Do they harmonize with all other fictions in the known Trek universe?). Things really get moving, of course, when there's a new movie, like *Generations*, to discuss. Visit beforehand to speculate (Star Trek VIII?), and after the release to opine. ✓**DELPHI**→*go* ent sta for→set tmp

Trek Movie Rate Results

Usenet readers can rate the *Star Trek* movies on a scale of zero to one. Ballots are averaged and new results are posted periodically. Unsurprisingly, *Star Trek V* finishes last. ✓**INTERNET**→*anon-ftp* rtfm.mit. edu→/pub/usenet-by-hierarchy/ rec/arts/startrek/misc→TREK_ RATE_results_(MOVIES)

Trekker_Movies (echo) Within weeks following the premiere of *Star Trek VII*, conference members had started collecting reports and rumors about *Star Trek VIII* (late-1996 release date?). If the lead time to *Generations* is anything to go by, members should start posting script plots they'd like to see, script plots think they think they'll see, and script plots that a conference member's friend who works for a company that sells office supplies to Paramount has guaranteed they'll see. So, who's been signed for the next movie? ✓**TREKKERNET**

Which Movie Was The Best

The Wrath of Khan is not everyone's favorite—but almost. This topic began in 1993 and offers a wide range of opinions on *Star Trek* movies, from eloquent arguments about directors and acting to statements of rather terse advocacy: "*Star Trek VI*, the most action, drama, suspense, and badass Klingons." ✓**AMERICA ONLINE**→*keyword* trek→Star Trek Message Boards→The Promenade→Which Movie Was the Best

WS_Movie (echo) The latest *Star Trek* movie *Generations* dominated discussion here for a while. Fans wanted to flood Paramount in April 1994 with faxes when they thought the Borg would be killed off. They were devastated when they learned that Spock wasn't appearing in the movie. And then, in the weeks before the film's release, they posted every plot spoiler they could find. Expect conversation to pick up again as soon as the rumors about *Star Trek VIII* begin to circulate. ✓**WARPSPEED**

The Motion Picture

Basic Information About Star Trek: The Motion Picture Use this huge movie data base to find out the particulars about *Star Trek: The Motion Picture* and as a link to other *Star Trek* and science fiction films. In addition to full (even set design and makeup) credits you can find an animated clip of the *Enterprise* in action, trivia, and movie "goofs." Did you know, for example, that while traveling in the V'Ger cloud Spock comes across Darth Vader and the porcine goddess Miss Piggy? Simply search on *Star Trek*. ✓**INTERNET**→*www* http://www. msstate.edu/M/title-exact?18E8EB

Decker & Ilia Shot of Decker

Ilia and Kirk—downloaded from CompuServe's Sci-Fi Media Forum

and Ilia embracing. ✓**PVG** *dial* 513-233-7993→<your username>→<your password>→F→*Download a file:* PVSTTMP2.GIF

Kirk and Ilia Image of Admiral Kirk and Lieutenant Ilia. GIF format. ✓**COMPUSERVE**→*go* sfmedia→Libraries→*Search by file name:* ST1ILI.GIF

Spock Image of Spock from the first movie. ✓**COMPUSERVE**→*go* sfmedia→Libraries→*Search by file name:* ST1SPO.GIF

Star Trek: The Motion Picture Promotional shot of *Star Trek: The Motion Picture.* ✓**PVG** *dial* 513-233-7993→<your username>→<your password>→F→*Download a file:* PVSTTMP.GIF

Star Trek: The Motion Picture Critical analysis occurs on two levels here—not only the grand aesthetic achievement, but also the plot minutiae. Did *Star Trek* make a good translation to the big screen, or did it lose itself and end up looking like *2001: The Trek Odyssey?* Critiques of the direction and lighting are joined by explanations of the size of the V'Ger cloud (82 AUs, or 82 times the

distance between the Earth and the sun?). Even the drawbacks in the film—boring, boring, boring—don't stop fans from tracking down missing outtakes as if they were the Ark of the Covenant. ✓**GENIE**→*keyword* sfrt2→SFRT2 Bulletin Board→set 26→read 8

Star Trek: The Motion Picture Quotes A short selection of lines from the first *Star Trek* movie. ✓**INTERNET**→*www* http://www. cosy.sbg.ac.at/ftp/pub/trek/ quotes/st1_tmp.txt

The Wrath of Khan

Basic Information about The Wrath of Khan Not only does this site provide acting and production credits, but new insight into the film. Check out the trivia section for an analysis of Khan's relationship to Captain Ahab from *Moby Dick*, as well as a technical explication of how the Cow Palace helped created that fantastic explosion scene. ✓**INTERNET**→*www* http://www.msstate.edu/M/title-exact?18E6BF

Dr. Carol Marcus Picture of Dr. Carol Marcus. ✓**PVG** *dial* 513-233-7993→<your username>→<your

password>→F→*Download a file:* CMARCUS.GIF

Khan Close-up of Ricardo Montalban as superhuman outlaw Khan. ✓**PVG** *dial* 513-233-7993→<your username>→<your password>→F→*Download a file:* KHAN 04.GIF

Khan Soundclip The very definition of bad mood, Khan-style: "I've done far worse than kill you. I hurt you, and I wish to go on hurting you." ✓**INTERNET**→*www* http://sunsite.sut.ac.jp/multimed/sounds/startrek/khan3.au

Khan Soundclip The dulcet tones of Shatner and Montalban mingle twine together like the finest threads in this aural tapestry from the finale between Kirk and Khan. ✓**INTERNET**→*www* http://sunsite.sut.ac.jp/multimed/sounds/startrek/khan5.au

Lt. Saavik Two pictures of Saavik (Kirstie Alley) in *Star Trek II.* ✓**COMPUSERVE**→*go* sfmedia→Libraries→*Search by file name:* SAVIK1.GIF *and* SAVIK2.GIF

Picture: Showdown In this JPEG format image, the *Enterprise* meets *Reliant* for all the marbles. ✓**INTERNET**→*www* http://www.cosy.sbg.ac.at/mirror/httpd/info/star_trek/ent_rel/.jpg

Star Trek II Crew Publicity shot of the crew from *Star Trek II,* including a stern-looking Kirstie Alley as Saavik. ✓**INTERNET**→*anon-ftp* ftp.cis.ksu.edu→/pub/pictures/jpg/Startrek→stII.jpg

Star Trek II: The Wrath of Khan What inspires the elegaic prose here? Well, the death of Spock, of course, and also the destruction of the *Enterprise.* In fact, the individual seems to draw less support than the ship, with some fans even suggesting that Spock would have been better left dead—especially since he seemed to have turned into an Eastern mystic. Discussion of the possible uses of the Genesis Device (the machine that creates life from nothingness) sparks a debate over animal rights, and the film receives generally good press—many here credit it with reviving *Star Trek* and ensuring funding for *The Next Generation.* ✓**GENIE**→*keyword* sfrt2→SFRT2 Bulletin Board→set 26→read 9

Star Trek II: The Wrath of Khan Photos A series of photos with four scenes each from *Star Trek II.* ✓**PVG** *dial* 513-233-7993→<your username>→<your password>→F→*Download a file:* ST2WK4.GIF *and* ST2WKQ02.GIF *and* ST2WKQ05.GIF *and* ST2WKQ06.GIF

Star Trek II: The Wrath of Khan Photos A series of photos with four scenes, each from *Star Trek II,* including pictures of a burned Khan, an activated Genesis device, Spock's hand on McCoy's head during the mind-meld, an angry Uhura, Khan on the Bridge, Saavik at the controls, Khan on the view screen, and Dr. Marcus. ✓**PVG** *dial* 513-233-7993→<your username>→<your password>→F→*Download a file:* ST2WK4.GIF *and* ST2WKQ02.GIF *and* ST2WKQ05.GIF *and* ST2WKQ06.GIF

Star Trek Poster Electronic version of the *Star Trek II: The Wrath of Khan* poster. ✓**PVG** *dial* 513-233-7993→F→*Download a file:* TREK 2PST.GIF

Star Trek II: The Wrath of Khan Quotes An extensive collection of great lines from the second movie. ✓**INTERNET**→*www* http://www.cosy.sbg.ac.at/rec/startrek/Quotes.html

The USS Enterprise Picture of the *Enterprise* in *Star Trek II* on its way to the planet created by the Genesis experiment. ✓**COMPUSERVE**→*go* sfmedia→*Search by file name:* ENTER1.GIF

The USS Reliant Picture of the *Reliant* from *Star Trek II.* ✓**COMPUSERVE**→*go* sfmedia→Libraries→*Search by file name:* RELIAN.GIF

The Search for Spock

Basic Information About Star Trek III: The Search for Spock Jump to the filmographies of all the stars and production staff from this synopsis page. Look in the quotes section for an example of Kirk's use of a famous foreign phrase, and even add your own favorite quotes. Did you see the foam rocks slither down in the rock slide scene? ✓**INTERNET**→*www* http://www.msstate.edu/M/title-exact?18E722

The Cast of Star Trek III GIF of Kirk, Spock, Uhura, and Scotty.

STARQUOTES

Spock: "You are my superior officer. You are also my friend. I have been and always shall be yours."

—Spock to Kirk, *Star Trek II: The Wrath of Khan*

Net Source: *Star Trek Quotes—http://www.cosy.sbg.ac.at/ftp/pub/trek/quotes/st2_twok.txt*

✓**COMPUSERVE**→*go* sfmedia→Libraries→*Search by file name:* ST3CAS.GIF

Star Trek III Four pictures from the movie. ✓**PVG** *dial* 513-233-7993→<your username>→<your password>→F→*Download a file:* TREK3.GIF

Star Trek III: The Search for Spock Was the mystique of Spock enhanced by this film? Or did the film create more questions than it answered about Vulcan burial ceremonies?

Vulcan ritual and culture is the subject of much discussion here—*Pon farr* just seems untenable to most (Why would you want to wait seven years between mating?). Enter the ongoing debate: Did finding Spock detract from the drama? ✓**GENIE**→*keyword* sfrt2→SFRT2 Bulletin Board→set 26→read 10

Star Trek III: The Search for Spock Quotes A short collection of memorable lines from the third movie. ✓**INTERNET**→*www* http://www.cosy.sbg.ac.at/ftp/pub/trek

/quotes/st3_tsfs.txt

The Voyage Home

Basic Information About Star Trek IV: The Voyage Home Not only will this site tell you all about the actors, but it will also give you some good lines for your next blind date. "So you're from outer space?" "No, I'm from Iowa, I just work there." Those troubling continuity gaffes are detailed in "goofs," and you can also link to other *Star Trek* movies and related films in the sci-fi genre. ✓**INTERNET**→*www* http://www.msstate.edu/M /title-exact? 18E783

Chekov & Uhura Image of Uhura and Chekov on the *Enterprise*. ✓**COMPUSERVE**→*go* sfmedia→Libraries→*Search by file name:* TVH04.GIF

Dr. McCoy Picture of McCoy in the hospital in *Star Trek IV*. GIF image. ✓**COMPUSERVE**→*go* sfmedia→Libraries→*Search by file name:* TVH07.GIF

Dr. McCoy Picture of McCoy at

the hearing in *Star Trek IV*. ✓**COMPUSERVE**→*go* sfmedia→Libraries→*Search by file name:* TVH13.GIF

GIF of Chekov Guards come to get Chekov on the *Enterprise*. GIF image. ✓**COMPUSERVE**→*go* sfmedia→Libraries→*Search by file name:* TVH05.GIF

Gillian and Kirk Picture of Gillian and Kirk flirting in *Star Trek IV*. ✓**COMPUSERVE**→*go* sfmedia→Libraries→*Search by file name:* TVH06.GIF

"Gracie's Pregnant" Picture of Gillian's reaction to Spock's announcement. ✓**COMPUSERVE**→*go* sfmedia→Libraries→*Search by file name:* TVH02.GIF

Kirk in San Francisco Image of Kirk in his San Francisco apartment. ✓**PVG** *dial* 513-233-7993→<your username>→<your password>→F→*Download a file:* KIRK-B.GIF

Kirk Reacts Picture of Kirk watching Spock and Gracie swim together. ✓**COMPUSERVE**→*go* sfmedia→Libraries→*Search by file name:* TVH01.GIF

Lt. Saavik Image of Lieutenant Saavik in ST IV. ✓**COMPUSERVE**→*go* sfmedia→Libraries→*Search by file name:* ST4SAA.GIF

Portrait of Captain Kirk Image of Kirk in ST IV. ✓**COMPUSERVE**→*go* sfmedia→Libraries→*Search by file name:* ST4KIR.GIF

Portrait of Scotty Image of Mr. Scott in ST IV. ✓**COMPUSERVE**→*go* sfmedia→Libraries→*Search by file name:* ST4SCO.GIF

Scotty Talks to a Mouse Picture of Scotty trying to use a Macintosh by talking to the mouse in

Mankind's saviors—downloaded from CompuServe's Graphics Corner

Star Trek IV. ✓**COMPUSERVE**→*go* sf-media→Libraries→*Search by file name:* TVH10.GIF

Scotty & the Whales Picture of Scotty preparing to beam up the whales. ✓**PVG** *dial* 513-233-7993→f→*Download a file:* TVH08.GIF

Spock Swimming with Gracie Picture of Spock and Gracie swimming in *Star Trek IV.* ✓**COMPUSERVE**→*go* sfmedia→Libraries→*Search by file name:* TVH03.GIF

Spock & the Whale Picture of Spock mind-melding with the whale. ✓**PVG** *dial* 513-233-7993→f→*Download a file:* TVH03.GIF

Spock & the Whale Picture of Kirk watching Spock in the whale tank. ✓**PVG** *dial* 513-233-7993→f→*Download a file:* TVH01.GIF

Star Trek IV Collage Collage of photos from *Star Trek IV.* ✓**PVG** *dial* 513-233-7993→<your username>→<your password>→F→*Download a file:* PVSTIV.GIF

Star Trek IV Crew Picture of the crew on the bridge (Uhura and Kirk have perms). ✓**INTERNET**→*anon-ftp* ftp.cis.ksu.edu→/pub/pictures/jpg/Startrek→st6crew.jpg

Star Trek IV: The Voyage Home Two 16-scene image collages from *Star Trek IV.* ✓**PVG** *dial* 513-233-7993→<your username>→<your password>→F→*Download a file:* ST4H01.GIF *and* ST4H02.GIF

Star Trek IV: The Voyage Home Much of this category is devoted to humor: What's the funniest line in the warmest and fuzziest of *Star Trek* films? As far as more serious topics go, conference participants love to talk about the nature of time and the pawning of Kirk's glasses, and they also like to

"Excuse me, but what does God need with a starship?"
—Kirk, *Star Trek VI: The Final Frontier*

Net Source: http://www.cosy.sbg.ac.at/ftp/pub/trek/quotes/st5_tff.txt

disparage those who insist on beating these topics to death. Newer concerns include the cultural differences between the 24th and 20th centuries, including Jacqueline Susann and baseball. ✓**GENIE**→*keyword* sfrt2→SFRT2 Bulletin Board→set 26→read 11

Star Trek IV: The Voyage Home Quotes Lines from the fourth movie. ✓**INTERNET**→*www* http://www.cosy.sbg.ac.at/ftp/pub/trek/quotes/st4_tvh.txt

Sulu Picture of Sulu at the hearing in *Star Trek IV.* ✓**COMPUSERVE**→*go* sfmedia→Libraries→*Search by file name:* TVH11.GIF

Uhuru Picture of Uhura at the hearing in *Star Trek IV.* ✓**COMPUSERVE**→*go* sfmedia→Libraries→*Search by file name:* TVH12.GIF

The Final Frontier

Basic Information about Star Trek V: The Final Frontier There are two different plot summaries included here, perhaps because the film was too discombobulated for anyone to really figure out. "The whole movies was a goof," proclaims the "goof" section. But there are also fun trivia facts along with detailed credits. Did you know that the surface of Shaka-Ra is an electron microscope picture of a lobster claw? Do you know which part was played by Shatner's daughter? Do you care? ✓**INTERNET**→*www* http://www.msstate.edu/M/title-exact?

18E7E5

Enterprise Photo of the *Enterprise* as it approaches a blue gaseous planet. Heaven? ✓**INTERNET**→*anon-ftp* ftp.cis.ksu.edu→/pub/pictures/jpg/Startrek→st-v-08.jpg

Klingon Ship Head-on shot of a Klingon ship. ✓**INTERNET**→*anon-ftp* ftp.cis.ksu.edu→/pub/pictures/jpg/Startrek→st-v-05.jpg

National Enquirer Article Article printed before the release of *Star Trek V: The Final Frontier*, revealing the plot. ✓**COMPUSERVE**→*go* sfmedia→Libraries→*Search by file name:* ENQUIR.DOC

Star Trek V: The Final Frontier "It is never a good idea to have God as a character in a major motion picture." Unfortunately, the creators of this film thought that a search for the ultimate Creator would be really neat. The debate here is never about whether or not this film is a disaster—no one suggests that it's even mediocre—but what makes it disastrous. Is it the plot? The special effects? Bad science? Direction? Overacting? Slapstick humor? If you want a sympathetic audience to commiserate, you'll find it here. Some Trek fans actually admit that they've seen the film more than once, perhaps hoping against hope that it would improve with age. ✓**GENIE**→*keyword* sfrt2→SFRT2 Bulletin Board→set 26→read 12

Star Trek V: The Final Fron-

tier Quotes Lines from the fifth movie. ✓**INTERNET**→*www* http:// www.cosy.sbg.ac.at/ftp/pub/trek /quotes/st5_tff.txt

Undiscovered Country

A Picture of Starbase An image of the the *Enterprise* crew being transported aboard shuttlepod *SB103* transporting to the Starbase in *Star Trek VI*. ✓**COMPU-SERVE**→*go* sfmedia→Libraries→ *Search by file name:* ST05.GIF

Bashing Klingons Image of the scene when the Klingons are being defeated. ✓**COMPUSERVE**→*go* sfmedia→Libraries→*Search by file name:* BASH.GIF

Basic Information about Star Trek VI: The Undiscovered Country Full cast and crew credits are accompanied by a searchable quote index, goofs, and trivia. Learn how Shatner thought his posterior was a bit too bulky and had some scenes airbrushed. Find out how Kirk and Spock shocked

Movie poster—downloaded from lajkonik.cyf-kr.edu.pl

Al Pacino. And discover why the sixth film was such a success with fans and critics alike. ✓**INTERNET**→ *www* http://www.msstate.edu/M /title-exact? 18E842

Christian Slater Filmography Bad-boy Slater, the Nicholson of the nineties, is also a Trek fan, and he made a cameo appearance in this film as an ensign who appears at Captain Sulu's chambers. In interviews since, Slater has admitted that he loved the Trek uniform so much that he tried to walk off the set while wearing it, much to the chagrin of Paramount guards. ✓**INTERNET**→*www* http://www.msstate. edu/M/person-exact?a3DZF30F

Enterprise Crew Picture of the *Enterprise* crew from *Star Trek VI*. ✓**COMPUSERVE**→*go* sfmedia→Libraries→*Search by file name:* TREK61.GIF

Enterprise Under Photon Torpedo Attack Image of a photon fired at the *Enterprise* by General Chang from the perspective of Chang's ship. ✓**COMPUSERVE**→*go* sfmedia→Libraries→*Search by file name:* ATTK1.GIF

"If I were human..." Soundclip of Spock's remarks after receiving the order for the *Enterprise* to be decommissioned. ✓**COMPUSERVE**→ *go* sfmedia→Libraries→*Search by file name:* HUMAN.ZIP *or* HUMAN. SIT

Kirk and McCoy Picture of Kirk and McCoy on the Klingon Ice Planet in *Star Trek VI*. ✓**COMPUSERVE**→*go* sfmedia→Libraries→ *Search by file name:* ST6-6A

Kirk, Spock and Azetbur Image of Klingon Ambassador Azetbur, Kirk, and Spock in *Star Trek VI*. ✓**COMPUSERVE**→*go* sfmedia →Libraries→*Search by file name:*

ST6-8A

Klingon General Chang Picture of the Klingon enemy, General Chang, in *Star Trek VI*. ✓**COMPUSERVE**→*go* sfmedia→Libraries→ *Search by file name:* ST6-2A.GIF

Michael Dorn in Star Trek VI Picture of the Klingon defense attorney, Worf's grandfather. ✓**COMPUSERVE**→*go* sfmedia→Libraries→ *Search by file name:* ST6-4A.GIF

Multi-View GIF of Captain James T. Kirk Kirk image with scenes from the movie *Star Trek VI* in the background. ✓**COMPUSERVE**→*go* sfmedia→Libraries→ *Search by file name:* KIRK2.GIF

Multi-View GIF of Dr. McCoy McCoy image with scenes from *Star Trek VI* in the background. ✓**COMPUSERVE**→*go* sfmedia→Libraries→*Search by file name:* MC-COY2.GIF

Multi-View GIF of Mr. Spock Spock image with scenes from *Star Trek VI* in the background. ✓**COMPUSERVE**→*go* sfmedia→Libraries→*Search by file name:* SPOCK2.GIF

Spock Takes in Yosemite A picture of Spock and Kirk in the sixth movie. ✓**COMPUSERVE**→*go* sf-media→Libraries→ST6.GIF *Search by file name:*

Star Trek VI Overture Sounclip of the orchestral overture to the sixth *Trek* film. ✓**INTERNET**→*gopher* president.oit.unc.edu→pub→ multimedia →sun-sounds→sound_ tracks→star_trek_6_overture.au

Star Trek VI: Paramount Press Release Press release announcing the movie. ✓**COMPUSERVE**→*go* sfmedia→*Search by file name:* TREK6.TXT

"Captain's log, stardate 9529.1. This is the final cruise of the starship *Enterprise* under my command. This ship and her history will shortly become the care of a new generation. To them and their posterity will we commit our future. They will continue the voyages we have begun, and journey to all the undiscovered countries, boldly going where no man...where no one, has gone before."

—Kirk's sign-off, *Star Trek VI: The Undiscovered Country*

Net Source: Star Trek Quotes—http://www.cosy.sbg.ac.at/ftp/pub/trek/quotes/st6_tuc.txt

Star Trek VI: The Undiscovered Country This film is especially beloved, in part because it went a long way toward redeeming the series after the *Star Trek V* debacle. The hawks ("We should have gone in and kicked some Klingon butt") dispute the negotiated peace portrayed in the film. Doves grapple with the question of whether the crew's attitudes toward Klingons exhibit some level of racism. And once again, the question of Gene Roddenberry's influence on the film comes to prominence. Did he really request the removal of Operation Rescue because it went against Federation ideals? Would he have written James T. Kirk as a racist? ✓**GENIE**→ *keyword* sfrt2→SFRT2 Bulletin Board →set 26→read 13

Star Trek VI: The Undiscovered Country Quotes A large collection of lines from the sixth movie. ✓**INTERNET**→*www* http:// www.cosy.sbg.ac.at/ftp/pub/trek /quotes/st6_tuc.txt

Sulu: "My God" Soundclip from *Star Trek VI* as Captain Sulu watches the energy wave approach. WAV file. ✓**COMPUSERVE**→*go* sfmedia→Libraries→*Search by file name:* SULU.WAV

"There is an old Vulcan proverb..." Spock explaining why Kirk was chosen to be the envoy to the Klingon peace talks. The first file is for IBM compatibles; the second for Macs. ✓**COMPUSERVE**→*go* sfmedia→Libraries→ *Search by file name:* PROVRB.ZIP *or* PROVRB.SIT

Two Important Klingons If this file were a song, it would be sung to the tune of "Some Enchanted Evening" ("Two important Klingons/Ridges in their forehead"). Instead, it's a picture, and it shows the imposing figures of Chancellor Gorkon and Ambassador Azetbur. ✓**COMPUSERVE**→*go* sfmedia→Libraries→*Search by file name:* ST6-1A.GIF

The USS Excelsior The *Excelsior* emerges from the energy field in *Star Trek VI*. ✓**COMPUSERVE**→*go* sf-media→Libraries→*Search by file name:* ST06. GIF

The USS Excelsior Firing on Bird of Prey An image of the *Excelsior* firing on General Chang's Klingon Bird of Prey in the movie *Star Trek VI*. ✓**COMPUSERVE**→*go* sf-media→Libraries→ *Search by file name:* ST07. GIF

PART 4

THE
NEXT
GENERATION

Episode guide

This is a list of all episodes of *Star Trek: The Next Genera-tion* in order of airdate, along with relevant Net sites. Addresses are sometimes given in shorthand (*<address x>*); instructions on constructing full addresses appear in the FAQ (page 20), and on the key in the back of the book.

Season 1

Encounter at Farpoint

Episodes 1 & 2
Writer: D.C. Fontana & Gene
             Roddenberry
Director: Corey Allen
Stardate: 41153.7

Summary: The *Enterprise-D* crew must investigate a starbase at Farpoint, which turns out to be an alien with the ability to change its shape. On the way to Farpoint, the crew meets the powerful Q, who puts them on trial for their humanity. Picard defends the crew.

Vidiot's Synopsis ✓ **INTERNET** ...→*www* <address 1a>farpoint. syn.htm ...→*www* <address 1b> sttng-1.html#721

21st-Century Court Picture of a mock 21st-century courtroom. ✓ **INTERNET** ...→*anon-ftp* <address 33>→sttng029.jpg ...→*anon-ftp* <address 34>→sttng029.jpg

Alien Life Forms Image of alien life forms at Farpoint station ✓ **IN-TERNET** ...→*anon-ftp* <address 33>→sttng058.jpg ...→*anon-ftp* <address 34>→sttng058.jpg

Crew Examining Tasha Picture of a frozen Tasha being examined by Data, Picard, and Troi in sickbay. ✓ **INTERNET** ...→*anon-ftp* <address 33>→sttng009.jpg ...→*anon-ftp* <address 34>→sttng009.jpg

Data and Dr. McCoy Photo of 137-year-old Dr. McCoy on the *Enterprise NCC-1701-D.* ✓ **INTERNET** ...→*anon-ftp* <address 33>→sttng039.jpg ...→*anon-ftp* <address 34>→sttng039.jpg

Deanna Troi on Bridge Image of Troi in her original uniform. ✓ **INTERNET** ...→*anon-ftp* <address 33>→sttng041.jpg ...→*anon-ftp* <address 34>→sttng041.jpg

The Enterprise Image of the *Enterprise* firing energy toward Farpoint station ✓ **INTERNET** ...→*anon-ftp* <address 33>→sttng057.jpg ...→*anon-ftp* <address 34>→sttng057.jpg

Enterprise Bridge Image of Picard and crew on the bridge. ✓ **INTERNET** ...→*anon-ftp* <address 33>→sttng004.jpg ...→*anon-ftp* <address 34>→sttng004.jpg

Farpoint Station Picture of the Farpoint station. ✓ **INTERNET** ...→*anon-ftp* <address 33>→sttng 028.jpg ...→*anon-ftp* <address 34>→sttng028.jpg

Old Man Image of an old man with long hair. ✓ **INTERNET** ...→*anon-ftp* <address 33>→sttng031. jpg ...→*anon-ftp* <address 34>→sttng031.jpg

Picard and Crew Picture of Picard and crew in twenty-first century courtroom. ✓ **INTERNET** ...→*anon-ftp* <address 33>→sttng024. jpg ...→*anon-ftp* <address 34>→sttng024.jpg

STARQUOTES

"Let's see what's out there..."
Picard—"Encounter at Farpoint"

Net Source: STTNG Quotes—http://www. ugcs.caltech.edu/htbin/werdna/fortune?sttng

Q the Judge Q as judge in mock 21st-century courtroom. ✓**INTERNET** ...→*anon-ftp* <address 33>→ sttng025.jpg ...→*anon-ftp* <address 34>→sttng025.jpg

---

Strangers on the Bridge. Image of intruders on the *Enterprise* Bridge. ✓**INTERNET** ...→*anon-ftp* <address 33>→sttng066.jpg ...→ *anon-ftp* <address 34>→sttng066.jpg

---

Troi Picture of Counselor Troi on the bridge. ✓**INTERNET** ...→*anon-ftp* <address 33>→sttng053.jpg ...→*anon-ftp* <address 34>→sttng 053.jpg

---

View from the Bridge Picture of Picard and *Enterprise* crew watching alien life forms on viewscreen. ✓**INTERNET** ...→*anon-ftp* <address 33>→sttng056.jpg ...→*anon-ftp* <address 34>→sttng 056.jpg

---

Web Image of the web used by Q to capture *Enterprise*. ✓**INTERNET** ...→*anon-ftp* <address 33>→sttng 005.jpg ...→*anon-ftp* <address 34>→sttng005.jpg

---

Worf Picture of Worf on the Bridge. ✓**INTERNET** ...→*anon-ftp* <address 33>→sttng018.jpg ...→ *anon-ftp* <address 34>→sttng018.jpg

The Naked Now

Episode: #3
Teleplay: J. Michael Bingham
Story: John D.F. Black & J. Michael Bingham
Director: Paul Lynch
Stardate: 41209.2

Summary: After they investigate the mysteriously empty starship *Tsiolkovsky*, the crew becomes ill with a varient of the Psi2000 virus that destroys all their inhibitions.

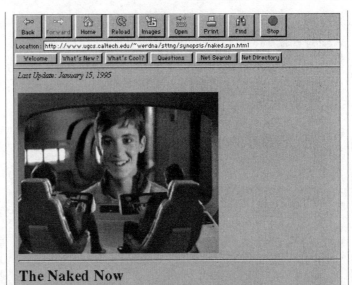

The Naked Now
synopsis from the Vidiot's TNG Program Guide

Screenshot–http://www.ugcs.caltech.edu:80/~werdna/sttng/synopsis/naked.syn.html

The known cure for the disease, found by the *Enterprise* crew in TOS's "Naked Time," is no longer effective.

Vidiot's Synopsis ✓**INTERNET**... →*www* <address 1a>naked.syn. html ...→*www* <address 1b>sttng-1.html#103

Beverly, Deanna, and Jean-Luc Image of Beverly, Deanna, and Jean-Luc examining tricorder readings in sickbay. ✓**INTERNET** ...→*anon-ftp* <address 33>→ sttng061.jpg ...→*anon-ftp* <address 34>→sttng061.jpg

---

Beverly with JLP in Sickbay Picard and Crusher talk in sickbay in the episode "The Naked Now." ✓**COMPUSERVE**→*go* sfmedia→Libraries→*Search by file name:* BJNKD.GIF

Kissing Couple A kiss between Tasha and Data. ✓**INTERNET** ...→*anon-ftp* <address 33>→ sttng064.jpg ...→*anon-ftp* <address 34>→sttng064.jpg

---

Natasha Yar Image of Natasha in a seductive outfit with Commander Data (unseen). ✓**INTERNET** ...→*anon-ftp* <address 33>→ sttng071.jpg ...→*anon-ftp* <address 34>→sttng071.jpg

---

Natasha Yar Picture of Tasha in sexy outfit seducing Data (unseen). ✓**INTERNET** ...→*anon-ftp* <address 33>→sttng069.jpg ...→ *anon-ftp* <address 34>→sttng069.jpg

---

Tasha Yar and Data Kissing Tasha and Data romantically linked due to a mysterious ship-wide intoxication. ✓**INTERNET** ...→ *anon-ftp* <address 33>→sttng070.jpg ...→*anon-ftp* <address 34>→ sttng070.jpg

---

Tasha Yar in Evening Wear Picture of Tasha Yar uncharacteristically attired—very sexy. ✓**INTERNET** ...→*anon-ftp* <address 33>→ sttng068.jpg ...→*anon-ftp* <ad-

dress 34>→sttng068.jpg

Wesley and Geordi LaForge

Picture of Wesley Crusher and Geordi LaForge in engineering. ✓**INTERNET** ...→*anon-ftp* <address 33>→sttng063.jpg ...→*anon-ftp* <address 34>→sttng 063.jpg

Wesley Crusher Picture of a young Wesley Crusher on the viewscreen. ✓**INTERNET** ...→*anon-ftp* <address 33>→sttng073.jpg ...→*anon-ftp* <address 34>→sttng073.jpg

Wesley Crusher Picture of Wesley Crusher, drunk, in Engineering section. ✓**INTERNET** ...→*anon-ftp* <address 33>→sttng067.jpg ...→*anon-ftp* <address 34>→sttng067.jpg

Code of Honor

Episode: #4
Writer: Katharyn Powers &
            Michael Baron
Director: Russ Mayberry
Stardate: 41235.25

Summary: Searching for a vaccine for the deadly plague Anchilles Fever, the *Enterprise-D* travels to Ligon II. There Tasha Yar is kidnapped by the planet's leader, and must do battle with his wife to win her freedom and obtain the vaccine.

Vidiot's Synopsis ✓**INTERNET** ...→*www* <address 1a>code.syn.html ...→*www* <address 1b>sttng-1.html#104

Haven

Episode: #5
Teleplay: Tracy Tormé
Story: Tracy Tormé &
            Lan Okunn
Director: Richard Compton
Stardate: 41294.5

Summary: The *Enterprise-D* travels to Haven to deliver Deanna Troi for her pre-arranged marriage. Deanna is torn between her career and her culture's customs, while her fiancé has second thoughts when he encounters the survivors of a biological war, including a woman he has been dreaming about for years.

Vidiot's Synopsis ✓**INTERNET** ...→*www* <address 1a>haven.syn.html ...→*www* <address 1b> sttng-1.html#105

Where No One Has Gone Before

Episode: #6
Writer: Diane Duane &
          Michael Reaves
Director: Rob Bowman
Stardate: 41263.1

Summary: A visiting engineer, Kosinski, causes the *Enterprise-D* to travel at excessive warp speed, throwing it into a universe where thoughts become real. A mysterious alien known as the Traveler works with Wesley to help the ship escape.

Vidiot's Synopsis ✓**INTERNET** ...→*www* <address 1a> nonegone.syn.html...→*www* <address 1b> sttng-1.html#106

The Last Outpost

Episode: #7
Teleplay: Herbert Wright
Story: Richard Krzemien
Director: Richard Colla
Stardate: 41386.4

Summary: In pursuit of a Ferengi cruiser bearing a stolen energy unit, the *Enterprise-D* is held in orbit around Delphi Ardu. It's soon discovered that it is not the Ferengi that are responsible, but

"The Enterprise visits Ligon II to obtain a rare vaccine needed to avert a plague on Stryis IV. As the Ligonian leader, Lutan, comes on board, he seems very arrogant, and more than slightly attracted to Tasha. In departing, he kidnaps Tasha from right under the Enterprise's noses. Data and Riker theorize that Lutan kidnapped Tasha as a display of 'counting coup'—by stealing the riskiest prize of all, he proved himself very brave for his followers. By Ligonian custom, Picard must ask to get Tasha back, in public, at a banquet. He does this, but Lutan says that he cannot part with her, thus breaking even his own customs. His wife, Yareena, challenges Tasha to a death-duel, which she must accept if the Enterprise is to obtain the vaccine. Lutan now cannot lose; if Yareena dies, he inherits her land (on Ligon, the women own the land), and if she lives, he loses nothing."

—from **Vidiot's Synopsis of "Code of Honor"**

ASK SPOT!

a) What is the name of the Benzite Wesley loses out to during the Starfleet Entrance Exam?

b) In what episode does Wesley serve as captain of the *Enterprise*?

(See answers on page 359)

Portal, the remaining sentry of the Tkon Empire, which ruled over the entire galaxy more than 600,000 years earlier.

Vidiot's Synopsis ✓**INTERNET** ...→*www* <address 1a>outpost. syn.html ...→ <address 1b>sttng-1. html#107

Ferengi Picture of three Ferengi on a rock. ✓**INTERNET** ...→*anon-ftp* <address 33>→sttng080.jpg ...→ *anon-ftp* <address 34>→sttng080. jpg

Ferengi Vessel Image of the *Enterprise* encountering a Ferengi vessel. ✓**INTERNET** ...→*anon-ftp* <address 33>→sttng08.jpg ...→ *anon-ftp* <address 34>→sttng08. jpg

Three Ferengi Image of three Ferengi laughing. ✓**INTERNET** ...→ *anon-ftp* <address 33>→sttng081. jpg ...→*anon-ftp* <address 34>→ sttng081.jpg

Lonely Among Us

Episode: #8
Teleplay: D.C. Fontana
Story: Michael Halperin
Director: Cliff Bole
Stardate: 41249.3

Summary: An energy being is caught in the ship's computer as the *Enterprise* moves through a mysterious cloud. The being moves from Worf to Crusher to Picard, through whom it tries desperately to get back to its own kind.

Vidiot's Synopsis ✓**INTERNET** ...→*www* <address 1a>lonely.syn. html...→<address 1b>sttng-1.html #108

Justice

Episode: #9
Teleplay: Worley Thorne
Story: Ralph Wills & Worley Thorne
Director: James L. Conway
Stardate: 41255.6

Summary: A pleasant shore leave on Rubicun III turns ugly when Wesley unknowingly violates the code of the host culture, the Edo, and is sentenced to death. Picard must decide between obeying the Prime Directive and saving Wesley's life.

Vidiot's Synopsis ✓**INTERNET** ...→*www* <address 1a>justice.syn. html...→<address 1b>sttng-1.html #109

The Battle

Episode: #10
Teleplay: Herbert Wright
Story: Larry Forrester
Director: Rob Bowman
Stardate: 41723.9

Summary: A Ferengi commander, DaiMon Bok, presents Cap-

tain Picard with the hulk of Picard's first ship, the *Stargazer*. What Picard does not realize is that Bok holds him responsible for the death of his son who was a Ferengi commander at the battle of Maxia. Aboard the *Stargazer* are thought-altering devices that make Picard believe that the *Enterprise-D* is an enemy ship.

Vidiot's Synopsis ✓**INTERNET** ...→*www* <address 1a>battle.syn. html...→*www* <address 1b>sttng-1. html#110

Hide and Q

Episode: #11
Teleplay: C.J. Holland & Gene Roddenberry
Story: C.J. Holland
Director: Cliff Bole
Stardate: 41590.5

Summary: Q returns and wreaks havoc by forcing the bridge crew to take part in a deadly game. Q offers Riker the chance to share his phenomenal powers, if Riker will become part of the Q Continuum.

Vidiot's Synopsis ✓**INTERNET** ...→*www* <address 1a>hideq.syn. html...→*www* <address 1b>sttng-1. html #111

How Rude Soundclip of Q: "How rude!" ✓**INTERNET**→ *anon-ftp* <address 35>→how-rude

Macrohead Soundclip: "Macrohead...(laughter)...microbrain." ✓**INTERNET**→ *anon-ftp* <address 35>→macrohead

Penalty Soundclip of Q: "Game penalty!" ✓**INTERNET**→*anon-ftp* <address 35>→penalty

Standing Order Soundclip of Picard: "There is a new ship standing order on the bridge: when one is in the penalty box, tears are permitted." ✓**INTERNET**→*anon-ftp* <address 35>→standing-order

Suffering and Dying Soundclip of Q: "Ahh, your species is always suffering and dying." ✓**INTERNET**→*anon-ftp* <address 35>→suffering-and-dying

Too Short a Season

Episode: #12
Teleplay: Michael Michaelian &
            D.C. Fontana
Story: Michael Michaelian
Director: Rob Bowman
Stardate: 41309.5

Summary: The *Enterprise-D* transports Admiral Jameson to Mordan IV to negotiate the release of Federation hostages. But the planet's leader really wants Jameson to pay for a civil war the admiral started on the planet forty years earlier.

Vidiot's Synopsis ✓**INTERNET**
…→*www* <address 1a>tooshort. syn.html…→*www* <address 1b>

---

sttng-1.html#112

The Big Good-Bye

Episode: #13
Writer: Tracy Tormé
Director: Joseph L. Scanlan
Stardate: 41997.7

Summary: In a film noir holodeck fantasy, Picard becomes a 1940s hard-boiled detective, Dixon Hill. While he is investigating a case, a short circuit in the holodeck system turns Picard's innocent pastime into deadly reality.

Vidiot's Synopsis ✓**INTERNET**
…→*www* <address 1a>goodbye. syn.html…→*www* <address 1b> sttng-1.html#113

Big Goodbye Scenes Three episode scenes. ✓**PVG** *dial* 513-233-7993→<your username>→ <your password>→F→*Download a file:* TNG016.GIF *and* TNG017.GIF *and* TNG018.GIF

Gloria and Dixon Hill Picture of Gloria (Guinan) and Dixon

Hill (Picard). ✓**PVG** *dial* 513-233-7993→<your username>→<your password>→F→*Download a file:* CLUES-C.GIF

Datalore

Episode: #14
Teleplay: Robert Lewin & Gene
            Roddenberry
Story: Robert Lewin & Maurice Hurley
Director: Rob Bowman
Stardate: 41242.4

Summary: While at Omicron Theta, Data's homeland, *Enterprise-D* discovers Data's twin, a duplicate android. They revive Data's "brother," Lore, only to discover that he was made too disconcertingly human, prone to megalomania and cruelty.

Trekker Review ✓**INTERNET**→ *www* <address 15>datalore.html

Vidiot's Synopsis ✓**INTERNET**
…→*www* <address 1a>datalore. syn.html …→*www* <address 1b> sttng-1.html#114

The Crystalline Entity Image of the deadly Crystalline Entity on the *Enterprise* viewscreen. ✓**INTERNET** …→*anon-ftp* <address 33>→ sttng325.jpg …→*anon-ftp* <address 34>→sttng325.jpg

Lore Picture of Lore, Data's evil twin. ✓**INTERNET** …→*anon-ftp* <address 33>→sttng047.jpg …→*anon-ftp* <address 34>→sttng047.jpg

Woman Smiling Picture of Carmen Davila, a colony engineer and friend of Commander Riker, who was killed in an attack by the Crystalline Entity. ✓**INTERNET** …→*anon-ftp* <address 33>→ sttng321.jpg …→*anon-ftp* <address 34>→sttng321.jpg

Screenshot—http://www.ugcs.caltech.edu/~werdna/sttng/synopsis/goodbye.syn.html

The Big Goodbye
synopsis from the Vidiot's TNG Program Guide

Angel One

Episode: #15
Writer: Patrick Barry
Director: Michael Rhodes
Stardate: 41636.9

Summary: On Angel One, the *Enterprise-D* finds the male survivors of the Odin living as second-class citizens under the rule of the planet's matriarchy. Meanwhile Picard and Worf suffer from a mysterious illness.

Trekker Review ✓**INTERNET**→
www <address 15>angel_one.html

Vidiot's Synopsis ✓**INTERNET**
...→*www* <address 1a>angel1.
syn.html ...→<address 1b>sttng-1.
html#115

Angel One Scene Scene from the episode. ✓**PVG** *dial* 513-233-7993→<your username>→<your password>→F→*Download a file:* TOWEL.GIF

Riker Image of Riker. ✓**COMPUSERVE**→*go* sfmedia→Libraries→*Search by file name:* TOWEL.GIF

11001001

Episode: #16
Writer: Maurice Hurley &
             Robert Lewin
Director: Paul Lynch
Stardate: 41365.9

Summary: The *Enterprise* undergoes servicing at Starbase 74, only to fall into the hands of the Bynars, who can communicate directly with computers. They trap Picard and Riker in a holodeck simulation and commandeer the ship in order to help repair their planet's computer system.

Trekker Review ✓**INTERNET**
→*www* <address 15>11001001.html

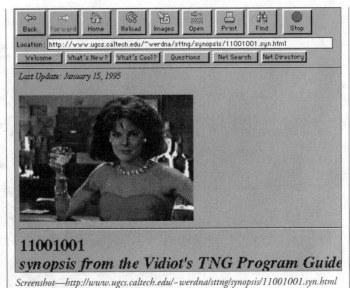

Back   Forward   Home   Reload   Images   Open   Print   Find   Stop

Location: http://www.ugcs.caltech.edu/~werdna/sttng/synopsis/11001001.syn.html

Welcome   What's New?   What's Cool?   Questions   Net Search   Net Directory

Last Update: January 15, 1995

11001001
synopsis from the Vidiot's TNG Program Guide

Screenshot—http://www.ugcs.caltech.edu/~werdna/sttng/synopsis/11001001.syn.html

Vidiot's Synopsis ✓**INTERNET**→
...→*www* <address 1a> 11001001.
syn.html...→*www* <address 1b>
sttng-1.html#116

Abandon Ship Soundclip: "Abandon ship. This is not a drill!" ✓**INTERNET**→ *anon-ftp* <address 35>→abandon-ship

Auto Destruct Soundclip of the computer: "Auto-destruct will detonate in four minutes and fifty-nine seconds." ✓**INTERNET**→*anon-ftp* <address 35>→auto-destruct

Awaiting Soundclip: "I'm awaiting inspiration." ✓**INTERNET**→ *anon-ftp* <address 35>→awaiting

Knock Out Like You Soundclip: "What's a knock out like you doing in a computer-generated gin joint like this?" ✓**INTERNET**→*anon-ftp* <address 35>→ knock-out-like-you

Not Programmed Soundclip: "I'm not programmed to give you that information." ✓**INTERNET**→ *anon-ftp* <address 35>→ not-pro-

grammed

Pride of the Enterprise Soundclip: "The pride of the *Enterprise* goes with you." ✓**INTERNET**→*anon-ftp* <address 35>→pride-of-the-enterprise

Problem Corrected Soundclip of Bynar voices from the episode 11001001: "We are almost done." "The deviation"—"caused by a previous"—"probe"— "has been corrected." "You may use the equipment"—"any time you wish." ✓**INTERNET**→*anon-ftp* <address 35>→problem-corrected

Under Control Soundclip of Picard: "Everything under control." ✓**INTERNET** →*anon-ftp* <address 35>→under-control

Valid Question Soundclip of the computer: "That is not a valid question." ✓**INTERNET** →*anon-ftp* <address 35>→valid-question

Home Soil

Episode: #17

Teleplay: Robert Sabaroff
Story: Karl Guers,
Ralph Sanchez &
Robert Sabaroff
Stardate: 41463.9

Summary: Some endangered species are so small you almost don't know they exist. While visiting terraformers on Velara III, the crew discovers a microscopic crystalline life form called "microbrains" about to be wiped out by the terraforming process. In desperation, the little aliens try to take the *Enterprise*, and the ensuing problems are anything but small.

Vidiot's Synopsis ✓**INTERNET**
...→*www* <address 1a>homesoil.syn.html ...→*www* <address 1b>sttng-1.html#117

Bag of Mostly Water Soundclip: "Bag of mostly water." ✓**INTERNET**→*anon-ftp* <address 35>→bag-of-mostly-water

I Had No Choice Soundclip: "Destroyed!...I had no choice." ✓**INTERNET**→*anon-ftp* <address 35>→i-had-no-choice

What Is It? Soundclip of Geordi: "Whoa...what is it?" ✓**INTERNET**→*anon-ftp* <address 35>→what-is-it

When the Bough Breaks

Episode: #18
Writer: Hannah Louise Shearer
Director: Kim Manners
Stardate: 41509.1

Summary: Although the Aldeans have the ability to hide their planet with an advanced cloaking device, they do not have the ability to reproduce. When their offer to trade this technology for children is refused, the Aldeans

Location: http://www.ugcs.caltech.edu/~werdna/sttng/synopsis/cmgofage.syn.html

Last Update: January 15, 1995

Coming of Age
synopsis from the Vidiot's TNG Program Guide

Screenshot—http://www.ugcs.caltech.edu/~werdna/sttng/synopsis/cmgofage.syn.html

kidnap six children from the ship.

Trekker Review ✓**INTERNET**→*www* <address 15>when_the_bough_breaks.html

Vidiot's Synopsis ✓**INTERNET**
...→*www* <address 1a>bough.syn.html...→*www* <address 1b>sttng-1.htm l#118

Coming of Age

Episode: #19
Writer: Sandy Fries
Director: Michael Vejar
Stardate: 41416.2

Summary: Wesley fails to pass his Starfleet entrance exams. Picard's old friend Admiral Quinn comes to the *Enterprise* to investigate Picard for conspiracy.

Trekker Review ✓**INTERNET**→*www* <address 1>coming_of_age.html

Vidiot's Synopsis ✓**INTERNET**

...→*www* <address 1a>cmgofage.syn.html ...→<address 1b>sttng-1.html#119

Heart of Glory

Episode: #20
Teleplay: Maurice Hurley
Story: Maurice Hurley, Herbert Wright & D.C. Fontana
Director: Rob Bowman
Stardate: 41503.7

Summary: Three Klingons are discovered aboard a Talarian ship in the Neutral Zone. Opposed to the Klingon peace with the Federation, they try to enlist Worf in their plan to take over the *Enterprise-D*.

Trekker Review ✓**INTERNET**→*www* <address 15>heart_of_glory.html

Vidiot's Synopsis ✓**INTERNET**
...→*www* <address 1a>glory.syn.html...→<address 1b>sttng-1.html

#120

Picture of Worf Worf in a scene from "Heart of Glory." ✓**COMPUSERVE**→*go* sfmedia→Libraries→ *Search by file name:* HOWL.GIF

Death Ritual Soundclip of a long howl from a Klingon death ritual. ✓**INTERNET**→*anon-ftp* <ad­dress 35>→death-ritual

Put Down the Phaser Soundclip of Worf: "Put down the phaser." ✓**INTERNET**→*anon-ftp* <address 35>→put-down-the-phaser

Seems Wrong Soundclip of Picard: "Everything about this seems wrong." ✓**INTERNET** →*anon-ftp* <ad­dress 35>→seems-wrong

True Test Soundclip of Worf: "The true test of a warrior is not without…it is within." ✓**INTERNET** →*anon-ftp* <address 35>→true-test

Why You Are Driven Soundclip: "Do you know why you are driven? Why you cannot relent or repent or confess or abstain?" ✓**INTERNET**→*anon-ftp* <address 35>→ you-are-driven

Arsenal of Freedom

Episode: #21
Teleplay: Richard Manning & Hans Beimler
Story: Maurice Hurley & Robert Lewin
Director: Les Landau
Stardate: 41798.2

Summary: On a weapons-manufacturing planet, the crew finds that weapons designers have been eradicated by their own products. The weapons, which have developed a life of their own, engage the *Enterprise* in a series of battles.

Trekker Review **INTERNET**→

www <address 15>the_arsenal_of_ freedom.html

Vidiot's Synopsis ✓**INTERNET** …→*www* <address 1a>arsenal. syn.html…→*www* <address 1b> sttng-1. html#121

Shields Up Soundclip: "Shields up. Photon torpedoes armed. Phasers standing by." ✓**INTERNET**→ *anon-ftp* <address 35>→ shields-up3

Skin of Evil

Episode: #22
Teleplay: Joseph Stefano & Hannah Louise Shearer
Story: Joseph Stefano
Director: Joseph L. Scanlan
Stardate: 41601.3

Summary: As they attempt to locate Deanna Troi, whose transport shuttle has crashed on Vagra II, the rescue team encounters Armus, an alien resembling a walking oil-slick. Armus assumes a humanoid shape and, just for the fun of it, kills Tasha Yar.

Vidiot's Synopsis ✓**INTERNET** …→*www* <address 1a>skin.syn. html…→*www* <address 1b>sttng-1. html #122

Tasha's Final Scene Tasha Yar's first "final" scene on the holodeck. ✓**PVG** *dial* 513-233-7993→<your username>→<your password>→F→ *Download a file:* NG06.GIF

Symbiosis

Episode: #23
Teleplay: Robert Lewin, Richard Manning & Hans Beimler
Story: Robert Lewin
Director: Win Phelps
Stardate: n/a

Summary: Responding to a dis

tress call from a freighter, the *Enterprise* discovers that the ship is a drug runner, shuttling between two planets, one of which supplies a powerful narcotic to the other, which is enslaved by drug use.

Vidiot's Synopsis ✓**INTERNET** …→*www* <address 1a>symbiosis. syn.html…→*www* <address 1b> sttng-1.html#123

We'll Always Have Paris

Episode: #24
Writers: Deborah Dean Davis & Hannah Louise Shearer
Director: Robert Becker
Stardate: 41679.9

Summary: Picard attempts to close a rift in the time/space continuum and discovers that an old lover from his Paris days has married the scientist whose research was responsible for the rift. Play it again, Sam.

Trekker Review ✓**INTERNET**→ *www* <address 15>well_always_ have_paris.html

Vidiot's Synopsis ✓**INTERNET** …→*www* <address 1a>paris.syn. html…→*www* <address 1b> sttng-1. html#124

Conspiracy

Episode: #25
Teleplay: Tracy Tormé
Story: Robert Sabaroff
Director: Cliff Bole
Stardate: 41775.5

Summary: Picard receives a secret message from an old friend apprising him of some bizarre Starfleet developments. Back on Earth, Picard discovers a number of Starfleet admirals have been taken over by alien parasites.

Vidiot's Synopsis ✓INTERNET ...→*www* <address 1a>conspiracy. syn.html...→*www* <address 1b>sttng-1.html#125

Admiral Quinn Picture of a contemplative Admiral Gregory Quinn. ✓INTERNET ...→*anon-ftp* <address 33>→sttng095.jpg ...→ *anon-ftp* <address 34>→sttng095. jpg

General Dexter Remmick Picture of an unsmiling General Dexter Remmick. ✓INTERNET ...→ *anon-ftp* <address 33>→sttng097. jpg ...→*anon-ftp* <address 34>→ sttng097.jpg

Quinn and Remmick Picture of Admiral Gregory Quinn and General Dexter Remmick on their visit to the *Enterprise NCC-1701-D*. ✓INTERNET ...→*anon-ftp* <address 33>→sttng086.jpg ...→*anon-ftp* <address 34>→sttng086.jpg

The Neutral Zone

Episode: #26
Teleplay: Maurice Hurley
Story: Deborah McIntyre & Mona Glee
Director: James Conway
Stardate: 41986.0

Summary: While investigating the destruction of outposts on the edge on the Neutral Zone, the *Enterprise* discovers a ship with three cryogenically frozen occupants. Once revived, the 20th-century earthlings find space-life 370 years in the future difficult to accept.

Vidiot's Synopsis ✓INTERNET ...→*www* <address 1a>neutral.syn. html...→*www* <address 1b>sttng-1. html#126

Claire Raymond Picture of cryogenically-frozen woman from the twenty-first century who dis-

covers she has living relatives in the twenty-fourth. ✓INTERNET ...→*anon-ftp* <address 33>→sttng1 14.jpg ...→ *anon-ftp* <address 34> →sttng114.jpg

Counselor Troi with Cleavage Picture of Troi counseling 21st century visitors, wearing a 24th century low-cut uniform. ✓INTERNET ...→*anon-ftp* <address 33>→ sttng118.jpg ...→*anon-ftp* <address 34>→sttng118.jpg

The Enterprise Picture of the *Enterprise* as it investigates the disappearance of outposts along the Neutral Zone. ✓INTERNET ...→ *anon-ftp* <address 33>→sttng205. jpg ...→*anon-ftp* <address 34>→ sttng205.jpg

Meeting in the Conference Room Image of a meeting to discuss strategy for possible encounter with the Romulans. ✓INTERNET ...→*anon-ftp* <address 33> →sttng113.jpg ...→*anon-ftp* <address 34>→sttng113.jpg

Picard in the Conference Room Image of Picard planning his strategy for meeting with the Romulans. ✓INTERNET ...→*anon-ftp* <address 33>→sttng112.jpg ... →*anon-ftp* <address 34>→sttng112. jpg

Ralph Offenhouse Picture of thawed person, Ralph Offenhouse, frozen with cryogenics in the 21st century aboard the *Enterprise*. ✓INTERNET ...→*anon-ftp* <address 33>→sttng115.jpg ...→*anon-ftp* <address 34>→sttng115.jpg

The Romulan Warbird Image of a Romulan Warbird: after encountering and threatening the Federation, the Romulans cloak themselves and return across the Neutral Zone. ✓INTERNET ...→ *anon-ftp* <address 33>→sttng120.

"Two admirals, Savar and Aaron, invite Picard and Riker down to dinner. The third, Gregory Quinn, asks to come up to the ship. Picard beams down, and Riker sees Quinn to his quarters. Quinn attacks Riker, showing incredible strength. He knocks Riker out, and even Worf shortly afterwards, before Beverly knocks him out with repeated phaser blasts. She examines him, and finds a parasitic creature has taken him over. She informs Picard about this. Picard goes in to dinner, where it is revealed that they've all been taken over. He tries to leave, but is caught by Riker, whom we earlier saw sneak up on Bev. As it happens, he's only faking, and they manage to stun everyone in the room, except for Aaron, who escapes. They catch him, and follow the creature that leaves hîs mouth to Remmick, who is the leader. They kill Remmick, and the mother-creature that crawls out of his ribcage.

—from **Vidiot's Episode Synopis of** "Conspiracy"

jpg ...→*anon-ftp* <address 34>→ sttng 120.jpg

Romulan Warbird Decloaking! A Romulan Warbird decloaks in the first encounter in half a century with the Romulans. ✓**INTERNET** ...→*anon-ftp* <address 33>→*anon-ftp* <address 34>→sttng 118.jpg ...→*anon-ftp* <address 34>→sttng 118.jpg

The Romulans Picture of the first Starfleet encounter with the Romulans in over 53 years! ✓**INTERNET** ...→*anon-ftp* <address 33>→sttng 119.jpg ...→*anon-ftp* <address 34>→sttng 119.jpg

Sonny Clemons Picture of one of the frozen guests aboard the *Enterprise*. ✓**INTERNET** ...→*anon-ftp* <address 33>→sttng 116.jpg ...→*anon-ftp* <address 34>→ sttng 116.jpg

Spacecraft Adrift Picture of the *Enterprise* encountering an unidentified craft and stopping to investigate. ✓**INTERNET** ...→*anon-ftp* <address 33>→sttng 111.jpg ...→*anon-ftp* <address 34>→sttng 111.jpg

---

Season 2

The Child

Episode: #27
Writers: Jaron Summers, Jon Povill & Maurice Hurley
Director: Rob Bowman
Stardate: 42073.1

Summary: Troi is impregnated by a mysterious alien creature which takes the form of a glowing light. Troi resists pressure to terminate the pregnancy and gives birth to a male child who develops rapidly.

Vidiot's Synopsis ✓**INTERNET** ...→*www* <address 1a>child.syn. html...→*www*<address 1b>sttng-2.html#127

Where Silence Has Lease

Episode: #28
Writer: Jack B. Sowards
Director: Winrich Kolbe
Stardate: 42193.6

Summary: In the Morgana quadrant, a curious alien called Nagilum traps the *Enterprise-D* in a space hole, hoping to learn more about humans—specifically, the ways in which they die.

Vidiot's Synopsis ✓**INTERNET** ...→*www* <address 1a>silence.syn. html...→*www* <address 1b>sttng-2.html#128

Elementary, Dear Data

Episode: #29
Writer: Brian Alan Lane
Director: Rob Bowman
Stardate: 42286.3

Summary: When re-creating Sherlock Holmes stories on the holodeck doesn't prove enough of a challenge for Data, Geordi orders the computer to create an opponent worthy of Data's intellect. The two are soon battling for real with a powerful new version of the evil Professor Moriarty.

Vidiot's Synopsis ✓**INTERNET** ...→*www* <address 1a>elementary. syn.html...→*www* <address 1b> sttng-2.html#129

Data as Sherlock Holmes Image of Data playing Sherlock Holmes in the Holodeck. ✓**COMPUSERVE**→*go* sfmedia→Libraries→ *Search by file name:* HOLMES.GIF

The Outrageous Okona

Episode: #30
Teleplay: Burton Armus
Story: Les Menchen, Lance Dickson and David Landsberg
Director: Robert Becker
Stardate: 42402.7

Summary: *Enterprise-D* picks up

Screenshot—http://www.ugcs.caltech.edu/~werdna/sttng/synopsis/neutral.syn.html

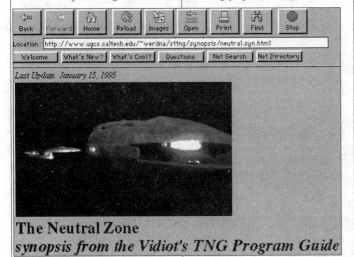

Last Update: January 15, 1995

The Neutral Zone
synopsis from the Vidiot's TNG Program Guide

Screenshot—http://www.ugcs.caltech.edu/~werdna/sttng/synopsis/whisper.syn.html

Okona, a cargo-ship captain with an engaging personality—so engaging, in fact, that Data decides to try to develop a sense of humor. At the same time, ships from other parts of the universe arrive, each demanding they be given Okona—the criminal.

Vidiot's Synopsis ✓ **INTERNET**
…→*www* <address 1a>okona.syn. html…→*www* <address 1b>sttng-2. html# 130

The Schizoid Man

Episode: #31
Teleplay: Tracy Tormé
Story: Richard Manning &
           Hans Beimler
Director: Les Landau
Stardate: 42437.5

Summary: A dying, brilliant scientist surreptitiously transfers his brain into Data, who begins displaying the symptoms of split personality.

Vidiot's Synopsis ✓ **INTERNET**
…→*www* <address 1a>schizoid. syn.html …→*www* <address 1b>

sttng-2.html# 131

Loud as a Whisper

Episode: #32
Writer: Jacqueline Zambrano
Director: Larry Shaw
Stardate: 42477.2

Summary: The *Enterprise-D* transports a deaf-mute mediator who speaks through a three-person "chorus" to a war-torn planet. When his chorus is killed, the mediator, with Troi's help, must learn to communicate.

Vidiot's Synopsis ✓ **INTERNET**
…→*www* <address 1a>whisper. syn.html…→ *www* <address 1b> sttng-2.html# 132

Unnatural Selection

Episode: #33
Writer: John Mason &
           Mike Gray
Director: Paul Lynch
Stardate: 42494.8

Summary: Genetically engineered children are the carriers of

a deadly disease that causes humans to age at a rapid rate. Dr. Pulaski contracts the disease and the crew races to find a cure.

Vidiot's Synopsis ✓ **INTERNET**
…→*www* <address 1a>unnatural. syn.html …→ *www* <address 1b> sttng-2.html# 133

A Matter of Honor

Episode: #34
Teleplay: Burton Armus
Story: Wanda M. Haight,
           Gregory Amos &
           Burton Armus
Director: Rob Bowman
Stardate: 42506.5

Summary: While taking part in an officer exchange program aboard a Klingon vessel, Commander William Riker is accused of treachery. The situation becomes even more complicated when the crew discovers a metal-craving bacteria feeding on the *Enterprise-D* and the Klingon ship *Pagh*.

Vidiot's Synopsis ✓ **INTERNET**
…→*www* <address 1a>honor.syn. html …→*www* <address 1b>sttng-2.html# 134

Dr. Pulaski Eats Klingon Dishes Dr. Pulaski finds Klingon cuisine most unappealing during dinner with Riker and Worf. ✓ **INTERNET** …→*anon-ftp* <address 33> →sttng 124.jpg …→*anon-ftp* <address 34>→sttng 124.jpg

Ensign Mendon Picture of a Benzite assigned to the *Enterprise*. ✓ **INTERNET** …→*anon-ftp* <address 33>→sttng090.jpg …→*anon-ftp* <address 34>→sttng090.jpg

Gok Image of one of the delightful delicacies of the Klingon World, Gok. ✓ **INTERNET** …→*anon-ftp* <address 33>→sttng 129.jpg

...→*anon-ftp* <address 34>→sttng 129.jpg

Klingon Cuisine Picture of Riker, Dr. Pulaski, and Worf sitting to feast on traditional Klingon cuisine in preparation for Riker's assignment to a Klingon vessel. ✓**INTERNET** ...→*anon-ftp* <address 33>→sttng 128.jpg ...→*anon-ftp* <address 34>→sttng 128.jpg

Klingon Cuisine Picture of Riker as he bravely consumes the Klingon delicacies he'll feast on during his tour aboard the Klingon vessel. ✓**INTERNET** ...→*anon-ftp* <address 33>→sttng 126.jpg ...→ *anon-ftp* <address 34>→sttng 126.jpg

Klingon feast Image of Worf helping Riker prepare for duty with the Klingons. ✓**INTERNET** ...→*anon-ftp* <address 33>→sttng 127.jpg ...→*anon-ftp* <address 34>→sttng 127.jpg

Klingon Stew Image of more appetizing Klingon creations from the *Enterprise*'s resident chef: Replicator 425. ✓**INTERNET** ...→ *anon-ftp* <address 33>→sttng 125. jpg ...→*anon-ftp* <address 34>→ sttng 125.jpg

Riker and Worf Picture of Worf giving advice to Riker prior to his tour aboard a Klingon vessel. ✓**INTERNET** ...→*anon-ftp* <address 33>→sttng 123.jpg ...→ *anon-ftp* <address 34>→sttng 123.jpg

The Measure of a Man

Episode: #35
Writer: Melinda M. Snodgrass
Director: Robert Scheerer
Stardate: 42523.7

Summary: A scientist who wishes to dismantle Data for study contends that Data is not a person and cannot resign from Starfleet to avoid a transfer to his command. In a trial to determine whether Data is a person or Starship property, Riker is forced to act as prosecutor and Captain Picard takes on the role of defense attorney.

Vidiot's Synopsis ✓**INTERNET** ...→*www* <address 1a>measure. syn.html ...→*www* <address 1b> sttng-2.html#135

The Dauphin

Episode: #36
Writers: Scott Rubenstein & Leonard Mlodinow
Director: Rob Bowman
Stardate: 42568.8

Summary: Wesley falls for Salia, the young ruler of Daled IV who is being transported to her homeworld to foster peace. The romance runs into problems when both Salia and her companion, Anya, turn out to actually be non-humanoid shape shifters.

Riker to Guinan in 10-Forward Transcript of the Riker/ Guinan scene in Ten-Forward lounge. ✓**COMPUSERVE**→*go* sfmedia →Libraries→*Search by file name:* BANTER.TXT

Vidiot's Synopsis ✓**INTERNET** ...→*www* <address 1a>dauphin. syn.html ...→*www* <address 1b> sttng-2.html#136

Contagion

Episode: #37
Writers: Steve Gerber & Beth Woods
Director: Joseph L. Scanlan
Stardate: 42609.1

Summary: The *Enterprise-D* travels to the aid of the *USS. Ya-mato*, which is experiencing computer failure. Before anything can be done, the ship explodes. The ship's logs shows that the *Yamato* contracted a computer virus from the planet Iconia, a virus that the *Enterprise* has just downloaded onto its own system.

Vidiot's Synopsis ✓**INTERNET** ...→*www* <address 1a>contagion. syn.html ...→*www* <address 1b> sttng-2.html#137

The Royale

Episode: #38
Writer: Keith Mills
Director: Cliff Bole
Stardate: 42625.4

Summary: Riker, Worf and Data become trapped in a world contained entirely in the Hotel Royale, a construct based on a 1930s novel left behind by a 20th-century astronaut.

Vidiot's Synopsis ✓**INTERNET** ...→*www* <address 1a>royale.syn. html ...→*www* <address 1b>sttng-2.html#138

Time Squared

Episode: #39
Teleplay: Maurice Hurley
Story: Kurt Michael Bensmiller
Director: Joseph L. Scanlan
Stardate: 42679.2

Summary: The crew finds a duplicate of Picard, apparently from six hours in the future, where he is the only survivor of the destruction of the *Enterprise-D*. The crew struggles to break the time loop before it becomes a reality.

Vidiot's Synopsis ✓**INTERNET** ...→*www* <address 1a>tsquared. syn.html ...→*www* <address 1b> sttng-2.html#139

The Icarus Factor

Episode: #40
Teleplay: David Assael & Robert
            L. McCullough
Story: David Assael
Director: Robert Iscove
Stardate: 42686.4

Summary: When Riker is offered the command of the *USS Aries*, he must confront his past and his estranged father, who has come to brief him on his new post.

Tim Lynch Synopsis & Review
✓ **INTERNET** ...→*anon-ftp* <address 2>icarus.rev ...→*gopher* <address 8>icarus.rev ...→*www* <address 14> icarus.rev.html

Vidiot's Synopsis ✓ **INTERNET** ...→*www* <address 1a>icarus.syn. html ...→<address 1b>sttng-2.html #140

Pen Pals

Episode: #41
Teleplay: Melinda M. Snodgrass
Story: Hannah Louise Shearer
Director: Winrich Kolbe
Stardate: 42695.3

Summary: Data breaks the Prime Directive when he responds to a radio signal and begins a friendship with a lonely little girl from a planet without exposure to alien cultures. Wesley has his first command.

Tim Lynch Synopsis & Review
✓ **INTERNET** ...→*anon-ftp* <address 2>→penpals.rev ...→*gopher* <address 8>→penpals.rev ...→*www* <address 14>penpals.rev.html

Vidiot's Synopsis ✓ **INTERNET** ...→*www* <address 1a>penpals. syn.html ...→*www* <address 1b> sttng-2.html#141

STARQUOTES

Data and His Pen Pal Picture of Data with his pen pal friend. ✓ **PVG** *dial* 513-233-7993→*<your username>→<your password>→F→ Download a file:* NG20.GIF

Q Who?

Episode: #42
Writer: Maurice Hurley
Director: Rob Bowman
Stardate: 42761.3

Summary: When Picard denies that the human race needs the assistance of the Q Continuum, an angry Q dispatches the ship to a remote part of the galaxy, thousands of light years away. This is the haunt of the deadly Borg, a race of cyborgs without individuality bent on assimilating all in their path. It's a new enemy for the Federation.

Tim Lynch Synopsis & Review
✓ **INTERNET** ...→*anon-ftp* <address 2>→qwho.rev ...→*gopher* <address 8>→qwho.rev ...→*www* <address 14> qwho.rev.html

Vidiot's Synopsis ✓ **INTERNET** ...→*www* <address 1a>qwho. syn.html ...→*www* <address 1b> sttng-2.html#142

The Borg ship Image of the *Enterprise* encountering an unknown ship. ✓ **INTERNET** ...→*anon-ftp* <address 33>→sttng203.jpg ...→*anon-ftp* <address 34>→sttng203.jpg

Q Picture of Q in ceremonial drag

on *Enterprise*. ✓ **INTERNET** ...→ *anon-ftp* <address 33>→sttng017. jpg ...→*anon-ftp* <address 34>→ sttng017.jpg

Q Picture of Q with long hair. ✓ **INTERNET** ...→*anon-ftp* <address 33>→sttng006.jpg ...→*anon-ftp* <address 34>→sttng006.jpg

Q in Uniform Picture of Q requesting an assignment aboard *Enterprise*. ✓ **INTERNET** ...→*anon-ftp* <address 33>→sttng014.jpg ...→ *anon-ftp* <address 34>→sttng014. jpg

Q on Bridge Image of Q in swashbuckler, Spanish armour garb on bridge. ✓ **INTERNET** ...→*anon-ftp* <address 33>→sttng 007.jpg ...→*anon-ftp* <address 34>→sttng007.jpg

Officer Q Q in Starfleet uniform. ✓ **INTERNET** ...→*anon-ftp* <address 33>→sttng055.jpg ...→*anon-ftp* <address 34>→sttng055.jpg

Samaritan Snare

Episode: #43
Writer: Robert L. McCullough
Director: Les Landau
Stardate: 42779.1

Summary: While Picard and Wesley travel to a starbase, one to take Starfleet exams, the other to undergo life-and-death heart surgery, cunning Pakleds try to kidnap Geordi in hopes of obtaining advanced technology.

Tim Lynch Synopsis & Review
✓ INTERNET ...→anon-ftp <address 2>→samaritan.rev ...→ gopher <address 8>→samaritan.rev ...→www <address 14> samaritan.rev.html

Vidiot's Synopsis ✓ INTERNET
...→www <address 1a> samaritan. syn.html...→<address 1b>sttng-2.html#143

Up the Long Ladder

Episode: #44
Writer: Melinda M. Snodgrass
Director: Winrich Kolbe
Stardate: 42823.2

Summary: Inhabitants of two earth outposts—one group living in a farming community and the other a highly advanced race of clones— must learn cooperation if they are to survive.

Tim Lynch Synopsis & Review
✓ INTERNET ...→anon-ftp <address 2>→ladder.rev ...→gopher <address 8>→ladder.rev ...→ www <address 14>ladder.rev.html

Vidiot's Synopsis ✓ INTERNET
...→www <address 1a>ladder.syn. html ...→www <address 1b>sttng-2.html#144

Manhunt

Episode: #45
Writer: Terry Devereaux
Director: Rob Bowman
Stardate: 42859.2

Summary: Deanna Troi's mother Lwaxana returns. She's hunting for a husband and fixes on Picard. Meanwhile there are other hunters aboard: Antedian delegates turn out to be assassins, determined to destroy the Federation conference.

Tim Lynch Synopsis & Review
✓ INTERNET ...→anon-ftp <address

2>→manhunt.rev ...→gopher <address 8>→manhunt.rev ...→www <address 14> manhunt.rev.html

Vidiot's Synopsis ✓ INTERNET
...→www <address 1a> manhunt. syn.html ...→www <address 1b> sttng-2.html#145

The Emissary

Episode: #46
Teleplay: Richard Manning &
             Hans Beimler
Story: Thomas H. Calder
Director: Cliff Bole
Stardate: 42901.3

Summary: Special Emissary K'Ehleyr, a Klingon/human and a former lover of Worf, joins the *Enterprise-D* crew on a special mission to intercept a Klingon warship that's been in suspended animation for decades. Worry is that the Klingons who are scheduled to revive on the ship will not know that the Klingon Empire is at peace with the Federation.

Tim Lynch Synopsis & Review
✓ INTERNET ...→anon-ftp <address 2>→emissary.rev ...→gopher <address 8>→emissary.rev ...→www <address 14> emissary.rev.html

Vidiot's Synopsis ✓ INTERNET
...→www <address 1a>emissary. syn.html...→www <address 1b> sttng-2.html#146

Peak Performance

Episode: #47
Writer: David Kemper
Director: Robert Scheerer
Stardate: 42923.4

Summary: Riker, in command of the *USS Hathaway*, engages the *Enterprise-D* in a war game. In the middle of the mock conflict, a Ferengi ship arrives with a more seri-

ous demand: control of the ship.

Tim Lynch Synopsis & Review
✓ INTERNET ...→anon-ftp <address 2>→peak.rev ...→gopher <address 8>→peak.rev ...→www <address 14>peak.rev.html

Vidiot's Synopsis ✓ INTERNET
...→www <address 1a>peak.syn. html ...→www <address 1b>sttng-2. html#147

Enterprise and Ferengi Ship
Picture of *Enterprise* encountering Ferengi warship. ✓ INTERNET ...→ anon-ftp <address 33>→sttng 084.jpg ...→anon-ftp <address 34>→sttng084.jpg

Shades of Grey

Episode: #48
Teleplay: Maurice Hurley,
             Richard Manning &
             Hans Beimler
Story: Maurice Hurley
Director: Rob Bowman
Stardate: 42976.1

Summary: On a remote planet, Commander Will Riker contracts a disease that paralyzes neural activity. Dr. Pulaski discovers that triggering unpleasant memories in Riker helps arrest the progress of the deadly disease.

Tim Lynch Synopsis & Review
✓ INTERNET ...→anon-ftp <address 2>→shades.rev ...→gopher <address 8>→shades.rev ...→ www <address 14> shades.rev.html

Trekker Review ✓ INTERNET→ www <address 16>shades_of_ gray.html

Vidiot's Synopsis ✓ INTERNET
...→www <address 1a>shades. syn.html ...→www <address 1b> sttng-2.html#148

Emissary
synopsis and review by Timothy Lynch

Screenshot—http://www.ugcs.caltech.edu/~werdna/sttng/synopsis/emissary.syn.html

Season 3

The Ensigns of Command

Episode: #49
Writer: Melinda M. Snodgrass
Director: Cliff Bole
Stardate: 43152.4

Summary: The Sheliak, a militant and powerful race, demand the removal of settlers on Tau Cygna V, a planet they can legally claim as their own. It is up to Data to try and convince the settlers to leave their homeland before they are destroyed and Captain Jean-Luc Picard to try and find a legal loophole.

Trekker Review ✓**INTERNET**→ *www* <address 17>the_ensigns_of_ command.html

Vidiot's Synopsis ✓**INTERNET** ...→*www* <address 1a>ensigns. syn.html ...→*www* <address 1b> sttng-3. html#149

Evolution

Episode: #50
Teleplay: Michael Piller
Story: Michael Piller & Michael Wagner
Director: Winrich Kolbe
Stardate: 43125.8

Summary: In the course of helping Dr. Paul Stubbs with experiments in astrophysics, Wesley inadvertently releases tiny robots that evolve into intelligent beings, creating complications for the scientist and the ship.

Trekker Review ✓**INTERNET**→ *www* <address 17>evolution.html

Vidiot's Synopsis ✓**INTERNET** ...→*www* <address 1a>evolution. syn.html ...→*www* <address 1b> sttng-3.html#150

Captain Picard Image of an unhappy Picard. ✓**COMPUSERVE**→*go* sfmedia→Libraries→*Search by file name:* PREM1.GIF

Picard & Riker Pictures of the Captain and first officer of the *Enterprise.* ✓**COMPUSERVE**→*go* sfmedia →Libraries→*Search by file name:* PREM2.GIF

USS Enterprise Doomed to Die *NCC-1701-D* is drawn into an area where binary stars are about to explode. GIF file. ✓**COMPUSERVE**→*go* sfmedia→Libraries→ *Search by file name:* EVOL1.GIF

The Survivors

Episode: #51
Writer: Michael Wagner
Director: Les Landau
Stardate: 43152.4

Summary: Visiting Delta Rana IV, the *Enterprise* discovers that all but two of the 11,000 inhabitants have been killed in an attack. The only survivors—an elderly man and wife—refuse offers of refuge on another planet. Picard discovers that all is not what it seems— the old man is really a "Douwd," a super being, embittered by the loss of the human he loved and tortured by the role he played in her death.

Trekker Review ✓**INTERNET**→ *www* <address 17>the_survivors. html

Vidiot's Synopsis ✓**INTERNET** ...→ *www* <address 1a>survivors. syn.html...→<address 1b>sttng-3. html#151

Who Watches the Watchers?

Episode: #52
Writers: Richard Manning & Hans Beimler
Director: Robert Weimer
Stardate: 43173.5

Summary: Federation anthropologists secretly observing a Bronze Age society are injured in an explosion, along with some of the humanoids. One treated aboard the *Enterprise* sees Picard and believes that he is the god that legends have foretold.

Tim Lynch Synopsis & Review
✓ **INTERNET** ...→*anon-ftp* <address 3>→watchers.rev ...→*gopher* <address 9>→watchers.rev ...→*www* <address 14>watchers.syn.html

Trekker Review ✓ INTERNET→
www <address 17>who_watches_the_watchers.html

Vidiot's Synopsis ✓ INTERNET
...→*www* <address 1a>watchers.syn.html ...→<address 1b>sttng-3.html#152

The Bonding

Episode: #53
Writer: Ronald D. Moore
Director: Winrich Kolbe
Stardate: 43198.7

Summary: When an archaeologist is killed on a mission, both Worf and the alien race responsible for her death vie for the right to care for her orphaned son. The aliens attract the boy with visions of his mother, while Worf makes plans for the Klingon bonding ritual.

Tim Lynch Synopsis & Review
✓ **INTERNET** ...→*anon-ftp* <address 3>→bonding.rev ...→*gopher* <address 9>→bonding.rev ...→*www* <address 14>bonding. rev.html

Trekker Review ✓ INTERNET→
www <address 17>the_bonding. html

Vidiot's Synopsis ✓ INTERNET
...→*www* <address 1a>bonding. syn.html...→ *www* <address 1b>

sttng-3.html#153

Booby Trap

Episode: #54
Teleplay: Ron Roman, Michael Piller, & Richard Danus
Director: Gabrielle Beaumont
Stardate: 43205.6

Summary: When the *Enterprise-D* becomes ensnared in a 1,000-year-old booby trap, Geordi calls up the ship's designer on the holodeck to help him figure a way out.

Tim Lynch Synopsis & Review
✓ **INTERNET** ...→*anon-ftp* <address 3>→booby.rev ...→*gopher* <address 9>→booby.rev ...→ *www* <address 14> booby.rev.html

Trekker Review ✓ INTERNET→
www <address 17>booby_trap. html

Vidiot's Synopsis ✓ INTERNET
...→*www* <address 1a>booby.syn. html ...→*www* <address 1b>sttng-3.html

The Enemy

Episode: #55
Writer: David Kemper & Michael Piller
Director: David Carson
Stardate: 43349.2

Summary: Geordi is accidentally left behind on the hostile Galordan Core and must cooperate with a stranded Romulan named Centurion Bochra to survive.

Tim Lynch Synopsis & Review
✓ **INTERNET** ...→*anon-ftp* <address 3>→enemy.rev ...→*gopher* <address 9>→enemy.rev ...→ *www* <address 14> enemy.rev.html

Trekker Review ✓ INTERNET→

www <address 17>

Vidiot's Synopsis ✓ INTERNET
...→*www* <address 1a>enemy.syn. html ...→*www* <address 1b>sttng-3.html#155

The Price

Episode: #56
Writer: Hannah Louise Shearer
Director: Robert Scheerer
Stardate: 43385.6

Summary: The Barzans have discovered a wormhole and several emissaries travel to the site where it will be sold. Troi falls for one of the bidders but soon discovers that he is part Betazoid and has been using his empathic powers to direct the negotiations in his favor.

Tim Lynch Synopsis & Review
✓ **INTERNET** ...→*anon-ftp* <address 3>→price.rev ...→*gopher* <address 9>→price.rev ...→*www* <address 14>price.rev.html

Vidiot's Synopsis ✓ INTERNET
...→*www* <address 1a>price.syn. html ...→*www* <address 1b>sttng-3.html#156

The Vengeance Factor

Episode: #57
Writer: Sam Rolfe
Director: Timothy Bond
Stardate: 43421.9

Summary: Commander Will Riker is attracted to a beautiful young woman taking part in peace negotiations settling an age old feud between the Acamarians and Gatherers. Tensions mount when during the negotiations a clan leader is murdered and the lovely Yuta is discovered to be a tool of revenge.

Tim Lynch Synopsis & Review
✓**INTERNET** ...→*anon-ftp* <address 3>→vengeance.rev ...→ *gopher* <address 9>→vengeance.rev ...→*www* <address 14>vengeance. rev.html

Trekker Review ✓**INTERNET**→ *www* <address 17>the_vengeance _factor.html

Vidiot's Synopsis ✓**INTERNET** ...→*www* <address 1a>vengeance .syn.html ...→*www* <address 1b> sttng-3.html#157

The Defector

Episode: #58
Writer: Ronald D. Moore
Director: Robert Scheerer
Stardate: 43462.5

Summary: The crew must decide whether or not to trust Setal, a Romulan defector who insists that the Romulans are planning a large scale offensive against the Federation.

Tim Lynch Synopsis & Review
✓**INTERNET** ...→*anon-ftp* <address 3>→defector.rev ...→*gopher* <address 9>→defector.rev ...→*www* <address 14>defector.rev.html

Trekker Review ✓**INTERNET**→ *www* <address 17>the_defector. html

Vidiot's Synopsis ✓**INTERNET** ...→*www* <address 1a>defector. syn.html ...→*www* <address 1b> sttng-3.html#158

The Hunted

Episode: #59
Writer: Robin Bernheim
Director: Cliff Bole
Stardate: 43489.2

Summary: While evaluating An-

gosia III for Federation membership, the crew joins in the search of an escaped prisoner. When they capture the fugitive, they discover that he has been imprisoned because the government had genetically altered him into a "perfect soldier," who cannot function in a state of peace. The crew must decide whether to intervene on behalf of the soldier or respect the government.

Tim Lynch Synopsis & Review
✓**INTERNET** ...→*anon-ftp* <address 3>→hunted.rev ...→*gopher* <address 9>→hunted.rev ...→ *www* <address 14>hunted.rev.html

Trekker Review ✓**INTERNET**→ *www* <address 17>the_hunted.html

Vidiot's Synopsis ✓**INTERNET** ...→*www* <address 1a>hunted. syn.html ...→*www* <address 1b> sttng-3.html#159

The High Ground

Episode: #60
Writer: Melinda M. Snodgrass
Director: Gabrielle Beaumont
Stardate: 43510.7

Summary: On Rutia IV, Crusher is kidnapped by a group of "terrorists" fighting for "freedom".

Tim Lynch Synopsis & Review
✓**INTERNET** ...→*anon-ftp* <address 3>→highground.rev ...→*gopher* <address 9>→highground.rev ...→*www* <address 14> highground.rev.html

Trekker Review ✓**INTERNET**→ *www* <address 17>the_high_ ground.html

Vidiot's Synopsis ✓**INTERNET** ... →*www* <address 1a>highground. syn.html ...→*www* <address 1b> sttng-3.html#160

Deja Q

Episode: #61
Writer: Richard Danus
Director: Les Landau
Stardate: 43539.1

Summary: Kicked out of the Q Continuum, Q arrives at the *Enterprise-D* naked and powerless, seeking refuge and hoping to learn how to be human. The Clamarians who follow are seeking something too: revenge for Q's previous exploits.

Tim Lynch Synopsis & Review
✓**INTERNET** ...→*anon-ftp* <address 3>→dejajq.rev ...→*gopher* <address 9>→dejajq.rev ...→*www* <address 14> dejaq.rev.html

Trekker Review ✓**INTERNET**→ *www* <address 17>deja_q.html

Vidiot's Synopsis ✓**INTERNET** ...→*www* <address 1a>dejaq.syn. html ...→*www* <address 1b>sttng-3.html#161

Aren't My Colors Soundclip of a whining Q: "These aren't my colors!" ✓**INTERNET**→*anon-ftp* <address 35> →arent-my-colors

Eat Any Good Books Soundclip of a sarcastic Q: "Oh, very clever Worf—eat any good books lately." ✓**INTERNET**→*anon-ftp* <address 35>→eat-any-good-books

Getting on My Nerves Soundclip of Q: "This is getting on my nerves....now that I have them." ✓**INTERNET**→*anon-ftp* <address 35>→getting-on-my-nerves

Not Good in Groups Soundclip of the arrogant Q: "I'm not good in groups. Difficult to work in groups when you're omnipotent." ✓**INTERNET**→ *anon-ftp* <address 35>→not-good-in-groups

Q and Worf Exchange between Worf and Q when Q appears on the bridge of the *Enterprise* as a human. Mac sound file. ✓**COMPUSERVE**→*go* sfmedia→Libraries→ *Search by file name:* Q-WORF.SIT

A Matter of Perspective

Episode: #62
Writer: Ed Zuckerman
Director: Cliff Bole
Stardate: 43610.4

Summary: Riker is accused of sabotage and murder in the wake of the explosion of the *Tanuga* Research Station. Picard, refusing to turn Riker over to Chief Investigator Krag, suggests that they use the holodeck to recreate the event and find the truth.

Tim Lynch Synopsis & Review
✓**INTERNET** ...→*anon-ftp* <address 3>→perspective.rev ...→*gopher* <address 9>→perspective.rev ...→*www* <address 14> perspective.rev.html

Trekker Review ✓**INTERNET**→ *www* <address 17>a_matter_of_ perspective.html

Vidiot's Synopsis ✓**INTERNET** ...→*www* <address 1a>perspective. syn.html ...→*www* <address 1b> sttng-3.html#162

Yesterday's Enterprise

Episode: #63
Teleplay: Steven Behr, Richard
            Manning, Hans Beimler
            & Ronald D. Moore
Story: Trent Christopher Gani-
            no & Eric A. Stillwell
Director: David Carson
Stardate: 43625.2

Summary: The *Enterprise-D* is confronted by the *Enterprise-C*, which has slipped through a time rift, and on which Tasha Yar is still alive and serving as Tactical Officer. Its appearance creates an alternate reality in which the Federation is losing a war to the Klingons and crew members are far less ethical.

Has Star Trek History Been Altered Forever? A short essay hypothesizing that the TNG episode "Yesterday's Enterprise" created an alternate time that redirected the chronological flow of the series and chronologically relocated all ensuing episodes. ✓**AMERICA ONLINE**→*keyword* trek→MORE ...→Star Trek Record Banks→Text/ Other Files→Upld: 10/19/94→ TEXT: Alternate Timeline (filename: TREKTIME.TXT)

Tim Lynch Synopsis & Review
✓**INTERNET** ...→*anon-ftp* <address 3>→yesterday.rev ...→*gopher* <address 9>→yesterday1.rev *and* yesterday2.rev ...→*www* <address 14> yesterday.rev.html

Time Loops, "Yesterday's Enterprise," and Tasha Yar Explained How did Tasha die twice? Questions about the episode "Yesterday's Enterprise," came up so often in the rec. arts.startrek* newsgroups that this FAQ was created. Offering four possible explanations (each of which depends on assumptions as to what timeline is real), the FAQ also examines and explains several other Trek episodes where time-loops were featured. ✓**INTERNET** ...→*anon-ftp* quepasa.cs.tu-berlin. de→/pub/doc/movies+tv-series/ StarTrek/FAQs→time.loops.gz ...→*www* http://www.cosy.sbg.ac. at/ftp/pub/trek/lists/timeloop.faq ✓**TFDN**→<address 23>

Trekker Review ✓**INTERNET**→

www <address 17>yesterdays_en
terprise.html

Vidiot's Synopsis ✓ **INTERNET**
...→*www* <address 1a>yesterday.
syn.html ...→*www* <address 1b>
sttng-3.html#163

Enterprise-C Three GIFs of the
Enterprise-C from the episode
"Yesterday's Enterprise." ✓ **COM-
PUSERVE**→*go* sfmedia→Libraries→
Search by file name: ENT-C.ARC

Picard and Tasha Yar Image of
Yar and Picard. ✓ **COMPUSERVE**→*go*
sfmedia→Libraries→*Search by file
name:* PICYAR.GIF

Picard and Enterprise Soundclip of Picard: "Let's make
sure...history never forgets...the
name...Enterprise. Picard Out."
WAV file. ✓ **COMPUSERVE**→*go* sfme-
dia→Libraries→*Search by file name:*
PICENT.WAV

The Offspring

Episode: #64
Writer: René Echeverria
Director: Jonathan Frakes
Stardate: 43657.0

Summary: After attending a cy-
bernetics conference, Data builds
himself an android daughter
named Lal. Starfleet wants to take

her to the Daystrom Institute for
further study, a plan to which her
"father" takes great exception.

Tim Lynch Synopsis & Review
✓ **INTERNET** ...→*anon-ftp* <address
3>→offspring.rev ...→*gopher* <ad-
dress 9>→offspring.rev ...→*www*
<address 14> offspring.rev.html

Trekker Review ✓ **INTERNET**→
www <address 17>the_offspring.
html

Vidiot's Synopsis ✓ **INTERNET**
...→*www* <address 1a>offspring.
syn.html ...→*www* <address 1b>
sttng-3.html#164

Data/Lal Image of Data showing
Lal to Troi. ✓ **COMPUSERVE**→*go* sf-
media→Libraries→*Search by file
name:* DATLAL.GIF

Sins of the Father

Episode: #65
Teleplay: Ronald D. Moore &
            W. Reed Moran
Story: Drew Deighan
Director: Les Landau
Stardate: 43685.2

Summary: Worf's younger brother, Kurn, arrives with the news
that their father has been accused
of treason. Worf returns to the
Klingon homeworld to defend his

father and restore the family's hon-
or. His is quite literally a do-or-die
mission: If Worf fails, he too will
be condemned and killed as a traitor.

Tim Lynch Synopsis & Review
✓ **INTERNET** ...→*anon-ftp* <address
3>→sins.rev ...→*gopher* <address
9>→sins.rev ...→*www* <address
14> sins.rev.html

Trekker Review ✓ **INTERNET**→
www <address 17>sins_of_the_fa
ther.html

Vidiot's Synopsis ✓ **INTERNET**
...→*www* <address 1a>sins.syn.
html ...→<address 1b>sttng-3.html
#165

Allegiance

Episode: #66
Writers: Richard Manning &
            Hans Beimler
Director: Winrich Kolbe
Stardate: 43714.2

Summary: The captain's odd behavior (singing in Ten Forward!)
raises questions of allegiance
among the crew, who do not realize that he has been replaced by a
duplicate. Meanwhile, Picard has
been imprisoned with three
aliens: one of whom is really the
captor.

Tim Lynch Synopsis & Review
✓ **INTERNET** ...→*anon-ftp* <address
3>→allegiance.rev ...→*gopher* <ad-
dress 9>→allegiance.rev ...→*www*
<address 14>allegiance.rev.html

Trekker Review ✓ **INTERNET**→
www <address 17>allegiance.html

Vidiot's Synopsis ✓ **INTERNET**
...→*www* <address 1a> allegiance.
syn.html ...→*www* <address 1b>
sttng-3.html#166

ASK SPOT!

a) Although Picard appoints Wesley to the position of
Acting Ensign, who helps him make this decision?

b) What is the legislation that rules that Data is the
property of Starfleet rather than an officer?

c) What is the name of the species interested in exploring the phenomenon of death with Picard's crew?

(See answers on page 359)

Captain's Holiday

Episode: #67
Writer: Ira Steven Behr
Director: Chip Chalmers
Stardate: 43745.2

Summary: While on vacation on the pleasure planet Risa, Picard gets involved with Vash, a beautiful archeologist searching for a 27th-century weapon. Things get complicated when a Ferengi shows up looking for the same device, followed by security agents from the future.

Tim Lynch Synopsis & Review
✓**INTERNET** ...→*anon-ftp* <address 3>→holiday.rev ...→*gopher* <address 9>→holiday.rev ...→*www* <address 14> holiday.rev.html

Trekker Review ✓**INTERNET**→
www <address 17>captains_holiday.html

Vidiot's Synopsis ✓**INTERNET**
...→*www* <address 1a>holiday.syn.html...→ *www* <address 1b> sttng-3.html#167

Tin Man

Episode: #68
Writer: Dennis Putman Bailey
             & David Bischoff
Director: Robert Scheerer
Stardate: 43779.3

Summary: Romulans and the Federation are attempting to contact an object orbiting a dying star. The empath who is to communicate with the alien maintains it is a living spaceship, a "Tin Man" who is literally dying of loneliness.

Tim Lynch Synopsis & Review
✓**INTERNET** ...→*anon-ftp* <address 3>→tinman.rev ...→*gopher* <address 9>→tinman.rev ...→*www* <address 14> tinman. rev.html

Last Update: January 15, 1995

Captain's Holiday
synopsis and review by Timothy Lynch

Screenshot—http://www.ugcs.caltech.edu/~werdna/sttng/synopsis/holiday.syn.html

Trekker Review ✓**INTERNET**→
www <address 17>tin_man.html

Vidiot Episode Synopsis ✓**INTERNET**...→*www* <address 1a>tin man. syn.html ...→*www* <address 1b>sttng-3.html#168

Scenes from "Tin Man" Five scenes from the episode, including the Tin Man on the viewscreen. ✓**PVG** dial 513-233-7993→<your username>→<your password>→F→ *Download a file: STTNG007.GIF and STTNG008. GIF and STTNG013.GIF and STTNG014.GIF and STTNG017.GIF*

Hollow Pursuits

Episode: #69
Writer: Sally Caves
Director: Cliff Bole
Stardate: 43807.4

Summary: Lieutenant Reginald Barclay, an engineer lacking social skills, spends his free time creating holodeck fantasies where he is an absolute monarch over his fellow crew members. In a subplot, mysterious malfunctions are the result of a chemical infection.

Tim Lynch Synopsis & Review
✓**INTERNET** ...→*anon-ftp* <address 3>→hollow.rev ...→*gopher* <address 9>→hollow.rev ...→*www* <address 14> hollow.rev.html

Trekker Review ✓**INTERNET**→
www <address 17>hollow_pursuits.html

Vidiot's Synopsis ✓**INTERNET**
...→*www* <address 1a>hollow.syn.html ...→*www* <address 1b>sttng-3.html#169

The Most Toys

Episode: #70
Writer: Shari Goodhartz
Director: Timothy Bond
Stardate: 43872.2

Summary: Data is thought to be dead after the shuttle he is piloting explodes. Actually, he has been kidnapped by an eccentric purveyor of stolen artifacts, who wants to add Data to his collection.

Tim Lynch Synopsis & Review
✓ **INTERNET** ...→*anon-ftp* <address 3>→toys.rev ...→*gopher* <address 9>→toys.rev ...→*www* <address 14> toys.rev.html

Trekker Review ✓ **INTERNET**→ *www* <address 17>the_most_toys. html

Vidiot's Synopsis ✓ **INTERNET** ...→*www* <address 1a>toys.syn. html ...→*www* <address 1b>sttng-3.html#170

Sarek

Episode: #71
Teleplay: Peter S. Beagle
Story: Mark Cushman & Jake Jacobs
Director: Les Landau
Stardate: 43917.4

Summary: After the Vulcan Ambassador Sarek arrives for a meeting with the Legarans, there are violent emotional outbursts among the crew members—the result of the telepathic influence of Sarek, who is suffering from a disease that destroys Vulcans' emotional control.

Tim Lynch Synopsis & Review
✓ **INTERNET** ...→*anon-ftp* <address 3>→sarek.rev ...→*gopher* <address 9>→sarek.rev ...→*www* <address 14> sarek.rev.html

Trekker Review ✓ **INTERNET**→ *www* <address 17>sarek.html

Vidiot's Synopsis ✓ **INTERNET** ...→*www* <address 1a>→sarek. syn.html ...→*www* <address 1b> sttng-3.html#171

Picard and Sarek Picture of Picard and Sarek on the *Enterprise*. ✓ **INTERNET** ...→*anon-ftp* <address 33>→sarek.jpg ...→*anon-ftp* <address 34>→sarek.jpg

Sarek and Perrin Image of Ambassador Sarek and his wife Perrin from the episode "Sarek's Last Mission." ✓ **COMPUSERVE**→go sfmedia→Libraries→*Search by file name:* SAREK2.GIF

Ménage à Troi

Episode: #72
Writers: Susan Sackett & Fred Bronson
Director: Robert Legato
Stardate: 43930.7

Summary: When Lwaxana Troi rebuffs the advances of the Ferengi DaiMon Tog, he kidnaps her, as well as Deanna and Riker. He hopes to profit from the telepathy and to convince Lwaxana to marry him.

Tim Lynch Synopsis & Review
✓ **INTERNET** ...→*anon-ftp* <address 3>→menage.rev ...→*gopher* <address 9>→menage.rev ...→*www* <address 14>menage. rev.html

Trekker Review ✓ **INTERNET**→ *www* <address 17>menage_a_troi. html

Vidiot's Synopsis ✓ **INTERNET** ...→*www* <address 1a>menage. syn.html ...→*www* <address 1b> sttng-3.html#172

Picnic Scene The picnic scene with Lwaxana and the Ferengi. ✓ **PVG** 513-233-7993→*<your username>→<your password>→F →Download a file:*PICNIC2.GIF

Transfigurations

Episode: #73
Writer: René Echevarria
Director: Tom Benko
Stardate: 43957.2

Summary: The sole survivor of a ship crash exhibits miraculous powers of recuperation. Dr. Crusher discovers that the humanoid is transforming itself into a non-corporeal form through energy bursts.

Tim Lynch Synopsis & Review
✓ **INTERNET** ...→*anon-ftp* <address 3>→transfig.rev ...→*gopher* <address 9>→transfig.rev ...→*www* <address 14>transfig.rev.html

Trekker Review ✓ **INTERNET**→ *www* <address 17>transfigurations. html

Vidiot's Synopsis ✓ **INTERNET** ...→*www* <address 1a>transfigura tions.syn.html ...→*www* <address 1b>sttng-3.html#173

The Best of Both Worlds, Part I

Episode: #74
Writer: Michael Piller
Director: Cliff Bole
Stardate: 43989.1

Summary: The Borg have arrived! The destruction of an outlying colony is the opening salvo in the conflict between the Borg and the Federation. After losing a battle with a Borg ship, Picard is kidnapped and transformed into a Borg called Locutus. His mission: to assimilate Earth. Riker's mission: to defend Earth.

Last Update: November 14, 1994

The Best of Both Worlds
synopsis from the Vidiot's TNG

Screenshot—http://www.ugcs.caltech.edu/~werdna/sttng/synopsis/best1.syn.html

Tim Lynch Synopsis & Review
√INTERNET ...→anon-ftp <address 3>→best.rev ...→gopher <address 9>→best11.rev and best12.rev ...→www <address 14> best1.rev.html

Trekker Review √INTERNET→ www <address 17>the_best_of_ both_worlds.html

Vidiot's Synopsis √INTERNET ...→www <address 1a>best1.syn. html ...→www <address 1b>sttng-3.html#174

Season 4

The Best of Both Worlds, Part II

Episode: #75
Writer: Michael Piller
Director: Cliff Bole
Stardate: 44001.4

Summary: The Borg continue on their destructive path toward Earth. As half of Starfleet is decimated, Riker attempts to rescue Picard.

Tim Lynch Synopsis & Review
√INTERNET ...→anon-ftp <address 4>→best2.rev ...→gopher <address 10>→best21.rev and best22.rev ...→www <address 14> best2.rev.html

Trekker Review √INTERNET→ www <address 18>the_best_of_ both_worlds_2.html

Vidiot's Synopsis √INTERNET →www <address 1b>sttng-4.html #175

Borg Ship GIF of a Borg cruiser. √COMPUSERVE→go sfmedia→Libraries→Search by file name: BORGSH.GIF

Enterprise Held by Borg Two

images of the *Enterprise's* first encounter with the Borg. √COMPUSERVE→go sfmedia→Libraries→Search by file name: EBORG1.GIF and EBORG2.GIF

Locutus of Borg Image of Picard as Locutus. √COMPUSERVE→go sfmedia→Libraries→Search by file name: LOCUTU.GIF √GENIE→keyword sfrt2→Text and Graphics Library→Download a file: 390

Picard as Locutus Image of Picard as the newest assimilated member of the Borg collective. √INTERNET ...→anon-ftp <address 33>→sttng201.jpg ...→anon-ftp <address 34>→sttng201.jpg

Picard Returning to the Enterprise Image of Picard, who had been kipnapped and tranformed by the Borg, returning to the *Enterprise*. √INTERNET ...→ anon-ftp <address 33>→sttng 200.jpg ...→anon-ftp <address 34>→sttng200.jpg

I am Locutus of Borg Memorable soundclip of Locutus (formerly Picard) voicing the Borg greeting: "I am Locutus of Borg. Resistance is futile. Your life as it has been is over." Another soundclip, "We have engaged the Borg," is also included. WAV file. √COMPUSERVE→go sfmedia→Libraries→Search by file name: LOCUTU.ZIP

Locutus Two very clear sound clips of Locutus' messages, including the brief threat "you will become one with the Borg" and the much longer speach with dramatic background music—"I am Locutus of Borg. Resistance is futile. Your life as it has been is over. From this time forward you will service...us." √INTERNET→anon-ftp sumex-aim.stanford.edu→/info-mac/snd→locutus.hqx

Family

Episode: #78
Teleplay: Ronald D. Moore
Story: Susanne Lambdin &
Bryan Stewart
Director: Les Landau
Stardate: 44012.3

Summary: After the battle with the Borg, Picard retreats to his family vineyard in France. Worf's adoptive parents, the Rozhenkos, pay him a visit. And Wesley contemplates viewing a hologram of his late father.

Tim Lynch Synopsis & Review
√ INTERNET ...→*anon-ftp* <address 4>→family.rev ...→*gopher* <address 10>→family.rev ...→*www* <address 14> family.rev.html

Trekker Review √ INTERNET→ *www* <address 18>family.html

Vidiot's Synopsis √ INTERNET →*www* <address 1b>sttng-4.html #178

Brothers

Episode: #77
Writer: Rick Berman
Director: Robert Bowman
Stardate: 44085.7

Summary: For no apparent reason, Data takes over the *Enterprise-D* and steers it to an isolated planet, where he discovers his creator, Dr. Soong. The scientist had summoned Data so he could install a chip allowing Data to experience emotions. One problem: Data's evil brother, Lore, responded, too.

Tim Lynch Synopsis & Review
√ INTERNET ...→*anon-ftp* <address 4>→brothers.rev ...→*gopher* <address 10>→brothers.rev ...→*www* <address 14>brothers.rev.html

Trekker Review √ INTERNET→ *www* <address 18>brothers.html

Vidiot's Synopsis √ INTERNET →*www* <address 1b>sttng-4.html #177

Scenes from Brothers Nine episode scenes featuring shots of Data, Crusher, and Dr. Soong. √ PVG *dial* 513-233-7993→<your username>→<your password>→F→ *Download a file:* STNGN302.GIF

Command Functions Soundclip: "Inquiries regarding command functions are no longer accepted from your present location." √ INTERNET→*anon-ftp* <address 35>→ com-functions

Data Whistle Soundclip of Data learning to whistle in the company of an impatient Lore. √ INTERNET →*anon-ftp* <address 35>→data-whistle

Lives Thrown Away Soundclip: "You don't give a damn about the people whose lives you're throwing away. We're not just machines." √ INTERNET→*anon-ftp* <address 35>→lives-thrown-away

Lore's Song Soundclip: "The sons of the prophet were valiant and bold / and quite unaccustomed to fear / but of all the most reckless, or so I am toooold (heh, heh, heh) / was Abdul Abulbul Amir." √ INTERNET→ *anon-ftp* <address 35>→lores-song

Suddenly Human

Episode: #76
Teleplay: John Whelpley & Jeri Taylor
Story: Ralph Phillips
Director: Gabrielle Beaumont
Stardate: 44143.7

Summary: The *Enterprise-D* discovers a human child aboard a Talarian ship who has been raised by an abusive Talarian father. Picard helps the child learn about being human, while he decides whether to take him to his human family or back to the Talarians.

Tim Lynch Synopsis & Review
√ INTERNET ...→*anon-ftp* <address 4>→human.rev ...→*gopher* <address 10>→human.rev ...→*www* <address 14>human.rev.html

Trekker Review √ INTERNET→ *www* <address 18>suddenly_human.html

Vidiot's Synopsis √ INTERNET →*www* <address 1b>sttng-4.html #176

Remember Me

Episode: #79
Writer: Lee Sheldon
Director: Cliff Bole
Stardate: 44161.2

Summary: Trapped in a rapidly contracting warp bubble, Dr. Crusher sees her fears about the loss of friends become reality.

Tim Lynch Synopsis & Review
√ INTERNET ...→*anon-ftp* <address 4>→remember.rev ...→*gopher* <address 10>→remember.rev ...→*www* <address 14> remember.rev.html

Vidiot's Synopsis √ INTERNET →*www* <address 1b>sttng-4.html #179

Trekker Review √ INTERNET→ *www* <address 18>remember_me. html

Shouldn't Have Happened Soundclip of Wes: "That shouldn't have happened." √ INTERNET→ *anon-ftp* <address 35>→wes-happen

Universe Soundclip of Beverly: "There's nothing wrong with me. There must be something wrong with the universe." ✓**INTERNET**→*anon-ftp* <address 35>→universe

Legacy

Episode: #80
Writer: Joe Menosky
Director: Robert Scheerer
Stardate: 44215.2

Summary: The *Enterprise-D* responds to a distress call from Turkana IV, Tasha Yar's home planet. There they find several feuding gangs—one led by Tasha's sister, Ishara.

Tim Lynch Synopsis & Review
✓**INTERNET** …→*anon-ftp* <address 4>→legacy.rev …→*gopher* <address 10>→legacy.rev …→*www* <address 14>legacy.rev.html

Trekker Review ✓**INTERNET**→*www* <address 18>legacy.html

Vidiot's Synopsis ✓**INTERNET** →*www* <address 1b>sttng-4.html #180

Reunion

Episode: #81
Teleplay: Thomas Perry, Jo Perry, Ronald D. Moore, Brannon Braga
Story: Drew Deighan, Thomas Perry & Jo Perry
Director: Jonathan Frakes
Stardate: 44246.3

Summary: K'mpec, the Klingon High Counsel, asks Picard to determine which of his successors, Duras or Gowron, poisoned him. Worf's former lover, K'Ehleyr, arrives with a surprise: a son he never knew existed.

Bite on the Cheek Soundclip of

K'ehleyr to Worf: "Not even a bite on the cheek for old times sake." ✓**INTERNET**→*anon-ftp* <address 35> →bite-on-the-cheek

Gwabje Najeel Soundclip: "Gwabje Nageel." ✓**INTERNET**→*anon-ftp* <address 35>→gwabje-nageel

Tim Lynch Synopsis & Review
✓**INTERNET** …→*anon-ftp* <address 4>→reunion.rev …→*gopher* <address 10>→reunion.rev …→*www* <address 14> reunion.rev.html

Trekker Review ✓**INTERNET**→*www* <address 18>reunion.html

Vidiot's Synopsis ✓**INTERNET** →*www* <address 1b>sttng-4.html #181

Future Imperfect

Episode: #82
Writer: J. Larry Carrol, David Bennett Carren
Director: Les Landau
Stardate: 44286.5

Summary: After succumbing to gas on Alpha Onias III, Riker wakes up in sickbay. It is 16 years later, he is captain of the ship and negotiating a treaty with the Romulans, but he can't remember anything after Alpha Onias.

Scenes from "Future Imperfect" 17 scenes from the episode, with Riker, Troi, Data, and the Romulans. ✓**PVG** *dial* 513-233-7993→<your username>→<your password>→F→*Download a file:* STNGN313.GIF *and* STNGN314.GIF

Tim Lynch Synopsis & Review
✓**INTERNET** …→*anon-ftp* <address 4>→future.rev …→*gopher* <address 10>→future.rev …→*www* <address 14>future.rev.html

Trekker Review ✓**INTERNET**→*www* <address 18>future_imperfect.html

Vidiot's Synopsis ✓**INTERNET** →*www* <address 1b>sttng-4.html #182

Screenshot—http://www.ugcs.caltech.edu/~werdna/sttng/synopsis/reunion.syn.html

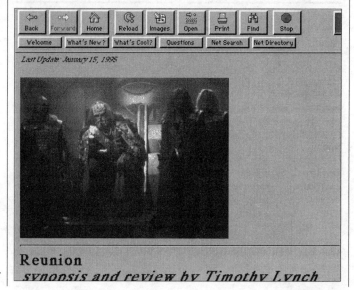

Last Update: January 15, 1995

Reunion
synopsis and review by Timothy Lynch

Final Mission

Episode: #83
Teleplay: Kasey Arnold-Ince
& Jeri Taylor
Story: Kasey Arnold-Ince
Director: Corey Allen
Stardate: 44307.3

Summary: After the shuttlecraft taking Wesley and Picard to Pentarus II crashes, Wesley works to save the captain's life. Riker attempts to save a planet from the effects of radiation.

Tim Lynch Synopsis & Review
√INTERNET ...→*anon-ftp* <address 4>→final.rev ...→*gopher* <address 10>→final.rev ...→*www* <address 14>final.rev.html

Trekker Review √INTERNET→ *www* <address 18>final_mission. html

Vidiot's Synopsis √INTERNET →*www* <address 1b>sttng-4.html #183

The Loss

Episode: #84
Teleplay: Hilary J. Bader, Alan J.
Adler, Vanessa Greene
Story: Hilary J. Bader
Stardate: 44356.9

Summary: The ship is trapped in a gravitational field which paralyzes all its systems. Troi looses her empathic powers and resigns her commission.

Tim Lynch Synopsis & Review
√INTERNET ...→*anon-ftp* <address 4>→loss.rev ...→*gopher* <address 10>→loss.rev ...→*www* <address 14>loss.rev.html

Trekker Review √INTERNET→ *www* <address 18>the_loss.html

Vidiot's Synopsis √INTERNET →*www* <address 1b>sttng-4.html #184

Scenes from "The Loss" 12 scenes from the episode, including scenes of Picard, the *Enterpise*, and the gravitational field. √**PVG** *dial* 513-233-7993→<your username> →<your password>→F→*Download a file:* STNGQ380.GIF *and* STNGQ381.GIF *and* STNGQ383. GIF

Data's Day

Episode: #85
Teleplay: Harold Apter,
Ronald D. Moore
Story: Harold Apter
Director: Robert Weimer
Stardate: 44390.1

Summary: Data details the events of a "typical" day in his life to Admiral Maddox: the wedding of Keiko and Miles O'Brien, and transporting a Vulcan ambassador to a meeting with the Romulans in the Neutral Zone.

Tim Lynch Synopsis & Review
√INTERNET ...→*anon-ftp* <address 4>→data.rev ...→*gopher* <address 10>→data.rev ...→*www* <address 14> data.rev.html

ASK SPOT!

a) **What items, and how many of them, does Q order from the food replicator to make himself feel better about being rendered merely human?**

b) **What is the Zha-Juc's role in Klingon politics?**

c) **What is the name of the fatal illness that overcomes Spock's father, Sarek?**

d) **What is the name of Will Riker's double?**

(See answers on page 359)

Vidiot's Synopsis √INTERNET →*www* <address 1b>sttng-4.html #185

Keiko and Miles Marry Picture of the O'Brien wedding. √**PVG** *dial* 513-233-7993→<your username>→<your password>→F→ *Download a file:* WED1.GIF *and* WED2.GIF

Scenes from "Data's Day" 12 scenes from the episode, including several from the wedding of Keiko and Miles. √**PVG** *dial* 513-233-7993→<your username>→<your password>→F→*Download a file:* STNGQ366.GIF *and* STNGQ367. GIF *and* STNGQ374.GIF

Bonding Rituals Soundclip of Worf: "Human bonding rituals often involve a great deal of talking...and dancing...and crying." √INTERNET→*anon-ftp* <address 35>→bonding-rituals

Humor and Sex Soundclip of Data: "There may be a correlations between humor and sex. The need for more research is clearly indicated." √INTERNET→*anon-ftp* <address 35>→humor-and-sex

Lunkhead Soundclip of a deadpan Data: "My hair does not require trimming, you lunkhead."

✓**INTERNET**→ *anon-ftp* <address 35>→lunkhead

Ornithoid Soundclip of Lieutenant Data: "I could be chasing an untamed ornithoid without cause." ✓**INTERNET**→ *anon-ftp* <address 35>→ornithoid

The Wounded

Episode:#86
Teleplay: Jeri Taylor
Story: Stuart Charno, Sarah
            Charno & Cy Chermax
Director: Chip Chalmers
Stardate: 44429.6

Summary: Picard must stop the commander of the *USS Phoenix*, Captain Maxwell, from undertaking his personal crusade—to attack the Cardassians and destroy the peace agreement. O'Brien, who served under Maxwell, must grapple with his conflicting allegiances.

Tim Lynch Synopsis & Review
✓**INTERNET** ...→*anon-ftp* <address 4>→wounded.rev ...→*gopher* <address 10>→wounded.rev ...→*www* <address 14> wounded.rev.html

Trekker Review ✓**INTERNET**→ *www* <address 18>the_wounded. html

Vidiot's Synopsis ✓**INTERNET** →*www* <address 1b>sttng-4.html #186

Devil's Due

Episode: #87
Teleplay: Philip Lazebnik
Story: Philip Lazbnik &
            William Douglas
            Lansford
Director: Tom Benko
Stardate: 44474.5

Summary: A woman called

Ardra, who claims to be the Devil, comes to exact payment from the Ventaxians, who exchanged their future for a thousand years of prosperity and peace. Picard takes on the Devil and tries to find a way to void the bargain.

Tim Lynch Synopsis & Review
✓**INTERNET** ...→*anon-ftp* <address 4>→devil.rev ...→*gopher* <address 10>→devil.rev ...→*www* <address 14>devil.rev.html

Trekker Review ✓**INTERNET**→ *www* <address 18>devils_due.html

Vidiot's Synopsis ✓**INTERNET** →*www* <address 1b>sttng-4.html #187

Arda Picture of Ardra. ✓**PVG** *dial* 513-233-7993→<your username>→ <your password>→F→*Download a file*: ARDRA.GIF

Scenes from "Devil's Due" Scenes from the episode, including shots of Ardra and the beast she turns into. ✓**PVG** *dial* 513-233-7993 →<your username>→<your password>→F→*Download a file*: STNGQ308.GIF *and* STNGQ311. GIF *and* STNGQ312.GIF *and* DEVIL.GIF

Clues

Episode: #88
Teleplay: Bruce D. Arthurs,
            Joe Menosky
Story: Bruce D. Arthurs
Director: Les Landau
Stardate: 44502.7

Summary: Investigating a wormhole, everyone in the crew except Data loses consciousness. When they awake, Data appears to be lying about what happened.

Tim Lynch Synopsis & Review
✓**INTERNET** ...→*anon-ftp* <address

4>→clues.rev ...→*gopher* <address 10>→clues.rev ...→*www* <address 14> clues.rev.html

Trekker Review ✓**INTERNET**→ *www* <address 18>clues.html

Vidiot's Synopsis ✓**INTERNET** →*www* <address 1b>sttng-4.html #188

Scenes from "Clues" Eight scenes, including Lt. Worf leading a martial arts class, Guinan and Picard on the holodeck, and several scenes on the bridge. ✓**PVG** *dial* 513-233-7993→<your username> → <your password>→F→*Download a file*: STNGQ319.GIF *and* STNGQ320.GIF

First Contact

Episode: #89
Teleplay: Dennis Russell Bailey,
            David Bischoff, Joe
            Menosky, Ronald D.
            Moore, Michael Piller
Story: Marc Scott Zicree
Director: Cliff Bole
Stardate: n/a

Summary: While investigating a planet that is developing space technology, Riker is captured by the local inhabitants who still believe themselves to be alone in the galaxy. Picard faces violating the Prime Directive by making the *Enterprise*'s presence known in order to save Riker.

Tim Lynch Synopsis & Review
✓**INTERNET** ...→*anon-ftp* <address 4>→first.rev ...→*gopher* <address 10>→first.rev ...→*www* <address 14> first.rev.html

Trekker Review ✓**INTERNET**→ *www* <address 18>first_contact. html

Vidiot's Synopsis ✓**INTERNET**

→*www* <address 1b>sttng-4.html
#189

Scenes from "First Contact"

12 scenes from the episode, including pictures of Chancellor Avel Durken and the conservative Minister of Internal Security of the planet Malcor III, Krola. ✓**PVG** *dial 513-233-7993→<your username>→<your password>→F→ Download a file: STNGQ328.GIF* and *STNGQ329.GIF* and *STNG Q335.GIF*

Galaxy's Child

Episode: #90
Teleplay: Maurice Hurley
Story: Thomas Kartozian
Director: Winrich Kolbe
Stardate: 44614.6

Summary: After accidentally killing a large pregnant alien, the crew acts as midwife, only to find that the baby believes the ship is its mother. Geordi, having fallen for an image of Dr. Leah Brahms he called up on the holodeck, meets the real Dr.Brahms.

Tim Lynch Synopsis & Review

✓**INTERNET** …→*anon-ftp* <address 4>→galaxy.rev …→*gopher* <address 10>→galaxy.rev …→*www* <address 14> galaxy.rev.html

Trekker Review ✓**INTERNET**→

www <address 18>galaxys_child. html

Vidiot's Synopsis ✓**INTERNET**

→*www* <address 1b>sttng-4.html #190

Scenes from "Galaxy's Child"

Eight scenes from the episode, including several featuring Geordi and Guinan. ✓**PVG** *dial 513-233-7993→<your username>→<your password>→F→ Download a file: STNGQ336.GIF*

and STNGQ339.GIF

Night Terrors

Episode: #91
Teleplay: Pamela Douglas,
 Jeri Taylor
Story: Shari Goodhartz
Stardate: 44631.2

Summary: While caught in a Tyken's Riff, Troi receives telepathic S.O.S. messages from an alien starship, which also cause the crew to go mad from sleep deprivation.

Tim Lynch Synopsis & Review

✓**INTERNET** …→*anon-ftp* <address 4>→night.rev …→*gopher* <address 10>→night.rev …→*www* <address 14> night.rev.html

Trekker Review ✓**INTERNET**→

www <address 18>night_terrors. html

Vidiot's Synopsis ✓**INTERNET**

→*www* <address 1b>sttng-4.html #191

Scenes from "Night Terrors"

Four scenes from the episode, including a terrified looking Troi and an anxious Dr. Beverly Crusher. ✓**PVG** *dial 513-233-7993→ <your username>→<your password>→F→Download a file:* STNGQ348.GIF

Identity Crisis

Episode: #92
Teleplay: Brannon Braga
Story: Timothy De Haas
Director: Winrich Kolbe
Stardate: 44664.5
Guest Star: Maryann Plunkett

Summary: Geordi and his friend Susanna Leijten are compelled to return to an outpost they visited while serving on the USS Victory. When they arrive they discover

other former shipmates are changing into invisible alien creatures. And they, too, are beginning to metamorphosize.

Tim Lynch Synopsis & Review

✓**INTERNET** …→*anon-ftp* <address 4>→identity.rev …→*gopher* <address 10>→identity.rev …→*www* <address 14> identity.rev.html

Trekker Review ✓**INTERNET**→

www <address 18>identity_crisis. html

Vidiot's Synopsis ✓**INTERNET**

→*www* <address 1b>sttng-4.html #192

Scenes from "Identity Crisis"

Four scenes from the episode. ✓**PVG** *dial 513-233-7993→<your username>→<your password>→F→ Download a file: STNGQ358.GIF*

The Nth Degree

Episode: #93
Writer: Joe Menosky
Director: Robert Legato
Stardate: 44704.2

Summary: Lt. Barclay gains superhuman powers after contact with an alien probe. He uses his new skills to take over the ship and direct her through the wormhole into uncharted space.

Tim Lynch Synopsis & Review

✓**INTERNET** …→*anon-ftp* <address 4>→nth.rev …→*gopher* <address 10>→nth.rev …→*www* <address 14> nth.rev.html

Trekker Review ✓**INTERNET**→

www <address 18>the_nth_de gree.html

Vidiot's Synopsis ✓**INTERNET**

→*www* <address 1b>sttng-4.html #193

Scenes from "Nth Degree"

12 scenes from the episode, including Geordi crawling through the ship shafts. ✓**PVG** *dial* 513-233-7993→*<your username>→<your password>→F→Download a file:* STNGQ350.GIF *and* STNGQ356.GIF *and* STNGQ357.GIF

Barclay Pass

Lt. Barclay makes a pass at Troi: "I don't need a counselor. What I need is the company of a charming, intelligent woman." ✓**INTERNET**→*anon-ftp* <address 35>→barklay-pass

Holodeck Fantasy

Soundclip of Lt. Barclay: "And maybe this is not any better than escaping into a holodeck fantasy." ✓**INTERNET**→*anon-ftp* <address 35>→holodeck-fantasy

Human Analysis

Soundclip: "Emotive. Electrochemical stimulus response. Cranial plate. Bipedal locomotion. Endoskeletal contiguous external integument. Hierarchical collective command structure. Interrogative." ✓**INTERNET**→*anon-ftp* <address 35>→human-analysis

I Understand

Soundclip of Barclay: "I understand...everything." ✓**INTERNET**→*anon-ftp* <address 35>→i-under stand

See So Much More

Soundclip of Barclay: "I can see so much more than you are capable of. You should trust that." ✓**INTERNET**→*anon-ftp* <address 35>→see-so-much-more

Q-Pid

Episode: #94
Teleplay: Ira Steven Behr
Story: Ira Steven Behr & Randee Russell
Director: Cliff Bole
Stardate: 44741.9

Last Update: January 15, 1995

Q-pid
synopsis and review by Timothy Lynch

Screenshot—http://www.ugcs.caltech.edu/~werdna/sttng/synopsis/qpid.syn.html

Summary: Captain Picard runs into his old flame Vash at an archeological conference. Q interferes with their reunion by transforming Picard into Robin Hood and the crew into the Merry Men who must rescue Maid Marian (Vash) from the evil Sheriff of Nottingham, Q.

Tim Lynch Synopsis & Review

✓**INTERNET** ...→*anon-ftp* <address 4>→qpid.rev ...→*gopher* <address 10>→qpid.rev ...→*www* <address 14> qpid.rev.html

Trekker Review

✓**INTERNET**→*www* <address 18>qpid.html

Vidiot's Synopsis

✓**INTERNET**→*www* <address 1b>sttng-4.html #194

Q-Pid Scenes

Four scenes of members of the *Enterprise* crew dressed as Robin Hood and his merry men. ✓**PVG** *dial* 513-233-7993→*<your username>→<your password>→F→Download a file:* QPID01.GIF ✓**INTERNET**→*anon-ftp* <address 34>→qpid01.jpg

Scenes from "Q-Pid"

12 scenes from the episode, including Picard as Robin Hood and Vash as Maid Marian. ✓**PVG** *dial* 513-233-7993→*<your username>→<your password>→F→Download a file:* STNGQ386.GIF *and* STNGQ390.GIF *and* STNGQ391.GIF

Nervous

Soundclip of Data: "I am not nervous. I am confused." ✓**INTERNET**→*anon-ftp* <address 35>→nervous-confused

Not a Merry Man

Soundclip of a very unhappy Worf: "I protest! I am NOT a merry man!" ✓**INTERNET**→*anon-ftp* <address 35>→not-a-merry-man ✓**COMPUSERVE**→*go* sf-media→Libraries→*Search by file name:* MERRYM.WAV

Throw Rug

Soundclip of Q: "You know, Worf, you'd make a perfect throw rug in Nottingham castle." ✓**INTERNET**→*anon-ftp* <address 35>→throw-rug

The Drumhead

Episode: #95
Writer: Jeri Taylor

Director: Jonathan Frakes
Stardate: 44769.2

Summary: Admiral Satie investigates a leak of information to the Romulans. When she discovers that crew member Simon Tarses is half-Romulan, she jumps to the conclusion that she has found the culprit. Picard jeopardizes his own career by attempting to stop the witch hunt.

Tim Lynch Synopsis & Review
⁄INTERNET …→*anon-ftp* <address 4>→drumhead.rev …→*gopher* <address 10>→drumhead.rev …→*www* <address 14>drumhead.rev. html

Trekker Review ⁄INTERNET→ *www* <address 18>the_drumhead. html

Vidiot's Synopsis ⁄INTERNET →*www* <address 1b>sttng-4.html #195

Half a Life

Episode: #96
Teleplay: Peter Allan Fields
Story: Ted Roberts,
              Peter Allan Fields
Director: Les Landau
Stardate: 44805.3
Guest Star: David Ogden Stiers

Summary: Lwaxana Troi become infatuated with a scientist who thinks he can save his culture from destruction. But even if he succeeds, he must obey a societal dictum that he commit suicide at 60.

Tim Lynch Synopsis & Review
⁄INTERNET …→*anon-ftp* <address 4>→half.rev …→*gopher* <address 10>→half.rev …→*www* <address 14> half.rev.html

Trekkker Review ⁄INTERNET→

www <address 18>half_a_life.html

Vidiot's Synopsis ⁄INTERNET →*www* <address 1b>sttng-4.html #196

Scenes from "Half a Life"
Four scenes from the episode, including shots of Lwaxana and Picard. ⁄**PVG** *dial* 513-233-7993→ <your username>→<your password>→F→*Download a file:* STNGQ395.GIF

The Host

Episode: #97
Writer: Michael Horvat
Director: Marvin V. Rush
Stardate: 44821.3

Summary: When a visiting ambassador dies aboard the *Enterprise-D*, the crew discovers that his body has been a host to a Trill. The parasite takes temporary refuge in Riker until it finds a new host.

Tim Lynch Synopsis & Review
⁄INTERNET …→*anon-ftp* <address 4>→host.rev …→*gopher* <address 10>→host.rev …→*www* <address 14> host.rev.html

Trekker Review ⁄INTERNET→ *www* <address 18>the_host.html

Vidiot's Synopsis ⁄INTERNET →*www* <address 1b>sttng-4.html #197

Beverly in Love Picture of Beverly in love. ⁄**PVG** *dial* 513-233-7993→<your username>→<your password>→F→*Download a file:* HOST2.GIF

Scenes from "The Host" Four scenes from the episode, including the stomach of a Trill. ⁄**PVG** *dial* 513-233-7993→<your username> →<your password>→F→*Download*

a file: STNGQ405.GIF

Every Second Digitized soundclip: "There are times when every second does count." ⁄INTERNET→ *anon-ftp* <address 35>→everysecond

The Mind's Eye

Episode: #98
Teleplay: René Echevarria
Story: Ken Schafer &
              René Echevarria
Director: David Livingston
Stardate: 44885.5

Summary: While the ship investigates Klingon claims that the Federation has been supplying rebels, Romulans kidnap and brainwash Geordi with the intent of sparking a war between the two states. On Romulan instructions, Geordi supplies weapons to the rebels and plans to assassinate the Klingon governor.

Tim Lynch Synopsis & Review
⁄INTERNET …→*anon-ftp* <address 4>→mindseye.rev …→*gopher* <address 10>→mindseye.rev …→*www* <address 14> mindseye.rev.html

Trekker Review ⁄INTERNET→ *www* <address 18>the_minds_eye. html

Scenes from "Mind's Eye" Four scenes from the episode, including several of the crew on the bridge. ⁄**PVG** *dial* 513-233-7993→ <your username>→<your password>→F→*Download a file:* STNGQ359.GIF

Vidiot's Synopsis ⁄INTERNET →*www* <address 1b>sttng-4.html #198

In Theory

Episode: #99

Writer: Joe Menosky,
 Ronald D. Moore
Director: Patrick Stewart
Stardate: 44932.3

Summary: A young woman on the rebound focuses her romantic interests on Data, who seeks advice from crew members as he attempts to experience love.

Tim Lynch Synopsis & Review
⁄INTERNET ...→*anon-ftp* <address 4>→theory.rev ...→*gopher* <address 10>→theory.rev ...→*www* <address 14> theory.rev.html

---

Trekker Review ⁄INTERNET→ *www* <address 18>in_theory.html

Vidiot's Synopsis ⁄INTERNET →*www* <address 1b>sttng-4.html #199

Redemption, Part I

Episode: #100
Writer: Ronald D. Moore
Director: Cliff Bole
Stardate: 44995.3

Summary: Picard and Worf travel to the Klingon homeworld, where Picard sparks a civil war by helping Gowron assume the throne. Worf and his brother continue their efforts to clear their father's name.

Tim Lynch Synopsis & Review
⁄INTERNET ...→*anon-ftp* <address 4>→redemption.rev ...→*gopher* <address 10>→redemption.rev ...→*www* <address 14>redemption. rev.html

---

Trekker Review ⁄INTERNET→ *www* <address 18>redemption.html

Vidiot's Synopsis ⁄INTERNET →*www* <address 1b>sttng-4.html #200

Blondes and Jazz Soundclip of Riker: "Blondes and jazz seldom go together." ⁄INTERNET→*anon-ftp* <address 35>→blondes-and-jazz

Request Denied Soundclip: "I understand your concerns. Request denied." ⁄INTERNET→*anon-ftp* <address 35>→ request-denied

Season 5

Redemption, Part II

Episode: #101
Writer: Ronald D. Moore
Director: David Carson
Stardate: 45020.4

Summary: Upon discovering that the Romulans are supplying the opposition in the Klingon civil war, Picard brings the Federation into the conflict. A Romulan commander claims to be Tasha Yar's daughter.

Tim Lynch Synopsis & Review
⁄INTERNET ...→*anon-ftp* <address 5>→redemption2.rev ...→*gopher* <address 11>→redemption2.rev ...→*www* address 19 redemption2.rev.html

---

Trekker Review ⁄INTERNET→ *www* <address 19>redemption_2.html

---

Vidiot's Synopsis ⁄INTERNET →*www* <address 1b>sttng-5.html #201

Bird of Prey in Orbit Image of a Bird of Prey. ⁄COMPUSERVE→*go* sfmedia→Libraries→*BOPORB.GIF* BOPORB.GIF

USS Sutherland—Nebula Class Image from the episode "Redemption, Pt. II" of the *USS Sutherland.* ⁄COMPUSERVE→*go* sfmedia→Libraries→*Search by file*

"With 17 minutes left, and Picard not yet found, the team has no choice but to start taking out the distribution nodes. They take out three, and as the ship drops out of warp (allowing the Enterprise to begin channeling that power to the dish and arming it), the Borg converge. Six Borg are taken out before they adapt to the new phasers, and the team prepares to beam back.

"Suddenly, Beverly sees Picard in profile (the right half of his face, as you'd see if you were facing him) and says, 'Jean-Luc!' He slowly turns, and the team sees with horror that he has been altered—into a Borg himself. Worf tries to grab him, but is repelled by a forcefield. The team is forced to beam back empty-handed. They tell Riker what's happened, and Geordi says the Borg ship is already beginning to regenerate.

"Riker tells them to prepare to fire."

—from **Tim Lynch's review of "The Best of Both Worlds, Part I"**

name: NEBULA.GIF

Worf Resigns to Fight GIF of Worf and Garon . ✓ **COMPUSERVE** →*go* sfmedia→Libraries→*Search by file name:* WORF.PCX

Celebrate Soundclip of a screaming Klingon: "Celebrate for tomorrow we all may die." ✓ **INTERNET**→*anon-ftp* <address 35>→ celebrate

Dies Well Soundclip: "I hope he dies well." ✓ **INTERNET**→*anon-ftp* <address 35>→dies-well

Klingon Desire Sounds of Klingon desire. ✓ **INTERNET**→*anon-ftp* <address 35>→klingon-desire

Darmok

Episode: #102
Teleplay: Joe Menosky
Story: Philip Lazebnik,
            Joe Menosky
Director: Winrich Kolbe
Stardate: 45047.2

Summary: Picard and a Tamarian captain, Dathon, are trapped together on a planet ruled by a savage beast. Their cooperation is hampered by the fact that Tamarians converse only in metaphors.

The Darmok Dictionary Sometimes, even after seeing the incredible range of *Star Trek* material online, you can still be awed. This glossary of Tamarian phrases, linked to soundclips and written translations of the Tamarian expressions, is truely impressive. Each significant phrase uttered by the Tamarian captain is translated and described. The document includes scene-by-scene descriptions of important conversations and appendices describing other unusual languages in science fiction and possible precedents for the Tamarian language. "Sokath! His eyes open!" ✓ **INTERNET**→*www* http://www.indirect.com/www/ raphael/darmok/darmok.html

Tim Lynch Synopsis & Review ✓ **INTERNET** ...→*anon-ftp* <address 5>→darmok.rev ...→*gopher* <address 11>→darmok.rev ...→*www* <address 14> darmok.rev.html

Trekker Review ✓ **INTERNET**→ *www* <address 19>darmok.rev.html

Vidiot's Synopsis ✓ **INTERNET** →*www* <address 1b>sttng-5.html #202

Darmok and Jellard Picture of Darmok and Jellard at Tenagra. ✓ **PVG** *dial* 513-233-7993→<your username>→<your password>→F→ *Download a file:* DARMOK.GIF

At Tenagra Soundclip: "Darmok and Jalad at Tenagra." This Tamarian phrase expresses an effort to understand another being through similar experiences. ✓ **INTERNET**→*anon-ftp* <address 35> →at-tenagre

Timber His Arms Wide Soundclip of a Tamarian: "Timber his arms wide." ✓ **INTERNET**→*anon-ftp* <address 35>→ timber-his-arms-wide

When the Walls Fell Soundclip: "Shaka, when the walls fell." ✓ **INTERNET**→*anon-ftp* <address 35>→ when-the-walls-fell

Ensign Ro

Episode: #103
Teleplay: Michael Piller
Story: Rick Berman,
            Michael Piller
Director: Les Landau
Stardate: 45076.3

Summary: On a covert mission to help capture a Bajoran terrorist group, Ensign Ro Laren—a Bajoran herself—discovers the attacks are really the work of the Cardassians.

Tim Lynch Synopsis & Review ✓ **INTERNET** ...→*anon-ftp* <address 5>→ensignro.rev ...→*gopher* <address 11>→ensignro.rev ...→*www* <address 14> ensignro.rev.html

Trekker Review ✓ **INTERNET**→ *www* <address 19>ensign_ro.html

Vidiot's Synopsis ✓ **INTERNET** →*www* <address 1b>sttng-5.html #203

Ro Laren Picture of Ensign Ro newly assigned to the Enterprise-D. ✓ **INTERNET** ...→*anon-ftp* <address 33>→ro2.jpg ...→*anon-ftp* <address 34>→ro2.jpg

Silicon Avatar

Episode: #104
Teleplay: Jeri Taylor
Story: Lawrence V. Conley
Director: Cliff Bole
Stardate: 45122.3

Summary: The Crystalline Entity attempts to destroy Melona IV, but Data and Riker's quick thinking saves some settlers. A doctor arrives to study the entity, and to exact vengeance for the Crystalline attack on Omicron Theta III.

Tim Lynch Synopsis & Review ✓ **INTERNET** ...→*anon-ftp* <address 5>→silicon.rev ...→*gopher* <address 11>→silicon.rev ...→*www* <address 14> silicon.rev.html

Vidiot's Synopsis ✓ **INTERNET** →*www* <address 1b>sttng-5.html #204

Do Not Understand Soundclip of Data's oft-spoken: "I do not

Location: http://www.ugcs.caltech.edu:80/~werdna/sttng/tlynch/silicon.rev.html

Guided Tour | What's New? | Questions | Net Search | Net Directory | Newsgroups

Silicon Avatar
synopsis and review by Timothy Lynch

Screenshot—http://www.ugcs.caltech.edu/~werdna/sttng/synopsis/avatar.syn.html

understand." ⏴INTERNET→*anon-ftp* <address 35>→ do-not-understand

Disaster

Episode: #105
Teleplay: Ronald D. Moore
Story: Ron Jarvis,
Philip A. Scorza
Director: Gabrielle Beaumont
Stardate: 45156.1

Summary: A quantum filament paralyzes the ship, isolating crew members. Troi takes command while Picard is trapped in a turbo-lift and Worf must deliver Keiko's baby in the Ten-Forward lounge.

Tim Lynch Synopsis & Review
⏴INTERNET ...→*anon-ftp* <address 5>→disaster.rev ...→*gopher* <address 11>→disaster.rev ...→*www* <address 14>disaster.rev.html

Vidiot's Synopsis ⏴INTERNET →*www* <address 1b>sttng-5.html #205

Trekker Review ⏴INTERNET→ *www* <address 19>disaster.html

The Game

Episode: #106
Teleplay: Brannon Braga
Story: Susan Sackett,
Fred Bronson,
Brannon Braga
Director: Corey Allen
Stardate: 45208.2

Summary: Riker returns from vacation with a game to which all crew members but Data quickly become addicted. The game stimulates the pleasure centers of the brain and is part of a conspiracy to take over the Federation.

Ted Brengle's IMHO Review
⏴TFDN→<address 23>→ arma.zip

Tim Lynch Synopsis & Review
⏴INTERNET ...→*anon-ftp* <address 5>→game.rev ...→*gopher* <address 11>→game.rev ...→*www* <address 14> game.rev.html

Trekker Review ⏴INTERNET→ *www* <address 19>the_game.html

Vidiot's Synopsis ⏴INTERNET

→*www* <address 1b>sttng-5.html #206

A Little Strange Soundclip: "Don't you think that's a little strange?" ⏴INTERNET→*anon-ftp* <address 35>→a-little-strange

Chocolate 1 Soundclip: "I never met a chocolate I didn't like." ⏴INTERNET→*anon-ftp* <address 35>→chocolate1

Chocolate 2 Soundclip: "Chocolate is a serious thing." ⏴INTERNET →*anon-ftp* <address 35>→chocolate2

Unification, Part I

Episode: #107
Teleplay: Jeri Taylor
Story: Rick Berman &
Michael Piller
Director: Les Landau
Guest Star: Leonard Nimoy
Stardate: 45233.1

Summary: In a cloaked Klingon ship, Picard flies to Romulus to discover what Ambassador Spock is doing on his clandestine visit to Romulan Senator Pardek. Meanwhile Riker and Geordi try to figure out how the Ferengi have obtained a Vulcan deflector unit.

Archived Discussion of "Unification, Part I" Should there be a *Star Trek* canon?—Roddenberry sanctioned only? (The discussion transpired before The Great Bird's death.) Should there be more attention paid to continuity with TOS? Background information on Spock's familial ties is brought up in the conversation. ⏴GENIE→*keyword* <address 22>→688

Tim Lynch Synopsis & Review
⏴INTERNET ...→*anon-ftp* <address 5>→unif1.rev ...→*gopher* <address 11>→unif1.rev ...→*www* <address

14> unif1.rev.html

Trekker Review ✓ INTERNET→ *www* <address 19>unification_1. html

Vidiot's Synopsis ✓ INTERNET →*www* <address 1b>sttng-5.html #208

Klingon Bird of Prey Image of a Klingon ship in Romulan space. ✓ INTERNET ...→*anon-ftp* <address 33>→sttng307.jpg ...→*anon-ftp* <address 34>→sttng307.jpg

Picard as a Romulan Picard and Data surgically altered to look like Romulans. ✓ INTERNET ...→ *anon-ftp* <address 33>→romulan1. jpg ...→*anon-ftp* <address 34>→ romulan1.jpg

The Romulan Empire A picture of the Romulan homeworld. ✓ INTERNET ...→*anon-ftp* <address 33>→sttng312.jpg ...→*anon-ftp* <address 34>→sttng312.jpg

Romulus View of Romulan empire headquarters. ✓ INTERNET ...→ *anon-ftp* <address 33>→sttng320. jpg ...→*anon-ftp* <address 34>→ sttng320.jpg

Classified Matter Soundclip of Picard: "I'm sorry. It's a classified matter." ✓ INTERNET→*anon-ftp* <address 35>→ classified-matter

Handsome Women and Co-operation Soundclip: "He probably figures that we don't get to see a lot of handsome women out this way and someone like you might get a little more cooperation from me. He's probably right." ✓ INTERNET→*anon-ftp* <address 35>→ handsome-women-and-cooperation

Jigsaw Puzzle Soundclip of Geordi: "You're going to be like putting together a big jigsaw puz-zle when you don't even know what the picture's suppose to be." ✓ INTERNET→ *anon-ftp* <address 35>→jigsaw

Look Sweet Soundclip: "Don't you two look sweet." ✓ INTERNET →*anon-ftp* <address 35>→dont-you-look-sweet

Peace and Long Life Sound-clip: "Peace and long life." ✓ INTERNET→ *anon-ftp* <address 35>→ peace-and-long-life

Welcome to Romulus Sound-clip of a Romulan: "Welcome to Romulus." ✓ INTERNET→*anon-ftp* <address 35>→welcome-to-romulus

Unification, Part II

Episode: # 108
Teleplay: Michael Piller
Story: Rick Berman &
               Michael Piller
Director: Cliff Bole
Guest Star: Leonard Nimoy
Stardate: 45245.8

Summary: Ambassador Spock's peace mission goes awry when Picard and Data learn Spock is being used as part of a Romulan plot to conquer Vulcan. Riker discovers that the Romulans are also behind the theft of Vulcan ships.

Archived Discussion of "Unification, Part II" Is there a 24th-century cloaking gap (missile gap)? How does Romulan's climate compare to Vulcan's? Can humans be happy in either home world? How could the Romulans hope to defeat the Vulcans with a mere 2,000 men—illogical! Is TNG selling the Romulans short? ✓ GENIE→*keyword* <address 22>→684

Tim Lynch Synopsis & Review ✓ INTERNET ...→*anon-ftp* <address 5>→unification2.rev ...→*gopher*

<address 11>→unification2.rev ...→*www* <address 14>unification 2.rev.html

Trekker Review ✓ INTERNET→ *www* <address 19>unification_2. html

Vidiot's Synopsis ✓ INTERNET →*www* <address 1b>sttng-5.html #207

Ambassador Spock Image of Spock on Romulus speaking to Captain Picard (unseen). ✓ INTERNET ...→*anon-ftp* <address 33>→ sttng313.jpg ...→*anon-ftp* <address 34>→sttng313.jpg

Ambassador Spock Picture of Ambassador Spock on Romulus. ✓ INTERNET ...→*anon-ftp* <address 33>→sttng13.jpg ...→*anon-ftp* <address 34>→sttng13.jpg

Mind Meld Spock and Picard mind-meld. ✓ PVG *dial* 513-233-7993→<your username>→<your password>→F→*Download a file:* MELD.GIF

Sela and Ambassador Spock Picture of Sela and Ambassador Spock confronting each other. ✓ INTERNET ...→*anon-ftp* <address 33> →sttng318.jpg ...→*anon-ftp* <address 34>→sttng318.jpg

Sela, Romulan Commander Image of Sela, daughter of Tasha Yar and Romulan Commander. ✓ INTERNET ...→*anon-ftp* <address 33>→sttng319.jpg ...→*anon-ftp* <address 34>→sttng319.jpg

Spock Picture of Spock in cave on Romulus ✓ INTERNET ...→*anon-ftp* <address 33>→spock.jpg ...→ *anon-ftp* <address 34>→spock.jpg

Spock and Data An image of Spock and Data in Sela's office. ✓ COMPUSERVE→*go* sfmedia→Li-

Back Forward Home Reload Images Open Print Find Stop

Location: http://www.ugcs.caltech.edu:80/~werdna/sttng/tlynch/unif2.rev.html

Guided Tour | What's New? | Questions | Net Search | Net Directory | Newsgroups

Last Update: November 14, 1994

Unification II
synopsis and review by Timothy Lynch

Screenshot—http://www.ugcs.caltech.edu/~werdna/sttng/synopsis/unif2.rev.html

braries→*Search by file name:* SPOK-DA.GIF

Spock on Romulus Image of Spock on Romulus. ✓**INTERNET** ...→*anon-ftp* <address 33>→sttng314.jpg ...→*anon-ftp* <address 34>→sttng314.jpg

Dreadful Noise Soundclip: "What is that dreadful noise?" ✓**INTERNET**→*anon-ftp* <address 35>→dreadful-noise

Exchange of Information Soundclip: "I'm afraid the exchange of information will have to flow in one direction only." ✓**INTERNET**→*anon-ftp* <address 35> →exchange-of-information

Fascinating Soundclip of Spock's "fascinating." ✓**INTERNET**→*anon-ftp* <address 35>→fascinating

I Hate Vulcans Soundclip:"I hate Vulcans." ✓**INTERNET**→*anon-ftp* <address 35>→i-hate-vulcans

Quite Right Soundclip of Picard to Riker: "Quite right number one:" ✓**INTERNET**→*anon-ftp* <ad-dress 35>→quite-right

Remove My Ears Soundclip: "Think I'll take this opportunity to remove my ears." ✓**INTERNET**→*anon-ftp* <address 35>→remove-my-ears

A Matter Of Time

Episode: # 109
Writer: Rick Berman
Director: Paul Lynch
Stardate: 45349.1
Guest Star: Matt Frewer

Summary: While helping Penthara IV cope with damage from an asteroid collision, the *Enterprise-D* encounters a time traveler. The man, who claims to be a professor from the future researching the *Enterprise-D* and its mission, is really a thief from the past.

Archived Discussion of "A Matter of Time" What is the morality of time travel? Is there ever a valid reason for changing the past or the future? Is Picard "being a Kirk" when he overacts? ✓**GENIE**→*keyword* <address 22>→690

Tim Lynch Synopsis & Review ✓**INTERNET** ...→*anon-ftp* <address 5>→matter.rev ...→*gopher* <address 11>→matter.rev ...→*www* <address 14> matter.rev.html

Trekker Review ✓**INTERNET**→ *www* <address 19>a_matter_of_time.html

Vidiot's Synopsis ✓**INTERNET** →*www* <address 1b>sttng-5.html #209

Everyone Dies Soundclip of the time traveller admonishing Captain Picard: "Everyone dies, captain. It's just a question of when." ✓**INTERNET**→*anon-ftp* <address 35>→everyone-dies

Indescribable Soundclip: "To experience the moment...to witness the nuances...indescribable." ✓**INTERNET**→*anon-ftp* <address 35>→indescribable

Keep Your Assumptions Soundclip: "Wouldn't it be best if you kept your assumptions to yourself...wouldn't it?" ✓**INTERNET** →*anon-ftp* <address 35>→keep-your-assumptions

Questionnaires Soundclip: "I hate questionnaires." ✓**INTERNET**→ *anon-ftp* <address 35>→question naires

Tasha Soundclip of Picard: "Tasha." ✓**INTERNET**→*anon-ftp* <ad-dress 35>→tasha

This is Wonderful Soundclip: "Oh, this is wonderful." ✓**INTERNET** →*anon-ftp* <address 35>→this-is-wonderful

Welcome Soundclip of Picard: "Welcome to the 24th century." ✓**INTERNET**→*anon-ftp* <address 35>→welcome-to-24

New Ground

Episode #110
Teleplay: Grant Rosenberg
Story: Sarah Charno &
Stuart Charno
Director: Robert Scheerer
Stardate: 45376.3

Summary: At Bilana III, the *Enterprise-D* takes part in tests of the soliton wave, which is designed to propel ships at warp drive without warp engines. Worf wrestles with the obligations of fatherhood when his mother brings Alexander back from Earth.

Archived Discussion of "New Ground" Many members of the discussion were annoyed with the "maladjusted child coming to terms with his father" theme of this episode. Where's the science fiction? Others want TNG to experiment: "Child psychology's fine, but would it have been better if the child psychology were more Klingon oriented?" ✓GENIE→*keyword* <address 22>→692

Tim Lynch Synopsis & Review ✓INTERNET ...→*anon-ftp* <address 5>→newground.rev ...→*gopher* <address 11>→newground.rev ...→*www* <address 14>newground.rev.html

Trekker Review ✓INTERNET→ *www* <address 19>new_ground.html

Vidiot's Synopsis ✓INTERNET →*www* <address 1b>sttng-5.html #210

Hero Worship

Episode #111
Teleplay: Joe Menosky
Story: Hilary J. Bader
Director: Patrick Stewart
Stardate: 45397.3

Hero Worship
synopsis and review by Timothy Lynch

Screenshot—http://www.ugcs.caltech.edu/~werdna/sttng/synopsis/hero.rev.html

Summary: A young boy who is the only survivor on a science vessel blames himself for his parent's deaths. Unable to handle the guilt and loss, the child decides he wants to be an android just like Data and represses all emotions.

Archived Discussion of "Hero Worship" What was the effect of Shakespearean training on Stewart: Is it too magnificent, too stark, too "dramatic"? A general discussion of children and trauma emerges from a debate over Troi's encouragement of young Timothy's repression of his feelings. There are also many reminiscences of Roddenberry. ✓GENIE→*keyword* <address 22>→702

Tim Lynch Synopsis & Review ✓INTERNET ...→*anon-ftp* <address 5>→hero.rev ...→*gopher* <address 11>→hero.rev ...→*www* <address 14>hero.rev.html

Trekker Review ✓INTERNET→ *www* <address 19>hero_worship.html

Vidiot's Synopsis ✓INTERNET →*www* <address 1b>sttng-5.html #211

Violations

Episode #112
Teleplay: Pamela Gray &
Jeri Taylor
Story: Shari Goodhartz, T.
Michael, Pamela Gray
Director: Robert Weimer
Stardate: 45429.3

Summary: Troi, Riker, and Dr. Crusher are traumatized by horrifying memories and lapse into comas. The crew determines that they have been mentally raped by a brutal empath.

Tim Lynch Synopsis & Review ✓INTERNET ...→*anon-ftp* <address 5>→violations.rev ...→*gopher* <address 11>→violations.rev ...→*www* <address 14> violations.rev.html

Trekker Review ✓INTERNET →*www* <address 19>violations.html

Vidiot's Synopsis ✓**INTERNET** →*www* <address 1b>sttng-5.html #212

The Masterpiece Society

Episode #113
Teleplay: Adam Belanoff,
             Michael Piller
Story: James Kahn,
             Adam Belanoff
Director: Winrich Kolbe
Stardate: 45470.1

Summary: A fragile, genetically engineered colony is threatened with destruction by the gravitational force of a stellar core fragment. The *Enterprise* crew tries to help the society, which is unwilling to be relocated, but creates additional havoc in the fragile social balance.

Tim Lynch Synopsis & Review ✓**INTERNET** ...→*anon-ftp* <address 5>→masterpiece.rev ...→*gopher* <address 11>→masterpiece.rev ...→*www* <address 14> masterpiece.rev.html

Trekker Review ✓**INTERNET**→ *www* <address 19>the_masterpiece_society.html

Vidiot's Synopsis ✓**INTERNET** →*www* <address 1b>sttng-5.html #214

Conundrum

Episode # 114
Teleplay: Barry Schkolnick
Story: Paul Schiffer
Director: Les Landau
Stardate   45494.2

Summary: Under the influence of an alien probe, crew members experience amnesia. When they regain consciousness, they are under orders to destroy a Lysian space station. The question: Will the crew go against the Prime Directive and annihilate a less technologically sophisticated society?

Archived Discussion of "Conundrum" A Trek-specific nature-versus-nurture discussion: if you take away the experiences and memories of people's lives, what is left? ✓**GENIE**→*keyword* <address 22>→703

Tim Lynch Synopsis & Review ✓**INTERNET** ...→*anon-ftp* <address 5>→conundrum.rev ...→*gopher* <address 11>→conundrum.rev ...→ *www* <address 14> conundrum.rev.html

Trekker Review ✓**INTERNET**→ *www* <address 19>conundrum.html

Vidiot's Synopsis ✓**INTERNET** →*www* <address 1b>sttng-5.html #215

Power Play

Episode #115
Teleplay: René Balcer,
             Herbert J. Wright &
             Brannon Braga
Story: Paul Reuben,
             Maurice Hurley
Director: David Livingston
Stardate: 45571.2

Summary: The spirits of exiled prisoners inhabit the bodies of Troi, Data, and O'Brien who return from an investigative mission with altered personalities.

Archived Discussion of "Power Play" The big questions: Why does it always seem that when you get taken over by an alien, you become immune to phasers? Given what hackers are able to do now, is it really that unbelievable that you could use the beverage computer in Ten Forward to take over the

"This episode generated conflicting emotions in me. On the one hand, yes, Alexander is partially human, and should be given the choice of following his mother's path of diplomacy rather than force. On the other hand, if he doesn't train as a warrior, he WON'T have the choice of following his father's path if he should wish it. The best example I can give is this--I plan to send my hypothetical children to an Orthodox Jewish Day School. Yes, I hope that this plus reinforcement from home will encourage them to stay observant, but I know from people around me that this is not necessarily so. What it WILL do is give them the choice to either remain observant or return to it later on without the difficulty I faced when I became observant as an adult. Equally, I want them to have a good secular education so that they can go to the college they choose. I want them to have CHOICE."

—from **GEnie's archived discussion of "First Born"**

ship? √GENIE→*keyword* <address 22>→667

Tim Lynch Synopsis & Review
√INTERNET ...→*anon-ftp* <address 5>→*powerplay.rev* ...→*gopher* <address 11>→powerplay.rev ...→*www* <address 14> powerplay.rev.html

Trekker Review √INTERNET→ *www* <address 19>power_play. html

Vidiot's Synopsis √INTERNET →*www* <address 1b>sttng-5.html #216

Ethics

Episode #116
Teleplay: Ronald J. Moore
Story: Sara Charno &
                   Stuart Charno
Director: Chip Chalmers
Stardate: 45587.3

Summary: When Worf's spine is crushed in an accident, he must choose among three unattractive options: a dangerous experimental procedure, ritual suicide, or living

life with a handicap. Worf asks Riker to assist him in ending his life.

Tim Lynch Synopsis & Review
√INTERNET ...→*anon-ftp* <address 5>→*ethics.rev* ...→*gopher* <address 11>→ethics.rev ...→*www* <address 14> ethics.rev.html

Trekker Review √INTERNET→ *www* <address 19>ethics.html

Vidiot's Synopsis √INTERNET →*www* <address 1b>sttng-5.html #216

The Outcast

Episode #117
Writer: Jeri Taylor
Director: Robert Scheerer
Stardate: 45614.6

Summary: Riker visits a planet where androgyny is the law and falls in love with a rebel, Soren, who has declared itself female.

Archived Discussion of "The Outcast" Is this a good analogy

for the plight of gays in American society? Is the female the baseline for humanoid biology/androgyny or would all have been upset if Riker fell for a more masculine-looking creature? Does the Federation protect human rights? (The episode elicited a tremendous amount of discussion from all corners of Cyberspace after it aired.)
√GENIE→*keyword* <address 22> →722

Tim Lynch Synopsis & Review
√INTERNET ...→*anon-ftp* <address 5>→*outcast.rev* ...→*gopher* <address 11>→outcast.rev ...→*www* <address 14> outcast.rev.html

Trekker Review √INTERNET→ *www* <address 19>the_outcast.html

Vidiot's Synopsis √INTERNET →*www* <address 1b>sttng-5.html #217

Cause and Effect

Episode #118
Writer: Brannon Braga
Director: Jonathan Frakes
Stardate: 45652.1
Guest Star: Kelsey Grammar

Summary: The *Enterprise*, slamming into another starship, gets caught in a "temporal causality" loop, forcing it to replay over and over again its own destruction.

Tim Lynch Synopsis & Review
√INTERNET ...→*anon-ftp* <address 5>→*cause.rev* ...→*gopher* <address 11>→cause.rev ...→*www* <address 14> cause.rev.html

Trekker Review √INTERNET→ *www* <address 19>cause_and_effect.html

Vidiot's Synopsis √INTERNET →*www* <address 1b>sttng-5.html #218

Screenshot—http://www.ugcs.caltech.edu/~werdna/sttng/synopsis/outcast.rev.html

The Outcast
synopsis and review by Timothy Lynch

Poker Game Picture of the episode's opening poker scene. ✓ **PVG** *dial* 513-233-7993→<your username>→<your password>→ F→*Download a file:* POKER.GIF

The First Duty

Episode # 119
Writers: Ronald D. Moore & Naren Shankar
Director: Paul Lynch
Stardate: 45703.9

Summary: A member of Wesley Crusher's squadron dies as a result of a reckless display of flight bravado. When Wesley and classmates at Starfleet Academy become involved in the subsequent cover-up, Picard and Dr. Crusher arrive to help get to the bottom of the incident.

Archived Discussion of "The First Duty" Wesley finally does something bad and by doing so "gets a character"—this was the overwhelming consensus following the airing of this episode. But, enjoyment over Wesley's fall from grace aside, debate focused on whether Wesley should have told the truth or shown solidarity with his mates. ✓ **GENIE**→*keyword* <address 22>→ 683

Tim Lynch Synopsis & Review ✓ **INTERNET** ...→*anon-ftp* <address 5>→firstduty.rev ...→*gopher* <address 11>→firstduty.rev ...→*www* <address 14> firstduty.rev.html

Trekker Review ✓ **INTERNET**→ *www* <address 19>the_first_duty. html

Vidiot's Synopsis ✓ **INTERNET** →*www* <address 1b>sttng-5.html #219

Boothby Picture of the wise groundskeeper, Boothby, of Starfleet Academy. ✓ **PVG** *dial* 513-233-7993→<your username>→ <your password>→F→*Download a file:* BOOTHBY.GIF

The Hearing Beverly and Picard at the Starfleet Academy hearing about the accident. ✓ **PVG** *dial* 513-233-7993→<your username>→ <your password>→F→*Download a file:* BEVPCRD.GIF

Cost of Living

Episode #120
Writer: Peter Allan Fields
Director: Winrich Kolbe
Stardate: 45733.6

ASK SPOT!

a) In the episode "Yesterday's Enterprise," who tells Tasha that she's dead?

b) What is genotonic replication?

c) Whose love interest is Countess Regina Bartholomew?

d) What ship is Commander Riker offered command of when the Enterprise is docked at Starbase Montgomery, and who arrives to brief him on the mission?

e) Who says "I will have to say that this morning I was the leader of the universe as I knew it. This afternoon, I am only a voice in a chorus. But I think it was a good day"?

f) What is the name of the scientist who eventually kills the Crystalline Entity?

g) What female human does Q explore the universe with?

h) What is the name of the proto-Vulcan race (still in its Bronze age) that the crew of the Enterprise mistakenly interfere with?

(See answers on page 359)

Summary: Wedding bells should be ringing for Lwaxana Troi when a planetary dignitary arrives to fulfill her well-publicized desires, but he balks at her society's custom of being married in the nude. Meanwhile Deanna Troi attempts to moderate Worf's gruff influence on Alexander.

Archived Discussion of "Cost of Living" Must *Star Trek* always have an action plot or is mother/ daughter conflict sufficient? The character of Lwaxana is subject to harsh criticism by GEnie members: "Lwaxana makes my teeth hurt." Lwaxana aside, the mud bath and dancing woman at the wedding banquet received much electronic applause. ✓GENIE→*key-word* <address 22>→808

Tim Lynch Synopsis & Review ✓INTERNET ...→*anon-ftp* <address 5>→cost.rev ...→*gopher* <address 11>→cost.rev ...→*www* <address 14> cost.rev.html

Trekker Review ✓INTERNET→ *www* <address 19>cost_of_living. html

Vidiot's Synopsis ✓INTERNET →*www* <address 1b>sttng-5.html #220

The Perfect Mate

Episode #121
Teleplay: Gary Perconte,
              Michael Piller
Story: René Echevarria,
              Gary Perconte
Director: Winrich Kolbe
Stardate: 45761.3

Summary: The *Enterprise* must deliver a peace offering—Kamala, a ravishing woman with the ability to transform herself to suit any man's desires. Male crew members are stunned by her beauty, but she only has eyes for Picard.

Archived Discussion of "The Perfect Mate" Why, oh why, can two beings perfect for each other never just say "Damn my duty, I love you" on Trek? Is Kamala's ability to transform herself into the perfect love object "co-dependency" run rampant? ✓GENIE→ *keyword* <address 22>→793

Tim Lynch Synopsis & Review ✓INTERNET ...→*anon-ftp* <address 5>→perfect.rev ...→*gopher* <address 11>→perfect.rev ...→*www* <address 14> perfect.rev.html

Trekker Review ✓INTERNET→ *www* <address 19>the_perfect_mate.html

Vidiot's Synopsis ✓INTERNET →*www* <address 1b>sttng-5.html #221

Episode Scene Four scenes from the episode, including a large shot of Kamala and another of Kirk giving away the bride. ✓PVG *dial* 513-233-7993→<your username>→ <your password>→F →*Download a file:* MATE.GIF

Imaginary Friend

Episode #122
Teleplay: Edith Swensen,
              Brannon Braga
Story: Jean Louise Matthias,
              Ronald Wilkerson &
              Richard Fliegel
Director: Gabrielle Beaumont
Stardate: 45852.1

Summary: Lonely little Clara's imaginary playmate, Isabella, turns out to be rather nasty and very real. The plasma-based life-form wreaks havoc as it attempts to find an energy source aboard the ship and considers humans through the eyes of a child.

Archived Discussion of "Imaginary Friend" TNG does *Rosemary's Baby*. Amidst complaints that the story-line bears an uncanny resemblance to *National Enquirer* headlines ("My best friend is an alien") and gripes that the "characterizations were so cardboard you could see the perforations," lie debates on the nature of sentience and how *Star Trek* can use the horror genre. ✓GENIE→*key-word* <address 22>→788

Tim Lynch Synopsis & Review ✓INTERNET ...→*anon-ftp* <address 5>→imaginary.rev ...→*gopher* <ad-

dress 11>→imaginary.rev ...→*www* <address 14> imaginary.rev.html

Trekker Review ✓ **INTERNET**→ *www* <address 19>imaginary_ friend.html

Vidiot's Synopsis ✓ **INTERNET** →*www* <address 1b>sttng-5.html #222

I, Borg

Episode #123
Writer: René Echevarria
Director: Robert Lederman
Stardate: 45854.2

Summary: The *Enterprise-D* captures an injured Borg and in the process of nursing it back to health, gives it a name (Hugh) and witnesses the devolopment of its character. Picard and Guinan confront their prejudices and the crew considers programming the Borg with a virus and sending him back to destroy the Borg race. The storyline is continued in "Descent."

Archived Discussion of "I, Borg" Is adherence to the "Prime Directive" reasonable in the face of genocide? And, when do fear and anger towards the Borg, cross the line and become mere prejudice? ✓ **GENIE**→*keyword* <address 22> →791

Tim Lynch Synopsis & Review ✓ **INTERNET** ...→*anon-ftp* <address 5>→iborg.rev ...→*gopher* <address 11>→iborg.rev ...→*www* <address 14> iborg.rev.html

Trekker Review ✓ **INTERNET**→ *www* <address 19>i_borg.html

Vidiot's Synopsis ✓ **INTERNET** →*www* <address 1b>sttng-5.html #223

Hugh and Geordi Picture of

Last Update: November 14, 1994

I, Borg
synopsis and review by Timothy Lynch

Screenshot—http://www.ugcs.caltech.edu/~werdna/sttng/synopsis/iborg.rev.html

Hugh, the Borg, and Geordi. ✓ **PVG** *dial* 513-233-7993→<your username>→<your password>→F→ *Download a file:* NEXTC08.GIF

Hugh in the Brig Picture of Hugh in the Enterprise brig. ✓ **PVG** *dial* 513-233-7993→<your username>→<your password>→F→ *Download a file:* HUGH.GIF

Next Phase

Episode #124
Writer: Ronald D. Moore
Director: David Carson
Stardate: 45892.4

Summary: When Geordi and Ro Laren are made invisible by a new Romulan cloaking device, the crew believes they are dead. To their dismay, the invisible duo— who can see and hear the crew— discover that the Romulans plan to destroy the *Enterprise.*

Archived Discussion of "Next Phase" The development of Ro Laren's character gets a thorough

analysis. And why do non-corporeal bodies have shadows? ✓ **GENIE** →*keyword* <address 22>→780

Tim Lynch Synopsis & Review ✓ **INTERNET** ...→*anon-ftp* <address 5>→nextphase.rev ...→*gopher* <address 11>→nextphase.rev ...→*www* <address 14> nextphase.rev.html

Trekker Review ✓ **INTERNET**→ *www* <address 19>the_next_phase. html

Vidiot's Synopsis ✓ **INTERNET** →*www* <address 1b>sttng-5.html #224

The Inner Light

Episode #125
Teleplay: Morgan Gendel,
            Peter Allan Fields
Story: Morgan Gendel
Director: Peter Lauritson
Stardate: 45944.1

Summary: Picard is rendered unconscious for a few minutes by an alien probe. During that time

Last Update: November 14, 1994

The Inner Light
synopsis and review by Timothy Lynch

Screenshot—http://www.ugcs.caltech.edu/~werdna/sttng/synopsis/innerlight.rev.html

he lives a whole other life on a planet extinct since the 14th century when a star in its system went nova.

Tim Lynch Synopsis & Review
✓**INTERNET** ...→*anon-ftp* <address 5>→innerlight.rev ...→*gopher* <address 11>→innerlight.rev ...→*www* <address 14> innerlight.rev.html

Trekker Review ✓**INTERNET**→
www <address 19>the_inner_light.html

Vidiot's Synopsis ✓**INTERNET**
→*www* <address 1b>sttng-5.html #225

The Inner Light
Several scenes from the episode. ✓**PVG** *dial* 513-233-7993→<your username>→<your password>→F→*Download a file:* INNER1.GIF ✓**INTERNET** ...→

anon-ftp <address 33>→inner1.jpg ...→*anon-ftp* <address 34>→inner1.jpg

Time's Arrow, Part I
Episode #126
Teleplay: Joe Menosky,
              Michael Piller
Story: Joe Menosky
Director: Les Landau
Stardate: 45959.1

Summary: Picard and Data are shocked to find Data's head along with artifacts that appear to be 500 years old. Data travels to 19th-century San Francisco to search for its origins, and, while there, meets Mark Twain.

Tim Lynch Synopsis & Review
✓**INTERNET** ...→*anon-ftp* <address 5>→arrow.rev ...→*gopher* <address

11>→arrow.rev ...→*www* <address 14> arrow.rev.html

Trekker Review ✓**INTERNET**→
www <address 19>times_arrow.html

Vidiot's Synopsis ✓**INTERNET**
→*www* <address 1b>sttng-5.html #226

Season 6

Time's Arrow, Part II
Episode #127
Teleplay: Jeri Taylor
Story: Joe Menosky
Director: Les Landau
Stardate: 46001.3

Summary: While in the 19th century, Data runs across an alien plot to drain human vitality. Picard and the crew travel back in time to rescue their friend.

Tim Lynch Synopsis & Review
✓**INTERNET** ...→*anon-ftp* <address 6>→arrow2.rev ...→*gopher* <address 12>→arrow2.rev ...→*www* <address 14> arrow2.rev.html

Trekker Review ✓**INTERNET**→
www <address 20>times_arrow_2.html

Vidiot's Synopsis ✓**INTERNET**
→*www* <address 1b>sttng-6.html #227

Double Heads
Picture of the two Data heads. ✓**PVG** *dial* 513-233-7993→<your username>→<your password>→F→*Download a file:* 2DTAHDS.GIF

Mark Twain
Picture of Mark Twain helping out. ✓**PVG** *dial* 513-233-7993→<your username>→<your password>→F→*Download a file:* TMSARW2.GIF

Realm of Fear

Episode #128
Writer: Brandon Braga
Director: Cliff Bole
Stardate: 46041.1

Summary: One of Lt. Reginald Barclay's many phobias becomes a reality when he is bitten by creatures living in the transporter beam.

Archived Discussion of "Realm of Fear" How does the transporter actually work? Is Barclay's behavior realistic? Members share their own battles with phobias. ✓GENIE→*keyword* <address 22>→429

Tim Lynch Synopsis & Review
✓INTERNET ...→*anon-ftp* <address 6>→realm.rev ...→*gopher* <address 12>→realm.rev ...→*www* <address 14> realm.rev.html

Trekker Review ✓INTERNET→ *www* <address 20>realm_of_fear. html

Vidiot's Synopsis ✓INTERNET →*www* <address 1b>sttng-6.html #228

Man of the People

Episode #129
Teleplay: Frank Abatemarco
Director: Winrich Kolbe
Stardate: 46071.6

Summary: Ambassador Alkar comes aboard the ship and begins to exert a very negative influence over Troi. As she begins to age at a rapid rate, it becomes clear that he is abusing her through her empathy.

Tim Lynch Synopsis & Review
✓INTERNET ...→*anon-ftp* <address 6>→man.rev ...→*gopher* <address

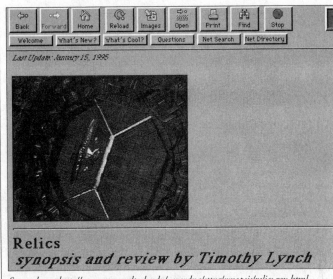

Relics
synopsis and review by Timothy Lynch

Screenshot—http://www.ugcs.caltech.edu/~werdna/sttng/synopsis/relics.rev.html

12>→man.rev ...→*www* <address 14> man.rev.html

Trekker Review ✓INTERNET→ *www* <address 20>man_of_the_ people.html

Vidiot's Synopsis ✓INTERNET →*www* <address 1b>sttng-6.html #229

Relics

Episode #130
Writer: Ronald D. Moore
Director: Alexander Singer
Stardate: 46125.3

Summary: While investigating a distress beacon emanating from a crashed ship on the surface of a Dyson Sphere, the *Enterprise-D* rescues Montgomery ("Scotty") Scott, who survived by remaining in a perpetual transporter beam. Scotty teaches Geordi how to be a miracle-worker as they save the *Enterprise* of the 24th century.

Archived Discussion of "Relics" How will Scotty handle

the fact that he's 30 years younger than his friends and technology has passed him by? What happened to Paramount's promise that no old members would be on the show? The necessity/value of the *Star Trek* canon is once again debated. ✓GENIE→*keyword* <address 22>→430

Tim Lynch Synopsis & Review
✓INTERNET ...→*anon-ftp* <address 6>→relics.rev ...→*gopher* <address 12>→relics.rev ...→*www* <address 14> relics.rev.html

Trekker Review ✓INTERNET→ *www* <address 20>relics.html

Vidiot's Synopsis ✓INTERNET →*www* <address 1b>sttng-6.html #230

Schisms

Episode #131
Teleplay: Brannon Braga
Story: Jean Louise Matthias &
             Ron Wilkerson
Director: Les Landau
Stardate: 46154.2

LaForge: "Everything was normal, and then, suddenly, it's like the laws of physics went right out the window."

Q: "And why shouldn't they? They're so inconvenient."

—"True Q"

Net Source: STTNG Quotes —http://www.ugcs.caltech.edu/htbin/werdna/fortune?sttng

Summary: A dimensional rift in the cargo bay caused by LaForge's experiment enables aliens from another time to board the ship. Crew members suffer emotional and physical exhaustion and all share a memory of a strange room with an examining table.

Archived Discussion of "Schisms" Why do they make so many aliens look like "mad space monks" and give them all bad hair? For those less concerned with alien hair (although it's a big issue here), this discussion also includes analysis of the "Ode to Spot" poem composed by Data. ✓ **GENIE** →*keyword* <address 22>→431

Data's Ode to Spot Full text of the ballad Data wrote for his cat Spot. ✓ **AMERICA ONLINE**→*keyword* trek→MORE...→Star Trek Record Banks→Text/Other Files→Upld: 11/08/92→TEXT:Ode to Spot (Filename: SPOTODE.DOC) ✓ **COMPUSERVE** →*go* sfmedia→Libraries →*Search by file name:* ODE2SP.TXT ✓ **INTERNET**→*www* http://www.eeng.dcu.ie/~stdcu/trek/spot.html

Tim Lynch Synopsis & Review ✓ **INTERNET** ...→*anon-ftp* <address 6>→schisms.rev ...→*gopher* <address 12>→schisms.rev ...→*www* <address 14> schisms.rev.html

Trekker Review ✓ **INTERNET**→ *www* <address 20>schisms.html

Vidiot's Synopsis ✓ **INTERNET** →*www* <address 1b>sttng-6.html #231

True Q

Episode #132
Writer: René Echevarria
Director: Robert Scheerer
Stardate: 46192.3
Guest Star: Olivia d'Abo

Summary: A young woman begins to exhibit telekinetic powers and Q informs her that she is a member of the Q Continuum raised as human. His constant goading leads to a battle of wills, and discovery of her true abilities.

Archived Discussion of "True Q" GEnie members try to understand the rules governing the Q continuum and its immense power which leads to a discussion about why omnipotent beings resort to physical violence. ✓ **GENIE** →*keyword* <address 22>→445

Tim Lynch Synopsis & Review ✓ **INTERNET** ...→*anon-ftp* <address 6>→trueq.rev ...→*gopher* <address 12>→trueq.rev ...→*www* <address 14> trueq.rev.html

Trekker Review ✓ **INTERNET**→ *www* <address 20>true_q.html

Vidiot's Synopsis ✓ **INTERNET** →*www* <address 1b>sttng-6.html

#232

True Q Scenes Scenes from the episode, including a shot of Q and Crusher. ✓ **PVG** *dial* 513-233-7993 →<your username>→<your password>→F→*Download a file:* TRUE Q1.GIF *and* TRUEQ2.GIF *and* TRUEQ.GIF

Rascals

Episode #133
Teleplay: Allison Hock
Story: Ward Botsford,
             Diana Dru Botsford &
             Michael Piller
Director: Adam Nimoy
Stardate: 46235.7

Summary: Picard, Guinan, Keiko, and Ro get turned into children by an energy field. The ship travels to Ligos VII in response to a false distress signal, and falls into the clutches of the Ferengi who want to sell the *Enterprise-D* and use the crew as slave labor.

Archived Discussion of "Rascals" "Why don't they just broadcast this show on Saturday mornings?" Good fun or a sign of ST decay? Not everyone enjoyed the episode, but GEnie members did have fun discussing whether the child versions of the crew were what they expected. ✓ **GENIE**→*keyword* <address 22>→432

Tim Lynch Synopsis & Review ✓ **INTERNET** ...→*anon-ftp* <address 6>→rascals.rev ...→*gopher* <address 12>→rascals.rev ...→*www* <address 14> rascals.rev.html

Trekker Review ✓ **INTERNET**→ *www* <address 20>rascals.rev.htm

Vidiot's Synopsis ✓ **INTERNET** →*www* <address 1b>sttng-6.html #233

Back Forward Home Reload Images Open Print Find Stop

Location: http://www.ugcs.caltech.edu:80/~werdna/sttng/tlynch/fistful.rev.html

Guided Tour | What's New? | Questions | Net Search | Net Directory | Newsgroups

Last Update: November 14, 1994

A Fistful of Datas
synopsis and review by Timothy Lynch

Screenshot—http://www.ugcs.caltech.edu/~werdna/sttng/synopsis/fistful.rev.html

A Fistful of Datas

Episode #134
Teleplay: Robert Hewitt Wolfe &
             Brannon Braga
Story: Robert Hewitt Wolfe
Director: Patrick Stewart
Stardate: 46271.5

Summary: While Worf and Alexander are playing sheriff and deputy in a holodeck re-creation of the Old West, a malfunction traps them and Troi in a world where everyone, including the villain, is a Data-clone.

Archived Discussion of "A Fistful of Datas" Why do so many sci-fi series go back to the Old West? What kind of humor succeeds on Trek—this episode is ranked high, along with the "Trouble with Tribbles." And, would you use the holodeck if given the opportunity? ✓GENIE→*keyword* <address 22>→429

Tim Lynch Synopsis & Review ✓INTERNET ...→*anon-ftp* <address 6>→fistful.rev ...→*gopher* <address 12>→fistful.rev ...→*www* <address 14> fistful.rev.html

Trekker Review ✓INTERNET→ *www* <address 20>a_fistful_of_ datas.html

Vidiot's Synopsis ✓INTERNET →*www* <address 1b>sttng-6.html #234

Worf and Alexander A picture of Worf and Alexander in costumes from the old Wild West. ✓PVG *dial* 513-233-7993→<your username>→<your password>→F→ *Download a file:* WEST.GIF

Worf the Sherrif A picture of Worf playing a sherrif in a holodeck program. ✓PVG *dial* 513-233-7993→<your username>→<your password>→F→*Download a file:* WESTWORF.GIF

Quality of Life

Episode #135
Writer: Naren Shankar
Director: Jonathan Frakes
Stardate: 46307.2

Summary: Lt. Commander Data refuses to send mining robots from the planet Tyrus VIIA to undertake a dangerous mission because he believes they have become sentient beings.

Archived Discussion of "Quality of Life" What constitutes being alive? Engaging discussion of Data's developing "humanity." Opinions are divided on whether he would have/could have disobeyed orders. ✓GENIE→ *keyword* <address 22>→441

Tim Lynch Synopsis & Review ✓INTERNET ...→*anon-ftp* <address 6>→quality.rev ...→*gopher* <address 12>→quality.rev ...→*www* <address 14> quality.rev.html

Trekker Review ✓INTERNET→ *www* <address 20>the_quality_of_ life.html

Vidiot's Synopsis ✓INTERNET →*www* <address 1b>sttng-6.html #235

Chain of Command, Part I

Episode #136
Teleplay: Ronald D. Moore
Story: Frank Abatemarco
Director: Robert Scheerer
Stardate: 46357.4
Guest Star: Ronny Cox

Summary: Along with Dr. Crusher and Worf, Picard is assigned to infiltrate a biological weapons installation. He is replaced in command by no-nonsense Captain Jellico, who seems intent on provoking a war with the Cardassians.

Archived Discussion of "Chain of Command, Part I"

Is Jellico a better warship commander than Captain Picard? Does Picard lack the qualities necessary to be a warrior? How close does the crew's behavior come to mutiny? ✓ **GENIE**→*keyword* <address 22>→448

Image of a Starfleet Admiral

Vice-Admiral Nechayev on Enterprise to reassign Picard. ✓ **INTERNET** ...→*anon-ftp* <address 33>→sttng208.jpg ...→*anon-ftp* <address 34>→sttng208.jpg

Riker and Superior Officers

Image of Riker sitting with Starfleet Vice-Admiral Nechayev and Captain Jellico. ✓ **INTERNET** ...→*anon-ftp* <address 33>→sttng 209.jpg ...→*anon-ftp* <address 34>→sttng209.jpg

Tim Lynch Synopsis & Review

✓ **INTERNET** ...→*anon-ftp* <address 6>→chain1.rev ...→*gopher* <address 12>→chain1.rev ...→*www* <address 14> chain1.rev.html

Vidiot's Synopsis ✓ **INTERNET**

→*www* <address 1b>sttng-6.html #236

Jellico, Troi, and Riker

Picture of Riker, Troi, and Jellico. ✓ **PVG** *dial* 513-233-7993→<your username>→<your password>→F→ *Download a file:* JELLICO.GIF

Riker & Jellico

Picture of Riker arguing with Jellico. ✓ **PVG** *dial* 513-233-7993→<your username>→

Last Update: November 14, 1994

Chain of Command, Part II
synopsis and review by Timothy Lynch

Screenshot—http://www.ugcs.caltech.edu/~werdna/sttng/synopsis/chain2.rev.html

<your password>→F→*Download a file:* JELLICO2.GIF

Chain of Command, Part II

Episode #137

Writer:	Frank Abatemarco
Director:	Les Landau
Stardate:	46360.8
Guest Star:	Ronny Cox

Summary: The secret military installation turns out to be a Cardassian ruse. Picard is captured and tortured. Back on the *Enterprise-D*, Riker chafes under Jelli-co's command.

Archived Discussion of "Chain of Command, Part II"

Long debate over whether the Cardassains are evil by nature or by virtue of their long warring history. Includes an emotional discussion of real-world torture. ✓ **GENIE** →*keyword* <address 22>→449

Tim Lynch Synopsis & Review

✓ **INTERNET** ...→*anon-ftp* <address 6>→chain2.rev ...→*gopher* <address 12>→chain2.rev ...→*www* <address 14> chain2.rev.html

Vidiot's Synopsis ✓INTERNET
→*www* <address 1b>sttng-6.html #237

Ship in a Bottle

Episode #138
Writer: René Echevarria
Director: Alexander Singer
Stardate: 46424.1

Summary: After Barclay mistakenly calls him up on the holodeck, the troublesome Professor Moriarty (first created in "Elementary, Dear Data") demands release from the computer and a body.

Archived Discussion of "Ship in a Bottle" Extensive discussion about the holodeck creation of Moriarty and the real-world royalty problems encountered using Conan Doyle's characters. Trek tech is never too far removed from any serious TNG discussion: What is Heisenberg's Uncertainty Principle and how does it affect space, time, and "reality"? ✓GENIE →*keyword* <address 22>→450

Tim Lynch Synopsis & Review
✓INTERNET …→*anon-ftp* <address 6>→bottle.rev …→*gopher* <address 12>→bottle.rev …→*www* <address 14> bottle.rev.html

Trekker Review ✓INTERNET→ *www* <address 20>ship_in_a_bottle.html

Vidiot's Synopsis ✓INTERNET →*www* <address 1b>sttng-6.html #238

The Professor and the Countess Picture of Professor Moriarty and the Countess Regina Bartholomew. ✓PVG *dial* 513-233-7993→<your username>→<your password>→F→*Download a file:* PVTNG05.GIF

Aquiel

Episode #139
Teleplay: Brannon Braga &
            Ronald D. Moore
Story: Jeri Taylor
Director: Cliff Bole
Stardate: 46461.3

Summary: "Aquiel" is the name of a beautiful young lieutenant who is suspected of murdering two crew members on her relay station. Geordi has fallen for Aquiel (sight unseen) through reading her logs and correspondence on the station's system.

Archived Discussion of "Aquiel" "Soap Trek" some disdainfully label this episode. The general, not-too-terrific state of *Star Trek* romance is discussed—especially Geordi's lagging love life. For those interested, members also rated "Star Trek Babes." ✓GENIE→*keyword* <address 22>→505

Tim Lynch Synopsis & Review
✓INTERNET …→*anon-ftp* <address 6>→aquiel.rev …→*gopher* <address 12>→aquiel.rev …→*www* <address 14> aquiel.rev.html

Trekker Review ✓INTERNET→ *www* <address 20>aquiel.html

Vidiot's Synopsis ✓INTERNET →*www* <address 1b>sttng-6.html #239

Face of the Enemy

Episode #140
Teleplay: Naren Shankar
Story: René Echevarria
Director: Gabrielle Beaumont
Stardate: 46519.1

Summary: N'Vek, a Romulan dissident, kidnaps Troi and disguises her as a Romulan intelligence officer in order to aid the es-

STARNOTES

"I, actually, know exactly where Mommy LaForge is: She's having a complementary cocktail with the Bluegill at the Dyson Sphere where they found Scotty, which, after it was discovered, the Federation turned into a rest home for all the interesting Trek stories and characters that won't ever get the follow-up they deserve... I actually had hope for a moment that the missing mom story might be something more than a trite plot device for another of 'There are aliens in our warp core!' stories, (Jeez, these sub-space aliens are worse than termites. Somebody get a can of 'Raid'...) but then came that inexcusable moment at the end and I shuddered. Geordi says with a straight face, 'Boy, I sure am glad those alien dopplegangers used my mother's image, so that I could say good-bye, come to a sense of emotional closure, and no longer have to give a damn about what happened to her.'"

—from **Ted Brengle's Review of "Interface"**

cape of Romulan defectors. De-Seve, a former Federation member, arrives with a plan, devised by Spock, to help the Romulan defectors.

Archived Discussion of "Face of the Enemy" The development of Romulan society throughout the Trek canon is explored. Impassioned criticism and defense of Troi's acting and empathic abilities. ✓ **GENIE**→*keyword* <address 22>→446

Tim Lynch Synopsis & Review ✓ **INTERNET** ...→*anon-ftp* <address 6>→face.rev ...→*gopher* <address 12>→face.rev ...→*www* <address 14> face.rev.html

Trekker Review ✓ **INTERNET**→ *www* <address 20>face_of_the_enemy.html

Vidiot's Synopsis ✓ **INTERNET** →*www* <address 1b>sttng-6.html #240

Tapestry

Episode #141
Writer: Ronald D. Moore
Director: Les Landau
Stardate: n/a

Summary: After a power surge damages Picard's mechanical heart, Q, á la *It's A Wonderful Life*, guides the Captain back through his formative years. Would Picard make the same choices in life again?

Archived Discussion of "Tapestry" "Tapestry" evoked a lot of interesting questions: Is Picard's willingness to resort to violence essential to command? Is there any value to past regrets? And, how can one remain self-conscious during time travel? Once again Q's motivations were questioned. What exactly is his agenda?

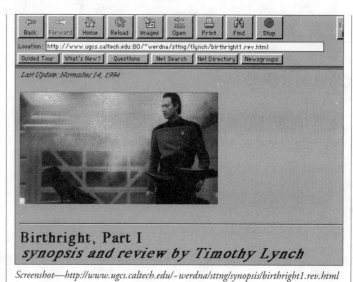

Birthright, Part I
synopsis and review by Timothy Lynch

Screenshot—http://www.ugcs.caltech.edu/~werdna/sttng/synopsis/birthright1.rev.html

✓ **GENIE**→*keyword* <address 22>→ 447

Tim Lynch Synopsis & Review ✓ **INTERNET** ...→*anon-ftp* <address 6>→tapestry.rev ...→*gopher* <address 12>→tapestry.rev ...→*www* <address 14> tapestry.rev.html

Vidiot's Synopsis ✓ **INTERNET** →*www* <address 1b>sttng-6.html #241

Birthright, Part I

Episode #142
Writer: Brannon Braga
Director: Winrich Kolbe
Stardate: 46578.4

Summary: While on DS9 rebuilding an aqueduct system, Worf discovers that his father may be alive—a Romulan P.O.W. Data has disturbing visions of Dr. Soong.

Archived Discussion of "Birthright, Part I" Are crossovers a wise decision? The link between stories—the search for a father—is explored. ✓ **GENIE**→*key-*

word <address 22>→492

Tim Lynch Synopsis & Review ✓ **INTERNET** ...→*anon-ftp* <address 6>→birthright1.rev ...→*gopher* <address 12>→birthright1.rev ...→*www* <address 14> birthright1.rev.html

Trekker Review ✓ **INTERNET**→ *www* <address 20>birthright_1.html

Vidiot's Synopsis ✓ **INTERNET** →*www* <address 1b>sttng-6.html #242

Birthright, Part II

Episode #143
Writer: René Echevarria
Director: Dan Curry
Stardate: 46759.2

Summary: Worf infiltrates the Klingon camp and to his horror discovers that they are living in peace with the Romulans. He attempts to rekindle the Klingon's warrior nature.

Archived Discussion of "Birthright, Part II" GEnie members explore the idea of Klingon dishonor in the context of the shame of Worf's father at being captured alive. Members also discuss Worf's inability to understand interracial marriage (obviously before his involvement with Deanna) and debate whether Worf was wrong to ruin the happy life of the villagers. ✓ **GENIE**→*keyword* <address 22>→504

Tim Lynch Synopsis & Review ✓ **INTERNET** ...→*anon-ftp* <address 6>→birthright2.rev ...→*gopher* <address 12>→birthright2.rev ...→*www* <address 14> birthright2.rev.html

Trekker Review ✓ **INTERNET**→*www* <address 20>birthright_2.html

Vidiot's Synopsis ✓ **INTERNET** →*www* <address 1b>sttng-6.html #243

Cmdr. Tokath Picture of the Romulan Commander Tokath. ✓ **PVG** *dial* 513-233-7993→<your username>→<your password>→F→ *Download a file:* PVTNG03.GIF

Starship Mine

Episode #144
Writer: Morgan Gendel
Director: Cliff Bole
Stardate: 46682.4

Summary: While the *Enterprise-D* is in dry dock, terrorists board seeking trilithium resin. They kidnap the remaining crew and commandeer the ship. Picard—now a stowaway on his own ship—must foil them.

Archived Discussion of "Starship Mine" "Be careful not to step in plot holes," warns one viewer. The nitpickers were out in force when discussing this episode: Why didn't the life form sensors

function? What happened to the injured crew member, or, for that matter, the second terrorist? ✓ **GENIE**→*keyword* address 22→495

Tim Lynch Synopsis & Review ✓ **INTERNET** ...→*anon-ftp* <address 6>→starship.rev ...→*gopher* <address 12>→starship.rev ...→*www* <address 14> starship.rev.html

Trekker Review ✓ **INTERNET**→ *www* <address 20>starship_mine.html

Vidiot's Synopsis ✓ **INTERNET** →*www* <address 1b>sttng-6.html #244

Lessons

Episode #145
Writers: Ronald Wilkerson & Jean Louise Matthais
Director: Robert Weimer
Stardate: 46693.1

Summary: Captain Picard hits it off with Commander Daren, the new head of Stellar Sciences. He is thrown into a quandary when he must assign her to a deadly mission.

Archived Discussion of "Lessons" How will the infatuation between Picard and the new science officer affect Beverly and Picard's relationship? And, was it indeed infatuation or was it love?

The debate over Data's sexual preference rages on. ✓ **GENIE**→*keyword* <address 22>→493

Tim Lynch Synopsis & Review ✓ **INTERNET** ...→*anon-ftp* <address 6>→lessons.rev ...→*gopher* <address 12>→lessons.rev ...→*www* <address 14> lessons.rev.html

Trekker Review ✓ **INTERNET**→ *www* <address 20>lessons.html

Vidiot's Synopsis ✓ **INTERNET** →*www* <address 1b>sttng-6.html #245

The Chase

Episode #146
Teleplay: Joe Menosky
Story: Ronald D. Moore & Joe Menosky
Director: Jonathan Frakes
Stardate: 46731.5

Summary: Picard's old archeology professor seeks his help in solving a 4-billion-year-old genetic mystery. Romulans, Klingons and Cardassians all race to find the answer. (Ahh, so that's why the universe has so many humanoid aliens.)

Archived Discussion of "The Chase" How does the explanation about the origin of so many humanoid aliens jibe with TOS's "preservers" theory? Includes a

a) **What is the name of the empathatic metamorph who bonds with Picard?**

b) **What is the name of Picard's love interest that shares his interest in music?**

(See answers on page 359)

long discussion of the place of evolution theories in Trek. ✓ **GENIE** →*keyword* <address 22>→494

Tim Lynch Synopsis & Review
✓ **INTERNET** ...→*anon-ftp* <address 6>→chase.rev ...→*gopher* <address 12>→chase.rev ...→ *www* <address 14>chase.rev.html

Trekker Review ✓ **INTERNET**→ *www* <address 20>the_chase.html

Vidiot's Synopsis ✓ **INTERNET** →*www* <address 1b>sttng-6.html #246

Frame of Mind

Episode #147
Writer: Brannon Braga
Director: James L. Conway
Stardate: 46778.1

Summary: In the midst of Dr. Crusher's production of a play about an insane man, Riker is captured and imprisoned in the Tilonus Institute for Mental Disorders.

Archived Discussion of "Frame of Mind" Imagine not being able to distinguish between reality and illusion. This chilling episode, reminiscent of "Twilight Zone," provoked a lot of discussion about the horror of such a circumstance. Members generally praised Jonathan Frakes' performance and a Paramount employee participated in the discussion, providing insider information about the filming. ✓ **GENIE**→*keyword* <address 22>→496

Tim Lynch Synopsis & Review
✓ **INTERNET** ...→*anon-ftp* <address 6>→frame.rev ...→*gopher* <address 12>→frame.rev ...→*www* <address 14> frame.rev.html

Trekker Review ✓ **INTERNET**→

www <address 20>frame_of_mind. html

Vidiot's Synopsis ✓ **INTERNET** →*www* <address 1b>sttng-6.html #247

Suspicions

Episode #148
Writer: Joe Menosky &
             Naren Shankar
Director: Cliff Bole
Stardate: 46830.1

Summary: Dr. Crusher supports a Ferengi scientist's controversial experimental device, but during the trial run the scientist is killed. Crusher faces a court-martial and the ruin of her career when she refuses to abandon the project.

Archived Discussion of "Suspicions" "Star Trek, She Wrote." Would any court of law in this galaxy believe Crusher's tale without hard evidence? ✓ **GENIE**→*keyword* <address 22>→497

Ted Brengle's IMHO Review
✓ **TFDN**→<address 23>→suspic.zip

Tim Lynch Synopsis & Review
✓ **INTERNET** ...→*anon-ftp* <address 6>→suspicions.rev ...→*gopher* <address 12>→suspicions.rev ...→*www* <address 14> suspicions.rev.html

Trekker Review ✓ **INTERNET**→ *www* <address 20>suspicions.html

Vidiot's Synopsis ✓ **INTERNET** →*www* <address 1b>sttng-6.html #248

Rightful Heir

Episode #149
Teleplay: Ronald D. Moore
Story: James E. Brooks
Director: Winrich Kolbe
Stardate: 46852.2

Summary: In a crisis of faith, Worf journeys to a planet where Klingons await the return of their spiritual leader, Kahless the Unforgettable. Kahless arrives, engendering fanatical devotion and deep mistrust.

Archived Discussion of "Rightful Heir" One of GEnie's own (an active member of the Science Fiction RoundTable) wrote the script for this episode. Discussion considers Kahless's role in the Klingon religion and in The Original Series. Members debate whether Kahless the Clone can

STARNOTES

"My father died when I was seven, in 1973. Shortly afterward, I adopted the Vulcan Mr. Spock as my role model and tried to suppress all my emotions. For two or three years, I was pretty successful at it, too—until I eventually decided that I wanted to be a normal kid.

"I never even knew why I had imitated the Vulcan, Spock, until many years later, when I saw 'The Wrath of Khan.' I was totally taken by surprise at Spock's death, and once I accepted it, I finally realized what I had done when I was a child."

—from **GEnie's Archived Discussion of the episode "Hero Worship"**

still be Kahless in spirit? ✓ **GE-NIE**→*keyword* <address 22>→498

Ted Brengle's IMHO Review
✓ **TFDN**→<address 23>→ rightful.zip

Tim Lynch Synopsis & Review
✓ **INTERNET** ...→*anon-ftp* <address 6>→rightful.rev ...→*gopher* <address 12>→rightful.rev ...→*www* <address 14> rightful.rev.html

Vidiot's Synopsis ✓ **INTERNET**
→*www* <address 1b>sttng-6.html #249

Second Chances

Episode #150
Teleplay: René Echevarria
Story: Mike Medlock
Director: LeVar Burton
Stardate: 46915.2

Summary: Unbeknown to Riker, eight years ago a transporter accident created a twin who now serves on the Starship *Potemkin* as Lt. Thomas Riker. The two meet when the *Enterprise-D* comes to Nervala IV. The duplicate Riker is still in love with Troi.

Archived Discussion of "Second Chances" Will they ever stop relying on "dopplegangers and doublemints" to drive a plot? Will Troi's unique opportunity to see the man she loved, and the man he has become, rekindle their romance? ✓ **GENIE**→*keyword* <address 22>→499

Tim Lynch Synopsis & Review
✓ **INTERNET** ...→*anon-ftp* <address 6>→second.rev ...→*gopher* <address 12>→second.rev ...→*www* <address 14> second.rev.html

Vidiot's Synopsis ✓ **INTERNET**
→*www* <address 1b>sttng-6.html #250

Timescape

Episode #151
Writer: Brannon Braga
Director: Adam Nimoy
Stardate: 46944.2

Summary: Picard, Geordi, Troi and Data return to the *Enterprise-D* to find it frozen in time along with a Romulan warship, minutes away from destruction.

Archived Discussion of "Timescape" Is the explanation of the time pockets existing in the frozen zone adequate or "cheesy"? Does this forebode a change in relations between the Federation and the Romulan Empire? ✓ **GENIE** →*keyword* <address 22>→500

Ted Brengle's IMHO Review
✓ **TFDN**→<address 23>→timscp.zip

Tim Lynch Synopsis & Review
✓ **INTERNET** ...→*anon-ftp* <address 6>→timescape.rev ...→*gopher* <address 12>→timescape.rev ...→*www* <address 14> timescape.rev.html

Vidiot's Synopsis ✓ **INTERNET**
→*www* <address 1b>sttng-6.html #251

Descent, Part I

Episode #152
Teleplay: Ronald D. Moore
Story: Jeri Taylor
Director: Alexander Singer
Stardate: 46982.1
Guest Star: Stephen Hawkings

Summary: A group of self-aware Borg endanger the *Enterprise-D*. Under the leadership of Data's evil brother, Lore, the Borg are engaged in a nefarious plan to turn Data against the Federation. Trekfan Stephen Hawkings makes a guest appearance in a poker game on the holodeck.

Archived Discussion of "Descent, Part I" Are the Borg even more terrifying with individual consciousness? What does Data's development of rage signify? ✓ **GE-NIE**→*keyword* <address 22>→501

Ted Brengle's IMHO Review
✓ **TFDN**→<address 23>→descent.zip

Tim Lynch Synopsis & Review
✓ **INTERNET** ...→*anon-ftp* <address 6>→descent.rev ...→*gopher* <address 12>→descent.rev ...→*www* <address 14> descent.rev.html

Vidiot's Synopsis ✓ **INTERNET**
→*www* <address 1b>sttng-6.html #252

A gathering of Borgs The Borg gather under Lore's command. ✓ **PVG** *dial* 513-233-7993 →<your username>→<your password>→F→*Download a file:* descent5.gif

Descent Scene Scene of Picard, Geordi, and Troi with phasers drawn. ✓ **PVG** *dial* 513-233-7993→ <your username>→<your password>→F→*Download a file:* DESCENT3.GIF

Season 7

Descent, Part II

Episode #153
Writer: René Echevarria
Director: Andrew Singer
Stardate: 47025.4

Summary: Dr. Crusher is left in command of the *Enterprise* as Riker and Worf attempt to free Troi, Picard, Geordi and Data from the Borg. Lore tries to convince Data to help him create a superhuman race to take over the galaxy. Hugh, the Borg who was given an individual identity during a stay on the Enterprise, comes to the crew's aid.

Archived Discussion of "Descent, Part II"

Do Data and Lore have the same rights as a human? Should Lore be punished by being dismantled or should he be imprisoned? What next for the Borg? ✓ **GENIE**→*keyword* <address 22>→1143

Ted Brengle's IMHO Review

✓ **TFDN**→<address 23>→descent2.zip

Tim Lynch Synopsis & Review

✓ **INTERNET** ...→*anon-ftp* <address 7>→descent2.rev ...→*gopher* <address 13>→descent2.rev ...→*www* <address 14> descent2.rev.html

Liaisons

Episode #154
Teleplay: Jeanne Carrigan Fauci & Lisa Rich
Story: Roger Eschbacher, Jaq Greenspon
Director: Cliff Bole

Summary: Crew members are chosen to chaperone Iyaarans to a meeting with the Federation. Worf, Picard, and Troi are all unknowingly tested as the Iyhaarans attempt to learn about love, anger, and pleasure.

Archived Discussion of "Liasons"

Is this the Trek version of Stephen King's Misery? Was the plot twist effective, or does Picard merely suffer from the Lois Lane (Gosh, I didn't realize!) syndrome? Is there anything admirable about experiencing extreme emotions? ✓ **GENIE**→*keyword* <address 22>→1144

Ted Brengle's IMHO Review

✓ **TFDN**→<address 23>→liasons.zip

Tim Lynch Synopsis & Review

✓ **INTERNET** ...→*anon-ftp* <address 7>→liaisons.rev ...→*gopher* <address 13>→liaisons.rev ...→*www* <address 14>liaisons.rev.html

Interface

Episode #155
Writer: Joe Menosky
Director: Robert Weimer
Stardate: 47215.5
Guest Star: Ben Vereen

Summary: The crew attempts to retrieve bodies from a research ship using an experimental "neural interface" that links the human nervous system with a probe. While using the probe Geordi has a vision of his mother, recently reported MIA.

Archived Discussion of "Interface"

What constitutes virtual reality and is this what the episode explores? ✓ **GENIE**→*keyword* <address 22>→1145

Ted Brengle's IMHO Review

✓ **TFDN**→<address 23>→interfac.zip

Tim Lynch Synopsis & Review

✓ **INTERNET** ...→*anon-ftp* <address 7>→interface.rev ...→*gopher* <address 13>→interface.rev ...→*www* <address 14> interface.rev.html

Gambit, Part I

Episode #156
Teleplay: Naren Shankar
Story: Christopher Hatton, Naren Shankar
Director: Peter Lauritson
Stardate: 47135.2

Summary: Captain Picard is missing and presumed dead. Riker, kidnapped by mercenaries looting archeological digs, discovers that Picard is an active, though unwilling, member of the group. Commander Data takes charge of the *Enterprise*.

Archived Discussion of "Gambit, Part I"

Do crew members' personalities change when their professional roles

Video capture from "Gambit"—downloaded from Perfect Vision Graphics BBS

change? And, why hasn't archeology changed at all by the 24th Century?— i.e., still loads of broken pots. ✓**GENIE**→*keyword* <address 22>→1146

Ted Brengle's IMHO Review
✓**TFDN**→<address 23>→gambit1.zip

Tim Lynch Synopsis & Review
✓**INTERNET** ...→*anon-ftp* <address 7>→gambit1.rev ...→*gopher* <address 13>→gambit1.rev ...→*www* <address 14> gambit1.rev.html

Gambit, Part II

Episode #157
Teleplay: Ronald D. Moore
Story: Naren Shankar
Director: Alexander Singer
Stardate: 47160.1

Summary: Picard and Riker try to escape the mercenaries, but first they make sure the ancient mind weapon stolen from the archeological site will not reach outlaw Vulcans.

Archived Discussion of "Gambit, Part II" Could Data ever be captain without the capacity to understand emotions? ✓**GENIE**→*keyword* <address 22>→1147

Ted Brengle's IMHO Review
✓**TFDN**→<address 23>→ gambit2.zip

Tim Lynch Synopsis & Review
✓**INTERNET** ...→*anon-ftp* <address 7>→gambit2.rev ...→*gopher* <address 13>→gambit2.rev ...→*www* <address 14> gambit2.rev.html

Phantasms

Episode #158
Writer: Brannon Braga
Director: Patrick Stewart
Stardate: 47225.7

Summary: Data's disturbing dreams lead the crew to deadly creatures infesting the Enterprise. But his nightmares are so real they lead him to attack Troi; for help, he turns to Sigmund Freud.

Archived Discussion of "Phantasms" Can Data have a subconscious mind? How much "hidden programming" could Dr. Soong have included in Data? ✓**GENIE**→*keyword* <address 22>→1148

Ted Brengle's IMHO Review
✓**TFDN**→<address 23>→phan.zip

Tim Lynch Synopsis & Review
✓**INTERNET** ...→*anon-ftp* <address 7>→phantasms.rev ...→*gopher* <address 13>→phantasms.rev ...→*www* <address 14>phantasms.rev.html

Dark Page

Episode #159
Writer: Hilary J. Bader
Director: Les Landau
Stardate: 47254.1

Summary: While serving as a language tutor for a telepathic race, Lwaxana remembers a horrifying incident that she has hidden from Deanna for 30 years. She suffers a breakdown and Troi enters her mother's mind to find the cause.

Archived Discussion of "Dark Page" Is the story merely a melodrama or a touching portrayal of grief and pain? Discussion of the universality of mother/daughter conflict. ✓**GENIE**→*keyword* <address 22>→1149

Ted Brengle's IMHO Review
✓**TFDN**→<address 23>→ dark.zip

Tim Lynch Synopsis & Review

✓**INTERNET** ...→*anon-ftp* <address 7>→darkpage.rev ...→*gopher* <address 13>→darkpage.rev ...→*www* <address 14> darkpage.rev.html

Attached

Episode #160
Writer: Nicholas Sagan
Director: Jonathan Frakes
Stardate: 47304.2

Summary: Dr. Crusher and Picard travel to KesPrit, a planet seeking Federation membership and discover the planet has two factions, the Kes, who want membership and the Prit, who abhor outsiders. The Prit kidnap the pair and create a telepathic link between the two with brain implants.

Archived Discussion of "Attached" Is there a future for the Beverly/Jean-Luc romance? Is the "let's be friends" campfire scene another cop-out—Trekkus Interruptus? ✓**GENIE**→*keyword* <address 22>→1150

Ted Brengle's IMHO Review
✓**TFDN**→<address 23>→attached.zip

Tim Lynch Synopsis & Review
✓**INTERNET** ...→*anon-ftp* <address 7>→attached.rev ...→*gopher* <address 13>→attached.rev ...→*www* <address 14> attached.rev.html

Force of Nature

Episode #161
Writer: Naren Shankar
Director: Robert Lederman
Stardate: 47310.2

Summary: While the *Enterprise* searches for a medical ship in the unstable Hekarran Corridor, scientists from a nearby planet complain that warp drives are destroying their planet's environment and the space-time continuum.

Archived Discussion of "Force of Nature"

Mankind (and others) are still struggling in the 24th century to reconcile progress with the environment. Transportation continues to be a particularly vexing problem. The focus of discussion for this episode was an analogy between cars in Los Angeles and the warp drives in the Hekarran Corridor. √GENIE→*keyword* <address 22>→1151

Ted Brengle's IMHO Review
√TFDN→<address 23>→ force.zip

Tim Lynch Synopsis & Review
√INTERNET ...→*anon-ftp* <address 7>→force.rev ...→*gopher* <address 13>→force.rev ...→*www* <address 14> force.rev.html

Inheritance

Episode #162
Teleplay: Dan Koeppel,
             René Echevarria
Story: Dan Koeppel
Director: Robert Scheerer
Stardate: 47410.2

Summary: Data discovers that Dr. Soong's wife, his "mother," is an android that Soong built to replace his wife when she was killed by the Crystalline Entity.

Archived Discussion of "Inheritance"
What is the relation of android to creator—parent, spouse, owner? √GENIE→*keyword* <address 22>→1152

Ted Brengle's IMHO Review
√TFDN→<address 23>→inher.zip

Tim Lynch Synopsis & Review
√INTERNET ...→*anon-ftp* <address 7>→inheritance.rev ...→*gopher* <address 13>→inheritance.rev ...→

www <address 14> inheritance. rev.html

Parallels

Episode #163
Writer: Brannon Braga
Director: Robert Wiemer
Stardate: 47391.2

Summary: After Worf gets back from a Klingon competition, a rift in the space-time continuum bounces Worf between alternate universes, including one in which he is married to Troi.

Ted Brengle's IMHO Review
√TFDN→<address 23>→ para.zip

Tim Lynch Synopsis & Review
√INTERNET ...→*anon-ftp* <address 7>→parallels.rev ...→*gopher* <address 13>→parallels.rev ...→*www* <address 14> parallels.rev.html

The Pegasus

Episode #164
Writer: Ronald D. Moore
Director: LeVar Burton
Stardate: 47457.1

Summary: Admiral Pressman, Riker's first commander, boards the *Enterprise-D* with the hopes of salvaging a secret cloaking device that was aboard The Pegasus when its crew mutinied.

Archived Discussion of "The Pegasus"
Why would the Federation make such a bad decision as signing an anti-cloaking device treaty with their enemies? Do the Trek writers and designers really not know what an asteroid looks like? √GENIE→*keyword* <address 22>→1282

Ted Brengle's IMHO Review
√TFDN→<address 23>→pegasus. zip

Tim Lynch Synopsis & Review
√INTERNET ...→*anon-ftp* <address 7>→pegasus.rev ...→*gopher* <address 13>→pegasus.rev ...→*www* <address 14> pegasus.rev.html

Homeward

Episode #165
Teleplay: Naren Shankar
Story: Spike Steingasser
Director: Alexander Singer
Stardate: 47423.9
Guest Star: Paul Sorvino

Summary: Worf's foster brother, Nicolai Rozhenko, has been studying a non-technological society on Baraal II. When their planet begins to die, Nicholai violates the Prime Directive by transporting inhabitants to a holodeck simulation until he can find them a new planet.

Archived Discussion of "Homeward"
When does the Prime Directive seem meaningless, even cruel? √GENIE→*keyword* <address 22>→1155

Ted Brengle's IMHO Review
√TFDN→<address 23>→homeward. zip

Tim Lynch Synopsis & Review
√INTERNET ...→*anon-ftp* <address 7>→homeward.rev ...→*gopher* <address 13>→homeward.rev ...→*www* <address 14>homeward. rev.html

Sub Rosa

Episode #166
Teleplay: Brannon Braga
Story: Jeri Taylor
Director: Jonathan Frakes

Summary: At her grandmother's funeral, Dr. Crusher is seduced by a mysterious and dangerous entity.

Last Update: January 15, 1995

Thine Own Self
synopsis and review by Timothy Lynch

Screenshot—http://www.ugcs.caltech.edu/~werdna/sttng/synopsis/thineown.rev.html

Archived Discussion of "Sub Rosa" Do women like this "gothic" episode more than men? Should Trek keep trying genres other than sci-fi? Has anyone dated Beverly and lived? ✓ **GENIE**→*keyword* <address 22>→1156

Ted Brengle's IMHO Review ✓**TFDN**→<address 23>→sub.zip

Tim Lynch Synopsis & Review ✓ **INTERNET** ...→*anon-ftp* <address 7>→subrosa.rev ...→*gopher* <address 13>→subrosa.rev ...→*www* <address 14> subrosa.rev.html

Lower Decks

Episode #167
Teleplay: René Echevarria
Story: Ronald Wilkerson, Jean Louise Matthais
Director: Gabrielle Beaumont
Stardate: 47566.7

Summary: Picard asks a young Bajoran junior officer to volunteer for a dangerous mission, which ultimately costs the promising youth her life.

Archived Discussion of "Lower Decks" Analysis of life at the bottom of the *Enterprise* crew roster. Discussion considers Vulcan emotions and gender roles. ✓ **GENIE** →*keyword* <address 22>→1157

Ted Brengle's IMHO Review ✓**TFDN**→<address 23>→lower.zip

Tim Lynch Synopsis & Review ✓ **INTERNET** ...→*anon-ftp* <address 7>→lowerdecks.rev ...→*gopher* <address 13>→lowerdecks.rev...→ *www* <address 14> lowerdecks. rev.html

Thine Own Self

Episode #168
Teleplay: Ronald D. Moore
Story: Christopher Hatton
Director: Winrich Kolbe
Stardate: 47611.2

Summary: Data suffers from amnesia when sent to retrieve a radioactive probe from a primitive planet, and struggles to defend himself against the image of a Typhoid Mary when the natives get radiation sickness. Troi decides to take tests for command.

Archived Discussion of "Thine Own Self" Are strangers considered "well poisoners" in all cultures? ✓ **GENIE**→*keyword* <address 22>→1158

Ted Brengle's IMHO Review ✓**TFDN**→<address 23>→ thine.zip

Tim Lynch Synopsis & Review ✓ **INTERNET** ...→*anon-ftp* <address 7>→thineown.rev ...→*gopher* <address 13>→thineown.rev ...→*www* <address 14> thineown.rev.html

Masks

Episode #169
Writer: Joe Menosky
Director: Robert Wiemer
Stardate: 47618.4

Summary: The *Enterprise-D* comes across an abandoned vessel built by a civilization dating back 87 million years and Data is overwhelmed by the mythology and personalities of the lost culture. The power of his mind begins to transform the ship into their temple.

Archived Discussion of "Masks" Discussion of the difficulty of evaluating a society from archeological remains. Analysis of the special effects. ✓ **GENIE**→*keyword* <address 22>→1159

Ted Brengle's IMHO Review ✓**TFDN**→<address 23>→ masks.zip

Tim Lynch Synopsis & Review ✓ **INTERNET** ...→*anon-ftp* <address 7>→masks.rev ...→*gopher* <address 13>→masks.rev ...→*www* <address 14> masks.rev.html

Eye of the Beholder

Episode #170
Teleplay: René Echevarria
Story: Brannon Braga
Director: Cliff Bole
Stardate: 47622.1

Summary: A crew member's suicide sends Troi and Worf on an investigation. They discover that a murder may have taken place during the construction of the *Enterprise-D*—and the two crew members also discover a mutual attraction.

Archived Discussion of "Eye of the Beholder" Is a position on the *Enterprise* a death sentence for relationships? What are the possibilities of a relationship between a Klingon warrior and an empath? ✓**GENIE**→ *keyword* <address 22>→1160

Tim Lynch Synopsis & Review
✓**INTERNET** ...→*anon-ftp* <address 7> →beholder.rev ...→*gopher* <address 13>→beholder.rev ...→*www* <address 14> beholder.rev.html

Genesis

Episode #171
Teleplay: Brannon Braga
Director: Gates McFadden
Stardate: 47653.2

Summary: "The operation was a success, but...." Dr. Crusher gives Lt. Barclay an injection with very negative side effects. Picard and Data return from seeking an errant photon torpedo to find the crew devolving into primitive species.

Archived Discussion of "Genesis" Well, on the upside, it could be considered a camp classic—shades of "Land of the Lost" and "Spock's Brain." As serious as

STARQUOTES

"You're wondering who we are...why we have done this ... how it has come that I stand before you, the image of a being from so long ago...Our civilization thrived for ages—but what is the life of one race, compared to the vast stretches of cosmic time? We knew that one day we would be gone, and nothing of us would survive—so we left you...Our scientists seeded the primordial oceans of many worlds, where life was in its infancy. The seed codes directed your evolution toward a physical form resembling ours: this body you see before you, which is of course shaped as yours is shaped, for you are the end result. It was our hope that you would have to come together in fellowship and companionship to hear this message—and if you can see and hear me, our hope has been fulfilled. You are a monument, not to our greatness, but to our existence."   —"The Chase"

Net Source: Timothy Lynch's review of The Chase—http://www.cosy.sbg.ac.at/ftp/pub/trek/ guide/tng/episode.145.txt

GEnie members could get about this discussion was to question whether Dr. Crusher could be sued for malpractice? ✓**GENIE**→*keyword* <address 22>→1161

Ted Brengle's IMHO Review
✓**TFDN**→<address 23>→genesis. zip

Tim Lynch Synopsis & Review
✓**INTERNET** ...→*anon-ftp* <address 7>→genesis.rev ...→*gopher* <address 13>→genesis.rev ...→*www* <address 14> genesis.rev.html

Journey's End

Episode #172
Writer: Ronald D. Moore
Director: Corey Allen
Stardate: 47751.2

Summary: When Wesley returns from Starfleet moody and uncertain, the Traveler arrives to help him plan his future. A new treaty leaves a Native American community inside Cardassian space, and

Wesley joins their struggle to remain in their homeland.

Archived Discussion of "Journey's End" Did Wesley betray the crew and Picard? Is the Native American storyline a valid analogy to American history or another example of political correctness? ✓**GENIE**→*keyword* <address 22>→1162

Ted Brengle's IMHO Review
✓**TFDN**→<address 23>→journey.zip

Tim Lynch Synopsis & Review
✓**INTERNET** ...→*anon-ftp* <address 7>→journey.rev ...→*gopher* <address 13>→journey.rev ...→*www* <address 14> journey.rev.html

First Born

Episode #173
Teleplay: René Echevarria
Story: Mark Kalbfeld
Director: Jonathan West
Stardate: 47779.4

Star Trek: The Next Generation Episode Guide

Summary: To Worf's dismay, Alexander expresses uncertainty about becoming a warrior. When Worf takes him to a festival to learn about Klingon culture they encounter a mysterious stranger who tries to convince Alexander to embrace his heritage.

Tim Lynch Synopsis & Review
✓INTERNET ...→*anon-ftp* <address 7>→firstborn.rev ...→*gopher* <address 13>→firstborn.rev ...→*www* <address 14> firstborn.rev.html

Archived Discussion of "First Born" Extensive analysis of Klingon culture and the importance of Klingon rituals. ✓GENIE→*keyword* <address 22>→1163

Ted Brengle's IMHO Review
✓TFDN→<address 23>→first.zip

Bloodlines

Episode #174
Writer: Nicholas Sagan
Director: Les Landau
Stardate: 47829.1

Summary: Picard's longtime Ferengi enemy, Daimon Bok, returns to exact retribution: In repayment for Picard's killing Bok's son at the Battle of Maxia, Bok will kill Jason, a son Picard never knew existed.

Archived Discussion of "Bloodlines" A U.S. navy battleship wouldn't go running off to find the commander's unknown son in the middle of a mission, so why does a Galaxy class starship? And why don't starship commanders ever have daughters they never knew? ✓GENIE→*keyword* <address 22>→1164

Ted Brengle's IMHO Review
✓TFDN→<address 23>→b-lines.zip

Tim Lynch Synopsis & Review
✓INTERNET ...→*anon-ftp* <address 7>→bloodlines.rev ...→*gopher* <address 13>→bloodlines.rev ...→*www* <address 14> bloodlines.rev.html

Emergence

Episode #175
Teleplay: Joe Menosky
Story: Brannon Braga
Director: Cliff Bole
Stardate: 47869.2

Summary: A magniscope storm causes the holodeck computer to gain artificial intelligence.

Archived Discussion of "Emergence" "I enjoyed watching it like I enjoy watching a train wreck," complained one GEnie member. The entire discussion of this episode was dominated by disgruntled viewers sick of holodeck/ship malfunction storylines. ✓GENIE→*keyword* <address 22>→165

Ted Brengle's IMHO Review
✓TFDN→<address 23>→emergenc.zip

Tim Lynch Synopsis & Review
✓INTERNET ...→*anon-ftp* <address 7>→emergence.rev ...→*gopher* <address 13>→emergence.rev ...→*www* <address 14>emergence.rev.html

Preemptive Strike

Episode #176
Teleplay: René Echevarria
Story: Naren Shankar
Director: Patrick Stewart
Stardate: 47941.7

Summary: Lt. Ro Laren returns to the Enterprise to undertake a secret mission. She must infiltrate the Maquis and end their attempts

═══ *STARNOTES* ═══

"To take two hours and step back, seeing all the patterns that have shifted down over the past seven years, appreciating how much water has gone under the bridge, even as the future beckons. In that way, the failure of the plot is wholly fitting, even as the episode's eventual triumph over that fact is even more so. This is an episode that wades into the center of TNG, into both its strengths and its weaknesses, leaving you reminiscing about the characters and the grand thrusts of their adventures. In other words, just what a last episode should so. To the Big Board. One last time. The Grade: A (A final celebration of Q, the promise of humanity, Fun With Time, the Enterprise blowing up, and Technobabble. In essence, everything that made Star Trek: The Next Generation great. Probably this episode only deserves and A- or a B+, but what the hell... They made me miss them, and that deserves something.)"

—**Ted Brengle's Review of "All Good Things"**

to provoke the Cardassians into war.

Archived Discussion of "Preemptive Strike" Should Ro Laren stay true to her heritage or to the Federation? How dangerous is the DMZ? And, how will the Maquis figure in the *Voyager* series? ✓**GENIE**→*keyword* <address 22>→1166

Ted Brengle's IMHO Review ✓**TFDN**→<address 23>→p-strike.zip

Tim Lynch Synopsis & Review ✓**INTERNET** …→*anon-ftp* <address 7>→preemptive.rev …→*gopher* <address 13>→preemptive.rev …→ *www* <address 14>preemptive. rev.html

All Good Things...

Episode #177
Writers: Ronald D. Moore &
            Brannon Braga
Director: Winrich Kolbe
Stardate: 47988.1

Summary: "All good things must come to an end"—especially in the final episode of the series. Things also come full-circle from the first episode as Q passes judgement on humanity. Picard travels between three time periods—his first meeting with Q, his first time aboard the *Enterprise*, and a future in which he suffers from a debilitating brain disease—to solve a paradox: Can actions in the future destroy the past?

All Good Things "All good things must come to an end" sound clip from the last episode TNG. ✓**COMPUSERVE**→*go* sfmedia→ Libraries→*Search by file name:* TOEND.WAV

Archived Discussion of "All Good Things" What did *you*

> "All good things must come to an end."—Q to Picard, "All Good Things..."

Net Source: STTNG Quotes—http://www.ugcs. caltech.edu/htbin/werdna/fortune?sttng

want to happen? Is it paradoxical that the timelines didn't affect each other? What does the future, or the past, hold for the *Enterprise-D*: warp 13? Did the open-ended nature of the episode leave you unfulfilled? ✓**GENIE**→*keyword* <address 22>→1167

Ted Brengle's IMHO Review ✓**TFDN**→<address 23>→ agt.zip

Tim Lynch Synopsis & Review ✓**INTERNET** …→*anon-ftp* <address 7>→allgood.rev …→*gopher* <address 13>→allgood.rev …→*www* <address 14> allgood.rev.html

Last Episode Pictures Images from the final episode of TNG. ✓**COMPUSERVE**→*go* sfmedia→Libraries→*Search by file name:* TNG-LA.ZIP

All Good Things Soundclip Collection Dozens of soundclips from the last TNG episode, "All Good Things," including Q's final

comments in the courtroom, Data's analysis of Q and Picard's relationship, and the *Enterprise* exploding. ✓**INTERNET**→*gopher* tiger.acs.appstate.edu→Tiger's Sound Archive→Star Trek Wav Files (mostly TNG)→tngagt*

All Good Things Waves Several soundclips from the last episode of TNG. ✓**COMPUSERVE**→*go* sfmedia→Libraries→*Search by file name:* ALLGOO.ZIP

Goodbye Soundclip of Q to Picard: "Goodbye Jean-Luc, I'm gonna miss you..." ✓**INTERNET**→*gopher* tiger.acs.appstate.edu→Tiger's Sound Archive→Star Trek Wav Files (mostly TNG)

Picard: "Dammit, I'm not Stupid!" Soundclip of Captain Picard speaking to Doctor Crusher in the final episode. WAV file. ✓**COMPUSERVE**→*go* sfmedia→Libraries→*Search by file name:* STU-PID.WAV

The voyage continues

Born in the computer age, *Star Trek: The Next Generation* **has been a presence in the**

online world from its earliest years, and as a result the Net is a veritable cornucopia of TNG materials. But for all the diversity, there's really only one place to start, and that's **Andrew Tong's ST:TNG Page**, the monumental set of TNG Web pages located at Cal Tech. Tong has information on Emmy nominations, Nielsen ratings, production credits, and Trek technology, and that's only the beginning. If comprehensive sites aren't your cup of tea, and you'd rather spend time talking things out, visit AOL's **The Next Generation**, which contains a set of message folders dealing with all aspects of the series. And finally, get the skinny through official channels with the **Interview with Executive Producers**.

On the Net

Across the board

Andrew Tong's ST:TNG Page
When you're talking TNG, you're talking Tong. And when you're talking Tong, you're talking Web pages galore. Fans of TNG are advised not to miss this page, which serves as a sort of world hub for the series. Currently maintained at

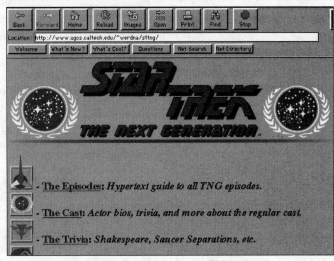

Andrew Tong's ST:TNG Page—http://www.ugcs.caltech.edu/~werdna/sttng

Cal Tech, where Tong is an undergraduate, these pages contain an incredible wealth of TNG material. Primary among the resources here is a detailed hypertext episode guide, chock-full of additional information like credits, Emmy nominations, snafus, Nielsen ratings, viewer comments, and Timothy Lynch's episode summaries and reviews.

The Cast takes you to actor biographies and filmographies; Trivia moves from Shakespeare references to mention of saucer separations; The Crew Behind the Crew is an informative interview with the show's creative team, Rick Berman, Michael Piller, and Jeri Taylor. Timeline Past, Present, and Future helps you grapple with loops, shifts, and temporal displacements; Science and *Star Trek* attempts to make sense of transporter technology; and the Random quote server spews up mem-

ories and pearls of wisdom.

But wait, there's more! Tong's super-duper search engine lets you search the TNG universe. For example, a search for "Spot" returned 37 citations, including Spot specific sites, episodes, the "Ode" and chronologies. ("sex" retrieved five entries, while "sex and Spot" turned up nothing) All this plus links to FAQs, the rec.arts. startrek archive, and the Star Trek List of Lists. ✓**INTERNET**→*www* http://www. ugcs.caltech.edu:80/ ~werdna/sttng/

The Next Generation This site spends much of its time (and much of yours) describing the achievements of TNG—its success with the "prime" audience of men 18-34; its wealth of Emmy nominations; its ratings triumph over *Wheel of Fortune*; and its multimillion dollar merchandise retail sales and its importance to the economy. The relentless sanctimony can begin to drag after a while, but the site also includes the TNG FAQ, in which cast members comment on their favorite episodes (Patrick Stewart's fave? "The Offspring"). **INTERNET**→*www* http://web.city.ac.uk/~cc103/tng.html

Roger James Hall Star Trek: The Next Generation Page

Roger James Hall provides *Next Generation* fans with a complete episode list, a connection to the Timothy Lynch reviews, and an attractive photo collage. Usenet ratings of each episode are included. And if you're in a linking mood, jump to the official Paramount Web page or Steve Norman's Page at City University in London. **INTERNET**→*www* http://http1.brunel.ac.uk:8080/~ph93rjh/sttng.html

Star Trek: The Next Generation Central

A Website turned image gallery for TNG cast pictures. Several excellent scans of publicity shots and magazine photos for the crew. **INTERNET**→*www* http://trill.pc.cc.cmu.edu/~jkoga/sttng_gallery.html

TNG Chat

Clubs: TNG If you're 16 or under and like the *Next Generation*, start your voyages here. "Hi! I'm 14. Just call me Will Riker." "I'm 15, the only thing I love more than U2 is *Star Trek*." Slightly older teens should check out the 14-16 Trekkies subject, and kids of all ages should keep in mind that new clubs, like the Awesome TNG club for 12-14 year olds, start up all the time. **PRODIGY**→ *jump* star trek bb→Choose a Topic→Clubs: TNG→14-16 Trekkies

The Next Generation The largest of AOL's Trek message

boards, the TNG discussion ranges from the popular Spot discussion (devoted to Data's cat) to the divisive Worf & Troi folder (Troi and Worf or Troi and Riker?) to the *Star Wars* vs. *Star Trek* debate folder. Folders come and go, but those for quotes, merchandise, and character analysis remain popular. When the Tasha Yar folder was created, members weighed in with their impressions of the rather "pushy" character. Was she a "bitch" or "the most powerful female character on the show"? As one participant remarked in the midst of the Tasha bashing, "Admittedly she had her personal problems, but so would you if you grew up on Turkana IV." **AMERICA ONLINE**→*keyword* trek→Star Trek Message Boards→The Promenade →The Next Generation

rec.arts.startrek.misc/rec.arts.startrek.current (ng)

TNG groupies are by far the most vocal r.a.s.* contingent and for good reason. Even if the *Next Generation* hasn't fully eclipsed the original series, it has certainly brought with it a wave of enthusiasts that far outreaches that of its dramatic forbear. It's only to be expected, then, that a solemn cry went out across the Net when TNG ended its TV run; the outpouring of bereavement posts still continues. "The 10 most intense Trek minutes ever?" says one mourner. "That's gotta be the end of 'Best of Both Worlds I,' when we find out that Picard is Borgi-

fied, the Federation is going to be pasted, and Riker has to fire on his captain; add to the fact that we had to wait the entire summer to see what happens next! I howled in a combination of frustration and delight when the words 'to be continued' flashed up on the screen....Well, that's my two strips of latinum anyway."

Other hot topics: What are the limits of Troi's empathic abilities? ("Why can't she sense all the minds on a cloaked ship? Of course it would ruin a lot of shows, but is there a technical reason why it doesn't work?" "Sure! Here's the technical reason: She's faking. That's right! She once claimed to be able to read a Ferengi's mind, but we all know that that's impossible. So it's clear: She fakes it, pure and simple. :-)")

Why does everyone hate Wesley Crusher? ("It is difficult to suspend disbelief when a 13-year-old kid—genius or otherwise—is able to quickly and effortlessly solve a problem that the entire engineering team of the flagship of the Federation couldn't solve. And, if Wesley is indeed The Smartest Human Being Ever™, his talents were wasted by having him 'driving the ship,' as Marina Sirtis puts it. Shouldn't he have been putting that brain to use doing research in quantum mechanics or warp drives or something?")

And most importantly, which of the TNG regulars are going to continue on the big screen, now that the series has passed through the Final Frontier? The Net line is that all the regulars are signed on for multi-pic deals, except Picard and Data, who will likely hold out for more money and perks—like directing. Make it so! ✓ **USENET**

Star Trek: The Next Generation When one member nominated the temporal loop show "The Inner Light" as the absolute worst TNG episode ever, suggesting that repeating the event sequence was a cheap way to film a show, many participants strongly disagreed. Not the most vocal Net spot for TNG discussion, this forum is still a good place to check in and log an opinion. ✓ **EWORLD** →sf→Star Trek→On the Small Screen→Star Trek: The Next Generation

Star Trek: The Next Generation Even after seven seasons, fans feel a need to justify their partiality to *The Next Generation*. Greater character development is often cited as an advance on the first series, and there are often digressions into amateur psychoanalyses of Picard, Worf, Data, Riker and Troi. Topic 17 gives fans the opportunity to get "things that drive them crazy" off their chests—for example, why are there never any lines for the holodeck? Do crew members make reservations? Topic 34 is a repository for your personal best—what made you laugh, cry (Tasha Yar's memorial), or swallow your heart. And the discussion in topic 18, family life on the *Enterprise*, sounds almost contemporary in its concern with child care and education. ✓ **GENIE**→*keyword* sfrt2→

SFRT2 Bulletin Board→ set 27

STTNG (echo) The seven-year run is over, but TNG fans gather in this conference for nonstop reminiscing, nitpicking, and fan gossip: Picard's uniform, the Romulan threat, the loss of the *Enterprise-D*, Marina Sirtis nudes. Don't quite understand Guinan? Other Trekkers here are willing to explain (but be wary of anyone who claims to completely understand the character). And, although the television series is the primary focus of discussion, anything about *The Next Generation* is up for discussion. (Warning: members have a difficult time restraining themselves from spilling over into other Trek series.) One avid fan just finished reading a *Trek* book where there were "a lot of races they obviously just made up for the book, like the Lactrans,

a race of giant slug people with telepathic powers and super IQs (How can anything have an IQ of 9000?)." She was reassured by another fan that books are a minor element in the *Star Trek* canon—behind TV episodes and movies. ✓ **FIDONET**→STTNG ✓ **TREKNET**→ TN_STTNG

TNG — The Next Generation Rob wonders about the emergence of non-traditional hairstyles among Vulcans. Don't most of them have bowl cuts? Lor thinks Wesley got more interesting as he was transformed from "a stereotypical wunderkind" to a more human, less two-dimensional, character. All things TNG rule in this active area, with the diehard enthusiasts pondering everything from Data's programming to the color of Klingon blood. One bizarre discussion focused on the issue of whether it would be wise to give birth by transporter. Debra said she'd be a mother by now if "beaming the kid out was a possibility." Others worried that beaming babies might have a "traumatic

Tasha Yar—downloaded from ftp.cis.ksu.edu

effect" on them. Needless to say, this idea merits further study. ✓**DELPHI** →*go ent sta for*→*set tng*

Trekker_TNG (echo) Sharing TNG memorable moments, bashing Berman for lame scripts, and championing their most beloved characters are favorite pastimes of TrekkerNet Net Trekkers. "Well, it would appear that I was right about Q all along," writes the frequent conference contributor Amanda. "Some people said I was wrong to think that Q cared for humanity, but HE was responsible for saving the human race." Yeah, yeah, yeah. But, while there's plenty of gushing fan commentary, the conference's hard data—episode guides and reviews—keep conference readers in the know. ✓**TREKKERNET**

TV: Next Generation Come here to whine about never seeing a Q-meets-Trelane story (you'll have to read the book *Q-Squared*), to celebrate the magic of Picard, to discuss your favorite episode, or to weigh in on the Troi vs. Crusher controversy (who's better looking? smarter? more talented?). ✓**PRODI-**

GY→*jump* star trek bb→Choose a Topic→TV: Next Generation

WS_STTNG (echo) Some of the smartest Trek talk on the Warp-Speed BBS network occurs in *The Next Generation* echo. How does TNG define life? Did the Klingons and Romulans or did the Earth Alliance and the Romulans sign a peace treaty? And, where can I find a female metamorph? (Well, perhaps not all the comments are stellar, but you can't let one bad apple spoil the whole orchard.) Episode information and critical reviews are also posted here. ✓**WARPSPEED**

Behind the scenes

Interview with Executive Producers Interviews with executive producers Rick Berman, Michael Piller, and Jeri Taylor. They discuss their debt to the original show, their departures from it, and their place within the Roddenberry universe. ✓**INTERNET** →*www* http://www.ugcs.caltech. edu/~werdna/sttng/iv.prod.html

Star Trek: The Next Genera-

tion Awards A list of Emmy nominations for the *The Next Generation* series from 1988 to 1993. Each nomination is linked to Mike Brown's synopsis of the nominated show. ✓**INTERNET**→ *www* http://www. ugcs.caltech. edu:80/~werdna/sttng/awards. html

TNG Awards A year-by-year list of Emmy nominations and wins for all seven years of the *The Next Generation's* run. ✓**INTERNET**→*www* http://web.city.ac.uk/~cc103/ emmys.html

TNG Emmy Nominations List of all the Emmy nominations and awards for *The Next Generation.* ✓**INTERNET**→*www* http://www. ugcs.caltech.edu/~werdna/sttng/ awards.html

TNG History Written like a Paramount press release, the history focuses on how well *Star Trek: The Next Generation* has done, commending the show as if it were a prize pupil. ✓**INTERNET**→*www* http: //web.city.ac.uk/~cc103/history. html

---

CYBERTREKKERS

Phil Kernick

Age 27; Adelaide, South Australia
Archives sarcastic Trek reviews on the Trekker Reviews Website

Time Online: All day

Favorite Character: Worf

Favorite Episode: "Yesterday's Enterprise" (TNG)

Mission Statement: "Trek culture is much like any other online culture—you are either in or you're not. It also tends to take Trek far too seriously—lighten up guys and have some fun!"

Email Address: phil@ringo.ssn.flinders.edu.au

Cast & crew

As any TNG fan knows, the crew of the *Enterprise-D* is both more diverse and more

complex than that of the original series. There's still a compelling captain, sure—although Picard's controlled demeanor is very different from Kirk's loose-cannon charisma—but Spock, Chekov, Sulu, Uhura, Scotty, and McCoy have been replaced by Riker, Worf, Deanna Troi, Data, Geordi, and the Crushers. Amidst the dozens of sites that contain pictures and filmographies of cast members, there are a few standouts. Listen to the **BBC Interview with Patrick Stewart** to discover the bald Captain's turn-ons and turn-offs. Debate the pros and cons of interstellar playboys in **Riker: Coverboy, Dork, or Anomaly?** And finally, drop in to **Wesley Jokes**, a collection of malicious anecdotes and riddles designed to mock the child genius everyone loves to hate.

The Next Generation *crew (video capture)—downloaded from ftp.cis.ksu.edu*

On the Net

Across the board

Beam them Down Picture of the TNG cast beaming down. ✓**PVG** *dial* 513-233-7993→F→ Download a File:→PVTNGPST.GIF

Crew of the Star Trek: The

Next Generation Image of Picard, Riker, Worf, Data, Crusher, Troi, and La Forge with the *Enterprise* in the background. ✓**COMPUSERVE**→*go* sfmedia→Libraries→ *Search by file name:* CAST.GIF

NCC_1701D Enterprise Home Page This homepage is a labor of love, still under construction. The creator wants this site to have the flavor of an official Starfleet document. Currently the "Starfleet Personnel Records" for each crew member are online, complete with picture, rank, rating, previous postings, decorations, quarters, and a brief biography. (Did you know Riker was eighth in his class at Starfleet?) If you want to help develop this site, sign on. ✓**INTERNET**→*www* http://lal.cs.byu.edu /people/black/StarTrek/ncc1701d /homepage.html

TNG Cast Click on the nose of your favorite cast member to find out all about both the character and the actor. A 8x10 glossy of

each player is accompanied by birthday, favorite episode, and an extensive biography. The important episodes for each character are listed with brief summaries and linked to the episode reviews. Other Roles suggests that there might be life beyond Trek. Each actor's endeavors in theater, movies and television are compiled for ease of checking: What's McCoy been up to for twenty years? Where should you look for Kira on a *McGyver* rerun? Not just the biggies—that nameless transporter technician has been on *NYPD Blue*, and Diana Muldaur was McCloud's girlfriend. Another option leads to a list of TNG guest stars —from the famous (Mick Fleetwood as an Antedian dignitary in "Manhunt") to the not yet famous (Liberty as Spot in "Data's Day"). ✓**INTERNET**→*www* http://www. ugcs.caltech.edu/~werdna/sttng/ cast.html

TNG Cast Birthdays Want to send a birthday card to Gates Mc-

Fadden? This site will tell you when to lick the stamp. ✓**INTERNET**→*www* http://www.ugcs.cal tech.edu/~werdna/sttng/misc2. html#22

TNG Crew *A picture of the entire Enterprise-D crew.* ✓**INTERNET**→ *www* http://www.cosy.sbg.ac.at /ftp//pub/trek/pics/tngcrew.jpg

TNG Crew Profiles Descriptions, biographies, and stats (height, weight, gender, haircolor, etc.) of each of the main TNG characters. The biographies are filled with bits of trivia and references to TNG episodes. Do you know the names of the women Picard became romantically involved with during the series? The date Ro Laren was born? How Dr. Crusher developed her interest in medicine? It's all here. ✓**AMERICA ONLINE**→*keyword* trek→MORE...→ Star Trek Record Banks→Text/Other Files→Upld: 07/09/94→TEXT: TNG Crew Profiles (filename: CREWTNG.TXT)

TNG: The Characters The key word here is "character"—these are not actor biographies. This site contains information on: Picard, Riker, Data, La Forge, Worf, Troi, Beverly, Wesley, O'Brien, Guinan, Tasha Yar, and Ro Laren. Look here for vital statistics, posts, *Enterprise* records, likes/dislikes and pet peeves. Just in case you want to date one of the stars. ✓**INTERNET** →*www* http://www.cms.dmu.ac. uk/~it2yh/tngch.html

Jean-Luc Picard

alt.sexy.bald.captains (ng) Dominated by a group calling itself the Patrick Stewart Estrogen Brigade ("that's PSEB, with a silent P, as in psychotic," according to one member), whose devotees post about their desire to "grope

him like a piece of meat." Three of the group's members visited New York to see Stewart in his one-man version of *A Christmas Carol*. After the show, they got to touch him! ("Yes, my shaking little hand reached out and gently stroked the captain's l-l-l-leather jacket. It was lovely.") Of course, Picard's not the only bald captain to lust after...there's always Captain Stubing. Certainly one of the strangest spots on the Net. Amusing territory for lurkers. ✓**USENET**

BBC Interview with Patrick Stewart He speaks a little Klingon, doesn't think "Make it so" jokes are funny, and, in real life,

probably couldn't program a VCR. Stewart was interviewed by BBC radio at the close of the sixth season of TNG and this is a transcript. ✓**INTERNET**→*anon-ftp* que pasa.cs.tu-berlin.de→/pub/doc/ movies+tv-series/StarTrek/Inter views→stewart-interview-bbc.gz ✓**TFDN**→TFDN—Fact Files→*Download a file:* psbbc1.zip

Captain Jean-Luc Picard Jean-Luc Picard likes Earl Grey tea, even through he's French. Not always a high achiever, he missed Starfleet on first attempt. And those are only two fascinating facts about the captain courageous in this brief bio that's accompanied

Patrick Stewart (from Death Train*)—downloaded from Perfect Vision Graphics BBS*

by a picture. ✓**INTERNET**→*www* http://www.cms.dmu.ac.uk/~it2yh /pic.html

Captain Jean-Luc Picard For those who thought Captain Jean-Luc Picard materialized out of thin air to command the *Enterprise-D* this biography should provide illumination on his stellar acting career as a Royal Shakespeare Company-trained stage and screen thespian. ✓**INTERNET**→*www* http:// www.ugcs.caltech.edu/~werdna /sttng/picard.html

Captain Jean-Luc Picard Picture of the Captain of the *Enterprise NCC-1701-D*. ✓**COMPUSERVE** →*go* sfmedia→Libraries→*Search by file name:* STNG 14.GIF

Captain's Log A soundclip of Picard saying, "Captain's Log supplemental. The *Enterprise* is back under control." WAV file. ✓**COMPUSERVE**→*go* sfmedia→*Search by file name:* PICARD.WAV

Dune Image of Stewart in the role of Gurney in the movie *Dune*. ✓**COMPUSERVE**→*go* sfmedia→Libraries→*Search by file name:* PS-DUNE.GIF

Excalibur Image of Patrick Stewart in the movie *Excalibur*. ✓**COMPUSERVE**→*go* sfmedia→Libraries→ *Search by file name:* PSXKBR.GIF

Jean Luc Picard Picture of the *Enterprise* Captain. ✓**COMPUSERVE**→*go* sfmedia→Libraries→ *Search by file name:* TNGPIC.GIF

Make It So Five different "make it so" audio clips. ✓**COMPUSERVE**→ *go* sfmedia→Libraries→*Search by file name:* makeitso.sit

Pat Chat For those who just can't seem to get enough of Starfleet's Bald God, you can sit around and

talk about him with fellow supplicants. Thursdays at 9 pm EST in the private room Picard. Contact moderators The Marge or Eyechik if you're interested. ✓**AMERICA ON-LINE**→*keyword* pc→Rooms→Available Room→Member Rooms→ Picard

Patrick GIF Stewart in a brown sweater. ✓**COMPUSERVE**→*go* sfmedia →Libraries→*Search by file name:* PA-TRIK.GIF

Patrick Stewart The bald captain, who was once voted by *TV Guide* as the sexiest man on television, has quite a devoted following. This is the board for the mostly female fans of Patrick Stewart and an information organ for the fan club IAAPS (International Audience Alliance For Patrick Stewart). All the latest news and gossip is here: when he will appear for an interview, when he will appear on television (not as Picard), when he will appear in the theater, when he will appear on film, and on and on. But the real unspoken question on everyone's mind is: When will he appear in his underwear? ✓**AMERICA ONLINE**→*keyword* trek→Star Trek Message Boards→The Next Generation→Patrick Stewart

Patrick Stewart Biography A profile of Stewart's professional career, including a list of play, film, and television credits. Also includes personal background and a bibliography. ✓**COMPUSERVE**→*go* sfmedia→Libraries→*Search by file name:* STEWAR.TXT

Patrick Stewart Filmography Get Stewart's complete filmography by plugging in his name. Up come all his endeavors, from *In Search of Dr. Seuss* to *Star Trek: Generations,* along with full credits, plot synopsis and even reviews.

Find out the name of that nasty plotting Roman soldier he played in *I, Claudius*. ✓**INTERNET**→*www* http://www.msstate.edu/Movies→Search the database for a person's name→*Search for the name(s):* stewart, patrick

---

Patrick Stewart in Bathrobe Image of Stewart drinking tea while wearing a bathrobe. ✓**COMPUSERVE**→*go* sfmedia→Libraries→*Search by file name:* PSROB.GIF

Patrick Stewart Interview Pictures Pictures from a 1993 *Tonight Show* appearance. ✓**COMPUSERVE**→*go* sfmedia→Libraries→*Search by file name:* PSTONI.GIF

Patrick Stewart Official Fan Club Information about Patrick Stewart's fan club. ✓**COMPUSERVE**→*go* sfmedia→Libraries→*Search by file name:* IAAPS.TXT

Patrick Stewart on TV Guide The cover of the 1993 issue of *TV Guide* featuring Patrick Stewart as Captain Picard. ✓**COMPUSERVE**→*go* sfmedia→Libraries→*Search by file name:* PS.GIF

Picard Sharp picture of the *Enterprise* captain. ✓**PVG** dial 513-233-7993→<your username>→<your password>→F→ Download a file:→ PV-SFST2.GIF

Picard at Starfleet Academy Picture of Captain Picard at Starfleet Academy. ✓**PVG** dial 513-233-7993→<your username>→<your password>→F→Download a file: PVTREK10.GIF

Picard GIF Another Picard picture. ✓**COMPUSERVE**→*go* sfmedia→Libraries→*Search by file name:* PICD.GIF

Picard on the Bridge Picard assumes his seat on the bridge.

✓**COMPUSERVE**→*go* sfmedia→Libraries→*Search by file name:* JLPBRG.GIF

Picard Wisdom Soundclip of Picard: "I think that when one's been angry for a very long time, one gets used to it, and it becomes comfortable like…like, old leather, and finally it's becomes so familiar that one can't ever remember feeling any other way." ✓**INTERNET**→*anon-ftp* smaug.cs.hope.edu→/pub/sound/trek→ picard-wisdom

---

"The Inner Light" Flute Music Soundclip of Picard playing the flute in the episode "The Inner Light." ✓**COMPUSERVE**→*go* sfmedia→Libraries→*Search by file name:* INNERL.ZIP

WAV of Picard WAV file of Picard saying, "Let's make sure history never forgets the name *Enterprise*. Picard out." ✓**COMPUSERVE**→*go* sfmedia→Libraries→*Search by file name:* PICENT.WAV

William Riker

Commander Riker Picture of TNG first officer William Riker. ✓**COMPUSERVE**→*go* sfmedia→Libraries→*Search by file name:* TNGRIK.GIF

Frakes Black-and-white photo of Jonathan Frakes. ✓**GENIE**→*keyword* sfrt2→Text and Graphics Library→*Download a file:* 1038

Jonathan Frakes A search on Frakes's acting credits reveals that he has made the best of America's inability to get over the Civil War, appearing in four miniseries on the subject. Here you can discover what Riker has in common with Armand Assante, Alec Baldwin, Kathleen Turner, Louse Lasser, Ellen Burstyn, and fellow Trekker Nana Visitor. They all got their

Will Riker—downloaded from lajkonik. kr-cyf.pl.edu

---

start on *The Doctor*s. ✓**INTERNET**→*www* http://www.msstate.edu/Movies→Search the database for a person's name→*Search for the name(s):* frakes, jonathan

Riker: Coverboy, Dork, or Anomaly? Riker's womanizing, suggests one fan, is as much a beard as his beard: "It's so obvious; he's gay and can't bring himself to admit it. So he overcompensates by hitting on anyone/thing vaguely female." After the flames are doused—most fans are unwilling to consider the possibility of machismo as self-deception—other TNG faithful carry out the difficult business of analyzing the character. What about his relationship with Deanna Troi? What about his relationship with his father? Is he a consistent personality or merely a foil for the more richly drawn characters. And does it matter that he's the playboy of the Western universe: "So what if he gets laid a lot? And so what if he's overbearing and histrionic? So was Kirk. Riker is obviously a Kirk carry-over because they probably weren't too sure how Picard would be received." ✓**AMERICA ONLINE**→*keyword* scifi→Star Trek/Comics/

Star Trek: The Next Generation Cast & Crew

TV/Star Wars Boards→Star Trek→ Riker: coverboy, dork, or nomaly?

"The Federation's Gone!" Sound clip of Riker's announcement that the Borg have taken over the Federation. WAV file. ✓**COMPUSERVE**→*go* sfmedia→Libraries→ *Search by file name:* FEDGON.ZIP

William Riker Fans learn that Riker never really recovered from the early death of his mother. It took Troi to "draw him out of his emotional darkness." Other factoids (fictionoids?) include a description of his birthplace, Valdez, Alaska, no doubt still recovering from Exxon. ✓**INTERNET**→*www* http://www.cms.dmu.ac.uk/~it2yh/rik.html

William Riker Jonathan Frakes gives his take on the military bearing of his character—Riker's perception of his role as "Number One." This brief biography contains tidbits about Frakes' actress wife Genie Francis and his years as a "contract player" on the soap *The Doctors.* ✓**INTERNET**→*www* http://www.ugcs.caltech.edu/~werdna/sttng/riker.html

Data

Brent Spiner A database search reveals Spiner hasn't always been an android. He played Democratic deal-maker Allard Lowenstein in a miniseries about Senator Robert F. Kennedy (alongside Shannon Dougherty no less!). Read his reviews here by just searching on his name. ✓**INTERNET**→*www* http://www.msstate.edu/Movies→Search the database for a person's name →*Search for the name(s):* spiner, brent

Brent Spiner What is it about the sexless that makes them so ir-

resistible? Lt. Commander Data, or Ol' Yellow Eyes, as his mostly female fans adoringly refer to him, follows in the tradition of Mr. Spock as the sexiest unsexy guy on TV. Brent receives more fan mail than any other character. With an adulation that evokes memories of John Hinckley and Jodie Foster, fans on AOL's Brent Spiner Board trade the latest news. Which conventions did Brent attend, and what was he wearing? Who is the mysterious Brenda who has been seen talking with him at several conventions? Was that really his girlfriend with him on *Entertainment Tonight* or merely a Paramount ploy to deflect rumors that he's gay? And what about that appearance as the pornographic film director on *Hill Street Blues*? It was so unDatalike! But what probably generates the most squishy reverence is Brent's album, appropriately titled *Ol' Yellow Eyes.* Unlike William Shatner and Leonard Nimoy, though, it would appear that Brent has genuine singing talent. ✓**AMERICA ONLINE**→*keyword* trek→ Star Trek Message Boards→The

Next Generation→Brent Spiner

Brent Spiner The Actors/Actresses topic is usually dominated by Brent Spiner discussions—even a year after TNG stopped filming new episodes. Loyal fans (primarily women) gather in subjects like "Brent is not boring" or "Brent as a topic" or "Club Brent." Brent die-hards check in regularly to exchange gossip about the hunky android. Writes Kay, "For the record, Brent is fine, still single and signed a contract with Paramount to do three more pictures that are NOT related to *Star Trek*...soooo, all we can do is wait. Data now has his 'emotion' chip and they think that it will give him the ability to age. And to that Brent says 'thank God.' Well, until next time...keep Club Brent alive!" ✓**PRODIGY**→ *jump* star trek bb→Choose a Topic→Actors/Actresses

Commander Data Picture Picture of the android Starfleet Commander. ✓**COMPUSERVE**→*go* sfmedia →Libraries→*Search by file name:* TNGDAT.GIF

Data (video still)—downloaded from lajkonic.cyf-kr.pl.edu

Cast & Crew **Star Trek: The Next Generation**

Data Data's DOB: Activated 2nd February 2336. A brief account of Data's elevation to the status of sentient being/Federation citizen is provided. Data's struggle with moral questions as an android is highlighted—he never told his own "mother" that she was really an android. ✓**INTERNET**→*www* http://www.cms.dmu.ac.uk/~it2yh /dat.html

Data Brent Spiner definitely doesn't take himself too seriously, releasing an album *Ol' Yellow Eyes is Back* featuring backup vocals on the Dataesque track "It's A Sin to Tell A Lie" by the Sunspots (Stewart, Frakes, Burton and Dorn). This site also includes a painstaking collection of all the times that Data has used contractions—in theory something his circuits won't allow. A careful viewer has also documented all the cats in Data's chambers from "All Good Things"—nine!! Could the tabby be the original Spot? ✓**INTERNET**→*www* http://www.ugcs.cal tech.edu/~werdna/sttng/data.html

Data 1 Great image of Data looking very serious. ✓**INTERNET**→*anon-ftp* wuarchive.wustl.edu→/graphics /gif/d→data 1.gif

Data Noises Do androids dream of electric noises? This one does. Listen to the sound of Data processing. ✓**INTERNET**→*www* http:// www.cosy.sbg.ac.at/rec/startrek /sounds.html

Data's Ode to Spot Full text of the ballad Data wrote for his cat Spot. ✓**INTERNET** ...→*www* http:// www.eeng.dcu.ie/~stdcu/trek/ spot.html ...→*gopher* chop.isca. uiowa.edu 8338→General Information→Star Trek Reviews→Data's Ode to Spot ✓**AMERICA ONLINE**→ *keyword* trek→MORE...→Star Trek Record Banks→Text/Other Files→

Upld: 11/08/92→TEXT:Ode to Spot (Filename: SPOTODE.DOC)

Spiner Spiner black-and-white publicity shot. ✓**GENIE**→*keyword* sfrt2→Text and Graphics Library→ *Download a file:* 1098

Brent Spiner Plays Guitar Picture of Spiner playing the guitar on the set. ✓**PVG** *dial* 513-233-7993→<your username>→<your password>→F→Download a file: DATA05.GIF

Brent Spiner Plays Guitar Picture of Spiner playing the guitar on the set. ✓**PVG** *dial* 513-233-7993→<your username>→<your password>→F→Download a file: BRENT.GIF *and* PVTNGP03.GIF *and* SPINER1.GIF

Data Collage of Data pictures. ✓**PVG** *dial* 513-233-7993→<your username>→<your password>→ F→Download a file: DATA07.GIF

Data Plays the Violin Picture of Data playing the violin. ✓**PVG** *dial* 513-233-7993→<your username>→<your password>→F→ Download a file: DATA01.GIF

Worf

Lt. Worf Worf image. ✓**COMPUSERVE**→*go* sfmedia→Libraries →*Search by file name:* WORF.GIF

Michael Dorn at a Convention Two images of Michael Dorn at the Vancouver Trekfest Convention. ✓**COMPUSERVE**→*go* sfmedia→Libraries→*Search by file name:* DORN1. GIF, DORN2.GIF

Michael Dorn Filmography Run out to rent

Jagged Edge to try and spot Worf incognito, or listen to a soundbite bitten from the opening credits of the 70's cop melodrama *CHiPs.* ✓**INTERNET**→*www* http://www. msstate.edu/Movies→Search the database for a person's name→ *Search for the name(s):* dorn, michael

Worf Four terrific soundclips of lines uttered by your favorite Klingon that can be used to identify general computer functions: "I'm beginning to see the appeal of this program;" "Computer freeze program;" "Computer...end program;" and "End program!" For Macs. ✓**INTERNET**→*anon-ftp* sumex-aim.stanford.edu→/info-mac/snd→ sttng-worf-datas.hqx

Worf Worf—the very name strikes the heart and produces a noble tone. Follow him through his proud days as the first Klingon at Starfleet, learn the history of his family's dishonor, and even feel a twinge of injustice on his behalf when his son Alexander is listed as a "bastard." Surely in the 24th century illegitimacy will have ceased to be an important issue. ✓**INTERNET**→ *www* http:// www.cms.dmu. ac.uk/~it2yh/ wor. html

Worf Michael Dorn got to play Worf's

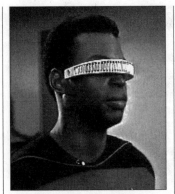

Geordi La Forge (video still)—downloaded from ftp.cis.ksu.edu

own grandfather in *Star Trek VI*. But what did Dorn do before? Well, even though it's hard to see the face under the forehead, you may recognize him as a *CHiPs* regular, and Andrew Tong's page also explains that the actor has fulfilled a lifelong dream of flying with the Blue Angels. ✓**INTERNET**→*www* http://www.ugcs.caltech.edu/~werdna/sttng/worf.html

Worf Klingon Opera Let the lovely sounds of Klingon opera flow into your Terran ears. ✓**INTERNET**→*anon-ftp* nic.switch.ch:→/mirror/vms/DECUS/lt93b/brodie/startrek/tng→worf-klingon-opera.au

Geordi La Forge

Burton Black and white photo of LeVar Burton. ✓**GENIE**→*keyword* sfrt2→Text and Graphics Library→*Download a file:* 1039

Geordi La Forge Blind at birth, Geordi can interpret electromagnetic waves through his Visual Instrument and Sight Organ Replacement (VISOR). A Starfleet brat, his father roams the Modine system, while his mom commands a ship in the Neutral Zone. ✓**INTERNET**→*www* http://www.cms.

dmu.ac.uk/~it2yh/geo.html

Geordi La Forge LeVar Burton's character was named after a disabled fan, now deceased, and this brief biography of actor and character emphasizes the civic responsibility behind the visor. First, of course, there's *Roots*, the miniseries that helped shape the consciousness of a nation, and this document stresses how young Burton was when he won the role of Kunta Kinte (a mere sophomore at USC). ✓**INTERNET**→*www* http://www.ugcs.caltech.edu/~werdna/sttng/geordi.html

Geordi the Techie Picture of Geordi La Forge. ✓**PVG** *dial* 513-233-7993→F→Download a File: PVLEVAR.GIF

LeVar Burton Picture of Burton at a Trek convention in NYC. ✓**COMPUSERVE**→*go* sfmedia→Libraries→*Search by file name:* LEVAR1.GIF

LeVar Burton Filmography Best known for his portrayal of the young Kunta Kinte in *Roots*, Burton is now a key member of the Trek universe, with directing credits on *Voyager*. Here's a list of his other film and TV appearances. ✓**INTERNET**→*www* http://www.msstate.edu/Movies→Search the database for a person's name→*Search for the name(s):* burton, levar

Beverly Crusher

Beverly Crusher Beautiful photo of Dr. Crusher. ✓**PVG** *dial* 513-233-7993→<your username>→<your password>→F→Download a file: PV-SFST1.GIF

Beverly Crusher Bev and Jack had been married six years when he was killed. What's a poor widow and brilliant doctor to do?

Does she really carry a torch for Picard or blame him for Jack's death? Answer these and more questions with this character biography. ✓**INTERNET**→*www* http://www.cms.dmu.ac.uk/~it2yh/bev.html

Beverly Crusher Did you know that Gates McFadden used to work hand in glove with the Muppets? Creatures with hairy faces and odd foreheads must have come as no surprise. This little bio is full of fun facts—McFadden earned her B.A. from Brandeis, teaches acting, and has a two-year old son. But don't expect to learn more about Bev and Picard—their relationship is described only as "emotionally charged." ✓**INTERNET**→*www* http://www.ugcs.caltech.edu/~werdna/sttng/beverly

Beverly Fans For more than two years, fans of Gates McFadden and her TNG character Beverly Crusher have been meeting in this subject. If the atmosphere is sometimes a little claustrophobic—fans know the names of each others children, for goodness sake—it's

Beverly Crusher—downloaded from CompuServe's Sci-Fi Media Forum

also productive, and there's a tremendous amount of back-patting over McFadden's new UPN series *Marker*. ✓ **PRODIGY**→*jump star trek bb*→Choose a Topic→Actors/Actress→Beverly Fans

Doctor Crusher Scenes of the doctor treating her patients. ✓ **PVG** *dial* 513-233-7993→<your username>→<your password>→F→ *Download a file:* BEVTRT.GIF *and* BEVTRT2.GIF *and* BEVTRT3. GIF

Gates McFadden Fans here think Gates McFadden is beautiful, funny, and underappreciated by the Trek higher-ups. Why didn't they develop Dr. Crusher's character more? Will she get a bigger part in the movies? Can she do no wrong? ✓ **AMERICA ONLINE**→*keyword* trek→Star Trek Message Boards→The Next Generation→ Gates McFadden

Gates McFadden Filmography When you trace McFadden's credits for *The Hunt For Red October*, you'll learn that $20,000 was spent on hairpieces for Sean Connery. What does this have to do with Beverly Crusher? Well, nothing, but it's fascinating nonetheless, and it's linked to a bio about your favorite red-headed Trek doc. ✓ **INTERNET**→*www* http://www. msstate.edu/Movies→Search the database for a person's name→ *Search for the name(s):* mcfadden, gates

Gates McFadden: Small Town Kid Makes Good A 1992 interview with McFadden in which she discusses her name, her childhood, her time studying in France, her hair, and her directing aspirations. ✓ **INTERNET**→*anon-ftp* quepasa.cs.tu-berlin.de→/pub/doc/movies+tv-series/StarTrek/Interviews→gates-interview.gz

"This is a banana split...and it's quite possibly one of the greatest things in the universe."
—**Troi, "Suddenly Human"**
Net Source: STTNG Quotes— http://www. cosy.sbg.ac.at/ftp/pub/trek/ quotes/st_tng4.txt

Glamourous Gates Glamour shot of Gates McFadden. ✓ **PVG** *dial* 513-233-7993→<your username>→ <your password>→F→ *Download a file:* PV-WOT02.GIF

Deanna Troi

Autographed Picture of Troi Autographed publicity photo of Troi from a Trek convention in Spokane, Washington. ✓ **COMPUSERVE**→*go* sfmedia→Libraries→ *Search by file name:* TROIAG.GIF

Deanna Troi Deanna Troi's character sketch includes brief psychoanalysis of both Deanna and Lwaxana. The dilemmas of an empathic half-breed are explored, as are the effects of loss on Betazoids. ✓ **INTERNET**→*www* http://www.cms. dmu.ac.uk/~it2yh/tro.html

Deanna Troi Of Greek extraction, raised in London, trained in classical music, married to musician Michael Lamper, Marina Sirtis cut her dramatic teeth in the European tour of the *Rocky Horror Picture Show*, and admits here that she created Troi's unplaceable accent to reflect the 24th century lack of national barriers. ✓ **INTERNET**→*www* http://www.ugcs.cal tech.edu/~werdna/sttng/troi.html

Deanna Troi She's a chocoholic, whipped into submission by her mother, muddled by occupational and romantic choices, and Deanna Troi is as stable as most Terran psychologists—which is to say not stable at all. As a result of her discombobulation, she draws the ill will of fans, who also disparage Trek creators for forcing her to wear a form-fitting bodysuit (the message board itself is subtitled "a place to discuss those huge @!@"). But most TNG regulars admit that Deanna improved greatly toward the end of the show, and many women check in to suggest that the character is the most realistic career woman in outer space—neurotic, imperfect, and yet still somehow compelling. ✓ **AMERICA ONLINE**→*keyword* scifi→ Star Trek/Comics/TV/Star Wars Boards→Star Trek→Deanna Troi

GIF of Troi Picture of Troi. ✓ **COMPUSERVE**→*go* sfmedia→Libraries→*Search by file name:* TROI.GIF

Marina Convention Photos Photos of Marina Sirtis at a Seattle convention. ✓ **COMPUSERVE**→*go* sfmedia→Libraries→*Search by file name:* MARINA1.GIF, MARINA4. GIF, MARINA5.GIF, *and* MARINA6.GIF

Marina Sirtis Filmography Some of the Trek fan world might say that Sirtis's role in *Waxwork II* accurately reflects her acting capabilities. Counselor Troi also once played a hooker in the slasher movie *Deadly Seduction*. Search here for plot summaries and further information. ✓**INTERNET**→ *www* http://www.msstate.edu/ Movies→Search the database for a person's name→*Search for the name(s):* sirtis, marina

Marina Sirtis in Black Lace Sirtis wearing a black lace dress at a Trek convention. ✓**COMPUSERVE** →*go* sfmedia→Libraries→ *Search by file name:* PVSRT2.GIF

Portrait of the Beautiful Marina Sirtis Sirtis in a black velvet evening dress at a Trek convention. ✓**COMPUSERVE**→*go* sfmedia→ Libraries→*Search by file name:* PVSRTS.GIF

Sirtis A view of Marina Sirtis. ✓**GENIE**→*keyword* sfrt2→Text and Graphics Library→*Download a file:* 1042

Troi Great head shot of Counselor Troi. ✓**INTERNET**→*anon-ftp* wu archive.wustl.edu→/graphics/gif /t→troi1.gif

Troi Meeting Goddess of Empathy Counselor Troi meets the

Deanna Troi (video still)—downloaded from ftp.cis. ksu.edu

Goddess of Empathy in a touching scene on the holodeck. ✓**COMPUSERVE**→*go* sfmedia→Forum→ *Search by file name:* TROI2.GIF

Upset Soundclip of Troi saying "I sense how upset you are." ✓**INTERNET**→*anon-ftp* smaug.cs.hope.edu→ /pub/sound/trek→upset

Wesley Crusher

Wesley Crusher "Wesley is a genius!" 'Nough said. ✓**INTERNET**→ *www* http://www.cms.dmu.ac.uk/ ~it2yh/wes.html

Wesley Crusher: Deep 6 Him Each message begins "Whack"! But that's not necessarily the method of murdering Wesley. It's an acronym for the group known as Wesley Haters And Creative Killers. And while some demonstrate the ability to differentiate between the actor Wil Wheaton and the child prodigy Wesley, most have an unbridled enthusiasm for bashing anything that looks like even vaguely Wesleic: "Let's hope he and the Traveler take a wrong turn somewhere and end up in the Wormhole." Or, "I just finished [the novel] *Q-Squared* and some of you will be happy to know that there's an alternate universe in which Wesley died as a small child..."

Too mean-spirited? Some are a little less violent in their thoughts about Wesley: "My guess is that Wesley earned our rancor by being a dry, boring, plastic non-character. And while I can accept the idea of a boy genius, I still don't think he could solve problems that befuddled the rest of the crew, who are supposedly composed of the best and brightest humanity has to offer." ✓**AMERICA ONLINE**→ *keyword* trek→Star Trek Message Boards→The Neutral Zone→Wesley Crusher: Deep 6 Him

Wesley Crusher (video still)—downloaded from ftp.cis.ksu.edu

Wesley Jokes No one takes more ribbing than the wonderboy of the *Enterprise-D*, and there's no better place to keep your finger on the pulse of Wesley crushing than AOL's Wesley Jokes folder. "Q: If Wesley Crusher and a Ferengi were dropped off the World Trade Center, who would hit the ground first? A: Who cares." "Q: Why did Wesley Crusher's girlfriend like to be on top? A: She heard he was a Crusher." With wit and wisdom from around the world, this message board is sure to appeal to anyone with a mean streak. And there are even some truly odd postings, such as this aggrieved revelation from a Trek fan: "When I go out in public in my uniform (it doesn't happen often enough), people call me...Wesley." ✓**AMERICA ONLINE**→ *keyword* scifi→Star Trek/Comics /TV/Star Wars Boards→Star Trek →Wesley Jokes

WHACK Wes Haters and Creative Killers still can't stop plotting against the character Trekkers most like to hate. "Oh Q, Oh Omnipotent Q, please kill Wes." Organized against the "24th century Doogie Howser," the topic is filled with poems and lyrics prophesizing the character's death, tasteless jokes about Crusher, and idea after idea for ways to kill the kid. One *Doom* fan is looking for a game patch so he can chainsaw Wesley Crusher instead of the monsters. Fun group! **PRODIGY**→*jump* star trek bb→Choose a Topic→Clubs: Other→WHACK

Wheaton Wheaton black-and-white publicity shot. **GENIE**→*keyword* sfrt2→Text and Graphics Library→*Download a file:* 1098

Wil Wheaton Filmography Nineteen credits since 1981 seems like an awful lot for so young an actor. The search shows that Wheaton has gone from playing the innocent pre-teen in *Stand By Me* to a teen losing his innocence to Sonia Braga in *The Last Prostitute*. Trek has even elevated Wheaton to the recognizability of cameo level (*She's Having A Baby*). **INTERNET**→*www* http://www.msstate.edu/Movies→Search the database for a person's name. →*Search for the name(s):* wheaton, wil

Guinan

Guinan It's hard to write a brief bio of someone more than 600 years old—luckily, "the details of her life will always remain her secret." A victim of the Borg, Guinan is wary, keeping her own counsel. But her fans are loyal, and keep hoping that she'll one day be voted universal mom. **INTERNET**→*www* http://www.cms.dmu.ac.uk/~it2yh/gui.html

Whoopi Goldberg Filmography Everybody knows Whoopi Goldberg, but a search on her name does turn up a few surprising Hollywood facts. Did you know she played Buckwheat's mother? This site is updated constantly, so you'll know ahead of time what Whoopi's making. **IN-**

TERNET→*www* http://www.msstate.edu/Movies→Search the database for a person's name→*Search for the name(s):* goldberg, whoopi

Tasha Yar

Denise Crosby Filmography Look here to find out what she's been up to since she left the galaxy —most recently in *Black Water* with Johnny Cash. Other credits include two *Pink Panther* movies and a spate of lame thrillers—*Relative Fear, Desperate Crimes.* **INTERNET**→*www* http://www.msstate.edu/Movies/→Search the database for a person's name→*Search for the name(s):* crosby, denise

Last Words of Lt. Natasha Yar Transcript of the scene in the holodeck following Yar's death where she gives her goodbye message. **COMPUSERVE**→*go* sfmedia→Libraries→*Search by file name:* TASHA.TXT

Tasha Yar Didn't understand it the first time around—or was it the second time around? This document is a sincere effort to clarify the complicated histories of Tasha Yar, complete with diagrams of the various timelines and their intersections. Admitting the complexity of the situation, the author invites questions and additions. Remember, here history has happened because of events in the future—get it? **INTERNET**→*www* http://www.cms.dmu.ac.uk/~it2yh/tas.html

Tasha Yar Image of Tasha Yar. **COMPUSERVE**→*go* sfmedia→Libraries→*Search by file name:* TNG-YAR.GIF

Sela GIFs of Denise Crosby as the Romulan Commander and Tasha Yar's daughter. **COMPUSERVE**→*go* sfmedia→Libraries→

Search by file name: BLONDE.GIF and SELA.GIF

Guest stars

TNG Guest Stars Who? Corbin Bernsen, Mick Fleetwood, Olivia D'Abo, David Ogden Stiers, John Tesh, Paul Winfield, James Doohan, Kelsey Grammer, and Ashley Judd. And even a Pataki (Michael) who played a Governor (Karnas, in "Too Short a Season"). **INTERNET**→*www* http://www.ugcs.caltech.edu/~werdna/sttng/gueststars.html

Alexander

Alexander Picture of Worf's son Alexander. **COMPUSERVE**→*go* sfmedia→Libraries→*Search by file name:* TNGALE.GIF

Barclay

Lt. Reginald Barclay Picture of Lt. Reginald Barclay. **PVG** *dial* 513-233-7993→<your username>→<your password>→F→Download a file: BARCLAY.GIF

Boothby

GIF of Boothby Picture of the gardener from Starfleet Academy who helped Picard when the Captain was a cadet. **COMPUSERVE**→*go* sfmedia→Libraries→*Search by file name:* TNGBOO.GIF

Mr. Homn

Carel Struycken Convention photo of Carel Struycken, who played Lwaxana Troi's valet. **COMPUSERVE**→*go* sfmedia→Libraries→*Search by file name:* CAREL1.GIF

K'Ehleyr

K'Ehleyr Picture of her first appearance. ✓ **COMPUSERVE**→*go* sfmedia→Libraries→*Search by file name:* KEHLAR.JPG

K'Ehleyr Publicity picture of K'Ehleyr. ✓ **COMPUSERVE**→*keyword* sfmedia→Libraries→*Search by file name:* TNGKLR.GIF

Ro Laren

Ro Photo of Ensign Ro, the Bajoran assigned to the *Enterprise-D*. ✓ **INTERNET** ...→*anon-ftp* ftp.cis.ksu. edu→/pub/pictures/jpg/Startrek→ ro.jpg ...→*anon-ftp* lajkonik.cyf-kr.edu.pl→/agh/reserve/gifs/star trek→ro.jpg

Ro Laren (video still)—downloaded from ftp.cis. ksu.edu

Michelle Forbes Filmography Before she was Ro Laren, Michelle Forbes was all over the map— from the gritty murder movie *Kalifornia* to the Irish morality tale *The Playboys*. She even worked with two of the oddest celebs in our particular universe, Judy Tenuta and Adam Ant, in *Love Bites*. But probe no further, lest you risk learning of the time she played twins on a soap opera. ✓ **INTERNET**→*www* http://www.msstate. edu/Movies/→Search the database for a person's name→*Search for the name(s):* forbes, michelle

Ro Laren Ro Laren was more than slightly disturbed by watching her father beg for his life while being tortured to death by Cardassians. This Bajoran trouble-maker has definite issues with authority. Find out here how far she's come —from court-martial to the first earring-wearing *Enterprise-D* officer. ✓ **INTERNET**→*www* http://www. cms.dmu.ac.uk/~it2yh/ro. html

Lwaxana

Majel Barrett Filmography Originally cast as Number One for the pilot episode of TOS and later to marry Gene Roddenberry and play the luscious Nurse Chapel and the irrepressible Lwaxana Troi, Barrett also accured a list of non-Trek film credits including *A Guide to the Married Men* and *Love in a Goldfish*. Here's the list. ✓ **INTERNET**→*www* http://www. msstate.edu/Movies/→Search the database for a person's name→ *Search for the name(s):* barrett, majel

Lwaxana Troi Collage of photos of Majel Barrett as Lwaxana Troi. ✓ **PVG** *dial* 513-233-7993→F→ Download a File: LWAXANA.GIF

Majel at a Convention Photos of Majel Barrett at a Seattle convention. ✓ **COMPUSERVE**→*go* sfmedia →Libraries→*Search by file name:* majel1.gif *and* majel2.gif

Miles O'Brien

Colm Meaney Filmography Meaney has played a doctor in *The Road to Wellville*, a cop in *Dick Tracy*, a major in the *Last of the Mohicans*, and Geronimo's dad in *War of the Buttons*—one of the most active movie careers of current Trek actors. ✓ **INTERNET** →*www* http://www.msstate.edu/ Movies/→Search the database for a person's name→*Search for the name(s):* meaney, colm

Miles O'Brien What makes Miles O'Brien tick? The massacre at Setlik III, when the simple engineer was forced to kill in cold blood, left him with a deep loathing of Cardassians, and a promotion to lieutenant. And then, of course, there's Ireland, still going strong in the 24th century. ✓ **INTERNET**→*www* http://www.cms. dmu.ac.uk/~it2yh/mil.html

Miles O'Brien Home Page Is Miles O'Brien just your normal chief engineer? Damned right, and that's what makes him so blinkin' extraordinary. This gushing fan page is devoted to the character, as well as other roles Colm Meaney has played. ✓ **INTERNET**→*www* http://www.astro.umd.edu/~sgeier /obrien.html

Dr. Pulaski

Diana Muldaur Brief Biographical Sketch Features a chronological list of acting credits and a short personal history. ✓ **COMPUSERVE**→*go* sfmedia→Libraries→*Search by file name:* MULDAU.TXT

Q

alt.fan.q (ng) Speculating on the future activities of an omnipotent

Q (video still)—downloaded from lajkonik.cyf-kr.pl.edu

being leaves everything wide open. In this moderately active newsgroup, fans of the troublesome and mischievous superbeing exchange ideas on the devilment Q may cause in the new *Voyager* series and *Star Trek* films. Trade your favorite Q jibes or expound your theories on the nature of the Q Continuum. ✓ **USENET**

De Lancie Picture of de Lancie at a *Star Trek* convention. ✓ **PVG** *dial* 513-233-7993→<your username> →<your password>→F→*Download a file:* DELANCIE. GIF

De Lancie at Dreamwerks Transcript of a Q&A session at a 1988 Trek convention in which John de Lancie reveals how he landed the role of Q. ✓ **COMPU-SERVE**→*go* sfmedia→Libraries→ *Search by file name:* Q.TXT

"I am Q" WAV file of Q saying "I am Q." ✓ **COMPUSERVE**→*go* sfmedia→Libraries→*Search by file name:* IAMQ.WAV

Interview with John de Lancie A transcript of a radio interview with John de Lancie in which he talks about college, his parents, his career, and Q. ✓ **TFDN**→TFDN— Trek Fact Files→*Download a file:* DELANCIE.ZIP

John de Lancie Filmography When looking up Q, place a space after the "de." Several popular recent movies, including *The Hand That Rocks the Cradle* and *The Fisher King*, have used his talents. And doesn't it seem fitting that de Lancie used to wreak havoc in the smaller universe of *Days of Our Lives?* ✓ **INTERNET**→*www* http:// www.msstate.edu/Movies→Search the database for a person's name.

→*Search for the name(s):* de lancie, john

Q the... Soundclip of an exchange between Q and Picard in the episode "Deja Q." Q: "Q, the ordinary." Picard: "Q, the liar. Q, the misanthrope." Q: "Q, the miserable. Q, the desperate." ✓ **INTERNET**→*anon-ftp* smaug.cs.hope.edu →/pub/sound/trek→q-the

Sarek

Sarek A picture of Sarek. ✓ **COMPUSERVE**→*go* sfmedia→Libraries→ *Search by file name:* SAREK1.GIF

The Traveler

The Traveler Picture of the mysterious Traveler. ✓ **PVG**→*dial* 513-233-7993→<your username>→ <your password>→ F→*Download a file:* TRAVELER.GIF

═══ CYBERTREKKERS ═══

Andrew C. Tong

Age 20; Pasadena, CA

The Star Trek:TNG Website.

"I'm having trouble getting into DS9, so I haven't been watching a lot of Trek...My dad has watched TOS for as long as I can remember."

Favorite Series: *The Next Generation*

Favorite Character: "Spock, because I can identify with him. Something common to a lot of nerds, I think, since we all get the kind of ribbing that Kirk and Bones put Spock through. He gives me the hope that someday, I'll be able to find my little niche, some place where all my differences and idiosyncracies will actually become assets, in a way."

Favorite Episode: "Tapestry" (TNG) and "Parallels" (TNG)
"I like 'Tapestry' because it was reassuring for me at a crucial point in my freshman year in college: it reminded me quite strongly that bad experiences, which I regret, can be transformed into something which makes me into a better person—that the crap in my life can really work for the greater good."

Other Interests: IRC

Email Address: werdna@ugcs.caltech.edu

24th-century guides

The longest-running of any Trek series, TNG has almost two hundred episodes to its

name, and it's no easy task to keep track of them. But that doesn't mean it's impossible, especially with the rich resources of the Net. First, pay a visit to **The Next Generation Episode Guide Hypercard Stack**, a downloadable guide to the series available on commercial services as well as the Internet. Then join the hundreds of other sharp-eyed fans sniffing around for continuity errors in **Operation Snafu**. And finally, check to see which TNG episodes earned the respect of fans, and which earned only derisive dismissal, with **TNG Episode Ratings**.

On the bridge (video capture)—downloaded from ftp.cis.ksu.edu

On the Net

Episode guides

The Next Generation Episode Guide Hypercard Stack A searchable HyperCard Stack of TNG episodes. Stack includes plot descriptions, the names of script writers and episode directors, cast information, and more. For Macintoshes eqipped with a Hyper-Card player. ✓**AMERICA ONLINE**→ *keyword* mac software→Search the Libraries→Search All Libraries→ *Search by file name:* Star Trek-TNG Guide 2.0.sea ✓**COMPUSERVE**→*go* sfmedia→Libraries→*Search by file name:* TNG21A.SIT ✓**INTERNET**→ *anon-ftp* ftp.u-tokyo.ac.jp→/.1/

mac/umich/hypercard/fun→star trektngguide2.0.cpt.hqx

Star Trek: The Next Generation List of Episodes, Plot Descriptions, and Major Characters Episode guide with *Next Generation* cast list and episode descriptions that include the date aired, stardate, and one-liner synopses. Miscellaneous trivia items are attached to the end of the document: Starfleet ranks and insignia; an explanation of stardates; the episodes in which Picard violates the Prime Directive; and the opportunities to be a ship captain that have been offered to Commander Riker. ✓**INTERNET**→*anon-ftp* rtfm.mit.edu→/pub/usenet-by-hierarchy/rec/arts/startrek/misc→ STARTREK_LISTS:_ st:tng_{biweekly}

Star Trek: The Next Generation Quick Reference Guide
Short summaries of each TNG episode. ✓**INTERNET**→*anon-ftp* ftp.cc.umanitoba.ca→/startrek→ quickref.tng

Star Trek TNG Episode Guide An introductory history of *The Next Generation*, and details of the seven seasons—including cast lists, production, direction, and writing credits for each show. ✓**INTERNET** …→*anon-ftp* elbereth.rutgers. edu→/pub/sfl→star-trek-tng.guide …→*gopher* dds.dds.nl→ De Biblio theek→boeken→Mass Media→Star Trek→Star Trek TNG Episode Guide

TNG Brief Episode Summaries One sentence summaries. "Counselor Troi becomes pregnant; a deadly cargo of plasma plague threatens the ship." Need we say more? ✓**INTERNET**→*www* http:// http1.brunel.ac.uk:8080/~ph93rjh/ briefs.txt

TNG Complete Episode List

The basic information—complete list of episodes with stardate and air date. ✓ **INTERNET**→*www* http://http1.brunel.ac.uk:8080/~ph93rjh/list.txt

TNG Episode Guide

Quick reference summaries of *The Next Generation*. One sentence lets you know if you want to see it again, or what to prepare for. ✓ **INTERNET**→*www* http://www.cms.dmu.ac.uk/~it2yh/tngep.html

TNG Episode Guide

A brief synopsis of each episode is accompanied by hypertext links that connect to Timothy Lynch's detailed reviews (many accompanied by an image from the particular episode), Emmy nominations for each episode, promos, credits, press releases, and comments and trivia added by readers. Nielsen and WWW ratings are provided so you can see how your opinion compares with the world at large. There are also links to the "snafu" list, making it easy to check if Troi's uniform did change color or if an alien ship uses Goodyear tires. A link to the "The Next Cliche" reviews is provided for those with the ability to handle gentle mocking of their favorite show. ✓ **INTERNET**→*www* http://www.ugcs.caltech.edu/~werdna/sttng/episodes.html

TNG Episode List

A full seven-season list of episodes with stardates, plot descriptions, and air dates. ✓ **DELPHI**→*go* ent sta dat→set tng→*read* TNG Episode List - Complete

TNG Episodes List

Titles-only list of episodes. ✓ **COMPUSERVE**→*go* sfmedia→Libraries→*Search by file name:* TNGEPS.LST

Vidiot's Star Trek: The Next Generation Program Guide

A guide with extensive credits and program synopses compiled by Trek fan Mike Brown. Although it's browsable in hypertext format at several Websites, the guide can also be downloaded as postscript files. The complete guide includes cast lists, each episode's *TV Guide* blurb, Nielsen ratings, and episode summaries. All the episodes are related in detail, even relaying the emotional tenor of each scene. For those truly obsessed there are TV log listings and teasers for each episode of the first six seasons. (Note: Though te Cal Tech site only lists the first four seasons, Mike Brown has promised to soon release a full seven-season program guide to TNG on his Website—Vidiot's.) ✓ **INTERNET** ...→*www* http://www.ugcs.caltech.edu:80/~werdna/sttng/raw/guide/ ...→*www* http://ringo.ssn.flinders.edu.au/vidiot/tng.html ...→*anon-ftp* quepasa.cs.tu-berlin.de→/pub/doc/movies+tv-series/StarTrek→Vidiots-TNG-Guide-NCSB-PSUK-6.04 ✓ **TFDN**→TFDN—Star Trek Facts→*Download a file:* STTNG-1.ZIP, STTNG-2.ZIP, STTNG-3.ZIP, STTNG-4.ZIP, STTNG-A.ZIP, STTNG-B.ZIP, STTNG-C.ZIP, STTNG-CT.ZIP, STTNG-CV.ZIP, STTNG-D.ZIP, STTNG-E.ZIP, STTNG-F.ZIP, STTNG-H.ZIP, STTNG-I.ZIP, STTNG-IN.ZIP, STTNG-J.ZIP, STTNG-M.ZIP, STTNG-N.ZIP, and STTNG-RM.ZIP

FAQs & lists

Star Trek: The Next Generation Series Information

The "general information" here begins with an essay on the history of TNG, and the Roddenberry dream. Very brief episode summaries, without cast or production information, provide a chronology for the series. The major aliens of the Trek universe are cataloged, and as an added bonus, linked to the episodes in which they appear—so get ready for BorgFest '95! ✓ **INTERNET**→*www* http://www.ee.surrey.ac.uk/Personal/STTNG/index.html

Star Trek TNG: The List of Lists

The ultimate nitpicking and trivia guide for *Next Generation* Trekkers. Episode-by-episode notes on inconsistencies, Treknicalities, and other "snafus" as well as huge character lists, plot summaries, international Trek information, species lists, and even a list of characters who've smoked on the series. Need a sample of the incredible wealth of information? Sure thing. "Changes from the pilot to the first season: Opening credits changed from actor's name only to actor and character name. Troi's outfit was changed from blue 'miniskirt' to non-uniform dress with rank pips removed." ✓ **INTERNET** ...→*www* http://www.cosy.sbg.ac.at/ftp/pub/trek/lists/tng.txt ...→*anon-ftp* ftp.cc.umanitoba.ca→/startrek/lol/lol.tng ...→*anon-ftp* quepasa.cs.tu-berlin.de→/pub/doc/movies→tv-series/StarTrek/lol_0494→tng0494txt ...→*anon-ftp* netcom.com→/pub/mholtz→tnglist_0494.Z

Star Trek: The Next Generation 24th-Century Guides

TNG FAQ List A short reference to TNG with a list of episodes (no description) and stardates, along with the colors of TNG Uniforms, a description of Gates McFadden's comings and goings, a history of the character Tasha Yar, the complete "Ode to Spot," and an explanation of cloaking devices and transwarp drives. ✓**AMERICA ONLINE**→*keyword* trek→MORE...→Star Trek Record Banks→Text/Other Files→Upld: 06/25/94→TEXT: TNG FAQ List (Filename: TNG-FAQ.TXT)

Nitpicking

Operation Snafu A list of episode-by-episode inconsistencies and discontinuities. In "Samaritan Snare," Wesley opens a communications channel and "says that Shuttle #2 is ready for takeoff. However, in the following scene, when the shuttle is seen powering up, there is a '01' on the outside of the shuttle." The nitpicking is never malicious, relying only on loving scrutiny of the show. In "Sins of the Father," the sound effects people "must have fallen asleep every time someone got slapped." ✓**INTERNET**→ *www* http://www.ugcs.caltech.edu/~werdna/sttng/snafus.html

TNG In-Jokes Sometimes inside jokes are hilarious, and sometimes they're just, well, inside. This document lists and analyzes the moments on *The Next Generation* where the cast and crew decide to have a little fun with the material. See if you spotted the veiled references to *Gilligan's Island* and *M*A*S*H*, the Japanese hidden in wall scroll, or the flux capacitor in the episode "Hollow Pursuits." ✓**INTERNET**→*www* http://www.ugcs.caltech.edu/~werdna/sttng/in-jokes.html

Plots

TNG Recurrent Behaviors Does watching TNG sometimes leave you saying: "Oh, no I can't believe they're dragging out that tired old thing again"? You are not alone. Compiled here is every instance that Picard has surrendered or violated the Prime Directive (9 times), every time Wesley has saved the day (10 times), and more. Each episode listed is linked to plot summaries, Lynch reviews, and ratings. ✓**INTERNET**→ *www* http://www.ugcs.caltech.edu/~werdna/sttng/misc2.html

Quotes

Next Generation Quote Quotes from seven seasons of *The Next Generation*. These lists sit between lists of quotes from the other TV series and the movies. ✓**INTERNET**→*www* http://www.cosy.sbg.ac.at/rec/startrek/Quotes.html

Random TNG quote Need some TNG to start your day? Try the Random Quote server—gems from seasons 1-6. Push the button to be rewarded with Worf sharing his view on sex with Riker (earth girls are "fragile") in "Justice." If you want to know more about the episode you click on the title to jump to the synopsis and review. Or ask for another quote and test your TNG recall. ✓**INTERNET**→ *www* http://www.ugcs.caltech.edu/htbin/werdna/fortune?sttng

Star Trek: The Next Generation Classic Quotes Quotes from 121 episodes of TNG beginning with "Encounter at Farpoint" (Picard: "Let's see what's out there.") and ending with "All Good Things." (Q: "Goodbye Jean-Luc. You had such potential, but then all things must come to an end.") ✓**AMERICA ONLINE**→*key-*

STARNOTES

"In 'The Drumhead,' it is recorded that Picard violated the Prime Directive nine times while in command of the Enterprise. These are believed to be [some of] the episodes containing these violations:

'Justice.' In order to save Wesley from the death penalty for (accidentally) violating one of the Edo laws.

'Angel One.' The crew barely managed to save the survivors of a Federation ship from death for trying to change the society of Angel One.

'Pen Pals.' Data communicates with a girl whose planet was slowly self-destructing.

'Up The Long Ladder.' Picard essentially forced the clone race to live and breed with the Bringloidi, despite the strong resistance of the clone race and the fact that this would completely destroy the non-sexual nature of the clone race.

'First Contact.' The Enterprise contacts a planet in order to rescue Commander Riker."

—from **TNG Recurrent Behavior**

word trek→MORE...→Star Trek Record Banks→Text/Other Files→ Upld: 12/06/94→TEXT: Star Trek: TNG Quotes V1.2 (Filename: NGQUOTES.TXT)

Star Trek: TNG Quotes Episode by episode (from "Encounter at Farpoint" to the seventh season episode of "Journey's End") listing of interesting quotes and brief scene transcripts. ✓**COMPUSERVE**→ *go* sfmedia→Libraries→*Search by file number:* NGQUOT. TXT

TNG Quote File "Let's make sure history never forgets the name *Enterprise.*" A file full of quotes from TNG. ✓**COMPUSERVE**→*go* sfmedia→ Libraries→*Search by file name:* ngquot.txt

---

Timothy Lynch Next Generation Episode Reviews Written by Timothy Lynch, a devoted *Next Generation* fan and large presence on the rec.arts.startrek* newsgroups, these reviews (which cover the second through the seventh seasons) offer an extensive plot summary and a large dose of unabashed enthusiasm for the show. In the articles, Lynch speculates about what he thinks is going to happen, lets you know what stories made him feel good (or lousy), and offers his opinion about which actresses make particularly good Klingons. For a trip back through the *Next Generation* years, Lynch can be fun reading. And, the detail in Lynch's summaries are fodder for any trivia buff. The Website and the gopher site offer search engines to scan reviews for specific references. ✓**INTERNET** ...→*anon-ftp* ftp.coe.montana.edu →/pub/mirrors/.startrek/Tim_ Lynch_stuff ...→*anon-ftp* ftp.alumni. caltech.edu→/pub/tlynch ...→*gopher* chop.isca.uiowa.edu:8338 →General Information→Star Trek Reviews ...→ *www* http://www.

ugcs.caltech.edu:80/~werdna/ sttng/tlynch/

TNG Episode Ratings The power of the WWW—19,787 votes to date, 111.461 average per episode. And the verdict thus far? "Best of Both Worlds" triumphs with 9.3 out of 10, "Shades of Gray" scrapes the bottom with 3.1. Production number and stardate are also included. ✓**INTERNET**→ *www* http://www.ugcs.caltech. edu/~werdna/sttng/ratings

---

TNG Rate Results The best is worth waiting for, or, at least, that's the consensus so far of Usenet readers who've cast ballots rating *The Next Generation* episodes. "All Good Things" finishes at the top of the list with a .940 rating (each episode is given a rating between zero and one according to an average of the ballots cast by Usenet readers.) ✓**INTERNET** →*anon-ftp* rtfm.mit.edu→/pub/ usenet-by-hierarchy/rec/arts/ startrek/misc→TREK_RATE_ results_(TNG)

Trekker TNG Reviews Sarcastic reviews and parodies of several *The Next Generation* episodes written by Phil Kernick and organized by season. ✓**INTERNET**→*www* http: //ringo.ssn.flinders.edu.au:80/ trekker/tng/

The IMHO End-of-TNG Blowout "It's time to take stock of what it all meant (if anything). So let loose. The Klingons are in the mosh pit, we've got fried tribbles shimmering on the hibachi, there's the 'Dunk-A-Worf' booth, and the band is starting up the TNG Rag to accompany our seven-year grand tour. Grab your partner." *Star Trek* fan Ted Brengle reviewed every episode of TNG during the show's seven-year run (they're individually available in the TFDN

Star Trek Facts/Info library). This review is his final curtain call, and with it, he not only takes readers on a journey back through the voyages of Picard's *Enterprise*, but also takes his share of parting shots at Rick Berman and Paramount. ✓**TFDN**→TFDN—Star Trek Facts→ *Download a file:* BLOWOUT.ZIP

Paramount Press Kit TNG plots, guests stars, milestones, new planets, races, and starships. Each season is summarized and defined with bits of trivia. Did you know that in the seventh season Gates McFadden became the first female cast member of *Star Trek* to direct an episode? ✓**TFDN**→TFDN Press Release Files→*Download a file:* PPK_TNGT.ZIP

Picard in his Ready Room—downloaded from ftp.cis.ksu.edu

Generations

The seventh of the Trek film series was a fan's wet dream—the two *Enterprise* crews

joining forces to save the universe from evil. And *Star Trek: Generations* was also a boon for the Net, with dozens of sites devoted to the film. Begin the tour at the **Generations FAQ**, which offers a chatty history of the film's development, and then move on to multi-media teasers like **Collide** and **Eternity**. And finally, if you've seen the film but can't remember all the lines, download the entire **Generations Script** and conduct practice readings of Kirk's death scene in the privacy of your very own spaceship. "Oh, my…"

On the Net

Across the board

Basic Information about Generations A plot summary and credit are accompanied by reviews of the most recent *Trek* film. *The San Francisco Chronicle* finds that all the vibrancy comes from Captain Kirk, and the *Eye Weekly of Toronto* finds that the mix of two casts resulted in unfermented grape juice. Add your own opinion by rating the film 1-10. Jump to other Trek and sci-fi films, or cast and crew filmographies. ✓**IN-TERNET**→*www* http://www.msstate.edu/Movies/→*Search the database for this movie title:* Generations

Generations (TNG Movie) This board grew so fat so fast, it almost surpassed the TNG board in size. In the months leading up to the movie, rumors flew across the board generating anxiety and anticipation among fans. Raging at the thought that Paramount was intending to destroy the *Enterprise-D*, fans created the Death of the Enterprise folder to commiserate. Following the release of *Generations* in November 1994, fans started submitting their reviews—hundreds of them.

While the movie may no longer be showing in theaters, in the Star Trek VII Redone folder members are still trying to troubleshoot the plot. Should Data have been more sensitive and less humorous, perhaps murmuring Tasha's name when he awoke with the emotion chip installed? Why couldn't Guinan and Uhura have met? Why do *Enterprises* just out of dry

Movie poster—downloaded from CompuServe's Sci-Fi Media Forum

dock keep failing? And, really, those gullible Klingon sisters give Klingons a bad name. The Trivia Notes folder and the Nitpickers Guide to Generations folder store several hundred messages that identify flaws and inconsistencies in the movie. The incompetent Captain Harriman (shown in the first scenes of the movie) also has a fan club here. Says one fan, "Harriman was just a bit too young and a bit too goobery to make a realistic captain of any starship. But you know, I kind of liked the lunkhead." ✓**AMERICA ONLINE**→*keyword* trek→Star Trek Message Boards→ The Promenade→Generations (TNG Movie)

Star Trek: Generations You've heard of the generation gap? How about the *Generations* Gap? In category 2—"He's Jim, Dead"—the newsgroup regulars engage in great lamentation over the passing of a hero. Well, except for those who express immense relief that Kirk and his raging emotions and toupee are gone from the universe. *Next Generation* fans also shoulder up against classic Trek partisans, each insisting they have better characters, Federation principles, or uniforms. Specifics are also addressed, and plot holes filled. ✓**GENIE**→*keyword* sfrt2→SFRT2 Bulletin Board→set 26→read 2 *or* 3 *or* 7

History & rumor

Generations FAQ Traces Net and media rumors (in detail) about the movie *Generations*— from 1992 when Shatner announced at a convention that he had submitted a script idea, to the January 1994 reports that Kirk would die and that Spock would not be in the movie, to the March 1994 leak of the script, to events shortly before *Generations* opened in November 1994. This FAQ is a

fascinating historical document— illustrating the fervent Trek rumor mill in action. Early chatter had it that Shatner tried to shop a script that had him winning a much younger woman (what a surprise!). *The Daily Mail* reported several months later that Stewart and Shatner were in mortal battle over top billing. The gossip continued fast and furious right up to the posting of several plot summaries which appear to have come from script drafts obtained by stealth. Now that the movie is out, there are no spoilers, but this document is valuable for its testament to Trek obsession. ✓**INTERNET**→*www* http://web.city.ac.uk/~cc103/new film.html ✓**COMPUSERVE**→*go* sfmedia →Libraries→*Search by file name:* stmovf.txt

Pics & sounds

Data: "It is revolting." A soundclip of Data after experiencing a drink he hated: "Oh, yes! I hate this! It is revolting!" Guinan then asks: "More?" Responds Data: "Please." ✓**COMPUSERVE**→*go* sfmedia→Libraries→*Search by file name:* REVOLT.ZIP

Data: "Magnetic Personality" Soundclip of Data, equipped with emotions: "You could say I have a magnetic personality—hahahaha—Humor! I love it!" ✓**COMPUSERVE**→*go* sfmedia→Libraries→*Search by file name:* MAGNET.ZIP

"Sounds Like Fun" Exchange as Picard attempts to convince Kirk to join him in defeating Soran. Says Kirk: "I take it the odds are against us and the situation is grim." Says Picard: "You could say that." Responds Kirk: "Sounds like fun." ✓**COMPUSERVE**→*go* sfmedia→Libraries→*Search by file name:* FUN.ZIP

Teaser The movie's teaser. ✓**COMPUSERVE**→*go* sfmedia→Libraries→ *Search by file name:* GEN.ZIP

Pictures

Generations Pictures Publicity shots from the movie *Generations*, including a close-up of Guinan, the three crew members from TOS being interviewed, Kirk alone, a pensive Picard, a worried Riker, Picard in civilian clothes, and the evil Soran. AOL's and eWorld's collections are the largest, with about 25 pictures, while CompuServe's is the smallest. ✓**AMERICA ONLINE**→*keyword* hollywood online→Pictures & Sounds→ Star Trek Generations ✓**COMPUSERVE**→*go* showbiz→Libraries→ *Search by keyword:* generations ✓**DELPHI**→*go* ent holly more sta →search→gif→read ✓**EWORLD**→ hollywood→Movie Photos/Publicity Stills→Star Trek Generations

Picard & Data Picture of Data and Picard in *Generations*. ✓**PVG** *dial* 513-233-7993→<your username>→<your password>→F→ *Download a file:* PVGEN006.GIF

Picard & Kirk on Horseback Picture of Picard and Kirk on horseback. ✓**PVG** *dial* 513-233-7993→<your username>→<your password>→F→*Download a file:* PVGEN001.GIF

Sea Captain Picard Picture of Captain Picard as a sea vessel captain. ✓**PVG** *dial* 513-233-7993→ <your username>→<your password>→F→*Download a file:* PVGEN004.GIF

Shatner & Stewart Review Script William Shatner and Patrick Stewart looking at the *Generations* script. ✓**PVG** *dial* 513-233-7993→<your username>→ <your password>→F→*Download a*

file: PVGEN002.GIF

Star Trek: Generations Image Page Browse a photo album of close to sixty *Generations* images (Graphical Web browser required). Whether you're interested in an anxious looking Guinan, a laughing Data, a crazed Soran, or a crashing *Enterprise*, just click on the 24-bit color image for a 620x364 picture. At the bottom of the picture page are links to information about and pictures of Paramount *Star Trek* products tied to the movie and the movie poster in JPEG and GIF format, as well as a reproduction of the full *Foxtrot* comic strip about the movie. ✓ **INTERNET**→ *www* http://www.ftms.com:80/st-ds9/gen_img.html

Promotions

Collide "Where past and future collide..." Movie teaser setting up a space disaster that imperils 230 million people. The first file at each site is for Windows and the second for Macs. ✓ **AMERICA ONLINE**→ *keyword* hollywood online→ Multimedia→Star Trek Generations →Upld: 10/28/94→WIN: 'Collide' AVI Clip (Filename: COLLID.AVI) *or* MAC: 'Collide' Quicktime Clip (Filename: Collide Quicktime) ✓ **DELPHI**→ *go* ent holly more star →search→video→read→ 1 *or* 4 ✓ **COMPUSERVE**→ *go* showbiz→Libraries→*Search by file name:* COLLID.AVI *or* COLLID.MQT ✓ **EWORLD** →hollywood→QuickTime Movie Clips→Star Trek Generations→Sent: 10/27→'Collide' Quicktime Clip (Filename: Collide Quicktime) ✓ **PRODIGY**→ *jump* star trek downloads→Downloads→Collide.AVI Clip

Eternity "I have an appointment with eternity and I don't want to be late."—Soran. The first file at each site is for Windows and the

second for Macintoshes. ✓ **AMERICA ONLINE**→ *keyword* hollywood online →Multimedia→Star Trek Generations →Upld: 10/28/94→WIN: 'Eternity' AVI Clip (Filename: ETRNTY.AVI) *or* MAC: Eternity' Quicktime Clip (Filename: Eternity Quicktime) ✓ **DELPHI**→ *go* ent holly more star→ search→ video→read→3 *or* 5 ✓ **COMPUSERVE**→ *go* showbiz→Libraries→ *Search by file name:* ETRNTY.AVI *or* ETERN.MQT ✓ **EWORLD**→hollywood →QuickTime Movie Clips→Star Trek Generations→Sent: 10/27→'Eternity' Quicktime Clip (Filename: Eternity Quicktime) ✓ **PRODIGY**→ *jump* star trek downloads→Downloads→ Eternity.AVI Clip

Help "Why would he destroy a star? I need help..." It's Kirk and Picard to the rescue. The first file at each site is for Windows and the second for Macs. ✓ **AMERICA ONLINE**→ *keyword* hollywood online →Multimedia→Star Trek Generations→Upld: 10/28/94→WIN: 'Help' AVI Clip (Filename: HELP. AVI) *or* MAC: 'Help' Quicktime Clip (Filename: Help Quicktime) ✓ **DELPHI**→ *go* ent holly more star→ search→video→read→2 *or* 6 ✓ **COMPUSERVE**→ *go* showbiz→Libraries→ *Search by file name:* HELP.AVI *or* HELP.MQT ✓ **EWORLD** →hollywood→QuickTime Movie Clips→Star Trek Generations→Sent: 10/27→Help' Quicktime Clip (Filename: Help Quicktime) ✓ **PRODIGY** →*jump* star trek downloads→Downloads→Help.AVI Clip

MPEG A short but high-quality clip from the movie. ✓ **INTERNET**→ *www* http://www.cosy.sbg.ac.at/ftp/pub/trek/films/tng.mpeg

Star Trek Generations Magazine Electronic promotional magazine with pictures and a dropdown menu table-of-contents. Features filmographies for *Generations* stars, biographies on the di-

rectors and producers, and a description of the movie. ✓ **AMERICA ONLINE**→ *keyword* hollywood online →Multimedia→Star Trek Generations→Upld: 10/29/94→MAC: 'Star Trek Generations Mag ✓ **DELPHI**→ *go* ent holly more star→ search→magazine→read ✓ **COMPUSERVE**→ *go* showbiz→Libraries→ *Search by file name:* trek.mag ✓ **EWORLD**→hollywood→Interactive Multimedia Kits→Star Trek Generations→Sent: 10/28→Star Trek Generations Magazine (Filename: Star Trek Generations Mag.sea)

Star Trek Interactive Take a tour of the *Enterprise*. Created by Paramount to publicize the movie *Generations*, the demo begins and ends with the *Next Generation* theme song. You'll begin at the turbo lift, where you can choose to visit Ten-forward, the Transporter room, the Battle Bridge, the Shuttle Bay, or the Holodeck. Each room offers new information about the movie *Generations*, *Star Trek*, and the characters. The Transporter room is a must see! Beam in your favorite characters. Windows users should download the first file; Mac users, the second. ✓ **AMERICA ONLINE**→ *keyword* hollywood online→Multimedia→ Star Trek Generations→Upld: 11/01/94→WIN: Star Trek Interactive (Filename: TREKZ.EXE) *or* MAC: Star Trek Interactive (Filename: Star Trek Interactive.sea) ✓ **DELPHI**→ *go* ent holly more star→ search→interactive→read→1 *or* 2 ✓ **COMPUSERVE**→ *go* showbiz→ Libraries→ *Search by file name:* TREKZ.EXE *or* 94STRK.MAG ✓ **EWORLD**→hollywood→Interactive Multimedia Kits→Star Trek Generations→Sent: 11/01→MAC: Star Trek Generations MM Kit (Filename: Star Trek Interactive.sea) ✓ **PRODIGY** →*jump* star trek downloads→ Downloads→Star Trek Multimedia

Quotes

Generations Quotes Famous lines from the movie for those who just can't get enough of the Kirk-Picard matchup. Okay. Here's one: "I have an appointment with eternity and I don't want to be late." ✓INTERNET→www http://www.maths.tcd.ie/hyplan/s/sj/stquotes.html

Reviews

A Nitpicker's FAQ for Star Trek: Generations Admiral Wombat's report on the inconsistencies and flaws in the movie *Generations*. This FAQ mimmicks the style used in author Phil Farrand's *Nitpicker's Guides*. Now for the test. Did you notice that "shortly after arriving at the Nexus, Ensign Sulu reports that the starboard, or right, vessel's hull is collapsing. On the viewscreen, the port, or left, ship explodes." ✓INTERNET→anon-ftp quepasa.cs.tu-berlin.de→pub/doc/movies+tv-series/StarTrek/FAQs→Generations-Nitpicker_s.FAQ.gz

Crew through Time The magazine *Entertainment Weekly* gave the movie *Generations* a "B": the full set of comments that accompanied this respectable grade are available here. ✓INTERNET→www http://www.timeinc.com/ew/941125/movies/generations.html

Generations Review Timothy Lynch, who for the past few years has posted episode-by-episode reviews of *Star Trek* shows to the rec.arts.startrek* hierarchy, wasn't overly impressed with the movie *Generations*, but that didn't stop him from writing a long plot summary and review. If you left the movie to use the bathroom, don't worry. Lynch is likely to have described it in excruciating detail—

the movie, of course. ✓INTERNET …→gopher chop.isca.uiowa.edu 8338→General Information→Star Trek Reviews→Star Trek: Generations Review→Star Trek Generations Review …→anon-ftp ftp.alumni.cal-tech.edu→/pub/tlynch/misc→generations.rev

IMHO Star Trek: Generations Review Ted Brengle's review of the movie *Generations*. Brengle is a Trek fan who has written more than a hundred reviews of Trek episodes. ✓TFDN→TFDN—Trek Fact Files→st7.zip

Satire

Star Trek Song Song about the final days of the *Enterprise-D* to the tune of Don McLean's "American Pie." ✓COMPUSERVE→go sfmedia→Libraries→Search by file name: SWANSO.TXT

Script

The Generations Script Here it is—the infamous script of the movie *Generations* that circulated on the Net before the movie was released. No guarantee that it'll be here for long or that it's accurate on a line by line basis, but it certainly includes some familiar scenes. ✓INTERNET→www http://www.unisuper.com.au/strek/generati.htm

Sequel

The Next Movie et al. Discussion about the next movie has already infiltrated the *Generations* folder (look for the folder to break away into its own message board in the upcoming months), with hundreds of messages speculating on whether Leonard Nimoy will direct, what the movies will be like without Kirk, and what the next plot will be like. One fan, disgrun-

tled with *Generations*, writes: "In fact, I'm writing an outline of just such a Romulan-related/Bev and Jean-Luc/big battle in space script right now. Of course, no one at Paramount will ever read it, but for me it will be a confidence-booster. After all, with the horrible job they did with *Generations*, why the hell can't a schmuck like me write something as good as one of those high-paid Hollywood writers?" ✓AMERICA ONLINE→keyword trek→Star Trek Message Boards →The Promenade→Generations (TNG Movie)→The Next Movie *and* Nimoy in ST8 *and* guinan in star trek 8?

STARNOTES

"Does it bother anyone that when Kirk is in the Nexus he is using a TOASTER? He's in the 23rd century, and people still use toasters, one of the worst designs of the 20th century? I thought that Star Trek was supposed to show a vision of the future that was positive. Also why was Picard living with a 19th century English family in the Nexus? I'm not a big fan of TNG, so maybe there's an explanation for this. And why did his wife offer him a cup of tea when he was drinking a glass of wine?"

—from **AOL's Generations—Trivia Notes**

PART 5

DEEP SPACE NINE

Episode guide

This is a list of all episodes of *Star Trek: Deep Space Nine* through "Past Tense" listed in order of airdate, along with relevant Net sites. Addresses are sometimes given in shorthand (*<address x>*); instructions on constructing full addresses appear in the FAQ (page 20), and on the key in the back of the book.

Season 1

Emissary

Episode #1 & 2
Teleplay: Michael Piller
Story: Rick Berman, Michael Piller
Director: David Carson
Stardate: 46379.1

Summary: Commander Sisko takes over DS9 and finds the wormhole. Major conflicts are introduced through flashbacks to the Federation's battles with the Borg and the death of Sisko's wife. The history of the Cardassian/Bajoran conflict is described.

Archived Discussion of "Emissary" A series intro and fans' opinions on special effects, hairstyles, uniforms. ✓ **GENIE**→*keyword* <address 22>→*Download a file: 45*

Tim Lynch Review ✓ **INTERNET** ...→*anon-ftp* <address 24>→ emissary.rev ...→*gopher* <address 27>→Emissary

Trekker Review ✓ **INTERNET**→ *www* <address 30>emissary.html

1701-D Docked at DS9 Docked *Enterprise NCC-1701-D.* ✓ **COMPU-**

Benjamin and Jake—downloaded from Perfect Vision Graphics BBS.

SERVE→*go* sfmedia→Libraries→ *Search by file name:* ENTDOC.GIF

Battle of Wolf 359 Locutus at the Battle of Wolf. ✓ **COMPUSERVE** →*go* sfmedia→Libraries→*Search by file name:* BORGBA.GIF

"The Emissary" Scenes Twenty scenes from the episode. ✓ **PVG** *dial* 513-233-7993→<your username> →<your password>→F→*Download a file:* DS001_Q1.GIF, DS001_Q2.GIF, DS001_Q3.GIF, DS001_Q4.GIF, *and* DS002_S4.GIF

A Man Alone

Episode #3
Teleplay: Michael Piller
Story: Gerald Sanford, Michael Piller
Director: Paul Lynch
Stardate: 46421.5

Summary: Odo has a violent encounter with a man from his past who is later found dead. The crew tries to clear him of murder charges. Keiko O'Brien opens a school.

Archived Discussion of "A Man Alone" Parallels between Bajoran and Islamic societies— from architecture to religion. ✓ **GE-NIE**→*keyword* <address 22>→ *Download a file: 453*

Tim Lynch Review ✓ **INTERNET** ...→*anon-ftp* <address 24>→ manalone.rev ...→*gopher* <address 27>→A Man Alone ✓ **TFDN**→<address 23>→manalone.rev

Trekker Review ✓ **INTERNET**→ *www* <address 30>a_man_alone. html

Past Prologue

Episode #4
Writer: Kathryn Powers
Director: Winrich Kolbe

Summary: Tahna Loss, a member of the Bajoran terrorist group Kohn-ma, plans to destroy the wormhole and render Bajor and DS9 useless. Kira is torn between her loyalties.

Archived Discussion of "Past Prologue" What are the properties of the wormhole? Must Odo conserve mass when he changes shape? ✓ **GENIE** →*keyword* <address 22>→*Download a file: 454*

Tim Lynch Review ✓ **INTERNET** ...→*anon-ftp* <address 24>→ prologue.rev ...→*gopher* <address 27>→Past Prologue ✓ **TFDN**→<address 23>→prologue.rev

Trekker Review ✓ **INTERNET**→ *www* <address 30>past_prologue. html

Babel

Episode #5
Teleplay: Michael McGreevey & Naren Shankar
Story: Sally Caves & Ira Steven Behr
Director: Paul Lynch
Stardate: 46423.7

Summary: Everyone on the space station is infected with a virus which leaves the crew speechless. The doctors race against time to find a cure before the disease becomes life-threatening.

Archived Discussion of "Babel" How is it that Federation members always seem able to communicate with newly encountered races—Babel fish in their ears? Discussion involved a comparison of the actual symptoms of aphasia and those shown in the episode. ✓ **GENIE**→*keyword* <address 22>→*Download a file: 455*

Tim Lynch Review ✓ **INTERNET** ...→*anon-ftp* <address 24>→ babel.rev ...→*gopher* <address 27>→*Babel* ✓ **TFDN**→<address 23>→*babel.rev*

Trekker Review ✓ **INTERNET**→ *www* <address 30>*babel.html*

"Babel" Scenes Several scenes from the episode, including one with Dr. Bashir and another with Commander Sisko. ✓ **PVG** *dial* 513-233-7993→<your username>→ <your password>→F→*Download a file:* DS005-S2.GIF *and* DS005-Q1.GIF *and* DS005-S3.GIF

Captive Pursuit

Episode #6
Teleplay: Jill Sherman Donner, Michael Piller
Story: Jill Sherman Donner
Director: Corey Allen

Summary: The station becomes a temporary refuge for a Gamma Quadrant resident who was raised to be prey in his culture's traditional hunt.

Archived Discussion of "Captive Pursuit" Should the Prime Directive be rethought in such a situation? Is the hunt a cultural tradition or cruel persecution? What if the quarry asks for help? Is Quark capable of becoming the traditional bartender/shrink? ✓ **GENIE**→*keyword* <address 22>→ *Download a file: 456*

Tim Lynch Review ✓ **INTERNET** ...→*anon-ftp* <address 24>→ captive.rev ...→*gopher* <address 27>→*Captive Pursuit* ✓ **TFDN**→<address 23>→*pursuit.rev*

Trekker Review ✓ **INTERNET**→ *www* <address 30>*captive_pursuit. html*

Q-Less

Episode #7
Teleplay: Robert Hewitt Wolfe
Story: Hannah Louise Shearer
Director: Paul Lynch
Stardate: 46531.2

Summary: A mission to Gamma Quadrant locates the archeologist Vash, last seen running off for adventures with Q in TNG "Qpid." Q follows her to DS9, attempting to convince her to rejoin his rambles. She, however, has no such wish and begins selling off her archeological finds through Quark, one of which houses a life-form that is creating a dangerous gravitron field.

Tim Lynch Review ✓ **INTERNET** ...→*anon-ftp* <address 24>→ qless.rev ...→*gopher* <address 27> →*Q-Less* ✓ **TFDN**→<address 23> →*qless.rev*

Trekker Review ✓ **INTERNET**→ *www* <address 30>*q_less.html*

Archived Discussion of "Q-Less" Good explanation of Q's background, for beginners, and comparison of Picard's and Sisko's

"Then there's Opaka. I don't know why, exactly, but I really found myself liking her a lot. So does everyone else, clearly—Sisko and Kira were almost *competing* for her attentions on the runabout. She's like Guinan in some ways— her calm acceptance of nearly everything, for one. While her main purpose was to bring out Kira's healing, she was interesting in her own right, and I'll miss seeing her in future episodes. I do have to wonder, though, where all this is going to lead. Opaka's loss is probably not going to be taken lightly by Bajor, and the combination of this plus the revelation about the orbs in 'Emissary' may lead to a major spiritual crisis there. I'll be intrigued to see where it goes. Some particular moments are worth watching for, including Opaka's calm anticipation of her own death (among the more striking elements of the episode."

—from **Tim Lynch's review of the episode "Battle Lines"**

reactions to Q. ✓GENIE→keyword <address 22>→Download a file: 457

Dax

Episode #8

Teleplay:	D. C. Fontana, Peter Allan Fields
Story:	Peter Allan Fields
Director:	David Carson
Stardate:	46910.1

Summary: Curzon Dax—Trill host prior to Jadzia Dax—is accused of the murder of his old friend Enina Tandro. Two problems: Curzon is dead and Jadzia refuses to defend herself. Sisko and Odo attempt to prove that Curzon Dax and Jadzia Dax are different entities, although inhabited by the same Trill, while Jadzia remains silent about an affair Curzon had with the Tandro's wife.

Archived Discussion of "Dax" Which should have primacy in a case against a Starfleet officer on DS9—Federation law, Trill law, or Bajoran law? And, as always when Trills are the focus of an episode, general Trill questions come up: e.g., are there ever newborn Trills that grow up in child hosts, or are they born mature and immediately enter adults? ✓GENIE → keyword <address 22>→Download a file: 458

Tim Lynch Review ✓INTERNET ...→anon-ftp <address 24>→ dax.rev ...→gopher <address 27>→ Dax ✓TFDN→<address 23>→dax.rev

The Passenger

Episode #9

Teleplay:	Morgan Gendel, Robert Hewitt Wolfe, Michael Piller
Story:	Morgan Gendel
Director:	Paul Lynch

Summary: After years of hunting, Ty Kajada is about to capture a scientific criminal, who is on his way to DS9 to steal diridium. When the felon dies in a fire aboard his ship, she has trouble believing he is really dead, although Dr. Bashir insists it is so.

Archived Discussion of "The Passenger" General chat about Dax. What does 300 years of experience mean for Dax? Does she react using that experience or the way her current, 28-year-old host might? ✓GENIE→keyword <address 22>→Download a file: 459

Tim Lynch Review ✓INTERNET ...→anon-ftp <address 24>→ passenger.rev ...→gopher <address 27>→The Passenger ✓TFDN→<address 23>→passenger.rev

Trekker Review ✓INTERNET→ www <address 30>the_passenger. html

Move Along Home

Episode #10

Teleplay:	Frederick Rappaport, Lisa Rich, Jeanne Carrigan-Fauci
Story:	Michael Piller
Director:	David Carson

Summary: Falow, the leader of the Wadi, takes exception to being cheated by Quark. He creates a real-life game to challenge the Ferengi, with real-life players—Sisko, Kira, Bashir, and Dax—but noone knows the rules.

Archived Discussion of "Move Along Home" Does Quark's real concern for Sisko, Kyra, Bashir, and Dax suggest a more sensitive nature than usual for a Ferengi? And what about those new aliens—the Wadis? "Cute, harmless...more long-hair bikers with forehead tattoos from the Gamma Quadrant." ✓GENIE→ keyword <address 22>→Download a file: 460

Tim Lynch Review ✓INTERNET ...→anon-ftp <address 24>→ movealong.rev ...→gopher <address 27>→Move Along Home ✓TFDN→<address 23>→movalhom. rev

Trekker Review ✓INTERNET→ www <address 30>move_along_ home.html

The Nagus

Episode #11

Teleplay:	Ira Steven Behr
Story:	David Livingston
Director:	David Livingston
Guest Star:	Wallace Shawn

Summary: Zek, the Ferengi Grand Nagus, comes to a trade conference to initiate new profit-making enterprises in the Gamma Quadrant. Ailing, he feels he cannot continue his duties and selects Quark as his successor, causing great consternation among other Ferengis, especially his son, Krax.

Archived Discussion of "The Nagus" Does the Ferengi lifestyle bear any resemblance to our century and its competitive business culture? And isn't the Grand Nagus reminiscent of the Godfather? ✓GENIE→keyword <address 22>→Download a file: 462

Tim Lynch Review ✓INTERNET ...→anon-ftp <address 24>→ nagus.rev ...→gopher <address 27>→The Nagus ✓TFDN→<address 23>→nagus.rev

Trekker Review ✓INTERNET→ www <address 30>the_nagus.html

The New Nagus GIF of Quark preparing to be the new Nagus.

✓**PVG** *dial* 513-233-7993→<your username>→<your password>→F→*Download a file:* PVQUARK2.GIF

Vortex

Episode #12
Writer: Sam Rolfe
Director: Winrich Kolbe

Summary: Odo arrests a thief from the Gamma Quadrant who tantalizes him with stories of other changelings and a necklace that provides a clue to Odo's origins.

Archived Discussion of "Vortex" Is Odo getting a new look? Does Odo have to conserve mass when he shape shifts? Does the improbability of Odo give the writers a license to be inconsistent? ✓**GENIE**→*keyword* <address 22>→*Download a file:* 463

Tim Lynch Review ✓**INTERNET** ...→*anon-ftp* <address 24>→vortex.rev ...→*gopher* <address 27>→Vortex ✓**TFDN**→<address 23>→vortex.rev

Trekker Review ✓**INTERNET**→*www* <address 30>vortex.html

"Vortex" Scenes Twelve scenes from the episode, including Kira and Dax, Odo, and the fugitive Croden. ✓**PVG** *dial* 513-233-7993 →<your username>→<your password>→F→*Download a file:* DS012-Q1.GIF *and* DS012-Q2.GIF *and* DS012-Q3.GIF

Battle Lines

Episode #13
Teleplay: Richard Danus & Evan
            Carlos Somers
Story: Hilary Bader
Director: Paul Lynch

Summary: The spiritual leader of the Bajorans, Kai Opaka, visits Deep Space 9. While on a tour of the wormhole, she is killed and resurrected on a moon where two races carry on eternal warfare. The microbes which restored Opaka's life prevent her from ever leaving the warring planet, to which she hopes to bring peace.

Archived Discussion of "Battle Lines" What is an acceptable level of violence for *Star Trek*? Is bringing a character back to life cheesy emotional manipulation, on par with that found in *ET* and *Lady and the Tramp*? What is behind Kira's increasing tendency to cry—downplaying the strong woman? ✓**GENIE**→*keyword* <address 22>→*Download a file:* 464

Tim Lynch Review ✓**INTERNET** ...→*anon-ftp* <address 24>→battle.rev ...→*gopher* <address 27>→Battle Lines ✓**TFDN**→<address 23>→batline.rev

Trekker Review ✓**INTERNET**→*www* <address 30>battle_lines.html

Kai Picture of Kai Opaka. ✓**PVG** *dial* 513-233-7993→<your user name>→<your password>→F→*Download a file:* DS013-S1.GIF

Kai Opaka—downloaded from Perfect Vision Graphics BBS

Storyteller

Episode #14
Teleplay: Kurt Michael Bensmiller
            & Ira Steven Behr

Story: Kurt Michael Bensmiller
Director: David Livingston
Stardate: 46729.1

Summary: Sisko is asked to mediate when the diversion of a river by the Cardassians leads to a Bajoran territory dispute. Jake and Nog ally themselves with Varis Sul, the child leader of one faction. Meanwhile, a dying spiritual leader appoints O'Brien as his successor, leaving him with the problem of chasing away a dangerous storm threatening the planet.

Archived Discussion of "Storyteller" Trek tech talk alert: is there an explanation, in our universe, for warp drive? Viewers thrill to their first glimpse of Odo's bucket. Insider explanations of the economics of syndication, ratings, and Paramount Productions. ✓**GENIE**→*keyword* <address 22>→*Download a file:* 465

Tim Lynch Review ✓**INTERNET** ...→*anon-ftp* <address 24>→storyteller.rev ...→*gopher* <address 27>→The Storyteller ✓**TFDN**→<address 23>→strytllr.rev

Progress

Episode #15
Writer: Peter Allan Fields
Director: Les Landau
Stardate: 46844.3
Guest Star: Brian Keith

Summary: Kira tries to evict a Bajoran farmer from the moon Heraddo, which will soon be awash in toxic gases, but meets with resistance from the man, who doesn't want to leave his land.

Archived Discussion of "Progress" Is this another Trek analogy to environmental devastation? Are episodes with a message too talky? Does Brian Keith actually chew scenery? ✓ **GENIE**→ *keyword* <address 22>→*Download a file:* 466

Tim Lynch Review ✓ **INTERNET** ...→*anon-ftp* <address 24>→ progress.rev ...→*gopher* <address 27>→Progress ✓ **TFDN**→ <address 23>→progress.rev

Jake & Nog Picture of Jake and Nog. ✓ **PVG** *dial* 513-233-7993→ <your username>→<your password>→F→ *Download a file:* JAKENOG.GIF

If Wishes Were Horses

Episode #16
Teleplay: Nell McCue Crawford,
              William L. Crawford,
              Michael Piller
Story: Nell McCue Crawford,
              William L. Crawford
Director: Robert Legato
Stardate: 46853.2

Summary: In an attempt to study human behavior, aliens from the Gamma Quadrant enable imaginations to run wild and wishes to come true on the station. Rumpelstiltskin starts things off in O'Brien's quarters, while Jake and Ben meet their baseball idols.

Archived Discussion of "If Wishes Were Horses" What's the future of baseball—baseball in the 24th century, in particular? The discussion included ruminations on the sexual tension between Bashir and Dax when the characters were "under the influence." ✓ **GENIE**→*keyword* <address 22>→*Download a file:* 467

Tim Lynch Review ✓ **INTERNET** ...→*anon-ftp* <address 24>→ wishes.rev ...→*gopher* <address 27>→If Wishes Were Horses ✓ **TFDN**

→<address 23>→wishes.rev

Scenes from "If Wishes Were Horses" Several multi-picture files with episode scenes, including Rumpelstilskin and Jake with a baseball glove. ✓ **PVG** *dial* 513-233-7993→<your username>→<your password>→F→*Download a file:* DS016-Q1.GIF and DS016-Q2. GIF and DS016-Q3.GIF and DS016-Q4.GIF and DS016-Q5.GIF and DS016-S1.GIF and DS016-S2. GIF and DS016-S5.GIF

The Forsaken

Episode #17
Teleplay: Don Carlos Dunaway,
              Michael Piller
Story: Jim Trombetta
Director: Les Landau
Stardate: 46925.1

Summary: A mysterious Gamma Quadrant probe causes problems as a "lost puppy" form takes over the station's computer. Lwaxana conceives a fondness for Odo after he retrieves a piece of stolen jewelry. To Odo's horror, the two are trapped in an elevator past the time he can hold his shape.

Archived Discussion of "The Forsaken" Can you imagine anyone in the entire universe you would less like to be stuck in an elevator with than Lwaxana? ✓ **GENIE**→*keyword* <address 22>→ *Download a file:* 468

Tim Lynch Review ✓ **INTERNET** ...→*anon-ftp* <address 24>→ forsaken.rev ...→*gopher* <address 27>→The Forsaken ✓ **TFDN**→ <address 23>

Lwaxana & Odo Two images of Odo and the Betazoid Lwaxana Troi. ✓ **PVG** *dial* 513-233-7993→ <your username>→ <your password>→F→*Download a file:* LWX-

NA2.GIF *and* LWXNA3. GIF

Dramatis Personae

Episode #18
Writer: Joe Menosky
Director: Cliff Bole
Stardate: 46922.3

Summary: A Klingon ship returning from the wormhole explodes and as the captain dies, he utters only "Victory." Now things get really strange, as the *Enterprise* crew starts acting out parts in an alien drama

Archived Discussion of "Dramatis Personae" Any ideas about how they could have done this episode right? Several members contributed their own plot revisions. Besides episode rewrites, the archive includes debate about Trek sexism provoked by the "Is Kira a lesbian or just one tough chick?" question. ✓ **GENIE**→ *keyword* <address 22>→*Download a file:* 469

Tim Lynch Review ✓ **INTERNET** ...→*anon-ftp* <address 24>→ dramatis.rev ...→*gopher* <address 27>→Dramatis Personae ✓ **TFDN**→ <address 23>→dramatis.rev

Scenes from "Dramatis Personae" Several multi-picture files featuring scenes from Quark's bar, a close-up of Kira, and others of O'Brien and Bashir. ✓ **PVG** *dial*

Quark—downloaded from Perfect Vision Graphics BBS

513-233-7993→ <your username>
→<your password>→F→*Download
a file:* DS018-Q1.GIF *and* DS018-
Q2.GIF *and* DS018-Q3.GIF *and*
DS018-Q4. GIF *and* DS018-Q5.GIF
and DS018-S1.GIF *and* DS018-
S2.GIF *and* DS018-S6.GIF

Duet

Episode #19
Teleplay: Peter Allan Fields
Story: Lisa Rich, Jeanne
            Carrigan-Fauci
Director: James L. Conway

Summary: An injured Cardassian comes to the station for medical help and is arrested by Kira,
who believes him to be a war
criminal who was in charge of a
forced labor mining camp where
many Bajorans lost their lives.

Archived Discussion of "Duet"
Is this a holocaust analogy or just
melodrama? Is there any justification on either the Bajoran or Cardassian side for the continuing violence and desire for vengeance?
√**GENIE**→*keyword* <address 22>→
Download a file: 470

Ted Brengle's IMHO Review
√**TFDN**→ <address 23>→duet. zip

Tim Lynch Review √INTERNET
...→*anon-ftp* <address 24>→duet.
rev ...→*gopher* <address 27>→
Duet √**TFDN**→<address 23>→duet.
rev

In the Hands of the Prophets

Episode #20
Writer: Robert Hewitt Wolfe
Director: David Livingston
Guest Star: Louise Fletcher

Summary: A candidate to become the next Kai, Vedek Winn
objects to the science taught in

Keiko's station school. Maintaining that it is in conflict with Bajoran religious teachings, she ignites
a controversy that could under-
mine the fragile alliance between
Bajorans and the Federation.

Archived Discussion of "In the Hands of the Prophets"
Does *Star Trek* exhibit an anti-religious
bias? Was Gene Roddenberry an
atheist or a humanist? The
episode's retelling of the Scopes
trial elicited responses among
members ranging from personal
definitions of spirituality to debate
over constitutional (Federation)
guarantees. √**GENIE** →*keyword* <ad-
dress 22>→*Download a file:* 471

Ted Brengle's IMHO Review
√**TFDN**→ <address 23>→hands. zip

Tim Lynch Review √INTERNET
...→*anon-ftp* <address 24>→
prophets.rev ...→*gopher* <address
27>→In the Hands of the Prophets
√**TFDN**→<address 23>→prophets.
rev

Season 2

The Homecoming

Episode #21
Teleplay: Ira Steven Behr
Story: Jeri Taylor,
            Ira Steven Behr
Director: Winrich Kolbe

Summary: In the first of three

parts, Kira discovers that Lee
Nalis, a famous Bajoran rebel
leader, is a Cardassian P.O.W., and
sets out to free him. In doing so,
she finds out that Nalis might not
be all that legend claims.

Archived Discussion of "The Homecoming"
Are Bajorans fa-
natics? Will "The Circle" under-
mine the peace process in the same
manner in which, for instance,
Hamas is attempting to subvert
peace in Israel? What is a hero?
√**GENIE**→*keyword* <address 22>→
Download a file: 1224

Scenes from "The Homecoming"
Several multi-picture files
with episode scenes, including a
close-up of the Bajoran hero Lee
Nalis, and another of Quark. √**PVG**
dial 513-233-7993→<your user-
name>→<your password>→F→
Download a file: DS021-S1.GIF *and*
DS021-S2.GIF *and* DS021-S3.GIF
and DS021-S4.GIF *and* DS021-S5.
GIF *and* DS021-S6.GIF

Ted Brengle's IMHO Review
√**TFDN**→<address 23>→home. zip

Tim Lynch Review √INTERNET
...→*anon-ftp* <address 25>→home
coming.rev...→*gopher* <address
28>→The Homecoming

The Circle

Episode #22
Writer: Peter Allen Fields
Director: Corey Allen

ASK SPOT!

a) How long can a Trill live outside a host?

b) What is Garak's first name?

c) Who was the one millionth customer in Quark's bar?

d) What unique capability does the *Defiant* possess?

(See answers on page 359)

Summary: Replaced as liaison officer by Lee Nalis, Kira leaves to spend time with the Bajoran spiritual leader Vedek Bareil. She is taken captive by "The Circle." The crew must rescue her, and determine who is supplying the terrorist group with arms.

Archived Discussion of "The Circle" Does the stateroom scene (ranked by many here as the best *Star Trek* scene ever!) remind you of the *Barber of Seville*? Will love soften Kira? ✓ **GENIE** → *keyword* <address 22> → *Download a file:* 1225

Ted Brengle's IMHO Review ✓ **TFDN** → <address 23> → circle. zip

Tim Lynch Review ✓ **INTERNET** ... → *anon-ftp* <address 25> → circle.rev ... → *gopher* <address 28> → The Circle

The Siege

Episode #23
Writer: Michael Piller
Director: Winrich Kolbe

Summary: Sisko and the crew disobey orders to turn over DS9 and the wormhole to the Bajorans. They hope to hold the station long enough to be able to convince the council that giving "The Circle" possession would be a dramatic mistake.

Ted Brengle's IMHO Review ✓ **TFDN** → <address 23> → siege. zip

Tim Lynch Review ✓ **INTERNET** ... → *anon-ftp* <address 25> → siege.rev ... → *gopher* <address 28> → The Siege

Invasive Procedures

Episode #24
Teleplay: John Whelpley, Robert
            Hewitt Wolfe
Story: John Whelpley
Director: Les Landau
Stardate: 47182.1

Summary: A space storm causes the evacuation of the station. While security is loosened, Verad, a renégade Trill, and his band of followers take control of the Deep Space 9 station. Verad demands that Bashir turn Dax's Trill entity over to him.

Archived Discussion of "Invasive Procedures" Is the Melville's novel *Moby Dick* a greater work than Roddenberry's *Star Trek*? Why did Quark's complicity in the takeover go unpunished? ✓ **GENIE** → *keyword* <address 22> → *Download a file:* 1227

Tim Lynch Review ✓ **INTERNET** ... → *anon-ftp* <address 25> → invasive.rev ... → *gopher* <address 28> → Invasive Procedures

Cardassians

Episode #25
Teleplay: James Crocker
Story: Gene Wolande, John
            Wright
Director: Cliff Bole

Summary: Garak pushes Bashir into investigating a Cardassian boy adopted by a Bajoran family. The ensuing custody battle reveals political intrigue involving the boy's father and former station commander Gul Dukat.

Archived Discussion of "Cardassians" What were Garak's motivations in turning in his fellow Cardassians? Discourses on the nature and permanence of prejudice—can it be unlearned? ✓ **GENIE** → *keyword* <address 22> → *Download a file:* 1228

Ted Brengle's IMHO Review ✓ **TFDN** → <address 23> → cards.zip

Tim Lynch Review ✓ **INTERNET** ... → *anon-ftp* <address 25> → cardassians.rev ... → *gopher* <address 28> → Cardassians

Melora

Episode #26
Teleplay: Evan Carlos Somers,
            Steven Baum, Michael
            Piller, James Crocker
Story: Evan Carlos Somers
Director: Winrich Kolbe
Stardate: 47229.1

Summary: Dr. Bashir falls for a disabled cartographer from a planet with lighter gravity. Quark encounters an old acquaintance bent on revenge.

Archived Discussion of "Melora" The author of this episode is wheelchair-bound. Does this add to the realism of the story?

What would be the effect of antigravity on human movement? ✓ **GENIE**→*keyword* <address 22>→ *Download a file:* 1229

Ted Brengle's IMHO Review
✓ **TFDN**→<address 23>→mel.zip

Tim Lynch Review ✓ INTERNET
...→*anon-ftp* <address 25>→ melora.rev ...→*gopher* <address 28>→Melora

Rules of Acquisition

Episode #27
Teleplay: Ira Steven Behr
Story: Hilary Bader
Director: David Livingston
Guest Star: Wally Shawn

Summary: The Grand Nagus Zek appoints Quark as his emissary to the Dozai, a Gamma Quadrant race who enjoy turning a profit almost as much as do the Ferengi. He is hampered in this exciting duty by his new assistant, Pel, who is burdened by a troublesome secret: he's a she.

Archived Discussion of "Rules of Acquisition" How many Rules of Acquisition can you recite? Are the Ferengi a commentary on anti-Semitism? Is greed genetic? ✓ **GENIE**→*keyword* <address 22>→*Download a file:* 1230

Ted Brengle's IMHO Review
✓ **TFDN**→<address 23>→rules. zip

Tim Lynch Review ✓ INTERNET
...→*anon-ftp* <address 25>→ acquisition.rev ...→*gopher* <address 28>→Rules of Acquisition

Necessary Evil

Episode #28
Writer: Peter Allen Fields
Director: James L. Conway
Stardate: 47282.5

Summary: An assault on Quark appears to be tied to a murder which took place years ago when DS9 was under Cardassian rule. Odo had initiated the investigation then as a new station constable, and must renew his efforts to find the culprit, who may be Kira.

Archived Discussion of "Necessary Evil" Are Odo's methods intentionally patterned on Colombo's? What lies in the future for Kira and Odo—romance? ✓ **GENIE** →*keyword* <address 22>→*Download a file:* 1231

Ted Brengle's IMHO Review
✓ **TFDN**→<address 23>→nec.zip

Tim Lynch Review ✓ INTERNET
...→*anon-ftp* <address 25>→ necessary.rev ...→*gopher* <address 28>→Necessary Evil

Second Sight

Episode #29
Teleplay: Mark Gehred-
             O'Connell, Ira Steven
             Behr, Robert Hewitt
             Wolfe
Story: Mark Gehred-
             O'Connell
Director: Alexander Singer
Stardate: 47329.4

Summary: Sisko falls in love with a mysterious woman, who is really the telepathic projection of an egocentric Federation Terraformer.

Archived Discussion of "Second Sight" Is this just another love affair sacrificed for the sake of mankind? And why is the galactic speed limit applied in such a haphazard fashion? ✓ **GENIE**→*keyword* <address 22>→*Download a file:* 1232

Ted Brengle's IMHO Review

✓ **TFDN**→ <address 23>→secsi. zip

Tim Lynch Review ✓ INTERNET
...→*anon-ftp* <address 25>→ second.rev ...→*gopher* <address 28>→ Second Sight

Sanctuary

Episode #30
Teleplay: Frederick Rappaport
Story: Gabe Essoe, Kelley
             Miles
Director: Les Landau

Summary: Refugees from the other side of the wormhole come seeking a promised land. The only problem is that they are convinced it's Bajor, which the Bajoran government believes is unable to sustain such a large immigration.

Archived Discussion of "Sanctuary" Were the Bajorans morally wrong to turn their backs on the refugees? How can the Universal Translator become immediately familiar with a new language? Is the new society a realistic portrayal of matriarchy? ✓ **GENIE**→*keyword* <address 22>→*Download a file:* 1233

Ted Brengle's IMHO Review
✓ **TFDN**→<address 23>→sanc.zip

Tim Lynch Review ✓ INTERNET
...→*anon-ftp* <address 25>→ sanctuary.rev ...→*gopher* <address 28>→ Sanctuary

Rivals

Episode #31
Teleplay: Joe Menosky
Story: Jim Trombetta, Michael
             Piller
Director: David Livingston
Guest Star: Chris Sarandon

Summary: Quark is troubled when a con man opens a gambling parlor, cutting into Quark's action. His new gambling machines have an odd effect on the very laws of probability, and a run of bad luck plagues the inhabitants of DS9.

Archived Discussion of "Rivals" Should beings with telepathic powers be prohibited from playing poker and should those with vast memories be allowed to count cards? √**GENIE**→*keyword* <address 22>→*Download a file:* 1234

Ted Brengle's IMHO Review √**TFDN**→<address 23>→rivals. zip

Tim Lynch Review √**INTERNET** ...→*anon-ftp* <address 25>→rivals.rev ...→*gopher* <address 28>→Rivals

The Alternate

Episode #32
Teleplay: Bill Dial
Story: Jim Trombetta, Bill Dial
Director: David Carson

Summary: The scientist who discovered the foundling Odo in the Denorios Belt finds a similar DNA structure on a dying planet —perhaps the key to Odo's mysterious origins. Another morphing being is brought aboard, but its imminent death releases a hostile life form.

Archived Discussion of "The Alternate" If Odo can become anything, why doesn't he look more "normal" in human form? Is the unexplained tension between Dr. Mora and Odo a father/son conflict? √**GENIE**→*keyword* <address 22>→*Download a file:* 1238

Ted Brengle's IMHO Review √**TFDN**→<address 23>→alter. zip

Tim Lynch Review √**INTERNET**

...→*anon-ftp* <address 25>→alternate.rev ...→*gopher* <address 28>→The Alternate

The Armageddon Game

Episode #33
Writer: Morgan Gendel
Director: Winrich Kolbe

Summary: O'Brien and Dr. Bashir make an unsuccessful attempt to help the T'Lani and Kellerans end their centuries-long war by destroying a biological weapon. Now infected, O'Brien and Bashir are stranded on a ravaged planet as the races finally ally—to kill them.

Archived Discussion of "The Armageddon Game" Men and women on GEnie take sides on the fate of the O'Brien marriage and treknologists speculate on alternative methods of disarming a biological weapon. √**GENIE**→*keyword* <address 22>→*Download a file:* 1235

Tim Lynch Review √**INTERNET** ...→*anon-ftp* <address 25>→armageddon.rev ...→*gopher* <address 28>→Armageddon

Whispers

Episode #34
Writer: Paul Robert Coyle
Director: Les Landau

Summary: The Paradans, exhausted by civil war, negotiate with O'Brien to hold a peace conference at the station. When he returns, he finds the crew behaving strangely. Are aliens controlling their minds to destroy the peace?

Archived Discussion of "Whispers" Were you guessing until the last few minutes of the broad-

"This episode gleefully dispatched a lot of my pet prejudices. First of all, I usually find the Cardassians the most hopelessly dull alien race ever created for Star Trek, and laughably inadequate when called in to act as Major Bad Guys (Boo, Hiss). So, what does this episode do? It gives us the most interesting, complex Cardassian ever portrayed. And what a character! An in-your-face series of reverses and counter-identities, his story resembles nothing so much as the meticulous removing of the many layers of an onion, and would have fallen apart without the knock-out performance of Harris Yulin as the chameleonic Cardassian. It says something about the Cardassians, though, that the strongest villain that they've ever contributed to Trek isn't even a real villain. And he is VERY effective as a villain. In 'Duet,' though, we see the subtle but earth-shaking difference."

—from **Ted Brengle's Review of the episode "Duet"**

cast? What did you think was going on? The wisdom of spoiler topics is hotly debated. ✓**GENIE**→ *keyword* <address 22>→*Download a file:* 1236

Ted Brengle's IMHO Review
✓**TFDN**→ <address 23>→whispers.zip

Tim Lynch Review ✓INTERNET
...→*anon-ftp* <address 25>→ whispers.rev ...→*gopher* <address 28>→Whispers

Paradise

Episode #35
Teleplay: Jeff King, Richard Manning, Hans Beimler
Story: Jim Trombetta, James Cricker
Director: Corey Allen

Summary: While searching for planets suitable for colonization, Sisko and O'Brien encounter a colony run by a woman who is militantly opposed to technology.

Archived Discussion of "Paradise" Demagogues David Koresh and Jim Jones are used in the discussion as anologies to the chilling episode. GEnie members struggle to understand what appeals to people about dark Edens in both the 20th and the 24th centuries. ✓**GENIE**→*keyword* <address 22>→*Download a file:* 1239

Ted Brengle's IMHO Review
✓**TFDN**→ <address 23>→paradise. zip

Tim Lynch Review ✓INTERNET
...→*anon-ftp* <address 25>→ paradise.rev ...→*gopher* <address 28>→Paradise

Shadow Play

Episode #36
Writer: Robert Hewitt Wolfe

Director: Robert Scheerer
Stardate: 47603.3

Summary: Sisko apprentices Jake to O'Brien in preparation for the academy. Meanwhile Dax and Odo discover a planet where the inhabitants are living holograms—and fast disappearing.

Archived Discussion of "Shadow Play" Speculation on the future of Kira and Vedek Bariel's romance. How did the villagers become omicron particles—were they once real? Is DS9 so self-sufficient that crew members can leave their stations on any whim? ✓**GENIE**→*keyword* <address 22>→*Download a file:* 1237

Ted Brengle's IMHO Review
✓**TFDN**→ <address 23>→shadow. zip

Tim Lynch Review ✓INTERNET
...→*anon-ftp* <address 25>→ shadowplay.rev ...→*gopher* <address 28>→Shadowplay

Playing God

Episode #37
Writers: Jim Trombetta & Michael Piller
Director: David Livingston

Summary: Dax is selected to initiate a new Trill into the symbiotic relationship. The two unknowingly bring back from the wormhole a proto-universe which begins to expand. They must destroy it, and all the life that may exist inside, before it destroys them.

Tim Lynch Review ✓INTERNET
...→*anon-ftp* <address 25>→ playing.rev ...→*gopher* <address 28>→Playing God

Profit & Loss

Episode #38

Writers: Flip Kobler, Cindy Marcus
Director: Robert Wiemer

Summary: A Cardassian warship pursues a dissident teacher and students who support democracy over the Cardassian military government. The teacher has come to the station seeking the aid of her old love, Quark.

Archived Discussion of "Profit & Loss" Why doesn't Trek tell us more about alien sexuality? Is the Cardassian state patterned on Iraq and its military government? ✓**GENIE**→*keyword* <address 22>→*Download a file:* 1241

Ted Brengle's IMHO Review
✓**TFDN**→ <address 23>→profit.zip

Tim Lynch Review ✓INTERNET
...→*anon-ftp* <address 25>→ profit.rev ...→*gopher* <address 28>→Profit and Loss

Blood Oath

Episode #39
Teleplay: Peter Allen Fields
Story: Andrea Moore Alton
Director: Winrich Kolbe

Summary: Three Klingons from the original series come to Deep Space 9 seeking Curzon Dax to help carry out a blood oath the four made to kill a pirate. Jadzia Dax feels honor-bound to keep the covenant and accompanies them on their hunt.

Archived Discussion of "Blood Oath" Are Trills emotionally or morally bound by the actions of past hosts? ✓**GENIE**→*keyword* <address 22>→ *Download a file:* 1249

Ted Brengle's IMHO Review
✓**TFDN**→ <address 23>→blood.zip

Tim Lynch Review ✓INTERNET

...→*anon-ftp* <address 25>→blood oath.rev ...→*gopher* <address 28>→ Blood Oath

Jadzia Dax—downloaded from CompuServe's SF-Media Forum.

Dax the Klingon Jadzia Dax dressed as a Klingon outside the Albino's hideout. ✓COMPUSERVE →*go* sfmedia→Libraries→*Search by file name:* DAX1.GIF

Dax: the Klingon Picture of Dax dressed in full Klingon gear. ✓PVG *dial* 513-233-7993→<your username>→<your password> →F→*Download a file:* DS9-008.GIF

The Maquis, Part I

Episode #40
Teleplay:	James Crocker
Story:	Rick Berman, Michael Piller, Jeri Taylor, James Crocker
Director:	David Livingston

Summary: A Cardassian truce leaves some colonies stranded on the wrong side of a neutral zone. Several settlers, led by Cal Hudson, try to arrange peace, but the Cardassians want no part of it. Sisko and the former commander of DS9, Gul Dukat, get pulled into the conflict when Bok'Nor is blown up by a saboteur.

Archived Discussion of "The Maquis, Part I" How successful is the Federation in this difficult political situation? The tie-in to *Star Trek: The Next Generation* episode "Journey's End" is explored. ✓GENIE→*keyword* <address 22>→*Download a file:* 1250

Ted Brengle's IMHO Review

✓TFDN→ <address 23>→maquis.zip

Tim Lynch Review ✓INTERNET

...→*anon-ftp* <address 25>→ maquis1.rev ...→*gopher* <address 28>→The Maquis, Part I

The Maquis, Part II

Episode #41
Teleplay:	Ira Steven Behr
Story:	Rick Berman, Michael Piller, Jeri Taylor, James Crocker
Director:	Corey Allen

Summary: Sisko must rescue Gul Dukat from the Maquis, at the same time obeying Starfleet orders to broker a peace agreement for the Volon colonies. His Federation orders also bring him into conflict with his old friend Hudson.

Tim Lynch Review ✓INTERNET

...→*anon-ftp* <address 25>→ maquis2.rev ...→*gopher* <address 28>→The Maquis, Part II

The Wire

Episode #42
Writer:	Robert Hewitt Wolfe
Director:	Kim Friedman

Summary: Dr. Bashir tries to aid his friend Garak, a Cardassian who is addicted to a device implanted in his brain by Cardassian Intelligence.

Tim Lynch Review ✓INTERNET

...→*anon-ftp* <address 25>→ wire.rev ...→*gopher* <address

28>→The Wire

Crossover

Episode #43
Teleplay:	Peter Allen Fields, Michael Piller
Story:	Peter Allen Fields
Director:	David Livingston

Summary: Kira and Bashir are accidently thrown into an alternate universe where the evil Kira threatens to kill the good Bashir, the two Kiras are strangely drawn to each other, and Bajorans are tyrants.

Ted Brengle's IMHO Review

✓TFDN→ <address 23>→cross. zip

Tim Lynch Review ✓INTERNET

...→*anon-ftp* <address 25>→cross over.rev ...→*gopher* <address 28>→ Crossover

Two Kiras Kira and the Intendant (Kira 2). ✓COMPUSERVE→*go* sfmedia→Libraries→*Search by file name:* KIRINT.GIF

The Collaborator

Episode #44
Teleplay:	Ira Steven Behr, Gary Holland, Robert Wolfe
Story:	Gary Holland
Director:	Cliff Bole

Summary: Vedek Winn and Vedek Bariel are competing for the post of Kai of Bajor. Winn arrives just before the election to tell Kira that her lover, Bariel, may have been a Cardassian collaborator responsible for the death of a number of Bajorans.

Ted Brengle's IMHO Review

✓TFDN→ <address 23>→col.zip

Tim Lynch Review ✓INTERNET

...→*anon-ftp* <address 25>→

collaborator.rev ...→*gopher* <address 28>→The Collaborator

Archived Discussion of "The Collaborator"
Examination of Bajoran religion and its social ramifications. Is it "ethical" to sacrifice 48 lives in order to save a thousand ones? ✓**GENIE**→*keyword* <address 22>→*Download a file:* 1264

Tribunal

Episode #45
Writer: Bill Dial
Director: Avery Brooks
Stardate: 47944
Guest Star: Fritz Weaver

Summary: The O'Briens' vacation is ruined when their runabout is captured by a Cardassian warship under the command of Gul Evek. Miles is put on trial for smuggling weapons to the Maquis on Cardassa Prime.

Archived Discussion of "Tribunal"
Trek does Kafka. Analogies are made to the famous show trials of the past. Are the Cardassian courts the space equivalent of Stalin's? Was O'Brien really tortured or, perhaps even worse, merely made to believe so? ✓**GENIE**→*keyword* <address 22>→*Download a file:* 1265

Tim Lynch Review ✓**INTERNET**
...→*anon-ftp* <address 25>→tribunal.rev ...→*gopher* <address 28>→Tribunal

The Jem Hadar

Episode #46
Writer: Ira Steven Behr
Director: Kim Friedman

Summary: Quark and Sisko take Jake and Nog to a planet on the other side of the wormhole to complete their science projects.

While assisting a fugitive, the adults are captured by the Jem Hadar, members of the Dominion, and the two boys must find a way to get help on their own.

Discussion of "The Jem Hadar"
Speculation on the nature of the "new" enemy, the Dominion. Just how evil are these guys—worse than the Borg? How well does Federation technology stack up against that of the Dominion? ✓**GENIE**→*keyword* sfrt2→SFRT2 Bulletin Board→set 29→read 2

Ted Brengle's IMHO Review
✓**TFDN**→ <address 23>→j.zip

Tim Lynch Review ✓**INTERNET**
...→*anon-ftp* <address 25>→jem hadar.rev ...→*gopher* <address 28>→Jem'Hadar

Season 3

The Search, Part 1

Episode #47
Teleplay: Ron Moore
Story: Ira Steven Behr & Robert Hewitt Wolfe
Director: Kim Friedman

Summary: Trouble at DS9—Odo may resign. Meanwhile, the new ship *Defiant* readies itself for battle with the Jem Hadar.

Discussion of "The Search, Part I"
Just how advanced a ship is the *Defiant*, and how will *Voyager* compare in firepower? Is it just the old "lock phasers and fire" dressed up? Is Sisko finally coming alive as a commander? ✓**GENIE**→*keyword* sfrt2→SFRT2 Bulletin Board→set 29→read 3

Ted Brengle's IMHO Review
✓**TFDN**→ <address 23>→search.zip

Tim Lynch Review ✓**INTERNET**→
gopher <address 29>→The Search, Part I

The Search, Part II

Episode #48
Teleplay: Ron Moore
Director: Jonathan Frakes

Summary: Odo's long search for his origins comes to an unexpected end. The "Founders" of the repressive Dominion may be his shapeshifter relatives.

Discussion of "The Search, Part II"
Was this episode just a "big cheat"? Did the Federation encounter the Founders too quickly? Are the Changelings really the founders of the Dominion or was it all a dream? How do the pointed ears come into it? ✓**GENIE**→*keyword* sfrt2→SFRT2 Bulletin Board→set 29→topic 4

Ted Brengle's IMHO Review
✓**TFDN**→ <address 23>→search2.zip

Tim Lynch Review ✓**INTERNET**→
gopher <address 29>→The Search, Part II

The House of Quark

Episode #49
Teleplay:* Ronald D. Moore
Story:* Tom Benko
Director: Les Landau

Summary: Quark, wanting to gain respect and business, embroiders a tale about killing a Klingon. His plan goes awry when the dead Klingon's family shows up and demands he marry the widow or "pay" for the death of the Klingon. Meanwhile Bashir helps Keiko with personal problems.

Discussion of "The House of

Quark" How does Klingon no-fault divorce work? Is there a Klingon administrative class as well as a warrior class? Is Dr. Bashir really sensitive enough to have diagnosed Keiko O'Brien's trouble? ✓**GENIE**→*keyword* sfrt2→SFRT2 Bulletin Board→set 29→read 5

Tim Lynch Review ✓**INTERNET**→ *gopher* <address 29>→The House of Quark

Equilibrium

Episode #50
Teleplay: Rene Echevarria
Story: Christopher Teague
Director: Cliff Bole

Summary: Sisko discovers that a crucial Trill belief—that only one Trill in ten is capable of joining—is untrue. Half the population can join, but the story has been handed down to keep Trills from wreaking havoc in search of a symbiont.

Discussion of "Equilibrium" Doesn't Sisko violate the Prime Directive by threatening to reveal the Trill secret if Dax is not saved? Is it ridiculous to assume the secret could have been kept from such an intelligent population? ✓**GENIE**→*keyword* sfrt2→SFRT2 Bulletin Board→set 29→ read 6

Ted Brengle's IMHO Review ✓**TFDN**→ <address 23>→equil.zip

Tim Lynch Review ✓**INTERNET**→ *gopher* <address 29>→Equilibrium

Second Skin

Episode #51
Story: Robert Hewitt Wolfe
Director: Les Landau

Summary: Kira is in for a shock when not only is she kidnapped by

Cardassians, but her captors insist that she not a Bajoran but one of them.

Discussion of "Second Skin" Will Kira ever accept that all Cardassians are not alike? The Cardassian underground is revealed in this episode and Garak's relationship to it is discussed. Will plastic surgery of the future let us all transform into our ideals? ✓**GENIE** →*keyword* sfrt2→SFRT2 Bulletin Board→set 29→read 7

Ted Brengle's IMHO Review ✓**TFDN**→ <address 23>→sskin.zip

Tim Lynch Review ✓**INTERNET**→ *gopher* <address 29>→Second Skin

The Abandoned

Episode #52
Story: D. Thomas Maio &
             Steve Warnek
Director: Avery Brooks

Summary: Odo tries to convince a young, violent Jem Hadar that there is more to life than fighting and killing.

Discussion of "The Abandoned" Debate over the budding relationship between Odo and Kira, and more speculation about the Jem Hadar. ✓**GENIE**→*keyword* sfrt2→SFRT2 Bulletin Board→set 29→read 8

Tim Lynch Review ✓**INTERNET**→ *gopher* <address 29>→The Abandoned

Civil Defense

Episode #53
Story: Mike Krohn
Director: Reza Badiyi

Summary: The fate of the station is in the hands of a flight crew when

an automated Cardassian security program is activated by mistake.

Discussion of "Civil Defense" The bad blood between Garak and Dukat is explained. Are there really only six plots in the universe, the malfunctioning computer being among the most popular? "Data processing professionals" applaud a realistic computer story. ✓**GENIE** →*keyword* sfrt2→SFRT2 Bulletin Board→set 29 →topic 9

Ted Brengle's IMHO Review ✓**TFDN**→<address 23>→civil.zip

Tim Lynch Review ✓**INTERNET** →*gopher* <address 29>→Civil Defense

Meridian

Episode #54
Story: Hilary Bader & Evan
             Carlos Somers
Teleplay: Mark Gehred-
             O'Connell
Director: Jonathan Frakes
Stardate: 48423.2

Summary: Dax finally falls in love. The only problem is that her love interest lives on a planet about to enter another dimension—for sixty years.

Discussion of "Meridian" Can the Meridians survive on their planet during the dimensional shift? Are Trek romances dull because viewers know that they can't last, or because they're badly written? ✓**GENIE**→*keyword* sfrt2→SFRT2 Bulletin Board→set 29→read 10

Tim Lynch Review ✓**INTERNET**→ *gopher* <address 29>→Meridian

Defiant

Episode #55
Story: Ronald Moore

Director: Cliff Bole
Stardate: 48467.3

Summary: Thomas Riker, the duplicate of Will Riker created by a transporter accident, returns, steals the *Defiant*, and begins a campaign of terror against the Cardassians. Sisko and Gul Dukat work together to stop him.

Discussion of "Defiant" Is Tom Riker a "bad guy" in this piece, or just misguided, searching for his own identity? Can he have his own identity? Should Tom Riker's fingerprints be altered to protect Will? Do Will and Tom share a soul? Can Sisko's and Dukat's love of the family serve as a bond between the two? √GENIE→*keyword* sfrt2→SFRT2 Bulletin Board→set 29→read 11

Tim Lynch Review √INTERNET …→*gopher* <address 29>→Defiant

Fascination

Episode #56
Story: Ira Steven Behr & James Crocker
Teleplay: Philip Lazebnik
Director: Avery Brooks

Summary: When the flamboyant Lwaxana Troi comes to DS9, love is in the air. Suddenly everyone is infatuated with everyone else.

Discussion of "Fascination" Does anyone in the universe like Laxwana Troi? How realistic is the Keiko and Miles O'Brien marriage? Can't Star Trek writers avoid the "kid stuff" and have characters really say how they feel? √GENIE →*keyword* sfrt2→SFRT2 Bulletin Board→set 29→read 12

Tim Lynch Review √INTERNET→ *gopher* <address 29>→Fascination

Past Tense, Part I

Episode #57
Story: Ira Steven Behr & Robert Hewitt Wolfe
Teleplay: Robert Hewitt Wolfe
Director: Reza Badiyi

Summary: Sisko, Bashir, and Dax return to San Francisco around 2024, altering history (and the Federation's history).

Discussion of "Past Tense, Part I" Is the episode too politically liberal?—"I'm surprised they didn't mention that the American President was Dan Quayle, and Newt Gingrich was his VP." And, were the anti-war messages of TOS series any less blatant? Warp drive and warp theory are major topics of conversation. √GENIE→ *keyword* sfrt2→SFRT2 Bulletin Board→set 29→read 13

Tim Lynch Review √INTERNET→ *gopher* <address 29>→Past Tense, Part I

Past Tense, Part II

Episode #58
Story: Ira Steven Behr & Robert Hewitt Wolfe
Teleplay: Robert Hewitt Wolfe & Rene Echevarria
Director: Jonathan Frakes

Summary: In order to prevent a change in the historical timeline, Sisko acts out the role of a man (recorded in history as a martyr) who died when the DS9 crew returned—earlier than he should have. The Net assumes a major role in the plot, serving as a communications system to broadcast the plight of the 21st-century homeless population.

Discussion of "Past Tense, Part II" Notice an inconsistency, something a little odd in this episode? And how about a lack of originality? The nitpickers were out in force for the second part of "Past Tense." Was the episode merely "The City on the Edge of Forever" retooled for the DS9 era? And what did O'Brien mean when he said, "I know Earth in the 21st century was rough, but not_that_ rough." Other fans were concerned about the chain of command on the space station—who is in charge of DS9 when all the commanding officers are off the premises? Quark? √GENIE→*keyword* sfrt2→SFRT2 Bulletin Board →set 29→read 14

STARNOTES

Space station hubsites

As the runt of the Trek litter, DS9 has a vexed status on the Net, with a distinct short-

age of diehard fans and a surplus of disgruntled Trekkers who insist that the show is falling short of its promise. The introductory materials online both confirm and give the lie to that assertion. Start at the **DS9 Information Link**, which offers the broadest overview of the series. Then spend some time in the various Cyberpockets devoted to DS9 chat. What will happen to the series now that *Voyager* is on the air, especially since DS9 has begun to change its own character with the addition of a ship? Is the spirituality of the Bajorans an asset or an annoyance? And is Jadzia Dax the hottest thing in space or what? Drop in to eWorld's **Star Trek: Deep Space Nine**, AOL's **Deep Space Nine Board**, or the **rec.arts. star trek*** hierarchy to share your opinions and analysis.

Vidiot's Deep Space Nine Page—http://www.ftms.com/st-ds9/

On the Net

DS9 101

Deep Space 9 Bible Excerpts from a speech about Deep Space Nine given by Majel Barrett Roddenberry, the wife of the late Gene Roddenberry, a few months before the series premiered. Several pas-

sages from the show's writers' guidebook, known as the *Deep Space Nine Writers Bible*, are quoted, and the speech also offers a fascinating overview of the initial conception of the show: "A brief journey through the Bajoran Worm Hole will take a starship to the Gamma Quadrant, normally a sixty-year journey at warp 9. The ride is a spectacular light show: very brilliant colors surround the ship, while inside, strange visual distortions affect perceptions as passengers tear through the space-time continuum. This wormhole is a new passageway to hundreds of unexplored sectors of space and it will turn Bajor into the leading center of commerce and scientific exploration in the sector, attracting travelers from all over the galaxy." ✓ **AMERICA ONLINE**→*keyword* trek→MORE...→Star Trek Record Banks→Text/Other Files→Deep Space Bible.txt ✓ **COMPU-**

SERVE→*go* sfmedia→Libraries→ *Search by file name:* DS9UPD.TXT ✓ **INTERNET**→*anon-ftp* wiretap.spies. com→Wiretap Online Library→ Media→Trek→deep9.bib

Across the board

Deep Space Nine British site that includes an episode guide, cast information, a brief FAQ, and other data. ✓ **INTERNET**→*www* http://web.city.ac.uk/~cc103/ds9. html

Deep Space Nine: General Where should the show go from here? Is Sisko's schtick played out? When will we learn the rest of the Rules of Acquisition? And what about education of teenage children on Trek? Fans remain proud of DS9's individuality and frequently discuss how it can best retain its unique perspective. In the general topics, they muse about how average Bajorans feel about average Cardassians. Temperatures rise in the inevitable Bajoran-inspired discussion about the place of religion in politics. And the Chief Engineer competition has devolved into an ongoing political correctness debate—is Colm Meaney better than James Doohan because his accent is real? Topic 6—"Where Should We Go From Here?"—proffers suggestions for upcoming plots, and DS9 meets *Babylon 5* in Topic 8, with each vying for the honor of best carrying on the Roddenberry dream of democracy in space. ✓**GENIE**→*keyword* sfrt2→SFRT2 Bulletin Board→Set 28

DS9 Information Link Want a brief description of the show? How about a regular cast list, an episode listing, or a list of video releases? All your wants and needs will be satisfied at the Surrey site, which also contains links to other DS9 pages. ✓**INTERNET**→*www* http://www.ee.surrey.ac.uk/Personal/STDS9/index.html

---

Deep Web Nine Finnish Trek fan Pekka Hulkkonen is obviously smitten with *Deep Space Nine,* and this mammoth, graphic-intensive Website serves as a monument to the series. The site carries—or links to—DS9 episode guides, official paramount information, interviews with cast members, image galleries, the Ferengi Rules of Acquisition, and Vidiot's DS9 Guide. But Hulkkonen doesn't limit himself to adventures on the edge of the wormhole. He has collected resources and links for each of the movies and the series, including the *Animated Series.* And then he has gone on to amass links to Trek information compiled by clubs on the Net, including the Klingon Language Institute, STARFLEET, the Terry Farrell

Fan Club, and the United Federation of Planets fan club. Under the heading Star Trek-home pages, he's brought together a long list of Trek-related home pages, many of them of European origin. Anyone looking for a home page for Data? How about Chief O'Brien? There are links to these pages from here. Finally, when you're sick of Trek (if you're ever sick of Trek), he's created home pages for other sci-fi series, such as *Star Wars* and *Babylon 5.* And—as always—you can get there from here. ✓**INTERNET**→*www* http://www.tut.fi/~pekka/trek.html

---

Vidiot's Deep Space Nine Page This Website's main feature are Paramount air schedules and episode press releases. Each release includes the names of cast members and guest stars, the copy for the *TV Guide* ad, and a sentence or two highlighting the episode's dilemma. Site also includes a DS9 quick reference guide with one-line summaries of each episode aired so far, a preview page with images from the next episode of DS9, images of the *Defiant,* and a copy of the Ferengi Rules of Acquisition. ✓**INTERNET**→*www* http://www.ftms.com:80/st-ds9/

DS9 chat

Deep Space Nine Board Fans and foes of Dax, Kira, Commander Sisko, Quark, Odo, and the Doctor can enter one of the many DS9 discussions here (usually there's a folder for each of these characters). You can also ask a question about the Cardassian military or the Dominion, trade DS9 collectibles, gather with other members of ENVY (the Nana Visitor fan club), or engage in the ongoing debate about getting gay characters on DS9. ✓**AMERICA ON-LINE**→*keyword* trek→Star Trek Mes-

sage Boards→Deep Space Nine Board

DS9=Boldly Going Nowhere The most maligned of Trek series has both adherents and detractors on this message board. Well, mostly detractors. "The first episodes of this season of DS9 were some of the weakest Trek scripts I have ever seen. What the hell is in Rick Berman's head?" When they're not attacking the show directly, fans are attacking it indirectly, suggesting that DS9 has moved beyond its fruitless adolescence into an equally fruitless adulthood. And sometimes they're defending it by attacking its fraternal twin, *Babylon 5:* "B-5 lacks the most important thing that makes or breaks a science-fiction show: credible dialogue. The stuff that comes out of the characters' mouths sometimes is so corny that it makes me sick." ✓**AMERICA ONLINE**→*keyword* scifi→Star Trek/Comics/TV/Star Wars Boards→Star Trek→DS9=boldly going nowhere

---

DS9—Deep Space Nine The regulars talk about *Deep Space Nine* like they've got a stake in the show's success. Hang out here and you'll read a lot of spontaneous, gut-level reactions to recent episodes, especially when there's a sense of the series faltering. The talk is laden with suggestions for future shows. With *Deep Space Nine,* part of the fun comes from the suspense of new material—something most people can't say about TOS or TNG. You can only guess where the series is headed, and lots of people do. Could the Romulans become "good guys"? It's possible, but not a prospect that pleases. "The Romulans are the scum of the Milky Way," one fan wrote, "and they always will be." "They keep taking away all our bad guys," another lamented.

Much attention is paid to the development of such characters as Sisko and Odo—though some fans are displeased with the way they've been handled, they are curious to see what happens to them. ✓**DELPHI**→*go ent sta for set ds9*

rec.arts.startrek.current/rec. arts.startrek.misc (ng) Fact: DS9 gets short shrift in the Usenet world. There are a few exceptions, of course, with Ferengis being the most noteworthy—a project to uncover all 285 of the Ferengi Rules of Acquisition is in full force, as attentive readers and viewers attempt to piece together a complete list of the spiritual/economic bylaws followed by the universe's most greedy and manipulative intelligent species. While fans seem divided over Sisko, the station commander played by Avery Brooks, a recent "Who's Your Favorite Captain?" thread drew a great number of lurking Siskoids out of the woodwork. And now that DS9 is the senior *Star Trek* series on the air, its Net worth is sure to improve. ✓**USENET**

Star Trek: Deep Space Nine Is Klingon blood red or pink? Pink, of course. And how do we know that? Well, we just know. In fact, one of eWorld's resident Trek experts notes that a former Trek plot turned on this very fact when an assassin revealed his non-Klingon identity by bleeding red blood. From DS9's theme music to the Ferengi Rules of Acquisition, there's a fearsome amount of nitpicking and trivia jockeying here, and gossip and rumors about cast members often generate more discussion than the show's actual plots and themes. ✓**EWORLD**→*sf*→ *Star Trek*→*On the Small Screen*→ *Star Trek: Deep Space Nine*

STDSN (echo) Several big names

in the Trek world hang out here, including Lists of Lists creator Mark Holtz. From the strength of Kira's character—watch as she metamorphoses from a "racist Cardassian hater to a more sympathetic and understanding woman" —to the spots on Dax that drive men wild, this conference treats the ins and outs of DS9 in lavish detail. ✓**FIDONET** ✓**TREKNET**→ TN_STDSN

Trekker_DS9 (echo) Heavy on DS9 news and information, the conference is filled with air schedules, FAQs, and lists of DS9 trivia. Summaries of television, radio, and newspaper interviews with cast members are also posted here, along with reports on convention appearances by the stars. One conference participant posted a loyal transcript of remarks made by Avery Brooks at a recent convention, including comments on relationships with other cast members: "He said that he and Colm spend all day laughing. He said he often spends time doubled over on the floor with laughter from something Colm said and then Colm will say, 'The commander's lost it again!'" When fans aren't transcribing, they're opining—"I hope if Q comes back to DS9 he actually does something. Last time all he did was mope about all lovesick over Vash. And she's not good enough for him!" And several regulars contribute detailed synopses, spoilers, and reviews, including Ted Brengle (the IMHO reviews) and Tim Lynch. Trek fan Charles Castevens posts incredibly detailed scene-by-scene descriptions of many episodes—although those readers not in the mood for spoilers should skip Castevens. ✓**TREK-KERNET**

TV: Deep Space Nine All of Prodigy's DS9 fans are here, lob-

bying for Q but fearing they'll lose him to *Voyager*, bickering over who Dax should be paired with (Sisko, Bashir, or Kira), and breaking off into factions for Cardassians and specific DS9 crew members. ✓**PRODIGY**→*jump star trek bb*→Choose a Topic→TV: Deep Space Nine

WS_STDS9 (echo) Episode lists, reviews, and cast information constitute a significant portion of the posts in this conference. Still, there's a motley crew of regulars that tries to steer the conference away from information and toward discussion—trying to decide, for instance, whether Jake Sisko is as worthy of scorn as Nog or Wesley Crusher. ✓**WARPSPEED**

Pictures

Deep Space Nine Station Picture of the DS9 space station and the wormhole. ✓**PVG** dial 513-233-7993→F→*Download a File:*→DSN-32.GIF

DS9 Station Picture of the *Deep Space Nine* space station. ✓**PVG** dial 513-233-7993→F→*Download a File:* DS9SPACE.GIF

Enterprise at DS9 Picture of the *Enterprise* docking at DS9. ✓**PVG** dial 513-233-7993→F→*Download a File:* ENTDOC.GIF

Station floorplan

DS9 Station Directory A copy of the station directory displayed during the television show "Science of Star Trek." There's Garak's Clothiers and Mrs. O'Brien's Schoolroom, but there are also the tongue-in-cheek references to Berman's Dilithium Supply. ✓**COMPUSERVE**→*go sfmedia*→*Libraries*→*Search by file name:*

Deep Space residents

Since its inception, *Deep Space Nine* has had a slightly different attitude toward its

characters than other *Star Trek* shows—in short, it has allowed its cast to be over-run by unsympathetic characters who are slowly (sometimes very slowly) exposed as complex and sympathetic beings. Take Dr. Julian Bashir. *Please.* When he first arrived at the space station he was a whiny and arrogant baby doc without a single redeeming characteristic. But as time has passed, Bashir has been written with more complexity, and he has developed quite a fan following. Fans have similar feelings about Kira Nerys, whose aggressive personality is at once offputting and endearing; and Quark, the avaricious Ferengi everyone loves to hate. And then there is Jadzia Dax—no matter how much the Net's male Trekkers discuss her beauty (and her beauty spots), they never seem to have their fill of Trill. Download a GIF of the DS9 Crew, read transcripts of a session with **Avery Brooks on Prodigy**, or scan the **Colm Meaney Filmography** to understand why Chief Engineer O'Brien may be leaving the show to pursue his film career.

Deep Space 9 *(video still)—from http://www.tut.fi/~pekka/trek.html*

On the Net

Cast info

Deep Space Nine A complete cast list with hypertext links to cast member filmographies. ✓**INTERNET**→*www* http://www.cm.cf.ac.uk/Movies/

Deep Space Nine Cast List Includes a list of regular cast and recurring guest roles. ✓**INTERNET**→*www* http://www.ee.surrey.ac.uk/Personal/STDS9/cast.html

Cast photos

Cast of Star Trek: Deep Space Nine Cast photo of DS9 characters. ✓**COMPUSERVE**→*go* sfmedia→Libraries→*Search by file name:* DS9001.GIF

Deep Space Nine Cast Photo Autographed shot of the first-season cast. ✓**COMPUSERVE**→*go* sfmedia→Libraries→*Search by file name:* CAST1.GIF

Deep Space Nine Central DS9 image gallery with photos of cast members in and out of character. ✓**INTERNET**→*www* http://trill.pc.cc.cmu.edu/~jkoga/stds9_gallery.html

DS9 Crew A GIF of the DS9 crew. ✓**COMPUSERVE**→*go* sfmedia→Libraries→*Search by file name:* DS9CRW.GIF

Benjamin Sisko

Avery Brooks Filmography A complete list of Brooks's TV and film credits, from *Roots: The Gift* to *Uncle Tom's Cabin* to a host of appearances as Hawk in the *Spencer For Hire* series. ✓**INTERNET**→*www* http://www.cm.cf.ac.uk/Movies/→Search the database for a person's name→*Search for the name(s):* brooks, avery

Avery Brooks on Prodigy No, Avery Brooks wasn't a *Star Trek* fan when growing up. He's not a captain—he's a commander.

Deep Space Residents Star Trek: Deep Space Nine

Commander Sisko—downloaded from Perfect Vision Graphics BBS

He's not Hawk—he's Sisko. And, in real life, he's also a tenured professor at Rutgers University. The first half of this file carries Brooks's answers to questions asked by Prodigy fans, while the second half is a Q&A session with Rick Berman, executive producer of all Trek series. ✓**TFDN**→TFDN - Fact Files→*Download a file:* dsntalk.zip

Benjamin Sisko Pictures of Commander Benjamin Sisko. ✓**PVG** dial 513-233-7993→<your username>→<your password>→F→ *Download a file:* DS9-SSKO.GIF *and* PVSISKO5.GIF *and* SISKO1. GIF *and* SISKO2.GIF *and* DSN-001.GIF

Commander Benjamin Sisko Though this message board doesn't have as much traffic as some of the others, the posts have a rare intensity and insight that seems fitting for fans of DS9's stol-id-on-the-outside, crying-on-the-inside Commander. While some fans of the show attack the performance of Avery Brooks—"my opinion is that Avery Brooks's act-ing and/or the directing of Sisko is the only major problem with the show"—many of the posts defend Sisko against the onslaught of crit-

icism, focusing on his difficult role as a single father and his complex past.

"Sisko gets the short end of the stick week after week. I really think that there is a lot of poten-tial in the Sisko character—if the writers would only wake up and give him something to do." ✓**AMER-ICA ONLINE**→*keyword* trek→Star Trek Message Board→Deep Space Nine Board→Commander Ben-jamin Sisko

Commander Benjamin Sisko A description of *Deep Space Nine's* widower commander, with a spe-cial focus on the complexity of his character. ✓**INTERNET**→*www* http://web.city.ac.uk/~cc103/cast/bensisko.html

Kira Nerys

3 Faces of Major Kira GIF of three different looks of Major Kira Nerys. ✓**COMPUSERVE**→*go* sfmedia →Libraries→*Search by file name:* KIRAS3.GIF

ENVY, a Nana Visitor Fan Club Information about Visitor's fan club, ENVY. ✓**COMPUSERVE**→*go* sfmedia→Libraries→*Search by file name:* ENVY.TXT

Kira Devoted to discussion of DS9's tough-as-nails Major and the woman who portrays her. Much of the talk focuses on the magnetism of the character, espe-cially the fond hope of fans that she will become the first bisexual character on *Star Trek.* "I've often noted how they have played Kira and Dax against one another." Sometimes, of course, the mes-sages veer off topics, and it's left to the more conscientious among the participants to bring the conversa-tion back in line: "No offense to you all but I thought this file was for and about Nana and her char-

acter Kira! Some people out there need to take a step back and grab hold of some reality. It is Fiction, Bajor does not exist." ✓**AMERICA ONLINE** →*keyword* trek→Star Trek Message Boards→Deep Space Nine Board→ Kira

Kira and Sisko First Encounter WAV file of Kira saying, "You're throwing it away...all of you... don't ask my opinion next time." ✓**COMPUSERVE**→*go* sfmedia→Li-braries→*Search by file name:* THROWA.WAV

Kira and the Intendant An image from the episode "The Crossover." GIF file. ✓**COMPU-SERVE**→*go* sfmedia→Libraries→ *Search by file name:* KIRINT.GIF

Kira Nerys Pictures of Major Kira. ✓**PVG** dial 513-233-7993→ <your username>→<your pass-word>→F→*Download a file:* DS9-KIRA.GIF *and* KIRA.GIF *and* KIRA02.GIF *and* KIRA3.GIF *and* PVDS900B.GIF *and* PVDSN02.GIF *and* PVKIRA01.GIF *and* PV-NANAV1.GIF *and* KIRAS3.GIF *and* NANAV.GIF

Kira—downloaded from Perfect Vision Graphics BBS

Major Kira Fans Aren't we all major Kira fans? Those who assemble here share a passion for fan fiction, writing Bajoran storylines for the fiery Major—often with a love angle. ✓**PRODIGY**→ *jump* star trek bb→Choose a Topic→Clubs: DS9→Major Kira Fans

Major Kira Nerys A picture of Kira Nerys, along with a brief essay that concentrates on her role within DS9's social structure and an explanation of her "aggressive nature." ✓**INTERNET**→*www* http://web.city.ac.uk/~cc103/cast/kira.html

Nana Visitor Filmography One of the last of the TV troupers, with a list of television series credits longer than a Buck Bokai home run. *Hooperman, Thirtysomething, L.A. Law, Matlock, Hotel, Hunter, Night Court, Knight Rider,* and more. ✓**INTERNET** →*www* http://www.cm.cf.ac.uk/Movies/→Search the database for a person's name→*Search for the name(s):* visitor, nana

Nana Visitor Pictures of actress Nana Visitor. ✓**PVG** *dial* 513-233-7993→<your username>→<your password>→F→*Download a file:* PV-SFST3.GIF *and* NANADNCE.GIF *and* NANACAKE.GIF

Nana Visitor GIF Image of Visitor from an issue of *Soap Opera Weekly.* ✓**COMPUSERVE**→*go* sfmedia →Libraries→*Search by file name:* NAN1.GIF

Nana Visitor in Dancing Shoes Photo of Nana Visitor dressed in a dancing outfit. ✓**COMPUSERVE**→*go* sfmedia→Libraries→*Search by file name:* NVDANC.GIF

Nana Visitor in TV Guide *TV Guide* image of Nana Visitor. ✓**COMPUSERVE**→*go* sfmedia→Libraries→*Search by file name:* NVLEGS.GIF

Nana Visitor Minneapolis Convention Photos Photos of Nana Visitor at a Minneapolis Trek convention. ✓**COMPUSERVE**→*go* sfmedia→Libraries→*Search by file name:* NANA1.GIF *or* NANA2.GIF *or* NANA3.GIF *or* NANA4.GIF

Nana Visitor Vancouver Convention Photos A series of photos of Nana Visitor at a 1993 Trek convention in Vancouver: Visitor getting on stage, Visitor listening to questions, Visitor sipping coffee, Visitor speaking, Visitor holding her baby, etc. ✓**COMPUSERVE**→*go* sfmedia→Libraries→*Search by file name:* NVAN1.GIF, NVAN3.GIF, NVAN4.GIF, NVAN5.GIF, NVAN7.GIF, NVAN8.GIF, NVAN9.GIF

What Has She Done? A collection of articles and reviews about Nana Visitor's other roles. ✓**COMPUSERVE**→*go* sfmedia→Libraries→*Search by file name:* NANA.TXT

Dax

Dax Pictures of the lovely Jadzia Dax. ✓**PVG** *dial* 513-233-7993→<your username>→<your password>→F→*Download a file:* DAX.GIF *and* DAX01.GIF *and* DAX4.GIF *and* DS9-JDAX.GIF *and* PVDS900C.GIF *and* DAXSMILE.GIF *and* DSN-005.GIF *and* STDS9005.GIF *and* TF01.GIF *and* TF02.GIF *and* TF03.GIF

Dax To some, her beauty spots mark her as the Cindy Crawford of deep space. To others, she's the source of speculation ("wondering what patterns the spots take on the rest of the body"). To others still, she's a woman under siege from oversexed teenage boys ("Dax is my favorite character, and yes, Terry is very attractive, but

Dax—downloaded from Perfect Vision Graphics BBS

does AOL *really need* a place for all of you to discuss seeing her naked?"). In the spaces between the discussions of Terry Farrell's pulchritude, there's the occasional analysis of her character, or Trill psychology. And remember—Dax marks the spots. ✓**AMERICA ONLINE**→*keyword* trek→Star Trek Message Boards→Deep Space Nine Board→Dax

Dax Photo of Terry Farrell's character. ✓**INTERNET**→*www* http://www.cosy.sbg.ac.at/ftp/pub/trek/pics/dax.jpg

Dax as a Klingon Image of Dax dressed in Klingon garb. ✓**COMPUSERVE**→*go* sfmedia→Libraries→*Search by file name:* DAX1.GIF

Farrell Gets Spots Spots are painted on Terry Farrell. ✓**PVG** *dial* 513-233-7993→<your username>→<your password>→F→*Download a file:* DAX2.GIF

I'm Not Submissive Dax saying "I'm not submissive" in the episode "If Wishes Were Horses." WAV file. ✓**COMPUSERVE**→*go* sfmedia→Libraries→*Search by file name:* SUBMIS.WAV

Lieutenant Jadzia Dax With more than three hundred years of experience and a body that would stop a clock, Jadzia Dax is one of the most beloved of DS9 characters, and this page offers a brief biography, along with an explanation of her personality. ✓ **INTERNET** →*www* http://web.city.ac.uk/~cc103/cast/jadzia.html

Terry Farrell FAQ Terry had a Tribble doll when she was seven! One FAQ contributor went to high school with Farrell, another had asked her a question at a convention, and another person saw nude pictures of her in the magazine *Women of Fantasy*. Besides collecting Farrell impressions from fans, the FAQ lists Farrell's other acting credits, her thoughts on *Star Trek*, Dax merchandise, and relevant biographical information. ✓ **INTERNET**→*www* http://panacea.library.ucsb.edu/~jkoga/tf.html ✓ **DELPHI**→*go* ent sta dat→set ds9→read terry farrell faq→down *or* list

Terry Farrell Filmography Ah, Terry. How do I watch thee? Let me count the ways. Appearances in *Family Ties* and *The Cosby Show*. A role in *Hellraiser III: Hell on Earth*. And then there are the numerous TV movies, ranging from *Beverly Hills Madam* to *Danielle Steel's Star*. ✓ **INTERNET**→ *www* http://www.cm.cf.ac.uk/Movies/→Search the database for a person's name→*Search for the name(s):* farrell, terry

Terry Farrell Internet Fan Club The beautiful Terry Farrell plays the beautiful Jadzia Dax. This site includes information on how to pay tribute to Farrell, along with a gallery of pictures—Terry getting her makeup done (how far do those spots stretch?), Terry in casual dress, etc. Note: There are no pictures of Terry completely in the buff. ✓ **INTERNET** →*www* http://trill.pc.cc.cmu.edu/~jkoga/tf.html

Odo

Morphing Odo Picture of Odo in mid-morph. ✓ **PVG** *dial* 513-233-7993→<your username>→<your password>→F→*Download a file:*→ PVDSN01.GIF

Odo Pictures of Odo, the Security Chief. ✓ **PVG** *dial* 513-233-7993 →<your username>→<your password>→F→*Download a file:* DS9-ODO0.GIF *and* DS012-S1.GIF *and* DSN-002.GIF *and* ODO4.GIF

Odo (quite simply) What is Odo, exactly? Is he a symbol? A concept? Or merely an interstellar hardass? Fans are split on the direction the shape-shifter's character should take, with some suggesting a broader emotional palette and others recommending playing to the tough-guy stereotype: "What the writers should do is give him some gritty, sobering scenarios that will make good use of his particular point of view. The show should stop trying to turn him into a better adjusted adult and use his neurosis for all it's worth." ✓ **AMERICA ONLINE**→*keyword* trek→Star Trek Message Boards→Deep Space Nine Board→

Odo—downloaded from Perfect Vision Graphics BBS

Odo (quite simply)

Rene Auberjonois Filmography Ever since the early seventies, when he was a recurring member of Robert Altman's ensemble films—*M*A*S*H, McCabe and Mrs. Miller, Brewster McCloud*—Auberjonois has been a fixture in American entertainment. Sadly, he's probably best remembered for playing the unctuous Clayton on the sitcom *Benson*, and not for his fine work in projects such as the 1991 TV adaption of David Leavitt's *The Lost Language of Cranes*. ✓ **INTERNET**→*www* http://www.cm.cf.ac.uk/Movies/→Search the database for a person's name→*Search for the name(s):* auberjonois, rene

Results of Phrenetic Analysis of Shapeshifter Species G-1 A mock physiological analysis of Odo, supposedly written by Dax and Dr. Bashir and based on the information known about Odo at the end of DS9's second season. ✓ **AMERICA ONLINE**→*keyword* trek→ MORE...→Star Trek Record Banks→Text/Other Files→Upld: 06/25/94 →TEXT: Scientific paper describing Odo (Filename: ODO.TXT)

Security Chief Odo Direct from Antos IV, it's Security Chief Odo, the shape-shifter with the law-and-order mind. This short essay analyzes Odo's character and situates him among the rest of the DS9 cast. ✓ **INTERNET**→*www* http://web.city.ac.uk/~cc103/cast/odo.html

Dr. Julian Bashir

Bashir Pictures of Julian. ✓ **PVG** *dial* 513-233-7993→<your username>→<your password>→F→ *Download a file:* BASHIR.GIF *and* BASHIR2.GIF *and* DS9-BSHR.GIF *and* PVDS900A.GIF *and* DSN-004.GIF

Julian—downloaded from Perfect Vision Graphics

Dr. Julian Bashir With a healthy eye for the ladies and a brilliant medical career ahead of him, Julian Bashir tends to the medical needs of the space station *Deep Space Nine* with confidence and aplomb. Is he arrogant? Is he sweet on Jadzia Dax? Has he become closer to O'Brien since the crisis on Bajor? ✓**INTERNET**→*www* http://web.city.ac.uk/~cc103/cast/julian.html

Siddig el Fadil Most of the messages on AOL's Siddig el Fadil board focus on the same old topics—love, lust, sex, and romance. Will Bashir finally connect Dax's dots?

Merek thinks the Trill will decline: "I don't think that Dax is not capable of romance. It's just that with a 300-year-old slug in her belly, romance plays a lesser role in her life just now." Others suggest that he is secretly interested in Garak, but Lida disagrees: "The father/son theory makes a lot more sense, and is not gross.... Bashir is firmly established as a man who loves women, so let's keep it that way…"

While some of the threads veer completely off course—there's an extended exchange between two women about faithless men that reads like a white paper for a country ballad—most of them try to diagnose the character of the good Doctor. ✓**AMERICA ONLINE** →*keyword* trek→Star Trek Message Boards→Deep Space Nine Board→Siddig el Fadil

Siddig el Fadil Filmography Well, Siddig el Fadil hasn't done very much for Hollywood yet, except for DS9—nothing, in fact, except for a role in an upcoming Lawrence of Arabia film. But that doesn't diminish his starpower as the handsome and confident Dr. Julian Bashir. ✓**INTERNET**→*www* http://www.cm.cf.ac.uk/M/person-exact?a16994E→Search the database for a person's name→ *Search for the name(s):* fadil

The O'Briens

Chief Ops Officer Miles O'Brien A brief biography of DS9's working-class hero, including an account of his accidental murder of a Cardassian while on patrol duty. ✓**INTERNET**→*www* http://web.city.ac.uk/~cc103/cast/miles.html

Colm Meaney Filmography Meaney has had small parts in a number of big films, including *Die Hard 2* and *Dick Tracy*, and slightly larger roles in such films as *The Last of the Mohicans*, *The Snapper*, and *The Commitments*. Keep track of his growing body of work with this list of film and TV credits. ✓**INTERNET**→*www* http://www.cm.cf.ac.uk/Movies/→Search the database for a person's name→ *Search for the name(s):* meaney, colm

Miles O'Brien Pictures of Chief of DS9's Operations Miles O'Brien. ✓**PVG** *dial* 513-233-7993 →<your username>→<your password>→ F→*Download a file:* DSN-003.GIF *and* OBRIEN1.GIF

Miles O'Brien Page A page entirely devoted to the character portrayed by Colm Meaney. Why? Well, the page comes with its own raison d'être. To wit: "It's astonishing, how much stuff you can find on the Net about pretty much every idiot who ever appeared in ST:TNG. But for whatever reason, Miles O'Brien seems to be ignored by most people." In rectifying this oversight, the page provides pictures of O'Brien, a list of all the DS9 episodes in which he appears, a chronology of his life with episode references, a Colm Meaney interview, and trivia about the actor and the character. ✓**INTERNET**→ *www* http://www.astro.umd.edu/~sgeier/obrien.html

Keiko O'Brien Picture of Keiko holding her daughter Molly. ✓**PVG** *dial* 513-233-7993→<your username>→<your password>→F→ *Download a file:* KEIKO.GIF

The O'Brien Family—downloaded from Perfect Vision Graphics BBS

The O'Briens Picture of Miles, Keiko, and baby. ✓**PVG** *dial* 513-233-7993→<your username> →<your password>→ F→*Download a file:* PVDSN01.GIF

Quark

Armin Shimerman Filmography Before he was Quark, he was nothing! Unless you count a diverse film and TV career that includes roles in Blake Edwards's *Blind Date*, the horror flick *The Hitcher*, and *Murder, She Wrote*. ✓**INTERNET**→*www* http://www.cm.

cf.ac.uk/Movie→Search the data-base for a person's name→*Search for the name(s)*: shimerman, armin

DS9 "The House of Quark" Teaser Quark killing a Klingon. WAV file. ✓**COMPUSERVE**→*go* sfme-dia→Libraries→*Search by file name*: HOUSEO.ZIP

Quark Pictures of Quark. ✓**PVG** *dial* 513-233-7993→<your user-name>→<your password>→F→ *Download a file*: QUARK.GIF *and* DS9-QURK.GIF *and* QUARK02.GIF

Quark The barkeep and Ferengi host gets the star treatment here, with a brief essay that explains his avaricious (and yet somehow sym-pathetic) nature. ✓**INTERNET**→*www* http://web.city.ac.uk/~cc103/cast /quark.html

Quark A relatively unfocused discussion on Armin Shimerman and the Ferengi profiteer he por-trays. Topics include a campaign to save the Ferengi family of Rom and Nog, the size of Ferengi Q-tips, and a fan's rosy assessment of Shimerman's instructional skills: "I saw Armin do a rather quick master class at a British Beauty and the Beast convention, he was wonderful. Everyone came away from it feeling like they had really learned something about acting." ✓**AMERICA ONLINE**→*key-word* trek→ Star Trek Message Boards→Deep Space Nine Board →Quark

Quark Fan Club Application to join OASIS, the Quark/Armin Shimerman fan club. ✓**AMERICA ONLINE**→*keyword* trek→MORE...→ Star Trek Record Banks→Text/Other Files→Upld: 07/02/94→TEXT: Quark Club Application (filename: QUARKCLB.APP)

Quark—downloaded from Perfect Vision Graphics BBS

Quarks The shape-shifter and the Ferengi are at it again. Sound-clip of a scene where Odo enters Quark's and makes a public re-quest that everyone at the bar "please refrain from using your imaginations." Quark mocks Odo, saying, "Just because you don't have an imagination—don't ruin it for the rest of us." For Macs. ✓**IN-TERNET**→ *anon-ftp* sumex-aim.stanford.edu→ /info-mac/snd→quark.hqx

Gul Dukat

Dukat Smiles Picture of Gul Dukat smiling sweetly. ✓**COM-PUSERVE**→*go* sfmedia→Libraries→ *Search by file name*: ducat.gif

Dukat's Women Though there's plenty of general discussion about Gul Dukat, the main purpose of this message board is to discuss the erotic and romantic potential of the Cardassian. "I like Garak as well, but there isn't enough infor-mation about him to develop an attachment. True, Andrew is a su-perb actor, and he makes Garak come to life, but he doesn't have an aura of animal magnetism that Alaimo exudes everytime he puts on that exoskeleton (slurp)." Though this topic might not seem particularly promising, it seems to hold the interest of most of the participants, even the bemused men who occasionally drift

through: "So, Tiff, does this mean I can't come in here? Is this board kind of like at high school dances when all the girls go running off into the bathroom? We menfolk could never figure that out..." ✓**AMERICA ONLINE**→*keyword* trek→ Star Trek Message Boards→Deep Space Nine Board→Dukat's Wo-men

Mark Alaimo Filmography Alaimo has appeared in a number of films, including *Tango & Cash*, *The Dead Pool*, *Total Recall*, *Hard-core*, and *Seems Like Old Times*. Hungry for more? Check out this comprehensive filmography. ✓**IN-TERNET**→*www* http://www.cm.cf.ac.uk/M/person-exact?aA1BE→ Search the database for a person's name→*Search for the name(s)*: alaimo, mark

Never Trust Cardassians Who Smile Too Much Picture of the smiling Cardassian bigshot, Gul Dukat. ✓**COMPUSERVE** →*go* sfmedia →Libraries→*Search by file name*: DUCAT.GIF

Jake Sisko

Cirroc Lofton Filmography Before he was Jake Sisko, Cirroc Lofton appeared as a skateboarder in Ivan Reitman's cute-dog hit *Beethoven*, which also starred Charles Grodin. ✓**INTERNET**→*www* http://www.cm.cf.ac.uk/Movies/→ Search the database for a person's name→*Search for the name(s)*: lofton, cirroc

Jake Sisko Is young Jake better than TNG's child prodigy Wesley Crusher? Is the plague better than a field of flowers? This page fur-nishes all the relevant information on the commander's teenage son. ✓**INTERNET**→*www* http://web.city. ac.uk/~cc103/cast/jake.html

Guided tours of DS9

Week after week, *Deep Space Nine* takes place at the edge of the Alpha Quadrant, where

the Cardassians have built a space station to control the Bajoran race, only to see the Bajoran resistance force the Cardassian government to abandon its outpost to the Federation. And week after week, *Deep Space Nine* also takes place on the Net, where various aspects of the show are presented, catalogued, and dissected. First, head over to the **Deep Space Nine Episode Guide**, which offers plot summaries and cast lists. And then, spend some time luxuriating in the expanse of the **Star Trek DS9 List of Lists**, which includes character profiles, ship lists, and the incomplete but constantly updated **Ferengi Rules of Acquisition**.

On the Net

Across the board

DS9-Information Link Includes a cast list, brief plot summaries, video release information, and programming information for TV showings worldwide. ✓**INTERNET** →*www* http://www.ee.surrey.ac.uk/Personal/STDS9/Head.html

Broadcast info

Current DS9 Schedule The names and airdates of the next few

Video—from http://www.ee.surrey.ac. uk/Personal/STDS9/video.html

episodes of *Deep Space Nine.* ✓**AMERICA ONLINE**→*keyword* trek→ current ds9 schedule

TV showings Airdates for the U.S., the U.K., Australia, and Germany. ✓**INTERNET**→*www* http://www.ee.surrey.ac.uk/Personal/STD S9/air dates.html

Video releases

Deep Space Nine Video Releases Not yet released on video in the U.S., DS9 episodes are already available in the United Kingdom and Australia. This document lists the available episodes, along with their catalog numbers, and a picture of several of the cartridge covers. ✓**INTERNET**→*www* http://www.ee.surrey.ac.uk/Personal/STDS9/video.html

Encyclopedia

Star Trek: Deep Space Nine Index and Encyclopedia A marvelous DS9 reference that comprises close to seventy pages of descriptions of episodes, characters, ships, worlds, food and drink, elements, diseases, games and sports, animals, and plants. ✓**TFDN** →TFDN—Trek Facts→*Download a file:* DS9E0994.ZIP

Episode guides

Deep Space Nine Episode Guide An up-to-date episode guide to the show, organized in episode tables. Check airdates, stardates, and summaries, and find your favorites, whether it's "Dax" or "If Wishes Were Horses." Each listing links to a slightly longer plot description. ✓**INTERNET**→*www* http://www.ee.surrey.ac.uk/Personal/STDS9/episodes.html

Deep Space Nine: Episodes This board has separate discussion topics for each and every episode of the current season. Also includes general chat about the seasons. If you want to muse on Odo's relationship with the Dominion as portrayed in the two-part episode "The Search," or nit-pick Trill psychology in "Dax," head here. ✓**GENIE**→*keyword* sfrt2 →SFRT2 Bulletin Board→set 29

Deep Space Nine Seasons Episode List A list of DS9 episodes and episode numbers. ✓**EWORLD**→sf→Star Trek→Captain's Log→Deep Space Nine Seasons Episode List

DSN Episode Guide Hypercard Stack Options for short, long, and note-like synopses for episodes from the first season of DS9. Director, stardate, airdate, episode number, guest stars, and cast member information also included. Generate reports, search the stack, and access hypertext links to other hypercard stacks for TOS and TNG. Requires Macintosh, system 6.05 or higher and 2.5 megs of RAM. ✓ **INTERNET**→*anon-ftp* ftp.u-tokyo.ac.jp→/mac/umich/hypercard/fun/startrek→dsnineguide2.0.cpt.hqx ✓ **COMPUSERVE**→*go* sfmedia→*Libraries*→*Search by file name:* DS921A.SIT ✓ **AMERICA ONLINE**→*keyword* mac software→Search the Libraries→Search All Libraries→*Search by file name:* Star Trek-DS9 Guides 2.0.sea

DSN-Episode Guide No-frills, brief descriptions of episodes. The site tends to be several episodes behind. ✓ **INTERNET**→*www* http://www.cms.dmu.ac.uk/~it2yh/dsnep.html

Episode Guide A list of episodes, their stardates, and one-line plot summaries from "Emissary" to "The Jem Hadar." For some reason, episodes are handled in pairs, which are called "volumes." ✓ **INTERNET**→*www* http://web.city.ac.uk/~cc103/ds9/episodes.html ✓ **DELPHI**→*go* ent sta dat set ds9→read DS9 Episode Guide→down *or* list

Program Guides Fairly detailed summaries of each episode of DS9. ✓ **INTERNET**→*www* http://ringo.ssn.flinders.edu.au/vidiot/ds9.html

Star Trek: Deep Space Nine Episode Guide Compiled by the moderator of the Science Fiction Lovers mailing list, this guide fea-

tures an overview of the show, a list of regular cast members, and an annotated list of episodes with paragraph-length plot summaries and the names of the producer, writers, directors, and cast members. ✓ **INTERNET**→*anon-ftp* elbereth.rutgers.edu→/pub/sfl→star-trek-ds9.guide

Star Trek: Deep Space Nine Episodes A straightforward list of episodes, stardates, and airdates. The list is often several episodes ahead of airing dates. ✓ **INTERNET**→*www* http://www.pt.hk-r.se/student/pt94ero/DS9.Episodes.html

The Star Trek: Deep Space Nine FAQ List A list of episodes and stardates from the first two seasons. ✓ **AMERICA ONLINE**→*keyword* trek→MORE...→Star Trek Record Banks→Text/Other Files→Upld: 06/25/94 →TEXT: DS9 FAQ List (DS9FAQ.TXT)

Star Trek: Deep Space Nine Quick Reference Guide Short plot summaries of each episode of DS9. ✓ **INTERNET**→*anon-ftp* ftp.cc.umanitoba.ca→/startrek→quickref.ds9

Episode reviews

Deep Space Nine Episode Reviews A collection of Net Trekker Timothy Lynch's detailed DS9 episode reviews. As often as not, the reviews are critical—"is it just me, or was the love story angle given some of the worst dialogue [DS9's] seen in a long time?"—and Lynch spares no spoilers, tossing in ample dialogue excerpts and plot analyses along with his own material.

Are Lynch's reviews worth reading? Well, they're chatty and unpretentious, and he doesn't shrink from strong opinions; "In the Hands of the Prophets," for in-

stance, earns kudos as "one hell of a good show." ✓ **INTERNET** ...→*anon-ftp* ftp.coe.montana.edu→/pub/mirrors/.startrek→Tim_Lynch_stuff ...→*gopher* chop.isca.uiowa.edu: 8338→General Information→Star Trek Reviews ...→*gopher* chop.isca.uiowa.edu:8338→General Information→Star Trek Reviews

Ted Brengle's IMHO Retrospective of DS9's First Season Review of the first season of DS9. ✓ **TFDN**→TFDN — Fact Files→ds9.zip

Trekker DS9 Reviews Phil Kernick's sarcastic reviews, which subject DS9 episodes to a constant stream of mocking patter. ✓ **INTERNET**→*www* http://ringo.ssn.flinders.edu.au:80/trekker/ds9/

Lists, trivia & quotes

Star Trek DS9 List of Lists Like most Lists of Lists, this massive DS9 document collects a cornucopia of series information and trivia, including episode summaries, the Ferengi Rules of Acquisition, ship lists, character profiles, and even continuity errors spotted by eagle-eyed fans. ✓ **INTERNET** ...→*anon-ftp* ftp.cc.umanitoba.ca→/startrek/lol→lol.ds9 ...→*anon-ftp* quepasa.cs.tu-berlin.de→/pub/doc/movies+tv-series/StarTrek/ lol_0494→dsn0494.txt ...→*anon-ftp* netcom.com→/pub/mholtz→dsnlist_0494.Z

Quotes from Star Trek: Deep Space Nine Who said, "My replicator or yours?" Julian Bashir asked Jadzia Dax in the episode "The Alternate," but odds are he wasn't the first. Stop by here for your *Deep Space Nine* quote fix. ✓ **INTERNET**→ *www* http://www.pt.hk-r.se/student/pt94ero/DS9.Quotes.html

PART 6

VOYAGER

Voyage of the damned

What would you do if you were stranded in the Delta Quadrant with more than 75 years

standing between you and your home? You'd probably hire a film crew and begin recording your adventures for broadcast on a fledgling television network. Or at least that was the decision of the crew of the *Voyager*. Trek's fourth series, *Star Trek: Voyager*, premiered this past January, and instantly became a major player in the world of sci-fi TV. On the Net, the impact was just as sudden. From the **Air Schedule and Press Release Web Page** to **Star Trek Voyager**, sites devoted to the new series began to proliferate, giving fans a chance to check on facts, share opinions, and learn about the production history of the show. And if you'd prefer a more formal approach to fan culture, check out Paramount Pictures' official **Voyager Page**.

Paramount's Voyager *Website—http://voyager.paramount.com/voyagermenu.html*

On the Net

Hubsites

Air Schedule and Press Release Web Page At the moment, one of the most comprehensive sites on the Net for *Voyager* information. Includes air schedules, cast profiles, an extensive collection of images from the premiere episode, and news articles about the show. ✓ **INTERNET→** *www* http://www.ftms.com/st-voy/

Entertainment Weekly Article A copy of EW's cover story on *Voyager*, with a special focus on actress Kate Mulgrew, who portrays the first female captain in Trek-space. Includes Mulgrew's assessment of the casting decision: "It took balls for these guys to hire me in this capacity. It's a bold choice, and an appropriate one for 400 years in the future." ✓ **INTERNET→** *www* http://www.timeinc.com/ew/950120/voyager/voyager1.html

Star Trek Voyager From the earliest speculation—an October 1993 message that asks if *Voyager* is "the *Next Generation* continuation featuring the brash Riker double and Troi on a new ship?" —to more recent reaction to the pilot, Trek fans lavish praise and (occasionally) scorn on the newest series. Kate Mulgrew's voice comes under fire, as does the quality of the writing, but most fans agree that the show's strengths are more evident than either TNG or DS9 at this stage in their evolution. ✓ **AMERICA ONLINE→** *keyword* scifi→ Star Trek/Comics/TV/Star Wars Boards→Star Trek→ST: Voyager

Star Trek: Voyager Character profiles, episode guides, and some phenomenal pictures of the *Voyager* ship. ✓ **INTERNET→** *www* http://www.armory.com/~bsc/voyager/voyager.html

Voyager A single-page site maintained by Michael Zecca, this document offers information on air schedules, the show's premise, advertising, and soundtrack information. As the show develops, coverage and features are sure to grow.

✓ **INTERNET**→*www* http://www. eeng.dcu.ie/~stdcu/voyager/voy ager.html

Voyager A longish document with assorted facts about the *Voyager* series. Highlights include a list of stations that will carry the show worldwide. ✓ **INTERNET**→*www* http://web.city.ac.uk/~cc103/voy ager.html

Voyager Page With an introduction from the holographic Dr. Zimmerman and a recorded message from star Kate Mulgrew, this is one of the fanciest sites—which is only fitting, since it's bankrolled by Paramount Pictures itself. ✓ **INTERNET**→*www* http://voyager.para mount.com/

Broadcast info

Air Schedule Official and unofficial air schedules for *Voyager,* with upcoming episode titles. ✓ **INTERNET**→*www* http://www.ftms. com/st-voy/AirSched1.html

Chat

rec.arts.startrek* (ng) These most public of forums—the newsgroups—allow for the most open (and some might even say vicious) discussions. Here the Vulcan of color and the Native American from another planet are mapped on the matrix of political correctness. Others include off-the-cuff speculations on how the ship can get back in less that 75 years ("just click your heels together three times") and analyses of the straight-man from Laurel and Hardy to Neelix and Tuvok. Get it of your chest here, since there are bound to be legions of fans, likeminded and dissenting, ready to take you on. ✓ **USENET**

Star Trek: Voyager On Com-

puServe, there's a riot going on, mostly because some unfrozen caveman Trek fan suggested that there's something "not nice" about a female starship captain. Set phasers on "Steinem." Others discuss the black Vulcan issue—is it just a result of natural evolution, or an indication that by the 24th century we have overcome any need to "explain away" multiracial casting? And can Tuvok, whatever his skin color, be "as good a Vulcan as Spock"? Finally, there's the issue of the array. Would Picard have stranded his crew in the middle of nowhere just to save a dependent race? Would Kirk? And since the ship is commanded by Kathryn Janeway, does it really matter? ✓ **COMPUSERVE**→*go* sfmedia→Browse Message→Star Trek

Star Trek: Voyager If you like Katherine Hepburn, you'll love the new *Star Trek* Captain Kathryn Janeway, whose voice and manners resemble those of the Hollywood legend. Hepburn fans find Captain Janeway very appealing, while those who can't even approach a golden pond have some reservations about her brittle manner. Trekkers on eWorld also turn their noses up at plot platitudes—there is plenty of criticism of "plasma storms and ships hiding in this or that nebula," but many seem willing to give the show a fair chance. And finally, there's a considerable amount of ship talk, everything from *Voyager's* warp potential to interior decor (some say that the bridge is "too cluttered"). ✓ **EWORLD**→sf→Star Trek→On the Small Screen→Star Trek: Voyager

Star Trek: Voyager If detailed analysis of every nanosecond of the *Voyager* show is your pleasure, search no further. The opening credits sequence has already gar-

nered over 70 messages. Under scrutiny this specific, *Voyager* doesn't always hold up—older Trekkers are suspicious of the show's relation to past series, and many viewers are hostile toward Kate Mulgrew's Captain Janeway. On the other hand, Ensign Harry Kim has made a big hit with the legions of brand new Trek fans, and there are plenty of technological discussions (*Voyager* v. *Defiant*) and ideological skirmiskes (the gays-in-space thread has yet to dwindle even three months after the "lesbians on ship" rumor proved to be false). Viewers also take the opportunity to lay out what they never want to see again. "No more mind-control episodes!" "No more Klingon honor tales." "No more lame doomed love affairs!" Paramount, are you listening? ✓ **AMERICA ONLINE**→*keyword* trek→Star Trek Message Boards→ Star Trek: Voyager

Star Trek: Voyager *Voyager* talk among these die-hard *Star Trek* fans focuses on a single dominant question—is the show too similar to TNG and TOS, or is it too different? Some fear for the future of the *Star Trek* franchise and others insist that the dream of the Great Bird still abides. Amidst gripes about aliens who don't have water—hard to believe that they could have fancy spaceships and the ability to travel to other planets, but somehow neglect to store the SINGLE MOST IMPORTANT FLUID IN THE ENTIRE GALAXY!—and complaints about the new Captain's voice ("Katherine Hepburn on helium," opines one wag), the conversation is packed with the sorts of Trek questions that occupy fans everywhere. Would a truthful Vulcan make a very good spy? Can the hologram doctor make conceptual leaps of logic? And was the Prime

Directive violated, or was the crew merely compensating for its earlier intervention? ✓GENIE→*keyword* sfrt2→SFRT2 Bulletin Board→set 30

Trek_voyager (echo) As anyone here is happy to point out, the *Voyager* is not the first Federation starship to be helmed by a female captain. Does anyone remember Captain Garrett of the *Enterprise-C*? Have we all gone nuts? In advance of the show's debut, most discussion focused on names that were floated as possibilities for Janeway—Patsy Kensit, Lindsay Wagner—especially after actress Genevieve Bujold walked off the set two days into production. While other threads moved into TNG territory—conversation on The Great Gates McFadden Autograph Scandal ("Gatesgate")—*Voyager* discussion picked up again after the series pilot, and some fans even took the time to reconsider the public trashing of Bujold, remarking that "Trek fandom is singularly unforgiving" to one's private life. ✓FIDONET

TV: Voyager How does *Voyager* stack up against old *Star Trek* series? Fans are grading it somewhere in the A-/B+ range, not shabby at all for a newcomer. Some sci-fi aficionados with longer memories find the premise a bit limited—"wasn't *Lost in Space* already done?" asks one fan, although no one mentions *Gilligan's Island* (feel free to break into individual discussion groups to compare Kate Mulgrew's competent management with the bumbling command of Alan Hale. Jr.). Then there are questions that nag at even the most casual fan. Is Janeway a captain with a conscience or a wimp with a fancy uniform? If Ocampas only live nine years, will that beautiful young thing be a shriveled hag be-

fore we know it? Throughout, the adjective "awesome" gets a workout from the show's younger fans. ✓PRODIGY→*jump* star trek bb→ Choose a Topic→TV: Voyager

Voyager These fans are really serious about the importance of *Voyager* to the *Trek* canon—they have enthusiasm to spare, and a few of them are even offering to mail tapes to the benighted areas of the country that don't get UPN. In addition, there's lots of speculation about the future of the *Voyager* crew—will they meet the Borg out there in the Gamma quadrant, or encounter Wesley Crusher on his travels? Participants are invited to take an online survey that rates the show and the its characters—here, Harry Kim wins hands down. And for everyone who has already decided on the show's merits, here's a corrective insight: "If *Voyager* was that bad how would you rate *My Mother the Car*?" ✓DELPHI→*go* ent star forum

Episode guide

Heart of Stone Teaser Soundclip for "Heart of Stone." ✓COMPUSERVE→*go* sfmedia→Libraries →*Search by file name:* heart.zip

Life Support Soundclip of the teaser for "Life Support." ✓COMPUSERVE→*go* sfmedia→Libraries →*Search by file name:* life.zip

Star Trek: Voyager (Episodes) Summaries of episodes, from "Caretaker" and "Parallax" through last week's stellar interstellar offering. ✓GENIE→*keyword* sfrt2→SFRT2 Bulletin Board→set 31

Synopsis of Voyager Pilot Episode A brief and not entirely accurate summary of the plot of the pilot episode of the series. ✓IN-

TERNET→*www* http://www.armory. com/~bsc/voyager/voyepisode. html

Time and Again Soundclip of the teaser for the episode "Time and Again." ✓COMPUSERVE→*go* sfmedia→Libraries→*Search by file name:* time.zip

Reviews & nitpicking

Published Articles About Voyager Articles about *Voyager* from *TV Guide, Variety,* and the *Wisconsin State Journal.* Also includes a special bonus—a *Parade* magazine Q & A session with Genevieve Bujold (the first Captain Janeway) about her decision to leave the show. ✓INTERNET→ *www* http://www. ftms.com/st-voy/articles. html

Trekker Treat *Entertainment Weekly* TV critic Ken Tucker hails the arrival of UPN and *Voyager* in a generally complimentary review of the newest *Trek* series. ✓INTERNET→ *www* http://www.timeinc. com/ew/950127/TV/259TVvoy ager.html

The ship

The Ship The *Voyager* ship, the latest model in the Trek starship fleet, has the ability to land on planets—and it's cool besides. These artists' renderings of the *Voyager* range from basic blueprints to elaborate raytraces. ✓INTERNET ...→*www* http://www. ftms.com/images/voyager_a.gif ...→*www* http://www.ftms.com/ images/voyager_b.gif ...→*www* http://www.armory.com/~bsc/ voyager/voyager.jpg ...→*www* http://www.armory.com/~bsc/ voyager/voyager1.gif ...→*www* http://www.armory.com/~bsc/ voyager/voyager2.gif

Delta Quadrant exiles

Like every other Trek series, Voyager is powered by the interaction between the cast

members. From Captain Kathryn Janeway to Lieutenant Tom Paris, from Chakotay to Kes, the new crew is filled with strong personalities, and most of them are well-represented online. Read *Entertainment Weekly*'s **Space Cadets**, a sidebar to a recent cover story on *Voyager* that offers brief character profiles along with photos. Keep track of the ever-expanding **Jennifer Lien Filmography**. And judge Captain Janeway's much-maligned voice—faux Hepburn, some say—by listening to soundclips (**Before You Sprain Something**, clipped from an at-ease order given to Ensign Harry Kim, is fast becoming a popular catchphrase).

The Making of Voyager—*http://www.ftms.com/st-voy/images/voy_26.jpg*

On the Net

Across the board

Captain and Officers GIF of Janeway, Chakotay, and Tuvok. ✓ **COMPUSERVE**→*go* sfmedia→Libraries →*Search by file name:* CAPT2.GIF

The Cast A trio of photos of the entire cast, along with individual publicity photos of the principal performers. ✓ **INTERNET**→*www* http://www.ftms.com/st-voy/Cast.html

Series Information Includes cast, credits, and additional information for *Voyager* series. ✓ **INTERNET**→*www* http://www.msstate.edu/M/title-exact? 1C0A3

Space Cadets Subtitled "The Shipshape cast of the *Voyager* reports for roll call," this *Entertainment Weekly* article, printed just after the series first aired, offers a gallery of the series' stars, along with brief profiles of their characters. ✓ **INTERNET**→ *www* http://www.timeinc.com/ew/950120/voyager/voyager_bar.html

Star Trek Voyager—The Characters Though this document originally contained some errors, they'll almost certainly be corrected during the first few weeks of the show's run. In addition, there are some fascinating rumors about characters who will be added to the show—most notably, Patty Yusutake, who is rumored to be tranferring from the *Enterprise*

NCC-1701-D. ✓ **INTERNET**→*www* http://deeptht.armory.com/~bsc/voyager/characters.html

Voyager Character List Compiled before the airing of the *Voyager* pilot, this is a list of the show's characters, along with a brief biography of each. ✓ **AMERICA ONLINE**→*keyword* trek→MORE...→ Star Trek Record Banks→Text/Other Files→Upld: 09/24/94 TEXT: Voyager Character Bios→VOYCRW.TXT ✓**EWORLD**→sf→Star Trek→Captain's Log→STVoyager→Character Info/list

Capt. Janeway

Before You Sprain Something Soundclip of Captain Janeway advising, "Mr. Kim—at ease before you sprain some-

thing." ✓**COMPUSERVE** →*go* sfmedia→Libraries→*Search by file name:* atease.zip

Bipedal Species Sound-clip of Captain Jane-way to the Caretak-er: "This minor bi-pedal species does not take kindly to being abduct-ed." WAV file. ✓**COMPUSERVE**→*go* sfmedia→Libraries→*Search by file name:* failed.zip

Captain Kathryn Janeway Photo of Kate Mulgrew in cos-tume for the role. ✓**INTERNET**→ *www* http://www.ftms.com/st-voy/images/voyper01.jpg

Janeway's Introduction A WAV file of Captain Janeway in-troducing herself to Neelix. ✓**COM-PUSERVE**→*go* sfmedia→Libraries→ *Search by file name:* cptjnw.wav

Kate Mulgrew Filmography Lists her credits, including *Roots: The Gift* (which also featured Av-ery Brooks, who plays DSN's Commander Benjamin Sisko). the soap opera *Ryan's Hope*, the film *Throw Momma from the Train*. And of course, *Mrs. Columbo*. ✓**INTERNET**→ *www* http://www. msstate.edu/Movies/→Search the database for a person's name→ *Search for the name(s):* Mulgrew, Kate

Capt. Janeway (NOT!)

Genevieve Bujold Filmogra-phy The long and storied career of the French-Canadian actress who would have been Captain, back through her roles in *Le Voleur* and *The Trojan Women*. ✓**INTERNET**→ *www* http://www. msstate.edu/Movies/→Search the database for a person's name→ *Search for the name(s):* Bujold, Genevieve

Chakotay

Chakotay A Native Ameri-can from another planet? How much sense does that make? And what do those mark-ings above his eye mean? A picture of the *Voyager's* First Officer. ✓**INTERNET**→*www* http://www.ftms.com/st-voy/images/voyper02a.jpg

Robert Beltran Filmography Usually typecast in an ethnic Latin role—from Lieutenant Delgado in *Crackdown* to Juan in *Scenes from the Class Stuggle in Beverly Hills*— Robert Beltran is perhaps best known for his role as Raoul in *Eating Raoul*. ✓**INTERNET**→*www* http://www.msstate.edu/Movies/ →Search the database for a per-son's name→*Search for the name(s):* Beltran, Robert

Tom Paris

Lt. Tom Paris Dashing in only the way a torment-ed ex-con can be, Tom Paris is confi-dent and cocky, even in this cast photo. ✓**INTERNET**→*www* http://www. ftms.com/st-voy/images/voyper09. jpg

Robert Duncan McNeill Fil-mography This veteran of *Star Trek: The Next Generation*, who appeared as Senior Cadet Nicholas Locano in "The First Duty," ap-pears as Tom Paris. Find out about his other roles with this filmogra-phy. ✓**INTERNET**→*www* http:// www.msstate.edu/Movies/→ Search the database for a person's name→ *Search for the name(s):* Mc-Neill, Robert Duncan

Tuvok

Tim Russ Filmography With appearances in *Bird, Spaceballs, Crossroads,* and *Mr. Saturday Night,* Tim Russ may be familiar to you even without the pointy Vulcan ears. ✓**INTERNET**→*www* http://www.msstate.edu/Movies/ →Search the database for a per-son's name→*Search for the name(s):* Russ, Tim

Tuvok Photo of the Vulcan Security Chief, described as a 24th century version of sleuth Her-cule Poirot. ✓**INTERNET**→ *www* http://www.ftms. com/st-voy/images/voyper03.jpg

Vulcan-L (ml) Tuvok adds new blood to this old mailing list. One Vulcan-watcher was "a bit con-fused with the Tuvok role—he seemed to act more as first offi-cer/science officer than a security officer." The participants go on to wonder about Tuvok's personali-ty—"Actually, he reminded me a lot of Odo, more than Spock. He seemed to have too much of an at-titude with Neelix"—and to hope that the *Voyager* writers remember *Pon farr.* ✓**INTERNET**→*email* major-domo@netcom.com ✍ *Type in mes-sage body:* subscribe vulcan-l <your email address>

B'Elanna Torres

B'Elanna Torres Nice photograph of chief engineer B'Elanna Torres. ✓**INTERNET**→*www* http://www.ftms. com/st-voy/ images/ voyper09. jpg

Roxann Biggs-Dawson Filmography She hasn't been in much before *Voyager*, but she's in *Voyager*, and that's enough to merit a filmography page for Roxann Biggs-Dawson. ✓**INTERNET**→*www* http://www.msstate.edu/Movies/→Search the database for a person's name→*Search for the name(s):* Biggs-Dawson, Roxann

Dr. Zimmerman

Doctor Replacement A soundclip of the holographic doctor: "A replacement must be ordered as soon as possible." ✓**COMPUSERVE**→*go* sfmedia→Libraries→*Search by file name:* replac.zip

Dr. Zimmerman Photo of the holographic doctor. ✓**INTERNET**→ *www* http://www.ftms.com/st-voy/images/voyper04a.jpg

Robert Picardo Filmography You know Coach Ed Cutlip on *The Wonder Years*? You know Eddie from *The Howling*? If you do, you also know Robert Picardo, who plays the holographic doctor aboard the *Voyager*. ✓**INTERNET**→ *www* http://www.msstate.edu/Movies/→Search the database for a person's name→*Search for the name(s):* Picardo, Robert

Harry Kim

Garrett Wang Filmography The young Asian-American actor is making his debut in the series, but if the popularity of Harry Kim is any indication, watch this spot for more information on what is sure to be a brilliant career. ✓**INTERNET**→*www* http://www.msstate.edu/Movies/→Search the database for a person's name→*Search for the name(s):* Wang, Garrett

Harry Kim Young enough to have a yearbook photo, this 21-year-old communications officer instead has a cast photo. ✓**INTERNET**→*www* http://www.ftms.com/st-voy/images/voyper08.jpg

Kes

Jennifer Lien Filmography *Voyager* marks the debut for this 20-year-old, who is bidding to become the Meg Ryan of the Delta Quadrant. ✓**INTERNET**→ *www* http://www.msstate.edu/Movies/→Search the database for a name→*Search for the name(s):* Lien, Jennifer

Kes If you were a beautiful and ethereal Ocampa with less than nine years to live, would you tag along with a ship with a 75-year sentence in the deepest reaches of space? Maybe not—but if you decide to take the trip, here's a nice picture that you can leave behind to remind your friends and loved ones of your smiling face. ✓**INTERNET**→*www* http://www.ftms.com/st-voy/images/voyper06.jpg

Neelix

Ethan Phillips Filmography From *Bloodhounds of Broadway* to *Green Card*, from *Glory* to *Lean on Me*, from *The Shadow* to *Ragtime*, Ethan Phillips has had a long career of short screen appearances, both in the movies and on the tube. ✓**INTERNET**→ *www* http://www.msstate.edu/Movies/→Search the database for a person's name→ *Search for the name(s):* Phillips, Ethan

Neelix Fast-talking, smelly, idiosyncratic, and enamored of all kinds of space garbage, Neelix also takes a great picture. ✓**INTERNET**→ http://www.ftms.com/st-voy/images/voyper05a.jpg

Neelix Greeting Soundclip of Neelix to the *Voyager* crew: "Good to meet you!" ✓**COMPUSERVE**→*go* sfmedia→Libraries→*Search by file number:* neelix.wav

STARNOTES

"The black Vulcan really was…fascinating. I can't recall any mention of other colors on Vulcan in any book or movie. But no reason why not. It stays much more with the Gene Roddenberry goal of an integrated and equal universe.

On to other things. In reply to the question about the Vulcan brain vs human brain, somewhere I recall the Vulcan brain actually has 4 parts, with each part being able to work independently of the other."

—from **Vulcan-L**

FREE KATE MULGREW!

Vox Populi on the Net

Late last summer, just before *Star Trek: Voyager* began production, rumors circulated that Paramount was reconsidering its decision to cast a female captain. Within days, the online world sprang to the defense of gender balance and equal opportunity in outer space. The first klaxon was sounded by Trek reviewer extraordinaire Tim Lynch, who posted messages on rec.arts. startrek* newsgroups that encouraged his fellow fans to contact Paramount executives and make their displeasure known. Within days, more than 200 Trekkers answered Lynch's call, flooding Paramount's offices with plaintive letters and pointed faxes. Eventually, Paramount opted to cast a woman in the role—Kate Mulgrew as Captain Kathryn Janeway, who took over the command of the *Voyager* in the series premiere January 16. Was the Lynch mob responsible for preserving this decision? Perhaps. Whatever the case, the letter-writing campaign was at the very least an illustration of the Net's ability to amplify fan voices, and it is in that spirit that we reprint Lynch's August 1994 post:

> Hi, folks. Sorry for the cross-posting, but this is a large enough topic that I felt it was appropriate. Follow-ups are set to r.a.s.fandom, as it seems the most likely venue.
>
> Based on some conversations I've had around town (casting agents, that sort of thing), I think the rumor of Paramount execs *wanting* to cast a man as Voyager captain is correct.
>
> However, filming hasn't started yet, which means there is a chance of the situation changing. As such, I have a suggestion.
>
> Someone's already posted Rick Berman's office phone number. DO NOT USE IT. It would probably be considered harassment and do at least as much harm as good.
>
> Let's go with the old standby: a letter-writing campaign. What the

hey, it's worked once, albeit years ago. I would strongly suggest the following criteria:

1) Do not, not, NOT make it confrontational. I know enough people in the industry to guarantee that any letter starting, "You money-grubbing bastards" will be tossed into a wastebasket unfinished.

2) Make it intelligent, but disappointed. Point out, for instance, that casting a woman as the lead role would open up dramatic areas left unexplored by Trek in the past, and that Trek has a nearly 30-year tradition of doing new and bold things. If it applies to you, it might not be a bad idea to point out that you were excited about the initial idea when you first heard it.

[IF your chances of watching the show change with the casting choice, then you should absolutely mention it—but be very, VERY careful. Don't phrase it as a threat; it'll get nowhere. Something like "I'm burning out a bit on the 'same old, same old' Trek formula, but a change in the lead would be radical enough to keep my interest" might be nice—but please change the wording. These letters shouldn't look identical.]

3) It should be sent to Kerry McCluggage (sp?), who is in charge of Paramount's television division.

4) DO NOT, UNDER ANY CIRCUMSTANCES, mention Trek anywhere on the envelope. If you do, the letters will head straight to the Trek building — Rick Berman et al. They're not the ones that need the letters.

Once again, that's:

— to Kerry McCluggage at Paramount, NOT anyone at Trek;

— disappointed, but intelligently written and NOT confrontational in the least;

— possibly mentioning Trek's past history of boldness and the dramatic potential of the casting choice.

One other thing: Given Voyager's scheduled premiere in January, the casting choice will have to be made very, VERY soon. Time is of the essence here; let's do it.

Tim Lynch

"If your chances of watching the show change with the casting choice, mention it—but be very, very careful. Don't phrase it as a threat."

PART 7

REAL
SPACE

Astronomy

From *Star Wars* to *Star Trek*, from *Starman* to *Star Search*, much of science fiction has

busied itself imagining what goes on beyond those tiny pinpricks of light that constellate the night sky. And in recent decades, astronomy has supplemented its age-old interest in optics—how can we devise new and better ways of seeing into distant space?—with other concerns that press against disciplines such as geology, physics, theology, and philosophy. What kinds of life are out there? Do we have any right to investigate? And what does it tell us about life on our own planet? On the Net, astronomy enjoys the richness and diversity of resources accorded to all major sciences. Blast off from **AstroWeb** and **The Star*s Collection**, debate the profession in **sci.astro**, or share your knowledge about gravitational fields and coilguns in **sci.space.tech**.

On the Net

Hubsites

Astronomy Hypertext Book With documents on inverse square law and planetary motion, this isn't the most basic of sites, but it is a useful resource for students of astronomy. In addition to its gen-

Total eclipse—downloaded from galaxy.uci.agh.edu.pl

eral resources, this site includes problem sets, syllabi, and reading lists for astronomy classes at the University of Oregon. ✓**INTERNET**→ *www* http://zebu.uoregon.edu /text.html

AstroWeb Weave your way through AstroWeb, which links to Internet astronomy resources of all types—Websites, gophers, telnet sites, FTP sites, and Usenet newsgroups. ✓**INTERNET**→ *www* http:// marvel.stsci.edu/net-resources.html

National Space Society Operated by the NSS—a "nonprofit, publicly supported organization promoting space research, exploration, development, and habitat" —this forum is anchored by an online version of *Ad Astra* maga-

zine; it includes articles about space activism, the NASA budget, and space shuttles. In addition, NSS maintains two bulletin boards, one devoted to general topics of interstellar interest, and the other focused on space politics. Threads in these boards range across the universe of discussion topics, from Mars missions to astronaut email to Gene Roddenberry ("By creating *Star Trek*, Gene opened the world of the future and the possibilities of life in space to the eyes of our country.") And if you're not in the mood to discuss, visit the online libraries— GIFs of pyramidal structures on Mars, notes on a space station redesign, space acronyms, and more. ✓**AMERICA ONLINE**→*keyword* space

The Star*s Collection A set of links to astronomy organizations, institutes, and projects across the globe. ✓**INTERNET**→*www* http://cdsweb.u-strasbg.fr/~heck/sf.htm

Astrochat

sci.astro (ng) Hard and soft astronomers meet here to debate the validity of new theories and old questions. During the Christmas season, for example, amateur astronomers, amateur Biblical scholars, and lots of others hashed out the question of what the star of Bethlehem really was. New ideas, such as a plan to reorbit Venus to make it conducive to life, get a hearing—if a somewhat skeptical one. Help is provided for those wanting to build their own telescope, or just needing some clarification, if possible, about the Big Bang, origin of the moon, or the age of the universe. ✓**USENET**

sci.astro.planetarium (ng) In addition to announcements for planetarium-related jobs and events, this group spends a fair amount of time discussing what's new in the field. The tone is more professionally oriented than many astronomy newsgroups—if you need to know an "algorithm to translate from equatorial coordinates (right ascension, declination) to galactic longitude and latitude," these people will more than likely know it by heart. ✓**USENET**

Basic astronomy

Astrotext An initiative to develop an online astronomy textbook with contributions from Net users. Currently in its planning stages, the textbook will be edited by astronomers from MIT. ✓**INTERNET**→*www* http://uu-gna.mit.edu: 8001/uu-gna/text/astro/index.html

Earth and Universe Billed as a comprehensive multimedia guide to our universe, this site links to educational programs about the Origin of the Universe, the Life Cycle of Stars, the Sun, the Galaxy, Nebulae, Planets, and Other Remarkable Sites. Proceed through the program with or without audio—either way, you'll come out knowing more about the stars than Carl Sagan, Jack Horkheimer, and Spock put together. ✓**INTERNET**→ *www* http://www.eia.brad.ac.uk/btl/

Frequently Seen Acronyms Learn these ASAP, from ASIS to FOS to FWHM to MECO to NASM to SOHO to SPAN to SSPS to XVV to YSO. OK? ✓**INTERNET**→*www* http://www.cis.ohio-state.edu/hypertext/faq/usenet/space/acronyms/faq.html

General Astronomy Information What is a star? Why do we have summer? What about leap years, pulsars, supernovae, sundials, and space shuttles? Get answers to basic questions of astronomy, including a list of the 25 brightest stars and the 30 stars closest to the Earth. ✓**INTERNET**→*www* http://cast0.ast.cam.ac.uk/RGO/leaflets/

sci.space.news (ng) Lots of information for those tracking the skies. There are space calendars, summaries of solar geophysical activities, space probe status reports ,and newsbriefs. This is also a good place to keep up with aerospace industry news through the frequent posting of corporate news releases. ✓**USENET**

Space FAQs Questions and answers on everything from mission schedules to planetary probes, from astronomical mnemonics to astronaut training. ✓**INTERNET**→

www http://www.cis.ohio-state.edu/hypertext/faq/usenet/space/top.html

Clubs

Bradley University Astrology Club Club information, membership benefits, club events, and a list of current members. ✓**INTERNET**→*www* http://lydia.bradley.edu/campusorg/astro/

Penn State Astronomy Club Information about the club, an event schedule, archives of sounds and images, and links to other astronomy pages on the Web. ✓**INTERNET**→*www* http://emb121.rh.psu.edu/astroclub/astroclubhome.html

The Planetary Society Founded by Carl Sagan and Bruce Murray, the society aims to ferret out the secrets of outer space. Learn about the Mars Rover Tests, visit the Center for Mars Exploration, or spend time investigating explorations with government and space agencies, scientists, engineers, students, and educators. ✓**INTERNET**→*www* http://wea.mankato.mn.us/TPS/

Observatories

List of Astronomical Observatories A complete list of world observatories, from Hungary's Konkoly Observatory to the Mt. Wilson Observatory to the Gemini 8m telescope. ✓**INTERNET**→*www* http://www.cfht.hawaii.edu/html/astro_observ.html

Solar system

A Guide to the Nine Planets Should actually be titled The Nine Planets and 61 Known Moons, Described and Presented With Multimedia Tools and Including

Chapters on Spacecraft, Terminology, and Space Science. From Mercury to Pluto (and Charon), the entire solar system is addressed. ✓**INTERNET**→*www* http://seds.lpl.arizona.edu/nineplanets/nineplanets/nineplanets.html

---

Guide to the Solar System After careful consideration and long hours of judging, the architects of this site have narrowed the set of planets in our solar system down to their favorite nine, and this site represents....What? There are only nine? Oh. Never mind. ✓**INTERNET**→*www* http://www.c3.lanl.gov/~cjhamil/SolarSystem/homepage.html

By planet

Mars Atlas The red planet is the source of so much sci-fi lore that it would be a shame not to have a Website devoted to its charms and myths, hard facts and cold scientific truths. And here it is, for your perusal—the Mars Atlas in all its crimson glory, a WWW-browsable, zoomable, and scrollable atlas of Mars, showing the locations (footprints) of thousands of high-resolution *Viking* Orbiter images. ✓**INTERNET**→*www* http://fi-www.arc.nasa.gov/fia/projects/bayesgroup/Atlas/Mars/

Mars Global Surveyor Project An overview of the project—press releases and regular updates. ✓**INTERNET**→*www* http://mgs-www.jpl.nasa.gov/

Saturn Events Planetary hula-hoop competitions? Games of Red Rover with its Jovian neighbors? This site offers basic documents on the Ringed Planet, along with plots, images, and animations. ✓**INTERNET**→*www* http://seds.lpl.arizona.edu/nineplanets/nineplanets/nineplanets.html

Space science

High Energy Astrophysics Space Research Center Located at the Goddard Space Flight Center, the High Energy Astrophysics Space Research Center is devoted to the study of, well, high-energy astrophysics. The Website includes a wealth of information about HEASRC projects, as well as links to other sites on the Internet. ✓**INTERNET**→*www* http://heasarc.gsfc.nasa.gov/

---

sci.space.policy (ng) The subtitle of this group could easily be "How to make a mint off the universe." The practicalities of funding a moon base through Hollywood film rights are discussed, alongside technical specifications for a machine to mine precious ores from fallen asteroids. Real "policy" discussion ranges around the perceived unwillingness of the government and the aerospace industry to make space travel economically feasible for the average entrepreneur. ✓**USENET**

---

sci.space.science (ng) Want to chat about ion engines, terraforming Venus, or the smallest known sun? While there are more technical terms floating around sci.space.science than other astronomy newsgroups, it isn't beyond the reach of most earthbound enthusiasts. Gentle jibing results when the uninformed wonder why Jupiter's orbit hasn't changed since being hit by the asteroids. (Evidently it's a matter of proportion—why doesn't the earth tilt when I jump off my desk?) ✓**USENET**

---

sci.space.tech (ng) Here aerospace techies plan the future with backyard inventors. Will a superconductor-powered motor function better in the frigid temperatures of space? There is in-depth analysis of the usefulness of railguns and coilguns, in which complex concepts like conductivity, mass, and projectile velocity make guest appearances. But there is also room for out-of-this-world speculation—a new version of the desert island scenario. "What would you need to move off the earth permanently?" ✓**USENET**

Space Science Information Systems This page has numerous hot links to a variety of NASA sites and international space science agencies, including the National Science Foundation (USA), Instituto Nacional de Pesquisas Espaciais (Brazil), Centre d'Études et de Recherches de Toulouse (France), Deutsche Forschungsanstalt für Luft- und Raumfahrt (Germany), Agenzia Spaziale Italiana (Italy), National Space Development Agency (Japan), and the United Nations Office for Outer Space Affairs. ✓**INTERNET**→ *www* http://www.igpp.ucla.edu/ssis.html

---

STARNOTES

"Unless we can find a sufficiently terrestrial environment in which we can start minimally, and at this time, only Mars is a possibility for habitation. We will need tools, the tools to make tools, and transportation to obtain the raw materials. It looks like we will need power sources to supplement solar power even within the solar system."

—from **sci.space.tech**

NASA

With a long history of space travel, the National Aeronautics and Space Administration

is the United States's version of *Star Trek*'s Starfleet, with a collection of spaceworthy vessels commissioned to probe the corners of the galaxy. In addition, NASA is also one of the most active government agencies on the Net, with dozens of Web-sites corresponding to the nation's major astrophysics facilities. Want to know more about the *Challenger* disaster (that's mission 51-L to NASA)? Check out **Shuttle Launches from the Kennedy Space Center**. Interested in learning about Houston's Mission Control? Drop into the **Johnson Space Center**. And if you're flummoxed by even a casual mention of the Zuni Rocket Vehicle, spend some time browsing the **NASA Thesaurus**.

Shuttle launch—downloaded from seds.lpl.arizona.edu-pub/images

On the Net

Hubsites

NASA Information Services
The main website for the National Aeronautics and Space Administration isn't fancy or slick, but it will help you move through the vast storehouse of NASA resources online. ✓**INTERNET**→*www* http://www.nasa.gov/

NASA Internet Connections

Link yourself silly with this document, which comprises the hundreds upon hundreds of NASA Net sites. ✓**INTERNET**→*www* http://www.jsc.nasa.gov/nasa/NASAInternet.html

Facilities

NASA Ames Research Center
Located at California's Moffett Field, in the heart of Silicon Valley, Ames Research Center is home to more than 30 of the U.S.'s principal technological facilities, including the world's most sophisticated wind tunnel complex and the most advanced supercomputing system on the planet. As you might expect, it has quite a presence on the Net, with more than a dozen Websites. This home page

unifies them all and gives some background information on the site. ✓**INTERNET**→*www* http://www.arc.nasa.gov/

NASA Dryden Flight Research Center *Top Gun* in outer space is more than just a fantasy—spacecraft need pilots just like jets do. The Dryden Flight Research Center in Edwards, California, trains pilots for space, and this site lists all current projects and tours the facility. ✓**INTERNET**→*www* http://www.dfrf.nasa.gov/dryden.html

NASA Goddard Space Flight Center WWW Home Page Learn more about the Earth by observing it through space. That's the shaping purpose of the Goddard Space Center in Greenbelt, Maryland. Goddard has more than sixty Websites, but this is a good starting point, with links to projects like Space Shuttle Small Payload and Hydrospheric Processes. ✓**INTERNET**→*www* http://www.gsfc.nasa.gov/GSFC_home page.html

NASA Johnson Space Center Perhaps most famous for Mission Control, Houston's Johnson Space Center remains one of the most venerable NASA facilities. Check out this Website for Johnson Space Center events, research projects, and directory information. ✓**INTERNET**→*www* http://www.jsc.nasa.gov/

NASA Kennedy Space Center President John F. Kennedy had a vision, that America should go bravely into space with its head held high and its eyes wide open, and the Kennedy Space Center in Florida stands as a testament to this idea. Similarly, the Kennedy Space Center Website testifies to the vision of Internet architects, with a wealth of resources for

space buffs. Want to know about KSC facilities? Interested in frequently asked space questions? Curious about linking to other international space sites? Get started here. ✓**INTERNET**→*www* http://www.ksc.nasa.gov/ksc.html

NASA Langley Research Center The Langley Research Center sits in Hampton, Virginia, in the CIA's backyard. Adorned with a graphic that celebrates the center's 75th anniversary (it occurred in 1992), this site offers press releases and documents. ✓**INTERNET**→*www* http://www.larc.nasa.gov/

NASA Lewis Research Center The highlight of this site is Internet NASA television coverage of shuttle mission STS-63, achieved through CU-See Me technology and broadcast real-time during the mission on February 2. But the page also contains links to other research projects currently in progress at this Cleveland facility. ✓**INTERNET**→*www* http://www.lerc.nasa.gov/

NASA Marshall Space Flight Center Located in Huntsville, Alabama, the Marshall Center is one of the most important NASA sites, and this Web page contains links to a wide variety of documents and press releases pertaining to the center's mission and research. ✓**INTERNET** *www* http://www.msfc.nasa.gov/

Space shuttles

Shuttle Launches from the Kennedy Space Center If you're a shuttle launch aficionado, this official NASA site is the place to be, with launch schedules, launch photos, detailed mission descriptions, and astronaut biographies. For a morbid frisson, check out the fate of 1986's mission 51-

L. "Launch Jan. 28 delayed two hours when hardware interface module in launch processing system, which monitors fire detection system, failed during liquid hydrogen tanking procedures. Explosion 73 seconds after liftoff claimed crew and vehicle. Cause of explosion was an O-ring failure in right SRB. Cold weather was a contributing factor." ✓**INTERNET**→*www* http://www.ksc.nasa.gov/shuttle/missions/missions.html

Space Shuttle Models A complete list of all space shuttle models available online, including information on how to retrieve plans and data from FTP sites. ✓**INTERNET**→*www* http://www-graphics.stanford.edu/~tolis/shuttle.html

Space stations

International Space Station Alpha The next time you're watching *Deep Space Nine* or *Babylon 5*, imagine that the United States had its very own space station. And then visit this site, which is NASA's official online repository for all data pertaining to the International Space Station Alpha project. The site includes an acronym list, a program overview, movies, still photos, white papers, a clickable map of the ISSA project, and a technical data guidebook. ✓**INTERNET**→*www* http://issa-www.jsc.nasa.gov/ss/Space Station_homepage.html

Terminology

NASA Thesaurus Thousands of terms pertaining to space science and travel, from the Ablestar Launch Vehicle to the Zuni Rocket Vehicle, along with classifications and related terms. ✓**INTERNET**→*www* http://www.sti.nasa.gov/nasa-thesaurus.html

Space shots

Some of the most breathtaking photographs in human history have come from cameras

borne into space by probes, satellites, and rockets. Pictures of our own planet taken from space force a radical recontextualization of human life, and images broadcast from beyond our own solar system provide visual correlatives for such abstract concepts as infinity and God. These Net sites are some of the best places in Cyberspace to download images of outer space, whether your tastes run toward Mars (**Mars Images Menu**), other planets (**Regional Planetary Facility**), or views of the earth taken from orbit by the Space Shuttle (**Space Shuttle Photos Repository**). Use them as startup screens or screen savers, or make astronomical printouts to paper your bedroom walls.

On the Net

Astronomical Pictures & Animations An astronomical number of astronomical pictures and animations, including images of novae, comets, Messier objects, and all the planets in this diverse and lovely solar system of ours. ✓ **INTERNET**→*www* http://www.univ-rennes1.fr/ASTRO/astro.english.html

CCD Images of Galaxies A

Galaxy—downloaded from seds.lpl.arizona.edu/pub

gallery of several kinds of galaxies, including the Fabry-Perot Gallery, Protoplanetary Disks, Digital Spectra of Different Kinds of Stars, and the Planetary Nebulae Gallery. ✓ **INTERNET**→*www* http://zebu.uore gon.edu/galaxy.html

Comet P/Shoemaker-Levy 9 Impact Home Page Shoemaker-Levy slams into Jupiter! That's right, a comet and a planet, making interstellar noise. Relive the music of impact with this wonderful home page, which includes computer animations and artist renderings, as well as FAQs and fact sheets about the comet, and links to other Shoemaker-Levy sites around the Web. ✓ **INTERNET**→*www* http://seds.lpl.arizona.edu/sl9/sl9.html

Images & Animations Astronomiques The earth and other interplanetary bodies look the same from French satellites, more or less, and this site collects French space images and animations. ✓ **INTERNET**→*www* http://www.univ-rennes1.fr/ASTRO/astro.french.html

Magellan Image Server Hun-

dreds and hundreds of images from the *Magellan* space probe. ✓ **INTERNET**→*www* http://delcano.mit.edu/cgi-bin/midr-query#load

Mars Images Menu Photos of Mars and its moons, taken from various probes and spacecraft, including a 1969 Mariner 6 view of the Sinus Sabaeus and Deucalionis Regio portion of Mars, and a view of Martian soil taken from the *Viking* probe. ✓ **INTERNET**→ *www* http://esther.la.asu.edu/asu_tes/TES_Editor/SOLAR_SYST_TOUR/Mars.html

MSSS Viking Image Archive Use the Web to view images from the *Viking* orbiters, which circled and photographed from 1976 to 1980. ✓ **INTERNET**→*www* http://barsoom.msss.com/http/vikingdb.html

Regional Planetary Facility A databank of images at the Center for Earth and Planetary Studies that serves as a reference library for all planetary mission and image data. Browse for press releases, search for images, and view. ✓ **INTERNET**→*www* http://ceps.nasm.edu:2020/rpif.html

Space Shuttle Photos Repository Not photographs of the space shuttles, but photographs taken from the space shuttles, including shots of the Rabaul Caldera volcanic eruption in Papua New Guinea, the Grand Canyon, the Namib Desert, Madagascar, and the San Francisco Bay area. ✓ **INTERNET**→*www* http://ceps.nasm.edu:2020/RPIF/SSPR.html

PART 8

GENRE: OTHER SCI-FI

The sci-fi universe

The human mind likes nothing more than wandering beyond its bounds, and since the

first science-fiction stories—Jules Verne's tales, perhaps, or maybe even Milton's *Paradise Lost*—futuristic and alien-life literature has seized readers' imaginations and kept them captive. And the closer we get to "the future," the more powerful and intricate the genre seems to become, in part because of the cooperation of new communication technologies such as the Net. Science-fiction fans will find that their drool cups runneth over at the **Rutgers Archive**, which contains a latinum mine of information on sci-fi authors, films, and television series, and then they can share their thoughts (without the benefit of a Vulcan mind meld, of course) in **GEnie's Science Fiction RoundTable**. Those fans who prefer the comfort of a good book to the blue glow of the tube might want to head for **alt.fan.philip-dick** or **alt.fan.douglas-adams**. And finally, if you've been dreaming that your 110 g Frisbee is a self-contained world, check out **alt.alien.visitors**.

Screenshot from http://www.microserve.com/~server/sf.html

On the Net

Across the board

Giant Science Fiction Gophers Ceaseless in their pursuit of links, these sci-fi gophers have created connections to archives of sci-fi zines, the full text of sci-fi novels, FAQs for every sci-fi discussion group on the Net, newsletters from publishing houses, convention schedules, fan-club information, author biographies, image and sound-clip collections, and lists galore. ✓ **INTERNET** ...→*gopher* gopher.lysator.liu.se→Science Fiction (Linköpings Science Fiction-Förening) *or* Science Fiction Archive ...→*gopher* marvel.loc.gov→ Employee Information→Clubs and Organizations→What IF...? LCPA Science Fiction Forum

Hyperion Science Fiction Archive A frequently updated collection of FAQs and guides related to science fiction, including the sci-fi TV titles list, the *Earth 2* FAQ, and a huge *Babylon 5* collection of lists, pictures, and episode guides. ✓ **INTERNET**→*anon-ftp* ftp. hyperion.com→/pub/TV

Mr. Data's Data (j) An electronic news column covering the sci-fi media—from *Doctor Who* to *Forever Knight* to *Star Trek*—on a monthly basis. Culls gossip, rumor, and hard news about shows from all the sci-fi newsgroups and mailing lists, off-line fan clubs and newsletters, and the press. What *DS9* actor will make his directorial debut this week? Where are the plot twists of your favorite show heading? What shows are being threatened with cancellation and which are being revived? ✓ **INTERNET**→*email* badnhoop@siucvmb. siu.edu ✍ *Write a request*

rec.arts.sf.misc (ng) Quantum mechanics, ballistic performance, and *Twilight Zone* remakes all have a home in this newsgroup. Not much focus here, and a fair dose of off-topic chatter, but that's what you'd expect in a grab-bag group like this one. It's a good place to draw on the knowledge of other sci-fi fans: Post a question and you're sure to get an answer in warp speed. You'll find quite a few posts about upcoming events, such as conventions and new TV shows. If you've got something sci-fi to say, and it doesn't seem right for one of the other rec.arts.sf groups, post it here. **✓USENET**

rec.arts.sf.science (ng) Private space exploration, cold fusion, personality cloning, and other candidates for the year 2000 edition of the Sharper Image catalog. Speculative science at its best—nowhere else outside of the physics lab do people argue as intelligently about "ways around the Heisenberg Uncertainty Principle" and other basic assumptions of modern science. The most skillful participants make the scientific seem absurd and the fictitious sound plausible. As they say on the like-minded Fox TV hit *The X-Files*, "The truth is out there." **✓USENET**

Rutgers Archive A huge collection of science-fiction episode guides, with entries on shows ranging from the immensely popular (*Star Trek*) to the barely remembered (*The Flash*). Annotated links to hundreds of sci-fi Internet sites organized into archives, authors, awards, bibliographies, bookstores, fandom, fiction, movies, publishers, reviews and criticism, role-playing games, television, Usenet news groups, and fanzines. In addition, the Rutgers Archive contains other documents of interest to science-fiction fans, including a UFO guide, a list of Nebula award winners, and a large archive of *SF*

Lovers digest. Simply put, one of the largest sites in Cyberspace, and one of the most comprehensive (and this isn't just an opinion—this incredible guide was the recipient of a Best of the Net Award). Bet your friends that they've never seen anything like it. **✓INTERNET**→*anon-ftp* gandalf.rutgers.edu→/pub/sfl →sf-resource.guide

Science Fiction and Cyber-punk Archive A collection of links to sci-fi and Cyberpunk fan clubs, resource guides, and role-playing games. **✓INTERNET**→*www* http://www.microserve.com /~server/sf.html

Science Fiction Fandom What does it take to be a science-fiction fan? Well, first of all, you need to follow a show. And not just any show. A science-fiction show. It can be classic Trek, or *Babylon 5*, or *The X-Files*, or even a lesser-known program like *Forever Knight* or *Highlander*. But you have to follow it regularly, and almost religiously. And then you have to talk about it—with your friends, with your neighbors, with anyone who will listen. AOL's Science Fiction Fandom board covers a broad spectrum of sci-fi topics, from general categories (the best and worst sci-fi movies of all time) to more specific concerns (Is *Babylon 5* better than *Battlestar Galactica*? Where can you see naked footage of David Duchovny?), and if it doesn't always go where no man has gone before, it does provide a friendly environment for discussion and gentle disagreement. **✓AMERICA ONLINE**→*keyword* scifi→Science Fiction Fandom Board

Science Fiction & Fantasy Forum Concentrates mostly on literature, which means there's heavy traffic for readers of popular authors from Stephen Donaldson to

William Gibson to Robert Heinlein. It also means that many of the postings are fans' notes—gushing appraisals of classic works ("Bradbury's *Martian Chronicles* is the most completely imagined science-fiction novel ever"), arguments over originality ("Should we credit the invention of robots to Karl Capek or Isaac Asimov?"), and even clarifications of picayune points in massive epics ("How exactly does mind reading work in Frank Herbert's *Dune*?"). Looking to read even more sci-fi adventures? The Member Fiction and Scripts Library (a subset of the Science Fiction Libraries) has stories, poems, and songs written by other AOL members. The literary orientation doesn't shut out related media, of course, and there are some fascinating discussions on film and TV, such as a running poll on the best sci-fi film ever. Curious? So far, it's *Blade Runner* by more than a nose, but you're welcome to weigh in. While critical favorites like Dick and Gibson may be winning in the polls, popular raves like Spielberg and Lucas rule the libraries: *Star Wars* fans

Sci-fi movie poster—downloaded from AOL's SciFi Channel Forum

have packed a separate library with images, timelines, FAQs, and newsletters. ✓ **AMERICA ONLINE**→ *keyword* scifi

Science Fiction RoundTables
The full set of Science Fiction RoundTables on GEnie comprise one of the biggest chat zones anywhere in Cyberspace, and it seems to be expanding at the rate of the universe itself. Divided into three gigantic bulletin boards—Written Word, Media, and Fandom—there are detailed and crowded discussions in progress on everything from Jules Verne to William Gibson. Real science, ethics and space exploration, science-fiction pulps, the economic health of the sci-fi publishing industry. Want to talk about authors? Well, every author has an individual category from A (Roger Allen) to Z (Roger Zelazny). Interested in the latest opus by Tappan King or Melinda Snodgrass, or do you just want to ask "What people think about Buckaroo Banzai, especially the dreadlocks"? Look no further. ✓ **GENIE**→ *keyword* sfrt

SF, Fantasy & Horror So, you're going to a convention and you need the perfect alien costume. Peruse the Science Fiction Costumes folder in the Fandom section. And, where is the nearest convention being held? Check out the forum's Event Calendar. The Alexandria Restored Library is beginning to fill with images, articles, and other sci-fi related material, including an active *Star Wars* folder. The forum also has links to areas devoted to *Star Trek*, comics, and animation. ✓ **EWORLD**→sf

SF-Lovers (ml) No, the name of this digest does not refer (specifically anyway) to the incestuous world of cyberpunk authors, Captain Kirk's seduction of green,

half-dressed planet princesses, or the late-night action at a science-fiction convention. It's lovers of the genre, you see. All science-fiction and fantasy themes are game, and much of the digest material comes from the rec.sf.* newsgroup hierarchy. Saul Jaffe, the moderator, speaks of the digest as a magazine, and brings a strong sense of decorum to his editorial choices. The flame-free result is really the only human way of keeping up with the hyperactive science-fiction newsgroups for literature, TV, and movies. The digest is still huge though—monthly compilations available from the immense FTP archive average about 1.25 meg. ✓ **INTERNET**→*email* sf-lovers-request@rutgers.edu ✍ *Write a request*

SF/Fantasy Forum The forum collects a sketchy, haphazard, and unflaggingly energetic group of posts on various science-fiction and fantasy literature and art—fanzines, novels, filking, and magazines. "I have a good plot idea for the *X-Files*," writes one fan, and proceeds to detail a wild plot that has something to do with paranormal phenomena infiltrating TVs from the inside out, using boob tubes as transmitters for alien agendas. Give it time! Sci-fi fans can also speak their piece both on the message boards and in live conferences on the great cultural milestones of their beloved genre—*Star Wars*, *Star Trek*, *Highlander*, and even Anne McCaffrey's *Pern* novels—and the forum includes workshops in which published sci-fi authors share their advice on writing effective speculative fiction. Libraries are filled with fan fiction, filks, and co-member criticisms. ✓ **COMPU-SERVE**→*go* sflit

SF/Media Forum Every indus-

try, medium, and genre has its "big players." Science fiction has *Star Trek*, *Star Wars*, *Doctor Who*, *Babylon 5*, *The X-Files*, and *seaQuest*—all commanding a steady following in this forum. So, while on the *Star Wars* message board the Dark Lord of *Star Trek* Knowledge points out that "Jabba isn't King-pin of the Galaxy for being (how did Ben put it?) weakminded," another member on the SF/Fantasy TV topic is describing watching episodes of *Lost in Space* that have been dubbed in Spanish. And, over on the *seaQuest* topic, last night's episode is being compared with *Star Wars*: "The creature coming out chasing Lucas and Dagwood reminded me of *Star Wars* when the creature chased the millennium Falcon when they were stranded on the asteriod, remember?" For FAQs, images, and archives of interesting discussions, head for the libraries. ✓ **COMPUSERVE**→*go* sfmedia

SFFAN (echo) A fun forum for debating sci-fi history (remember George Lucas' lawsuit against *Battlestar Galactica* for plagiarizing from *Star Wars*?) and the plot twists of current print and screen favorites like *Highlander*, *The X-Files*, *Pern*, and *Discworld* novels. The participants are willing to follow a winding path from the author Piers Anthony to the British sci-fi comedy TV show, *Red Dwarf*. ✓ **FIDONET**

Books

alt.books.derenyi (ng) The genetic theories of the cult science-fiction novelist Katherine Kurtz inspire her adoring fans. They debate whether a "half-Deryni" can acquire the powers by training and conclude that "either a person is Deryni, or he isn't." Kurtz is exploring the "genetic basis of learned vs. instinctive," according to a long thread. They see analogues in social issues from "the Royal House of England" to the "race struggle" in America. Pipelined to Del Ray Books, her publisher, they speculate about the forthcoming Childe Morgan trilogy and wonder about a Deryni film in the works. ✓USENET

---

alt.books.isaac-asimov (ng) There's a lot of talk puzzling out the lineage of Asimov story lines now that they're being farmed out to other science-fiction writers à la the post–Fleming 007. The most soulful participants wonder out loud about character motivations in the new "Asimov" novels with the kind of active curiosity that would make a high-school English teacher think she had been transported to a parallel universe. Maybe it's because so many of the group members have shared experiences treading through Asimov's work, but the conversation is extremely polite and reasoned, even when debating the data storage potential of black holes. ✓USENET

---

alt.fan.douglas-adams (ng) If consciousness is a kind of dense, blurry fog, then the humor of Douglas Adams is an out-of-control lorry that emerges out of that fog against the red, rebounding off of street signs and the occasional pedestrian before crashing through the window of a fish-and-chips shop. Of course, if you've read Adams's five-volume *Hitchhiker's Guide* trilogy, you know this already. Vogon poetry. Pan-Galactic Gargle Blasters. The end of EOEAWKI (Existence On Earth As We Know It) and the answer to the question of life, the universe, and everything. Alt.fan.douglas-adams, where the *Guide* series and other snarky bits of Adams insanity are discussed, showers readers

with incredibly unenlightening points of philosophy, anecdotes of how the number 42 has influenced/changed/ended their lives, and lots and lots of Favorite Lines. It's moderately trafficked, begging to be read no more than two or three times a week at most, and almost exclusively male. Like its cousin alt.fan.pratchett, it has an extensive international following, with posters chiming in from all parts of the Crown and its colonies in addition to the good old U.S. of A. While old reports suggested that Adams himself was not a presence on the group, new surveillance has revealed that the head loon himself does occasionally drop by for a hoot or two. That is, when he's not in the bath. ✓USENET

---

alt.fan.philip-dick (ng) Philip K. Dick's works were among the most visionary science-fiction novels written, and they've earned the late writer quite a cult following. These self-proclaimed Dickheads spend a great deal of time worrying about the infrastructure of Dick-related Usenet traffic (Should the group be cross-indexed with alt.books.philip-dick? And what about that alt.fan.bladerunner splinter group?), so much so that they almost obscure the more substantive traffic—postings about Dick's epilepsy, critical reviews of his novels, and birthday wishes (December 21) from tenderhearted fans. ✓USENET

Philip K. Dick A list of the writings of sci-fi author Philip K. Dick, whose works were used as the basis for the films *Total Recall* and *Blade Runner*. ✓INTERNET→ *anon-ftp* gandalf.rutgers.edu→ /pub/sfl/authorlists→Dick.Philip

---

Philip Kindred Dick FAQ Born a twin, treated for agoraphobia,

BOOKS

A Princess of Mars By Edgar Rice Burroughs. ✓INTERNET→ *anon-ftp* mrcnext.cso.uiuc.edu→ /gutenberg/etext93→pmars10. txt

---

Around the World in Eighty Days By Jules Verne. ✓INTERNET→*anon-ftp* mrcnext.cso.uiuc. edu→/gutenberg/etext94→80 day10.txt

---

At the Earth's Core By Edgar Rice Burroughs. ✓INTERNET→ *anon-ftp* mrcnext.cso.uiuc.edu→ /gutenberg/etext94→ecore10.txt

---

From the Earth to the Moon and a Trip Around It By Jules Verne. ✓INTERNET→*anon-ftp* mrc next.cso.uiuc.edu→/gutenberg/ etext93→moon10.txt

---

The Gods of Mars By Edgar Rice Burroughs. ✓INTERNET→ *anon-ftp* mrcnext.cso.uiuc.edu→ /gutenberg/etext93→gmars11.txt

---

Paradise Lost By John Milton. ✓INTERNET→*anon-ftp* mrc next.cso.uiuc.edu→/gutenberg/ etext92→ plrabn12.txt

---

Paradise Regained By John Milton. ✓INTERNET→*anon-ftp* mrcnext.cso.uiuc.edu→/guten berg/etext93→rgain10.txt

---

The Time Machine By Herbert George Wells. ✓INTERNET→ *anon-ftp* mrcnext.cso.uiuc.edu→ /gutenberg/etext92→timem0. txt

---

The War of the Worlds By Herbert George Wells. ✓INTERNET→*anon-ftp* mrcnext.cso.uiuc. edu→/gutenberg/etext92→ warw10.txt

addicted to amphetamines, prone to paranoia and mystical experiences, Philip K. Dick was one of the most compelling sci-fi writers of the century, and this FAQ answers most everything about PKD that you're likely to ask, providing information on his complete works, newsletters, movies, and even pop songs that contain references to Dick. ✓**INTERNET**→*www* http://www.interport.net/~regulus /pkd/pkd-int.html

rec.arts.sf.reviews (ng) Wanna be a critic? Here's your chance. Ply your trade in a group devoted to reviews and criticism of science-fiction, fantasy, and horror works. You can review a short story, an album, a magazine, a TV series, a movie—anything, in essence, related to science fiction. For better or worse, the group's not dominated by Trekkers, like some other sci-fi areas on the Net, and books, rather than movies or TV shows, get reviewed more than anything else. The works reviewed include *Foreigner* by C.J. Cherryh ("The story, such as it is, consists of a not-very-interesting character trying to cope with a situation he doesn't understand"), *Of Tangible Ghosts* by L.E. Modesitt, Jr. ("Some good ideas here, but this particular mixture just doesn't work"), and *The Cult of Loving Kindness* by Paul Park ("This novel has much more of art than entertainment in it, and the art failed to reach me"). The reviewers don't trash the works savagely, but they don't write puff pieces either. Interesting reading. ✓**USENET**

rec.arts.sf.written (ng) Fan fiction and professional sci-fi writing meet without colliding. Many of the newsgroup's contributors struggle with the fact that sci-fi has expanded so much that it's no longer possible for fans to keep up

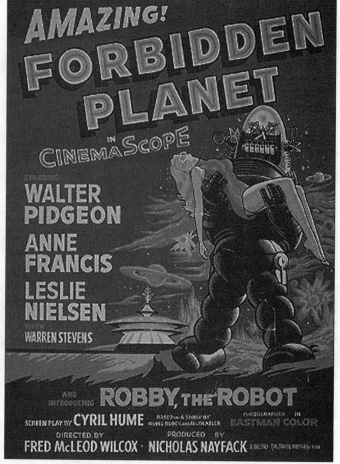

Sci-fi movie poster—downloaded from AOL's SciFi Channel Forum

with everything that's published. A large number of semiregular participants therefore rely on reader reviews—both brief and not—posted here for advice on what sci-fi, fantasy, cyberpunk, or horror novel to look forward to in new releases.

At its best, this newsgroup is a terrific sci-fi book club. A senior editor at Tor Books, one of the most important sci-fi publishers today, occasionally throws his two cents in. ✓**USENET** *Archives:* ✓**INTERNET**→*anon-ftp* rtfm.mit.edu→ /pub/usenet-by-hierarchy/rec/

arts/sf/written

Science Fiction and Fantasy Gopher A mix of sci-fi FAQs and reading lists, including the *Blade Runner* FAQ, the Isaac Asimov Fiction Timeline, the Bad Guide to *Star Wars*, and a science fiction books bibliography. ✓**INTERNET**→ *gopher* dds.dds.nl→De Bibliotheek→ boeken→Mass Media→Science Fiction and Fantasy

Useful Books and Periodicals for Writers of Science Fiction and Fantasy A list of books to read and places to publish sci-fi writing. ✓**INTERNET**→*www* http://www.timeinc.com/twep/Aspect/Interviews/sourceBUTLER.html

Conventions

rec.arts.sf.announce (ng) A useful group to check out now and then. Lots of posts about sci-fi-related events. Planning a trip? How about going to "FrankCONstein" at the Radisson Hotel Clayton in St. Louis? According to a post about the con, the event will feature "the left earlobe of Jon 'Mr. Wonderful' Stadter, weenie-boy artist," and "the right pinkie toe of Mickey Zucker Reichert, famous author and toastmistress."

Not your thing? Then how about a Trek convention in Memphis with James Doohan? Okay, that's more like it, right? This group's not just for convention addicts. Other announcements include the Top 100 Science Fiction List, a collection of recommended readings ("The Moon Is a Harsh Mistress" was at the top followed by *Dune*), and news of writing workshops. ✓**USENET**

rec.arts.sf.fandom (ng) The political nature of the Hugo and other science-fiction awards is a regular theme, but the real use of this newsgroup is planning your next trip to a science-fiction convention (con). Just about every serious American, Canadian, and British con—and there are dozens —is announced here with a list of the featured guests.

The denizens of this group put a lot of sweat into being serious sci-fi fans by publishing zines and attending (and running) conventions. For a while, the emphasis on conventions led to a minor flame war, with some contending there was too much "con" news. Others disagreed, questioning what would

happen to fandom without cons. "Fandom is cons, parties at cons, parties with people you meet at cons, zines about cons, clubs that run cons, clubs that wish they ran cons, clubs that run discussion groups in between going to cons," wrote one con lover.

"Without cons, fandom might still exist, but there would be precious little of it, and someone would invent cons in about ten minutes." In other words, cons rule. Diss cons, and you diss fandom. ✓**USENET**

Sci-fi show The Bionic Woman—*from AOL's SciFi Channel Forum*

Definitions

Authors Definitions of Science Fiction Sci-fi literary greats have not only wrestled with the limits of the universe (or lack there of), but also the definition of the genre. This is an archive of the definitions some—Isaac Asimov, Alvin Toffler, and Frank Herbert, to name a few—have offered. ✓**INTERNET**→*gopher* gopher.lysator.liu.se→Science Fiction (Linköpings Science Fiction-Förening)→Definitions of "science fiction"

Merchandise

rec.arts.sf.marketplace (ng) What's the story with the X-rated C-3PO card? "I believe that's due to a printing error," wrote one col-

lector, "C-3PO looks like he has a …um, male member." Another disagreed: "Printing error, nothing. Somebody *airbrushed* a little manhood onto that droid." Whatever the case, the card goes for $50. Any takers? Looking for *Star Wars* figures in mint condition? How about a complete set of *Star Trek* cards? If you're in the market for such wares, you've come to the right place, as long as you've got a credit card, cash, or something to trade. This is the place to visit if you want to buy, trade, or just chat about sci-fi stuff—everything from Harlan Ellison books to videos of Gene Roddenberry. You know you're dealing with serious fans when they're spending money like these Netheads. ✓**USENET**

Publishing houses

The Del Rey Internet Newsletter (j) A monthly newsletter about Del Rey science fiction and fantasy novels, including book descriptions, news about upcoming releases, author bibliographies, and features. The archive includes back issues of the newsletter as well as order information, manuscript submission requirements, and sample chapters of Del Rey Books. ✓**INTERNET**→*email* ekh@panix.com ✍ *Write a request Archives:* ✓**INTERNET**→*gopher* gopher.panix.com →Del Rey Books (Science Fiction and Fantasy)

Sci-fi & sci-fact

alt.alien.visitors (ng) The group that optimizes the kook ecosystem, alt.alien.visitors is almost equal parts True Believers, Scientifics, Net bystanders, and Kookwatchers—existing, if not in harmony, then in synchronicity. Discussion of crop circles, the "Greys" (insectoid ETs whose activities have been documented, sort of), Erich Von Däniken, and biblical proof of aliens exists side by side with utterly hilarious posts mocking the UFO party line. One ongoing, somewhat paranoid thread concerns whether alt.alien. visitors is now "moderated," i.e., screened for improper—or overly revelatory?—posts.

The conclusion anyone might draw from actually reading alt.alien.visitors is: No. If you're a True Believer or Scientific, watch for the posts of Earl Dumbrowski, an even-headed, empirical researcher and enthusiast of UFOs; if you're more inclined to see the whole thing as a gas, watch for the posts of the so-called Hastings UFO Society, which claim to be channeled onto the group by a psychic named Madame Thelma. The posts, documenting the activities and beliefs of a UFO club somewhere out in Hooterville, are so strange and well written that you might just believe—for a second—that the UFO Society exists, before you fall down laughing. ✓USENET

---

alt.paranet.* (ng) Believers, skeptics, experts, and amused bystanders jump between the family of paranet newsgroups—alt.paranet.abduct, alt.paranet.paranormal, alt.paranet.science, alt.paranet.skeptic, and alt.paranet.ufo—in ongoing discussions about the possibility of aliens and a world beyond. Discussion on these groups tends to be scientific and serious. ✓USENET

Encounters Forum Associated with the Fox network's *Encounters: The Hidden Truth*, this forum sets out to prove that the world is not a rationalist prison, and that things happen every single day that simply cannot be explained by reasonable scientific minds. The most common phenomenon

"Welcome To The Edge"

What's On...

- 📄 About the Sci-Fi Channel
- 📄 Promotions & Briefings
- 📁 Cartoon Quest
- 📁 Episode Titles
- 📁 Inside Space
- 📁 Series Descriptions
- 📁 Sci-Fi Buzz
- 📁 Movies & Specials
- 📁 Weekly Programming Schedule
- 🔍 Search the Online Area

Keyword: SciFi Channel

The Fan Dome

FTL Newsfeed

The Lab

Graphic Inter-Mission

Check out the Sci-Fi Channel Online and get all the schedule and program information you need plus a whole lot more

Screenshot of AOL's SciFi Channel Forum

---

is alien abduction, generating roughly a dozen messages daily. The subscribers seem dead serious about their lunch dates with aliens; as one man says, "When my wife started coming up with memories and dream recollections that made me suspect she was a possible abductee, I couldn't ignore it any more. Funny how a thing like that turns your thinking around."

Encounters also covers ghosts, spiritualism, possession, and spoon bending. (Bob announced his upcoming bending party.) The staff of the *Encounters* television show frequents this forum looking for stories (strange kangaroo behavior in Australia, sidewalk eating blobs from the sky in San Francisco). ✓COMPUSERVE→ go encounters

---

UFO-L (ml) Biblical references to UFOs, the recent disappearance of the Mars observer, lost Soviet probes. What on earth can it all mean? This bunch approaches the idea of extraterrestrial life thoughtfully and seriously. A relatively flameless list for the curious and the almost convinced to figure it

all out together. ✓INTERNET→*email* listserv@psuvm.bitnet ✍ *Type in message body:* subscribe ufo-l <your full name>

Television & film

A Viewers' Guide to Sci-Fi's Greatest Hits A list, compiled by *Entertainment Weekly*, of "highlights, milestones, and oddities" in science-fiction television and film. The dates of each show and a brief description are included. ✓INTERNET→*www* http://www.timeinc.com/ew/941202/scifi/251scifitimeline.html

---

Digital Obsessions With more sci-fi links than you can shake a Klingon d'k tahg at, from *Trek* to *Dune* to *Battlestar Galactica*, this site also contains dozens of interesting links to shared-fantasy sites. Whether you want to learn, lecture, or luxuriate in role-playing environments, this is an excellent starting point, and the Website graphics alone are worth the trip. ✓INTERNET→*www* http://iocom/user/blade/digital.html

---

Other Shows *Dune? Space*

Precinct? Not *Trek*, but certainly of interest to *Trek* fans, or anyone hungry for the food for thought of science fiction. Fans have a wide range of interests and a wide variety of opinions, and they bristle at the suggestion that the sci-fi world is as monolithic as, say, the obelisk in *2001: A Space Odyssey.* Speaking of *2001,* the breakthrough Kubrick movie gets a lot of play here, with dozens of explanations preferred for the last hour of the movie, and at least one viewer asking if "the no-gravity toilet on the PanAm transport really worked." ✓**DELPHI**→*go* ent sta for set oth

rec.arts.sf.movies (ng) Sure, there's the usual chatter about *Blade Runner* and *Alien,* but there's also talk of strange and obscure flicks, like *Attack of the Mushroom People* and other lost classics. The group's FAQ asks that Trekkers post to the appropriate *Trek* newsgroup, rather than here, but the request isn't heeded—not by a long shot. You'll find discussions of the Khan character, of William Shatner's ego and acting ability, and a lot of thrashing about concerning the relative merits of the six *Star Trek* films. You'll even find talk of *Deep Space Nine,* and it's not even a movie yet! Oh, well. So much for the *Star Trek* exclusion rule.✓**USENET**

rec.arts.sf.tv (ng) With so many different allegiances, you'd think it would be hard to make your way through the flame wars in a place like this, but it's not. Sci-fi fans can find common ground now and then, and they do more often than not, in this freewheeling newsgroup. *Battlestar Galactica, Lost in Space, Space: 1999*—it's all fair game here (along with all types of *Trek,* of course). But if you criticize *The X-Files,* watch out. One guy called the popular

Fox series "a waste of time," saying the show's trashy approach to the paranormal belongs alongside *The Weekly World News* in the supermarket checkout line. The response? Much anger against his "wild ravings." It's a good spot to talk about the shows you still love, or want to discuss, even if they were only on the air for a season or two. ✓**USENET**

The Sci-Fi Channel Part television guide, part press release, part convention. Check out the Episode Titles folder to see what's playing this month on your favorite series. Slightly terrified of missing your favoritie sci-fi show? The other folders are filled with announcements and publicity about programming on the Sci-Fi Channel. Head to the Lab—home of the Sci-Fi Channel Message Board—for the most interesting part of the forum.

Perhaps nowhere else in Cyberspace does *The Bionic Woman* generate more discussion than *Star Trek.* Offbeat is the key here although the forum holds more than its fair share of sci-fi fans with crushes on late-seventies sci-fi stars. ("Does anyone know whatever happened to Maren Jensen, Starbuck's first girlfriend?") Animated sci-fi, British sci-fi, and *Quantum Leap* are also big favorites, and since you've got their ear, why not post your programming request (several hundred people already have) for Sci-Fi Channel execs: "I would like to see an *Aliens* and *Predator* movie marathon! Please do it, Sci-Fi Channel big bosses." ✓**AMERICA ONLINE**→*keyword* scifi channel

Sci-Fi Invades Hollywood The lead story for *Entertainment Weekly*'s science fiction issue reprinted electronically, and including links to other sci-fi articles

on sci-fi legacy, *X-Files,* and *Earth 2.* ✓**INTERNET**→*www* http://www.timeinc.com/ew/941202/scifi/251scifimain.html

Sci-Fi TV Archive From *Buck Rogers in the 25th Century* to the *Six Million Dollar Man* to *Planet of the Apes,* the site is home to a huge collection of information about sci-fi television and sometimes movies. Here you'll find an archive of the *seaQuest Newsletter,* pictures of Nana Visitor, the *Earth 2* FAQ, an episode guide for *The X-Files,* and a list of *V* titles. Popular programs like *Babylon-5, Quantum Leap, Alien Nation,* and *Star Trek* (of course) have entire directories of the archive devoted to them. ✓**INTERNET**→*anon-ftp* doc.ic.ac.uk→/pub/media/tv/collections/tardis/us/sci-fi

Science Fiction TV Series Episode Lists Lists of episodes for the current season of science-fiction television programs. ✓**INTERNET**→*anon-ftp* ftp.hyperion.com→/pub/TV→sftv-titles

Titles of Upcoming Episodes Titles of upcoming episodes for many sci-fi shows. ✓**INTERNET**→*www* http://www.hyperion.com/ftp/pub/TV/sftv-sched

Trekker_FX (echo) Whether you're enamored of the cheesy spaceships in *Battle Beyond the Stars* (you can see the strings!), enraptured by the Death Star and the X-Wing fighter, or entranced by the state-of-the-art computer animation in *Babylon 5,* you'll feel special in this effects conference. ✓**TREKKERNET**

Trekker_Previews (echo) Episode summaries, as well as air dates and times, for a broad spectrum of sci-fi shows. ✓**TREKKERNET**

Alien(s)

Of all the sci-fi film series in America, the *Aliens* movies have perhaps the best pedigree,

as well as the most varied palette of pleasures for fans of the genre. First, there's Ridley Scott's 1979 film *Alien*, a gloomy story of extraterrestrial menace erupting aboard a manned spacecraft. Then there's *Aliens* (1983), the hugely successful James Cameron sequel that trumps the original by moving beyond an atmospheric opening into an extended crescendo of special effects and gonzo Marines. While the third installment (1992's *Alien³*, which some fans jokingly refer to as *Alienses*) slipped off the mark with a half-baked prison-colony plot and David Fincher's all-style, no-substance direction, it remains a curiosity, especially given the producers' decision to discard an early script by cyberpunk godfather William Gibson. No matter how they feel about the third film, most fans admit that the series rests upon the capable back (and neck, and arms, and cheekbones, and eyes, and thighs) of Sigourney Weaver as Ripley; the excellent support of Weaver's costars; and the canny management of gen-

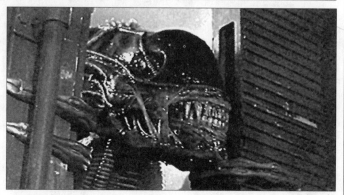

Aliens' Alien—dowloaded from http://dutial.twi.tudelft.nl/~alien/aliensmovie.html

der themes. In the online world, the films are ably represented by the **Aliens WWW Page**, which links to material from all three films. Collectors of *Aliens* apocrypha will have a field day with **William Gibson's Alien³ Script**, and fans with creative notions of their own can contribute to the ongoing collection of **Alien 4 Story Ideas**. In Cyberspace, no one can hear you scream, but scream anyway—it's good for you.

On the Net

Hubsites

Aliens WWW Page Under an ominous slogan—"Alien, the beast, worse than your fantasies could create"—and images from the first film, Ridley Scott's semi-

nal sci-fi film gets the star treatment, along with James Cameron's sequel and H.R. Giger's drawings. The site links to information about sequels, ideas for extending the story, and excerpts from reviews of *Alien³*. ✓**INTERNET**→*www* http://dutial.twi.tudelft.nl/~alien/alien.html

Cast & crew

Who Said What About Alien³ Ranging from the fawning (Charles Dance describing *Alien³* director David Fincher as "a genius, basically, for whom I would jump off London Bridge") to the catty but thought-provoking (H.R. Giger's comment that "I read in the papers that she got something like $5.5 million for playing Ripley again. Imagine what could've been possible if all that money was spent on the creature!"), this file contains a variety of quotes from the cast and crew about the third film in the series. ✓**INTERNET**→*www* http://dutial.twi.tudelft.nl/~alien/whosaidwhat.html

FAQ

Aliens FAQ A gigantic four-part FAQ that covers all the *Aliens* films and associated media. Investigate the finer points of the first film with questions on everything from film production (How can I get a longer version of *Alien*?) to plot (How come Ripley managed to survive in the shuttle without the coolant that Lambert and Parker were collecting?) to plausibilities (Does the alien have eyes? How does it see?). Plumb the trivia of the sequel (What does "Sulaco" mean? Is Ferro's first name "Mira"?) Learn about movie-watching rituals and William Gibson's *Alien³* script. ✓**INTERNET**...→ *www* http://dutial.twi.tudelft.nl/~alien/alientext.html ...→ *anon-ftp* rtfm.mit.edu→/pub/usenet/byhierarchy/rec/arts/movies→Movies:Alien_FAQ*

Molecular biology

Origins of the Hivequeen Have you noticed that the aliens change shape from film to film, despite the fact that they are supposedly part of the same menace? This document, written by a molecular biologist, attempts "to explain the different alien body types between the films without invoking genetic transfer between species, as well as the difference in gestation time between films." ✓**INTERNET**→*www* http://dutial.twi.tudelft.nl/~alien/alien-origin.hivequeen

Scripts

Alien Script A loyal fan's faithful transcription of the entire first film, from the opening pan across the red planet to the climactic closing scene. Spend hours reliving the excitement with Ripley, Kane, Dallas, Parker, Ash, and the other crew members. And remember—

"Good God! That crap's gonna eat through the hull!" ✓**INTERNET**→ *www* http://dutial.twi.tudelft.nl/~alien/texts/Alien-script

Aliens Script James Cameron's original script for *Aliens,* which redefined forever the meaning of maternal instinct. For fans of the film or Cameron's oeuvre, this is a must; there's something particularly satisfying about watching an entire movie script scroll scene by scene across your Netscape window. ✓**INTERNET**→*www* http://dutial.twi.tudelft.nl/~alien/texts/Aliens-script

William Gibson's Alien³ Script Cyberpunk godfather William Gibson, the author of *Neuromancer* and *Mona Lisa Overdrive,* was commissioned to write the script for *Alien³.* Though Gibson's script was eventually abandoned, it remains a compelling fiction. This is the revised first draft of Gibson's screenplay, which was written from a story by David Giler and Walter Hill. ✓**INTERNET** →*www* http://dutial.twi.tudelft.nl/~alien/texts/gibson-script

William Gibson's Alien³ Script—Short Version An earlier and shorter version of William Gibson's abandoned script for

Alien³. ✓**INTERNET**→*www* http://dutial.twi.tudelft.nl/~alien/texts/gibsons-script2

Sequels

Alien 4 Story Ideas When superfan Eelko de Vos asked for ideas for the fourth *Aliens* film on rec.arts.sf.movies, other *Aliens* fans responded in force. Here's a selection of his favorites, which range from brief scenarios ("a ship carrying eggs/FH's/whatever originally destined for The Company's research facilities crashes in the Great African Plains") to complete stories. ✓**INTERNET**→ *www* http://dutial.twi.tudelft.nl/~alien/A4-stories/alien4-stories.html

Terminology

EEVs When the members of the Interstellar Commerce Commission moved to standardize all starship escape systems in service, did they expect that dedicated Netsurfers would summarize and analyze the technological repercussions of this decision? Probably not. But they did, and now they're available online. ✓**INTERNET**→*www* http://dutial.twi.tudelft.nl/~alien/EEV-tech-info.html

Ripley—downloaded from http://dutial.twi.tudelft.nl/~alien/aliensmovie.html

Babylon 5

What is this *Babylon 5*, and why does it seem so similar to *Star Trek: Deep Space*

Nine?—that same fringe-of-the-galaxy outpost, that same easy travel to other sectors, that same sense of ongoing negotiation among alien cultures. More than any other sci-fi show currently on the air, *Babylon 5* seems to speak the same language as DS9, and speak it more fluently—its fans assert that it has better writing, stronger characters, and more exciting special effects than the *Trek* version. If you're new to the world of Babylonian culture, you'll probably want to start with **The Lurker's Guide to Babylon 5** and the **Hyperion Babylon 5 Archive**. If you're a seasoned vet, check out the B5 **Stories** written by fans, and maybe even try your own hand. And if you're a resident of Oz, don't miss the B5 **Australian Air Dates**. In addition, don't forget that *Babylon 5* is as much a Net phenomenon as a television one—series creator Straczynski makes canny use of the online environment, with regular postings on B5 newsgroups and frequent appearances on GEnie and IRC Channels.

Babylon 5 *station—downloaded from http://www.uml.edu/Babylon-5/*

On the Net

Hubsites

Babcom Includes links to sound clips, fan fiction, news and reviews, and miscellaneous series materials. ✓**INTERNET**→*www* http://www.nueva.pvt.k12.ca.us/~akosut/b5

Babylon 5 News A site that supplies newly minted information on the series, including air schedules and a quote generator. ✓**INTERNET**→*www* http://www.cgd.ucar.edu/cms/zecca/b5/B5news.html

Babylon 5 Resources A set of *Babylon 5* links, including connections to the Lurker's Guide, the electronic press kit, and Paul Hess's *Babylon 5* newsgroup. ✓**INTERNET** →*www* http://www.astro.nwu.edu/lentz/sci-fi/b5/home-b5.html

Hyperion Babylon 5 Archive "Satai—an honorific applied to members of the Grey Council" is one of the many terms listed in the *Babylon 5* Dictionary. The Unofficial Babylon 5 Encyclopedia is an A-Z list (with explanations) of characters, ships, and locations in the *Babylon 5* universe. And besides these resources, there are the episode-by-episode reviews and synopses, actor lists, technical explanations, FAQs, multimedia resources, transcripts of radio interviews, 3-D models, archives of B5 discussions on CompuServe and GEnie, and an interview with Harlan Ellison about his role on the show. ✓**INTERNET** ...→*www* http://www.uml.edu/Babylon-5 ...→*anon-ftp* ftp.hyperion.com →/pub/Babylon-5

The Lurker's Guide to Babylon 5 Unlike some other TV series, which have a handful of home pages scattered throughout Cyberspace, this site is maintained with the cooperation of series creator J. Michael Straczynski. The Lurker's Guide is vast, with links not only to series materials but related science-fiction, historical, and literary sites, and it's so comprehensive that even series addicts may find themselves reeling from the wealth of information. ✓INTERNET→*www* http://www.hyperion. com/lurk/lurker.html

Other Sources of Babylon 5 Information Part of the Lurker's Guide, this page links to convention data, newsletter descriptions, and other sources for *Babylon 5* information such as Websites and GEnie features. ✓INTERNET→*www* http://www.hyperion.com/lurk/other-sources.html

Your Fresh Air Waiter's Babylon 5 Pages Includes a second season episode guide and a comprehensive list of series merchandise, including novels, comics, laserdiscs, and an interactive CD-

ROM. ✓INTERNET→*www* http://poe.acc.virginia.edu/~dss2k/b5.html

Broadcast info

B5 Australian Air Dates Down Under, *Babylon 5* airs at 7:30 p.m. Saturdays, and if you want to find out what episodes are on in Oz, check out this page. ✓INTERNET→*www* http://www.hyperion.com/lurk/misc/au-eplist.html

B5 Local Stations Lists all local stations that broadcast *Babylon 5*, along with guidelines for fans wishing to urge local station managers to carry the show (Rule Number One: "Be Polite"). ✓INTERNET ...→*www* http://www.hyperion. com/b5/b5tvaddresses.txt ...→ *anon-ftp* ftp.hyperion.com→/pub/TV/Babylon-5→b5tvaddresses.txt

B5 UK Air Dates Turn to Channel 4 for the British broadcasts of *Babylon 5*, which began in early February of this year. And to find out which episode is playing this

Tuesday at 6 p.m., just dial up this URL. ✓INTERNET→*www* http://www.hyperion.com/lurk/misc/uk-eplist.html

Cast & creators

Character Appearance Charts Was Susan Ivanoca in "A Distant Star"? How about Londo Mollari? And did Kosh Naranek put in an appearance in "The Long Dark"? Discover the answers with these easy-reference charts, which list all major characters and their appearances. ✓INTERNET ...→ *www* http://www.hyperion.com/lurk/misc/b5-appearances1.html ...→*www* http://www.hyperion.com/lurk/misc/b5-appearances2.html

The Official Babylon 5 Cast List A complete list of roles in the first season of the show, sorted both by cast and by character. ✓INTERNET ...→ *www* http://www.hyperion.com/b5/cast.txt ...→*anon-ftp* ftp.hyperion.com→/pub/TV/Babylon-5→cast.txt

Other Works of J. Michael Straczynski Before he created *Babylon 5*, Straczynski was a well-known journalist, journeyman scriptwriter, and author of sci-fi and fantasy fiction, and this document offers a comprehensive list of his accomplishments, right down to the episodes of *Jake and the Fatman* that he wrote. ✓INTERNET ...→*www* http://www.uml.edu/Babylon-5/jms.credentials ...→ *anon-ftp* ftp.hyperion.com→/pub/TV/Babylon-5→jms.credentials

Radio Interview with J. Michael Straczynski A July 1994 radio interview with *Babylon 5*'s creator, conducted by Chuck Lavazzi and broadcast on KDHX-FM, St. Louis. ✓INTERNET ...→ *www* http://www.uml.edu/Babylon-5/jms.radio.7-24-94 ...→*anon-*

Screenshot —*http://www.cgd. ucar.edu/cms/zecca/b5/B5news.html*

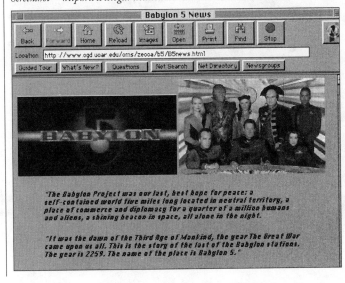

Babylon 5 Genre: Other Sci-Fi

ftp ftp.hyperion.com→/pub/TV /Babylon-5→jms.radio.7-24-94

Supporting and Recurring Characters Stephen Furst, Mary Kay Adams, Bill Muni, and all your other favorite *Babylon 5* actors are here, with photos of them in costume and descriptions of the characters they play. ✓**INTERNET**→ *www* http://www.hyperion.com /lurk/misc/recur-2.html

Chat

alt.tv.babylon-5 (ng) Less active and more off-topic than its sibling, alt.tv.babylon-5 has lots of speculation about what's going to happen next in the series. "In *Star Trek*, they had a story for every episode," one newbie wrote. "In B5 there is a story line that carries on from show to show." Uh, really? This group's crowded with cerebral sci-fi fans bent on discussing the show's philosophical foundations and the characters' motivations. One lengthy thread concerned the supposed bisexuali-

ty of a certain character. Frustrated with the discussion, one fan posted, "What, you haven't shut up yet? Take it elsewhere, please. This is not alt.tv.babble.religiously." ✓**USENET**

Babylon 5 No, it's not a *Star Trek* spinoff, but yes, it's part of the Delphi Trek forum. Why? Well, *Babylon 5* talk, among Treksters, always seems to devolve into comparisons with the real thing. It's a habit they can't kick. These sci-fi fans have to wean themselves of their Trek biases, and they know it: "I told myself to quit looking for Trekisms in B5 and accept the show on its own merits."

Talk here drifts to *Deep Space Nine* and assorted Trek lore now and then, but the regulars take *Babylon 5* seriously, and so should intrepid travelers to this cyberspot. Unless you want to be pegged as a newbie, don't ask who JMS is. (For the uninitiated, JMS is J. Michael Straczynski.) Be forewarned: Those posting spoilers may be punished in this group.

Do it, and you risk having an irate fan threaten to "beat the living narn" out of you ("May you commit a crime and end up in a Centauri prison!"). ✓**DELPHI**→*go ent sta* for set bab

Babylon_5 (echo) Would Patrick McNee make a better Narn or Centauri? The relationship between the Trek and B5 universes makes up most of the threads in this BBS echo for the discussion of the *Babylon 5* TV show that charges along in the wide path cut by *Star Trek*. The tightly knit group of core participants is at work on its own nitpicker's guide ("gravity is produced by rotating the station, but is it just one arm that actually moves?"), which will no doubt draw on the scientific bent of several key participants ("do aliens necessarily have DNA?").

If the guide follows the drift of many posts, there should be some interesting sections trying to explain the sexuality of the two strong women characters, Talia and Susan. ✓**FIDONET**

Babylon 5 With lots of discussion about the computer graphics on the show, the new CD-ROM companion to the series, and individual decisions made by the show's creative directors (Bill Mumy: Why Minbari?), this is a busy and spirited discussion area for fans of *Babylon 5*. With so many changes from season to season, all but the most dedicated fans need a helping hand, and this is a good place to begin. ✓**AMERICA ONLINE**→*keyword* scifi→Science Fiction Fandom Board→Babylon 5

Babylon 5 Bulletin Board The *Babylon 5* bulletin board can accumulate up to 100 messages a day in any number of topics. With categories entitled "No kids or

Babylon 5 *cast (1st season)—downloaded from http://www.uml.edu/Babylon-5/*

G'Kar—downloaded from http://www. uml.edu/Babylon-5/

cute robots ever,""Discussions of Minbari hormones and Varion gender," and "Sex on Babylon 5," its chat takes on a decidedly sardonic tone.

Babylon 5 creator J. Michael Straczynski is active on the board, and can be venerated, not to mention compared to the Great God Roddenberry, in "The First Amalgamated Church of Joe" (Category 8). There may not be more "action" on *Babylon 5,* but there is a good deal of speculation on space sex on this board (what is the place of the missionary position in space?), and ribald humor centering on the physical attributes of Centauris.

Fans also meet here to talk conventions, make plans to meet in this dimension, and discuss how best to create digital aliens. For those who like to speculate on the future, Category 29 discusses, with spoilers, "The Master Plan," the five-year mission of the series. ✓**GE-NIE**→*keyword* sfrt2→SFRT2 Bulletin Board→set 18

Digests of B5 Mailing List

Though it no longer exists, this once-popular mailing list is still available in archive form, and includes a variety of interesting dis-

cussions about the series. ✓**INTERNET** ...→*www* http://www.uml. edu/Babylon-5/Digests/...→*anon-ftp* ftp.hyperion.com→/pub/TV/Babylon-5/Digests

rec.arts.sf.tv.babylon5 (ng) J. Michael Straczynski, the show's creator and executive producer, not only lurks in this group, he posts, and posts with frequency, often responding to questions from fans. If you want to ask JMS a question, put "JMS:" in the subject line. But don't post story ideas! JMS would have to withdraw for legal reasons, according to the group's FAQ.

While this outpost is certainly energized by the presence of JMS ("Really love your posts, please keep us informed!"), that's not to say other things don't get discussed here. They do. Aside from the usual character/plot chatter, you'll find serious talk about the spirituality of the Minbari and the merits of the Earth Alliance's weapon systems. ✓**USENET**

Episode guides

Babylon 5 Episode Discussion

Sometimes it's difficult being the new kid on the block. *Babylon 5* has had to prove itself to several generations of Trekophiles and it has been waging its battle episode by episode. There are definite favorites: "Soul Hunter," "Signs and Portents," and "Babylon Squared" each gather nearly 300 messages. You can get an answer to that question about cobra bays, or why you should wear a helmet when traveling in space. Or just muse over the motivations of your favorite characters, and their new dos, uniforms, or loves. ✓**GENIE**→*keyword* sfrt2→SFRT2 Bulletin Board→set 19

Babylon-5-Reviews-L (ml)

"No one walks away from this episode without some moral taint," Allan wrote of "Believers." Andy was really turned off by "Born to the Purple": "I'm hoping, *praying*, that this is as bad as B5 gets." These reviewers write comprehensive and contemplative critiques of the show they love. You're likely to find phrases like "moral ambiguity," "scientific rationalism," and "religious extremism" in them, along with ratings of plots and performances. Even when a writer skewers a show, it's with the hope of seeing something better the following week. ✓ **INTERNET**→*email* listserv@cornell.edu ✍ *Type in message body:* subscribe b5-review-l <your full name>

Episode Guide for Babylon 5 A concise guide to B5 episodes. ✓ **INTERNET**→*anon-ftp* ftp.hyperion.com→/pub/Babylon-5/uk-guide/uk-b5-epguide.txt

Babylon 5 Episode List A list of original airdates, episode numbers, production numbers, and titles, along with links to fuller descriptions of most of the episodes. The description of the first episode in season two, for instance ("Points of Departure"), includes a detailed plot summary, a transcription of the onscreen credits, a list of guest stars, and a viewer rating. ✓ **INTERNET**→*www* http://www.hyperion.com/lurk/eplist.html

Episode List A full list of *Babylon 5* episodes, with links to synopsis and cast information. ✓ **INTERNET**→*www* http://web.uml.edu/Babylon-Enc/enc.html

Fan fiction & clubs

B5 Stories A list of fan fiction using the characters and locations of *Babylon 5.* ✓ **INTERNET**→*anon-ftp* ftp.digex.net→/pub/access/hess/b5/Stories

FAQ & basic info

Babylon 5 FAQ A text version of the series FAQ. ✓ **INTERNET** ...→ *www* http://www.uml.edu/Baby

Ambassador Delenne—downloaded from http://www.uml.edu/Babylon-5/

lon-5/babylon-5-faq ...→*anon-ftp* ftp.hyperion.com→/pub/TV/Babylon-5→babylon-5-faq ...→*anon-ftp* rtfm.mit.edu→/pub/usenet-by-hierarchy/rec/arts/sf/tv/babylon5

Babylon 5 Technical Manual Starfuries? Minbari Rings? Vorlons? If this sounds like a foreign language, you're in luck—this document explains the gadgets, gizmos, and weird science occurring on everybody's favorite five-mile-long space station. ✓ **INTERNET** ...→*www* http://www.uml.edu/Babylon-5/b5.tech...→*anon-ftp* ftp.hyperion.com→/pub/TV/Babylon-5→b5.tech

Grid Epsilon Log Excerpted from the GEnie postings of the show's creator, J. Michael Straczynski, this document offers a complete guide to the characters and history of the show, suggesting that "if *Star Trek* was *Wagon Train to the Stars*, then *Babylon 5* is *Casablanca* in space." ✓ **INTERNET**→ *www* http://www.uml.edu/Babylon-5/b5log.txt

JMS Answers File Half FAQ, half interview, this file contains actual quotes by *Babylon 5* creator J. Michael Straczynski from Usenet and commercial service postings. Topics range from comparisons between B5 and *Twin Peaks* ("I loved *Twin Peaks* dearly," says Straczynski, "but if you missed one episode, you were screwed") to descriptions of alien races ("The Drazi are a very violent, ill-tempered spe-cies"). ✓ **INTERNET**→*www* http://www.uml.edu/Babylon-5/b5_jms_answers.txt

The Making of Babylon 5 With questions ranging from the basic ("What is *Babylon 5*?") to the contentious ("What makes JMS think he can do a good science fiction TV show?"), this document is an FAQ to the series. Learn about series creator J. Michael Straczynski and how the show's vaunted special effects are created on home computers, and explore links to literary and historical works used as allusions by *Babylon 5* scriptwriters (Mark Twain's *The War Prayer*, Shakespeare's *King Lear*). ✓ **INTERNET**→ *www* http://www.hyperion.com/lurk/production.html

The Unofficial Babylon 5 Encyclopedia An alphabetical list of the main terms, characters, planets, and plot elements from the series, with hypertext links across the encyclopedia. Jump from "Eyes," the slang term used by Earth Alliance for Internal Affairs, to the Earth Alliance itself, the political organization based on Earth that includes the Mars Colony, all the Jovian moons, and Orion. ✓INTERNET ...→*www* http://web.uml.edu/Babylon-Enc/enc.html...→*anon-ftp* ftp.hyperion.com→/pub/TV/Babylon-5→b5encyc.txt

History

History of Ancient Babylonia Are there parallels between the plot of the B5 series and the history of ancient Babylonia? Find out through this document which explores the relationship between the two. ✓INTERNET ...→*www* http://www.hyperion.com/b5/History.Babylonia ...→ *anon-ftp* ftp.hyperion.com→/pub/TV/Babylon-5→History.Babylonia

Humor

Directory of Babylon 5 Humor Parodies, satires, and Letterman-style top tens that gently mock the series. ✓INTERNET→*anon-ftp* cco.caltech.edu→/pub/humor/babylon5

Everything I Ever Needed to Know I Learned From Babylon 5 A humorous list of lessons learned from the show, including "Don't argue with superior beings," "Know what you want in case somebody asks," and "Don't shoot people: The paperwork is a pain in the butt." ✓INTERNET→*www* http://www.cas.usf.edu/dforms/b5everything.html

Multimedia

Babylon 5 Sound and Vision Mark Mecca's site has roughly a dozen sound clips, a handful of images, and the opening title sequence from the second season. ✓INTERNET→*www* http://www.microserve.com/~meccamw/

Babylon 5 Images A collection of images, mainly ships and characters. ✓INTERNET→*www* http://www.public.iastate.edu/~selowthe/b5.html

Season Two Title Sequence GIFs of the title sequence from the second season of *Babylon 5*. ✓INTERNET→*www* http://www.scp.caltech.edu/~nathan/b5.season2.html

Babylon 5 Sounds From Ivanova's mantra ("Ivanova is always right...you will listen to Ivanova") to Garibaldi's battle-cry ("Win, lose, or draw, this thing's gonna know it was in a fight"), this archive contains various sounds from the series, in both Macintosh and .wav formats. ✓INTERNET→*anon-ftp* ftp.digex.net→/pub/access/hess/b5/sounds

Quotes

Information on Random Quote Generator Learn all about the random quote generator from the program's new author, Heiji Horde. ✓INTERNET→*www* http://www.reed.edu/~horde/b5/b5Quote.html

Quote Generator This Website has a program that generates a randomly selected quote from the popular science-fiction series *Babylon 5*. ✓INTERNET →*www* http://www.cs.dartmouth.edu/~crow/b5quote.html

Swapping email

Babylon 5

with B5's Guru

I n many ways, the Net itself seems like a sci-fi invention—millions upon millions of individuals connected invisibly, communicating at the speed of electricity. The online world has created new forms of identity, new forms of punishment, new forms of culture. So you'd think that sci-fi media big shots—the authors, directors, producers, and other visionaries who make fantasy reality—would eagerly embrace electronic communication. You'd be wrong.

Sure, some science-fiction luminaries make use of the Internet. Novelist Douglas Adams frequents the newsgroup devoted to discussion of his work. *The X-Files* producer/writer Glen Morgan has participated in IRC chats about the popular Fox series. And Trek honcho Rick Berman has appeared as a guest on AOL's Center Stage. But the electronic world is conspicuously short on big names.

Novelist William Gibson, who coined the phrase Cyberspace, doesn't hang out online. Neither does George Lucas or James Cameron. In fact, if you took a online census of sci-fi big shots, you'd find only one name recurring consistently, and that name is J. Michael Straczynski. Straczynski is the creator of *Babylon 5*, one of the most popular and inventive sci-fi shows currently on the air, and since the beginning of the series he has spent much of his work-week online, responding to fans' questions and concerns on CompuServe, GEnie, and Usenet. You may have seen him online: He signs his messages with a simple "jms."

Equipped with a computer he calls his "Deathstar 2000 megasystem" (a Dell with mucho memory, two CD-ROMs, and four megs of VRAM), Straczynski receives 500 to 600 messages a day and tries to respond to them all. Straczynski's posts convey a real sense for his love of writing, television, and science fiction—not to mention his devotion to the fans of *Babylon 5*. Just don't post original story ideas—for obvious legal reasons, Straczynski would be obligated to leave newsgroups if fans started suggesting plots. Interviewed via email, Straczynski discussed the Net's influence on the creative process, his affinity with his fans, and his undying passion for quality science fiction.

Q: How did you start using email and participating in Usenet discussion groups, and when?

JMS: I've been on the Net since about 1985, logging on to CompuServe via an old Kaypro II. I was one of the first writers I knew plugged into the system. So I didn't really get into it for B5; I've just sorta always been here, and I've always tried to use the medium to help inform people about how television really works. The scenario now is simply an extension of that, albeit writ large.

Q: Does the Net help in the creative process? How so?

JMS: The Net helps in the creative process not by suggesting things (which is verboten), but mainly by asking me 10 zillion questions about my show, the story, the characters, that I'd never even considered. The more I can answer these questions, the more I can suss out my

own characters, the better the resultant show.

Q: Can you think of specific questions that have helped?

JMS: The most helpful are questions about alien cultures, or the histories of our characters, which make me have to define these in very specific terms than the sometimes general notion in the back of my head.

Q: It's an understatement to say that you're much more open and responsive to fans and fan concerns than Paramount. Why?

JMS: I think I'm generally more responsive to fans because I'm a fan myself. You almost always hear producers appointed to SF series saying, "Oh, no, no, I never watched any of the stuff myself, I'm just doing it now, and of course, my version isn't really science fiction." I'm a fan of the genre; I grew up reading Bradbury and Heinlein and Asimov and Ellison and Lovecraft and Tolkien and Clarke. Where now I stand on the stage at a convention, I used to sit in the seats along with everybody else there in the trenches. I think that gives me a good understanding for how SF fans are generally

> "I think I'm generally more responsive to fans because I'm a fan myself. I think that gives me a good understanding for how SF fans are generally exploited."

exploited by Hollywood—told to line up, buy the products, and shut up.

Q: Does your reluctance to comment on *Star Trek* have to do with the similarities between *Deep Space Nine* and your show, or do you just have problems with the way *Star Trek* has been transformed into a franchise and an industry?

JMS: My problem with *Star Trek* is that I'm conflicted; yes, I do feel that they have become too entrenched, and too much a franchise, so that they miss great opportunities to do challenging material. There is some difficulty between the history of *Babylon 5* and *Deep Space Nine,* but we're trying to treat that like blood under the bridge, and just move on to make the best show we can. At the same time, there are some very good people over at Trek, like Jeri Taylor, Brandon Bragah, and a couple others, and I don't want to cause them problems. So in general I just say nothing and just nod a lot.

Q: What drew you to science fiction? And what are your favorite SF novels?

JMS: I was drawn to SF because it had for me that sense of wonder that is appealing to all kids. And we moved around a lot, once a year, while I was growing up, so the only continuity in my life came via my books. My favorite books would be the *Lord of the Rings* trilogy, the *Foundation* books, *The Color Out of Space, The Martian Chronicles, Men Martians and Machines, The Haunting (of Hill House),* and *Alas Babylon.*

Q: Given the amount of email you get, do you have anyone helping you read/screen/reply to it?

JMS: I read all my email myself; there's nobody in between. And there will come some point (I'm near it now) where the simple volume of mail becomes such that I have to choose between cutting back, and doing the show that generates the email in the first place. But as Ted Kennedy might've said, but never did, "I'll drive off that bridge when I come to it."

Q: What advice would you give a 15-year-old kid who wants to write SF?

JMS: Hold onto your dreams. The world will try to take them from you. The world is wrong.

Battlestar Galactica

A fairly long time ago in a galaxy not so far away, it was the seventies, and *Star Wars*

had swept America off its feet. Kids were jumping their parents for money to buy Landspeeder toys. Alec Guinness was the subject of erotic dreams. And the American television market was begging for a facsimile. Of all the shows to jump into the post-*Star Wars* TV sci-fi market, the best known was Glen A. Larson's *Battlestar Galactica*. If you were a kid, or an adult without a particularly demanding job, you'll have no trouble remembering the adventures of Starbuck, Apollo, Adama, Cassiopea, and Muffit the Daggit. Campy, formulaic, and often as poorly written as the back of a cereal box, *Battlestar Galactica* was also immensely enjoyable, and few shows since have matched it for pure entertainment value. When it was cancelled after a year, America mourned, and attempts to revive the series couldn't bring back the magic. Start your own journey at the **Galactica Home Page**, speak your mind on the **Battlestar Galactica Mailing List**, learn the **Pyramid Card Game rules**, and then jump on the BSG bandwag-

Apollo and Starbuck—http://www.carleton. edu/BG/images/

on with the **Battlestar Galactica Revival Campaign**, which has apparently caught the eye of stars Richard Hatch and Dirk Benedict.

On the Net

Hubsites

Galactica Home Page Maintained by Mark Heiman at Carleton College, this site aims to someday become the central repository for all things *Battlestar Galactica*. With a complete series

FAQ, episode guides, a fan registry, fan club information, sounds, images, miscellany, crossover stories between Galactica and Trek, archives of the Battlestar Galactica Collection at TARDIS, and important information from the *Battlestar Galactica* revival campaign, it's well on its way. ✓ **INTERNET**→ *www* http://www.carletonedu/BG/

Galactica Miscellanea All things that don't fit elsewhere fit here, like AP news articles about the show, the rules of the Pyramid card game, filk songs, and a detailed analyis of the Colonial collar insignia. ✓ **INTERNET**→*www* http://

www.carleton.edu/BG/misc

History & revival

Battlestar Galactica Revival Campaign An update on Fox's campaign to revive the *Battlestar Galactica* series that includes a more concentrated version of the John LaRocque series chronology. ✓**INTERNET**→*www* http://www.carleton.edu/BG/campaign.html

John P. LaRocque's Brief History of Battlestar Galactica A timeline of the show's history, from the pilot to the final episode, "The Hand of God," this document also includes news of a possible mid-nineties revival with original stars Dirk Benedict and Richard Hatch. ✓**INTERNET**→*www* http://www.carleton.edu/BG/misc/revival_faq.html

Characters

Colonial Uniform Analysis An attempt to "make some sense out of the Colonial Uniforms which seem to defy all laws of rank/award/unit designation as well as most items of consistency," this analysis focuses on the all-important collar pins, tiny dress-uniform adornments that may or may not hold the secret to Galactica's military hierarchy. In the end, the inquiry proves inconclusive, and the author suggests that we may never know the answer unless "someone takes the original film and scans it in with a 5000 dpi $45,000 scanner." ✓**INTERNET**→*www* http://www.carleton.edu/BG/misc/pins.html

Cylon History The original Cylons were a "technologically advanced reptilian race from a far corner of the galaxy," far different from the modern humanform examples. Learn how these canny baddies develop acute reasoning abilities, and how they can monitor electronic telemetry from up to fifty sources simultaneously. ✓**INTERNET**→*www* http://www.carleton.edu/BG/misc/cylons.html

Chat

Battlestar Galactica Mailing List (ml) Catch any instances of "regular English," rather than "BSG-speak," in your taped episodes? Ever notice the similarities between the control panels of the space shuttle and those of the Viper? And what about all those religious references? Such matters concern the active participants in this mailing list. These people like BSG, sure, but they're also capable of serious discussions about atheism and pop culture, and they've got an uncanny way of connecting their seemingly off-BSG discussions to matters pertinent to the show.

You've got a lot of science whizzes on this list; it's not uncommon for the talk to devolve into a discussion of amino acids and the emergence of complex life forms. But, lest you think you're signing up for chemistry class, the list is also social and chatty. Who had a crush on Starbuck? Who preferred Apollo? Who can't tell the difference between Lorne Greene and Lloyd Bridges? ✓**INTERNET**→*email* majordomo@cairo.anu.edu.au ✍ *Type in message body:* subscribe star *Archives:* ✓**INTERNET**→*anon-ftp* ftp.doc.ic.ac.uk→/media/tv/collections/tardis/us/sci-fi/BattlestarGalactica/digests

Episode guides

Battlestar Galactica Episode Guides Recall the high-flying adventures of Apollo, Starbuck, Adama, and the rest of the characters that populated the *Wings* of outer space. This episode guide provides airdates, plot summaries, and full credits for every single *Galactica*, from the premiere (with guest stars Jane Seymour, Rick Springfield, and Lew Ayres) onward. Remember Muffit the Daggit? How about those special appearances by Britt Ekland, Fred Astaire, and Randolph Mantooth? No? Well, refresh your memory at these sites. ✓**INTERNET** ...→*www* http://www.carleton.edu/BG/guide.html ...→*anon-ftp* gandalf.rutgers.edu→/pub/sfl→galactica.guide ...→*gopher* dds.dds.nl→De Bibliotheek→boeken→Mass Media →Television→Battlestar Galactica Episode Guide

Galactica 1980 Episode Guide Revived after a season's cancellation, *Battlestar Galactica* changed its face for the eighties, and this episode guide details the new look. Apollo is dead. Starbuck and Tigh are gone. Adama has a beard. But the space hijinks go on. ✓**INTERNET**→*www* http://www.carleton.edu/BG/guide80.html

Fan clubs

The Battlestar Galactica Fandom Registry An annotated list of fanzines and fan clubs, both electronic and postal. ✓**INTERNET**→*www* http://www.carleton.edu/BG/registry-fandom.html

The Battlestar Galactica Periodicals Registry A complete list of the books, comics, and magazines associated with the series. ✓**INTERNET**→*www* http://www.carleton.edu/BG/registry-periodicals.html

Fan fiction

StarTrek and Galactica Crossover Stories Five pieces of fan fiction based on imagined crossover between the fictional worlds of *Battlestar Galactica* and *Star Trek*. ✓**INTERNET**→*gopher* depot.cis. ksu.edu→Star Trek Stories→Cross over

FAQ

Battlestar Galactica FAQ When did the show air? How much did it cost? What are the other alien races? Did Commander Cain survive in "The Living Legend"? Did the *Galactica* eventually find Earth? Who is Glen Larson? Who is John Dykstra? From queries about the show's broadcast history to questions about its fictional universe, this document satisfies all elementary *Galactica* curiosities. ✓**INTERNET**→ *www* http://www.carleton.edu/ BG/FAQ-index.html

Filk songs

Galactica Drinking Filk A song that invites fans to combine outer-space themes and huge amounts of alcohol. ✓**INTERNET**→*www* http:// www.carleton.edu/BG/misc/filk-drinking.html

Galactica Filk Song Sung to the tune of "My Favorite Things," this song pokes gentle fun at the show, and contains at least one hilarious verse: "Centares, cylons, imperious leaders, if you were a book, you would lose all your readers. Great loards of COBOL have lead you astray. Don't you know Earth is the opposite way?" All together now! ✓**INTERNET**→*www* http:// www.carleton.edu/BG/misc/filk-roast.html

Games

Battlestar Galactica Drinking Game One of the "more deadlier" (and less grammaticallier) drinking games ever devised. Drink every time someone gets in-

jured, or a Cylon raider flies directly into the laser blasts from a Viper. Take two drinks whenever Cassiopea loses her temper, or anytime a character with a name gets killed. And down a whopping seven drinks at any reference to how Boxey would feel if Apollo remarried. There are also rules for comic books and novels. For those who wonder what no-gravity vomit looks like. ✓**INTERNET**→*www* http://www.carleton.edu/BG/ misc/drinking-game.html

Pyramid Card Game Rules Remember the game Starbuck was always playing and losing? Here are the rules. ✓**INTERNET**→*www* http://www.carleton.edu/BG/misc /pyramid_rules.html

Multimedia

Battlestar Galactica Images A set of *Galactica* images. ✓**INTER-NET**→*www* http://www.carleton. edu/BG/images/

Battlestar Galactica Sounds A set of *Galactica* sounds. ✓**INTER-NET**→*www* http://www.carleton. edu/BG/sounds/

News & reviews

Galactica 1980 Revival Article Written by Associated Press television critic Jerry Buck, this article explains ABC's decision to rescue *Galactica* from cancellation limbo with a three-hour movie. ✓**INTERNET** → *www* http://www.carleton.edu/ BG/misc/1980_article.html

Galactica Suicide Article A reprint of an Associated Press article about a Minnesota teenager who committed suicide after the original series was cancelled. ✓**IN-TERNET**→*www* http://www.carleton. edu/BG/misc/suicide.html

Russian Reaction to Galactica This *Izvestia* article suggests that the outer-space series is rife with anti-Soviet propaganda, and also takes polemical potshots at other seventies TV shows such as *Buck Rogers in the 25th Century* and *The Six Million Dollar Man*. ✓**INTERNET**→*www* http://www. carleton.edu/BG/misc/izvestia_re view.html

STARNOTES

"Fox television has recently let it be known that it wants input on their shows on the Net, in particular, the Alien Nation revival, and The X-Files. There has never been a better time for Galactica fans. People who want a revival with the surviving original cast of the series, and who have waited 15 years for it! Fox has shown a willingness to revive once- dead properties in the form of the recent Alien Nation two-hour movie, and may make more. If people show enough interest, Fox could easily regain interest in Battlestar Galactica. So help bring Galactica back! Send your letters of support to:

foxnet@delphi.com"

-from **Important Info on Galactica Revival Campaign**

Blade Runner

In 1982, Harrison Ford took a break from his megabuck roles in *Star Wars* and *Raiders*

of the Lost Ark to take the lead role in this piece of sci-fi noir, a futuristic mood piece directed by Ridley Scott and based on Philip K. Dick's *Do Androids Dream of Electric Sheep?* Only Scott's third film (after *The Duellists* and *Alien*), *Blade Runner* became a seminal piece of American science fiction, brilliantly mixing provocative ideas, gratuitous violence, and twenty-first-century cheesecake (Ford and Rutger Hauer for the women, Sean Young and Daryl Hannah for the men). A 1991 director's cut of the film corrected some of its most flagrant imperfections and firmly installed the film at the top of the sci-fi film pantheon, permitting it the rare luxury of both cult status and mass acceptance. **Off-World (A Blade Runner Page)** collects links to resources about the film; the **Blade Runner References List** sketches its debts to other works of film and literature; and the brief article "Sequels to Blade Runner?" offers some insight into the perfidious idiocies of Hollywood—Arnold Schwartzenegger in the lead role?

Blade Runner

Synopsis

Blade Runner (a term borrowed from William S. Burroughs) is a Ridley Scott adaptation of the Philip K. Dick novel *Do Androids Dream of Electric Sheep?* It is perhaps one of the most popular cult films ever covering

Screenshot of Blade Runner *site—http://bau2.uibk.ac.at/perki/films/brunner/br.html*

On the Net

Hubsites

Blade Runner A solid *Blade Runner* home page that includes a synopsis of the film's plot, a cast list, a summary of the controversy surrounding the Vangelis score, and even two video clips from the film—in .AVI format, though, and consequently playable only on a Windows machine. ✓**INTERNET**→*www* http://BAU2.uiBk.ac.at/per ki/films/brunner/br.html

Blade Runner References List A comprehensive list of periodicals, books, and journals related to *Blade Runner*. ✓**INTERNET**→*www* http://kzsu.stanford.edu/uwi/br/br-stuff.html

Off-World (A Blade Runner Page) A growing archive of material related to *Blade Runner*, including sounds, sights, discussions, and links to other home pages. ✓**INTERNET**→*www* http://kzsu.stanford.edu/uwi/br/off-world.html

Chat

The Blade Runner File: Compilation of Discussion About Blade Runner Hundreds of pages of discussion on the Ridley Scott film, including a review of the film's visual sense, listings of alternate endings, missing footage, and little-known details. Warning: This document contains many spoilers, and anyone who hasn't seen the film yet should probably not read it. ✓**INTERNET**→*www* http://kzsu.stanford.edu/uwi/br/br-file.html

FAQ

Blade Runner FAQ What is *Blade Runner*? What book is it based on? Is the sound track available? What are replicants? And is Decker really a replicant? This list of frequently asked questions (and frequently given answers) is overseen by Australian Murray Chapman, and seeks both to satisfy the entry-level curiosities of *Blade Runner* neophytes and to address the complex questions of die-hard fans. The sites are slightly different; the Ohio State site also contains information on translations of the document into German, Japanese, and Spanish. ✓**INTERNET** ...→*www* http://www.vir.com/ VideoFilm/Blade/brfaq_0.html# TOC ...→*www* http://www.cis. ohio-state.edu/hypertext/faq/ usenet/movies/top.html ...→ *anon-ftp* rtfm.mit.edu→/pub/ usenet/news.answers/movies→ bladerunner-faq

Blade Runner's Literary Sources

As everyone knows, *Blade Runner* is loosely based on Philip K. Dick's book *Do Androids Dream of Electric Sheep?* But do you know how loosely? And do you know what other literary figures contributed to the birth of the Ridley Scott film? This document traces the literary genealogy of the original script, reviewing the various drafts, rewrites, and contributors. ✓**INTERNET**→*www* http://www.vir.com/ VideoFilm/Blade/brfaq_2.html

International

Dossier Blade Runner This site, which originally started as a gopher, brings together an incredible range of information and detail about the sci-fi classic *Blade Runner*: its setting, characters, author, and even the concepts of replication, memory, and artificial humanity undergirding the plot. The text is primarily in Spanish—"Yo soy Deckard"—however, so bring along a translator. ✓**INTERNET**→*www* http://www.uji. es/CPE/dossiers/br/index.html

Multimedia

Blade Runner Sounds A set of sound clips from the film. ✓**INTERNET**→*anon-ftp* calypso-2.oit.unc. edu→/pub/multimedia/sun-sounds /movies/bladerunner

Sequels

Sequels to Blade Runner? More than a decade after the release of the original film, K. W. Jeter wrote two novels that extended the plotline of the original film. Within minutes, both were snapped up by Bantam Spectra publishing, and movie deals seem to be in the works. Oddly enough, this document includes a transcript of a press release that claimed that actor Arnold Schwarzenegger starred in the original film. "Hasta la vista, replicants." ✓**INTERNET**→*www* http://kzsu.stanford.edu/uwi/br/ sequels.html

Sound track

Blade Runner Soundtrack Samples For the longest time, there was no official *Blade Runner* sound track available, a situation that greatly disconcerted fans of the movie. This Website reviews the outcry and furnishes excerpts of the score digitized for Windows and UNIX formats. ✓**INTERNET**→ *www* http://www.nets.com/site/ Vangelis/films/brunner/brunner. html

Blade Runner Soundtrack An excerpt from the FAQ, this document explains why the haunting Vangelis theme music was unavailable to fans for so long, and addresses the better-late-than-never release of the official sound track. ✓**INTERNET**→*www* http://www.vir. com/VideoFilm/Blade/brfaq_3. html

Doctor Who

With a television series that ran for more than 20 years, countless novels and stories,

and even two feature films, *Doctor Who* is a huge entertainment franchise in Britain, where long scarves, Daleks, and striking female companions are as commonplace as crumpets. On this side of the pond, the penetration isn't quite as good, but the international character of the Net ensures that American Whozits can get their fix whenever they wish. From the extremely broad (the **Doctor Who Home Page** and the **Main Who Archive**) to the extremely narrow (**People Related to Doctor Who Who Have Died** and **The Doctor Who Interesting Quote List**), online resources will cure what ails information-starved fans.

Doctor Who *logo—from http://www.ee.surrey.ac.uk/Personal/DrWho/index.html*

On the Net

Hubsites

Doctor Who A hot spot for all things *Doctor Who*, whether you're into *Who* books, the TV series, or *Who*-related conventions. Topics include *Doctor Who* autographs, *Who* books for sale, and *Who* reruns. A number of experts can be found here, and they've got strong opinions on everything from the BBC and its handling of the show to the various doctors and their companions. Yet this is a newbie-

friendly spot. If you're seeing *Who* for the first time, you'll get advice on what to look for in the episodes. The libraries have some good stuff, including "Missing Without Trace," an in-depth report on the missing *Who* episodes; a file with the latest news on a U.S. revival of *Doctor Who*; a PC-based "photonovel" for the missing episode "The Tenth Planet 4," and a color GIF of Tom Baker. **✓COMPUSERVE**→*go* sfmedia→*Libraries or* Messages→*doctor who*

Doctor Who An index of *Doctor Who* sites that includes general information about the series, episode details, and biographical information on all the major cast members. **✓INTERNET**→*www* http://www.ee.surrey.ac.uk/Personal/DrWho/index.html

Doctor Who Home Page A

large site that includes the *Doctor Who* FAQ, a program guide, other roles of series actors, and a current list of stations carrying the show. **✓INTERNET**→*www* http://nitro9.earth.uni.edu/doctor/homepage.html

Main Who Archive Series information, graphics, and sounds. **✓INTERNET**→*anon-ftp* frontiosDoctor.niagara.edu→/pub/Doctor_Who

Trans-Dimensional Junk/Doctor Who Sites Maintained by *Doctor Who* fan Loren Peace, this site contains a huge number of valuable resources for other fans, including fan fiction, pictures, sounds, quotes, working titles, and "the ultimate guide" to the series. **✓INTERNET**→*www* http://www.phlab.missouri.edu/ccpeace_www/Dr.Who/

Tom Baker—from http://www.phlab.missouri.edu/ccpeace_www/Dr.Who/pics

Cast

Cast Information A list of all the actors who have played *Doctor Who*, as well as other major cast members. ✓ **INTERNET**→*www* http://www.ee.surrey.ac.uk/Personal/ Dr-Who/cast.html

Other Roles of Doctor Who Actors A list of the other roles of the dozens of actors who have participated in the *Doctor Who* series. ✓ **INTERNET**→*www* http://nitro9. earth.uni.edu/doctor/roles. html

People Related to Doctor Who Who Have Died Any necrology for a series with a 23-year run is bound to be substantial, and this document lists the *Doctor Who* alums who have passed on to that big junkyard in the sky, including William Hartnell (the first Doctor), Pat Troughton (the second Doctor), writers, script directors, and film editors. ✓ **INTERNET**→*www* http://nitro9.earth.uni.edu/doctor/dead. html

Chat

Doctor Who *Doctor Who* fans are so enthusiastic that many have been known to produce their own audio and video sequels to the long-running British show. These people really live the "Whoniverse" (topics 22 and 23 tell you where to find them). There is a slight cultural divide in evidence here—the Atlantic Ocean. Brits accuse the Americans of not being creative enough to fill in for the obvious technical gaps between socialized TV and Hollywood. Americans resent the disbelief that the new American produced *Who* can never measure up to the original. Because the series was so long running, episode discussion is divided by who played Who. Fans range in age and taste from an 11-year-old girl seeking plot explication to longtime followers praising the sexy companion or the *Midsummer Night's Dream* quality of their personal favorites. ✓ **GENIE**→*keyword* sfrt2→SFRT2 Bulletin Board→set 13

rec.arts.drwho (ng) More *Who* than you'll know how to handle, from the subsequent careers of the stars of the show to the latest in *Who* publications and paraphernalia. You'll hear endless debate about rumors of a new series, with lots of hope for a purported two-hour TV pilot for Fox. Will it include an eighth Doctor? Or will it be a remake of the original series? Lots of guesses, but no real answers. Some fans, apparently, have limits to their devotion. One *Who*-man decided to sell his *Doctor. Who* scarf, which was made by a friend's mother; he was looking for the best offer ("Looks like the real thing—incredibly cool for the Tom Baker look-alike"). It helps if you know the lingo for this group. These people like acronyms, especially NA (New Adventures, referring to *Doctor Who* novelizations) and MA (*Missing Adventures*, another series of books). ✓ **USENET**

Episode guides

Doctor Who Episode List A list of all the episodes, with brief plot summaries. Episodes are divided according to the actor playing Doctor Who. ✓ **INTERNET** ...→*www* http://www. ee.surrey.ac.uk/Per sonal/DrWho/

episodes.html …→*gopher* dds.dds.nl→De Bibliotheek→boeken→Mass Media Television→Doctor Who Episode List

Doctor Who Program Guide Compiled by Matthew Newton, this site has complete cast and credit information for the series up through the thirteenth season, and promises to fill in missing information shortly. In addition, Newton has annotated his credits, and included related novelizations. √**INTERNET**→*www* http://nitro9.earth.uni.edu/doctor/program.html

Dr. Who in Detail Review each of the past 26 seasons of the show, or have the episodes sorted alphabetically by title. √**INTERNET**→*www* http://www.phlab.missouri.edu/ccpeace_www/Dr.Who/dwid/

Dr. Who's Canonical List of Sluts A list of all of the Doctor's companions from 1963 to 1989. The list describes and rates the companions, and lists the episodes in which he or she appeared. √**IN-TERNET**→*gopher* dds.dds.nl→De Bibliotheek→boeken→Mass Media Television→Doctor Who's Canonical List of Sluts

Lost and Missing Episode Information How do episodes get lost? Well, sometimes it's the fault of film archivists, and sometimes they slip through a rip in the fabric of time. But with so many devoted *Doctor Who* fans working to rescue them, they won't stay away long. This site has a dual function, serving as both a warehouse of information on episode retrieval and rescue, and as a headquarters for the ongoing recovery effort. √**IN-TERNET**→*www* http://nitro9.earth.uni.edu/doctor/lost.html

The Ultimate Guide to Dr. Who A complete and compre-hensive episode and story guide to the show, with cast listings, direc-torial credits, plots, original air-dates, and more trivia than you'll be able to digest, even if you can travel through time. √**INTERNET**→*www* http://www.phlab.missouri.edu/ccpeace_www/Dr. Who/ultimate_guide

Fan fiction

alt.drwho.creative (ng) *Doctor Who* fans have kept the show alive with original scripts posted to this newsgroup of fervent followers. In these episodes, as on the series, you'll find the Doctor and the TARDIS and lots of strange hap-penings. Some of the writers invite their comrades in *Who*-dom to add to ongoing story lines, so you can even get a piece of the action yourself. The group focuses on the creative side of *Doctor Who*, but occasionally you'll hear rumors of revivals and questions about what stations carry the show. √**USENET**

Doctor Who Fiction List A full list of *Doctor Who* fan fiction. √**IN-TERNET**→*www* http://usacs.rutgers.edu/~edharel/drwho.html

The Net Adventures of Dr. Who An immense collection of fan stories, some of which were originally posted on alt.drwho.cre-ative. Follow the good Doctor through the twists and turns of time, through the world of Daleks and junkyards, with "Third Times the Charm," "Cyberhunter," and "A Little Game of Chess," among others. √**INTERNET**→*www* http://www.phlab.missouri.edu/cgi-bin/storylist

FAQ & basic info

Doctor Who Background and Setting Brief essay explaining the premise of the series. For beginners only. ✓**INTERNET**→*www* http://www.ee.surrey.ac.uk/Personal/Dr-Who/setting.html

Doctor Who Books Books related to the series, including novelizations and reference guides. ✓**INTERNET**→*www* http://nitro9.earth.uni.edu/doctor/books.html

Doctor Who FAQ How can I write to the actors who have played *Doctor Who*? I write *Doctor Who* fiction in my spare time. Who can I show it to? And what is this *K9 and Company* show we keep seeing? This is a copy of the rec.arts.drwho FAQ, which includes answers to everything you always wanted to know but were afraid to ask. ✓**INTERNET** …→*www* http://www.phlab.missouri.edu/ccpeace_www/Dr.Who/FAQ...→ *www* http://nitro9.earth.uni.edu/doctor/faq.html

Games

Dr. Who Puzzle Game This is a 16-piece puzzle game for people who can't get enough of the series. While image loading slows down play—the puzzle must reload all 16 pictures after each move—the game can become very addictive. Winners are treated to a large picture of the cast. ✓**INTERNET**→*www* http://www.phlab.missouri.edu/HOMES/ccpeace_www/game/game-who.html

Humor

List of Doctor Who Top Ten Lists Top Ten signs you have been watching too many bad *Doctor Who* episodes? ("Whenever anyone yells at you, you reply by saying 'My name is <insert name here> and I can yell just as loud as you!'") Top ten things that the Time Lords still can't do? ("Have an interesting conversation.") Top

ten things overheard in American households after the first new episodes? ("Cybermen? They're just like the Borg!") A collection of more than 20 top ten lists relating to the good Doctor. ✓**INTERNET**→*www* http://nitro9.earth.uni.edu/doctor/topten/topten.html

Multimedia

Doctor Who Pictures Images from the series. ✓**INTERNET**→*www* http://www.phlab.missouri.edu/ccpeace_www/Dr.Who/pics/

Doctor Who Sounds What? Sounds. Where? Here. Who? Yes. ✓**INTERNET**→*www* http://www.phlab.missouri.edu/ccpeace_www/Dr.Who/sound

Doctor Who: The Key To Time Key to time model created by Austrian sci-fi fan Brigitte Jellinek. ✓**INTERNET**→*www* http://www.cosy.sbg.ac.at/~bjelli/Who/index.html

Images of Daleks Andrew Marriott's raytraces of Daleks in Australia. ✓**INTERNET**→*www* http://www.cs.curtin.edu.au/~raytrace/unnatural_terrain_images.shtml

Quotes

The Doctor Who Interesting Quote List "I know that travel through the fourth dimension is a scientific miracle I didn't expect to find solved in a junkyard." "Doctor, we've got our clothes on!" "Never mind about me, Harry. There's a man in danger!" Noteworthy quotes from the show, divided into a number of different topics, including art, destruction, Daleks, the future, history, judgment, politics, resistance, strategy, and (of course) time. ✓**INTERNET**→*www* http://www.mit.edu:8001/people/dasmith/Who/Quotes.html

Doctor Who Quotes Dozens and dozens of pages of quotes, dialogue excerpts, and favorite scenes, transcribed and indexed. ✓**INTERNET**→*www* http://www.phlab.missouri.edu/ccpeace_www/Dr.Who/quotes.html

Reviews & nitpicking

Dr. Who Bloopers Do you remember the time in "An Unearthly Child" when the noise of a falling cameraman is clearly audible? Or how about in the Aztec episodes, when an overhead camera crashes into a sacrificial altar? If you're laughing so hard at these memories that you have to hold your sides to keep them from splitting, you'll love this document, which offers a comprehensive list of bloopers, blunders, mix-ups, screwups, and anything else that gets in the way of seamless entertainment. ✓**INTERNET**→*www* http://www.phlab.missouri.edu/ccpeace_www/Dr.Who/bloopers

Jo Grant—from http://www.phlab.missouri.edu/ccpeace-www/Dr.Who/pics/asst.html

Dune

Like other classics of science-fiction, Frank Herbert's *Dune* novels have long been

beyond reproach, and this elevated reputation is a mixed blessing—if it ensures that the books receive critical respect, it also limits their vitality. That's why David Lynch's 1984 film adaption was such a boon to *Dune*; while the narrative was frequently convoluted and unsatisfying, masterful visuals and a strong cast—Sting, Kyle MacLachlan, Jurgen Prochnow, and Patrick Stewart (later to earn fame as the captain of some space barge)—elevated it above standard sci-fi fare. Online *Dune* culture is well represented by one excellent home page (**DUNE II**) and a reasonably active newsgroup (**alt.fan.dune**). But the best *Dune* on the Net is the role-playing *Dune*. There are a multitude of MUDS such as **DuneMUSH II** and **Revenant** that allow Internet users to mentally gussy themselves up as Turennes and Wikkheisers.

On the Net

Hubsites

DUNE II Get your just des(s)erts at this Website, which links to sounds, pictures, definitions, and other information about the Duniverse. ✓**INTERNET**→*www*

Paul and Friend—http://www.ksu.ksu.edu:/~kxb/dune/dunegifs.html

http://www.ksu.ksu.edu:/~kxb/dune.html

Books

Dune Books Frank Herbert's *Dune Chronicles* existed long before the David Lynch film, and this is a complete list of all original publications, along with tapes, comics, and movies related to the chronicles. ✓**INTERNET**→*www* http://www.ksu.ksu.edu:/~kxb/dune/dunebooks.html

Chat

alt.fan.dune (ng) "After reading the scene in *Dune Messiah* when the stone burner blinds Paul and a bunch of his Fedaykin," one fan wrote, "I'm wondering, What IS a stone burner?" These fans all scurry to their much-valued copies of *The Dune Encyclopedia* whenever there's a question like that one.

Sometimes, they're hard up for an answer. Stone burner?

Perhaps it was just a "plot device," an exotic way to cause blindness without massive cultural justification. And perhaps not. Not a heavily trafficked group, but one with knowledge of all aspects of Dunedom, whether it's Frank Herbert's books, the movie *Dune*, or the MUSH simulations of the *Dune* universe. ✓**USENET**

FAQ

Dune FAQ Basic questions and answers about the *Dune* universe and DuneMUSH. ✓**INTERNET** …→*anon-ftp* rtfm.mit.edu→/pub /usenet/alt.answers→dune-faq

Dune Terminology Don't go out onto the *bleg* without your *bourka*, kids, and be sure to take along your copy of this document, which includes a full *Fremen* glossary. Whether you're marveling at the *Coriolis Storm*, dodging the *fedaykin*, or watching a *cielago* sail across the sky, one way or the other you'll have to come to terms with the language. ✓**INTERNET**→ *www* http://www.ksu.ksu.edu:/ ~kxb/dune/duneterms.html

Games

Dune 2: The Battle for Arrakis Help the forces of good triumph over evil, or something like that, as you rescue the desert planet Arrakis. This document introduces the game, outlines rules, and offers both an FAQ and tips for better play. ✓**INTERNET**→ *www* http://wcl-rs.bham.ac.uk/Games Domain/dune2/dunefaq1.html

MUDs

DuneMUSH Connection Instructions So you've read all about DuneMUSHing, and you're eager to try, but you just don't know where to go. Well, never fear. With this handy-dandy collection of telnet addresses and instructions, you'll learn how to MUSH in the blink of an eye. ✓**INTERNET**→ *www* http://www. ksu.ksu.edu:/~kxb/dune/dune mush_connect.html

DuneMUSH II It's 10,181, a full decade before the ascension of Paul Muad'Dib Atreides, and you're standing on as the Head of House Major Moritani, Broncalo, presents a gift to His Majesty, the Sublime Padishah Emperor Shaddam IV.

What will you do? With DuneMUSH II you can relive the events of Frank Herbert's novels, and even change them, although you should try to respect local customs and regulations. This page includes information on all the factions participating in this roleplaying game—the Moritani, the Turenne, and the Wikkheiser—as well as hosting seminars designed to improve DuneMUSH play. In addition, it links to the MUSH archive, rules, MUSH news, and events. ✓**INTERNET**→ *www* http:// www.princeton.edu/~cgilmore/ dune/mush/

DuneMUSH ReadMe A catalog of the DuneMUSH archive, including an events file, a guide to Arrakeen building, and forms for submitting behavior and situations to the judges. ✓**INTERNET**→*anon-ftp* mellers1.psych.berkeley.edu→/pub /DuneMUSH/README

Revenant After the August 1994 close demise of DuneMUSH, Revenant rose from the ashes. Set one millennium after the close of Herbert's final novel, *Chapterhouse: Dune*, the MUSH uses the characters, settings, and traditions of the fictions to create a speculative and interactive computer world.

You'll have to be a Wizard or a builder to enter Revenant, but this page gives background information and status updates for the MUSH. ✓**INTERNET**→*www* http:// www.artsci.wustl.edu/~revenant/

Multimedia

Dune Images Images from the film. ✓**INTERNET**→*www* http:// www.ksu.ksu.edu:/~kxb/dune/ dunegifs.html

Dune Sounds Sounds sampled from the film, including "Father, the sleeper has awakened," "I must not fear," and the ever-popular "It is by will alone I set my world in motion." ✓**INTERNET**→*www* http:// www.ksu.ksu.edu:/~kxb/dune/ dunesounds.html

Feyd—http://www.ksu.ksu.edu:/~kxb/dune/dunegifs.html

Forever Knight

Drop a thirteenth-century vampire into the heart of a modern metropolis and you've got

Forever Knight, a late-night syndication hit that trades on the popularity of other sci-fi and fantasy series—most notably the immortals-and-swords action series *Highlander* and Anne Rice's *Vampire Chronicles*—but manages to retain some cheap thrills of its own. Nick Knight is the aforementioned vampire, who has come to the twentieth century hoping to exorcise his dark side by joining the police force. Covering for his vampirism by feigning a severe allergy to sunlight (now there's the very definition of a strained plot device), Knight roams the city's streets, fighting both human criminals and blood-sucking foes. Derided as a *Highlander* rip-off, *Forever Knight* has found a niche among fans who don't like Conan and Kinnear, and it seems to be holding its own against newer syndicated cult shows. Begin your Knight moves with the *FK* mailing list (**Forkni-L**), the *FK* newsgroup newsgroup (**alt.tv.forever-knight**), and a host of minor treasures, including a **List of Known Vampires**.

Forever Knight *logo from http://www.hu.mtu.edu/~gjwalli/fktoc.html*

On the Net

Hubsites

Forever Knight For whatever reason, these *Forever Knight* fans talk French now and then: *"Bon soir mon petit chat, comment ça va?"* Lots of night owls among this crowd—appropriate for fans of a vampire show. One frequenter of the group, home from school, claimed he rarely saw daylight. "It made watching *FK* seem somehow more real, if you see what I mean," he wrote, "because here I could see that a person almost COULD conduct life normally on a nocturnal schedule." The libraries have a selection of screen captures, like Nick Knight brooding in the episode "Dark Knight" and Janette looking through a curtain at her club, the Raven. You can also pick up a copy of *Nick News*, a fanzine. ✓**COMPUSERVE**→*go* sfmedia→Libraries *or* Messages→Forever Knight

Forever Knight home page

This site includes history and background for the show, information on the cast and crew, episode guides, information on fan clubs, and links to related sites. ✓**INTERNET**→*www* http://www.hu.mtu.edu/~gjwalli/fktoc.html

Broadcast info

Forever Knight Air Times Syndicated shows like *Forever Knight* tend to get stranded in the limbo of late-night television, sandwiched between David Letterman and infomercials about the ground-glass diet ("Pass one meal and you'll never want to eat again!"). So it takes an expert to find them on the air—or an ordinary mortal armed with this comprehensive airtimes guide, which lists hundreds of American cities along with station call letters, network affiliation, and airtimes. ✓**INTERNET**→*www* http://www.hu.mtu.edu/~gjwalli/air_times_text.html

Cast & crew

Cast Information From Geraint Wyn Davies, who plays Nick Knight himself, to other cast members, such as Catherine Disher and Nigel Bennett, this site links to pages for each performer that contain full stage and screen credits as well as large in-line photos." ✓**INTERNET**→*www* http://www.hu.mtu.edu/~gjwalli/credits.html

Crew Information Biographical and professional information on production crew members, including cocreator Barney Cohen and director of photography Bert Dunk. ✓**INTERNET**→*www* http://www.hu.mtu.edu/~gjwalli/crew_credits.html

Chat

alt.tv.forever-knight (ng) These fans don't have the fervor typical of Trekkers, but they do flock to *Forever Knight* for its unique and witty take on the world of vampires. Talk revolves around best episodes, the depth of the characters, references to the show in magazines, and plaintive requests for help finding *Forever Knight* on the tube. ✓**USENET**

Forkni-L (ml) Lots of theories about everything related to *Forever Knight*, many of which center on romantic issues. Is LaCroix in love with Nick? Is he in love with Janette and jealous of Nick? Or are the three of them involved in one of those eon-spanning triangular affairs that cannot be understood by mere mortals? Join the never-ending debate. Or maybe your tastes run toward cultural issues, like the amount of sleep required by a vampire. "Perhaps an *FK* vampire needs less sleep as he gets older and more

powerful," wrote one of the regulars. But they're willing to joke about it, too: "I want Janette's wardrobe and am willing to lend her my hairdresser in return!" ✓**INTERNET**→*email* listserv@psuvm.psu.edu ✉ *Type in message body:* subscribe forkni-l <your full name>

Episode guide

Episode Guide Contains a good summary of the series premise and a detailed episode guide that includes episode titles, airdates, cast lists, production credits, plot summaries, and interesting facts pertaining to the episode. This is the only place you're likely to discover that Carl Ciartalio created the role of Pure Melrose. ✓**INTERNET**→*anon-ftp* elbereth.rutgers.edu→/pub/sfl→forever-knight.guide

Forever Knight Episode Guide Plots, airdates, cast information, and production credits for the entire run of *Forever Knight*. ✓**INTERNET**→*www* http://www.hu.mtu.edu/~gjwalli/episode_guide.html

Fan fiction

Fiction Bibliography A massive alphabetical list of fan fiction—stories, novel ideas, and scripts—much of it drawn from the *FK*-fic list, and some of it available by mail. Check out the wealth of material generated by Lady of the Knight Susan Garrett. ✓**INTERNET**→*www* http://www.hu.mtu.edu/~gjwalli/fiction.html

FKfic-L (ml) An electronic journal devoted to fan fiction that imagines further—if not forever—adventures for the characters of *Forever Knight*. ✓**INTERNET**→*email* listserv@psuvm.psu.edu ✉ *Type in message body:* subscribe fkfic-l <your full name>

Fans

Forever Knight Fan Clubs Lists of fan clubs for major cast members, including Nigel Bennett, Catherine Disher, Gary Farmer, John Kapelas, Deborah Duchena, and Natsuko Ohama, and (of course) Geraint Wyn Davies, along with general info on other *Forever Knight* fan clubs in the U.S. and Canada. ✓**INTERNET**→*www* http://www.hu.mtu.edu/~gjwali/fan clubs.html

List & trivia

Flashback Timeline In "For I Have Sinned," Nick travels to fifteenth-century France. In "Dead Issue," he's in Holland at the beginning of the sixteenth century. And in "Only the Lonely," he's smack-dab in the middle of present-day Toronto. Follow the bouncing time-traveling vampire with this document, which indexes flashbacks both by episode and by century. ✓**INTERNET**→*www* http://www.humtu.edu/~gjwalli/FK_timeline.html

List of Known Vampires There's no Dracula, no Count Chocula, and no Lestat, but plenty of other bloodsuckers, from the 1000+-year-old Janette to the young Richard Lambert, make the grade in this registry of *Forever Knight* immortals. ✓**INTERNET**→*www* http://www.hu.mtu.edu/~gjwalli/vampire_list.html

Merchandise

Forever Knight Merchandise You can buy T-shirts, books, posters, photos, fake fangs, and scary music for time-traveling vampire fans. ✓**INTERNET**→*www* http://www.hu.mtu.edu/~gjwalli/merchandise.html

Highlander

Starring Sean Connery and French heartthrob Christopher Lambert, the original High-

lander was the surprise hit of 1986, winning audiences over with its mix of immortal camp and flashy special effects. Four years later, director Russell Mulcahy and the two principals reunited for *Highlander II—The Quickening*. The mother of all indigestable sequels, *The Quickening* soon became the proverbial bullet that die-hard fans occasionally must—if not love to—bite in front of their VCRs and then spit out on the Net. With a television series and a third movie (*Highlander 3: The Final Dimension*) added to their banquet of pleasure, online Connor fans gather at **The Gathering**, cluster in **alt.tv.highlander**, and drown their sorrows in the **Highlander Drinking Game**.

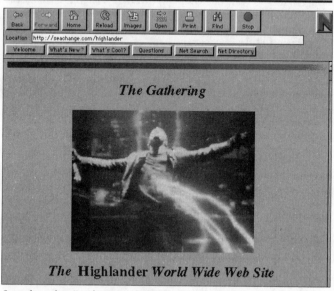

The Gathering

The **Highlander** *World Wide Web Site*

Screenshot —*http://seachange.com/highlander*

On the Net

Hubsites

The Gathering A comprehensive *Highlander* site that includes FAQs, film summaries, series episode guides, a timeline, lists of immortals, fiction, and even rules for a drinking game. ✓ **INTERNET** → *www* http://seachange.com /highlander

Highlander "Could someone ex-

plain this to me?" Kyle wrote. "Either you are all die-hard fans, immortal, or just plain crazy." What do you think, Kyle? This is the place to talk about *Highlander* on CompuServe. "Guilty on the first count," Elaine replied. "On the second I wish. On the third, weeell maybe just a little." A fun and dedicated group, with lots of talk of the *Quickening* and plot sequences. In the libraries, you'll find goodies like a timeline covering the events in the *Highlander* world. ✓ **COMPUSERVE** → *go* sfmedia → Libraries *or* Messages → Highlander

Highlander WWW Site The official and unofficial Web page for all things *Highlander*, including the two existent films, the TV series, and the third film, which is scheduled to be released stateside

sometime in the near future. ✓ **INTERNET** → *www* http://www.acm.iit. edu/highlander/

Chat

alt.tv.highlander (ng) "Is it me," wrote one *Highlander* fan, "or do a lot of the immortals that Duncan deems to be his close friends go crazy, turn against him, etc., and thus he ends up having to kill 'em all?" Nope, someone responded, it's just that the turncoats and the psychos "make for more interesting story lines." A reasonable theory. You'll find lots of talk about airdates, time inconsistencies, and debates over "the Quickening" (a mystical process that's got something to do with beheading immortals). These fans don't talk about the *Highlander* movies and TV shows like they're high art, but they're not likely to agree with the reviewer who called the latest movie "brainless fodder for undiscriminating audiences." The review, posted to the group, got a blow-by-blow refutation ("H3 gets bad rap" was the title of the post). Not a group dominated by sci-fi fans. One of the regulars jokingly referred to *Star Trek* as *Star* What? ✓**USENET**

Highla-L (ml) Why didn't Duncan have a scar when he got slashed? And what happens to bullets when an immortal gets shot? "I like to think that somehow their internal Quickening dissolves the bullet and heals the wound," Adam wrote. "After all, the Quickening is what *makes* them immies, right?" Right, I guess, although Ellis said it had already been determined that "bullets are ejected from the wound when it heals" (that's in the TV series, at least). Lots of Quickening theories and talk of the latest *Highlander* buzz, whether it's about a new film or the TV show. Much mulling over details, like why Kurgan's left—or was it right?—arm was always covered. ✓**INTERNET**→*email* listserv@psuvm.psu.edu ✍ *Type in message body:* subscribe highla-l <your full name>

Highlander (echo) Share your views on immortals, beheadings, quickenings, Connerys, Lamberts, Kurgans, Duncans, swords, and other pertinent topics. ✓**FIDONET**

Episode guides

Series Episode Guide Episode guides for the first three seasons of the *Highlander* series, these documents contain detailed information on cast, plots, and technical credits. ✓**INTERNET** ...→*www* http://seachange.com/highlander/one.html ...→*www* http://seachange.com/

highlander/two.html ...→*www* http://seachange.com/highlander/three.html

Fan fiction

Highlander Stories Two stories written by Wendy L. Miler that continue the *Highlander* legacy, "The Quick and the Dead" and "Questionable Beginning." ✓**INTERNET** ...→*www* http://seachange.com/highlander/quick.html ...→*gopher* http://seachange.com/highlander/begin.html

FAQ

Highlander FAQ How many immortals were in the movies? What are the differences between the American and British releases? What other names has Connor used? And what the hell is the Quickening, anyway? Like most FAQs, this document answers the most pressing questions about its topic. ✓**INTERNET**→*www* http://www.acm.iit.edu/highlander/FAQ/highlander_toc.html

Highlander FAQ It's billed as "a comprehensive source of information on all aspects of the *Highlander* universe," and it's exactly that, with questions and answers for the film, the series, and the role-playing game. ✓**INTERNET**→*www* http://seachange.com/highlander/faq.html

Games

Highlander Drinking Game Get drunk with your favorite immortals with these rules, which key common events in the series to alcoholic responsibilities. Invented in Carbondale, Illinois, this game is for viewers of legal drinking age only. ✓**INTERNET**→*www* http://seachange.com/highlander/drinking.html

Highlander: The Gathering If you're participating in a role-playing game using the White Wolf storytelling system, this module will allow you to take part in the world of *Highlander*. ✓**INTERNET**→*www* http://www.acm.iit.edu/highlander/Rules/

Lists & trivia

Highlander Flashback Timeline When you're trying to follow a show filled with the twists and turns of time-travel, it's hard to keep your temporal balance. And that's why we need more documents like this timeline, maintained by Velia Tanner and Julie Beamer.

Starting in late sixteenth-century Scotland and continuing through the present, this timeline is annotated with episodes and also justifications for its chronological guesses. ✓**INTERNET**→*www* http://seachange.com/highlander/timeline.html

Highlander Immortals List Who wants to live forever? Well, George Burns for one, and also the *Highlander* immortals, who are more familiarly known as "immies." Maintained by Brian Hayden, this list includes the name of each and every immortal, the actor or actress who played the role, the appearances, and the approximate age. ✓**INTERNET**→*www* http://seachange.com/highlander/immies.html

Swords used by Immortals The pen is mightier than the sword, but the sword is no slouch either, and this is a complete list of the blades used as weapons in the series, ranging from katanas to sabers to daggers. ✓**INTERNET**→*www* http://seachange.com/highlander/swords.html

MST3K

MST3K, of course, is *Mystery Science Theater 3000*, the sci-fi camp/cult hit that began

as a local cable-access show in Minnesota and rose to national fame on the wings of cable, and particularly Comedy Central. Ostensibly the story of a man stranded in an abandoned space station, the robots he has built to keep him company, and the bad movies inflicted upon them by the devilish Gizmonic Corporation, *MST3K* is in fact a demonstration of criticism at its finest—incisive, unpredictable, unrelenting, and hilarious, the *MST3K* team (Joel, Mike, Crow, and Tom Servo) rails against cheesy cinema with an attitude that is equal parts Pauline Kael and Bill Hicks. Unabashedly intelligent, sometimes to the point of snobbery, *MST3K* has found a second home on the Net, where no less than five major sites testify to the show's popularity. Weigh in with opinions about recent episodes on **alt.tv.mst3k**, dip into the **MST3K List of Lists,** or download a robot pinup from **MST3K Images.** And if you can't get enough of the corrosive satire, visit the **Mystery Usenet Theater at Web**

Watching Gamera—*from gynko.circ.upenn.edu/pub/rsk/mst3k*

Site Number 9, in which MAKE.MONEY.FAST posts and other Usenet atrocities are subjected to mocking marginalia that would make Servo proud.

On the Net

Hubsites

Deep 13 A wealth of *MST3K* links, including cast information, an episode guide, an FAQ, and a gateway to alt.tv.mst3k. ✓**INTERNET**→*www* http://alfred1.u.washington.edu:8080/~roland/mst3k/mst3k.html

Experimental MST3K In addition to the standard array of FAQs—on the series, on rock-climbing—this site links to a

quote generator and also contains Mac and Windows screensavers for downloading. ✓**INTERNET**→*www* http://www.publiciastate.edu/~hunter/mst3k.html

Index for Mystery Science Theater 3000 A well-maintained introduction to the show, with excerpts from the FAQ, air schedules, an episode guide, and links to other pages, all lavishly illustrated with images from the show. Unfortunately, since page architect Rob DeMillo has recently moved from MIT to Brown University, the address of the Index may change. ✓**INTERNET**→*www* http://jaquenetta.wx.ll.mit.edu/MST3K/Index.html

John's Mystery Science Theater 3000 Page Information files, drinking games, images, trivia quizzes, air schedules, and selected Usenet postings. ✓**INTER-**

NET→*www* http://www.engin. umich.edu/~jgotts/mst3k.html

MST3K Billed as a "pool-o-links," this site includes airtimes, FAQs, fan fiction, pictures and sounds, and links to Usenet newsgroups. ✓**INTERNET**→*www* http://www.ee. pdx.edu/cat/chaos/html/mst3k. html

MST3K Archive A clearinghouse of archival material, including FAQs, episode guides, a list of lists, and a short description of the series. ✓**INTERNET**→*www* http:// www.cis.ohio-state.edu/hypertext/ faq/bngusenet/alt/tv/mst3k/top. html

MST3K Stuff Includes links to a few other home pages, as well as two Mac downloads—a screensaver and the famous Stack O'Love database, which includes a huge amount of information about the show (episode guide, tape cataloger, drinking game rules, and a cookbook) and has incurred the wrath of *MST3K*'s legal representatives. An FAQ linked to the site reviews the legal situation surrounding the Stack O'Love ✓**INTERNET**→*www* http:// www.teleport.com/~lynsared/ mst.html

Website Number 9 Links to other *MST3K* sites, along with pictures from the show and an explanation of the Internet version of *MST3K*, Mystery Usenet Theater 3000, where bad Internet posts ranging from get-rich-quick schemes to hapless fan fiction are given the full *MST3K* treatment. ✓**INTERNET**→*www* http://www.engin. umich.edu/labs/mel/mneylon /mst3k/mst3k.html

Website o' Love One of the earlier and largest *MST3K* Websites, this site includes episode ratings,

summaries, newsletters, links to FTP sites, FAQs, and lyrics to the show's musical numbers. If there is anything wrong with the Website O' Love, it's the presentation, which forgos graphics entirely and as a result tends toward the pedestrian. ✓**INTERNET**→*www* http:// www.cs.odu.edu/~warren/mst3k /MST3K.html

Cast

Cast A page of large images and small descriptions of the *MST3K* cast, from Crow to Gypsy to Tom Servo to Cambot. ✓**INTERNET**→ *www* http://www.c3.lanl.gov/~ adelson/funlinks/mst_cast.html

Chat

alt.tv.mst3k / alt.fan.mst3k / rec.arts.tv.mst3k (ng) A cynical and hilarious set of newsgroups, much like the show itself. Fans of *Mystery Science Theater 3000* revel in their ruthlessness. After all, the show relies on viewer disdain for movies like *Invasion USA*, *The Creeping Terror*, and *Teenagers from Outerspace*.

One fan, upset by recent fare like *Racket Girls* and *Red Zone Cuba*—they weren't bad enough? —posted a plea for "dumb Japanese monsters" and "stupid alien movies": "We want to leave the sleazy 50s-60s underworld films (YAWN!) mercifully buried and happily decaying into a puddle of ooze!" Newbies, beware. Post a sincere question to this group and you're asking for a flame. Plenty of talk of sci-flicks like *Logan's Run*, *Nightfall*, and *Fire Maidens of Outer Space*.

Celebrity mentions should be particularly severe, with posts judged by their level of ridicule. After Kathy Ireland was called "the dumbest celebrity," one regular wrote: "If you ever get a chance,

listen to Nancy Sinatra. She makes Tony Danza and Sylvester Stallone look like Mensa members." ✓**USENET**

Mystery Science Theater 3000 A great hangout for MSTies and MSTics, with folders called "Joel vs. Mike," "Satellite of Love," "Favorite Running Gags," and lots of other goodies. The quotes in the "Favorite Quotes" folder include "Bite me, it's fun," and "We come bearing honey-bakes yams."

Check out the "Itchy Mango" folder for an "add-on story": "Create absurd situations, zany characters, and disgusting plot conveniences. In jokes—a plus. You (all of you) are responsible to keep the wacky adventures of Ms. Itchy Mango alive and kicking. Post away!"

This is a raucous and fun-loving bunch. Never a dull moment, with caustic comments appreciated. One MSTy's thoughts on "Kitten With a Whip": "My, this movie was putrid....What cheese!" ✓**AMERICA ONLINE**→*keyword* scifi→ Star Trek/Comics/TV/Star Wars Boards→Mystery Science Theater 3000

Conventions

About ConcentioCon An article from *Time* magazine about the 1994 *MST3K* convention. ✓**INTERNET**→*www* http://www.c3.lanl. gov/~adelson/funlinks/time_mst_ con.html

MST3K ConcentioCon-Expo-Fest-A-Rama Pictures Photos from the September 1994 *MST3K* convention. ✓**INTERNET**→*www* http://www.c3.lan1.gov/~adel son/funlinks/mst_con_pix.html

Texas NonCon Plans for a June 1995 convention to compensate for the lack of official conventions. This site contains information about the event. ✓ **INTERNET**→*www* http://www.c3.lanl.gov/~adel son/funlinks/mst_non_con.html

Episode guide

Brief Episode Guide A checklist of episodes from every season of the show. ✓ **INTERNET**→*www* http://www.cis.ohio-state.edu/hypertext/faq/usenet/tv/mst3k/brief-episode-guide/faq.html

Episode Guide A guide to every *Mystery Science Theater 3000* episode that includes titles, air-dates, summaries of the pre- and post-film skits, and descriptions of some of the major jokes in the show. ✓ **INTERNET**→*www* http://www.cis.ohio-state.edu/hypertext/faq/usenet/tv/mst3k/episode-guide/faq.html

FAQ

FAQs A five-part FAQ that covers every aspect of the show, from plot twists and song lyrics to broadcast history and future episodes. Long live the Weinerman song! ✓ **INTERNET** ...→*www* http://www.cis.ohio-state.edu/hypertext/faq/usenet/tv/mst3k/part1/faq.html ...→*www* http://www.cis.ohio-state.edu/hypertext/faq/usenet/tv/mst3k/part2/faq.html ...→*www* http://www.cis.ohio state.edu/hypertext/faq/usenet/tv/mst3k/part3/faq.html ...→*www* http://www.cis.ohiostate.edu/hypertext/faq/usenet/tv/mst3k/part4/faq.html ...→*www* http://www.cis.ohio-state.edu/hypertext/faq/usenet/tv/mst3k/part5/faq.html

MST3K Most Frequently Asked Questions Learn all about *Mystery Science Theater*, from Joel's escape from the ship to the reasons Frank is leaving the show, and also explore links to additional Websites and newsgroups. ✓ **INTERNET**→*www* http://www.cis.ohio-state.edu/hypertext/faq/usenet/tv/mst3k/most-faq/faq.html

---

Mystery Science Theater 3000: Frequently Asked Questions Can you order episodes directly from the producers? How do the show's creators find the bad films with which they torture Joel? And what about rock climbing? This FAQ contains basic information, song lyrics, fan-club data, electronic forums, props and sets, robot biographies, and obscure trivia about *MST3K* and the source films it lampoons. ✓ **INTERNET**→*www* http://www.cis.ohio-state.edu/hypertext/faq/usenet/tv/mst3k/faq/faq.html

Games

MST3K Drinking Game Ed Dravecky's drinking-game rules, with different categories for "Sip," "Drink," "Guzzle," and "Hook an IV and Call the Doctor." Even robots will enjoy this game. ✓ **INTERNET**→*www* http://www.engin.umich.edu/~jgotts/mst3k/drink-game.html

Lists & trivia

MST3K List of Lists There are details, and then there are details. What color jumpsuit is Joel wearing in episode 214? What guest characters have appeared in more than one episode? And how does Heather Locklear feel about her performance in "The Lingerie Justice Files"? If these don't strike you as pathologically specific questions, you may enjoy the *MST3K* List of Lists. ✓ **INTERNET**→*www* http://www.cis.ohio-state.edu/hypertext/faq/usenet/tv/mst3k/list-of-lists/faq.html

Multimedia

MST3K Images Images of the *MST3K* gang. ✓ **INTERNET**→*anon-ftp* gynko.circ.upenn.edu→/pub/rsk/mst3k

STARNOTES

"My, this movie was putrid! Talk about nothing happening... but nothing happened in a sort of deceptive way...cause I kept thinking something was going to happen, but really, it didn't, did it? Know what I mean?

<G>

"As for John Forsythe, well, his acting hasn't improved much over time, has it? And, I just loved the part where Ann Margaret was pulling on the phone cord when he was talking to his wife. What cheese!

<G>

"I've gotta watch it again to pick up some favorite lines.
"I liked Kevin as the Kitten with a Whip...I was so disappointed that Ann M. didn't whip John Forsythe a few times!

<VBG>"

—from **Mystery Science Theater 3000** on AOL

Quantum Leap

During its five-year run on NBC (1989-1993), *Quantum Leap* leapt into the hearts of

quality-television fans everywhere. With Scott Bakula as the superintelligent (six doctorates, 11 languages, one Nobel Prize) Dr. Samuel Beckett and Dean Stockwell as the rough-and-tumble Rear Admiral Albert Calavicci, the show took one simple science-fiction concept—a hero who time-travels through his own lifetime, inhabiting other bodies—and spun out dozens of quality playlets. Though the plots sometimes fell into formula—"as a stuntman, Sam is to save the life of his younger brother"—the strongest *Leap*s insisted on the importance of American history, whether the Civil Rights movement or the assassination of John F. Kennedy. At its best, *Quantum Leap* was public TV with a twist and fans fondly remember that aspect on **The Quantum Leap Mailing List**, the **Leaps Unbound** fanzine, and the **alt.ql.creative** newsgroup, which is devoted to fan fiction. There's even a **QL Drinking Game** that lets the faithful reward themselves for inside jokes with a hit of the hard stuff.

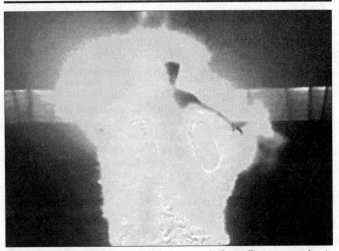

Opening sequence—http://www-usacs.rutgers.edu/funstuff/tv/quantum-leap/

On the Net

Hubsites

The Accelerator Channel And how do you leap through Cyberspace? With a well-designed Website devoted to *Quantum Leap*, especially one that includes general information, fan-club listings, and fan fiction. ✓**INTERNET**→*www* http://www-usacs.rutgers.edu/funstuff/tv/quantum-leap/

Information Roadmap A hypertext copy of the introduction to rec.arts.sf.tv.quantum-leap. Includes related Web pages, rebroadcast schedules, reviews of CDs and cassettes, videos, companion books, and original novels, and fan fiction. ✓**INTERNET**→*www* http://www-usacs.rutgers.edu/fun-stuff/tv/quantum-leap/roadmap. html

Quantum Leap Archive *QL* guides, mailing list archives,

drinking game rules, tape lists, interview transcripts, and FAQs. ✓**INTERNET**→*anon-ftp* ftp.doc.ic.ac.uk→/pub/media/tv/collections/tardis/us/sci-fi/QuantumLeap

Quantum Leap FTP Site A large archive of material about the series, including basic information, sounds, and fan fiction. ✓**INTERNET**→*anon-ftp* ftp.cisco.com→/ql-archive

The Quantum Leap Information Page Follow the adventures of Sam Beckett with this excellent home page, which includes leaps—er, links—to basic information, an episode guide, sound bites, images, and broadcast schedules. ✓**INTERNET**→*www* http://lumchan.ifa.hawaii.edu/ql/ql.html

Broadcast info

Quantum Leap Rerun Schedules If you've wasted hours flipping through channels looking for the show, waste no more with this rerun schedule, which furnishes showtimes for the USA Network and the Sci-Fi Channel. ✓**INTERNET** →*www* http://www-usacs.rutgers. edu/fun-stuff/tv/quantum-leap/re-run-sched.html

Chat

Quantum_Leap (echo) Most conversation follows whatever episode the USA cable channel is up to in its repeats of the sci-fi drama. A small cadre of enthusiasts often acts as a kind of unofficial help desk for the less regular participants who come here to iron out their understanding of Sam Beckett's time travel. There are also several *Quantum Leap* novels and comic books that get treated like extra episodes of the show. ✓**FIDONET**

Quantum Leap One of the regulars became worried when one of her comrades started to take this "leaping" business a bit too seriously. "You are aware that this is just a TV show," she wrote. The response? "What do you mean by 'just a tv show.' Is your brain swiss-cheesed :-) It's real! Isn't it?" Uh, is there such a thing as a straitjacket for Netizens of Cyberspace?

Lots of arguing and analyzing of individual episodes. In the libraries, you'll find a listing of QL fan stuff, a file on "the people, places, or things you won't see Sam 'leaping' into," and the "Quantum Leap Episode Index." ✓**COMPUSERVE**→*go* sfmedia→Libraries *or* Messages→Quantum Leap

Quantum Leaper (ml) *Quantum Leap* fiction, convention queries, spottings of the show's stars—it's all fair game for The

Quantum Leaper, a mailing list/ newsletter for *Leap* lovers. Subscribing will keep you up-to-date on any news in the world of QL. You can, for instance, discuss Sam's leaping into a black man ("This was a pioneering move when it was done, and they pulled it off"), the QL soundtrack ("It is *definitely* worth getting"), or trade stories about episode-taping snafus (and learn, via an off-topic thread, that snafu is a war acronym that stands for "situation normal, all fucked up"). ✓**INTERNET**→*email* cs-leap-request@durham.ac.uk ✍ *Write a request Archives:* ✓**INTERNET**→*anon-ftp* ftp.doc.ic.ac.uk→ /pub/media/tv/collections/ tardis/us/sci-fi/QuantumLeap/ QuantumLeaper

Episode guide

Episode Guide A complete list of the show's episodes, including production number, original airdate, plot summaries, production credits, and a ready-reference index for the historical time covered by the episode. ✓**INTERNET**→*www* http://www-usacs.rutgers.edu/fun-stuff/tv/quantum-leap/episode-index.html

Fan fiction

alt.ql.creative (ng) Let your imagination run wild—and into another era—with stories based on the TV show *Quantum Leap*. Fans write their own *Quantum Leap* stories and post them here, where they find a small-but-devoted audience.

If you're not into writing your own fiction, read the stories posted here. Some of them are quite good, like "Ace," in which Sam finds himself as a World War I fighter pilot. Aside from the stories, there's a fair amount of discussion about many aspects of the

series—what, for instance, are the rules of "leaping?" ✓**USENET**

Fans

Fanzine List A large list of *Quantum Leap* newsletters, letterzines, zines that are being published and, zines that are in the works, fan clubs, and ordering addresses. ✓**INTERNET**→*www* http:// www-usacs.rutgers.edu/fun-stuff/ tv/quantum-leap/fanzines.html

Leaps Unbound Information about the *Quantum Leap* fanzine edited by Cheryl Belucci, Tracy Finifter, and Gina Goff, including story titles and descriptions. ✓**INTERNET**→*www* http://www-usacs. rutgers.edu/fun-stuff/tv/quantum-leap/leaps-unbound.html

FAQ & basic info

Quantum Leap FAQ Does Scott Bakula do his own singing on the show? Is Scott Bakula really as nice as he seems to be? If Al is a hologram, why does he cast shadows? All this and more basic information about the show that put the humanity back in time travel. The second version of the FAQ is an extended one, and contains additional information about broadcast schedules, among other topics. ✓**INTERNET**...→*www* http:// www-usacs.rutgers.edu/fun-stuff/ tv/quantum-leap/faql.html ...→ *www* http://www-usacs.rutgers. edu/fun-stuff/tv/quantum-leap/ faql-2.html

The Mission of Project Quantum Leap A transcript of the show's opening voice-over. ✓**INTERNET**→*www* http://www-usacs. rutgers.edu/fun-stuff/tv/quantum-leap/saga-sell.html

The Quantum Leap Primer Taken from the SF-Lovers archive at Rutgers, this document offers a basic introduction to the time travels of Dr. Sam Beckett. ✓**INTERNET** →*gopher* wiretap.spies.com→Wiretap Online Library→Mass Media →Television→quantum.prm

Spoiler FAQL If you don't mind ruining plots—or having others ruin them for you—check out this FAQ, which is maintained by Robin Chi-Woon Kwong and addresses such pressing questions as "Do two different actresses play Donna?" and "Can Sam hear the Imaging Chamber door or the handlink?" ✓**INTERNET** →*www* http://www.usacs.rutgers.edu/fun-stuff/tv/quantum-leap/spoiler-faql.html

Games

Quantum Leap Drinking Game How can you have a cult television show without an accompanying drinking game? What would fans do if they couldn't sit at home doing shots every time Sam looks in the mirror, gives an inspirational speech, or speaks in a foreign language?

If you've ever wanted to yell out "Keep the Leap!" and chug all remaining alcohol whenever someone offers an explanation of the string theory of quantum leaping, this is the document for you. But remember—keep the revelry to a minimum, and be responsible rather than foolish. Friends don't let friends leap drunk. ✓**INTERNET** →*www* http://www.usacs.rutgers.edu/fun-stuff/tv/quantum leap/drinking-game.html

Lists & trivia

Quantum Leap Directors Are you a fan of Anita Addison's work on "Ghost Ship"? And how about the time choreographer-to-the-stars Debbie Allen dropped by to helm "Private Dancer"? Complete lists of QL directorial credits, along with episode names and numbers. ✓**INTERNET**→*gopher* wire tap.spies.com→Wiretap Online Library→Mass Media→Television→Quantum Leap Directors

Quantum Leap List of Lists Past episode summaries, general series information, airdates and airtime listings, working titles, characters who have seen Al and Sam, characters who have spent time in the chamber, and scenes with continuity errors that could possibly be considered bloopers, all lovingly compiled and presented by loyal *Quantum Leap* fans. ✓**INTERNET**→*gopher* wiretap.spies.com→Wiretap Online Library→Mass Media→Television→Quantum Leap List of Lists

Quantum Leap Quotes Witty and memorable sayings that once flowed from the lips of Scott Bakula, Dean Stockwell, and the rest of the QL cast. ✓**INTERNET**→*anon-ftp* ftp.cisco.com→/ql-archive/text→ql.quote

Multimedia

Quantum Leap Imaging Chamber See Sam leap! See Al mug! See history change! An archive of images from the show. ✓**INTERNET**→*www* http://lumchan.ifa.hawaii.edu/ql/images/qlpix.html

Quantum Leap Sounds From special effects to snippets of dialogue, the wealth of sounds contained in this archive are guaranteed to transport you into the wonderland of *Quantum Leap*. Feast your ears on the past. ✓**INTERNET**→*www* http:/www-usacs.rutgers.edu/fun-stuff/tv/quantum-leap/sounds.html

Red Dwarf

The loopiest of loopy British sci-fi shows, *Red Dwarf* **has brought new meaning to the**

word "smeg," and new life to the laugh-out-loud parody. Set aboard the mining ship *Red Dwarf*, the show takes to ludicrous extremes the stranded-man premise used by such shows as *The Prisoner*. Dave Lister, the only survivor of a radiation leak, must content himself with the companionship of his talking cat, a computer named Holly, and Arnold Rimmer, a hologram simulation of one of the dead crewmen. Deliriously plotless and ingeniously moronic, *Red Dwarf* revels in bad moods and implausibilities; Lister and Rimmer don't always get on like the best of buddies, and even their friendly conversations can veer off into digressions so pointless they make your average dorm-room bull session seem like a policy debate. Online, fans can talk about the extinction of the buffalo on **alt.tv.red-dwarf**, download sounds and theme songs, and even review the premise of the third season (**Series III Text**), in which Lister discovers that he is pregnant after a liaison with his female self in a parallel universe.

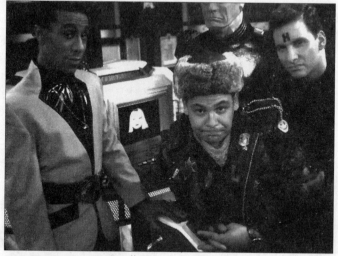

Cast of Red Dwarf—*from www.hal.com/~markg/docs/RedDwarf/ images/*

On the Net

Hubsites

Red Dwarf Home Page Laugh yourself sick with this site, which includes an episode guide, an FAQ, quotes, lots of images, sounds, and more. ✓ **INTERNET→** *www* http://www.hal.com/~ markg/docs/RedDwarf/rd-home_ page.html

Red Dwarf Website A large collection of *Red Dwarf* information, including a series FAQ, images, sounds, quotes, and a script archive. ✓ **INTERNET→** *www* http:// http2.brunel.ac.uk:8080/home. html

Chat

alt.tv.red-dwarf (ng) Given the hilarious weirdness of *Red Dwarf*, it's no surprise this group's full of off-topic banter about everything from the destruction of the buffalo to weevil-infested bread. A conversation about the origin of the show's generic and oft-used profanity, "smeg" led to a lengthy, flame-filled argument about the differences between smegma, semen, and sebum. "Are there any reported incidents of sex on *Red Dwarf*?" one potential viewer asked. "You see, I only want to watch it if there are." "Well, not much sex," one of the regulars responded, but in one episode there's a "fantastic scene where Lister was passionately kissing the giant cockroach which intended to suck his brains out with a straw." For those interested in the more serious side of this group, you'll find lots of discussion of Brit slang, and talk about whether American fans can understand the class nuances of the relationship between Dave Lister and Arnold Rimmer. Even if you know nothing of the show, this is a fun, fun place to hang out. ✓**USENET**

Interactive Talk A Website that lets subscribers participate in talk about *Red Dwarf*. Topics range from the problem of purchasing *Red Dwarf* videotapes to friendly disputes over favorite episodes. ✓**INTERNET**→*www* http://http3. brunel.ac.uk:10000/wit

FAQ

FAQ The most frequently asked questions about Britain's favorite science-fiction comedy series. Is there an episode guide? Did *Red Dwarf* start on radio? Why is Holly now a woman? And what about star Craig Charles, who was jailed on rape charges last July? The sites listed below are nearly identical, except for formatting (the first two are hypertext and the third consists of plain text). ✓**INTERNET** ...→*www* http://http2.brunel.ac. uk:8080/faq.html ... →*www* http://www.cis.ohio-state.edu/ hypertext/faq/usenet/tv/red_ dwarf-faq/faq.html ...→*anon-ftp* rtfm.mit.edu→/pub/usenet/news. answers/→red_dwarf-faq

Multimedia

Red Dwarf Images A handful of images from the show, displayed in miniature on the page and available for viewing in larger sizes. ✓**INTERNET**→*www* http:// http2.brunel.ac.uk:8080/images. html

Red Dwarf Image Collection A GIF of the cast, show logos in two easy-to-use sizes (large and small), and a few Starbug images. ✓**INTERNET**→*www* http://www.hal. com/~markg/docs/RedDwarf/rd-images.html

Red Dwarf Sound Archive A

large archive of .au format sounds from the show, including Holly's options for disabling the self-destruct sequence, Cat going fish-crazy, and the Rimmer directive. ✓**INTERNET**→*www* http://http2. brunel.ac.uk:8080/sounds/sounds. html

Red Dwarf Sounds The theme song, and plenty of salacious and entendre-filled sound bites from the show, including "Bonk Anything,""Groinal Socket," and "Novelty Condom Head." ✓**INTERNET**→*www* http://www.hal.com/ ~markg/docs/RedDwarf/rd-sounds.html

Quotes

Red Dwarf Favorite Quotes Quotes from the series, from Lister's "Where's me coffee cup with the mold in it?" to Kryten's cry, "It's a small, off-duty Czechoslovakian traffic warden!" ✓**INTERNET**→*www* http://http2.brunel.ac. uk:8080/quotes.html

Series III Text "Three million years in the future, Dave Lister, the last human being alive, discovers he is pregnant after a liaison with his female self in a parallel universe..." The opening text from the third season of the show. ✓**INTERNET**→*www* http://http2. brunel.ac.uk:8080/quotes/series3 start.html

Scripts

Red Dwarf Script Archive More than 30 scripts from the series, along with fan fiction that relies heavily on cross-pollinating the show with others, including *Star Trek* and *The Rocky Horror Picture Show*. ✓**INTERNET**→*www* http://http2.brunel.ac.uk:8080/ scripts.html

seaQuest DSV

Okay, okay, you have to listen to this pitch. It's concept. It's high concept. It's higher

than high concept. There have been plenty of sci-fi shows about outer space. Outer space is tired. Outer space is done. So guess where we go next? That's right, down. Down under. No, not Australia! Underwater. We can have a special submarine, an underwater vessel equipped to the nines, and a crew that represents the diversity the above-water civilization has to offer. We can have intrigue, romance, discovery, even horror. And we can crib the plots from other shows—it's instant success. Just add water. What? You're not convinced? Have I mentioned that the crew will have a pet? A talking dolphin? What? You're still not convinced? Well, our marketing people tell us that the show will be big with the kids on the Net, that it will provoke lots of talk (**alt.tv. seaquest**) and maybe even get a cult following (**sea-Quest FAQ**). Still uncertain? Have I mentioned that Steven Spielberg will executive produce? Good. I'll send the papers right over. And you won't be sorry. It's going to make a big splash. Bigger than *Supertrain*.

seaQuest *crew—from www.hyperion.com-80/ftp/pub/TV/seaQuest/Characters/*

On the Net

Hubsites

Nathan Evans's Page Created by a *seaQuest* fan who promises to link to *seaQuest* sites as they appear on the Internet. Currently, Evans's page links only to the *seaQuest* archive at hyperion.com. ✓ **INTERNET**→*www* http://nmt.edu/ ~seaquest/

seaQuest Archive Includes the *seaQuest* newsletter, a timeline, a mini-guide, and an FAQ. ✓ **INTERNET**→*anon-ftp* ftp.doc.ic.ac.uk→ /pub/media/tv/collections/tardis /us/sci-fi/seaQuest_DSV

seaQuest Directory Carries back issues of the now-defunct Talking Dolphins Newsletter, images of *seaQuest* characters, FAQs and episode guides, character bi-ographies, and a huge selection of soundclips from the show. ✓ **INTERNET**→*anon-ftp* ftp.hyperion.com →/pub/TV/seaQuest

seaQuest DSV Home Page The official MCA Website for *seaQuest*. Features international station listings, a short description of each upcoming episode, star profiles, a picture gallery, production information and credits, and a series overview. ✓ **INTERNET**→*www* http://www.mca.com/tv/seaquest/

Chat

alt.tv.seaquest (ng) David wants the writers of *seaQuest DSV* to have enough creativity not to steal characters and episodes from *Star Trek: The Next Generation.* "If you're going to steal stories," he writes, "at least don't make them WORSE than the original!" Another viewer—not a fan, exactly—dubbed this show "Fish Trek 90H20" for its combination of hardbodied hunks and salvaged Trek plots.

You'll find ample comparisons of Captains Kirk and Picard to *seaQuest*'s Captain Bridger. "Let's face facts," one person writes, "Bridger doesn't and can't compare to either of those captains." Aside from the Trek references, this group is heavy on science, with plenty of arguments about proper air pressure and vertebrates with gills. ✓USENET

seaQuest DSV When Katie, a 14-year-old, saw a post from Admiral Randy, she wanted to know if he was "REALLY an admiral?" Nope. He got the nickname in junior high, when he was fascinated with Admiral Nelson from *Voyage to the Bottom of the Sea*. Well, this is an appropriate spot for a sea-lover, right? Not the most active area, but it's got its devotees. Off-topic talk veers to sea-oriented sci-fi and fantasy. One argument concerned Dr. Smith: "She's a butt, and the day I start to like her will be the day *seaQuest* gets better ratings than *Star Trek*." The libraries have a meager selection, but they do include a heavily edited GIF of the show's logo, a Wav file, and an NBC press release about the second season. ✓**COMPUSERVE**→*go* sf media→Libraries *or* Messages→seaQuest DSV

Episode guide

seaQuest Mini-Guide Short plot summaries for *seaQuest* episodes with the episode authors, directors, and guest stars also noted. ✓**INTERNET** ...→*anon-ftp* ftp.hyperion.com→/pub/TV/seaQuest/Guides→sq_guide.txt.Z ...→ *anon-ftp* gandalf.rutgers.edu→/pub/sfl→seaquest.mini.guide

FAQ & trivia

seaQuest FAQ There's one burning question on everyone's mind, of course—How does the dolphin talk? But there are plenty of other important *seaQuest* topics covered in this document of frequently asked questions, including a discussion of the scientific conceits behind the series and clarifications of character and plot issues. Not only basic information for the show—cast, crew, premise, and a complete episode guide—but also the onscreen transmission code in the "Hide and Seek" episode, which guest-starred William Shatner; a list of the foreign languages spoken by communications officer Tim O'Neill; and the truth about Darwin, the Talking Tusriops Truncatus. ✓**INTERNET** ...→*anon-ftp* gandalf.rutgers.edu→/pub/sfl→seaquest.faq ...→*anon-ftp* ftp.hyperion.com→/pub/TV/seaQuest/Guides→sq_faq.txt.Z

seaQuest Trivia and Timeline Children are immune to attacks of the paranormal. Dead astronauts float in the distant reaches of the Milky Way. Water assists telepaths in concentrating. And other interesting facts from the world of *Seaquest DSV*, along with a detailed 21st-century timeline. ✓**INTERNET** ...→*anon-ftp* gandalf.rutgers.edu→/pub/sfl→seaquest.timeline ...→ *anon-ftp* ftp.hyperion.com→/pub/TV/seaQuest/Guides→sq_time.txt.Z

Merchandising

seaQuest DSV Merchandising FAQ Catalogs and describes merchandise available for *seaQuest DSV*, including novelizations, comics, action figures, trading cards, and calendars. ✓**INTERNET**→*anon-ftp* ftp.hyperion.com→/pub/TV/seaQuest/Guides→sq_mer_

faq.txt.Z

Multimedia

seaQuest Opening Soundclip: "The 21st century. Mankind has colonized the last unexplored region on the earth, the ocean." ✓**INTERNET**→*www* http://ai.eecs.umich.edu/people/kennyp/sounds/shows/seaquest.au

STARNOTES

"I have one other complaint about recent episodes: they've been much more predictable than some of the earlier episodes. Especially the killer weeds, the giant crocodile, and the one with two Dagwoods. What I enjoyed about the early episodes this season was that they'd take all sorts of cliches and dump them together so that I wasn't sure what was going to happen next, or even what direction the episode was going to be taking. Unfortunately, most of the plot twists in the three episodes I just mentioned were pretty easy to see coming. As opposed to the early episodes which took elements I've seen before but somehow combined them in a way that seemed new."

—from **alt.tv.seaquest**

Star Wars

After May 25, 1977, it was hard to find anyone in the Western world who wasn't pros-

trate in front of the altar of George Lucas's sci-fi mono-myth *Star Wars*. Luke, Han, Leia, Chewie, Vader, Obi-Wan, C3PO, and R2D2 became household names, and obscenely large box office receipts became Hollywood's new Holy Grail. The undisputed king of sci-fi marketing and media frenzy, *Star Wars* had coattails long enough for dozens of television shows and films across the world, not to mention two sequels of its own. Online fans can download not only scripts for all three films, but an incredible number of documents on merchandising and collecting, most of which are linked to the massive **Star Wars Home Page at UPenn**—including the **Star Wars Drinking Game** and an **Explanation of Hyperspace**. Images, sounds, role-playing games, **Memorable Star Wars Quotes**, and bloopers are all well represented, and as 1997 approaches, George Lucas's plan for the first volume of the second trilogy looks like it might be more than an idle fantasy. Pick a site, and make no mistake—these *are* the droids you're looking for.

Cast & Crew—from http://trill.pc.cc.cmu.edu:80/~jkoga/sw_gallery.html

On the Net

Hubsites

David Jansen's Star Wars Page Begun as a personal *Star Wars* home page, this site is now one of the most complete lists of Lucas-related materials on the Internet. In addition to links to all major *Star Wars* Websites, the Jansen page contains some material of its own, most notably GIFs captured from the *Star Wars* computer game and a "fortune cookie" program that generates random quotes from the trilogy. How random? Try C3PO's abashed expla-

nation to Han in *Return of the Jedi*: "I'm rather embarrassed, General Solo, but it appears you are to be the main course at a banquet in my honor." ✓**INTERNET→** *www* http://www.strw.leidenuniv. nl/~jansen/sw.html

Star Wars Website Maintained by Michael Sherman at Carnegie-Mellon, this general site includes information on all three films in the original trilogy, as well as sounds, pictures, movie scripts, and news clippings about upcoming LucasFilms projects. ✓**INTERNET→***www* http://www.cs.cmu.edu :8001/afs/andrew.cmu.edu/usr18/

Millennium Falcon—ftp.rus.uni-stutt gart.de‹/pub/graphics/pictures/tv+film/ mset/www/starwars.html

Star Wars If you're in the *Star Wars* message area and you see a topic on the best movie ever made, don't say it's *Jurassic Park*. Sure, these fans like Spielberg and those awesome special effects, but *The Empire Strikes Back* rules here. Got it? "I mean, I can sit down and watch ESB a thousand thousand times and still be awake," one SW-lover said. "I watch *Jurassic Park* three times and I'm out cold." Sometimes it seems like everyone in this place has watched Empire a "thousand thousand times." That doesn't mean these fans limit themselves to movie-watching: other active topics include *Star Wars* books and toys. Rumors about new *Star Wars* films get discussed at length, as you'd expect. In the libraries, you'll find The Complete Star Wars Chronology, a dissertation on Jedi grammar, and a Yoda start-up screen, among other goodies. ✓**COMPUSERVE**→*go* sfmedia→Libraries *or* Messages→Star Wars

Star Wars Home Page at UPenn So, you want an explanation of hyperspace travel, a list of Kenner action figures, a catalog of missing scenes from the trilogy, or the rules of the *Star Wars* drinking game? This huge (and we mean Jabba-size) home page includes *Star Wars* news, scripts of the trilo-

gy, images and sound files, information on the trilogy and *Star Wars* collectibles, guides to *Star Wars* role-playing games, nitpicking and bloopers lists, trivia, Lucas Arts pages, and a guest book. Also features a huge section of news and FAQs about the series. ✓**INTERNET**→*www* http://force.stwing. upenn.edu:8001/~jruspini/info/ starwars.html

Star Wars Multimedia WWW Archive Another massive *Star Wars* site with information on movies, novelizations, television, reference, music, and other related topics. The Bantha archive has large images, and as a result screens take quite a while to load, but this is one of the most comprehensive sources of *Star Wars* info, and maybe the best SW site apart from the home page at UPenn. ✓**INTERNET**→*www* http:// bantha.pc.cc.cmu.edu:1138/SW_ HOME.html

Star Wars Page Movie scripts, sounds, images, FAQs, and addresses for all *Star Wars* actors,

from Mark Hamill to James Earl Jones. ✓**INTERNET**→*www* http:// www.mgmt.purdue.edu/~vkoser/ starwars/star.html

Star Wars—The Greatest Movie Ever Made? A gushing fan page that agrees to agree that *Star Wars* is the greatest movie ever made. Includes links to Websites, rumors on upcoming films, and the opportunity to leave messages for other fans of the films. ✓**INTERNET**→*www* http://info.cern.ch/ wit/Topic1192

Star Wars 101

George Lucas's Message in New Star Wars Screensaver Users of the *Star Wars* screensaver already know that George Lucas has planted a message in the software about the history of the trilogy and its future. Those who have never heard of the screensaver may still want to read about Lucas's plans for continuing the drama. Here's a hint: "Much of the drama...will revolve around betrayal." ✓**INTERNET**→*www* http://force.

Screenshot from force.stwing.upenn.edu:8001/~jruspini/info/starwars.html

---

Star Wars Home Page at UPENN

Back | Forward | Home | Reload | Images | Open | Print | Find | Stop

Location: http://force.stwing.upenn.edu:8001/~jruspini/starwars.html

Welcome | What's New? | What's Cool? | Questions | Net Search | Net Directory

A long time ago in a galaxy far, far, away...

STAR WARS

The Star Wars Home Page

stwing.upenn.edu:8001/~jruspini/info/message.txt

Chat & fans

rec.arts.sf.starwars (ng) Much talk about *Star Wars* toys and the next trilogy. Would you buy a Darth Vader carrying case for $200? No?! Well, someone will. One thread was titled, "Why hasn't Luke gotten laid yet?" "I think it's about time," Anton wrote. "Heck, I bet even the Wookie sneaks out for a little nookie. Luke gets the award for being the most sexually repressed hero ever." But, soap-opera-like worries aside, this is a sci-fi savvy group of regulars with lots of Star Wares. When the conversation veers away from Obi-Wan and Luke, it often turns to *Star Trek*, with Corey contending a battle between the Enterprise and the Star Destroyer would be "very close" while Joshua trashes transporters as "the most contrived and moronic devices, ever." Hey, try and say that in rec.arts.startrek. fandom, bud! ✓ **USENET**

Star Wars Standing head and shoulders above all other sci-fi action movies, George Lucas's 1977 film, along with its two sequels, forever changed the habits and expectations of movie audiences worldwide. In the AOL *Star Wars* discussion, fans fret over rumors of new *Star Wars* films ("The only thing definite about this movie is that nothing is definite"), point out inside jokes in other Lucas efforts (in *Indiana Jones and the Temple of Doom*, there's a nightclub named for Obi-Wan Kenobi), and bemoan the diminished employment prospects of *Star Wars* star Mark Hamill ("Time has not been kind to Hamill...and neither was *Corvette Summer*"). This message board is one big love-in that

embraces Luke Skywalker, Darth Vader, Princess Leia, Han Solo, et al. ✓ **AMERICA ONLINE**→*keyword* scifi→Star Trek/Comics/TV/Star Wars→Star Wars

FAQs

Julie Lim's Name FAQ From Han Solo to Darth Vader to Boba Fett, much of the fun of *Star Wars* lies in its names, and this FAQ offers correct spellings for all major names in the *Star Wars* universe, along with explanations of the characters' genealogies (where known). ✓ **INTERNET**→*www* http://bantha.pc.cc.cmu.edu:1138/StarWars/Other/SW_LINEAGE_20.html

---

Star Wars FAQ Version 4.10 of the Star Wars FAQ. Includes the answers to such questions as, "Was *Return of the Jedi* originally titled *Revenge of the Jedi*?" (yes); "Is *Hardware Wars* part of the *SW* canon?" (no); and "Isn't *Star Wars* a ripoff of a Japanese film titled *The Hidden Fortress*?" (yes and no). ✓ **INTERNET**→*www* http://force.stwing.upenn.edu:8001/~jruspini/info/faq410.txt

Games

Board, Electronic, and Video Games Useful for collectors and players alike, this document lists all the games related to *Star Wars*, from the Kenner board and electronic games to state-of-the-art video cartridges. ✓ **INTERNET**→*www* http://force.stwing.upenn.edu:8001/~jruspini/info/swgames.txt

---

Star Wars Drinking Game Keyed to the entire trilogy, this is one of the most enjoyable sci-fi drinking games on the Net, with a good grasp of both obsession and absurdity. Drink whenever someone "has a bad feeling about this."

Drink whenever a Jedi is much more powerful than he looks. Drink whenever someone exclaims

STARNOTES

LEIA: Lord Vader, I should have known. Only you could be so bold. The Imperial Senate will not sit for this, when they hear you've attacked a diplomatic...

VADER: Don't play games with me, Your Highness. You weren't on any mercy mission this time. You passed directly through a restricted system. Several transmissions were beamed to this ship by Rebel spies. I want to know what happened to the plans they sent you.

LEIA: I don't know what you're talking about. I'm a member of the Imperial Senate on a diplomatic mission to Alderaan...

VADER: You're a part of the Rebel Alliance...and a traitor. Take her away!

"Princess Leia is marched away down the hallway and into the smoldering hole blasted in the side of the ship.

"An Imperial Commander turns to Vader."

—from **Script of A New Hope**

Han & Luke—from ftp.rus.uni-stuttgart. de/pub/graphics/pictures/tv+film/starwars

"No!" According to the rules, "the game ends when a bunch of Ewoks start dancing. No matter what you've been drinking, you will remember this image." ✓**INTERNET**→ *www* http://force.stwing. upenn.edu:8001/~jruspini/info/drinking.txt

Role-playing

Blank Character Attribute Form Furnishes a character template for role-playing, including name, player, species, sex, age, height, weight, physical description, personality, a quote, background, connection with other characters, skills, special abilities, equipment, and weapons. ✓**INTERNET**→ *www* http://force.stwing. upenn.edu:8001/~jruspini/info/charsheet.txt

Character Skills Chart Dexterity skills, strength skills, technical skills, knowledge skills, perception

skills, and how to integrate them into a role-playing game. ✓**INTERNET**→ *www* http://force.stwing. upenn.edu:8001/~jruspini/info/skills.txt

Explanation of Hyperspace The hyperdrive, of course, is a miracle of futuristic technology, powered by fusion generators that throw ships into a dimension where they can travel faster than light. This brief essay is West End Games' explanation of the intricacies of hyperspace and the technology of faster-than-light travel. ✓**INTERNET**→ *www* http://force. stwing.upenn.edu:8001/~jruspini/info/hyperspace.txt

Lightsaber Technology For all the twenty-somethings who had toy lightsabers as kids, this one's for you: West End Games' tech report on the latest in futuristic/atavistic weaponry. ✓**INTERNET**→ *www* http://force.stwing.upenn.

edu:8001/~jruspini/info/lightsabers. txt

Reviews of Available Role-Playing Games How good is the West End Games module? How about the boxed game Star Warriors? These two documents offer brief but informative reviews on all available *Star Wars* role-playing games. And while it may not exactly thrill you to learn that the reviewers played *Assault on Hoth* "four times and found the game moderately exciting," it's exactly this kind of consumer reportage that prospective buyers need. ✓**INTERNET**→ *www* http://force.stwing.upenn.edu:8001/~jruspini/rpg-rev.txt

Star Wars Role-Playing FAQ Can you still get in on the *Star Wars* role-playing game? No, not really. But this FAQ will help you feel like you were there, providing information about game construction, major characters, and even information on where stories produced by the game are archived. ✓**INTERNET**→ *www* http://force. stwing.upenn.edu:8001/~jruspini/info/rpg-faq.txt

Star Wars Source Book A lengthy and comprehensive introduction to the second edition of the *Star Wars* role-playing game, with sections devoted to weapons and equipment, ships, new skills, new aliens, and new planets. ✓**INTERNET**→ *www* http://force.stwing.upenn.edu:8001/~jruspini/info/source.txt

Star Wars MUSH: A New Threat The main Website for this SW MUSH, which picks up after "the New Emperor, Angmar, has reunited the scattered aristocratic houses of the Empire and founded a New Order of his own." Continue the struggle between light and dark, or just look at the related pictures. ✓**INTERNET**→*www* http://ix.urz.uni-heidelberg.de/~jradelef/swmush.html

Humor

List of Failed Star Wars Toys Next Christmas, you might want to think about buying your niece or nephew some of these hilarious *Star Wars* toys.

How about the Incredible Shavable Han Solo ("Sprouted real hair; failed miserably when tested on real kids"), the Nit-Laden Chewbacca, or the Dissect an Ewok Kit. And after a few minutes with the list, you'll learn to make your own jokes. ✓**INTERNET**→*www* http://force.stwing.upenn.edu:8001/~jruspini/info/joketoys.txt

Mad Magazine Parody of Star Wars Hilarious and stupid, this *Mad* Magazine parody of the *Star Wars* trilogy takes the series through its other films, *Send in the Clones, Makin' Wookie, Hiya Leia, A Matter of Life and Darth,* and *Cut and Droid*. ✓**INTERNET**→*www* http://force.stwing.upenn.edu:8001/~jruspini/info/madmag.txt

Top Ten Sexually Tilted Lines From the Trilogy This list relies more on willful juvenile misunderstanding than true double entendre (C3PO's "Curse my metal body, I wasn't fast enough" is saddled with sexual meaning, as are lines like "You came in that thing?" and "There's an awful lot of moisture in here"). But if you're looking for a crescendo of dim innuendos, this document will put a smile on your face. ✓**INTERNET**→*www* http://force.stwing.upenn.edu:8001/~jruspini/info/sexline.txt

Collectibles

Complete Price Guide to Kenner Toys You know that Chewbacca action figure in the back of your closet, the one where the Wookie is toting a green crossbow? Well, don't throw it out—it could be worth almost fifty dollars. This collector's guide to the Kenner *Star Wars* action figures includes descriptions of the toys, an explanation of the different value tiers, and a brief FAQ on action figures that includes the fascinating fact that the first Han Solo action figure released had a "ridiculously small head." ✓**INTERNET**→*www* http://force.stwing.upenn.edu:8001/~jruspini/info/swprice.txt

Diecast Models Kenner's vehicles and miniatures. ✓**INTERNET**→*www* http://force.stwing.upenn.edu:8001/~jruspini/info/diecast.txt

Gus Lopez's Star Wars Collector's Archive One of the main online sites for *Star Wars* collectors, the Lopez archive includes price lists, product descriptions, and a brief history of merchandise related to the film. Though this site concentrates on Kenner action figures, it also lists other toys, and much of the collectors' information is nicely illustrated. ✓**INTERNET**→*www* http://www.cs.washington.edu/homes/lopez/collectors.html

How to Spot Fake Movie Posters Tips from a collector on how to spot ripoffs, shams, and charlatans in the movie-poster collection business. Includes information on the artwork, descriptions of all known reprints and forgeries, and pricing guidelines. ✓**INTERNET**→*www* http://force.stwing.upenn.edu:8001/~jruspini/info/fakepost.txt

Luke & Leia—from http://trill.pc.cc.cmu.edu:80/~jkoga/sw_gallery.html

List of Kenner Action Figures They first arrived in 1978, blister-packaged on small color-photo headers, and since then, the toy world has never been the same. From Greedo to Hammerhead, from Walrus Man to Weequay, all the characters in the Kenner series are listed, along with catalog numbers. ✓**INTERNET**→*www* http://force.stwing.upenn.edu:8001/~jruspini/swfigrs.txt

List of Kenner Playsets Accessories and more for Kenner action figures, from Chewbacca's Bandolier Strap to the Cloud City Playset. ✓**INTERNET**→*www* http://force.stwing.upenn.edu:8001/~jruspini/swsets.txt

Micromachine Checklist A checklist of Galoob's Micromachines, 28 ships and 49 figures in all. ✓**INTERNET**→*www* http://force.stwing.upenn.edu:8001/~jruspini/microm.txt

MPC Models Snap-together models, vinyl character models, and Estes rockets related to *Star*

Wars. ✓ **INTERNET**→*www* http://
force.stwing.upenn.edu:8001/~
jruspini/info/swmodels.txt

Star Wars Collectors' Bible
Maybe you have all the Kenner
toys and the 20th-Century Fox
publicity materials, but have you
laid your hands on *Star Wars: A
Collection of Ten Prints* by Gene
Day, published in Canada only by
Aardvark-Vandheim Press? Hurry
on over to the Collector's Bible, a
detailed list of *Star Wars* merchandise organized alphabetically by
company. ✓ **INTERNET**→*www* http://
www.cis.ohio-state.edu/~thurn
/SWB/

Topps Trading Cards A brief list
of *Star Wars* trading cards. ✓ **INTERNET**→*www* http://force.stwing.
upenn.edu:8001/~jruspini/info/
topps.txt

Multimedia

Purdue Picture Archive Pictures of characters and ships, as
well as miscellaneous pictures,
with miscellaneous defined as "pictures not of ships or people." ✓ **INTERNET**→*www* http://www.mgmt.
purdue.edu/~vkoser/starwars/
pics.html

Quicktime of Energizer Bunny Commercial That cute and
cuddly Energizer Bunny just keeps
going and going and going, and
sometimes he stops along the way
to do battle with Darth Vader. In
this 1994 television commercial,
Vader's light-saber fizzles and sputters thanks to (you guessed it!) bad
batteries, and the little rabbit escapes with his pink fur unsinged
and his toy drum intact. This file,
a 14M *Quicktime* movie of the
commercial, lets the force of marketing be with you. ✓ **INTERNET**→
www http://bantha.pc.cc.cmu.
edu:1138/StarWars/Pictures/QT/

energizer.mo

Star Wars ASCII Art ASCII images of major figures from the trilogy. ✓ **INTERNET**→*www* http://force.
stwing.upenn.edu:8001/~jruspini/
ascii.txt

Star Wars Graphics C3PO and
R2D2 by Jabba the Hut's palace?
An artist's conception of the Hoth
battle? The snow-walkers? This
site includes large images, both
photos and illustrations. ✓ **INTERNET**→*www* http://www.mit.edu:
8001/people/davidw/swgraph.
html

Star Wars WWW Pictures Images from the trilogy. ✓ **INTERNET**→
www http://bantha.pc.cc.cmu.
edu:1138/StarWars/Pictures/SW
Pictures.html

Uni-Stuttgart Starwars Picture Archive *Star Wars* images
from a German site—*Der Krieg
der Sterne.* ✓ **INTERNET**→*anon-ftp*
ftp.rus.uni-stuttgart.de→/pub/
graphics/pictures/tv+film/starwars

UPenn Starwars Sound Archive An ocean of .wav files,
from Han's witty rejoinders from
the first film ("What an incredible
smell you've discovered" and "It's
not wise to upset a Wookie") to
Luke's anguished cry in *The Empire Strikes Back* ("No! No! That's
not true! That's impossible!").
✓ **INTERNET**→*www* http://force.
stwing.upenn.edu:8001/~jruspini/
swsounds.html

WPI Star Wars Picture Site
JPEGs and ASCII art from the
trilogy. ✓ **INTERNET**→*anon-ftp* wpi.
wpi.edu→/starwars/Pictures

WPI Star Wars Sound Library
From soundtrack samples to dialogue bites, this library includes a
number of audio clips from the

Star Wars trilogy. ✓ **INTERNET**→
anon-ftp sounds.sdsu.edu→/sounds/
movies/starwars

Music

Critique of Available Star Wars Recordings Whether you
are looking for John Williams's
original score for *Star Wars* or the
rerecorded *Return of the Jedi* music
soundtrack conducted by Charles
Gerhardt, you'll find it in this document, a short list of all domestic
and foreign soundtrack recordings
for the entire trilogy. ✓ **INTERNET**→
www http://force.stwing.upenn.

edu:8001/~jruspini/info/cdlist.txt

Listing of the Musical Scores of the Trilogy That haunting snatch of melody is echoing in your head, and you know it has something to do with the sale of R2D2, but you can't for the life of you remember what it's called. Or at least you couldn't before you downloaded this document, which lists the entire scores for all three films. Thrill to "Cantina Band." Feel the cold chill of "The Walls Converge." And try to hold back the tears when you hear "Rescue of the Princess, Part 1." ✓**INTERNET**→*www* http://force.stwing. upenn.edu:8001/~jruspini/info/scores.txt

Music Missing From Box Set If the phrase "obsessive fan" has started to lose its meaning, restore your faith with Tom Lentz's list of music missing from the box set. In other words, music from the score that somehow failed to appear on the soundtrack recording. In other words, music whose detection required minute comparisons of hours of videotape and audio CDs. ✓**INTERNET**→*www* http:// force.stwing.upenn.edu:8001/~jruspini/cdmiss.txt

Off the silver screen

List of Books With Timeline All novelizations, along with a timeline that organizes their events. ✓**INTERNET**→*www* http:// force.stwing.upenn.edu:8001/~jruspini/booklist.txt

List of Star Wars-related Books Fill your shelves with The Force, and do it with the help of this document, which lists titles, publisher's information, and LC and ISBN numbers for original hardbacks, pocket editions, coffee-table books, and children's books.

Han, Leia, & Luke—from http://trill.pc.cc.cmu.edu:80/~jkoga/sw_gallery.html

✓**INTERNET**→*www* http://force. stwing.upenn.edu:8001/~jruspini/info/swbooks.txt

Mark Martinez's Complete List of Star Wars Comics A long and annotated list of *Star Wars* comics. ✓**INTERNET**→*www* http://force.stwing.upenn.edu:8001/~jruspini/info/comics1.txt

The Radio Dramas With detailed information about the *Star Wars* radio drama broadcast on National Public Radio, this document is most useful for its fascinating casting tidbits—while Mark Hamill played Luke throughout the broadcasts, Yoda was voiced by John Lithgow, and up-and-coming actors such as Adam Arkin, David Allan Grieg, and David Paymer also worked on the production. ✓**INTERNET**→*www* http://force.stwing.upenn.edu:8001/~jruspini/info/radio.txt

Scott Streeter's List of Star Wars Comics All *Star Wars* comics, from the main Marvel set to the lesser-known Dark Horse

and Blackthorne editions. ✓**INTERNET**→*www* http://force.stwing. upenn.edu:8001/~jruspini/info/comics.txt

Star Wars Books Shipping dates and descriptions of upcoming *Star Wars* books—taken from the pages of Advance Comics. ✓**INTERNET**→ *www* http://force. stwing.upenn.edu:8001/~jruspini/info/futurebc.txt

Quotes & trivia

Guide to Star Wars Trivia Though there's plenty of *Star Wars* trivia here (the revelation that Darth Vader is Luke's father was added in the dubbing stages of *The Empire Strikes Back*; crew members filming the barge scene for *Return of the Jedi* pretended to be working on a horror movie called *Blue Harvest*), the highlights of this document are the lists of *Star Wars* references in other films (Harrison Ford playing a character named G. Lucas in *Apocalypse Now*, for instance). ✓**INTERNET**→ *www* http://force.stwing.upenn.

edu:8001/~jruspini/info/swtrivia.txt

Memorable Star Wars Quotes

"These aren't the droids you're looking for." "Help me, Obi-Wan Kenobi: You're my only hope." "Luke, I am your father." Relive the greatest moments in the trilogy with this list of *Star Wars* quotes, which is formatted as a single text file. ✓**INTERNET**...→ *www* http://force.stwing.upenn.edu:8001/~jruspini/info/swquotes.txt...→*anon-ftp* quepasa.cs.tu-berlin.de→/pub/doc/movies+tv-series/StarWars→Quote_List

Reviews & nitpicks

A Catalog of Missing Scenes from the Trilogy

Comparing the trilogy to audio tapes, comics, novelizations, and the painstaking dissection of theatrical trailers, this document lists the scenes missing from the officially released versions of the films, including the Biggs subplot in the first film and Lando Calrissian's death in *Return of the Jedi*. ✓**INTERNET**→*www* http://force.stwing.upenn.edu:8001/~jruspini/info/swmiss.txt

A Paper on Star Wars

A long essay on George Lucas's debt to the Western, the self-interest of Han Solo, and the remaking of the traditional mythical hero for the outer-space setting. ✓**INTERNET**→ *www* http://force.stwing.upenn.edu:8001/~jruspini/info/paper.txt

Brandon Gillespie's Bad Guide

Bloopers and miscues from the film, in both a hypertext version and a text file for downloading. Remember C3PO, king of the Ewoks? How about the continuity errors after Han is frozen in carbonite? ✓**INTERNET** ...→*www* http://www.declab.usu.edu:8080/StarWars/BadGuide.html ...→ *www*

http://force.stwing.upenn.edu:8001/~jruspini/info/badguide.txt

Hey, Wasn't That a Blooper Too?

Everybody knows the biggest mistakes in the trilogy, like Han's nonsensical claim in *Star Wars* that the Millennium Falcon made the Kessel Run in less than 12 parsecs (parsecs are units of distance, roughly equal to 3.25 light years). But do you know the explanation for the error? (George Lucas claims he made the blunder on purpose.) Or for the nine other gaffes in the trilogy? ✓**INTERNET**→*www* http://force.stwing.upenn.edu:8001/~jruspini/info/bloopers.txt

Roger Ebert's Review of A New Hope

A copy of Roger Ebert's thumbs-up review of the original 1977 film, which contains a number of insights that are fascinating for their pre-hype naiveté ("The golden robot, lion-faced space pilot, and insecure little computer on wheels must have been suggested by the Tin Man, the Cowardly Lion, and the Scarecrow in *The Wizard of Oz*"), and does not include a complaint that the film has too few scenes of characters eating Twinkies. ✓**INTERNET**→*www* http://force.stwing.upenn.edu:8001/~jruspini/info/anh-rvw.txt

Scripts

A New Hope

Though it's more commonly known as *Star Wars*, the 1977 film that kicked off Skywalker fever is actually called *Star Wars, Episode IV: A New Hope*. And this is the film's script, which moves from the opening scenes on Tattooine to the final battle over the malign Death Star. ✓**INTERNET**→ *www* http://force.stwing.upenn.edu:8001/~jruspini/info/anh.txt

The Empire Strikes Back

Where's Luke? He went out with his tauntaun hours ago, and if we don't find him soon, they're going to have to close the station for the night. Those are the breaks here on Hoth. But maybe he'll return, and maybe he'll learn to master the ways of the Jedi with the help of a Muppet. Find out with this script. ✓**INTERNET**→*www* http://force.stwing.upenn.edu:8001/~jruspini/info/tesb.txt

The Return of the Jedi

Many *Star Wars* fans consider the third film the weak link, and it's true that Jabba the Hut's prurient imprisonment of Princess Leia, not to mention the cuddly Ewoks, sometimes fall below the level of inspiration set by the first two movies. But that doesn't mean that the script isn't an important document in its own right. ✓**INTERNET**→*www* http://force.stwing.upenn.edu:8001/~jruspini/info/rotj.txt

Darth Vader—from http://trill.pc.cc.cmu.edu:80/~jkoga/sw_gallery.html

Twin Peaks

Cults don't get much more cultish than this. When director David Lynch, the king of the

eerie feature, announced that he was bringing his warped vision to the small screen, America didn't know exactly what to expect. What it got was *Twin Peaks*, a soap opera on acid that soared for one brilliant season and then sink so low that it was virtually unrecognizable. Weird for the sake of weird? You bet. Hilarious? Yes, ma'am. Exploitive of nubile young actresses? Welcome to Hollywood. And welcome to *Twin Peaks*, where a murdered high-school girl can be the trigger on a double-barrelled rifle of borderline psychosis and paranormal intrigue. Midgets speaking backwards while the button-down G-man dreams, and it's not even a Dylan lyric? You'd better catch your breath. And, while you do, check out the **Twin Peaks FTP Server** and the **Black Widow's Web**. Coffee? Pie? Sherilyn Fenn's Secret Space? You're not going to believe this.

Sherilyn Fenn—downloaded from audrey.levels.unisa.edu.au/twin-peaks/JPGS

On the Net

Hubsites

Black Widow's Web Maps of Twin Peaks, images of the charac-ters, the Twin Peaks FAQ, and more. ✓**INTERNET**→*www* http://www.seas.upenn.edu/~nbr/Black Widow.htm

David Lynch Resource Various resources related to the show and its creator David Lynch, including a guide to the town of Twin Peaks, Laura Palmer's secret diary, the screenplay to *Fire: Walk With Me*, and a biography of Agent Dale Cooper. ✓**INTERNET**→*www* http://web.city.ac.uk/~cb157/lynchres.html

Twin Peaks Billed as the "Ultimate Twin Peaks Reference Page," this site is maintained by Jon Yager, who admits in his introduction that "over the years [he] has become obsessed with the show, and with the other works of David Lynch," and that he's planning on using his Website to "spread the 'gospel' of *Twin Peaks*." If only the page lived up to its self-description. It does contain a number of links, and Yager's enthusiasm is admirable, but ultimately this is little more than the same collection of links available at other Peaks sites. ✓**INTERNET**→*www* http://www.xmission.com/~jon yag/TP/Twin-Peaks.html

Twin Peaks FTP Server Named after the only character ever to tie a cherry stem in a knot on television, this FTP server holds a large *Twin Peaks* archive—movie scripts, episode guides, an interview with Ray Wise, quotes, press kits, and filmographies for all performers. There are dozens of documents here, all of which are guaranteed to "peak" the interest of any hardcore fan. ✓**INTERNET** → *www* audrey.levels.unisa.edu. au→/twin-peaks

Welcome to Twin Peaks A good general site, with series information and FAQ, rebroadcast schedules, cast biographies and filmographies, and an image gallery. ✓**INTERNET**→*www* http://pogo. wright.edu/TwinPeaks/TPHome. html

Cast

Actors' Oeuvres For all the oddness in *Twin Peaks*, the show managed to include some show-business luminaries in its cast, including acclaimed film and stage vets such as Joan Chen, Piper Laurie, and Richard Beymer. And don't forget the fistful of new pin-ups the show created—Madchen Amick, Lara Flynn Boyle, and especially Sherilyn Fenn. This document offers a complete list of all known roles of the actors who appeared in *Twin Peaks*. ✓**INTERNET**→ *anon-ftp* audrey.levels.unisa.edu. au→/twin-peaks→oeuvre.actor %28A-L%29.tp *or* oeuvre.actor %28M-Z%29.tp

The Complete Guide to Twin Peaks Includes actor biographies (listed by character) for all major players in *Twin Peaks*, including Kyle McLachlan, Richard Beymer, Sheryl Lee, Lara Flynn Boyle, and Sherilyn Fenn. ✓**INTERNET**→*www* http://web.city.ac.uk/citylive/twin-peaks/

Sherilyn Fenn's Secret Space "Dedicated to the goddess, her life, and her work," this fan club (or Fenn club, as the case may be)

is also dedicated to softcore shots of everybody's favorite prime-time vixen. But don't get any ideas about ulterior motives; as the site manager explains, "I consider the contents of this page to be art.... If you take offense to it, leave now." ✓**INTERNET**→*www* http:// www.vsl.ist.ucf.edu/~kendall/ fenn.html

Chat

alt.tv.twin-peaks (ng) For such a strange TV show, a rather dull group. Sure, there's plenty of talk of the Log Lady, Bob, and Laura, but the group's mainly devoted to discussions about the times of re-runs, where to acquire videos, and appearances by the TP characters in other TV shows, like *Beverly Hills 90210*. Now and then participants will weigh in with opinions about Eraserhead, David Lynch's cult classic. Off-topic talk veers to *The X-Files*, Philip Dick novels, and anything else with that wacky two-worlds-within-one flavor. ✓**USENET**

Twin Peaks Final Episode An archive of the messages that flew across the wires in the days following the broadcast of the final episode of *Twin Peaks*. Was McLachlan's acting bad? How many inside jokes were there? And did you see the guy humping the deer? ✓**INTERNET**→*anon-ftp* audrey. levels.unisa.edu.au→/twin-peaks→ final.episode

Episode guide

Twin Peaks Episode Guide Remember September 30, 1990, the broadcast date for the now-famous Episode 8 ("May the Giant Be With You")? This episode guide lists all 29 episodes of the show, with titles, original airdates, plot summaries, cast, director, and

writers. If you continued watching long enough to see the final show, in which Nadine regains her senses and Donna confronts her parents about Ben, this document will make your dreams (and your nightmares about midgets and giants) come true. ✓**INTERNET**→*anon-ftp* audrey.levels.unisa.edu.au→ /twin-peaks→ episode.guide

Fan fiction

Directory of Fan Fiction Includes a number of stories written by fans of the show, including "Passion Play" and "Vanished." ✓**INTERNET**→*anon-ftp* audrey.levels.unisa. edu.au→/twin-peaks/Creative

FAQ

Twin Peaks FAQ What was the deal with the midget? How crazy was Benjamin Horne? And did the show get much, much worse as it went on, or did America hallucinate? A hypertext version of the Twin Peaks FAQ, with questions and answers about the TV series,

Agent Dale Cooper—from audrey.levels. unisa.edu.au/twin-peaks/JPGS

the film *Fire: Walk With Me*, related books, and cocreators David Lynch and Mark Frost. ✓**INTERNET**→*www* http://ara.kaist.ac.kr /tp.html

Lists & trivia

Log Lady Intros A collection of the introductions spoken by the odd but prescient Log Lady character. ✓**INTERNET**→*anon-ftp* audrey. levels.unisa.edu.au→/twin-peaks→ log.lady.intros

Twin Peak Quotes Promo dialogue and even entire scenes from the David Lynch show that was so weird it made your teeth ache. ✓**INTERNET**→*anon-ftp* audrey.levels. unisa.edu.au→/twin-peaks→twin-Quotes

Twin Peaks Allusions Want to know how David Lynch and Mark Frost came up with the name *Twin Peaks*? Try these explanations on for size: "Supposedly a fairly obvious sexual reference, I hadn't heard it used before, although SPY's *Separated At Birth?* book (published 1988) commented on the "Twin (widow's) Peaks" of Bob Eubanks and Butch (Eddie Munster) Patrick.

"As well, for a town even more obssessed with lumber, TP has nothing on Lumberton from *Blue Velvet*. Also, Blake Edward's 1962 thriller *Experiment In Terror* features Lee Remick as a bank clerk terrorized by a psycho into stealing from her employers. She lives in Twin Peaks (in San Francisco) and the psycho's name is Red Lynch!!"

As this excerpt indicates, this is a document long on archivist's perseverance, with mini-essays on everything from Dale Cooper's name to Ben Horne's Civil War fantasies. ✓**INTERNET**→ *gopher* wiretap.spies.com→Wiretap Online Library→Mass Media→ Television→

Twin Peaks Allusions

Twin Peaks Pilot—Every Second of It A confusing but possibly rewarding document that chronicles every single event, character, and movement in the Peaks pilot. ✓**INTERNET**→*gopher* wiretap. spies.com→Wiretap Online Library →Mass Media→Television→Twin Peaks Pilot - every second of it

Twin Peaks Symbolism Traffic lights, owls, coffee, pie. Characters with similar characteristics differing only in intensity. Twins. Opposites. Yin-yang pairs. This document details the universe of Peaks symbolism, with categories on everything from furry animals ("Josie Packard's vicuña coat") to animal heads ("the mounted deer head in the Book House"). ✓**INTERNET**→*gopher* wiretap.spies.com →Wiretap Online Library→Mass Media→Television→Twin Peaks Symbolism

Twin Peaks Timeline When were the Bookhouse Boys formed? How long has Wyndham Earl been looking for the Black Lodge? Find out with this document, which attempts a chronology of the events of the series. ✓**INTERNET** →*gopher* wiretap.spies.com→Wire tap Online Library→Mass Media →Television→Twin Peaks Timeline

Multimedia

Twin Peaks GIFs Pictures from the series. ✓**INTERNET**→audrey.levels. unisa.edu.au→/twin-peaks/GIFS

Twin Peaks JPEGs More pictures from the series. ✓**INTERNET** →audrey.levels.unisa.edu.au→/ twin-peaks/JPGS

Twin Peaks Sounds Sound effects and sound bites from the series. ✓**INTERNET**→audrey.levels.

unisa.edu.au→/twin-peaks/Sounds

Scripts

Twin Peaks: Fire Walk With Me Written by David Lynch and Robert Engels, this theatrically released *Twin Peaks* prequel had a particularly rough time with critics, getting stomped like a narc at a biker rally. But since it holds substantial interest for Peaks cultists, it seems only right that the script be online. ✓**INTERNET** →*www* http://web.city.ac.uk/ ~cb157/FWWM.script

STARNOTES

Ray Wise: I didn't want [Laura Palmer's killer] to be me. I grew to love Leland Palmer and his strange ways and I didn't want it to be him.

Terry Gross: Did it ease the pain though, knowing that in a way he was innocent? Because after all, he was possessed, it wasn't his own motivation that killed Laura Palmer.

Ray Wise: Absolutely. Leland is a true innocent, in a sense, because he was totally possessed by this evil spirit BOB. So when they told me that it really took the edge off. I was able to accept it a lot better.

—from the **Twin Peaks FTP Server**

The X-Files

For a generation raised on the Kennedy assassination, Watergate, and *Close Encounters*

of the Third Kind, *The X-Files* represents a perfect culmination, a show that twines big government, big media, and big secrets, all the while insisting that the paranormal is the norm. A hipper, smarter, sexier, and savvier version of the UFO series *Project Bluebook*, *The X-Files* has earned its keep with sharp scripts and smooth performances from both of its principals, David Duchovny (who plays Agent Fox Mulder) and Gillian Anderson (the skeptical Dr. Dana Scully). Perhaps predictably, the online world has flipped over Mulder, Scully, Deep Throat, and company—there's an immense amount of activity on Delphi's **X-Files SIG** and a comprehensive Australian home page (**The X-Files Page**). And finally, there are dozens and dozens of offerings from the world of **Fan Fiction**—many written by women, many featuring erotic elements, and many (surprise!) quite good.

On the Net

Hubsites

X-Files Home Page Audio clips

X-Files *opening title—http://www.rutgers.edu/x-files.html*

of the theme music and second-season promo, along with dozens of links to FAQs, FTP areas, episode guides, cast information, and fan-club data. ✓**INTERNET**→ *www* http://www.rutgers.edu/x-files.html

The X-Files Page Is there something about Australians that gives them special insights into the world of conspiracies and the paranormal? Decide for yourself at this side, which is the largest *X-Files* site Down Under, and one of the largest in the English-speaking world. Links include cast information, FAQs, fan-club data, and numerous other resources. ✓**INTERNET**→ *www* http://rschp2.anu.edu.au:8080/XFiles.html

Cast

A Genuine X-Centric *Entertainment Weekly*'s profile of David Duchovny, who plays Special agent Fox "Spooky" Mulder on *The X-Files*. As if you didn't know that already. ✓ **INTERNET**→ *www* http://www.timeinc.com/ew/9412

02/scifi/251scifiXbar.html

Cast Information Did you know that David Duchovny appeared in *Twin Peaks* as the cross-dressing Fed Denise? And what about the rumors that Gillian Anderson once had red hair? You won't find those answers here, but fans of the show should be accustomed to unanswered questions—and in the meantime, they can look at the photographs of the stars. ✓**INTERNET**→ *www* http://www.rutgers.edu/test/x-files/cast.html

David Duchovny FAQ Who does David Duchovny think he is? And who is he really? Biographical and professional information on the actor. ✓**INTERNET**→ *www* http://rschp2.anu.edu.au:8080/DDfaq

Duchovny-L (ml) A mailing list devoted to David Duchovny and his fans, who have dubbed themselves "Duchovniks" in his honor. ✓**INTERNET**→ *email* listserv@cornell.edu ✍ *Type in message body:* subscribe duchovny-l <your full name>

Gillian Anderson FAQ Ah, Gillian. Sometimes when I am alone at night, with only the television standing between me and oblivion, I think of you. You give me hope. You lift me up. You are the wind beneath my wings. And now I can find out all about you with this wonderful FAQ. Information about your life, your career, your character. The FAQ doesn't, however, answer the question I most frequently ask: Gillian, will you marry me? (I guess in some sense it does answer the question, if indirectly, by explaining to me that you are married and a new mother. But a man can still hope.) ✓**INTERNET**→*www* http://rschp2.anu.edu.au:8080/GAfaq

Gillian Anderson Interview A fan transcript of an interview with the lovely and talented Gillian Anderson, taken from *West* magazine, the Sunday supplement of the *San Jose Mercury News*. In the interview, Gillian discusses her pregnancy, the chance of a romantic entanglement between Dana Scully and Fox Mulder, and the gender dynamics on the show.

Includes Anderson's analysis of Scully's personality: "She has a very strong belief system, a very strong dedication to her background, which is medical and scientific. That belief system is always going to be the first thing that she turns to when she has to come up with explanations for situations—when she's doing an autopsy, or making any kind of decision, or presenting a hypothesis.

There is always going to be—not necessarily skepticism—but her rational mind will always be jumping to the forefront, before she accepts any idea or hypothesis of Mulder's. She is, I will say, more open-minded now and not

so judgmental of Mulder and his ideas." ✓**INTERNET**→*www* http://rschp2.anu.edu.au:8080/GAinter

Chat

alt.tv.x-files How to pass those meaningless seven days between *X-Files* episodes? Tune your Usenet dial to this newsgroup. ✓**USENET**

#x-files It's ten o'clock. It's Friday night. You've just watched the heart-stopping final moments of *The X-Files*. You're short of breath. You're long on opinions. You're full of questions. You're the perfect candidate for the X-Files IRC channel. Feel free to put

your two cents into the *X-Files* rating pool, which lets channel members rate shows on a 1 to 10 scale for several factors such as gore, scariness, and predictability. ✓**INTERNET**→*irc* channel #x-files

X-Files List of Mailing Lists Names, descriptions, and subscription instructions for all mailing lists pertaining to *The X-Files*. ✓**INTERNET**→*www* http://rschp2.anu.edu.au:8080/maillist

Summary of IRC Chat This Website summarizes the weekly action on the X-Files IRC channel, and does so thematically. Collect the thoughts of fans across the world on such pressing

Agents Dana Scully & Fox Mulder—from http://www.rutgers.edu/x-files.html

topics as chemistry, Cancerman, handcuffs, *Earth 2*, and (of course) the unstoppable pulchritude of Gillian Anderson. ✓**INTER-NET**→*www* http://rschp2.anu. edu.au:8080/IRCchat

Transcript of IRC Chat with Glen Morgan Glen Morgan, co-executive producer and writer for *The X-Files*, appeared on IRC in December of 1994 to discuss the series. That much is known. Everything else is mysterious. Who is Mr. Morgan, really? Why doesn't he use emoticons? And why is he so vehement in his insistence that Mulder is a porn addict ("YES!! YES!! YES!!")? ✓**INTER-NET**→*www* http://rschp2.anu.edu. au:8080/morganchat

The X-Files Not much strangeness here, considering the subject matter, but it's a hot spot for X-fans, nonetheless. Topics include "Why we like Mulder," "Top 10 *X-Files* Eps Poll," "anti-Philes," and "You converted me!" Mulder's got lots and lots of fans here. If he ever shows up at a CompuServe face-to-face, he'd better wear rip-proof clothing. Opinions of the guy? "Gorgeous." "Incredibly cute." "Cute buns in his Speedo." Enough already!

These fans have a cultlike allegiance to their show, and they want others to share it; they brag about getting their friends hooked. The libraries include an episode guide, a glossary for acronyms often used in posts about the show (a handy document for newbies), and *X-Files* lyrics for Christmas carols like "Silent Night" and "Frosty the Snowman"(sounds subversive, don't you think?). ✓**COMPUSERVE**→*go* sfmedia→Libraries *or* Messages→ The X-Files

The X-Files X-Philes like to get to know one another (in Topic 1),

perhaps because the series takes place in our world and reinforces the idea that you can never be sure who is dangerous and who isn't. As one fan admitted "I Love Paranoia, I Love Conspiracy." In Topic 9, (X-Files in Real Life) fans post modern mysteries the show should delve into—the Nazca lines, ancient astronauts, Florida's skunk ape and where the socks disappear to.

Real devotees have already evolved their own set of online acronyms for episode discussion which include shortcuts like PTDT—Pass The Drool Towel and IDDG—Intellectually Drop Dead Gorgeous. (A complete list can be found in topic 4 - YAXA.) Topic 11, the Jacuzzi Room, is for Topic Drift, and drift it does from Barry Manilow to cherry blossom festivals to ice dancing (frightening). Stay in the General or Cast topics for actual show chat. ✓**GENIE** →*keyword* sfrt2→SFRT2 Bulletin Board→set 18

X-Files Is *The X-Files* better than *Trek*? Does David Duchovny expose his entire derriere in Kalifornia? And does X-fandom necessarily correspond with paranoia? This message folder, one of the busiest on AOL's large sci-fi fandom board, reads like a friendly meeting of similar minds, with mostly chatty conversation and only occasional forays into the finer points of paranormal investigation. ✓**AMERICA ONLINE**→*keyword* scifi→ Science Fiction Fandom Board→X-Files

X-Files Conference Section leader Marilyn Wilkerson has announced a weekly conference for fans of the *X-Files*. Join the "X-Philes" of CompuServe every Sunday evening at 6:30 p.m. PST /9:30 p.m. EST /2:30 a.m. GMT in Conference Room 7 ("The

Phile Cabinet") in SFMEDIA. Be ready for scattershot *X-Files* talk, with lots of X-influenced chatter—some mindless, some hilarious. "Who here cried on Friday?" one X-Phile asked. "I misted," Robert said. Mary got a lump in her throat, but didn't cry. Pam cried her eyes out. Appropriately, one attendee was watching JFK during the conference, with others telling him to turn it off. ("Our theories make the JFK stuff look like *Sesame Street*," someone said.) There's plenty of talk of specific episodes in this conference, sure, but there's also a lot of off-topic typing, with suggestions for games of Nude Twister and Trivial Pursuit. ✓**COMPUSERVE**→*go* sfmedia→Conference→The Phile Cabinet

Episode guide

X-Files Episode Guide Cliff Chen's *X-Files* episode guide includes episode titles, airdates, cast information, production credits, and plot summaries, in addition to a FAQ for newcomers, cast information, a complete broadcast history, and links to other Internet *X-Files* resources. ✓**INTERNET**→*www* http://www.seas.upenn.edu/~cliff/xfiles-ep-guide.html

X-Files Episode Survey From the impossibly good ("The Erlenmeyer Flask") to the passable ("Lazarus," "Roland") to the piss-poor ("Space"), here are fan ratings for all *X-Files* episodes, along with information on writers and directors. ✓**INTERNET**→*www* http://www.rutgers.edu/test/x-files/survey-results.html

Fan fiction

alt.tv.x-files.creative Since the series has a nasty habit of leaving its plots open-ended, fans

Mulder's close encounter—from http://www.timeinc.com/ew/941202/scifi/

are wont to fill in the blanks with creative efforts of their own. While some stick close to formula—madmen, extraterrestrials, and the paranormal—others strike out for parts unknown. ✓**USENET**

X-Files Fan Fiction Mostly written by women, these stories run the gamut from short sketches ("Partners") to novella-length works with complex symbolism and accomplished writing ("Phoenix"). While much fan fiction takes advantage of its unauthorized status to thrust the characters into sexual situations, this archive includes sex-free versions alongside the more risqué narratives ("Over and over again his mouth caught a nipple, sucking gently until it was hard and sensitive, then letting it go and moving to some other suddenly alert part of her").

Then there are the hilarious crossover stories ("X-feld," in which Scully and Mulder meet Jerry and the gang) and even poetry (quasi-limericks devoted to Gillian Anderson). If you can't get enough of Fox and Mulder, or you want to assemble your own list of

dos and don'ts for TV writing, spend time browsing through this generous archive. ✓**INTERNET**→ *www* http://rschp2.anu.edu:8080/XFfanfic.html

X-Files Creative FAQ and Fan Fiction List Overseen by Pat Gonzales, this document answers the burning questions of would-be *X-Files* scriptwriters, including "What can be posted to alt.tv.x-files.creative?" and "How do I know what I've missed?" In addition, Gonzales maintains an ongoing list of fan stories. ✓**INTERNET**→ *www* http://rschp2.anu.edu.au:8080/xfcfaq

Fans

Australian Fan Club Information on the Australian *X-Files* fan club. ✓**INTERNET**→*www* http://rschp2.anu.edu:8080/AusXFfans

Fan Clubs Fan-club addresses and benefits. ✓**INTERNET**→*www* http://www.rutgers.edu/test/x-files/fan-club.html

X-Philes *X-Files* fans like *Star Trek*, *The Simpsons*, and *Seinfeld*. *X-Files* fans are 60 percent male.

X-Files fans are mostly college undergraduates. Or so says a survey conducted by two university professors. Review their data in tables, bar graphs, and pie charts, compare the fan demographics with general Internet demographics, and decide if this is an accurate portrait of a bona fide subculture or merely a distortion produced by inexplicable paranormal forces. ✓**INTERNET**→*www* http://www.rutgers.edu/test/x-files/survey-report.html

FAQ

X-Files Acronyms EBE? GATB? MIB? *The X-Files* is full of acronyms, some official, some not, some coined by fans of the show, and this document glosses them. Includes RSD (Red Shoe Diaries), the Showtime series that has employed *X-Files* regular David Duchovny, UST (Unresolved Sexual Tension), and EIHPs (Enemies in High Places). ✓**INTERNET**→*www* http://rschp2.anu.edu.au:8080/YAXA

Deep Throat FAQ Top-Secret Eyes-Only Dispatch. Destroy After Reading. Why? Because this document concerns Deep Throat (Jerry Hardin), the mysterious informer who sometimes helps Scully and Mulder explain the inexplicable. ✓**INTERNET**→*www* http://rschp2.anu.edu.au:8080/dtfaq

X-Files FAQ Who is an Oxford-trained psychologist with a photographic memory? Who is a medical doctor with an undergraduate degree in physics? What about pregnancy? Sexual tension? Special effects? Merchandise? Fanzines? Read all about your X-favorites in this FAQ. ✓**INTERNET**→*www* http://rschp2.anu.edu.au:8080/xffaq.html

Agent Scully—from http://www.rutgers.edu/x-files.html

X-Files Twenty Questions A list of 20 questions and answers dealing with the rudimentary aspects of *The X-Files*. ✓**INTERNET**→*www* http://rschp2.anu.edu.au:8080/twentyq

Multimedia

Collection of Audio Snippets Mulder: "I'm wondering which lie to believe." Scully: "You keep unfolding like a flower." Not a dialogue, but a catalog—and there are more audio clips where these came from. ✓**INTERNET**→*www* http://www.rutgers.edu/test/x-files/audio.html

Fan Art Drawings of Fox and Scully by fan Art Tucco, along with an *X-Files*-inspired piece created by Tatsubiro Ikeda. ✓**INTERNET**→*www* http://www.rutgers.edu/test/x-files/fan-art.html

Title Collage A series of images and sounds that recreate the show's opening—mandatory for any X-Phile. ✓**INTERNET**→*www* http://www.rutgers.edu/test/x-files/title/title.html

UFO GIF They shoot UFOs, don't they? Sure they do, and sometimes they upload the evidence onto the Net for all to see. Check it out for yourself. Your eyes will be as wide as (flying) saucers. ✓**INTERNET**→*www* http://rschp2.anu.edu:8080/ufogif

X-Files Sounds Sounds from the series. ✓**INTERNET**→*www* http://rschp2.anu.edu:8080/XFsounds/sounds.html

Music

X-Files Top Ten So the other day that old Blondie song came on the radio, that "Rapture," and all of a sudden everything became as clear as Crystal Pepsi: that Deborah Harry is talking about aliens! You know, the men from Mars, who eat cars, bars, and guitars? This interesting intersection between the world of X-Philia and the world of pop music not only lists songs mentioned on the show, but also catalogs other rock and pop compositions dealing with alien encounters. ✓**INTERNET**→*www* http://rschp2.anu.edu.au:8080/XFTops

Nitpicking

Netpicker's Guide to X-Files Written by X-Phile supreme Kimberlee Ricke, this is the first draft of an online nitpicker's guide, which raises plot problems and continuity errors from the series, and then attempts to resolve them. For instance, in "Ghost in the Machine," how did the Erisko computer manage to turn on Sully's machine? And in "Erlenmeyer Flask," did anyone notice the conspicuous (but accidental) shot of a Vancouver Drydock sign? ✓**INTERNET**→*www* http://www.rutgers.edu/test/x-files/netpickers-guide.html

Space junk: other shows

No matter how abruptly a television series might have been yanked from the air, or how

poorly a feature film might have been received, there's always room for fans and their obsessions on the Net. A **Space: 1999 mailing list**? A **Max Headroom Episode Guide**? A **Quatermass Archive**? Hell, there are even a handful of sites devoted to *The Adventures of Brisco County*, the time-travel Western that came and went so quickly you'd need a time machine to prove that it existed at all. So revel in the **Alien Nation Archive**. Celebrate the **Alf Episode Guide**. Hitch your wagon to the **alt.tv.robotech** newsgroup. And thank your deity of choice for the opening-credits MPEG on the **Lost in Space Page**.

Lost in Space *opening credits—http://www.mgmt.purdue.edu/~vkoser/lost_in_space/*

Alf

Alf Episode Guide Remember Gordon Shumway, that vaguely piglike Alien Life Form who came to Earth to crack jokes and wreak havoc on an ordinary suburban family? A complete four-season guide to *Alf* episodes with brief plot synopses of each show that aired. ✓**INTERNET**→*gopher* dds. dds.nl→De Bibliotheek→boeken→ Mass Media→Television

Alien Nation

Alien Nation First, there was the movie, with James Caan and Mandy Patinkin and a tough-as-nails story about future gangsters. Then there was the TV series. And now there's the Internet presence! ✓**INTERNET**→*anon-ftp* ftp.doc.ic.ac. uk→/pub/media/tv/collections/ tardis/us/sci-fi/AlienNation/

Blake's Seven

A Plethora of Blake's 7 Files Scripts, pictures, quotes, puzzles, a program guide, miscellany, and "audio bits," as well as humorous comparisons between *Blake's 7* and *Star Trek*. ✓**INTERNET**→*www* http:// www.phlab.missouri.edu/c621052_ www/Blakes7/

Blake's Seven Abbreviated Program Guide An episode guide for *Blake's 7* that includes

the original airdate, writer, director, and brief plot summary for each eposde. ✓**INTERNET**→*anon-ftp* ftp.doc.ic.ac.uk→/pub/media/tv/ collections/tardis/us/sci-fi/Alien Nation/

Brisco County

alt.tv.brisco-county (ng) Ah, the travails of a jilted Brisco addict. Whaddaya do when your show gets canceled? Post, post, post. These fans have worked themselves into a frenzy over the cancellation of *The Adventures of Brisco County, Jr.* One of them, wondering if Brisco could be rescued with a last-minute reprieve, wrote: "I can't stand it. I need some kind of answer. Will we ever see Brisco again? I think I'll write *TV Guide* or something. I've gotta know before I go insane…and I'm pretty damn close as it is!" Another suggested trying to pull a few strings at "the big 5 sided building"—i.e., the Pentagon—to "convince the brass that the return of *The Adventures of Brisco County Jr.* is essential for national security." You've got to give these people credit: They're loyal, if a bit wacky. And who knows? Maybe in 2014, the children of the 21st century will line up to eat cyberpopcorn and watch the summer smash *Brisco County: Generations.* ✓ **USENET**

Brisco County Archive A Western with time-travel? Sounds like the pages of two different scripts got mixed up. But as fans of *Brisco County* will tell you, these are two great tastes that sometimes taste great together, and this archive details the recipe, with an episode guide and other files pertaining to the series. ✓ **INTERNET**→*anon-ftp* ftp.doc.ic.ac.uk→/pub/media/tv/ collections/tardis/us/drama/Brisco County

Episode Guides A complete episode guide to that *Brisco* thing, with titles, original airdates, and plots. ✓ **INTERNET**→*anon-ftp* elbereth. rutgers.edu→/pub/sfl→brisco-county. guide

Buck Rogers

Buck Rogers Remember those halcyon days of Buck Rogers? Handsome, wry Gil Gerard? Bewitching, seductive Erin Grey? And how about that little computer that sounded like the Knight Rider car and hung around the old guy's neck? Less serious than *Battlestar Galactica* and less sophisticated than *The Six Million Dollar Man, Buck Rogers in the 25th Century* was still a huge hit, and has embedded itself in the consciousness of all twentysomethings. Relive the magic. ✓ **INTERNET**→*anon-ftp* ftp.doc.ic.ac.uk→/pub/media

/tv/collections/tardis/us/sci-fi/ BuckRogers

Earth 2

Earth 2 Refugee Camp What if they gave a second Earth and nobody came, except for a bunch of mediocre actors and writers who tried to shape the concept into a successful sci-fi series, succeeding only as a result of the undiscriminating palates of American television viewers? That's only one of the questions hovering over this page, which includes an *Earth 2* FAQ and a variety of episode and credit guides. ✓ **INTERNET**→*www* http://www.io.com/user/ftmexpat /e2/e2-camp.html

TV's Earth Mother *Entertainment Weekly's* profile of the actress Debrah Farentino, who plays the commander of a terrestrial expedition to a new habitable planet. ✓ **INTERNET**→*www* http://www. timeinc.com/ew/941202/scifi/ 251scifiE2bar.html

Welcome to Planet G889 "This time, *we* are the aliens." But we're happy aliens so long as we have Websites like this one, which is MCA's official page for its new series. Cast biographies, program guides, even exclusive information on the alien races and technological developments in the show. ✓ **INTERNET**→*www* http://www.mca. com/tv/earth2

Lost in Space

Lost in Space Episode Guide Marvel as the show degenerates from a legitimate sci-fi offering to the *Gilligan's Island* of outer space. Another guide to the show's episodes, from the black-and-white first season to later, sillier episodes ("The Thief From Outer Space," "Princess of Space," and even "The

Vegetable Rebellion," in which the Robinsons are turned into giant plants. ✓**INTERNET** ...→*www* http://www.twilight.com/lostspace ...→*www* http://www.galcit.caltech.edu/~joe/lis/episode.html ...→*gopher* dds.dds.nl→De Bibliotheek→boeken→Mass Media→Television

Lost in Space Page The poor Robinson family, lost in space in 1997. That's right, 1997—just around the corner now, but it must have seemed like a distant future when the show was first televised in 1965. This sci-fi comedy-adventure, which was aired earlier than the original *Star Trek*, has become a cult classic in its own right, with such luminaries as June Lockhart (*Lassie*) and Billy Mumy (*Babylon 5*) providing the high adventure and low comedy in deep space. ✓**INTERNET**→*www* http://www.mgmt.purdue.edu/~vkoser/lost_in_space/lost_in_space.html

Opening Credits Quicktime and MPEG movies of the show's opening credits, including the haunting and beautiful theme music. ✓**INTERNET**→*www* http://www.mgmt.purdue.edu/~vkoser/lost_in_space/movies.html

Max Headroom

Max Headroom Episode Guide Wild, hyperkinetic, and far ahead of its time, *Max Headroom* was the Reagan age's greatest creation, a high-tech stutter of postmodern irony. Shown in both Britain and the United States—with different casts, no less—the program featured Matt Frewer as a fast-talking guide to tomorrow, and confronted such issues as media ruthlessness, cutting-edge security, and computer conspiracy. ✓**INTERNET**→*anon-ftp* gandalf.rutgers.edu→/pub/sfl→max-headroom.guide

Earth 2—*from http://www.timeinc.com/ew/941202/scifi*

Outer Limits

Outer Limits Episode Guide From 1963 to 1965, *Outer Limits* terrified television viewers with its *Twilight Zon*-ish plots and its chilling ironies. This guide offers a complete list of all episodes, along with ratings. ✓**INTERNET**→*anon-ftp* gandalf.rutgers.edu→/pub/sfl→outerlimits.guide

The Prisoner

alt.tv.prisoner (ng) If there's a movie version of the cult series *The Prisoner*, who should play the main roles? Crispin Glover for Number 6? How about Gary Oldman? One fan thinks Christopher Walken would be the right choice. Walken reminds him of Patrick McGoohan, the creator and star of the original, but he admits, "He's a little too psycho, and his voice is a little annoying sometimes." The fans of this series from the sixties want everyone to watch it. They obsess about what episodes to share with their friends. They talk about directions to the real-life setting for the show, and the de-

tails of the Lotus Seven auto. They know their stuff, and if you post a faux pas among this crew, you'll be ordered to "Go directly to Town Hall. Do not pass the Green Dome." Certainly a spot for the devoted. ✓**USENET**

The Prisoner-Episode Guides An episode-by-episode guide to the late-sixties sci-fi cult show, in which a man known only as Number 6 (Patrick McGoohan) is stranded in a deserted town. ✓**INTERNET** ...→*www* http://itdsrv1.ul.ie/Entertainment/Prisoner/episodes.html ...→*anon-ftp* gandalf.rutgers.edu→/pub/sfl→prisoner.guide

Quatermass

Quatermass Archive You know, *Quatermass*. Or maybe you've never heard of Nigel Keane's character, Dr. Bernard Quatermass—a button-down Brit rocket physicist who spent his time in the limelight repelling alien invaders. Featured in various TV and film incarnations from 1953 to 1979, Quatermass was a plum role for Andre Morell, Brian Donlevy, Andrew Keir, and John Mills, and this page discusses various issues from the entire life span of the character. ✓**INTERNET**→*www* http://www.nick.med.usf.edu/quatermass.html

Robocop

alt.tv.robocop (ng) A cool hangout for serious *Robocop* fans. Where else can you find "The Definitive Robocop Schedule"? It's not one of the busiest spots on the Net, but the fans have a fun time talking about their love of all things Robo. Newbies can ask questions like this one: "Can anybody explain to me who the cyberbabe is, the one who appears in a swirling digital mist and acts like

Robocop's therapist or something?" Rumors of the show's demise get taken seriously, with letters sent swiftly to the producers. ✓**USENET**

Robotech

alt.tv.robotech (ng) Limited-edition art books, conventions, games—it's all here, in this intensely partisan group devoted to what one fan called "the glorious saga of *Robotech*." One interesting thread was titled "Robotech Brawns and Babes poll."

What kinds of mates do Robo-fans want? Well, they want a brawny guy who's "a relentless pilot and killer when the need arises," and a babe who's "beautiful, tough, resourceful, stubborn, and very loyal to her compatriots."

And if you're looking to meet the group's cosmetics standards, green hair helps—a frustrating fact for at least one female fan: "What IS it with you male Robotechers and GREEN-HAIRED WOMEN?! If you male Robotechers like it so much, I may have to get a bottle the next time I go down to the punk section of town!" ✓**USENET**

Robotech A mega-series created from the combination of three other Japanese animation series, *Robotech* is the most sprawling sci-fi cartoon currently available on this or any other planet, with a growing franchise that includes films, comic books, novelizations, and tons of merchandise. This page includes a *Robotech* FAQ, an episode guide, images, sounds, and links to fan fiction. ✓**INTERNET** →*www* http://www2.ncsu.edu/eos/users/r/rkswamy/www/robotech.html

Space 1999

Space 1999 One fan says that he

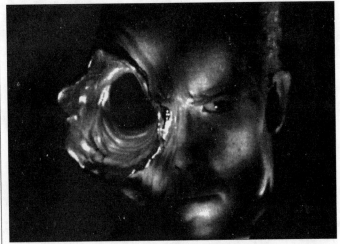

Terminator 2—*http://www.maths.tcd.ie/pub/films/terminator/*

holds out hope that with time, *Space 1999* will begin to shine like a newly found gem. Then, slightly wiser, he sighs and admits that it's "still horse excrement."

For a group of supporters, the *Space 1999* camp is pretty negative, but negative in an affectionate way. Remember the episode where the crew "passed through some weird gas and devolved into cavemen"? They do. Does anyone know where to get die-cast models of the series? They do. How about pictures, videocassettes, novelizations, and laserdiscs? Yep. ✓**AMERICA ONLINE**→*keyword* scifi→Star Trek/Comics/TV/Star Wars Boards →Television→Space 1999

Space 1999 Mailing List *Space 1999* wasn't on the air for long, but it's got some devoted followers. And if you're one of them, get thee to this list. Topics include announcements of upcoming fan events, talk of *Space 1999* models and merchandise, and mentions of film and TV appearances by the show's stars, like one by Martin Landau on *Leno* ("Didn't mention *Space*, but he did mention some of the crappy movies he's appeared

in"). Where else can you find great offers like a complete set of first year videotapes for $55, or a bunch of *1999* books, ranging in price from $2.50 to $4, depending on the condition.

Discussion of other sci-fi works is generally tolerated here, especially if Gerry Anderson had any involvement. Disputes center around technical issues, like why Alpha couldn't send an all-is-well message in the first episode, "Breakaway" ("Systems on Alpha had been badly damaged by the explosion," one person guessed). ✓**INTERNET**→*email* space-1999-request@quack.kfu.com ✍ *Write a request*

Space Precinct

Space Precinct While other shows load up with cultural significance and futuristic philosophies, *Space Precinct* relies on a more tried-and-true formula—cops and robbers. Like *CHiPs*, or *Dragnet*, or *Starsky and Hutch*, it's a classic story of good guys and bad guys, except that both groups are in the future. This Website offers a general introduction to Gerry Anderson's show, along with some multi-media materials and links to an Anderson FAQ. ✓**INTERNET**→*www* http://printnet.com/SpcPnct.html

The Terminator

Robocop vs. The Terminator A favorable *GameBytes* review of this game, which pits the futuristic toughies against one another in a battle to the death. ✓**INTERNET**→ *www* http://wcl-rs.bham.ac.uk/GameBytes/issue20/creviews/roboterm.html

Terminator 2 FAQ A *T2* FAQ, presented in hypertext form that includes explanations of different movie versions, detailed listings of available soundtracks, and speculation on whether or not there will be a third sequel. ✓**INTERNET**→ *www* http://www.maths.tcd.ie/pub/films/T2.html

Terminator 2 Trailer Download Instructions Want a complete trailer for the *Terminator 2* film? Well, you've got it. Experience the magic of a really long download or just read this informational file for fun. ✓**INTERNET**→ *anon-ftp* princeton.edu→/pub/t2demo→Terminator2.README

Time Trax

alt.tv.time-traxx Is Dale Midkiff, the actor who plays Darien Lambert, the time-traveling cop, an asset to *Time Trax*? Amy thinks Midkiff exudes "this sort of silent toughness." She likes him. Bruce disagrees: "I don't think he can act very well. This group wouldn't make anyone's Ten Most Active list (how many would?), but the fans have a strong allegiance to *Time Trax*. When a TV special on sci-fi shows ignored *Time Trax* in its time-travel segment, the regulars

vowed to start a letter-writing campaign. ✓**USENET**

Episode Guide "It began in the future. A scientist turning to evil, a time machine called TRAX, criminals who vanish, and a lawman with a mission. He has one weapon and a computer called Selma. With her, he will travel to a time more innocent than his own. Now he is among us, a special breed of man, traveling through our world, searching for fugitives from his own, knowing he cannot go home until he has found them all. His name is Darien Lambert and this is his story."

And this is the episode guide to his story, with episode titles, airdates, plot summaries (often quite lengthy), writing and directing credits, and a key to recurring elements in the series. Whether Darien is losing his memory, traveling to Japan, or hunting koala bears, he's covered by this guide. ✓**INTERNET**→*www* http://www.hyperion.com/ftp/pub/TV/timetrax.txt

Twilight Zone

New Twilight Zone Episode Guide A list of new *Twilight Zone* episodes supplemented by an episode-by-episode list of actors and the roles they played. ✓**INTERNET**→*gopher* dds.dds.nl→De Bibliotheek→boeken→Mass Media →Television

Rod Serling's From the Twilight Zone Order Rod Serling's books from The Virtual Bookshop. ✓**INTERNET**→*www* http://www.virtual.bookshop.com/auth/SerlingRod.html

T-Zone A mailing list devoted to the spooky side of life, the dark side of human nature, and plots

that go bump in the night. ✓**INTERNET**→*email* tzone-request@hustle.rahul.net ✍ *Write a request*

Twilight Zone Episode Guides Remember the first *Twilight Zone* ever, back in 1959? That would have been "Where is Everybody?" with Earl Holliman, which told the story of a man stranded in a deserted city. Or maybe you'd rather spend your time reviewing classics like "Stopover in a Quiet Town," or hit-and-miss efforts like "Caesar and Me."

This document lists all the episodes from the original run of the show, along with credits for writers, directors, and actors, a brief synopsis, and a capsule review. ✓**INTERNET** …→*www* http://www.twilight.com/twilight-zone.guide …→*anon-ftp* elbereth.rutgers.edu→/pub/sfl→twilight-zone.guide

Twilight Zone Theme Sound clip of the eerie opening music to the original *Twilight Zone* series. For Macs. ✓**INTERNET** …→*anon-ftp* sumex-aim.stanford.edu→/info-mac/snd→twilight-zone-tune.hqx …→*gopher* gopher.med.umich.edu →Entertainment→Sounds→Twilight-Zone.au

V

V Archive Less a miniseries than a TV event, this sci-fi thriller combined humans, aliens, and reptilian babies, coming up big in the ratings. And if *V* isn't exactly in the pantheon of American sci-fi, it was nevertheless one of the highlights of the eighties. This archive, with Gzipped documents galore, lists *V* novels, collects information about *V: The Rebirth*, and furnishes credits. ✓**INTERNET**→*anon-ftp* ftp.doc.ic.ac.uk→/pub/media/tv/collections/tardis/us/sci-fi/V

APPENDICES

A selection of the biggest, smartest, and snazziest Trek stops in Cyberspace

Boldly Go To These Sites First

rec.arts.startrek * ✓**USENET**

Star Trek Club ✓**AMERICA ONLINE**
→*keyword* trek

Star Trek Server ✓**INTERNET**→
www http://www.cosy.sbg.ac.at/
rec/startrek/star_trek_resources.
html

Vidiot Home Page ✓**INTERNET**→
www http://www.ftms.com:80/
vidiot/

Best Place to "Engage!"

The Neutral Zone ✓**AMERICA
ONLINE**→*keyword* trek→Star Trek
Message Boards→The Neutral
Zone

Star Trek ✓**FIDONET**

Ten Forward ✓**PRODIGY**→*keyword* star trek bb→Choose a
Topic→Ten Forward

Best Trek Tech Sites

rec.arts.sf.science ✓**USENET**

Relativity and FTL Travel FAQ
✓**INTERNET**→ ...*anon ftp* rtfm.mit.edu

→/pub.usenet-by-hierarchy/rec/
arts/startrek/tech→Relativity_
and_FTL_Travel ...*anon ftp* ftp.cc.
umanitoba.ca→/startrek→Relativity
_and_FTL.txt

Technical Talk ✓**DELPHI**→*go* ent
sta for→*set* tech

Best Alien Berlitz Course

**The Klingon Language Insti-
tute** ✓**INTERNET**→*www* http://
www. kli.org/KLIhome.html

Best Alien Blitzkrieg

The Borg ✓**INTERNET**→*www* http:
//www.cms.dmu.ac.uk/~ it2yh/
borg.html

Begin Your Trek Day with...

Star Trek Clock ✓**AMERICA ON-
LINE**→*keyword* trek→MORE...→Star
Trek Record Banks →Text/Other
Files→Upld: 07/19/92→Star Trek
clock Filename: TREKCLOCK.ZIP

Finnish Your Trek Day with...

Deep Web Nine ✓**INTERNET**→
www http://www.tut.fi/~ pekka/
trek.html

Most Logical Choice

Vulcan-L (ml) ✓**INTERNET**→*email*
majordomo@netcom.com ✍ *Type
in message body:* subscribe vulcan-l
<your full name>

Going Straight to the Source

Ask Mr. Shatner ✓**DELPHI**→*keyword* ent sta→ask shatner

If There Were No Trek...

Babylon 5 Resources ✓**INTER-
NET**→*www* http://www.astro.nwu.
edu/lentz/sci-fi/b5/home-b5.html

Raciest

alt.sex.fetish.startrek ✓**USENET**

Spaciest

The Star*s Collection ✓**INTERNET**
→*www* http://cdsweb.ustrasbg.fr/
~heck/sf.htm

Daxiest

Terry Farrell Internet Fan Club
✓**INTERNET**→*www* http://trill.pc.cc.
cmu.edu/~jkoga/tf.html

SPOT'S ANSWERS!

Pg. 32: a) Kataan b) Alpha Centauri c) "Pen Pals" d) Deneb IV e) "The Doomsday Machine"
Source: Star Trek Locations

Pg. 40: "Never insult a Ferengi's mother."
Source: Ferengi Rules of Acquisition

Pg. 51: a) 2,000,000 B.C. b) 2712 B.C. c) 1368 B.C. d) 20th Century (they seize power in 1993) e) 2249—January 20, to be precise. He reprograms the computers. f) Under Kirk's command (2259) g) 2237 (stardate 44001.4) h) 46424.1; Dr. Moriarty i) 2087 j) 8130.3 (real date January 28, 2287) k) 43489.2 l) 2222 (stardate 1268.5) m) 2355 n) 2292 o) 2349 p) 2245
Source: Star Trek Timeline

Pg. 134: "By Any Other Name," "Let That Be Your Last Battlefield."
Source: Star Trek List of Lists

Pg. 138: "The Corbomite Maneuver"
Source: The Hack-Man TOS Guide

Pg. 140: a) Television's first interracial kiss b) Commander Loskene c) "This Side of Paradise"
Source: The Hack-Man TOS Guide

Pg. 169: a) Mordock, "Coming of Age" b)"The Naked Now"
Source: Vidiot's Synopses

Pg. 184: a) The Traveler, "Where No One Has Gone Before" b) Acts of Cumberland, "The Measure of a Man" c) The Nagilum, "Where Silence Has Lease"
Source: Vidiot's Synopses

Pg. 190: a) Chocolate sundaes, 10, "Deja-Q" b) Competition for leadership, "Reunion" c) Bendii Syndrome, "Sarek" d) Thomas Riker, "The Second Chances"
Source: Vidiot's Synopses, Tim Lynch Reviews

Pg. 203: a) Guinan, "Yesterday's Enterprise" b) Experimental procedure to repair Worf's spine, "Ethics" c) Professor Moriarty's, "Ship in a Bottle" d) The USS Aries, his father Kyle Riker, "The Icarus Factor" e) Durken, "First Contact" f) Kyla Marr, "Silicon Avatar" g) Vash, "QPid" h) Mintakans, "Who Watches the Watchers"
Source: Vidiot's Synopses, Tim Lynch Reviews

Pg. 213: a) Kamala, "The Perfect Mate" b) Daren, "Lessons"
Source: Tim Lynch Reviews

Pg. 254: a) 93 hours, "Dax" b) Elim, "The Wire" c) Kira, "Meridian" d) cloaking, "Defiant"
Source: Tim Lynch Reviews

Spot found all his answers on the Net, as indicated by the source lines.

Trek and sci-fi Boards

General

Starbase Thompson	204-778-6302
DSC BBS	215-443-7430
PC Ohio	216-381-3320
Faster-Than-Light	404-292-8761
The Simple Board	504-664-2524
Perfect Vision Graphics BBS	513-233-7993
The Observatory BBS	519-679-5747
Space City Grafix	708-748-4025
The Movie BBS	718-939-5462

TFDN

Hal 9000	203-934-8432
The Wacko Board	203-261-3130
IKV Hailing Freq. of Terror	209-251-7529
Last Chance TBBS	210-822-7519
MegaCity One BBS	219-426-7015
Chicago Confuzion	312-986-0974
Skip's Doghouse	314-240-7547
Thew Final Frontier BBS	403-279-7696
Arrakis	405-752-8955
U.S.S. Proxima	416-265-3867
Deep Space	417-781-0178
Dimension 7	503-687-5991
The Kingdom of Cormac	513-731-4493
Oniris	514-681-9782
Starship Enterprise BBS	519-358-1561
The Black Stallion	602-649-0310
MACatastrophe BBS	610-779-1259
Critics Choice	619-467-0335
Our House BBS	619-460-8507
The Rebel BBS	702-435-0786
The Fat Angus BBS	705-497-3057
XybyX Technologies BBS	805-583-0299
Fire & Ice	810-887-0156
The Dark Side	904-645-6293
Digital Data Com. System	905-837-2149
CompuTech BBS	910-895-1214
LightSpeed BBS	910-697-2998
Omni	916-386-2521

TrekkerNet

The Last Resort	214-293-0022
The Message Board	214-293-0243
Arbor Ridge	301-797-5495
Confusion Central	301-868-3025
The Andromeda BBS	301-283-3746
The Middle River Exchange	410-391-5846
TheShareware Exchange	410-391-1088

Trekker's Tavern	413-737-2260
Lion's Den	613-392-8896
The Viking's Cove	613-394-5919
Inkwell	703-684-1397
Pen and Brush Post	703-644-6730
The Electric Oracle BBS	713-690-2851
The Richmond Connection	804-740-1364
Asylum	808-456-8541
Pacific Isle	808-395-0656
Paradise BBS	808-625-5120
Robotech	808-456-7745
The Bogtrotter's Haven	808-624-1527
Warp Speed BBS	808-486-0253
Cat-Tastrophe Corner BBS	918-663-6304

TrekNet

Blackstar!	201-335-6132
Chronicles InfoNet BBS	203-445-0607
The Star Quest BBS	203-569-2879
U.S.S. Nautilus BBS	203-827-0280
Federation Space	205-361-6140
Free Enterprise BBS	205-856-9809
The World According To...	205-633-5875
Quicksilver	206-780-2011
TrekNet Region 6005	206-868-5924
Check Six. BBS	207-945-2612
Last Outpost	207-384-5949
Union Pacific BBS	209-738-1370
Wolfstar BBS	209-582-5685
After Hours	210-492-6152
Star Trek: The Next Gen.	210-509-3272
House Atreides AMIGA	214-494-3702
DSC	215-443-5838
The Steel Valley BBS	216-545-0093
TrekNet Region 6001	216-345-5807
USS Paramount	216-494-6340
Farpoint BBS	301-593-4629
Deep Space Nine BBS	303-494-8447
LandTrek	305-370-0374
Star*Bank	305-975-5540
Nordic Exposure	402-734-0923
The Atomic Dustbin Node 2	402-291-8827
TrekNet Region 6006	402-291-2896
Calanost BBS	403-468-1741
The Bear Board	403-245-6189
Starbase Atlanta BBS	404-270-1373
Warp Factor BBS	404-773-7966
Echomail Hub 11	405-360-6082
USS Starfire BBS	405-262-7739
The Cultural Wasteland BBS	406-782-7941

AmiTrek BBS	407-348-3365
IKV Hovqul	407-633-1026
NCC-1701	407-380-1701
Sci-Fi Spaceport Collectibles	407-690-1808
Starfleet Command BBS	407-366-8735
Starship Enterprise	407-383-9820
The Empire	407-790-7345
Mission Control BBS	409-283-7778
Beacon Hill CBIS	412-962-9514
The Eagles Landing BBS	415-386-0124
The Final Frontier BBS	415-397-1422
ATRIBBS	416-867-3144
Echomail Hub 10	416-787-2582
Intro to Insanity	416-281-3441
Mount Olympus BBS	416-425-9288
Scruples!	416-661-5426
The Cat House BBS	416-665-0395
The Klingon Board of Prey	416-229-1378
The Next BBS	416-431-4529
TrekNet E. Canada Sector	416-265-3867
The Serial Connection BBS	501-785-0477
LiveWire	502-933-4725
Starlink! BBS	502-964-7827
Metallica City	503-744-0542
StarBase 1	505-425-1863
Areacode 508 Mass Hub	508-372-5482
Asylum	508-372-2258
Dreamer's Online	508-991-6058
Access! BBS	513-921-7623
Spock's Adventure	513-779-9717
The TowneHouse BBS	513-232-8042
The Silicon Garden	516-736-7010
The Difference Engine	519-766-4288
UFP	519-853-1508
Lightspeed Space Station	602-325-6674
Paramount Remote	604-937-0983
Red-Line	604-588-2181
Stargazer BBS	604-572-8213
TrekNet Region 6010	604-584-5964
Tunnel-Vision BBS	604-535-9826
USS Nexus	604-574-1523
Ferengi Emporium BBS	613-831-1412
Heavy Metal BBS	613-828-7854
The Eclectic BBS	613-230-0979
The Kanata BBS	613-831-4082
The Pixel Palace BBS	613-925-3086
XT Central	613-226-6533
Collector's Corner BBS	615-487-2229
The Lost Galaxy Multi-Line	616-329-4371
TrekNet North East Sector	617-739-9246

TrekNet Vice Coordinator	617-739-9246	The Smile Line BBS!	901-685-0017	The Tholian Web	914-227-4402
The Access	618-746-0916	Dreadnought	904-757-0640	The Wizard's Tower BBS	914-758-3055
S.T.A.R. One	619-697-4073	Echomail Hub 11	904-241-9537	Galactic Crossroads	916-334-5641
TrekNet Region 6017	702-786-2741	The Basement	904-376-8835	Life the Universe & Everything	916-334-7414
Castles Information Net	707-429-9789	The Warlock's Castle	904-378-6403	Ten Forward	916-338-4622
The Neutral Zone	716-865-8884	TrekNet Region 6002	904-249-8368	The Itchy and Scratchy Show	916-721-1701
The Next Generation BBS	718-236-8105	USS Phoenix	904-779-7411	IKE-2000	918-583-9456
Cybernet BBS	719-544-5652	Kronos (Quo'oS)	905-578-5048	Deep Space Nine	919-563-6199
Starbase 294	803-797-7584	Pan-Galacticomm	905-820-3897	The Cool World BBS	919-848-8904
The Trading Post	803-731-0690	Spectrum BBS	905-388-2542		
ASTRO	813-275-0414	Xaminex BBS	905-934-6203	**WarpSpeed**	
Echomail Hub 13	813-574-4707	The Key Board	910-282-6957	Fleet Commander	303-985-5903
The Dark Side of Town BBS	813-585-2934	Starbase 210 BBS	913-441-0603	Praxus BBS	318-237-7657
The Quantum Leap BBS	813-848-7363	Starship Excalibur	913-681-2423	USS Sports and More	610-995-2155
TrekNet Mid West Sector	817-467-7103	TrekNet Region 6012	913-384-1577	Diesel Smoke BBS	613-259-5213
Alpha Colony BBS	901-323-6429	Druid's Grove BBS	914-876-2237	USS Hermites	901-387-0469
The Electric Fox	901-327-1008	New York & New Jersey Hub	914-463-6160		

Internet Providers (Voice Numbers)

National

AlterNet/UUNet Techn.	800-488-6384	On-Ramp Technologies,Inc.	214-746-4710	N.J. Computer Connection	609-896-2799
BIX	800-695-4775	VoiceNet/DSC	215-674-9290	MRNet	612-342-2570
CERFNet	800-876-2373	APK Public Access	216-481-9436	North Shore Access	617-593-3110
CR Laboratories	415-837-5300	Prairienet	217-244-1962	The World	617-739-0202
Delphi	800-695-4005	IMS Intercom	301-856-2706	NEARnet	617-873-8730
Express Access	800-969-9090	SSNet	302-378-1386	NEARnet	617-873-8730
Global Enterprise Services	800-358-4437	Col. SuperNet, Inc.	303-273-3471	E & S Systems Public Access	619-278-8124
Internet Express	800-748-1200	CyberGate, Inc.	305-428-4283	CTS Network Services	619-637-3637
Netcom	800-353-6600	MCSNet	312-248-8649	XNet Information Systems	708-983-6064
NovaLink	800-274-2814	Merit Network, Inc/MichNet	313-764-9430	The Black Box	713-480-2684
PSILink	800-827-7482	MSen	313-998-4562	NeoSoft	713-684-5969
YPN—Your Personal Network	800-NET-1133	The IDS World Network	401-884-7856	South Coast Comp. Serv.	713-917-5000
		a2i communications	408-293-8078	KAIWAN Internet Services	714-638-2139
By Area Code		Telerama Public Access	412-481-3505	The Dorsai Embassy	718-392-3667
INTAC Access Corporation	201-944-1417	The Well	415-332-4335	Zone One Network Exchange	718-884-5800
CAPCON Library Network	202-331-5771	Institute for Global Com.	415-442-0220	Old Colorado City Com.	719-632-4848
Nuance Network Services	205-533-4296	UUnorth	416-225-8649	IslandNet	800-331-3055
Eskimo North	206-367-7457	UUNET Canada, Inc.	416-368-6621	Vnet Internet Access, Inc.	800-377-3282
Olympus Net	206-385-0464	Teleport	503-223-0076	The Portal System	800-433-6444
Halcyon	206-455-3505	Rain Drop Laboratories	503-452-0960	Iowa Network Services	800-546-6587
Maestro Technologies	212-240-9600	New Mexico Technet	505-345-6555	MIDnet	800-682-5550
Echo Communications	212-255-3839	HoloNet	510-704-0160	Clark Internet Services, Inc.	800-735-2258
The Pipeline	212-267-3636	Real/Time Communications	512-206-3124	InfiNet	800-849-7214
PANIX	212-741-4400	Illuminati Online	512-462-0999	DialMIDWEST	800-947-4754
Mordor Public Access	212-843-3451	Comm. Accessibles Montreal	514-288-2581	InterAccess	800-967-1580
Escape	212-888-8780	HookUp Comm. Corp.	519-747-4110	YPN—Your Personal Network	800-NET-1133
Interport	212-989-1128	Internet Direct, Inc.	602-274-0100	Global Connect	804-229-4484
MindVox	212-989-2418	Data Basix	602-721-1988	DFW Net	817-332-5116
Texas Metronet	214-705-2900	Evergreen Communications	602-926-4500	DPC Systems	818-305-5733
		MV Communications, Inc.	603-429-2223	Magibox	901-757-7835

@	Separates the **userid** and **domain name** of an Internet address. Pronounced "at."
anonymous FTP	Method of logging in to public file archives over the **Internet**. Enter "anonymous" when prompted for a **userid**. See **FTP**.
Archie	A program that lets you search **Internet FTP** archives worldwide by file name. One variant is called **Veronica**.
ASCII	A basic text format readable by most computers. The acronym stands for American Standard Code for Information Interchange.
bandwidth	The data transmission capacity of a network. Used colloquially to refer to the "size" of the Net; some information transmittals (e.g. multitudes of graphic files) are considered to be a "waste of bandwidth."
baud	The speed at which signals are sent by a **modem**, measured by the number of changes per second in the signals during transmission. A baud rate of 1,200, for example, would indicate 1,200 signal changes in one second. Baud rate is often confused with **bits per second (bps)**.
BBS	"Bulletin-board system." Once referred to stand-alone desktop computers with a single modem that answered the phone, but can now be as complicated and inter-connected as a commercial service.
binary transfer	A file transfer between two computers that preserves binary data—used for all non-text files.
bits per second (bps)	The data-transfer rate between two **modems**. The higher the bps, the higher the speed of the transfer.
bounced message	An **email** message "returned to sender," usually because of an address error.
bye	A log-off command, like "quit" and "exit."
carrier signal	The squeaking noise that modems use to maintain a connection. See also **handshake**.
cd	"Change directory." A command used, for example, at an **FTP** site to move from a directory to a subdirectory.
cdup	"Change directory up." Can be used at an **FTP** site to move from a subdirectory to its parent directory. Also **chdirup**.
chdirup	See **cdup**.
client	A computer that connects to a more powerful computer (see **server**) for complex tasks.
commercial service	General term for large online services (e.g., America Online, CompuServe, Prodigy, GEnie).
compression	Shrinkage of computer files to conserve storage space and reduce transfer times. Special utility programs, available for most platforms (including DOS, Mac, and

Amiga), perform the compression and decompression.

cracker A person who maliciously breaks into a computer system in order to steal files or disrupt system activities.

dial-up access Computer connection made over standard telephone lines.

dir "Directory." A command used to display the contents of the current directory.

domain name The worded address of an **IP number** on the **Internet**, in the form of domain subsets separated by periods. The full address of an **Internet** user is **userid@domain name**.

email "Electronic mail."

emoticon See **smiley**.

FAQ "Frequently asked questions." A file of questions and answers compiled for **Usenet newsgroups**, **mailing lists**, and games to reduce repeated posts about commonplace subjects.

file transfer Transfer of a file from one computer to another over a network.

finger A program that provides information about a user who is logged into your local system or on a remote computer on the Internet. Generally invoked by typing "finger" and the person's **userid**.

flame A violent and usually ad hominem attack against another person in a **newsgroup** or message area.

flame war A back-and-forth series of **flames**.

Free-Net A community-based network that provides free access to the **Internet**, usually to local residents, and often includes its own forums and news.

freeware Free software. Not to be confused with **shareware**.

FTP "File transfer protocol." The standard used to transfer files between computers.

get An **FTP** command that transfers single files from the **FTP** site to your local directory. The command is followed by a file name; typing "get file.name" would transfer only that file. Also see **mget**.

GIF Common file format for pictures first popularized by CompuServe, standing for "graphics interchange format." Pronounced with a hard *g*.

gopher A menu-based guide to directories on the **Internet**, usually organized by subject.

GUI "Graphical user interface" with windows and point-and-click capability, as opposed to a command-line interface with typed-out instructions.

hacker A computer enthusiast who enjoys exploring computer systems and programs, sometimes to the point of obsession. Not to be confused with **cracker**.

handle The name a user wishes to be known by; a user's handle may differ significantly from his or her real name or **userid**.

handshake The squawking noise at the beginning of a computer connection when two modems settle on a protocol for exchanging information.

Home Page The main **World Wide Web** site for a particular group or organization.

hqx File suffix for a BinHex file, a common format for transmitting Macintosh binary files over the **Internet**.

hypertext An easy method of retrieving information by choosing highlighted words in a text on the screen. The words link to documents with related subject matter.

IC "In character." A game player who is IC is acting as his or her **character**'s persona.

Internet The largest network of computer networks in the world, easily recognizable by the format of Internet **email** addresses: **userid@host**.

Internet provider	Wholesale or retail reseller of access to the **Internet**. YPN is one example.
IP connection	Full-fledged link to the **Internet**. See **SLIP**, **PPP**, and **TCP/IP**.
IP number	The unique number that determines the ultimate **Internet** identity of an **IP connection**.
IRC	"**Internet** relay chat." A service that allows **real-time** conversations between multiple users on a variety of subject-oriented channels.
jpeg	Common compressed format for picture files. Pronounced "jay-peg."
ls	"List." A command that provides simplified directory information at **FTP** sites and other directories. It lists only file names for the directory, not file sizes or dates.
lurkers	Regular readers of messages online who never post.
lynx	A popular text-based **Web browser**.
mailing list	Group discussion distributed through **email**. Many mailing lists are administered through listserv.
mget	An **FTP** command that transfers multiple files from the **FTP** site to your local directory. The command is followed by a list of file names separated by spaces, sometimes in combination with an asterisk used as a wild card. Typing "mget b*" would transfer all files in the directory beginning with the letter *b*. Also see **get**.
Net, the	A colloquial term that is often used to refer to the entirety of Cyberspace: the **Internet**, the **commercial services**, **BBSs**, etc.
netiquette	The rules of Cyberspace civility. Usually applied to the **Internet**, where manners are enforced exclusively by fellow users.
newbie	A newcomer to the **Net**, to a game, or to a discussion. Also called **fluxer**.
newsgroups	The **Usenet** message areas, organized by subject.
newsreader	Software program for reading **Usenet newsgroups** on the **Internet**.
port number	A number that follows a **telnet** address. The number connects a user to a particular application on the telnet site. LambdaMOO, for example, is at port 8888 of lambda.parc.xerox.com (lambda.parc.xerox.com 8888).
posting	The sending of a message to a **newsgroup**, bulletin board, or other public message area. The message itself is called a **post**.
pwd	A command used at an **FTP** site to display the name of the current directory on your screen.
real-time	The **Net** term for "live," as in "live broadcast." Real-time connections include **IRC** and **MUDs**.
remote machine	Any computer on the **Internet** reached with a program such as **FTP** or **telnet**. The machine making the connection is called the home, or local, machine.
RL	"Real life."
server	A software program, or the computer running the program, that allows other computers, called **clients**, to share its resources.
shareware	Free software, distributed over the **Net** with a request from the programmer for voluntary payment.
sig	Short for **signature**.
signature	A file added to the end of **email** messages or **Usenet** posts that contains personal information—usually your name, email address, postal address, and telephone number. **Netiquette** dictates that signatures, or **sigs**, should be no longer than four or five lines.
SLIP and PPP	"Serial line **Internet** protocol" and "point-to-point protocol." Connecting by

SLIP or PPP actually puts a computer on the Internet, which offers a number of advantages over regular **dial-up**. A SLIP or PPP connection can support a graphical **Web browser** (such as Mosaic), and allows for multiple connections at the same time. Requires special software and a SLIP or PPP service provider.

smiley
Text used to indicate emotion, humor, or irony in electronic messages—best understood if viewed sideways. Also called an **emoticon**. The most common smileys are :-) and :-(

snail mail
The paper mail the U.S. Postal Service delivers. The forerunner of **email**.

spam
The posting of the same article to multiple **newsgroups** (usually every possible one) regardless of the appropriateness of the topic (e.g., "Make Money Fast").

sysop
"System operator." The person who owns and/or manages a **BBS** or other **Net** site.

TCP/IP
The "transmission control protocol" and the "**Internet** protocol." The basis of a full-fledged Internet connection. See **IP Connection**, **PPP**, and **SLIP**. Pronounced "T-C-P-I-P."

telnet
An **Internet** program that allows you to log into other Internet-connected computers.

terminal emulator
A program or utility that allows a computer to communicate in a foreign or non-standard **terminal mode**.

terminal mode
The software standard a computer uses for text communication—for example, ANSI for PCs and **VT-100** for UNIX.

thread
Posted **newsgroup** message with a series of replies. Threaded **newsreaders** organize replies under the original subject.

timeout
The break in communication that occurs when two computers are talking and one takes so long to respond that the other gives up.

URL
"Uniform resource locator." The **World Wide Web** address of a resource on the **Internet**.

Usenet
A collection of networks and computer systems that exchange messages, organized by subject in **newsgroups**.

userid
The unique name (often eight characters or less) given to a user on a system for his or her account. The complete address, which can be used for **email** or **fingering**, is a userid followed by the @ sign and the **domain name** (e.g., Bill Clinton's address is president@whitehouse.gov).

Veronica
See **Archie**.

VT-100 emulation
Widely used terminal protocol for formatting full screens of text over computer connections.

WAIS
"Wide area information server." A system that searches through database indexes around the **Internet**, using keywords.

Web browser
A **client** program designed to interact with **World Wide Web servers** on the **Internet** for the purpose of viewing **Web pages**.

Web page
A **hypertext** document that is part of the **World Wide Web** and that can incorporate graphics, sounds, and links to other **Web pages**, **FTP** sites, **gophers**, and a variety of other **Internet** resources.

World Wide Web
A **hypertext**-based navigation system that lets you browse through a variety of linked **Net** resources, including **Usenet newsgroups** and **FTP**, **telnet**, and **gopher** sites, without typing commands. Also known as WWW and the Web.

zip
File-compression standard in the DOS and Windows worlds.

Index

Index

Index

Index

Index

Index

Index

Index

Index

Index

NOTES

Uncaptioned images:

Jupiter, page 23, http://www.stsci.edu:80/ftp/stsci/epa/gif/; Sun, page 23, http://seds.lpl.arizona.edu/pub/images/; Brigitte Jellinek, page 30, http://www.cosy.sbg.ac.at/rec/startrek; Picard as Locutus, page 37, ftp.cis.ksu.edu; Picard as a Borg, page 37, Perfect Vision Graphics BBS; Gul Ducat, page 38, CompuServe's SFmedia Forum/Star Trek; The Romulans , page 40, ftp.cis.ksu.edu; Lursa, page 46, AOL's Entertainment Weekly/Star Trek; The Enterprise, page 58, ftp.cis.ksu.edu; The Enterprise, page 59, lajkonik.cyf-kr.edu.pl; The Borg, page 60, lajkonik.cyf-kr.edu.pl; The Enterprise, page 60, Perfect Vision Graphics BBS; The Enterprise, page 60, Perfect Vision Graphics BBS; The Enterprise, page 61, ftp.cis.ksu.edu; U.S.S. Enterprise, page 61, ftp.cis.ksu.edu; Enterprise-A, page 61, ftp.cis.ksu.edu; The U.S.S. Defiant, page 62, CompuServe's SFmedia Forum/Star Trek; Klingon Bird of Prey, page 62, ftp.cis.ksu.edu; The Romulan Warbird, page 62, ftp.cis.ksu.edu; Shuttlecraft, page 62, ftp.cis.ksu.edu; Star Trek at 25, page 63, Perfect Vision Graphics BBS; TV Guide—Stewart, page 63, Perfect Vision Graphics BBS; TV Guide—DS9, page 63, Perfect Vision Graphics BBS; Trek Magazine, page 63, Perfect Vision Graphics BBS; Entertainment Magazine, page 63, http://www.tut.fi/~pekka/trek.html; Time Magazine, page 63, http://www.tut.fi/~pekka/trek.html; Picard's head, page 65, ftp.cis.ksu.edu; Kirk's Head, page 65, http://www.uvm.edu/~jfabian/tos70.jpg; Data, page 67, ftp.cis.ksu.edu; Tasha Yar, page 73, ftp.cis.ksu.edu; Jean-Luc and Beverly, page 74, ftp.cis.ksu.edu; Kirk, page 75 and page 131, CompuServe's Bettmann Archives; Spock, page 75 and page 131, CompuServe's Bettmann Archives; Nana Visitor, page 77, http://www.tut.fi/~pekka/trek.html; Earth, page 82, http://seds.lpl.arizona.edu/pub/images/; Hand, page 82 and page 115, http://www.cosy.sbg.ac.at/rec/startrek; Rick Berman, page 87, http://voyager.paramount.com; Paramount mountain, page 88, http://www.paramount.com; Michael Piller, page 89, http://voyager.paramount.com; Worf screaming, page 93, ftp.cis.ksu.edu; TNG Icons, page 96, ftp.u-tokyo.ac.jp; DS9 Icons, page 97, AOL's Mac Software; Star Trek Icons, page 98, AOL's Mac Software; Gates McFadden, page 112, Perfect Vision Graphics BBS; MST3K, page 115, http://alfred1.u.washington.edu:8080/~roland/mst3k/mst3k.html; Joel Robinson, page 116, http://www.cs.odu.edu/~warren/mst3k/newbies.html; Chekov, page 131, CompuServe's Bettmann Archives; Gene Roddenberry, page 131, CompuServe's Bettmann Archives; Uhura, page 131, CompuServe's Bettmann Archives; Dr. McCoy, page 131, CompuServe's Bettmann Archives; Sulu, page 131, CompuServe's Bettmann Archives; TNG Cast, page 165, http://www.astro.lsa.umich.edu:80/users/sewin/continuum; Picard, page 166 and cover, ftp.cis.ksu.edu; Q, page 222, ftp.cis.ksu.edu; Image of Captain Picard, page 225, ftp.cis.ksu.edu; Worf, page 232, ftp.cis.ksu.edu; Troi, page 234, Perfect Vision Graphics BBS; DS9 Opening Page, page 247, Perfect Vision Graphics BBS; DS9 Poster, page 271, http://www.ee.surrey.ac.uk/Personal/STDS9/video.html; U.S.S. Voyager, page 273, http://voyager.paramount.com/images/voyshpo1.gif; Captain Janeway, page 277, http://www.ftms.com/st-voy/images/voy_d2.jpg; Chakotay, page 278, http://www.ftms.com/st-voy/images/voy_36.jpg; Lt. Tom Paris, page 278, http://www.ftms.com/st-voy/images/voy_f8.jpg; Tuvok, page 278, http://www.ftms.com/st-voy/images/voy_f5.jpg; B'Elanna Torres, page 278, http://www.ftms.com/st-voy/images/voy_07.gif; Dr. Zimmerman, page 279, http://www.ftms.com/st-voy/images/voy_28.jpg; Kes, page 279, http://www.ftms.com/st-voy/images/voy_05.gif; Harry Kim, page 279, http://www.ftms.com/st-voy/images/voy_f2.jpg; Neelix, page 279, http://www.ftms.com/st-voy/images/voy_f7.jpg; Kate Mulgrew, page 280, http://www.ftms.com/st-voy/images/voy_d8.jpg; Voyager ship, page 281, http://www.ftms.com/st-voy/images/; Enterprise Shuttle, page 283, http://seds.lpl.arizona.edu/pub/images/; Galaxy, page 283, http://seds.lpl.arizona.edu/pub/images/; Babylon 5 Poster, page 291 and cover, http://www.microserve.com/~meccamw/; J. Michael Straczynski, page 309, http://www.hyperion.com/lurk/production.html; Babylon 5 Cast, page 310, http://www.cgd.ucar.edu/cms/zecca/b5/B5news.html; K-9, page 317, http://www.phlab.missouri.edu/ccpeace_www/Dr.Who/pics; Star Trek Ships Expanded, cover, http://www.ee.umanitoba.ca/~djc/startrek/ships.expanded.html; Three Klingons, cover, ftp.cis.ksu.edu; Kirk with Tribbles, lajkonic.cyf-kr.edu.pl; Dax, cover, CompuServe's SFMedia Forum/Star Trek; Voyager Web Shot, cover, http://voyager.paramount.com

Saturn from Starnotes, http://seds.lpl.arizona.edu/pub/images/planets/saturn
Jessica the Cat from Ask Spot, CompuServe's Graphics Corner

Michael Wolff & Company, Inc., digital publisher and packager, specializing in information presentation and graphic design, is one of the leading providers of information about the Net. The company's book *Net Guide*, published with Random House, has spent almost a year on bestseller lists, and is now a monthly magazine published by CMP Publications.

MW& Co., and its team of Net surfers, is embarked upon a project to map all corners of the Net. This means that the growing community of Net adventurers can expect a steady flow of new Net baedekers. *Net Guide* has now been joined by *Net Games, Net Chat, Net Money*, and *Net Trek,* and will shortly be followed by *Net Sports, Net Tech*, and *Net Music.* MW&Co.'s Internet service, YPN—Your Personal Network, features a hypertext version of the entire series. It is the most comprehensive Net source available anywhere.

Among the company's other recent projects are *Where We Stand—Can America Make It in the Global Race for Wealth, Health, and Happiness?* (Bantam Books), one of the most graphically complex information books ever to be wholly created and produced by means of desktop-publishing technology, and *Made in America?*, a four-part PBS series on global competitiveness, hosted by Labor Secretary Robert B. Reich.

Kelly Maloni, who directed the *Net Trek* project, is the managing editor of MW&Co. Senior editor Ben Greenman has written pop-culture criticism for many publications, including *Miami New Times*, the *Chicago Reader*, the *Village Voice*, and *Rolling Stone*, and has taught in the English department at Northwestern University. Senior editor Kristin Miller has taught in the history department at Columbia University, and contributed to many books, among them *Where We Stand, Net Chat, Net Games*, and *Net Money*. Jeff Hearn has served as art director for *Net Chat* and *Net Money*, and has been a desktop-publishing consultant for several publications, including *Spy*. He has a cat who looks just like Spot.

COLLECTOR'S ALERT!

Own the 2-hour series premiere on video for **$4.95!**

STAR TREK ®
THE NEXT GENERATION ™

The U.S.S. Enterprise™ has completed its final mission. Now you can relive the whole exciting story!

Take your station on the bridge after the ENTERPRISE™ completes its seventh and final tour of duty. You have a reserved seat for every action-packed mission to the far frontiers of space with this special Collector's Edition of the sci-fi classic on videocassette. Accelerate to warp speed and prepare for daring and dangerous encounters with fantastic beings in the remote corners of the universe.

Own the adventure-packed 2-hour series premiere, ENCOUNTER AT FARPOINT
— yours for just $4.95! You'll face the first of many deadly games of wit with the unforgettable superbeing "Q." You'll savor every suspense-packed moment of this double episode just as it originally aired — unedited, uncut in the exclusive Collector's Edition available only from Columbia House Video Library. Preview this fascinating 2-hour series premiere for 10 full days, risk-free. You must be absolutely thrilled or simply return the video for a full refund or credit to your charge account and be under no further obligation.

Forge ahead... into the farthest reaches of the universe!

If you decide to keep your first video and become a subscriber, you'll receive another thrilling 2-hour, 2-episode video every 4 to 6 weeks under the same risk-free terms. In future videos, you'll travel into the past, as a time rift sweeps you back for a face-to-face meeting with an earlier Starship Enterprise™ and crew. You'll see the cybernetic Borg capture Captain Picard and use him to try to conquer the human race ... plus many other gripping adventures. Keep only the videos you want for just $19.95 each plus shipping and handling. There is no minimum to buy and you may cancel your subscription at any time. Don't miss out on this specially packaged Collector's Edition from Columbia House Video Library... mail the coupon or call today!

Clip this coupon and mail today!
Or for faster service, use your credit card and call toll-free!
1-800-538-7766, Dept. W3H

STAR TREK© is a registered trademark of Paramount Pictures. All Rights Reserved.
STAR TREK®: THE NEXT GENERATION™ and associated characters and marks are trademarks of Paramount Pictures.
All Rights Reserved. TM and Copyright ©1994 Paramount Pictures. All rights reserved.
©1994, The Columbia House Company

Yes!

I want to voyage through space with Captain Picard and the crew. Rush my first 2-hour videocassette, ENCOUNTER AT FARPOINT, for only $4.95 plus $2.45 shipping and handling and enter my subscription to STAR TREK®: THE NEXT GENERATION™ —The Collector's Edition under the terms described above. If I do not choose to keep my introductory videocassette, I will return it within 10 days for a full refund or credit to my charge account with no further obligation. **Available on VHS only.**

CHECK METHOD OF PAYMENT:

❏ My check is enclosed for $4.95 plus $2.45 shipping and handling (total is $7.40) plus applicable sales tax made payable to Columbia House Video Library. P26

❏ Charge this and any future series purchases to my credit card: P27
❏ AMEX ❏ VISA ❏ MasterCard
❏ Diners Club ❏ Discover

Account No.

(   )

Exp. Date   Phone Number

Signature

NAME   (Please Print)

ADDRESS   APT.

CITY   STATE   ZIP

Mail coupon to: Columbia House Video Library, Dept.W3H, P.O. Box 1112, Terre Haute, IN 47811

Note: All subscriptions subject to review. Columbia House Video Library reserves the right to cancel any subscription. Canadian residents will be serviced from Toronto; offer may vary. **Applicable sales tax** added to all orders.

COLUMBIA HOUSE
VIDEO LIBRARY

The ultimate online navigation tool!

MAKE THE RIGHT COMPUTER CONNECTION! PAGE 41

NetGuide

THE GUIDE TO ONLINE SERVICES AND THE INTERNET   DECEMBER 1994

GET ONLINE!

203 Money-Saving Reviews

SHOP Day and Night

Hot games to download

Safe sites for **kids**

DOOM Booms!

PLUS
Graham Nash,
Adam Curry and
Ralph Nader on World
Peace and the INTERNET

Explore Cyberspace

with the new monthly guide to the online world of information and entertainment!

What's new online? Which Internet newsgroups, chat lines, and bulletin boards are hot? Where's the online action—and how do I get there?

Find out with NetGuide, the first-ever program guide to Cyberspace!

There's never been a magazine like NetGuide! Every month NetGuide points you to the best and brightest places to be and things to see online—more than a hundred listings <u>broken</u> <u>down</u> <u>by</u> <u>areas</u> <u>of</u> <u>interest</u> for quick and easy access.

• News, Arts & Entertainment! • Sports!
• Business & Finance! • Travel! • Reference Sources! • Science & Technology!
• Computers & Software! • Games!
• Romance • Lifestyles! • Politics!
• The Media! • And much more!

These aren't ordinary listings — they're reviews.
Before we publish them, our expert staff researches each listing. How easy is it to access? If it's a bulletin board, is the line always busy? How expensive is it? Is it worth the cost?

Navigate like a pro...
NetGuide isn't only a "where to" guide. It's also a "how-to" manual. You'll learn how to get around cyberspace and valuable techniques to make you a more cost-effective explorer on the information superhighway.

Be one of the first to try NetGuide!
Call **1-800-336-5900.**

Charter Offer
3 FREE ISSUES!

OFFER: You will receive a COMPLIMENTARY 3 ISSUE TRIAL SUBSCRIPTION to NetGuide. We will also send a Charter discount invoice for 12 additional issues (15 issues in all) for only $14.97 — less than a dollar an issue, and a Charter savings of 65% off the newsstand rate. If you aren't *amazed* by what NetGuide shows you, return the invoice marked "cancel." You will owe nothing and your three free issues will be yours to keep.

5 MINUTES TO FREEDOM

INSTANT INTERNET ACCESS

CONNECT TO THE INTERNET IN LESS THAN 5 MINUTES

7-DAY FREE TRIAL FOR WINDOWS

Internet Inside!™

Forget on-line services; InterRamp connects you <u>directly</u> to the Internet. That's the <u>BIG</u> difference.

In less than 5 minutes, you'll have access to MOSAIC, Gopher, WAIS, Veronica, Archie, ftp, E-Mail, NEWS and other hot Internet applications. You have the entire worldwide Internet at your fingertips.

Just a few clicks of your mouse, you're connected.

All applications are automatically configured for immediate use. It's that <u>SIMPLE</u>.

We're so sure you'll love Instant InterRamp, we'll let you try it absolutely <u>FREE</u> without any obligation.

All you need is a computer and a modem; we'll send you the Instant InterRamp software.*

PSI also offers high-performance LAN Internet solutions for your organization. Ask your sales representative for more information.

MACINTOSH® & UNIX VERSIONS ARE ALSO AVAILABLE

CALL NOW FOR FREE DEMO

1.800.PSI.0852

PREFERRED CUSTOMER NUMBER #00135

PSI Net — THE INTERNET STARTS HERE

FaxBack Info: 1.800.fax.psi.1 • Internet E-Mail: interramp-info@psi.com • World Wide Web: http://www.psi.net/
Download the software from the Internet: http://www.psi.net/indivservices/interramp/instaramp.html/
ftp: ftp.psi.com/iiramp/inetcham/

*Restrictions apply. Call PSI a Sales Representative for details. • PERFORMANCE SYSTEMS INTERNATIONAL, INC. • 510 HUNTMAR PARK DRIVE • HERNDON, VA 22070 • USA • ©1995 Performance Systems International, Inc. The PSINet logos is a registered trademark. All other trademarks and service marks are used with their permission and remain the property of their respective owners. [Rev. 2/7/95]

Find out who's trading with the Ferengi in the Gamma Quadrant.

Ever wonder what the business world will be like in 2370? Climb aboard Hoover's Company Profiles and transport your business knowledge into the Star Trek universe. You'll find the answers to:

* What's Quark's annual take in bars of latinum?
* What's the biggest trading house in The Federation?
* What's Starfleet's ownership interest in the Utopia Planitia Fleet Yards?
* What company does Bill Gates XIII work for?
* What's The Federation's most profitable mining company?

This selection of humorous Star Trek-based company profiles contains information on some of the most important businesses of the 24th century, including an overview of their operations, brief histories, details on the people, products, and places, and much more.

And for those of you who need company information a little closer to home, we offer over 1,200 profiles of 20th century companies as well.

Hoover's Company Profiles are available on America Online and as part of Hoover's Online on the Internet.

AMERICA ONLINE
keyword: hoovers

http://www.hoovers.com

THE UNIVERSE IS EXPANDING

STAR TREK® COMMUNICATOR™

...ENGAGE

A PUBLICATION OF THE OFFICIAL STAR TREK FAN CLUB ™

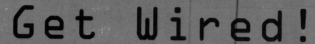

BUSINESS REPLY MAIL
FIRST CLASS MAIL PERMIT NO. 25363 SAN FRANCISCO, CA

Postage will be paid by addressee

PO Box 191826
San Francisco CA 94119-9866

GET WIRED!

GET WIRED!
AND STAY WIRED
BY READING NET SURF,
EXCLUSIVELY
IN WIRED.

If you want to keep up with the Digital Revolution, and the dozens of new sites that are appearing on the Net monthly, you need *Wired* and its Net Surf column – *Wired*'s guide to the best of the Net.

From its online presence (gopher, WWW, Info-rama@wired.com, WELL, and AOL) to its focus on convergence and the communications revolution, *Wired* is one of the most Net-savvy publications in America today.

That's because *Wired* is the only place where the Digital Revolution is covered by and for the people who are making it happen – you.

Since its launch in January 1993, *Wired* has become required reading for the digerati from Silicon Valley to Madison Avenue, from Hollywood to Wall Street, from Pennsylvania Avenue to Main Street.

But *Wired* may be hard to find on newsstands (we're printing almost 250,000 copies and still can't satisfy demand).

So if you want to get *Wired* regularly and reliably, subscribe now – and save up to 40 percent. If for any reason you don't like *Wired*, you can cancel at any time, and get your full subscription price back – that's how sure we are that you will like *Wired*.

If you want to connect to the soul of the Digital Revolution, our advice to you is simple.

--- **PLEASE FOLD ALONG THIS LINE AND TAPE CLOSED. (NO STAPLES)** ---

I want to get Wired – reliably and regularly. Begin my subscription immediately, if not sooner, saving me up to 40% off the newsstand price. If for any reason, I don't like Wired, I can cancel at any time, and get my full subscription back. I would like (check one below):

Individual subscription

		Can/Mex	Other
1 Year (12 issues)	☐ $39.95 (33% off single copy of $59.40)	☐ US $64	☐ $79
2 Years (24 issues)	☐ $71 (40% off single copy of $118.80)	☐ US $119	☐ $149

Corporate/Institutional subscription*

		Can/Mex	Other
1 Year (12 issues)	☐ $80	☐ US $103	☐ $110
2 Years (24 issues)	☐ $143	☐ US $191	☐ $210

Foreign subscriptions payable by credit card, postal money order in US dollars or check drawn on US bank only.
* We have a separate rate for corporate/institutional subscribers because pass-along readership is higher. We felt it would be unfair for individual readers to, in effect, subsidize corporate/institutional purchasers.

Name

Job title

Company

Street

CityStateZipCountry

Phone   This is your ☐ home ☐ office ☐ both

E-mail address
Very important! This is by far the most efficient way to communicate with you about your subscription and periodic special offers, and to poll your opinion on *WIRED* subjects.

Payment method   ☐ Check enclosed   ☐ Bill me (for corporate/institutional rates only)
                        ☐ American Express   ☐ Mastercard   ☐ Visa

Account number   Expiration date   Signature

Please Note: The "Bill Me" box above is only for corporations and institutions needing an invoice – which will be for the higher corporate/institutional rates. There is no "Bill Me" option for individuals.

WIRED rents its subscriber list only to mailers that we feel are relevant to our readers' interests. To remove your name from the rental list, please check this box ☐.

AGL